2/11

D1538531

DATE DUE

CHILD ANXIETY DISORDERS

A Guide to Research and Treatment

Second Edition

DEBORAH C. BEIDEL & CANDICE A. ALFANO

Routledge
Taylor & Francis Group
New York London

Routledge
Taylor & Francis Group
270 Madison Avenue
New York, NY 10016

Routledge
Taylor & Francis Group
27 Church Road
Hove, East Sussex BN3 2FA

© 2011 by Taylor and Francis Group, LLC
Routledge is an imprint of Taylor & Francis Group, an Informa business

Printed in the United States of America on acid-free paper
10 9 8 7 6 5 4 3 2 1

International Standard Book Number: 978-0-415-87373-4 (Hardback)

Library of Congress Cataloging-in-Publication Data

Beidel, Deborah C.
    Child anxiety disorders : a guide to research and treatment / by Deborah C. Beidel, Candice A. Alfano. -- 2nd ed.
        p. ; cm.
    Rev. ed. of: Childhood anxiety disorders / Deborah C. Beidel & Samuel M. Turner, c2005.
    Includes bibliographical references and index.
    ISBN 978-0-415-87373-4 (hardback : alk. paper)
    1. Anxiety in children. I. Alfano, Candice A. II. Beidel, Deborah C. Childhood anxiety disorders. III. Title.
    [DNLM: 1. Anxiety Disorders. 2. Adolescent. 3. Child. WM 172]

RJ506.A58B45 2011
618.92'8522--dc22   2010026869

Visit the Taylor & Francis Web site at
http://www.taylorandfrancis.com

and the Routledge Web site at
http://www.routledgementalhealth.com

This book is dedicated to our mentor and eternal friend Samuel M. Turner. Among the many gifts he shared with his patients, colleagues, students, and friends, perhaps no other has been as influential as his dedication to knowledge and truth. His legacy lives on not only in the hundreds of papers, chapters, and books he contributed to the science of clinical psychology but also in those of us fortunate enough to miss his brilliance, wit, and laughter.

Candice A. Alfano
Deborah C. Beidel

Contents

SECTION II   ANXIETY DISORDERS IN CHILDREN

About the Authors

Deborah C. Beidel received her PhD in 1986 from the University of Pittsburgh. After serving on the faculty at the University of Pittsburgh, the Medical University of South Carolina, the University of Maryland–College Park, and The Pennsylvania State University College of Medicine, she joined the doctoral program in clinical psychology at the University of Central Florida (UCF) in 2007. In addition to her appointment as professor of psychology, she is director of the doctoral program in clinical psychology and director of the UCF Anxiety Disorders Clinic. She was the 1990 recipient of the New Researcher Award from the Association for Advancement of Behavior Therapy, the 1995 Distinguished Educator Award from the Association of Medical School Psychologists, and the 2005 Samuel M. Turner Clinical Research Award from the Society of Clinical Psychology of the American Psychological Association. Dr. Beidel holds the American Board of Professional Psychology (ABPP) Diplomate in Clinical Psychology and Behavioral Psychology and is a Fellow of the American Psychological Association and the Association for Psychological Science. Her academic, research, and clinical interests focus on child and adult anxiety disorders, including their etiology, psychopathology, and behavioral treatment. She is the associate editor of *Journal of Anxiety Disorders*. In addition to several professional books, Dr. Beidel is the author (along with Cynthia Bulik and Melinda Stanley) of the undergraduate textbook, *Abnormal Psychology: A Scientist-Practitioner Approach*. She has been the recipient of numerous grants from the National Institute of Mental Health (NIMH) addressing the development and efficacy of behavioral interventions for adults and children with anxiety disorders.

Candice A. Alfano received her PhD in clinical psychology in 2005 from the University of Maryland at College Park. After completing a postdoctoral research fellowship at the Johns Hopkins University School of Medicine, she joined the faculty at the Children's National Medical Center (CNMC) in Washington, D.C. Dr. Alfano is assistant professor of psychiatry and pediatrics at the George Washington University School of Medicine. She founded and directs the Child and Adolescent Anxiety Program (CAAP) at CNMC, which provides comprehensive clinical services for anxious youth and training for psychology interns and child psychiatry fellows. Dr. Alfano has received several awards for her research, including awards from the Anxiety Disorders Association of America (ADAA), Division 53 of the American Psychological Association, and a 2008 New Investigator Award cosponsored by the NIMH. She received awards in 2009 and 2010 for Outstanding Teaching at CNMC. Dr. Alfano serves on the editorial board of several scientific journals, including the *Journal of Anxiety Disorders*, and has authored numerous peer-reviewed papers and chapters. She is coeditor (with Dr. Beidel) of the book *Social Anxiety Disorder in Adolescents and Young Adults: Translating Developmental Science Into Practice*. Her primary academic, research, and clinical interests focus on the early etiology, pathogenesis, and treatment of childhood anxiety, including the role of early sleep abnormalities. Dr. Alfano is the recipient of a 5-year Mentored Career Development Award from the NIMH to study sleep disturbances in children with anxiety disorders, including potential targets for psychosocial intervention.

Preface

It is now recognized that childhood anxiety disorders are among the most common psychological disorders in the United States. These debilitating disorders continue to have an impact on the lives of many children and result in both short- and long-term impairments. Research aimed at understanding their manifestations continues to emerge, and since the publication of the first edition of this book, many efficacious treatment programs have been developed. However, this literature often does not make its way into the hands of the health and mental health professionals, who every day attempt to manage and treat children with these conditions.

Over the years, we have provided many workshops on treating childhood anxiety disorders, and we often are asked for clinical materials (e.g., treatment plans, treatment manuals, sample fear hierarchies, self-monitoring forms) that we use in our clinical practice and in our ongoing treatment protocols. Thus, in this book, we discuss the research results of many investigators and describe our clinical experience in treating children with anxiety disorders. We hope that by including these clinical materials we can make more vivid the scientific descriptions and illustrate the range, severity, and functional impairment that childhood anxiety disorders can impart. In addition, we hope that these clinical materials illustrate the creative process of fitting appropriate treatments to individual cases, the necessity for understanding the nature of these conditions and how they affect youth who are afflicted, and the need for an understanding of the scientific literature. Indeed, it is unlikely, in our view, that childhood anxiety disorders can be effectively and appropriately treated if any of these components are missing. Hence, one objective was to discuss the material presented in such a manner that this would be unabashedly clear. We trust we were successful in this regard.

Because fears are so common in children, we felt that it was important that this book include not only anxiety disorders but also the developmental background necessary to place childhood anxiety disorders in their proper context. Therefore, we have divided this book into two parts. Part I, consisting of the first five chapters, provides an overview of children's fears, children's anxiety disorders, developmental considerations, the role of sleep in the development and maintenance of anxiety, and etiological factors that cut across specific disorders. Many of the interventions used to treat anxiety disorders in children emerged from the literature on adult disorders, and as such, sometimes are neither developmentally sensitive nor appropriate for children or adolescents. For graduate students and clinicians who are just beginning to do research or clinical interventions in this area, it is important to have a clear understanding of how these developmental factors affect both clinical presentation and the construction and implementation of efficacious treatment plans. Part II includes chapters on all of the identified childhood anxiety disorders.

New to this edition is a chapter on sleep and anxiety disorders. We included this chapter for several reasons. First, while there is considerable evidence that sleep problems are common across different forms of child psychopathology, and a majority of children presenting with a primary complaint of insomnia meet criteria for a psychiatric problem or disorder, a relationship with anxiety is perhaps most robust. Accumulating evidence suggests that sleep problems that begin during early childhood presage the later development of anxiety disorders. Further, since inadequate sleep impairs both physical and emotional health, the presence of these problems can significantly affect our attempts to treat childhood anxiety disorders. Since sleep disorders in children are complex, requiring understanding of both developmental and environmental factors that affect sleep patterns, sleep architecture, and sleep behaviors, we include a discussion of these unique considerations. Overall, the role of sleep disorders as an etiological factor, a clinical symptom, and a possible barrier to efficacious treatment is becoming clearer. Given the impact of sleep on physical, mental, and emotional functioning, we believe that the time is right to present the research examining the relationship between sleep and childhood anxiety.

Throughout the chapters, we endeavor not only to emphasize the developmental focus but also to present the literature on variations in clinical presentation by age, sex, race or ethnicity, and culture. As we noted in the first edition, data regarding the role of culture remain sparse, and we continue to encourage researchers to consider this area of research.

As authors, we are responsible for the veracity of the material contained in this book. However, with the assistance of others, its completion would not have been possible. First, we would like to thank our editor, George Zimmar, for his encouragement, good humor, and patience. Second, to Marta Moldvai, senior editorial assistant, thank you for your guidance and help with this second edition. We also want to acknowledge the assistance of Franklin Mesa in supervising the collection and editing of the references. Special thanks to Ed Beidel and Miguel Buddle, and the rest of our families and friends, who show never-ending patience for the long hours needed to produce the book. Finally, we thank our patients and their parents, who never fail to teach and inspire us in so many ways. It is our privilege to work with and learn from you.

Overview of Childhood Anxiety Disorders

CHAPTER 1

An Introduction to Children's Fears

Terrence is a happy 4-year-old preschooler. Until recently, he had no problems going to bed or falling asleep. However, last month, he had the same nightmare on two separate occasions: that "scary aliens were trying to take him away." Now, he insists that his parents stay with him in his room at night to protect him from the aliens.

Alyssa is a cheerful 18-month-old baby with a brand new baby brother. Although she has always been comfortable interacting with other adults and children, she now clings to her mother's side when new or unfamiliar people are present. Since the birth of her brother, Alyssa follows her mother around the house, wanting to be with her at all times.

These case descriptions illustrate just two of the myriad fears that exist among children and adolescents. Fearful reactions are widely recognized as common (Jersild & Holmes, 1935; Lapouse & Monk, 1959; MacFarlane, Allen, & Honzik, 1954; Ollendick, 1983); often, certain fears are considered part of normal development (Barrios, Hartmann, & Shigetomi, 1981; Fonseca, Yule, & Erol, 1994). For many years, fears and anxiety in children were not considered serious. As a consequence, parents often were advised by medical and mental health professionals not to worry because children would outgrow their fears (Poulton et al., 1997). In fact, many children do overcome some fears with time. However, as illustrated throughout this book, not every child outgrows or overcomes fear responses, and in a number of instances, these "fears" are not minor matters. Rather, they are manifestations of serious and often chronic conditions; alternatively, they may be the harbinger of more serious disorders. When fears are part of a serious condition, they sometimes create unreasonable emotional distress or result in functional limitations, such as academic or social impairment (e.g., Woodward & Fergusson, 2001).

A meta-analytic study suggested that anxiety in the general population increased over the years 1954 to 1981, and children's average scores on a standard child anxiety inventory, the Children's Manifest Anxiety Scale, increased by one standard deviation (i.e., an average increase of 5–6 points for both boys and girls; Twenge, 2000). Interestingly, by the 1980s, children who were considered to be without a psychiatric disorder (i.e., normal children) had higher scores on this inventory than did children diagnosed with a psychiatric disorder in the 1950s. Increases in anxiety scores were strongly correlated with increases in the divorce, birth, and crime rates. There was no relationship between anxiety and economic conditions in general. There was a positive relationship between anxiety and unemployment rates but a negative relationship with poverty (the author speculated that this was perhaps due to the sharp decrease in poverty levels during the 1960s). Although additional factors probably contributed to these increased scores, the data clearly indicate that anxiety was becoming an increasingly common phenomenon in the general child population.

When reaching the level at which they interfere with social, emotional, and academic development, fears and anxiety often are more appropriately termed *anxiety disorders*. Anxiety disorders consist of many overlapping and interrelated diagnostic categories that are among the most common psychiatric disorders in the United States and throughout the world (e.g., Costello, Costello, Edelbrock, & Burns, 1988; Kessler et al., 2009; McGee et al., 1990). This book focuses on anxiety disorders, their clinical presentation and development, as well as factors associated with their maintenance and treatment. To facilitate an understanding of the anxiety disorders, particularly in children, some background on normal fears and their prevalence, development, and stability is necessary.

WHAT IS FEAR?

Fear is a basic human emotion usually considered to be a response to objects or situations that threaten physical safety or emotional well-being (e.g., Marks, 1969; Miller, 1983). Fear is multidimensional, consisting of an outer behavioral expression, inner subjective distress, and associated physical or physiological changes (Marks, 1969). In addition to its ubiquitous nature, fearful reactions sometimes are adaptive, serving to keep one alert in dangerous situations (Korte, 2001). Similarly, the word *anxiety* has become part of everyday vocabulary and can have different meanings depending on the context in which it is used. Children might use the term *anxious* to represent excitement, for example, when

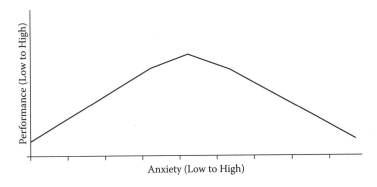

FIGURE 1.1   The relationship between anxiety and performance.

talking about a birthday party. In this instance, the child's interpretation of anxious is one of positive expectation.

To illustrate the relationship between anxiety and optimal performance, examination of the classic anxiety and performance curve is instructive (Figure 1.1). Consider the example of test anxiety. A small-to-moderate amount of anxiety often enhances motivation and helps one recall answers or concentrate on details required to solve certain problems. When anxiety exceeds a certain point, however, it has the opposite effect. Thus, in competitive situations, a moderate amount of anxiety improves the ability to excel, but severe anxiety interferes with the ability to concentrate and acts to decrease performance. Of course, there are individual differences with respect to the amount of anxiety one can tolerate before performance is affected (McDonald, 2001).

In most cases, however, the word *anxiety* describes a negative emotional state, such as the anxiety that one feels before an important testing situation. During a test, children can be fearful that they will forget the answers, for example, or that their mind will go blank. If called to the blackboard or asked to recite in front of the class, they might worry that they will not know the answer, that they will say the wrong thing, or they will not be able to talk at all and so will embarrass themselves. In short, anxiety in children most often is a negative emotion and one that they seek to eliminate. The precipitants of anxiety are usually less clear and predictable than for fear. In fact, sometimes anxiety has no easily identifiable cause—it is just an uncomfortable, ill-defined feeling of apprehension. Therefore, although technically fear sometimes is considered to be the immediate defensive reaction to a threatening stimulus, anxiety, on the other hand, often is defined as apprehension about some future event (Johnson & Melamed, 1979). In reality, however, these terms often are used interchangeably, as is done throughout this book. Throughout each of the ensuing chapters, specific issues with respect to clinical presentation, etiology, maintenance, and treatment of specific childhood anxiety disorders are addressed. We begin with a general review of fears in children.

THE EPIDEMIOLOGY OF FEARS IN CHILDREN AND ADOLESCENTS

For many years, there was a propensity on the part of parents and professionals to regard most fear responses as part of normal development. Indeed, there is a high probability that any child will, at some time, manifest some type of fearful behavior. In the earliest report on prevalence (Jersild & Holmes, 1935), nonreferred children displayed a number of fears. Interviews with mothers of 2- to 6-year-olds revealed that their children displayed between four and five different fears and exhibited a fearful reaction once every 4½ days. In one of the first longitudinal studies (MacFarlane et al., 1954), 90% of the sample demonstrated at least one fearful reaction at some time between the ages of 2 and 14. In a classic study of childhood fears, 43% of children (ages 6 to 12) had seven or more fears and worries, leading the authors to conclude that fears are common at this age (Lapouse & Monk, 1959). In addition, 15% of the mothers reported that their children had three or more anxious behaviors, such as nail biting, teeth grinding, and thumb sucking.

Miller, Barrett, Hampe, and Noble (1971) surveyed parents of 249 children selected from the general population. Using the Louisville Fear Survey Schedule, parents rated their child's response to each situation as no fear, normal fear, or extreme fear. Each specific object or event evoked excessive fear in less than 5% of the sample. For each fear stimulus, 84% of the children showed no fear, 5–15% demonstrated what was judged to be a normal fear, and 0–5% showed an excessive fearful reaction. Furthermore, even when the reactions were judged to be excessive, the fears still were considered to be part of normal development. However, there were a number of specific objects and events for which the distribution of parental ratings more closely approximated a normal curve. This group included snakes, rats, lightning, fire, tornados, being wounded, getting injections, and being seen naked. With respect to social and performance fears, 25% of the children (boys and girls) were rated as having some fear of attending social events due to worries of rejection or embarrassment. Fully 50% of the children were rated as having normal or extreme fears of being criticized, reciting in class, making mistakes or doing something wrong, and tests and examinations, a fear that Campbell (1986) also noted as predominant among school-age children.

In more recent years, an interview survey of 190 school-age children (Muris, Merckelbach, Gadet, & Moulaert, 2000) revealed that 75.8% of the sample reported fear of an object or situation, 67.4% endorsed the presence of worry, and 80.5% reported the presence of a "scary dream." The most common fears endorsed by the children included animals, imaginary creatures, being kidnapped, and social threats. The most frequent worries included thoughts of harm, death, performance at school, and being separated from their parents. The most common content of the scary dreams included imaginary creatures, harm, being kidnapped, dangerous animals, and death.

One limitation of these early studies is that the data were based solely on parental report; thus, it is not entirely clear if the children perceived themselves to be anxious or fearful. There are some data to suggest that the actual incidence of fearful reactions in children may be much higher than parental estimates. A validity study, conducted as part of the study by Lapouse and Monk (1959), indicated that maternal reports underestimated fear prevalence by as much as 41%. Similarly, comparison of mothers' and children's responses on the Fear Survey Schedule for Children (FSSC) revealed only moderate agreement between the mothers' rank-ordered estimates of their child's fears with the child's own estimate (Bondy, Sheslow, & Garcia, 1985). Mothers discerned their child's "main" fear but could not accurately report on secondary fears. In addition, mothers' overall estimates of their children's general fearfulness were correlated only with their daughters' general fearfulness, not their sons'. Thus, data generated by parental report alone may underestimate the prevalence of fears, and mothers appear to be more accurate in judging fears of their daughters than those of their sons.

STABILITY OF CHILDHOOD FEARS

As noted in the introduction, at least some fearful reactions are not stable over time. For example, Eme and Schmidt (1978) assessed the stability of fears in fourth-grade children. One year later, 83% of the objects or events initially identified as fear producing were still regarded as fearful by the children. However, the stability of the relative rank of the feared events within the group was low ($r = .38$). That is, although after 1 year children still endorsed the same objects or events as fearful, the severity of the fear had changed. In another study of stability, phobic children aged 6–15 were reassessed 2 years after the initial evaluation. Only 7% still had a "severe phobia," while 80% were symptom free. Spence and

McCathie (1993) reported a 2-year follow-up of Australian primary school children (Grades 3 or 4 at Time 1 vs. Grades 5 or 6 at Time 2). Among those boys and girls who initially scored above one standard deviation on the FSSC-II (Fear Survey Schedule for Children–II), 40% of the boys and 36% of the girls remained highly fearful (above one standard deviation) 2 years later. In contrast, only 6.5% of the boys and 12.8% of the girls who were not fearful at Time 1 scored in the highly fearful range at Time 2. Thus, both the prevalence and the severity of fearfulness are somewhat unstable over time, and for any individual child, the absolute level of fearfulness can wax and wane in intensity.

In one of the few studies to examine fears in adolescents (Poulton et al., 1997), the frequency and content of specific fears remained relatively stable from ages 13 to 15. However, when viewed as a function of change in age, few adolescents who reported fears at age 13 also endorsed these fears 2 years later. One potential criticism of such research, however, is that age-related changes in specific fears should be examined in light of the overall decrease in general fearfulness that occurs with age (Gullone, 2000; Weems & Costa, 2005). For example, Weems and Costa (2005) examined developmental differences in childhood fears among a sample of youth ages 6–17 years; fears were assessed using the revised version of the FSSC. Relative to a consistent decrease in overall fearfulness/anxiety, social fears steadily increased with age and were the predominant fear among midadolescents (ages 14–17 years). Similarly, in a longitudinal study examining the continuity of fears between 7 and 18 years of age, an increase in social fears was found even after accounting for an overall decrease in general fear levels (Westenberg, Gullone, Bokhorst, Heyne, & King, 2007). Thus, although common across all ages, there appears to be an overall instability in the fears of most children: Fears that manifest at one point in time may not be present at another. The exception to this rule of thumb, however, may be for social fears during the teenage years.

THE MEDIA AND CONTEMPORARY FEARS IN CHILDREN

In addition to the changing developmental appropriateness of many fears (e.g., fear of monsters is common among young children but not adolescents), the influence of one-time (global or local) events may account, to some extent, for the instability of some fears. For example, after September 11, 2001, childhood fears of terrorist attacks were highly common (Burnham, 2007; Burnham & Hooper, 2008). In the 1990s, during which the AIDS epidemic received considerable media attention, fear of AIDS was commonly reported by children (Gullone, 2000;

Gullone & King, 1992). Indeed, television, together with the Internet and other forms of media exposure, has surely emerged as a salient factor in children's contemporary fears. In addition to images and information about one-time events, information about more gradual societal changes and pressures, such as racial tensions, global warming, and world hunger, can serve to shape children's fears. As such, TV-induced fears are not uncommon (Cantor & Nathanson, 1996; Korhonen & Lahikainen, 2008). While limiting a child's exposure to such media is likely the most effective way to prevent the development of such fears, the American Academy of Pediatrics Committee on Public Education (2001) also suggests that parental coviewing and involvement are effective ways to prevent the negative effects of TV on children.

One-time events and societal changes also provide evidence of the continual need to update children's standardized fear scales. For example, Burnham (2005) examined the prevalence of 20 contemporary fears added to the FSSC-II (Gullone & King, 1992) among U.S. children ages 7 to 18 years. Specific items are presented in Table 1.1. Findings indicated that six of the new items were among children's top 20 fears. In another study, the most common fears reported by children and adolescents between 2001 and 2004 were examined using the same measure (Burnham, 2009). In addition to the standard FSSC-II items, youth were asked to respond to an open-ended question at the end of the survey: "What else makes you or people your age afraid, scared, or fearful?" While the overall results revealed that many of the fears of today's children parallel those identified in previous decades, influence of current events on self-reported fears also was evident (e.g., anthrax, explosives, snipers, Osama Bin Laden, and obesity).

DEMOGRAPHIC CHARACTERISTICS OF CHILDREN'S FEARS

Although a few early studies failed to identify gender differences (Mauer, 1965; Miller, Barrett, Hampe, & Noble, 1971; Nalvern, 1970), the majority of studies consistently found that girls reported a greater number of fears compared to their male counterparts (e.g., Croake & Knox, 1973; Lapouse & Monk, 1959; Poulton et al., 1997; Scherer & Nakamura, 1968; Spence & McCathie, 1993). Parents also attribute a greater level of fear to their daughters (Bondy et al., 1985). The higher incidence of fears in girls appears to be a reliable finding, yet why this is so is yet to be determined (Graziano, DeGiovanni, & Garcia, 1979). One explanation is that young girls legitimately experience a greater range of fears than boys. The same observations have been made with adults (Agras,

TABLE 1.1　Contemporary Fear Items Added to the FSSC-II

Contemporary Fear	Rank (of 98 items)
Being raped	3
Drive-by shootings	13
Having to fight in a war	14
My getting pregnant or getting my girlfriend pregnant	16
Car wreck/car accident	18
Shootings	20
Drowning/deep water	22
Going to jail	24
Terrorist attacks	27
Cults/satanic worship/voodoo	30
People carrying guns, knives, weapons	31
Gangs	34
Violence near my home	35
Being poor	36
Crime	37
My parents losing their jobs	41
Being a failure/not successful	42
Riots	43
Robberies	45
Not having enough money	60

Source: Based on U.S. children ages 7–18 years (from Burnham, J. J., *Measurement and Evaluation in Counseling and Development, 38,* 78–91, 2005).

Sylvester, & Oliveau, 1969). Conversely, cultural or gender role expectations may have an impact on how boys and girls report fears and perhaps how parents judge them as well. Thus, girls may appear more fearful than boys based on a greater willing to *report* fears, not because they actually *have* more fears. Consistent with this notion, Muris, Meesters, and Knoops (2005) found that a child's sex had minimal influence on fear and anxiety, whereas gender role orientation (i.e., socialization toward the development of feminine or masculine behaviors) was a strong determinant of fear. In particular, femininity and a preference for girls' toys were positively associated with fear and anxiety, whereas the opposite relation was found for masculinity and a preference for boys' toys. Thus, it is likely that socialization factors serve to shape greater fear in at least some girls. As one example, maternal overly controlling parenting has been shown to predict fear levels among girls but not boys (Ollendick & Horsch, 2007). Further discussion of the role of overcontrolling parenting is presented in Chapter 4.

Although self-reports indicated gender differences, these differences were not always apparent when physiological reactivity was assessed. When taking tests, for example, test-anxious boys and girls showed equal increases in blood pressure and pulse rates, both reactions considered indicative of anxiety (Beidel & Turner, 1988). This would suggest that when measures of fear not under a child's voluntary control (e.g., heart rate) are used to determine fear, boys and girls react equally (at least in test-taking situations), even though boys may not admit their anxiety as readily as girls. Thus, these data support the hypothesis that social appraisal or role expectations influence the self-report of fear and self-report data collected from boys and girls. Although the gender difference finding appears to be reliable, the reason for the difference remains unclear.

Socioeconomic status (SES) has been associated with the frequency and intensity of children's fears. Among early studies, the most reliable variation related to fear content. Fears most often reported by children of lower SES included physical injury and events such as violence, whippings, drug dealers, switchblades, drunks, rats, and cockroaches, whereas children with higher SES were more likely to experience school-related fears and fear of heights, car accidents, train wrecks, and more abstract categories of stimuli such as poisonous insects or dangerous animals (Angelino, Dollins, & Mech, 1956; Nalvern, 1970; Staley & O'Donnell, 1984). When differences were examined in terms of the total number of fears rather than simply fear content, children with lower SES reported more fears. Graziano et al. (1979) concluded that children of lower SES perceived their immediate environment as much more hostile and fearful than children of higher SES, which probably reflected their reality. Fear survey schedules often equate total number of fears with fear intensity. Although someone who fears a variety of stimuli is likely to be more generally fearful than someone with a particularly circumscribed fear, the description of the stimuli (as illustrated by the type of fears listed) undoubtedly affects self-report. Children of lower SES reported highly specific categories of fears, while children of higher SES identified more abstract categories of fearful stimuli. Equating number of reported fears with fear intensity becomes even more problematic when children must freely generate the names of objects they fear rather than endorse a list of items. If indeed this level of abstraction, based on SES, were a reliable finding, the differences in fear intensity would be an artifact of the child's level of abstraction, not a valid measure of their overall fear state (Graziano et al., 1979). In summary, differences in childhood fears that are considered to be a function of SES are more likely to result from the vastly different type of environments in which the children live and perhaps the different kinds of educational experiences available to them.

Fears appear to occur relatively consistently across various racial and ethnic groups within the United States as well as internationally. For example, African American and Caucasian children fear similar objects and situations; most commonly, they are afraid that they or a family member will be harmed in some way (Neal, Lilly, & Zakis, 1993). Test anxiety also seems to be about equally common for the two groups (Turner, Beidel, Hughes, & Turner, 1993). However, these racial groups rank their fears in a slightly different order.

ETHNIC AND RACIAL DIFFERENCES IN FEAR

Research on the fears of Hispanic youth is somewhat mixed. Some data suggest Mexican children and Mexican American youth report more fears and worries than Caucasian children, including fears of the unknown and fears of danger or death (Varela, Sanchez-Sosa, Biggs, & Luis, 2008). Blakely (1994) also reported greater fears among Hispanic compared to non-Hispanic boys in the United States, although this study only included maternal reports of children's fears. In contrast, Owen (1998) did not find any differences in the frequency, content, or intensity of fears between Hispanic and non-Hispanic youth. Among all youth, danger, death, and injury were the most common fears reported.

Internationally, children in different countries, including Australia, China, England, and South Africa, endorse the same fears as American children (Dong, Yang, & Ollendick, 1994; Loxton, 2009). Specifically, 6 of the top 10 fears of Chinese children are also among the top 10 fears of Australian and American children. Similarly, young South African children commonly endorse fear of the dark and physical harm (Loxton, 2009). Fears of physical danger are common, as are fears of situations involving people (social fears such as giving an oral report or having to speak to an authority figure such as the school principal; Dong et al., 1994). The fears of Kenyan and Nigerian children, as assessed using the Fear Survey Schedule for Children–Revised (FSSC-R), also have been examined (Ingman, Ollendick, & Akande, 1999). Children from Nigeria had a significantly higher level of fear than children from Kenya. Furthermore, both groups appeared to have higher scores on the FSSC-R than those previously reported for British, American, Australian, or Chinese children. However, a direct statistical comparison was not conducted and perusal of the means does not clearly indicate if these differences would be statistically significant. In addition to an analysis by country of origin,

Ingman et al. (1999) examined differences based on religion, gender, and age. However, unlike results from other cultures, there was no difference in the level of fear reported by children and that reported by adolescents. Furthermore, there was no main effect for gender, which also is inconsistent with findings from the majority of other studies that used the same methodology and the same assessment instrument.

To explain these disparate findings, Ingman et al. suggested that the relatively poorer socioeconomic conditions of these African countries may create higher levels of stress and more fears. Furthermore, depending on where these children lived, they might face different everyday dangers. For example, white South African children more frequently reported fears related to gangs and crime, whereas black South African children more often reported fears of animals such as snakes and crocodiles, underscoring the influence of the immediate environment and living conditions (Muris, du Plessis, & Loxton, 2008). Either hypothesis would be consistent with earlier research on the difference in fears among children from various SES groups within the United States (Graziano et al., 1979). In addition, with respect to gender, the suspected cultural difference that might affect reports in the United States and Europe might not be operative in some African countries. For example, Kenyan children showed sex segregation in peer groups at an age later than American children (Ingman et al., 1999). Perhaps this later emphasis on gender-specific activities also relates to gender-typical behaviors such as willingness to endorse fears. In summary, the study of African children notwithstanding, across a variety of cultures and countries, younger children appear to be more fearful than adolescents, and girls express more fears than boys (Dong et al., 1994; Gullone & King, 1993, 2001, Poulton et al., 1997; Spence & McCathie, 1993). Fear, then, seems to be a universal childhood experience.

To more adequately examine the potential impact of ethnicity on childhood fears, Meltzer and colleagues (2008) examined the fears of almost 8,000 children (5–16 years of age) of various ethnic groups living in Great Britain. Further, since broad categories (e.g., Black, South Asian) are largely inadequate in capturing the significant differences in religious and cultural beliefs that exist within these groups, the authors examined ethnicity based on the specific region or country of origin. Results showed that all non-White groups were more likely than White children to have a fear of animals, with the highest likelihood for Bangladeshi and Black Caribbean children. Pakistani and Bangladeshi children were more likely than White children to have a fear of animals, the dark, or the natural environment. Also, Bangladeshi, Pakistani, and Black African children were more likely to have fears of imaginary or supernatural beings than White children (see Table 1.2 for odds ratios).

TABLE 1.2 Odd Ratios of Childhood Fear Categories Based on Ethnicity

Fear Category	White (n = 6993)	Black/ Caribbean (n = 112)	Black/ African (n = 76)	Indian (n = 176)	Pakistani (n = 170)	Bangladeshi (n = 52)
Animals	1.0	3.64***	2.28**	1.81**	2.75***	5.32***
Blood/ injection/ injury	1.0	1.42	1.04	1.15	2.23***	1.85
The dark	1.0	1.43	0.66	1.18	2.23***	2.24**
Dentists/ doctors	1.0	1.07	0.80	0.71	2.04**	0.78
Natural environment	1.0	0.80	0.66	0.52	25.55**	3.42**
Vomiting/ choking/ disease	1.0	1.03	.34	2.04**	1.62	1.68
Imagined/ supernatural beings	1.0	1.63	3.15**	1.29	3.86***	4.28***

Source: From Meltzer, H., Vostanis, P., Dogra, N., Doos, L., Ford, T., & Goodman, R., *Child: Care, Health and Development, 35,* 781–789, 2008.
*p < .05. **p < .01. ***p < .001.

These data suggest that children's fears differ to some extent across different ethnic groups within the same country, and that cultural factors play a specific role in the type and level of fears experienced.

AGE-RELATED DIFFERENCES IN FEAR

Of all the reported normative differences, the most important variable appears to be the age-related nature of children's fears. Not only are different fears more salient at different ages, but also there is a normal developmental sequence. In the most widely used research paradigm, investigators administer fear surveys to children of different ages or the children's parents and examine the natural course by extracting those fears most commonly reported for each age group. Fears that are typical at each age are presented in Table 1.3 (Ollendick, Matson, & Helsel, 1985).

Several studies have examined the relationship of age to specific objects or events. There is an overall decline in children's fears with increasing age and differing predominant fears associated with each age (Barrios et al., 1981). Young infants are frightened by loss of support;

TABLE 1.3   Typical Fears at Specific Ages

Age	Fears
Infancy	Loss of physical support Sudden, intense, and unexpected noises Heights
1–2 years old	Strangers Toileting activities Being injured
3–5 years old	Animals (primarily dogs) Imaginary creatures Dark Being alone
6–9 years old	Animals Lightning and thunder Personal safety School Death
9–12 years old	Tests Personal health
13 years and older	Personal injury Social interaction and personal conduct Economic and political catastrophes

sudden, intense, and unexpected noise; and heights. One- and 2-year-old children are afraid of strangers, toileting activities, and being injured. Preschool children fear imaginary creatures, animals, and the dark. Younger elementary school children are fearful of animals and natural events such as lightning and thunder and report concerns for their own safety. In addition, school- and health-related fears become common at this age. Older children are fearful of injury, economic and political catastrophes, and social rejection. In discussing their developmental nature, Miller (1983) reported that around age 2, fear of the toilet is common. Dogs seem to provoke the most fear at age 3, while fear of the dark is most salient at age 4. At age 6, school-related anxiety becomes predominant, then decreases somewhat in intensity until around age 11, when there is another increase. Fears of injury and social anxiety remain stable throughout the life span from the time of their first appearance in early childhood.

Similar to the universality of the range of fear, this developmental sequence also appears to cut across culture. Australian children aged 7–10 years had higher fear scores than those 11–14 or 15–18 years (Ollendick et al., 1985). Consistent with other studies, younger children reported more fears of animals, whereas older children reported more fears of social evaluation and psychic stress. Similarly, older adolescents (16- to 17-year-olds) in Spain had more social fears than early (12- to 13-year-olds) or midadolescents (14- to 15-year-olds; Garcia-Lopez, Ingles, & Garcia-Fernandez, 2008). All of these developmental studies consistently demonstrate that younger children fear specific events, particularly those related to physical danger, whereas older children are more likely to endorse social fears and general distress.

From Grades 3 and 4 to Grades 5 and 6, girls reported decreased fears related to getting sick, parental criticism or punishment, the dark, and bears or wolves (Spence & McCathie, 1993). Boys showed decreases in fear of physical injury, parental criticism, the dark, meeting a stranger, and being left at home with a babysitter. The only fear that increased to any significant degree was "giving a spoken report," which was more frequently endorsed when boys were in Grades 5 and 6 than when they were in Grades 3 and 4. There was an increase in overall fears, as well as social fears, in children initially assessed at age 13 and again 2 years later (Poulton et al., 1997), based on 17 fearful situations listed in the Diagnostic Interview Schedule for Children (DISC; Costello, Edelbrock, Kalas, Kessler, & Klaric, 1982). Interestingly, the primary fear at both ages was "speaking in front of the class," which increased in prevalence from age 13 to 15. The authors concluded that although the overall percentage of fears increased from Time 1 to Time 2, this was primarily due to the increase in social fears.

Among 4- to 6-year-old children, fears were reported by 71% of the sample, whereas nightmares were reported by 67.7% (Muris et al., 2000). These prevalence rates increased to 87% and 95.7%, respectively, among 7- to 9-year-olds and then returned to somewhat lower levels (67.8% and 76.3%, respectively) among 10- to 12-year-old children. Worry, however, showed a different developmental pattern. Whereas 46.8% of 4- to 6-year-olds reported the presence of worry, the percentage was significantly higher among 7- to 9-year-olds (78.3%) and continued at the same level in 10- to 12-year-old children (76.3%). This different developmental pattern for worry probably reflects children's emerging cognitive development.

This entire developmental hierarchy may, in part, be a function of cognitive development. Vandenberg (1993) compared fears of children with mental retardation to those of children with at least normal intelligence. The fears of children ages 4 through 12 years were classified into one of four categories (fears of imaginary things, fears of animals, fears of events in the physical world, and fears of events involving humans, such as being hurt by someone). Consistent with all other studies of fears in children with at least average intelligence, fears of imaginary things were more prevalent at the younger ages, whereas fears of people-related events were more prevalent at the older ages. A comparison of the fears of children with mental retardation and children of at least average intelligence at the same chronological age revealed significant differences in fear content. Specifically, children with mental retardation were significantly more fearful of imaginary things and significantly less fearful of people-related events than children of the same chronological age but with at least normal intelligence. However, fears of children between the ages of 7 and 12 who had mental retardation were not different from the fears of children between the ages of 4 and 6 with at least average intelligence. Thus, it appears that the fears of children with mental retardation are more likely to reflect their level of cognitive development than their chronological age.

In summary, fearful reactions in children are common and tend to follow a consistent developmental sequence. Younger children are more fearful of physical events and imaginary creatures, whereas older children and adolescents are more fearful of social events. Girls are more likely than boys to express fears, but it remains unclear if this is a true difference or if it reflects cultural and role expectation parameters. Furthermore, although most childhood fears dissipate over time, some fears, particularly those that are social in nature, tend to remain constant.

WHEN DOES FEAR BECOME A PROBLEM?

Even if fear appears extreme, some fearful reactions disappear within a short period of time. For example, children who move to a new neighborhood may be fearful of a new school and initially refuse to go. If they watch a horror movie, they may be afraid of "monsters" for a few nights. However, as noted, fears involving social situations may not dissipate without professional intervention (Achenbach, 1985; Davidson, 1993). Furthermore, some fears may interfere with a child's or a family's functioning so seriously that waiting for it to dissipate is not an option. If a child needs surgery, for example, a parent cannot wait to see if the child will outgrow a fear of needles or doctors. Therefore, the challenge to parents, educators, and health care professionals is to decide when a fear is a problem, even if it is not acknowledged as such by the child. Following are several points to consider when attempting to determine if a child's fear is abnormal and if intervention is necessary (Miller et al., 1974):

1. **Is the fear out of proportion to the demands of the situation?** Some anxiety before a final exam would be considered normal. However, fear so severe that it inhibits the ability to study, causes nausea or vomiting on the morning of the exam, or makes the child forget all the answers that were so well known the previous night would be considered out of proportion to the situation.

2. **Can it be explained or reasoned away?** A child may hear and even be able to repeat a logical explanation about why monsters do not exist, but that does little to calm the child's fear. Despite parents' best attempts to explain or demonstrate that there are no monsters under the bed, the child still refuses to sleep in his or her own room. Reason and logical explanations do not make the fear go away.

3. **Is the fear beyond voluntary control?** Fearful thoughts keep returning despite parental reassurances that these worries are groundless. Similarly, crying, rapid heart rate, or rapid respiration cannot be controlled, no matter how hard the child tries. If telling a child "Just relax" seems useless, the fear is probably beyond voluntary control.

4. **Does the fearful reaction persist unchanged for an extended period of time?** Many childhood fears disappear within several weeks or months after their first appearance. If a fear persists intensely for more than 6 months, intervention may be required (American Psychiatric Association, 1994). However, if the fear involves refusal to attend school or prevents needed surgery or other medical attention, treatment should be initiated much sooner.

5. **Does the fear lead to avoidance of the situation?** A child whose separation or social fears are so severe that he refuses to attend school, social activities, or family outings would be considered a problem. Similarly problematic would be refusing medical intervention because of a fear of needles.

6. **Is the fear unadaptive?** As noted, moderate anxiety may enhance performance and help a child adapt to a stressful situation. However, severe fear does not allow a child to adapt or perform. In fact, it prevents adjustment to a changing situation, hence the common expression "frozen with fear."

7. **Is the fear appropriate for the child's age or stage?** A 4-year-old child's fear of the dark and insistence on a night-light would not be considered a significant problem (although it may seem that way to other family members at the time). However, such fear could be problematic for a 12- or 13-year-old.

8. **Does the fear interfere with social, emotional, or academic functioning?** This can happen in multiple ways, and some of these may not appear to be obviously related. Excessive fears

and anxiety can result in limited academic achievement, poor self-concept, deficient social skills and inhibited knowledge of social role expectations, extensive social isolation, and restrictions in play activities, loneliness, and depression (e.g., Beidel, Turner, & Morris, 1999; Kovacs, 1998). Anxious children sometimes have difficulties falling or staying asleep, which can have a significant impact on their daytime functioning. Anxiety also can result in true physical symptoms, such as headaches or stomach pain. These somatic symptoms can further impair or limit functioning and can create or increase emotional distress. Impairment of functioning is probably the most important consideration when deciding if treatment is needed.

As noted, perhaps the most important question to consider is whether the child's fear interferes with school, social, or emotional adjustment. For example, does a child who is afraid of snakes but lives in New York City have a snake phobia? Although expressing a fear of snakes, the real question is this: Does the fear prevent the child from doing what he or she would like to do? What if the child's grandparents lived in the country and the child refuses to visit because the grandparents once told the child that they saw a snake in the backyard? In this situation, the fear might require treatment because it prevents the child from visiting and spending time with grandparents. However, if the child rarely goes to a place where snakes are found, treatment probably is not necessary.

Interestingly, there are few actual data on the relationship of self-reported fears and functional impairment. Among a sample of Australian adolescents, overall, there was a significant relationship between level of fear and level of functional interference as a result of that fear (Ollendick & King, 1994). Across the 10 most common fears (8 of which related to physical danger and 2 of which were social-evaluative fears), 13% reported that their fears created little or no distress, 26% indicated that their fears resulted in some distress, and 61% reported that their fears resulted in maximal distress. Reviewed in greater detail in Chapter 5, nighttime fears are a common cause of significant interference for both children and families, including sleep loss and daytime fatigue, daytime behavioral problems, and increased parental stress. Of course, most data are based solely on subjective measurement, and assessment of functional interference via more objective and standardized procedures would illuminate these relationships more clearly.

The crucial issue is whether the fear creates functional interference. Like adults, children have "work" to do; they must go to school, learn, and participate in activities such as athletic events, dance practice, or groups such as Boy Scouts or Girl Scouts. As often noted, the work of children is play. They should attend parties, have friends, and be comfortable with domesticated animals. The list goes on and on. Why is participation in these activities important? In addition to a general sense of self-efficacy, playing with other children, for example, teaches rules of social interaction. Without socialization experiences, children may not learn the social skills necessary to develop friendships and establish the foundation for adult social behavior. Also, a child without friends suffers from loneliness, which can lead to other social and emotional problems. Treatment is needed if a child's fears prevent participation in or enjoyment of activities appropriate for his peer group and last for more than a few months.

SUMMARY

Although the prevalence of fears and anxiety disorders in children appears to be common, research devoted to understanding and treating these childhood disorders remains sparse. This is unusual because the study of childhood fear was instrumental in the development of theories of general human behavior (Barrios et al., 1981). Freud's analysis of Little Hans's fear of horses (1909/1975) marked the beginning of child psychoanalysis. Approximately 11 years later, Watson and Rayner (1920) published the case study of Little Albert. This study gave credence to Watson's treatise on behaviorism and provided an empirical test of a conditioning theory of human behavior. Despite these auspicious beginnings, the scientific study of fears and anxieties in children made little progress for many years, perhaps because fears were considered normal and transient or because it was assumed that interventions developed for adults would also be useful for children. Whatever the reason, until the mid-1970s it was appropriate to say that childhood fears and anxieties remained in the "prescientific era" (Miller et al., 1974). Since that time, there has been an exponential increase in interest regarding childhood anxiety disorders; currently, there is fairly substantive literature regarding the clinical presentation of children's fears and anxieties. Many childhood fears represent a normal reaction to environmental events; others represent what are considered normal stages of development, and still others are clearly unadaptive. Many fearful reactions will dissipate fairly quickly, and the challenge to clinicians is to determine the difference between those that are part of normal development and thus transitory and those that are maladaptive, likely to be chronic, and part of a more significant anxiety disorder.

CHAPTER 2

An Introduction to Childhood Anxiety Disorders

Jack was so exited to be starting kindergarten. His older brothers all went to school; they always called him a "baby" because he did not go to school. But now, he was 5 years old and a kindergartner! Over the summer, he visited his new classroom and got new clothes and a new bag to carry art supplies. His stomach felt kind of funny that first day of school, and he had tears in his eyes as his dad walked him to his classroom. But, as his dad turned to leave, Jack burst into tears. He clung to his father's leg and cried: "Don't leave me." Jack's father hoped that this was jitters on the first day of school and not the beginning of anxiety-based school refusal.

Amami was 9 years old. Her parents were killed in an automobile accident, and she went to live with her grandparents. Her grandmother was recently diagnosed with breast cancer, and her grandfather was doing the best he could. Amami was frightened: What if grandpa got sick, too? Everyone said grandma was doing great, but what if she died? With no other relatives, who would care for her when her grandparents died? What if she (Amami) got sick, too? What if grandpa could not work any more? Would they have enough money? She could not get the thoughts out of her mind—causing her to lose sleep, have daily headaches, and have nails that were bitten to the quick. Amami could be suffering from generalized anxiety disorder.

Sixteen-year-old Linda did not know what was happening. She was in the shopping mall, laughing with her friends in the food court. Now, she was having a hard time breathing. Her heart was racing; she felt dizzy and sweaty. Her friends were laughing and did not seem to know anything was wrong. Linda was sure that she was having a heart attack. She did not know that in reality she had just experienced her first panic attack.

The "modern" conception of childhood anxiety disorders often is tied to the descriptive cases of Little Hans (Freud, 1909/1975) and Little Albert (Watson & Rayner, 1920). However, childhood fears apparently have a much longer history; even Hippocrates (460–370BC) described the existence of fears in young children (Treffers & Silverman, 2001). Yet, prior to the 19th century, little attention was paid to childhood fears until the introduction of the book *On the Mental Peculiarities and Mental Disorders of Childhood* (West, 1860, cited in Treffers & Silverman, 2001). Since the 1980s, there has been growing interest; in the last quarter century, there has been enormous attention to the substantive issues of the psychopathology and treatment of childhood anxiety disorder. In subsequent chapters, the different anxiety disorders are reviewed in detail. Here, an overview of issues that cut across specific disorders is provided as well as their most prevalent conceptual models. In addition, epidemiology, comorbidity, and functional impairment related to anxiety are reviewed. Finally, general assessment issues to assist clinicians in determining the presence and severity of anxiety disorders are presented.

GENERAL CONCEPTUALIZATION OF ANXIETY DISORDERS

With respect to clinical presentation, the tripartite model (Lang, 1968) has been the dominant conceptualization of anxiety disorders since its development. In this model, anxiety is conceptualized as consisting of three components: physiological responses, subjective distress (more recently referred to as cognition), and behavioral responses (see Figure 2.1). Each of these three dimensions is reviewed next.

Physical and Somatic Distress

The physical aspects of fear encompass virtually any bodily response, although among children, headaches and stomachaches (or butterflies in the stomach) are common complaints (e.g., Beidel, Christ, & Long, 1991). Other physical symptoms include sweating, difficulty breathing, hot or cold flashes, dizziness, numbness or tingling in the hands or feet, chest pains or nausea, muscle aches and pains, and vague physical complaints such as a sore throat. Even children without anxiety disorders report various physical symptoms when they become frightened (Beidel, Christ, et al., 1991), but children with anxiety disorders endorse a greater number of physical symptoms. They also endorse a significantly higher

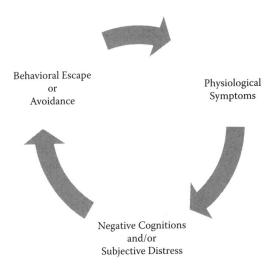

Behavioral Escape
or
Avoidance

Physiological
Symptoms

Negative Cognitions
and/or
Subjective Distress

FIGURE 2.1   Patterns of onset for childhood anxiety disorders. (Reprinted from Beidel, D. C., & Turner, S. M. (2005). *Child Anxiety Disorders.* New York: Routledge. With permission.)

frequency of specific physical symptoms, including hot flashes or cold chills, fear of fainting, and feeling like dying.

It is important to note that each anxious child does not experience every possible physical symptom or even any physical complaints. Among children, just like adults, certain symptoms appear to be characteristic of specific anxiety disorders. Children with panic disorder or separation anxiety disorder are significantly more likely to report somatic complaints than children with phobic disorders (Last, 1991). Among children and adolescents diagnosed with generalized anxiety disorder, social phobia, or separation anxiety disorder, virtually every child reported at least one physical symptom, and on average, children endorsed the presence of at least six symptoms (Ginsburg, Riddle, & Davies, 2006). The most common complaints were restlessness, stomachaches, blushing, heart palpitations, muscle tension, sweating, and trembling/shaking. Among children with obsessive-compulsive disorder (OCD), only 3.5% of children did not endorse the presence of any symptoms, and 67% of the sample reported five or more symptoms. Tension and feeling restless were most commonly reported. Even when two children have the same anxiety disorder, they will not necessarily have the same physical symptom profile, although headaches and stomachaches appear to cut across all disorders. Whereas one study reported higher rates of somatic complaints among girls than boys (Storch et al., 2008), another study did not find sex differences (Ginsburg et al., 2006). Older children are more likely than younger children to report somatic complaints (Ginsburg et al., 2006; Storch et al., 2008), and a greater number of somatic complaints is correlated with overall severity of anxiety (Ginsburg et al., 2006; Storch et al., 2008).

In addition to broad physical complaints, children react to specific anxious events or situations with heightened physiological responses. Rather than simply examining self-report of symptoms, some investigators have assessed physiological responses directly. Early studies focused on heart rate reactivity when infants were placed in situations designed to elicit anxious distress. These studies examined heart rate reactivity when infants were in a normal resting state and then when exposed to a fear-producing situation. Infants' heart rates accelerated when placed in several distressful situations: over the deep end of the visual cliff task (Schwartz, Campos, & Baisel, 1973), when in the presence of a stranger (Campos, Emde, Gaenbauer, & Henderson, 1975), or when approached by a stranger in an unfamiliar environment (Sroufe, Waters, & Matas, 1974). In other investigations, imagination of idiosyncratic, emotionally arousing scenes (as opposed to resting quietly) was accompanied by increases (over baseline) in heart rate and respiration in a group of asthmatic children (Tal & Miklich, 1976). Thus, even at an early age basic physiological reactivity patterns in infants and children are similar to adult patterns.

Initial comparative group studies of children focused on dental anxiety. Higher dental fear was associated with higher heart rate (Striker & Howitt, 1965; Venham, Bengston, & Cipes, 1977) and greater galvanic skin response (Melamed, Yurcheson, Fleece, Hutcherson, & Hawes, 1978). Similarly, children self-described as test anxious had significantly higher heart rates (averaging 95.5 beats per minute) when taking a test or reading aloud in front of a small audience in comparison to their non-test-anxious peers (averaging 90.7 beats per minute; Beidel, 1988). In addition, the heart rates of test-anxious children were consistently elevated across the 10-minute duration of the task. In contrast, non-test-anxious children had a brief, initial increase in heart rate that then returned to baseline by task completion. Increased heart rate and less heart rate variability were also present among children with separation anxiety disorder, overanxious disorder, panic disorder or panic attacks, or social phobia when compared to normal controls (Monk et al., 2001). Also, children with anxiety disorders had smaller overall changes in heart rate variability during baseline and during a carbon dioxide inhalation challenge task, although results were not reported separately by diagnosis.

These heart rate variability data are consistent with those reported for infants with behavioral inhibition (see Chapter 4) and for adults with social phobia (Turner, Beidel & Larkin, 1986). Furthermore, the data are consistent with data collected from rhesus monkeys when placed in anxious or stressful situations (Suomi, 1986). Specifically, when placed in an unfamiliar living colony, monkeys bred to be socially anxious reacted with increased heart rate reactivity that did not dissipate during their time in the unfamiliar situation. The consistency of these reactivity data (across rhesus monkeys, behaviorally inhibited infants, test-anxious children, and adults with social phobia) suggests that it may not be just initial increased heart rate but a persistent increase throughout the duration of the task (i.e., the individual does not habituate) that differentiates those with maladaptive anxiety from those without anxiety disorders. In summary, the presence of physical complaints and a pattern of physiological reactivity to anxious or distressing events appear common among children with fears and anxiety disorders.

Cognitive and Subjective Distress

In addition to somatic distress, cognitive features are a prominent part of the clinical syndrome of adult anxiety disorders; indeed, there has been much theorizing about the role of maladaptive cognitions in the etiology, maintenance, and treatment of anxiety states. In contrast, maladaptive and negative thoughts are not consistently part of the clinical presentation for all clinically anxious children, particularly those with phobic disorders (e.g., Beidel, 1991; Bogels & Zigterman, 2000; Kendall & Chansky, 1991; Treadwell & Kendall, 1996). One challenge when examining the cognitive component of childhood anxiety disorders is that cognition can be defined in different ways: as a specific process or as the outcome of that process (Alfano, Beidel, & Turner, 2002). We first examine the evidence that children with anxiety disorders demonstrate maladaptive cognitive processes. Following that, we examine the evidence that negative cognitions (thoughts) are part of the clinical presentation of anxiety disorders in children.

A simple information-processing model may be conceptualized as follows: A situation is encountered; information about the situation is encoded; finally, this information is interpreted. Depending on the manner in which this information is interpreted, anxiety may result. Based on a review of the information-processing model (Muris & Field, 2008), youth with anxiety disorders may manifest maladaptive encoding in the form of attention bias. They may also display interpretation deficits in the form of interpretation or memory biases. Potential attentional biases have been studied using either the Stroop task or a dot-probe task. In the Stroop task, attentional biases in anxious children would be demonstrated by longer latencies to name the color of a "threat" word (such as snake) than to a nonthreat word (such as sunshine). In the dot-probe task, children with anxiety disorders would exhibit faster latencies to detect a probe following threatening stimuli than nonthreatening stimuli. Overall, the literature in this area is sparse, and results were ambiguous. A meta-analysis (Bar-Haim et al., 2007) suggests that attentional biases exist among children who are highly anxious or who have anxiety disorders; however, some negative studies also exist (see Muris & Field, 2008, for a review).

Interpretation biases describe the tendency to associate threat with ambiguous or neutral stimuli. The existence of interpretation biases is usually assessed by counting the frequency with which negative interpretations are offered or by determining the amount of time or information required before a child or adolescent decides that a situation is dangerous or threatening. The available literature suggests that, in comparison to children with no disorder, children with anxiety disorders or high anxiety make more threatening interpretations of ambiguous external or internal cues and require less information about an event before deciding that the situation is dangerous (Muris & Field, 2008). Although virtually all of the research has been conducted in the United States and Europe, there is emerging evidence that this bias is cross cultural, existing among Chinese youth as well (Lu, Daleiden, & Lu, 2007).

There is little information that memory biases (selectively recalling memories that are congruent with an emotional state) are present in youth with anxiety disorders (Muris & Field, 2008), although a study of memory deficits in children with various anxiety disorders found that children with social phobia had significantly lower visual memory but not verbal memory scores on the Wide Range Assessment of Memory and Learning than children with generalized anxiety disorder or separation anxiety disorder (Vasa et al., 2007). These two memory tasks are considered "nonemotional" memory tasks. The reason for this finding is unclear, but the authors proposed that it may result from a primary dysfunction within the memory process of the brain or secondarily from biased attention processes. Another issue yet to be addressed is why this deficit was only found among children with social phobia and why it was present only during the visual, but not the verbal, memory task. Clearly, much more research is needed to understand the cognitive processes of youth with anxiety disorders before any general conclusions can be drawn.

Moving from conceptualizing cognition as a process to cognition as a specific thought, the manner in which negative thoughts are assessed appears to affect whether negative cognitions are detected. Whereas differences between anxious and nonanxious children are often found on self-report measures of cognition (e.g., Micco & Ehrenreich, 2009), these differences are not always replicated when thought listing or free-recall strategies are utilized. Clinically, children with phobic disorders (e.g., specific phobias or social phobias) report that when in a distressing situation, they are so overwhelmed by emotion that they are unable to think. Other times, when asked what they were thinking in the situation, preadolescent children will say "I don't know; I just felt scared." Among younger anxious children, it is not uncommon for emotional states (e.g., "I was thinking I was nervous") to be reported in place of specific thoughts (Alfano, Beidel, & Turner, 2006).

One explanation for the disparity between scores on a self-report inventory and free recall is that young children's cognitive abilities have not matured to the extent necessary to monitor their own cognitions (i.e., they do not yet have the ability to "think about thinking"). Thus, the presence of negative cognitions in children with anxiety disorders may be age related. Specific negative thoughts may not appear until adolescence, when youth reach the age at which they can monitor and report their thoughts.

To date, studies of basic cognitive development have had only limited impact on understanding the cognitive dimension of anxiety. For example, children's ability to reflect on their own mental activity increases with age and much of this increased reflection is verbal (Flavell, Green, Flavell, & Grossman, 1997). It is not until age 6 or 7 that children understand the concept of "talking to oneself" as a mental activity (Flavell, Flavell, & Green, 2001). Younger children are not capable of detecting, and therefore reporting, negative cognitions. Thus, as a result of basic cognitive immaturity, the cognitive dimension of anxiety may be absent in very young children; at the very least, it probably does not exist in the same format as that of older children, adolescents, and adults.

In addition to the basic question of their existence, the qualitative features of children's cognitions also are a function of physical and cognitive maturation (Graziano et al., 1979; Vasey, 1993). As noted, young children's fears tend to center on physical, external events (dogs, burglars). With increasing age, they develop the ability to consider the future, and their thoughts include catastrophic events and concerns about social evaluation. With cognitive maturity, fears and worry become more internal and abstract (Vasey, 1993), a reflection of cognitive development.

When negative cognitions and worry are possible, some children with anxiety disorders report excessive worries and catastrophic thoughts. Among children with specific phobia, these thoughts are central to the feared object or situation and usually occur when the child confronts or anticipates contact with the phobic stimulus. Before performing in a school play, for example, children may worry that they will forget their lines and make fools of themselves, even though they are well prepared. A child who fears dogs may worry that any dog, even a puppy, will bite, creating a need for stitches or hospitalization. Similarly, a child who is afraid of elevators may fear that the elevator will get stuck between floors, and that he will be unable to get out. Typical negative thoughts reported by anxious children include concerns that something may happen to their parents, that they themselves may be killed or kidnapped, that their home may be robbed, or that they may do poorly on a test. Thus, in most instances, thoughts reported by anxious children typically are specifically related to the feared object or event.

For some children, however, negative thoughts and worries are not specific to one object or situation. Rather, there are myriad worries, including those regarding future events ("Where will I work?" "Will I get into a good college?" "Will I get married?"); past behavior ("Did I make my best friend mad?"); social or academic abilities ("I'm not good enough."); their own health ("Do I have cancer?"); or the health of someone they love ("Were my parents in a car accident?"). Worries are usually associated with both common and uncommon probabalistic events or situations. Although worry may occur among children with any anxiety disorder, it is most often found in children with generalized anxiety disorder and separation anxiety disorder (Prins, 2001).

Despite the fact that worries appear to be common and often exist in children without anxiety disorders (Bell-Dolan, Last, & Strauss, 1990), to date, there is little research on childhood worry. One study (Last, Hersen, Kazdin, Orvaschel, & Perrin, 1991) assessed the construct of worry in children with anxiety disorders, attention deficit/hyperactivity disorder (ADHD), or children without a disorder. There was no difference in the content of the worries across diagnostic groups. However, children with anxiety disorders reported more frequent worrying than children in the other groups. Thus, it is the frequency and not the content of worry that seems to specifically characterize children with anxiety disorders, an outcome that is consistent with other studies of frequency and severity of worry in children with anxiety disorders (Bell-Dolan et al., 1990; Rachman & de Silva, 1978; see Chapter 6).

Relatedly, some youth suffer from obsessions, which are specific, persistent intrusive thoughts, often of an unrealistic nature. *Obsessions* are defined as recurrent and persistent thoughts, impulses, or images that are intrusive and inappropriate and cause marked distress (*Diagnostic and Statistical Manual of Mental Disorders, Fourth Edition* [DSM-IV]; American Psychiatric Association [APA], 1994, p. 418). Unlike worries, the content of obsessions is highly unusual. For example, a 14-year-old girl with obsessions had intrusive thoughts that her heart would stop beating, and that she would die. However, like worries, obsessions cannot be reasoned away, and the child's concern usually is much greater than the situation requires. Furthermore, children feel that they cannot control their thoughts. Children who express worry across many different spheres of functioning are most likely to be suffering from generalized anxiety disorder (see Chapter 6), and those with specific and recurrent cognitions likely suffer from OCD (see Chapter 11). Here, again, children, particularly young children, may not be able to clearly articulate specific thought content associated with their fears. Sometimes, children just describe a general feeling that something will go wrong, or that it is "just a feeling." Because children under age 12 may have trouble articulating their thoughts (Alfano et al., 2002), they may not be able to adequately or clearly express their concerns but only make vague statements about "not feeling well" or express physical complaints, such as presence of a headache.

In summary, the cognitions of anxious children may vary in content, severity, frequency, and controllability. Age and cognitive development appear to play a larger role in the cognitive dimension than in the expression of physical symptomatology. In some children, cognitions may be absent. Others may express vague concerns, and still others may have thoughts that resemble those found in adults with the same disorder.

Behavioral Response and Avoidance

In children, the behavioral dimension of anxiety is the easiest to observe, and behavioral signs may be the first indication that a child is fearful. As noted, developmental immaturity may alter the way that children express their anxiety—when compared to adults. Children may cry, cling to a parent, or have a tantrum in certain situations. Although less frequent, children sometimes demonstrate anxiety through disobedience or oppositional behavior. They may refuse to follow parental instructions if they involve contact with a feared event or object. In extreme cases, a child may refuse to go to school because of a school-related fear or separation fear (see Chapters 8 and 9) or refuse to speak because of social fears (see Chapter 10).

Other anxious behaviors may be less recognizable but just as debilitating (Beidel, Neal, & Lederer, 1991). Children may "play sick" to avoid taking a test. In school, children may avoid eye contact with the teacher in an effort to avoid being asked a question that requires a verbal reply. Other signs may include delay tactics such as taking an inordinate amount of time to prepare for an event (in the hope of missing it). Children with social fears may choose to stay inside and read rather than ride bicycles and play outside with other children. Children with performance anxiety may refuse to participate in school plays, recitals, or athletics (Beidel, 1991). In some cases, fearful situations or events occur suddenly and without warning. For example, on days when an oral report is expected, a child may "play sick" and stay home. If suddenly called on to read in front of the class, the child may still try to avoid the situation by "freezing" or refusing to speak. Thus, avoidance is another behavioral expression of fear.

Children also may express anxiety through repetitive behaviors or rituals (see Chapter 11). Common repetitive behaviors include extensive periods of time bathing, washing, cleaning, or performing repetitive acts (Thomsen, 2000). A child who fears that burglars will break into the house or that the house will catch fire sometimes spends hours checking door locks, windows, and oven knobs. Although these behaviors may appear nonsensical, they represent a child's attempt to decrease distress about feared events or consequences.

Escaping or avoiding situations often brings temporary relief from anxiety and fear. However, over time, avoidance or escape behavior actually strengthens anxiety and reinforces avoidance through the process of negative reinforcement (Mowrer, 1947). In the short term, avoidance or escape eliminates distress and acts as a powerful reinforcer. However, it also strengthens the avoidance response as well as the fear response (Mowrer, 1947). As is evident throughout this book, the psychosocial interventions with the most extensive empirical support are those that expose the child to the fearful situation or object. Thus, a primary goal of behavioral treatment is to reverse the pattern of avoidance or escape by exposure to the feared situations.

EPIDEMIOLOGY OF ANXIETY DISORDERS

As noted, anxiety disorders are common among children and adolescents. Table 2.1 depicts worldwide prevalence rates. As illustrated, rates increase with age (Costello & Angold, 1995; Essau, 2000), and disorders are more commonly reported among females than males (Beesdo, Knappe, & Pine, 2009; Essau, 2000). Initially, epidemiological studies focused on children who were school age or older. More recently, two epidemiological studies (Egger & Angold, 2006; Lavigne, LeBailly, Hopkins, Gouze, & Binns, 2009) investigated the presence of a subset of anxiety disorders in preschool children (see Table 2.1). As depicted in Figure 2.2, anxiety disorders in youth can occur at any time prior to adulthood, although the average age of onset differs depending on the particular diagnosis. The most frequently occurring disorders in children and adolescents are separation anxiety disorder, specific phobia,

TABLE 2.1   Prevalence Rates for Anxiety Disorders in Children and Adolescents

Study and Location	Age (years)	Range	Subject N	Prevalence
Germany				
Essau (2000)		12–17	1,035	8.6%
New Zealand				
Fergusson, Horwood, & Lynsky (1993)	15		961	12.8%
McGee et al. (1990)	15		943	10.7%
McGee, Feehan, Williams, & Anderson (1992)	18		930	12.4%
Newman et al. (1996)	21		961	20.2%
China				
Leung et al. (2008)	13.8		541	16.4%
United States				
Costello et al. (1988)		7–11	789	15.4%
Costello, Stoudhamer-Loeber, & DeRosier (1993)		12–18		17.7%
Costello et al. (after 1996)	9, 11, 13		4,500	5.7%
Egger & Angold (2006)[a]		2–5	307	8.9%
Kashani et al. (1987)		14–16	150	8.7%
Lavigne et al. (2009)[a]	4.4		796	0.8%

Source: Modified from Beidel, D. C., & Turner, S. M. (2005). *Child Anxiety Disorders.* New York: Routledge. With permission.

[a] These studies assessed only for generalized anxiety disorder and separation anxiety disorder.

and social phobia (Beesdo et al., 2009). Panic disorder and agoraphobia are rare in childhood but increase in prevalence during adolescence.

Anxiety disorders in children rarely occur in isolation (e.g., Costello & Angold, 1995). Many children diagnosed with one anxiety disorder often display symptoms of other anxiety disorders. Furthermore, many children meet criteria for a second anxiety disorder and sometimes even more, whereas others may suffer from a different secondary emotional or behavioral disorder. In Table 2.2, rates of comorbidity from several studies are presented. Most commonly, anxiety disorders often are comorbid with depressive disorders or externalizing disorders. Rates of depression and anxiety comorbidity ranged from 15.9% to 61.9% across

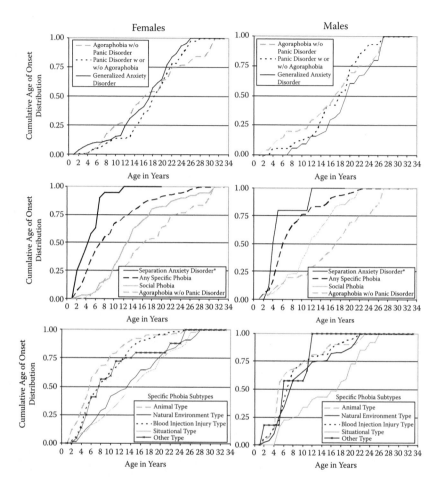

FIGURE 2.2   Patterns of age of onset of anxiety disorders (EDSP; N = 3,021). (Note: In phobias, impairment was required among subjects aged 18 years or older. *Separation anxiety disorder was only assessed in a subsample at Time 1.) (Reprinted from Beesdo, Knappe, & Pine, Anxiety and Anxiety Disorders in Children and Adolescents: Developmental Issues and Implications for DSM-V, 42. *Psychiatric Clinics of North America*, Vol. 32/3. © 2009, with permission from Elsevier.)

various studies (Brady & Kendall, 1992). Anxiety frequently is present prior to the onset of depression (Strauss, Last, Hersen, & Kazdin, 1988). In addition, when both disorders are present, the overall symptom picture and functional impairment are more severe.

Comorbidity rates for anxiety and behavioral disorders such as ADHD or ODD are lower than for anxiety and other internalizing

TABLE 2.2 Comorbidity Rates for Samples of Children Diagnosed
With a Primary Anxiety Disorder

Study	Age of Sample (years)	Overall Percentage With Comorbidity	Type and Percentage of Comorbidity
Essau et al. (2000)	2–17	51	None: 49
			Anxiety: 48
			Depression: 30.2
			Somatoform: 26.6
			Substance use: 11.5
Ginsburg & Silverman (1996)	6–17		
Hispanic subsample		91	
Caucasian subsample		83	
Kendall et al. (2001)	9–13	79	None: 21
			Anxiety: 49.7
			Depression: 4.6
			Externalizing: 25.4
Silverman, Saavedra, & Pina (2001)	7–16	67	None: 33
			Anxiety: 53.2
			Depression: 4.8
			Externalizing: 9.7
Kendall et al. (2010)	7–17	79	None: 21
			Anxiety: 78
			Depression: 5
			Externalizing: 21

Source: Modified from Beidel, D. C., & Turner, S. M. (2005). *Child Anxiety Disorders.* New York: Routledge. With permission.

disorders, ranging from 16.7% to 36.4% (Last, Hersen, Kazdin, Finkelstein, & Strauss,1987). An important issue, one discussed in the ensuing chapters, is the need to differentiate between children who have two distinct disorders and those who have overlapping symptoms but only one disorder. For example, if anxious children refuse to do as their parents' request because of their fear, their behavior may appear oppositional. However, in this case, the oppositionality is part of a pattern of avoidance and fear, not an entirely separate disorder.

Comorbid disorders may in part be a function of age. Specifically, several studies report that comorbidity is more often found among older children (Stavrakaki, Vargo, Boodoosingh, & Roberts, 1987;

Strauss et al., 1988). Rates of comorbidity also vary across the specific anxiety disorders. In one study, children with a primary diagnosis of separation anxiety disorder had higher rates of comorbidity than children with primary social phobia or primary generalized anxiety disorder (Verduin & Kendall, 2003). Overall, 47% of this sample had a comorbid diagnosis of specific phobia, and this disorder was more common among those with primary separation anxiety disorder or primary generalized anxiety disorder than among those with primary social phobia. In contrast, comorbid mood disorders were more common among those with primary social phobia or generalized anxiety disorder than children with separation anxiety disorder; overall, boys were more likely to have comorbid diagnoses of attention deficit disorder and oppositional defiant disorder than girls.

It is unclear if the presence of comorbid disorders has an effect on treatment outcome. Rapee (2000) reported that comorbid externalizing symptoms did not affect treatment outcome for children and adolescents with anxiety disorders. However, symptoms of secondary depression did appear to predict treatment response among another group of children with anxiety disorders (Berman, Weems, Silverman, & Kurtines, 2000). Similarly, the presence of comorbid disorders (not just symptoms) does not appear to affect treatment outcome for the primary (targeted) disorder (e.g., Beidel et al., 2007; Kendall, Brady, & Verduin, 2001; Rapee, 2003).

As with epidemiological prevalence data, specific comorbidity rates and their effect on treatment outcome are reviewed in the chapter for each specific anxiety disorder, where other issues, such as how to determine the presence of secondary disorders, also are addressed. The issue is raised here to alert the reader that children often present with myriad fears as well as other emotional and behavioral difficulties.

LONGITUDINAL COURSE OF ANXIETY DISORDERS

In addition to their substantial prevalence, further evidence that anxiety disorders in children merit serious attention comes from several longitudinal studies. Although many children with specific phobia appear to recover from or outgrow their diagnosis (Agras, Chapin, & Oliveau, 1972; Ollendick, 1979), the long-term outcome for other types of anxiety disorders is less positive.

Most of the available data indicate that anxiety disorders (perhaps with the exception of specific phobias) are chronic conditions with diagnostic retention rates ranging from 20% to 50%, depending on the age of the child at the time of the initial diagnosis, the specific disorder, and the length of the follow-up (Bernstein, Hektner, Borchardt, & McMillan, 2001; Cantwell & Baker, 1989; Cohen, Cohen, & Brook, 1993; Costello & Angold, 1995; Feehan, McGee, & Williams, 1993; Keller et al., 1992; McGee et al., 1992). For example, among children with a lifetime diagnosis of overanxious disorder (now called generalized anxiety disorder) or separation anxiety disorder, lifetime estimates indicated that the cumulative probability of remaining ill 8 years later was 46% (Keller et al., 1992), suggesting a moderate level of continuity, beyond what would be expected by chance alone. Across a 6-year period of adolescence, girls have more anxiety symptoms than boys, and the general course of the various disorders can be characterized as a decrease in symptom severity from late childhood through early adolescence, followed by symptom stability (Van Oort, Greaves-Lord, Verhulst, Ormel, & Huizink, 2009). For generalized anxiety disorder, social phobia, or separation anxiety disorder, symptoms increase again slightly during middle adolescence. This same increase occurs in late adolescence for panic disorder and OCD. The reasons for this particular trajectory are not clear, but life stressors are known to exacerbate anxiety symptoms in general. In this particular case, the timing of these symptom exacerbations may be related to developmental and life transitions, such as from childhood to adolescence and then from adolescence to adulthood (Van Oort et al., 2009).

Other studies indicated moderate stability for the later presence of an anxiety disorder, even though it might not be the same as the initial diagnosis (e.g., Cantwell & Baker, 1989). In a prospective study, 82% of children initially diagnosed with an anxiety disorder did not have the same disorder 3–4 years later (Last, Perrin, Hersen, & Kazdin, 1996). However, 30% had developed a new psychiatric disorder, including 15.5% who developed a new anxiety disorder, 13.1% a new depressive disorder, and 7.1% an externalizing disorder such as ADHD, oppositional defiant disorder, or conduct disorder. In the most extensive longitudinal, epidemiologic study (including 906 participants), the diagnosis of separation anxiety disorder during childhood predicted the presence of separation anxiety disorder in adolescence (Bittner et al., 2007). Overanxious disorder in childhood predicted the presence of overanxious disorder, panic attacks, depression, and conduct disorder in adolescence, whereas the presence of generalized anxiety disorder in childhood predicted the presence of conduct disorder in adolescence. Social phobia in childhood predicted the presence of overanxious disorder, social phobia, and ADHD disorder in adolescence.

Clearly, although some children recover from an anxiety disorder, to date it is not clear when or how such a recovery occurs; clinically, it appears that spontaneous remission may be negatively correlated with severity of the anxiety symptoms at baseline. When symptoms do not remit at follow-up, they tend to take one of two forms. For one sub-group, the same disorder that was present at baseline is still present at the follow-up assessment. This is referred to as *homotypic continuity* (Beesdo et al., 2009). A second type of continuity, *heterotypic continu-ity*, refers to people at follow-up who do not have the same disorder as at baseline but have a related disorder. Therefore, children who continue to suffer from a disorder, although not necessarily with the same initial diagnosis, are considered to have cases of heterotypic continuity. When both forms of continuity are considered, it is clear that a substantial percentage of youth initially diagnosed with an anxiety disorder will continue to suffer from an emotional disorder at follow-up. Again, the factors that predict why the form of the disorder changes in some chil-dren but not others are not clear.

To summarize, anxiety disorders in youth appear to be stable over substantial periods of time. Although rates are somewhat variable (likely the result of differing diagnostic practices and sample variances), about 40–50% of children exhibit homotypic continuity across follow-up peri-ods ranging from 6 months to 6 years. In addition, a sizable percentage of children (ranging from 25% to 30%) exhibit heterotypic continuity. As noted, it is not clear if the change in diagnosis reflects a change in diagnostic practices or developmental maturation or an actual change in the form of the disorder. In any case, the important factor is that the child still suffers from an anxiety disorder. Another group of children (about 20–25%) has no disorder at follow-up. Overall, these data sug-gest that, with the exception of specific phobias, there is moderate tem-poral stability for anxiety disorders and a high level of stability for the continuing presence of some type of anxiety state.

As noted, one criterion for the determination of an anxiety disorder is that the fears or anxiety must result in functional impairment. Often, it is difficult to determine exactly how to make this determination. If a child expresses anxiety in social situations but has a "best friend," is that child impaired? Exactly how few friends are necessary for one to be considered impaired in social functioning? Although these issues must be considered by the clinician during the individual diagnostic process, there is substantial evidence that, as a group, children with anxiety dis-orders suffer from social and academic impairment. In comparison to their peers, children with anxiety disorders often are socially neglected by their peers (Strauss, Lahey, Frick, Frame, & Hynd, 1988). Specifically, children without psychiatric disorders were significantly more likely to be nominated by their peers as "most liked," and children with conduct disorders were significantly more likely to nominated as "least liked." Children with anxiety disorders received few nominations of either type, suggesting that they had limited social impact on their classmates. They were not most liked or least liked. Rather, it was as if they were invisible to other children in the classroom.

Social impairment also exists among adolescents with anxiety disorders (Essau, Conradt, & Petermann, 2000). Across a 4-week period, 32% reported impairment in their social contacts. In addition, 35% reported impaired school performance, and 41% reported impairment in their leisure activities. Similarly, as depicted in Table 2.3, the frequency and severity of anxiety disorders in adolescence are significantly related to negative outcomes at age 21 (Woodward & Fergusson, 2001). Specifically, as the number of anxiety disorders at ages 14–16 increased, so did the risk for the presence of anxiety disorders, major depression, and illicit drug dependence at age 21. Rate increases were highest for youth with three anxiety disorders and decreased linearly for those with two disorders and then one disorder. To illustrate, for youth with three or more anxiety disorders in midadolescence, rates of anxiety disorders at age 21 were 3.5 times higher, depression was 2.0 times higher, and illicit drug use was almost 4 times higher than for youth without anxiety disorders. Anxiety disorders take a toll on the family and society as well (Bodden, Dirksen, & Bögels, 2008). When families recorded their various costs of living over a 2-week period (psychological and medical care, daycare, afterschool care, productivity losses due to parental work absence, loss of household activity time or leisure time, children's school absences, and out-of-pocket expenses), costs of families in which a child was being treated for an anxiety disorder were more than 20 times higher than the costs of families in the general population (12% of whom had a psychiatric diagnosis including anxiety disorders).

TABLE 2.3   Relationship of Adolescent Anxiety Disorders to Social Impairment in Adulthood

No. of Anxiety Disorders in Adolescents	Percentage of Anxiety Disorders in Adulthood	Percentage of Depression in Adulthood	Percentage of Illicit Drug Dependence	Percentage Entering the University at Age 21
0	17.4	28.5	3.0	34.2
1	28.8	38.2	4.8	26.0
2	43.7	49.2	7.5	19.0
3	62.0	60.5	11.2	13.4

Source: Reprinted from Essau, C. A., Conradt, J., & Petermann, F., *Journal of Clinical Child Psychology, 29,* 221–231, 2000; from Beidel, D. C., & Turner, S. M. (2005). *Child Anxiety Disorders.* New York: Routledge. With permission.

In summary, anxiety disorders create significant impairment across various domains of life functioning. Furthermore, these impairments are evident from an early age and continue throughout adolescence and early adulthood. Longer follow-up studies currently are not available except for several studies of shy children, which are addressed in the chapter on social phobia (Chapter 10).

OVERVIEW OF TREATMENTS FOR ANXIETY DISORDERS

Overall, behavioral, cognitive-behavioral, and pharmacological interventions have received the most empirical support in the treatment of childhood anxiety disorders (Reinblatt & Riddle, 2007; Silverman & Ollendick, 2005; Silverman, Pina, & Viswesvaran, 2008). Although discussed briefly here, specific outcomes are examined for each anxiety disorder in its respective chapter. Overall, an evidence-based medicine review (Compton et al., 2004) identified medium-to-large effect sizes for symptom reduction across primary outcome measures. There are now several intervention trials that include comparative and combination study designs. These outcome data confirm the efficacy of these individual interventions but do not provide consistent support for the use of combination therapies.

Several treatment issues cut across specific diagnostic categories. These issues include the need to educate parents and children about the particular disorder and expectations regarding treatment, familial psychopathology, parental concerns about the intervention, and specific treatment modifications based on developmental age. Although many of these issues have not been addressed empirically, substantial clinical experience suggests that they contribute to a successful treatment outcome.

Despite the particular diagnosis, or the particular intervention, treatment outcome will be significantly enhanced if both the child and the parent understand, to the best of their ability, the specific disorder and the proposed intervention. Prior to initiating treatment, the clinician should spend time educating the family about the disorder, including its etiology, demographics, and clinical presentation. The discussion should also address the current available pharmacological and psychosocial treatment outcome data, an overview of the proposed treatment package, the details of the proposed treatment package (including specific procedures and the time commitment), and an assessment of motivation to participate in the treatment program. Some of these issues may be covered in an informed consent procedure, but families often are ill-informed about the particular aspects of the child's disorder, and thus the relevance of the intervention often is unclear. A particular challenge for treatment providers is parental acceptance of a specific intervention. To date, two investigations (Brown, Deacon, Abramowitz, Dammann, & Whiteside, 2007; Young et al., 2006) suggest that parents prefer behavioral or cognitive-behavioral treatment approaches rather than pharmacological interventions. This preference is relative as both forms of treatment are perceived positively. However, the greater preference for psychological treatments may have an impact on families' willingness (e.g., motivation or compliance) to participate in a particular form of intervention or a randomized clinical trial. As illustrated in Figure 2.3, among parents who refused to participate in a randomized clinical trial comparing pharmacological treatment or behavior therapy for social phobia, the possibility of being assigned to the pharmacological treatment arm was the most common reason for study refusal—significantly more common than child refusal, distance from the clinic, or time involved in the study. Treatment preference may also affect the type of families who agree to allow their children to participate in randomized controlled clinical trials.

Children with anxiety disorders (or any other disorder) rarely independently seek treatment. Rather, adults recognize the child's distress and seek intervention on their behalf. Thus, children may have less motivation for treatment, and establishing a therapeutic relationship may be a formidable task. The emphasis on the need for a strong therapeutic relationship differs according to the theoretical basis of an intervention, but the need for cooperation and motivation cuts across intervention

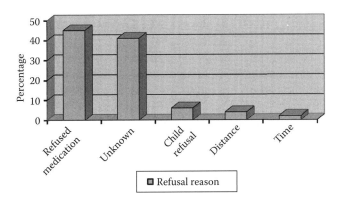

FIGURE 2.3 Reasons parents refuse participation in a randomized controlled trial. (Modified from Young et al., 2006. Pretreatment attrition and childhood social phobia: Parental concerns about medication. *Journal of Anxiety Disorders, 20,* 1133–1147.)

type. A meta-analysis examining treatment outcome for child and adolescent interventions identified several factors affecting the formation and
strength of the therapeutic relationship (Shirk & Karver, 2003). These
factors included patient variables, intervention type, or research design
characteristics. Overall, there was only a modest correlation between the
therapeutic relationship and treatment outcome ($r = .24$), similar to that
found for adult patients. Patient factors, mode of intervention, structure
of the intervention, and the context in which treatment was delivered
(individual, group, or family) did not play a role in moderating the effect
of treatment outcome. Interestingly, a strong therapeutic relationship
was important for obtaining a positive outcome when children presented
with externalizing, rather than internalizing, disorders. Thus, these data
indicate that although a positive therapeutic relationship plays a modest
role in treatment outcome, it is not the most important factor for positive
treatment outcome for childhood anxiety disorders.

In Chapter 4, we examine the important role of familial pathology
on the etiology of childhood anxiety disorders. How does the presence
of parental psychopathology have an impact on a child's treatment program? In some forms of behavioral intervention, for example, parents
may have to assist in their child's homework assignments (e.g., a parent
may have to take the child to the park to interact with other children).
However, if the parent suffers from agoraphobia, the ability to assist
the child may be impaired. Thus, treatment may fail because homework
assignments cannot be carried out as prescribed.

Some parents of anxious children have a tendency to be cautious, to
avoid taking risks, and to reinforce avoidance (Barrett, Rapee, Dodds,
& Ryan, 1996; see Chapter 4). Particularly for behavioral interventions,
such behavior would be counterproductive to therapeutic procedures that
attempt to place the child in contact with fearful or anxiety-producing
situations. Sometimes referred to as the *protection trap* (Silverman &
Kurtines, 1996), clinicians need to work with parents to assist them
in understanding that (a) exposure to the feared situation is necessary
if intervention is to be effective; (b) like adults, children's anticipatory
anxiety often is more intense than anxiety actually experienced when
in the distressing situation; and (c) the anxiety experienced during the
exposure sessions is rarely as intense as what parents imagine (particularly if a graduated procedure is used). In the last case, inviting the parents to observe an exposure session (through a one-way mirror or via a
videotape) will help the parent understand the intervention and decrease
their concerns.

Within each specific chapter, the literature on effective interventions
for that disorder is reviewed. Here, however, it is important to acknowledge the overall state of the literature and point out some avenues for

future directions. In the 1990s, there were few randomized, controlled trials. There were many case studies, single-case designs, and a wealth of clinical literature that suggested that both medication and behavioral interventions should be effective. Since that time, there has been a significant increase in the number of published controlled trials, both for pharmacological and for psychosocial interventions. Yet, there are still many basic issues that are unresolved. First, there is the intriguing issue that many children have a positive response to interventions that were designed as placebos. Educational support groups (designed as a psychological placebo) also have been reported to be effective for children with phobic disorders (Silverman & Berman, 2001) but not necessarily for other diagnostic categories, such as social anxiety disorder or OCD. Furthermore, the issue of functional impairment must also be considered when evaluating the effect of a placebo. Even among a group of children, all of whom meet diagnostic criteria for a disorder, the degree of functional impairment often ranges from mild to severe. It may be that those children who are less severely impaired may benefit from a less-specific intervention strategy, such as an educational support group. In support of this hypothesis, classes such as those offered by the Dale Carnegie Institute often are useful for adults who have mild speech anxiety but are rarely effective for those with severe social phobia. Therefore, level of impairment or severity of the disorder might provide an explanation for the placebo response rates reported in the empirical literature. Finally, it should be noted that few studies have attempted to examine the "permanence" of behavioral change as a result of placebo. It may be that placebo effects wear off, returning the child to his or her previous state of distress.

Few studies to date have examined issues of predicting treatment outcome and prescribing treatments. With respect to predicting treatment outcome, demographic variables such as age and gender are an obvious important consideration, although to date the findings in this area are unclear (see Silverman & Berman, 2001, for a review). There are some emerging data addressing factors that moderate or mediate treatment outcome (see individual chapters), but to date, the data are inconsistent.

The issue of prescribing treatments in some ways evolves from an understanding of the factors that affect treatment outcome. In addition, it requires an acknowledgment that certain behaviors, such as social withdrawal or school refusal, represent symptomatic behaviors that may be the product of different etiologies. Social withdrawal, for example, may be an indication of social phobia, depression, early-onset schizophrenia, or perhaps just a temperamentally inhibited disposition. Obviously, these conditions require different types of interventions.

Some interventions for children with social phobia include social skills training as this has been established as an element of the clinical presentation of the disorder. Other children may have social skills deficits as a result of oppositional disorders or pervasive developmental disorders such as autism or Asperger's disorder. Although all these children have difficulties with social skills, the specific deficits often differ markedly; thus, the content of the intervention needs to be much different, even if the specific strategy (i.e., social skills training) remains the same. School refusal is another behavior that can result from various etiologies and for whom prescriptive treatments may be appropriate (Kearney & Silverman, 1999). In this case, the intervention differs depending on the specific factors that lead to the problematic behavior (e.g., phobic reaction, tangible reinforcement).

Other factors, such as parental pathology, treatment credibility, and illness severity, may affect treatment efficacy but have not yet received adequate attention in the scientific literature (Silverman & Berman, 2001). Additional areas of needed intervention research include the need for moving beyond wait-list control conditions, improving our measurement strategies, increasing attention to developmental issues, and increasing minority representation, among many others (Silverman et al., 2008). Clearly, there is much work yet to be done.

Finally, there is the issue of treatment efficacy versus treatment effectiveness. Some researchers defined effectiveness in terms of the transfer of an intervention from the research clinic to a community clinic setting (e.g., Weisz, Donenberg, Han, & Weiss, 1995). One issue that has plagued the transfer of empirically supported treatments is the belief that patients in research settings are not representative of children in traditional outpatient clinics. However, examination of the demographics of children with anxiety disorders (e.g., Southam-Gerow, Weisz, & Kendall, 2003) revealed few differences between children recruited in a research clinic and children who sought treatment in a community-based service clinic. In fact, there were no group differences on any measure of internalizing symptomatology, although community clinic patients had more externalizing symptoms and diagnoses than patients in the research setting. Among the numerous demographic variables examined, only income and family structure differentiated the groups. Specifically, those treated in the community setting were more likely to be from lower-income, single-parent families. Although differences in treatment outcome were not examined in this report, the available data suggest that, at least in terms of patient characteristics, children with anxiety disorders treated in research clinics are similar to those seeking treatment in community service settings.

Another way to define effectiveness is in terms of the clinical impact of the intervention on the child's or adolescent's life functioning. That is, even if an intervention decreases the self-report of a presenting problem (such as anxiety), does this symptom decrease translate into enhanced daily functioning? For example, if an intervention results in decreased self-report of anxiety about attending school, does enhanced functioning also occur (the child joins afterschool activities requiring her to stay after school rather than leaving the school grounds as soon as possible)? Currently, data regarding the effectiveness of empirically supported treatments are lacking and should be targeted for future research.

SUMMARY

In summary, anxiety disorders appear to be prevalent in the general child population. The characteristic clinical presentation of these disorders includes physical symptoms, subjective (cognitive) distress, and behavioral avoidance. Unlike the common childhood fears discussed in Chapter 1, anxiety disorders represent a more serious psychological disorder; often, they do not dissipate over time without appropriate intervention. Therefore, contrary to the old adage—they will grow out of it—many children with an anxiety disorder do not grow out of their disorder. Moreover, these severe and chronic conditions also have the potential to significantly impair academic, emotional, and social development. Thus, as the understanding of these disorders has evolved, the need to recognize and effectively treat these conditions has become more salient. In this chapter, overarching considerations with respect to the conceptualization, assessment, and treatment of anxiety disorders in children and adolescents have been presented. Furthermore, areas of intervention in which more research is necessary have been highlighted. Following the chapters on developmental considerations and etiology, the remainder of this book is devoted to the various child and adolescent anxiety disorders, their clinical presentation, and effective intervention strategies.

CHAPTER 3

Developmental Considerations

Sara is 7 years old. She speaks only to her mother, father, and brother. At home, she is a happy, even boisterous, child. However, when anyone other than her immediate family is present (even her grandparents), she runs and hides. Even at 1 year of age, Sara would cry if others tried to make eye contact. She often cries now if others try to talk to her. Sara sometimes carries a small stuffed animal, and on rare occasions, the animal will "talk" aloud in a voice that is very different from Sara's own voice.

At age 12, Sara is considered "shy" at school. She has only one close friend and does not make eye contact with other students or teachers. Her grades are excellent—her teachers do not require her to give presentations in front of the class. She is allowed to give them privately to the teacher after school. Her social interactions are limited. She will go to her friend's house but will not "sleep over" if other girls are there.

Sara is now 17. She has never had a date. She did not go to her high school prom. Despite her academic record, which resulted in scholarship offers from several large universities, she has chosen to attend a small, local college "because of the people." She did not feel comfortable when she toured the dorms, and she wanted to remain at home. She volunteers with her church, if her mother is there, and spends hours on the Internet "chatting" with people she does not know. Her career goal is to be a Web page designer; she feels that she can do this from home.

As noted in the previous chapters, anxiety disorders exist at all ages. The currently accepted diagnostic system, the *Diagnostic and Statistical Manual of Mental Disorders, Fourth Edition, Text Revision* (*DSM-IV-R*; American Psychiatric Association [APA], 2000) considers childhood anxiety disorders as downward extensions of adult anxiety disorders (Schniering, Hudson, & Rapee, 2000). Only separation anxiety disorder is listed in the section "Disorders First Diagnosed in Infancy, Childhood and Adolescence," suggesting something unique about this disorder to the time of childhood. Otherwise, anxiety syndromes commonly diagnosed in children are found in the general section on anxiety disorders in the manual, in recognition that the disorders exist across all ages. However, as an acknowledgment to developmental immaturity, the criteria sometimes contain specific descriptors for how the disorder might manifest itself in children. Furthermore, as illustrated by the clinical vignettes that opened this chapter, even within childhood and adolescence, the clinical expression of a particular disorder may vary depending on the child's particular age. At each age, Sara met diagnostic criteria for social phobia even though the outward expressions are different. In this chapter, issues of physical, cognitive, and behavioral maturation as they relate to the expression of anxiety disorders in children are explored.

CLINICAL PRESENTATION

As noted, only separation anxiety disorder is included in the *DSM-IV-TR* section, "Disorders First Appearing in Infancy, Childhood and Adolescence," and is considered to have an onset solely in childhood. However, the diagnostic criteria for several other anxiety disorders do contain descriptors of how the disorder might be expressed in youth. For example, children often display fear differently from adults. The diagnostic criteria for social or specific phobia acknowledge these differences by noting that children may display excessive fear and distress by crying, tantrums, freezing, or clinging, behaviors not commonly displayed by adults with phobic disorders. Similarly, one of the diagnostic criteria of posttraumatic stress disorder is recurrent and intrusive distressing recollections of the traumatic event, including images, thoughts, or perceptions. In young children, the criteria note that this symptom may be expressed by repetitive play during which themes of the trauma are reenacted. These examples function to remind clinicians of the need to be aware of developmental factors that might influence how the disorder is expressed across the life span.

ARE ADULT ANXIETY DISORDERS
RELEVANT TO CHILDREN?

In addition to including behavioral descriptors specific to children, certain diagnostic categories acknowledge developmental immaturity by requiring a different number of symptoms necessary to meet diagnostic criteria. For an adult to meet diagnostic criteria for generalized anxiety disorder (GAD), three of six symptoms of anxiety and worry are necessary. However, only one of the six symptoms is necessary for a child to meet diagnostic criteria. It is important to note that although these specific descriptors acknowledge differences in how the disorder might be expressed, there is still the assumption that the disorder may exist across the life span.

Whereas separation anxiety disorder is considered to occur only among children, one anxiety disorder commonly found in adult patients, panic disorder with or without agoraphobia, is rarely diagnosed in youth. Some (Nelles & Barlow, 1988) have suggested that children may experience the physiological symptoms usually associated with panic but do not possess the cognitive maturation necessary to experience the cognitive component of panic disorder. The cognitive aspect of panic is the attribution that some symptoms of panic are specific thoughts of losing control, going crazy, or dying. These thoughts require the ability to conceive of the future. Young children may not have yet developed the cognitive ability to consider future events ("What if I die?" "What if I lose control?"). Without the presence of these cognitive symptoms, some investigators have suggested that children do not experience panic disorder (Chorpita, Albano, & Barlow, 1996). However, the limited number of children diagnosed with panic disorder may reflect the cognitive bias of clinicians rather than a true lack of prevalence among children.

> Melissa was 5 years old and a worrier. At school one day, she choked on a hot dog. Later that week, the family was scheduled to fly to California; the morning of the flight, Melissa had heart palpitations, light-headedness, and shortness of breath. She told her mother that she thought she would "fall over and die." At age 7, she had similar symptoms before a trip to Kansas. Melissa never worried about the panic attacks, although she had myriad other worries. At age 9, her worries became severe enough to warrant a diagnosis of GAD.

Melissa's symptoms are discussed in detail in Chapter 6. However, the panic she experienced clearly illustrates that panic features do occur even in very young children. The question remains, however, whether young children experience panic disorder. Interestingly, there is a condition termed *child hyperventilation syndrome* that includes symptoms such as difficulty breathing, dizziness, tingling sensations, headache, chest pain, and nausea, symptoms similar to those reported by individuals with panic disorder. In addition to the similarities in clinical presentation, the interventions used to treat child hyperventilation syndrome also are similar to those for panic disorder. In fact, successful interventions for hyperventilation syndrome include breathing into a paper bag, supportive therapy, and propranolol for the most severe cases. Despite the similarities in clinical presentation and intervention strategies, there do appear to be differences in the cognitive dimension of these syndromes. For example, prior to the age at which children achieve the cognitive developmental stage of formal operations, children diagnosed with hyperventilation syndrome make external attributions for their physical symptoms. The use of external attributions is in contrast to the "out-of-the-blue" phenomenon characteristic of adults with panic disorder. This situation has become even more muddled as a result of the most recent version of the *DSM* criteria (*DSM-IV-TR*). Currently, panic attacks can be (a) situationally bound, (b) situationally cued, or (c) uncued. In fact, children such as Melissa clearly experience panic attacks in relation to specific objects or situations (i.e., situationally bound or situationally cued). However, controversy remains regarding whether children, particularly young children, can meet the current diagnostic criteria for panic disorder.

DO CHILDREN SEE THEIR FEARS AS UNREASONABLE?

Another difference in children's expression of anxiety is the recognition that, unlike adults, children may not view their fears as unreasonable (APA, 1994). In fact, the decision to seek treatment for an anxiety disorder usually is not that of the child, but that of a parent or guardian, often after the advice of a physician, teacher, relative, or friend.

> Michael is a 14-year-old boy with obsessive-compulsive disorder (OCD). He worries about contracting a fatal disease. He feels that his clothes are never clean enough and washes them six times a day. His parents report that he runs the washing machine 16 hours per day, and over the past year, they have had to replace the washer three times because of overuse. Michael does not understand the problem and cannot understand why his parents just do not "buy another machine."

Adults with OCD may engage in the same cleaning behaviors and have the same intrusive thoughts regarding germs and death as does Michael. However, they usually clearly recognize the unreasonable nature of their fear. Thus, even though suffering from its effects, some children may not be aware that their behavior is abnormal.

A study of adult recall of the existence of childhood anxiety disorders is relevant to this issue of symptom recognition (Masia et al., 2003). Adults previously diagnosed with anxiety or mood disorders (approximate average age at initial intake was 9 years) were reinterviewed about their childhood histories. At the time of the first interview, childhood diagnoses were assigned after a strict diagnostic procedure, suggesting that these disorders were indeed present at the time that they were first assigned. However, when the subjects (now adults) were reassessed approximately 12.4 years later, recall of the earlier anxiety disorders was poor. Interrater reliability coefficients between anxiety diagnoses assigned at the initial assessment and lifetime anxiety diagnoses assigned at follow-up ranged from $r = .30$ to $r = .33$. Sensitivity estimates indicated that only 40–44% of those originally diagnosed with an anxiety disorder recalled that diagnosis at follow-up. Interestingly, interrater reliability for mood disorders was moderate ($r = .55$ to $r = .58$), suggesting that it is not gross memory deficit that accounts for the participant's inability to recall the earlier presence of anxiety disorders. As noted by the authors, the inability of adults to recall documented episodes of childhood anxiety disorders poses difficulties for epidemiological investigations. However, the inability of the individual to recall the presence of a previous anxiety disorder may be related to the use of the *DSM* diagnostic qualifier that among children, it is not necessary to view the fear as unreasonable. That is, if as children, individuals do not recognize that their symptoms are excessive or unreasonable, then as adults, they may not "recall" these episodes. In effect, the child never recognized the existence of the disorder even though its presence was clear to others. These data illustrate the need for multiple informants when assessing anxiety disorders in youth, particularly with respect to (a) determining severity or functional impairment and (b) understanding that children may not acknowledge the existence of a disorder. In addition to increasing the accuracy of the diagnostic process, children who do not acknowledge the presence of a disorder present significant challenges for implementation of a treatment program.

ASSESSMENT OF ANXIETY DISORDERS IN CHILDREN

In addition to similarities in diagnostic categories and the diagnostic process, the strategies used to assess anxiety in adults also are used with children (Beidel & Stanley, 1993; Fonseca & Perrin, 2001). These approaches include diagnostic interviewing, self-report measures, and behavioral assessment. Attention to developmental considerations also is needed throughout the assessment process. Given the rapidity of physical and cognitive development during childhood and adolescence, assessment strategies appropriate for 8-year-olds may differ from those required for 12-year-olds, which in turn may be different from what is needed for 16-year-olds. Furthermore, because many children may not recognize the presence and seriousness of anxiety disorders, the importance of collateral data from adults is inversely related to the age of the child. In the ensuing chapters, measurement strategies and assessment instruments useful for each specific disorder are discussed. General assessment issues that cut across the disorders are presented here.

A cogent review of developmental factors identified several important issues that merit consideration when assessing anxiety disorders in youth (Schniering et al., 2000), including limited parent–child agreement on diagnostic interviews and lack of adequate reliability and discriminant validity for both interview and self-report strategies. Although the reasons for these discrepancies in the assessment process are not readily apparent, cognitive maturation probably plays a critical role in the process of accurate data collection.

Developmental Considerations When Conducting Diagnostic Interviews

Assessment typically begins with a diagnostic interview, usually conducted with both parent and child. There are several different structured and semistructured diagnostic interviews used for this purpose. The most comprehensive interview schedule for the assessment of anxiety disorders is the Anxiety Disorders Interview Schedule for DSM-IV: Child and Parent Versions (ADIS-C/P; Silverman & Albano, 1996). The ADIS-C/P consists of two semistructured interview schedules, one designed to interview the child and the second for the parent. The parent schedule is more extensive and is the only version that assesses for oppositional defiant disorder, conduct disorder, and enuresis. Each diagnostic section has a series of screening questions, and positive responses lead to a more in-depth evaluation of that particular area. The ADIS-C/P has good-to-excellent test-retest reliability (Silverman et al., 2001), with kappas ranging from 0.61 to 1.00. It has strong convergent validity between ADIS-C/P diagnoses of social phobia, separation anxiety disorder, and panic disorder (Wood, Piacentini, Bergman, McCracken, & Barrios, 2002) and the corresponding empirically derived factor scores on the Multidimensional Anxiety Scale for Children (MASC; March, Parker, Sullivan, Stallings, & Conners, 1997). There was no convergence between MASC scores and the ADIS-C/P diagnosis of GAD, suggesting that children with GAD are not easily differentiated from children with other anxiety disorders (see Chapter 6 for a fuller discussion of this issue). One reason for the lack of discriminant validity for the diagnosis is that, consistent with most of the diagnostic literature pertaining to GAD, children with this disorder had more comorbid anxiety disorders than other diagnostic groups. Thus, they had a complicated clinical presentation, and the reported lack of validity for the diagnosis may be due to "noise" created by the presence of other disorders (or at least the presence of overlapping symptoms) rather than the inability of the assessment measures to distinguish between clearly defined and independent conditions.

A major issue with respect to diagnostic interviewing is poor parent–child agreement. More often than not, parents and children provide different, and sometimes conflicting, information regarding the child's clinical presentation. A thorough discussion of the issue is beyond the scope of this chapter; however, there are several variables that may affect diagnostic agreement (Grills & Ollendick, 2002). These factors include child variables such as age (younger children are usually less-reliable reporters, although adolescents may hide information from their parents), social desirability (the child's attempts to conceal emotional problems), and type of disorder (there is generally better parent–child agreement for externalizing disorders). Parental and familial characteristics that may affect diagnostic agreement include social desirability (parents concealing behavioral problems), parental psychopathology (parents with psychopathology tend to overreport their children's symptoms), impatience or boredom with the interview, and lack of communication or familial conflict. Maternal psychopathology and distress potentially influence maternal reports of children's behaviors (Langley, Bergman, & Piacentini, 2002), with symptom endorsement regarding the child's behavior higher than expected. In addition to child and family influences, interviewer and interview characteristics may function to decrease parent–child agreement. Potential factors that may affect validity include the inability of the interviewer to establish rapport, the different interpretations between parent and interviewer with respect to the meaning of a word such as *sometimes*, and the structured nature of the interview process. Furthermore, as noted in Chapter 1, when evaluating children, clinicians need to be aware of normative development so that "normal fears" are not considered abnormal behaviors (Langley et al., 2002).

There are practical, as well as theoretical, issues to consider when conducting interviews with children. First, as noted, diagnostic interviews of children and some adolescents require interviews not only with the child but also with one or both parents or other significant caregiver. In some instances, young children may not be able to give specific factual information such as age at onset, dates of significant life events, or other information that may be relevant to the diagnostic process. In other cases, contradictory data may be provided by parents and children. Parent–child agreement is only modest, ranging from 7.7% for depressive disorder to 32% for GAD (Grills & Ollendick, 2003). Percentage agreement rates for other anxiety disorders were 25% for separation anxiety disorder, 24.5% for social phobia, and 29.3% for specific phobia. However, these low agreement rates are not specific to anxiety disorder diagnoses. Percentage agreement for attention deficit/hyperactivity disorder (ADHD) inattentive subtype was 25% and for ADHD combination type was 25.3%. Thus, in general, to determine the most valid diagnosis, interviewing requires a consensus meeting, followed by the clinician's synthesis and integration of all available information.

A second practical consideration when conducting diagnostic interviews, particularly with adolescents, is placing limits on confidentiality and age of consent, which may vary across states. Specifically, as the age of the adolescent increases, the interviewer must consider whether interviewing the parents is necessary or advisable. Furthermore, the limits of confidentiality on the information disclosed during the interview must be carefully explained to both adolescents and parents.

A third clinical consideration is that interviewing may be an artificial situation, particularly with young children. Some young children prefer to be interviewed in the presence of their parents. Others are more comfortable if, rather than just sitting and answering questions, an activity such as a coloring book and crayons is used to lessen the formality of the interview process. In addition, using reinforcers (in the form of stickers or another small token) as acknowledgment for participation in the interview can help engender a positive therapeutic relationship.

Developmental Considerations When Using Self-Report Inventories

One of the most popular methods to assess anxiety in children and adolescents is the self-report inventory; again, several practical issues must be considered (Beidel & Stanley, 1993). These considerations include (a) the child's cognitive ability to describe himself or herself as anxious; (b) if terms such as fear, embarrassment, and worry have the same meaning for a child that they do for an adult; and (c) even if this distinction is possible, can the child accurately rate variations in intensity and frequency of these concepts? In general, self-report instruments rarely are administered to children under age 6. More commonly, they have a lower limit of age 8, an age when children appear capable of reading, and responding to, the inventories independently (Beidel & Stanley, 1993). As with diagnostic interviewing, an overall rule of thumb is that the younger the child, the more likely it is that information will have to be gathered from alternative sources such as parents or teachers. However, parent–child agreement also is poor with respect to self-report inventories (Schniering et al., 2000); thus, the same caveats regarding lack of agreement on diagnostic interviews also apply to self-report inventories.

As is the case for the prevailing diagnostic criteria, most self-report measures are downward extensions of equivalent adult measures (Schniering et al., 2000). In recognition of this issue, developers of child anxiety inventories have given careful attention to the developmental appropriateness of scale content. Less attention has been devoted, however, to examining the developmental appropriateness of instructions and administrative procedures. Specifically, can instructions used by adults when completing a self-report inventory also be used with children? For example, adults defined *worry* as the frequency of a particular thought. Thus, high scores on adult anxiety scales usually indicate the frequency of an aversive event. Most children's fear inventories ask children to rate fears using a 3-point scale, anchored with words such as "never," "some," and "a lot." In such cases, "a lot" is supposed to reflect frequency of the worry. However, frequent fears and worries of children appear to reflect aversive but extremely low-frequency events (e.g., dying, AIDS), suggesting that children, particularly those children age 10 and younger, may define *a lot* in terms of the aversiveness of the event, not how often the fearful thought occurred (Campbell, Rapee, & Spence, 1996, as cited in Schniering et al., 2000). They hypothesized that if children, particularly young children, are responding to the instructions of self-report inventories using a definition different from the intention of the constructors of the scale, then a child's idiosyncratic definition may result in data that reflect something different from the original intent of the scale. To illustrate this issue, recall that children consistently rate fears of injury, illness, death, and danger as the most feared situations on fear inventories, despite the fact that these threats rarely occur (McCathie & Spence, 1991). In one sample of children, 56.9% reported extreme fear of AIDS despite the fact that most had never been exposed to the virus (King & Gullone, 1990). These inconsistencies led several investigators (King & Gullone, 1990; McCathie & Spence, 1991) to conclude that children's endorsement of a list of potentially fearful events, such as those on the Fear Survey Schedule for Children–Revised (FSSC-R), reflected their opinion of the aversiveness of a specific event, not the frequent occurrence of these events in their daily life.

To empirically assess the issue of aversiveness or frequency, the fears of 102 children between the ages of 8 and 12 years were assessed using three different methods (the standard FSSC-R inventory [Ollendick, 1983], a fear-listing procedure, and a daily diary method [Muris et al., 2002]). Based on scores on the FSSC-R, "not being able to breathe," "being hit by a car or truck," "falling from high places," "bombing attacks or being invaded," and "fire or getting burned" were among the 10 most commonly endorsed fears. When given a blank piece of paper and asked to write down their fears, the children listed 49 different situations. "Bombing attacks/being invaded," "falling from high places," "being hit by a car or truck," and "fire/getting burned" were among the items, but they were less prevalent and not as highly ranked as on the FSSC-R. Finally, when daily diary data were examined, only 5.9% of the children reported fearing "not being able to breathe," 7.8% reported fearing "being hit by a car or truck," 2.9% reported fearing "bombing attacks/being invaded," 6.9% reported fearing "fire/getting burned," and 11.8% reported fearing "falling from high places." In most cases, children reported a short duration of these fears ("just for a moment"), and the intensity was rated as only moderate. In summary, these data suggest the need for careful consideration of the wording of instructions, particularly on self-report inventories. Rather than just handing the child the form, it would be advisable to spend a few moments with the child, clearly defining the instructions. The use of several examples may be necessary to ensure that children are completing the form in a valid manner.

Keeping this caveat in mind, children as young 2 to 3 years old can describe themselves as anxious, afraid, or scared (Bretherton, Fritz, Zahn-Waxler, & Ridgeway, 1986), and children as young as age 6 can make quantitative ratings of anxiety that correlate reasonably well with observers' ratings of the same emotional state (LeBaron & Zeltzer, 1984). Researchers or clinicians often are challenged to find ways to elicit accurate estimates of anxious severity or the frequency with which children encounter anxiety-producing situations. Practically, administering self-report measures in a group format may be inappropriate for 6- or 7-year-olds, who often have many questions about the meaning of particular words or may be unable to read a particular word. Individual administration of self-report inventories may be more appropriate for younger children.

Another issue that merits consideration is that many self-report inventories use numerical rating scales that embody concepts (e.g., descriptors such as "several" or "often") and require making discriminations that may be unfamiliar to preadolescent children. See Table 3.1 for two versions of a self-report inventory for social phobia, one version validated for preadolescents and young adolescents and the second version validated for adolescents age 14 and older.

Rating scales that contain more than three anchor points can be developmentally inappropriate for young children, possibly reducing the reliability and validity of the scales (Ollendick, 1983). For example, during the development of a scale to measure social phobia in preadolescent children, reliability and validity were substantially improved when the rating scale was reduced from 4 to 3 discrimination points (Beidel, Turner, & Morris, 1995). An alternative or additional method

TABLE 3.1   Comparable Items From the Social Phobia and Anxiety Inventory (SPAI) and the Social Phobia and Anxiety Inventory for Children (SPAI-C)

SPAI Item						
I feel anxious when speaking in front of						
	Never		Infrequent		Frequent		Always
Strangers	0	1	2	3	4	5	6
Authority figures	0	1	2	3	4	5	6
Opposite sex	0	1	2	3	4	5	6
People in general	0	1	2	3	4	5	6

SPAI-C Item		
I feel scared when speaking (giving a book report, reading in front of the class) in front of		
	Never or Hardly Ever	Sometimes	Most of the Time or Always
Boys and girls I know	0	1	2
Boys and girls I don't know	0	1	2
Adults	0	1	2

for increasing validity would be the substitution of numerical or verbal descriptors with visual stimuli that illustrate concepts such as "mild anxiety" or "severe anxiety" (LeBaron & Zeltzer, 1984).

Visually appealing self-monitoring forms also increase compliance with tasks such as daily diaries (Beidel, Neal, et al., 1991; see Figures 3.1 and 3.2 for examples of visual format rating scales useful with adolescents and children, respectively). In recognition of the need to develop instruments that are developmentally sensitive to the needs of young children, especially preschool children, researchers have introduced standardized instruments such as the Picture Anxiety Test (Dubi & Schneider, 2009) and Mood Assessment via Animated Characters (Manassis et al., 2009). Both self-report instruments are language free, requiring the child to rate their emotions consistent with pictorial displays. Preliminary psychometric properties are promising but require further empirical validation.

In summary, developmental differences exist in children's ability to differentiate anxiety from other affective and nonaffective states. Furthermore, as children's general cognitive abilities mature, so do their abilities to (a) differentiate between cognitions and affect and (b) apply

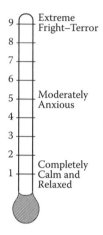

FIGURE 3.1   Self-rating of anxiety scale suitable for older children and adolescents. (From Beidel, D. C., & Turner, S. M. (2005). *Child Anxiety Disorders*. New York: Routledge. With permission.)

PUT AN X UNDER THE PICTURE THAT SHOWS HOW SCARED
YOU WERE WHEN THIS HAPPENED

FIGURE 3.2   Self-rating of anxiety scale suitable for younger children. (From Beidel, D. C., & Turner, S. M. (2005). *Child Anxiety Disorders*. New York: Routledge. With permission.)

quantitative concepts such as frequency or severity to accurately describe the extent of their emotional state. All of these issues merit careful consideration in the assessment of children's anxiety disorders.

Developmental Considerations During Behavioral Assessment

In general, overt (i.e., behavioral) expressions of anxiety often are the first indicators that an anxiety disorder exists. Although many researchers and clinicians are aware of developmental differences that may limit children's ability to report subjective distress, fewer are aware of differences in motoric-behavioral maturation that may affect the valid assessment of anxiety. In fact, level of physical maturation will limit a child's

range of behavioral expressions. Overall, physical development pro-
ceeds in a cephalocaudal and proximodistal manner; thus, children can
hold up their heads before they can walk (i.e., they gain control of neck
muscles before leg muscles). Furthermore, gross motor behaviors evolve
before subtler control is possible; mirroring this, behavioral expressions of fearfulness evolve from gross motoric responses such as crying
and running away to more controlled expressions such as gaze aversion
(Beidel & Stanley, 1993). Consistent with these findings, the ability of
children (ages 5, 9, and 13) to imitate elemental and complex behavioral
expressions (fear, anger, happiness, sadness) in humans increases with
increasing age (Ekman, Roper, & Hager, 1980). However, even at age
13, facial actions necessary to produce expressions of fear, sadness, and
anger were difficult for the adolescents to imitate, indicating that control
over facial expressions had not yet reached adult levels of functioning.

The inhibition of gross overt behaviors as an expression of fear
occurs throughout the developmental maturation of infant and adolescent rhesus monkeys as well as among humans (Mineka, Suomi, &
Delizio, 1981). Specifically, fearful behaviors in infant rhesus monkeys
are characterized by panic, vocalizations, and high activity, whereas in
adolescents, typical fearful behaviors are stereotypic activity and silence.
Although there are, of course, many differences between rhesus monkeys
and humans, these examples illustrate how developmental changes lead
to greater impulse control, gratification delay, and the ability to more
readily inhibit extreme motoric responses. Physical maturation and its
effect on behavioral assessment is presented here, with specific attention
to the impact of maturation on the construction and utility of behavioral
rating scales.

Actually, differences in cognitive and physical maturation may function synergistically to affect behavioral expressions of fear and anxiety.
Among pediatric cancer patients ages 2 to 20 undergoing bone marrow
aspiration, a behavioral observation checklist was used to rate anxiety
and distress (Jay, Ozolins, Elliott, & Cladwell, 1983). Children between
the ages of 2 and 7 were rated as more likely to exhibit overt distress,
such as crying, screaming, and having to be physically restrained. At age
6 or 7, distress levels appeared to decrease dramatically; according to
Piagetian theory, this is consistent with the age at which children develop
a more logical and realistic understanding of medical procedures. The
decreased overt expressions of fear exhibited by older children might
lead to the conclusion that older children are less fearful, at least according to their scores on the observational checklist. However, if one is not
developmentally sensitive to expressions of fear, a behavioral checklist
could lead to inaccurate conclusions. Specifically, using another sample
of children undergoing bone marrow aspiration and a similar behavioral

checklist (LeBaron & Zeltzer, 1984), children between the ages of 6 and 9 were more likely to cry, scream, express verbal anxiety, and need physical restraint than children between the ages of 10 and 18. Again, using this checklist, older children had lower scores, which might indicate less distress. However, there were two items, groaning and flinching, that were not on the original behavioral checklist but were coded in this study. These behaviors were significantly more common in the older children, and when the frequency of these behaviors was added to the original checklist scores, group differences in distress scores disappeared (i.e., the groups were equally anxious or distressed). Similarly, older children undergoing painful medical procedures displayed fewer overall overt anxious behaviors than younger children but were more likely than the younger children to exhibit muscle tension and specific verbal expressions of pain (Katz, Kellerman, & Siegal, 1980). Thus, observational scales must be sensitive not only to the behaviors of young children but also include items designed to capture the developmentally sophisticated fearful expressions of older adolescents (if the scale will be used across a broad age range).

To summarize, developmental factors are important in the assessment of each of the primary dimensions of fear, but attention to behavioral, physical, and cognitive maturation is not always considered when assessing children's anxious emotional states. Maturational processes do not occur in isolation; thus, improved cognitive abilities, for example, can affect behavioral expressions (Reznick et al., 1986). Furthermore, although the issue of social development was not addressed in this chapter, it must be noted that as children learn societal norms regarding emotional expression (e.g., "boys don't cry," "big girls don't cry"), this in turn may affect responses to fearful events (provided that they have achieved the physical and cognitive abilities necessary to inhibit their behavior). Thus, these factors likely function in a synergistic fashion to affect emotional expression (Beidel & Stanley, 1993) and therefore need to be considered in any efforts to accurately assess anxiety in children and adolescents.

DEVELOPMENTAL ISSUES IN THE TREATMENT OF ANXIETY DISORDERS

It is important to reemphasize that prior to treatment, clinicians need to be assured that they have differentiated transient or normal fear responses from true disorders. Furthermore, the design of the treatment plan must include information from multiple informants. Children often overlook impairment or interference that results from their disorder (Langley et al., 2002). Even if they admit somatic distress, they may not recognize how the disorder affects their daily functioning. Interviewing parents, and sometimes even teachers, is important in overall treatment planning.

Developmental factors are most often considered when designing or implementing treatment for preadolescent children. Adolescence, however, presents its own set of challenges. As adolescents strive to achieve autonomy, they may be reluctant to admit the need for treatment or accept help (Sauter, Heyne, & Westenberg, 2009). Parents may be able to physically bring young children to treatment; with physical maturation, it is less likely that parents will be able to force adolescents to go to treatment.

At the risk of becoming repetitive, most of the interventions developed for children with anxiety disorders also are downward extensions of successful adult treatments, and most empirical data exist for interventions that are cognitive-behavioral in approach. However, in children, cognitive interventions are not the sole interventions; rather, cognitive strategies are used in combination with behavioral interventions. It is unclear if this is a conscious decision based on knowledge of children's actual cognitive abilities or simply reflects the downward extensions of adult interventions. The latter explanation appears more parsimonious because the literature on the content and processes of cognition in children with anxiety disorders has not been thoroughly investigated and remains inconclusive (Alfano et al., 2002; Sauter et al., 2009). Among the issues noted are the significant differences with respect to the existence and types of cognitions reported by children with anxiety disorders (when compared with adults), results that are difficult to interpret due to methodological variance across studies and the issue of clinical versus statistical significance of reported outcomes. Furthermore, nonspecific cognitive assessment procedures do not allow for an assessment of changes in cognitive process (as opposed to cognitive content), which is the goal of cognitive-behavioral treatment (CBT). Finally, the majority of CBT studies fail to determine if changes in children's cognitions were instrumental in the therapeutic process (Powell & Oei, 1991). Thus, it is not clear that cognitive-behavioral interventions are changing the cognitive mechanisms that are hypothesized to underlie, and play an etiological role in, child anxiety disorders.

Others also have addressed developmental factors that need to be considered when selecting an appropriate intervention for children with anxiety disorders. There is a body of literature examining stages of cognitive development, particularly with respect to the capacity for introspection (Schniering et al., 2000), which is not fully developed until adolescence (e.g., Harter, 1990) This finding raises the issue of whether young children have the capacity to monitor their own thoughts, a key limitation for CBT interventions, which require metacognitive skills such as identification, monitoring, and modification of negative thoughts. Some clinicians (e.g., Kendall, 1994) use cartoon thought bubbles to help children learn to recognize and report anxious cognitions (see Chapter 6 for a detailed discussion of this intervention). Others (Piacentini & Bergman, 2001) also have noted a number of developmental considerations when attempting to implement CBT with young children. For example, in addition to less-developed cognitive abilities, children have poorer recognition and understanding of different emotional states, poorer future orientation, and greater variability in motivation for participating in treatment.

With respect to emotional states, children have only a limited ability to identify and differentiate between emotional states (Izard, 1994). In the social skills training program used for preadolescent children with social phobia (Social Effectiveness Therapy for Children [SET-C]; Beidel, Turner, & Morris, 2000), children are trained to recognize various facial expressions and to relate these expressions to particular emotions (see Chapter 10 for a description of SET-C). Other aspects of emotion also have been the subject of investigation. Children with anxiety disorders (children with GAD, separation anxiety disorder, and social phobia) and normal controls were assessed for the presence of four skills: knowledge about the cues for emotions, understanding of multiple emotion combinations (Can one be happy and sad at the same time?), knowledge of hiding of feelings, and knowledge about changing emotions (Can one change his or her feelings?; Southam-Gerow & Kendall, 2000). Children with anxiety disorders had a less-developed understanding of hiding and changing their emotions, two domains that are related to the modulation or regulation of emotion. These data suggest that certain aspects of CBT, such as replacing negative thoughts with positive coping statements, might be useful in altering the child's anxious emotional state. This type of direct intervention, however, need not be the only manner in which changes in anxiety can be produced. In young children, limited cognitive maturation results in the exclusive use of behavioral strategies (Piacentini & Bergman, 2001; Sauter et al., 2009). Strictly behavioral interventions such as SET-C also result in high rates of improvement even among children as young as age 8 (e.g., Beidel, Turner, & Morris, 2000). In the case of adolescents, particularly older adolescents, imaginal exposure procedures, perhaps delivered at high intensity, may be appropriate and useful. Furthermore, with cognitive maturity, the use of cognitive strategies may be more appropriate.

SUMMARY

In summary, developmental factors play an important role in all aspects of childhood anxiety disorders and will become even more important as researchers begin to investigate the presence of anxiety disorders in younger children (e.g., ages 2–5; Egger & Angold, 2006). As illustrated by the different descriptions of Sara, age affects the clinical presentation and expression of the disorder, the manner in which assessments can be reliably and validly conducted, and how the interventions are conceptualized and implemented. In the ensuing chapters, these issues are explored as the specific anxiety disorders are examined.

CHAPTER 4

Etiological Factors in the Development of Anxiety Disorders

INTRODUCTION

Some of the most common questions parents ask when a child is diagnosed with an anxiety disorder pertain to causal factors. "How did this condition develop?" "Is it hereditary?" "Is it something I did or didn't do?" Although there have been considerable advances in understanding childhood anxiety disorders as well as in the development of successful treatment strategies, there still is no definitive answer regarding questions of etiology. However, in recent years there has been substantial advancement in understanding the roles of genetic, neurobiological, and environmental factors in facilitating the development of maladaptive anxiety states. For example, behavioral genetic studies indicated that, on average, 30% of the risk in developing an anxiety disorder can be attributed to genetic factors (Bolton et al., 2006; Eley, Rijsdijk, Perrin, O'Connor, & Bolton, 2008; Gordon & Hen, 2004). Thus, in addition to possible heritable risk, it is clear that certain learning and environmental factors also are implicated in the development of anxiety in children. However, it is important to highlight from the outset that genetic, neurobiological, and environmental risk factors do not operate in isolation, and it is well accepted that multiple etiological pathways, including various combinations of factors, exist. Accordingly, a growing body of research is now rooted in the examination of gene–environment interactions in the development of child psychopathology, including anxiety disorders. At a basic level, a gene–environment interaction occurs when an environmental experience moderates the effect of a child's genotype or when a child's genotype moderates the effect of the environment on emotional and behavioral outcomes (Moffitt, Caspi, & Rutter, 2005). It also is becoming increasingly recognized that both genes and environment exert an influence on child behavior. While it is not feasible to consider all possible gene–environment interactions in this chapter, specific factors and pathways for which there is the most empirical evidence are discussed.

PSYCHOLOGICAL AND ENVIRONMENTAL PATHWAYS TO FEAR

Although there are a number of psychological theories about the nature of maladaptive anxiety in children, mechanisms described by Rachman (1977), including three specific pathways to fear acquisition, have received a good deal of empirical support. These pathways include direct conditioning (i.e., the experience of an extremely traumatic episode resulting in fear behavior and anxiety); observational learning (i.e., observing someone else experience a traumatic event or otherwise manifesting fear behavior toward certain stimuli); and verbal information transfer (i.e., receiving information that certain situations are dangerous or should be feared). A fourth mechanism through which fears may be acquired, nonassociative learning (Poulton & Menzies, 2002), has been proposed to address the widely held view (for which there are some data) that, in some cases, fears cannot be traced back to a conditioning experience. Nonassociative theory postulates that some fears have an evolutionary basis because they contribute to species survival. Each of these various mechanisms is discussed and evaluated in turn.

Direct Conditioning

Ten-year-old Mathew has traveled by air on several occasions and never expressed any fear. In fact, he was always eager to fly. On his last trip, however, as he flew with his parents to Miami, the pilot announced during the descent that there was some trouble with the landing gear, and that he would try to "bounce" the gear into place. The flight attendant walked through the cabin, instructing everyone to assume a "brace" position in case of a crash landing. There were a few frightening moments while the pilot tried to bring the gear down. Finally, he was able to land, using only the right landing gear. No one was injured, but Mathew refuses to go on a plane again.

When most adults try to understand the development of fears, they assume that, like Mathew, the child must have had a frightening experience with the object or event now avoided or feared. Similarly, psychological theories of phobia acquisition also have invoked primarily mechanisms of classical or associative conditioning, but of course, in many cases the details are not as obvious as the ones associated with Mathew's fear. Specific details of the conditioning experience are important to the development of fear and its subsequent treatment. To illustrate, consider the following example: A child was frightened by a brown German shepherd. The child develops a fear of large brown dogs but still may be comfortable with the family's white poodle. In cases like this, the child's fear does not include all dogs but is specific to the type of dog involved in the negative experience.

The acquisition of fears through conditioning mechanisms has been the subject of psychological inquiry throughout the 20th century. The story of Little Albert (Watson & Rayner, 1920) is the best-known example of fear acquisition. In this now-classic study, Watson and Rayner demonstrated how fear of a white rat could be acquired through conditioning principles. The subject was 11-month-old Albert, who had never shown fear of white rats. In this case, the white rat was the neutral stimulus. Through a series of conditioning trials, the white rat was paired with a loud aversive noise (unconditioned stimulus). This noise startled and frightened young Albert. After sufficient pairings of the rat and the loud noise, Albert would cry as soon as he was exposed to the white rat alone and would avoid any contact with it (i.e., the white rat was now a conditioned stimulus capable of evoking fear). As a result of this series of conditioning trials, Albert developed a fear of white rats. In other words, the conditioning experience produced a conditioned fear response. Furthermore, his fear generalized to other white furry objects, such as a Santa Claus beard. This research was conducted in the 1920s, and although the methods would not meet today's ethical standards for research, it was a powerful demonstration of how the principles of associative conditioning, derived largely from laboratory animal work, were applicable to humans. Moreover, it illustrated the rapidity of the conditioning process and its rapid generalization to many similar stimuli. Similarly, in the case of Mathew, the conditioned fear response was avoidance, accompanied by indices of sympathetic arousal and emotional distress.

Sometimes a fear, such as Mathew's fear of flying, develops after only a single incident. At other times, as in Albert's case, several repetitions of the conditioning event may be necessary. Thus, a child's fear of dogs, for example, may not develop after a single traumatic (conditioning) episode but result from the additive effects of several smaller but still frightening encounters with dogs. For example, a dog, in the excitement about visitors coming to the house, may jump on a small child who is visiting at the home. Although the dog merely jumps on the child and then runs away, the child is frightened by the sudden movements of the dog. After four or five such greetings by the dog, the child becomes tearful on entering the house and clings to his mother. Once the fear develops, it frequently leads to avoidance behavior that can persist for an indefinite period of time. Thus, what is illustrated here is the acquisition of an avoidance response through cumulative conditioning rather than a single aversive episode (see LeDoux & Muller, 1997, for a discussion of this issue).

Watson and Rayner's (1920) study illustrated the onset of fear through the process of classical conditioning, and a number of subsequent studies supported this mechanism as at least one avenue for fear acquisition (Delprato & McGlynn, 1984). An important extension of this theory was the two-factor theory of learning (Mowrer, 1947), which hypothesized that initially there is an association between a stimulus and an aversive outcome that results in the acquisition of a fear through classical conditioning. Then, the individual learns that avoidance of the stimulus reduces anxiety and fear. Thus, avoidance behaviors are strengthened through the process of negative reinforcement (i.e., avoidance of the negative stimulus terminates fear and hence reinforces the avoidant response), resulting in a behavior that is shaped by both associative and operant conditioning.

Even with the contribution of Mowrer's (1947) two-factor theory, it is clear that traditional conditioning theory cannot account for the acquisition of all fears. Several criticisms of this model have been discussed and are well known. First, aversive events are not found in the histories of all patients with fears or anxiety disorders (e.g., King, Eleonora, & Ollendick, 1998). Second, as Rachman (1990) noted, even under circumstances ideal for the acquisition of fear via an aversive event, some individuals fail to acquire the fear (e.g., DiNardo et al., 1988). Third, this model cannot explain the unequal distribution of fears reported in the general population (Agras et al., 1969). For example, a substantial number of individuals endorse fears of snakes or heights, yet few can report an aversive experience with these stimuli. Fourth, the traditional incremental-decremental conditioning model would suggest that after fear acquisition, subsequent nonreinforced presentations of the conditioned stimulus should result in fear attenuation (as demonstrated in laboratory experiments). For example, a spider bites a child, and the child acquires a fear. However, there are many spiders in the child's environment, and the child is never bitten again (i.e., there are no more aversive events). Yet, the child's fear does not extinguish but actually increases in intensity. To explain this phenomenon, Eysenck (1979) proposed the concept of incubation, by which fear increases over subsequent, nonreinforced presentations of the conditioned stimulus. Fifth, there is substantial evidence that fears can be acquired through observational learning. A review of various etiological studies among children illustrates this point (King et al., 1998). As depicted in Table 4.1, data from retrospective studies indicate that only a certain percentage of fears could be attributed to associative conditioning or an aversive event. Even within the category of specific phobia, the percentage of parents or children who reported that the child's fears began following an aversive event ranges from a high of 91% to a low of 0%. In fact, as noted by these authors, the most common method of fear acquisition among children appears to be observational learning, to which we now turn our attention.

Development of Fear Through Observational (Vicarious) Learning

> Several years ago, Michele's older brother had leukemia and had to undergo several medical procedures, including intravenous chemotherapy. Michele's mother wanted to be in the room when he was being treated. Because she could not always find a babysitter, Michele often saw her older brother crying whenever he had to have an intravenous needle inserted to receive the chemotherapy. Now, Michele is at the doctor's office and needs a tetanus booster shot. As the nurse approaches, she screams and cries uncontrollably.

In addition to conditioning events in which the child directly experiences some kind of aversive event, fears also can develop through vicarious experiences. For example, if a child observes someone acting fearfully, he or she subsequently may react with fear when in a similar situation. In the example, her older brother's emotional response was evident to Michele. However, there also are clinical examples for which fears are acquired even when individuals attempt to hide their emotional response.

> Mrs. Smith brought Jimmy to the anxiety clinic because he was afraid of thunderstorms. He would cry uncontrollably even when there were just a few dark clouds in the sky. During the interview, Mrs. Smith confided that she also was terribly afraid of thunderstorms, but she had never spoken of her fear to her son. When Jimmy was interviewed alone, however, we learned that he was well aware of his mother's fear because she sat in a darkened hallway during thunderstorms to reduce the chance of seeing lightning.

Just as in Michele's case, nothing aversive happened to Jimmy, or even to his mother; he only observed his mother's fearful behavior.

TABLE 4.1 Etiology of Fears Based on Psychological Theories of Fear Acquisition in Children

Study	Sample Size Unknown (%)	Type of Fear	Direct Conditioning (%)	Modeling (%)	Information (%)	Unknown
Doogan & Thomas (1992)	30	Dogs	91	73	82	—
King et al. (1997)	30	Dogs	27	53	7	13
Graham & Gaffan (1997)	36	Water	0	0	0	100
Menzies & Clarke (1993)	50	Water	2	26	0	72
Merckelbach, Muris, & Schouten (1996)	22	Spider	41	19	5	46
Ollendick & King (1991)	1,092	10 common fears	37	56	39	—

Source: Modified from Beidel, D. C., & Turner, S. M. (2005). Child Anxiety Disorders. New York: Routledge. With permission.

Furthermore, unlike Michele's brother, Jimmy's mother did not exhibit a strong emotional response. She merely sat quietly in a hallway, away from windows, to reduce her chance of seeing lightning. Even so, Jimmy had a fear of thunderstorms.

Some of the strongest data on observational learning comes from a series of studies by Susan Mineka and her colleagues on fear acquisition in rhesus monkeys. Although there are some difficulties in generalizing from animal behavior to human behavior, these data are an instructive model for fear acquisition through behavioral observation. Rhesus monkeys reared in the wild are afraid of snakes, whereas rhesus monkeys reared in the laboratory show no fear of snakes. This suggests that the fear must be acquired rather than biologically based. In a series of carefully controlled laboratory studies (Cook & Mineka, 1991; Mineka, 1987; Mineka & Cook, 1988), laboratory-bred monkeys (which demonstrated no fear of snakes) observed wild-bred monkeys behaving fearfully in the presence of a snake. After observation of the wild-bred monkeys, the laboratory-bred monkeys were placed in the presence of a snake and began to exhibit fearful behavior. In fact, after only 4–8 minutes of behavioral observation, the laboratory-bred monkeys demonstrated fear on both behavioral and emotional levels. These studies demonstrated that not only can fear be acquired, but also that it can be acquired through observation and in a short period of time. Importantly, the monkeys not only acquired avoidance behavior but also acquired emotional responses similar to those characteristic of human anxiety states. This indicates not only that the behavior response can be acquired in this fashion but also that the entire emotional complex can be acquired.

Although vicarious conditioning can explain why some individuals develop fears even though they have not experienced an aversive event directly, it does not answer all of the criticisms of the conditioning theory model of fear development (e.g., fears of some objects are more easily acquired than others). For example, using the same observational conditioning procedure described, Cook and Mineka (1989) demonstrated that fearful reactions were more easily acquired when laboratory monkeys observed wild monkeys behaving fearfully in the presence of snakes or lizards (fear-relevant objects) than when the monkeys were behaving fearfully in the presence of flowers or rabbits (fear-irrelevant objects). In each case, the videotape of a monkey behaving fearfully in the presence of a stimulus was spliced and edited to ensure that the reaction of the "fearful" monkey was identical; only the object eliciting the fearful reaction (toy snake, toy lizard, toy rabbit, or flower) was different. However, acquisition of fear was stronger when the objects were toy snakes and lizards (than when they were toy rabbits or flowers), suggesting that some stimuli are more subject to conditioning than others. However, it is not clear that these findings are readily transferable to humans. For example, humans are exposed to various types of information regarding their environment such that they may have preconceived notions about certain stimuli. For example, humans begin to learn early about the danger, and indeed the evilness, of snakes. This could make people much more prepared to be conditioned to snake stimuli. Also, the notion of biological preparedness (Seligman, 1971) enjoyed a brief period of consideration. This hypothesis simply stated that, through genetic transmission, humans are predisposed to be fearful of some objects more than others because they are related to survival. However, this hypothesis lost favor because there were few data to support such a conjecture, and importantly, the model had no predictive value for treatment outcome.

In addition to acquiring fears through observation, other data indicate that prior experiences with a specific object or event can *prevent* the acquisition of fear through a process similar to biological inoculation. Mineka and Cook (1988) demonstrated that prior experiences or information (in the form of prior exposure to "nonfearful" models) could inoculate monkeys against acquisition of fear. Laboratory-bred monkeys were first exposed to other laboratory-bred monkeys behaving nonfearfully in the presence of a snake. Then, these laboratory-bred monkeys observed wild-bred monkeys, which behaved fearfully in the presence of a snake, using the paradigm described. When the observer monkeys were exposed to the snake, they did not behave fearfully. In other words, acquisition of fear did not occur. This is extremely important because it suggests not only that psychological and environmental factors might interact to produce fearful states but also that environmental factors could be important in preventing them.

As a clinical example, imagine two 4-year-old children, Nicole and Adam. Nicole has a dog and has lots of positive experiences with her dog. Adam does not have a dog and only rarely has been in the presence of a dog. One day when Nicole and Adam are playing in the park, a large dog runs toward another child and jumps on him. The child cries loudly but is not hurt. Adam and Nicole see this event happen. Now, Adam cries whenever he sees a large dog and says "Doggie jump on me." Nicole does not. Why did Adam develop a fear and Nicole did not? One hypothesis is that Nicole had lots of experiences with her own dog (which might have jumped on her on occasion). Therefore, watching this negative event did not have the same effect on Nicole that it did on Adam (i.e., Nicole's positive experiences with dogs inoculated her against the development of fear following this event).

As depicted in Table 4.1, the existence of a substantial percentage of people with various specific fears indicates that the fear began after a vicarious conditioning experience, and in some cases, it was the primary agent of onset (e.g., Ollendick & King, 1991). Of course, conclusions from these studies are limited by the retrospective nature of the reports. However, there are data that directly examined the potential transmission of fear via modeling (vicariously). In one study, the extent to which a mother's open expression of her own fears was related to the severity of her child's fear was examined (Muris, Steernman, Merckelbach, & Meesters, 1996). Mothers rated their fearfulness on a 3-point scale, and children completed a standardized self-report measure of fear. There was a positive relationship between mothers' and children's fearfulness, suggesting that the more openly the mother expressed her own fears, the greater the level of fearfulness in the child. Similar findings have been reported in relation to child anxiety following traumatic events. Although data are limited to questionnaire-based studies, parental expression of anxiety in the aftermath of trauma is a strong predictor of children's posttraumatic stress symptoms (McFarlane, 1987; Swenson et al., 1996). Although intriguing, studies using more extensive and standardized assessment, particularly of mothers' fears, are needed before these findings can be accepted as conclusive.

A number of observational studies have examined the effects of parental modeling on infant behavior. In one study, mothers who acted fearfully in response to two novel toys influenced the same responses in their 15- to 20-month-olds (Gerull & Rapee, 2002). Similarly, Rosnay, Cooper, Tsigaras, and Murray (2006) found that after viewing their mother act in a socially anxious manner in the presence of a stranger, infants were significantly more fearful and avoidant of the same stranger compared to control infants. Not surprisingly, the impact of maternal modeling on infant behavior also was influenced by infant temperament; highly fearful infants were significantly more avoidant than low-fear infants in the social anxiety condition. The effects of parental modeling of socially fearful behaviors have also been examined longitudinally. In a study including mothers with and without social phobia, at 10 and 14 months of age infants observed their parent interacting with the same stranger (Murray et al., 2008). Maternal expression of social anxiety, which was greater among socially phobic mothers, at the infant age of 10 months predicted increased infant avoidance 4 months later. In addition, nonanxious mothers were observed to encourage greater positive social interaction with the stranger than socially phobic mothers, highlighting the potential of a gene–environment interaction.

To summarize the theory of vicarious fear acquisition, if a parent fears germs, public speaking, thunderstorms, or anything else and if the child observes the parent's fearfulness (even if it is passive avoidance, as in the case of Jimmy's mother), the child may also acquire the fear.

However, characteristics of the model can be important (e.g., Bandura, 1969). In short, observational learning (modeling) is a powerful method of fear acquisition. Furthermore, it could be an alternative explanation (in addition to biology, discussed separately in this chapter) for why fears seem to run in families. For example, if several family members have the same specific fear or are generally fearful, it may not be because of a particular gene that is transmitted from parent to child but a result of observational learning from a lifetime of vicarious experiences.

The role of observational learning in the acquisition of fear responses both enhances and complicates understanding of the etiology of childhood anxiety disorders. In some cases, children's phobias might result from firsthand aversive experience. However, they also might result merely because the child has observed someone else behave fearfully (even subtle fearfulness). Observational learning also can be a positive force. By observing others who are not fearful but who cope positively in frightening situations, fears might be prevented and eliminated (Bandura, 1969).

Development of Fear by Information Transfer

> Seven-year-old Jennifer has two older brothers who like to tease her. Over the past several weeks, they have been telling her stories about the bogeyman and monsters that come out at night to hurt little girls. They have been so convincing that Jennifer now will not sleep in her room alone; she has nightmares and cries uncontrollably. Her parents have tried to reason with her, but without success.

The provision of information is a third mechanism through which fears and avoidance behavior might develop. In an elegant study of the impact of parents on the fearful and avoidant behavior of their children, children with anxiety disorders were presented with a series of ambiguous events designed to tap into social or generally anxious situations (Barrett, Rapee, et al., 1996). One such vignette asked the child to imagine walking down the street when he sees a group of children playing a "great game." The child is asked what he would do in that situation. Initially, many children with anxiety disorders indicated that they would attempt to join the group of children and participate in the game. Next, these children were presented with the same situation in the presence of their parents. When queried about their response in the presence of their parents, they again initially said yes. Then, parents and children were asked to discuss the situation. Verbatim transcripts of the familial discussion revealed that parents made statements such as "Maybe they won't let you play" and "You are not very good at games, you know." After hearing these comments, anxious children were significantly more likely to change their answer in a direction indicating social avoidance of the situation than either control children or those with an externalizing disorder (i.e., rather than indicating they would try to join the group, they indicated that they would avoid the group). This study provides data clearly indicating that parental behavior (in this case, mothers' verbal comments) exerts substantial control over anxious children's behaviors and may serve to shape or maintain anxious responses. These data are further strengthened by retrospective accounts of adults with anxiety disorders who frequently indicated that their own parents often instructed them about fearful and anxious situations.

Of course, it should be noted that questions of etiology cannot easily be addressed by these studies inasmuch as children already were suffering from anxiety disorders. Thus, it cannot be adequately determined if the parents' behaviors precipitated or were the result of their child's anxiety. In fact, both possibilities have been supported by research. For example, Moore, Whaley, and Sigman (2004) observed anxious and nonanxious mothers with and without an anxiety-disordered child and found that irrespective of maternal anxiety disorder status, mothers of anxiety-disordered children openly predicted negative outcomes during parent–child interactions. In addition, however, anxiety-disordered mothers also were more likely to predict more negative outcomes than nonanxious mothers and tended to express these predictions while interacting with their children. Thus, transmission of fear between parents and children may occur via one (or more) multiple pathways.

Although a majority of information transfer research has focused on parents, a few studies have examined the provision of information from sources other than parents in the development of anxiety. In a series of studies (Field, Hamilton, Knowles & Plews, 2003; Field & Lawson, 2003; Lawson, Banerjee, & Field, 2007) in which children received negative, positive, or no information about a novel animal from experimenters, children given negative information exhibited more fearfulness and were avoidant of the animal, and these effects persisted over several months. In a similar study, children were shown a picture of a novel animal about which they received negative, ambiguous, positive, or no information from experimenters and then were asked to complete a series of measures assessing fear beliefs (Muris et al., 2009). Children who received negative information displayed the greatest fear beliefs about the animal, followed by children receiving ambiguous information, no information, and positive information. Importantly, although children with high levels of general fearfulness reported more fear beliefs overall, highly fearful children were no more sensitive to the effects of negative or ambiguous information than children low on general fearfulness, suggesting that information transfer was a more potent factor in generating fear beliefs than preexisting levels of fear. Although the long-term durability of these effects remains to be tested, experimental data among both anxious and nonanxious children clearly illustrated the potential impact of verbal information on the development of childhood anxiety.

Nonassociative Fear Acquisition

Although the most prominent views of fear acquisition have involved some form of associative conditioning, the various weaknesses associated with this model (e.g., the nonrandom distribution of fears, spontaneous emergence of fear) have led to the conceptualization of nonassociative theories of fear acquisition. Although discussion of nonassociative approaches have appeared in the literature over the years (e.g., preparedness; Seligman, 1971), they have not become prominent because, overall, there has not been an experimental base to support the construct, and variables associated with this approach have not proven useful in treatment. The essence of the nonassociative model is that conditioning experiences are not necessary for the development of fear. Rather, fears of some stimuli are biologically determined and passed down through evolutionary processes because they serve survival purposes for the species. Some of the hypothesized fears falling into this category include fear of darkness, heights, snakes, and strangers. These theories largely are consistent with views expressed much earlier by Charles Darwin (see Poulton & Menzies, 2002, for a more complete discussion).

In a cogent review of nonassociative theory, Mineka and Öhman (2002) addressed two of the basic tenets of the theory. First, nonassociative theory asserts that retrospective reviews of fear onset indicate that a number of individuals do not report a specific conditioning experience but rather that the fear has "always been there." However, just because an event cannot be recalled does not mean it did not occur. Furthermore, there is extensive literature demonstrating that retrospective recall is an extremely unreliable method of data collection (Mineka & Öhman, 2002). A second tenet of nonassociative conditioning is that many nonphobics recall relevant associative learning experiences, as do phobics. However, there again is extensive empirical literature demonstrating that there are many experiential and personality vulnerability (and invulnerability) factors that may mediate the impact of the conditioning experience (e.g., Mineka & Cook, 1988; see Mineka & Öhman, 2002, for an extensive rebuttal of this tenet). More recently, twin studies have been used to examine the potential genetic and environmental contributions of human fear conditioning for different types of fears. Available data, while somewhat limited, suggest the differential heritability of evolutionary-relevant stimuli, such as snakes, compared to other stimuli (Hettema et al., 2003), consistent with the notion that humans may be biologically prepared to selectively attend to certain environmental stimuli, including those with strong implications for survival. The expression of this genetic vulnerability may nonetheless require a specific conditioning experience.

One variable that is known to be associated with development of fear is environmental controllability or predictability. In essence, when one has the ability to predict, alter, or otherwise have an impact on his or her environment, the risk of fear development is lower. For example, 6-month-old rhesus monkeys reared from an early age (2 months) in an environment that permitted them to control the delivery of food, water, and treats displayed less fear and more exploratory behavior than monkeys who received food, water, and treats on a noncontingent basis or those reared without access to this broad variety of reinforcers. The results suggest that less fear could be attributed to their experiences with increased control over environmental events. In summary, although there are still many questions to be answered regarding the etiology of anxiety disorders, unlike the other pathways reviewed in the previous discussion, nonassociative theory currently does not rest on a solid experimental literature base that would support its theoretical contentions.

ENVIRONMENTAL AND PARENTING FACTORS

In addition to threatening verbal information, observational studies of interactions between anxious parents and children highlight the presence of unique parenting factors. Overall, findings from these studies indicated that when discussing argumentative or anxiety-laden topics, anxious parents were observed to be highly critical of their child's behavior (Hirshfeld, Biederman, Brody, Faraone, & Rosenbaum, 1997). Furthermore, anxious parents showed less positive regard and less affection, smiled less, and were more critical and catastrophizing (Whaley, Pinto, & Sigman, 1999) than parents of children with no disorder. They also were less likely to encourage psychological autonomy, which was described as solicitation of their child's opinion, toleration of differences of opinion, acknowledgment of and respect for the child's view, avoidance of being judgmental or dismissive, encouragement of the child to think independently, and use of explanation and inductive techniques (Whaley et al., 1999). While the vast majority of this research has been conducted among mothers, interactions between fathers and anxious children also have been characterized by less warmth when compared to control children (Barrett, Fox, & Farrell, 2005). Collectively, these data provide some confirmation for retrospective accounts of interactions of adults with anxiety disorders and their parents.

However, an important issue that merits further consideration is that it is not clear if these behaviors characterize all parent–child interactions or only those involving highly emotional or conflictual topics. Thus, it is unclear how anxious and nonanxious parents might differ in their interaction with their children around noncontentious issues. In the study by Moore and colleagues (2004) in which contentious topics were not the focus of parent–child interactions, degree of maternal warmth was significantly related to child anxiety disorder, suggesting that a child's level of anxiety, more than specific topics, may have an impact on the level of parental warmth. Nonetheless, much like existing research on verbal information transfer, these data cannot adequately establish whether these parental behaviors precipitated children's anxiety.

The notion of controlling parenting (i.e., overly involved, intrusive behavior that grants little autonomy) has received much attention in relation to the development of childhood anxiety disorders as it has consistently been identified among parents of anxious youth (see Wood, McLeod, Sigman, Hwang, & Chu, 2003). Theoretically, overcontrol may exert influence on child fearfulness in a number of ways, including discouraging independent problem solving and coping, fostering the perception of uncontrollability, or limiting a child's sense of competence. In two separate observational studies in which parents and children were observed working together on problem-solving tasks, mothers of children with anxiety disorders were more controlling than mothers of nonanxious children (Hudson & Rapee, 2001, 2002). Results from other studies suggested the presence of overcontrol, albeit in different forms, among both mothers and fathers of anxious children. For example, Greco and Morris (2002) examined the verbal responses and behaviors of fathers of children with high and low levels of social anxiety and found that the former group displayed more physical control during an origami task. However, fathers of anxious children did not display more verbal control than fathers of nonanxious children. In another study, parent–child interactions involving both mothers and fathers were compared among anxious children, the anxious child's nonsymptomatic sibling, and control children (Barrett et al., 2005). Interactions between parents and anxious children were characterized by more paternal control and less maternal reward of coping behaviors compared to controls. Thus, although overcontrol may present differently among mothers and fathers of anxious children, both may be significant in influencing children's anxiety.

Turner, Beidel, Roberson-Nay, and Tervo (2003) constructed a semi-structured interview, the Parent Behavior Interview (PBI), to more closely address aspects of "overprotective parenting." The interview consisted of 25 questions that assessed both the parents' willingness to allow their children to engage in typical childhood activities (skateboarding, playing contact sports, going to overnight camp, going to school unaccompanied) and their level of comfort when allowing their children to engage in these activities. Based on a factor analysis, four dimensions of activities were identified: separation from parents, physical activities, dangerous activities, and being away from home. Parents with anxiety disorders were no more likely to restrict their children's participation in any of the activities included in these four factors. However, they were significantly more likely to feel anxious when allowing their children to participate in physical activities (contact sports, gymnastics, climbing trees, amusement rides, skateboarding, or going on a field trip) or when they were physically separated from their children (child slept overnight with friends or relatives, attended summer camp, crossed the street alone, or when the child stayed with a babysitter). A second part of this investigation involved the actual observation of parent behavior when the child played on playground equipment such as a cargo net and a jungle gym. Whereas parents without an anxiety disorder were more likely to join their children in the physical play activities, parents with anxiety disorders were more likely to sit and watch from a distance. In addition, parents with anxiety disorders reported a higher level of peak distress while observing their child play on the equipment, although they did not prevent their children from engaging in the activities. Interestingly, by their own report, the children did not perceive their parent's distress. Thus, these results do not support the retrospective reports of anxious adults who describe a history of "parental overprotectiveness" and criticism; they do provide behavioral assessment of parenting behaviors of anxious adults in "normal" rather than emotionally charged situations. In short, it appears that by their own self-report and on direct behavioral observation, anxious parents do not necessarily inhibit the activities of their children even though they feel significantly more distressed when their children engage in these activities.

The need to instruct children about potential dangers, such as poisonous snakes or mushrooms, swimming during a thunderstorm, or sticking a knife into an electrical outlet is clear; indeed, it has been suggested that most harm avoidance behaviors of this sort are learned primarily through vicarious and verbal mechanisms (Bandura, 1969). But, if these cautions are extended to less-dangerous objects or situations or include highly fearful expressions of fear, children may develop abnormal fears. Parents, brothers and sisters, or others may make statements that lead to the development of fear. If parents say that getting a shot will hurt or that the bogeyman will come if the child does not behave, the child could learn that everyday objects and situations are to be feared. Overall, a collective body of research is suggestive of strong reciprocity between parent and child factors, necessitating the examination of more complex interactive models of the transmission of fear.

BIOLOGICAL PATHWAYS TO ANXIETY

There is substantial evidence to indicate that anxiety disorders run in families. If one family member has an anxiety disorder, the percentage of relatives who also will have fears and maladaptive anxieties is significantly higher than the percentage found among relatives of a normal control group (Crowe, Noyes, Persico, Wilson, & Elston, 1988). Among patients treated for specific phobias, for example, about 31% of the relatives also had specific phobias (Fyer, Mannuzza, Chapman, Martin, & Klein, 1995), a significantly higher percentage than the rate of 11% found among the relatives of normal controls. These figures suggest that specific phobias, like other forms of fear, are more common in some families than in others, although they do not explain the reason why these family clusters occur.

Rates of anxiety disorders among relatives are even more substantial when only parents and children are considered (in contrast to studies that include all available relatives). Among parents with anxiety disorders, available data indicate that approximately 38% of their children also have anxiety (Turner, Beidel, & Costello, 1987). In contrast, among children with anxiety disorders, 70% of parents have abnormal fears compared to 21.3% of parents of children without a disorder (Last, Hersen, Kazdin, Orvaschel, & Perrin, 1991). Similar to observation studies, however, a limitation of these data is that most research has been conducted among mothers only. In one of the few studies in which the presence of current and lifetime anxiety disorders was examined in both mothers and fathers of children with anxiety disorders, elevated risk of current maternal but not current paternal anxiety disorder was identified (Cooper, Fearn, Willetts, Seabrook, & Parkinson, 2006). However, an elevated risk of lifetime paternal anxiety disorder was found, although only for lifetime social anxiety disorder. Other data support the hypothesis of a more general familial relationship for anxiety disorders (Beidel & Turner, 1997; Mancini, Van Amerigen, Szatmari, Fugere, & Boyle, 1996; Weissman, Leckman, Merikangas, Gammon, & Prusoff, 1984).

In general, although the number of relatives who meet criteria for an anxiety disorder is somewhat dependent on the specific disorder, this familial relationship is well supported. As noted, it is not clear if the basis for the familial relationship is psychological, biological, or some combination of the two. A biological explanation is what often is first considered, and the fact that these disorders are familial has led to the hypothesis that anxiety disorders are genetically determined. However, it is important to remember that in most studies, even if more than one family member is fearful, the fears expressed by another family member often are not the same as that of the proband.

> Angela had fears of dying by eating contaminated food. She avoided eating many types of foods and felt that she had to wash repeatedly to avoid germs and contamination. Her father did not have these fears, but he suffered unexpected panic attacks. He also had a fear of crowds and airplanes.

Before turning to the literature on genetic studies, several "high-risk" investigations have examined the concept of familiality by assessing the psychophysiological reactivity of the offspring of anxious parents. Using this paradigm, children of parents with anxiety disorders, considered a group at high risk for the development of anxiety disorders, and children of parents with no disorder, are exposed to various stimuli hypothesized to be fear producing (e.g., loud tones, picture of snakes). Across several studies (Grillon, Dierker, & Merikangas, 1997; Grillon, Dierker, & Merikangas, 1998; Turner, Beidel, & Epstein, 1991; Turner, Beidel, & Roberson-Nay, 2005), offspring of anxious parents displayed physiological responses suggestive of hyperarousal. These behaviors were evident during both tonic and phasic conditions. Although the particular physiological response is somewhat dependent on the stimuli used and the variable selected for assessment, the results consistently indicated differences when the reactivity of these offspring was compared to offspring of parents without a disorder. Furthermore, the results were consistent regardless of whether the offspring of anxious parents had themselves been diagnosed with an anxiety disorder; that is, those children with no disorder but who had a parent with a disorder displayed the same pattern of reactivity as children with an anxiety disorder. One potential limitation of these data is that, to date, few psychiatric control groups have been included in the studies. This limits the conclusions that can be drawn regarding the uniqueness of these results to offspring of anxious parents (rather than being more generally characteristic of offspring of parents with a psychiatric disorder). With respect to this issue, preliminary data (Grillon et al.,

1998; Merikangas et al., 1999) reported that this pattern of heightened physiological reactivity was not evident in offspring of parents with alcohol disorders.

Twin Studies

Twin studies are important in trying to understand the role of family factors in the development of anxiety disorders. When the presence of fear is more common among monozygotic (MZ or identical) twins than dizygotic (DZ or fraternal) twins, these data are taken as an indication that the disorder has a genetic component (Andrews, Stewart, Allen, & Henderson, 1990; Kendler, Neale, Kessler, Heath, & Eaves, 1992b). However, as in the case of the family data presented, often the specific fears or anxiety disorders of one MZ twin is not the same as the fear or anxiety disorder in the co-twin. For example, one twin might experience sudden and unexpected episodes of extreme anxiety, including shortness of breath, hyperventilation, dizziness, hot or cold flashes, nausea, and chest pains. The other twin might have a strong fear of speaking in public (e.g., Torgersen, 1983). Accordingly, one study using a large sample of 6-year-old twin pairs to examine the genetic and environment contributions of specific phobia, separation anxiety disorder, and social anxiety disorder, found that specific phobia was most likely to be influenced by genetic factors, whereas separation and social anxiety disorders were more likely to be influenced by shared and nonshared environmental experiences (Eley et al., 2008). Thus, in a majority of cases what appears to be inherited is a tendency to develop anxiety disorders rather than the presence of a specific disorder. If this analysis is correct, one inherits a tendency to be anxious, and other factors likely determine the specific expression of the disorder. Such a conceptualization helps to explain why members of families with an anxious proband often do not have the same anxiety disorder. To summarize, anxiety disorders do appear to run in families. However, because relatives concordant for anxiety disorders often are not concordant for the same anxiety disorder, it is unlikely that each anxiety disorder per se can be linked to a specific gene (i.e., a "fear-of-heights" gene). What is more parsimonious (and more consistent with current data) is the concept known as anxiety proneness, or a general tendency toward fearfulness and anxiety. Although longitudinal outcome data are necessary prior to drawing firm conclusions, the heightened psychophysiological response seen in offspring of anxious parents may be one manifestation of anxiety proneness, and that may be what is inherited. Data addressing the biological components of anxiety disorders are reviewed next.

Neurobiological Predispositional Factors

Neuropsychiatric studies represent a relatively new area of investigation into the etiology of childhood anxiety disorders. As knowledge gleaned from adult studies continues to inform child researchers and as assessments in the form of magnetic resonance imaging (MRI), functional magnetic resonance imaging (fMRI), computed tomography (CT), and positron emission tomography (PET) scans become more available, these technologies are being used to further understand childhood anxiety disorders. A thorough review of the neurological and neurobiological bases of emotion and anxiety is well beyond the scope and aim of this chapter. In this section, some of the main findings to date are highlighted. Those interested in a more extensive discussion are referred to the work of Sallee and March (2001) and Pine (2007).

Studies of the biology of childhood anxiety disorders may be divided conceptually into two broad areas: neuroanatomy and neurobiology. With respect to neuroanatomy, MRI studies have examined the structure of various areas of the brain, including the amygdala, which has long been associated with complex fear states. However, neuroanatomical studies to date have produced mixed results. Larger amygdala volumes have been reported to exist among a small sample of children with generalized anxiety disorder (GAD) when compared to children without a disorder (De Bellis, Keshavan, Shiffleti, Iyengar, Dahl, Axelson, et al., 2002). With respect to another area of the brain, children with GAD were found to have larger superior temporal gyrus (STG) volumes than control children. Differences were evident for several specific areas, including total STG volume, right- and left-side STG volume, and STG white and gray matter (De Bellis, Keshavan, Shifflett, Iyengar, Dahl, et al., 2002). Differences in STG volume also have been reported for children with posttraumatic stress disorder (PTSD) (as a result of child maltreatment) when compared to children with no disorder (De Bellis, Keshavan, Frustaci, et al., 2002). However, children with PTSD had larger STG gray matter asymmetry (right vs. left), whereas children with GAD had larger STG white matter asymmetry (right vs. left). In addition, although some research has failed to find differences in the amygdala volumes of children with PTSD and children without a disorder (De Bellis et al., 1999), more recent work suggests that hippocampal volume deficits may develop in the months and years following a traumatic event (Carrion et al., 2007). These findings suggest that at least some differences in neuroanatomy may be a consequence rather than an etiological factor in PTSD. Among children with obsessive-compulsive disorder (OCD), increased thalamus volumes (Gilbert et al., 2000) and reductions in gray matter volumes of the dorsolateral prefrontal cortex

(Gilbert et al., 2009) have been found in comparison to children with no disorder.

Thus, in general, studies of children with anxiety disorders suggest some differences in brain structure. However, the areas where statistically significant differences have been identified are not always consistent across investigations or across specific anxiety disorders. The extant studies have several additional limitations as well. First, the number of children with a disorder included in most studies is small, raising questions about the representativeness of the sample. In several studies, only 12 or 13 children were included in the clinical group, whereas the number of children in the control group was twice or five times as large (De Bellis et al., 2000; De Bellis, Keshavan, Shifflett, Iyengar, Dahl, et al., 2002). Uneven group membership often presents problems for parametric statistical analyses, potentially leading to inaccurate conclusions regarding the statistical (and clinical) significance of the findings. A better data analytic strategy would have been to match each child with an anxiety disorder to a suitable control subject and conduct the data analyses using equivalent group sizes. A second limitation of the extant literature is that current MRI strategies assess many possible areas of the brain (sometimes as many as 20 areas are examined), and differences are usually detected in only 1 or 2 areas (De Bellis et al., 2000; De Bellis, Keshavan, Shifflett, Iyengar, Dahl, et al., 2002). This raises the question of experiment-wise error rate, a factor that may explain why different studies report different significant findings. In short, conducting a large number of statistical analyses without controlling for the probability of chance outcomes increases the likelihood of statistically significant, but erroneous, outcomes. A third limitation is that, in the majority of cases, abnormalities in brain structure are not associated with levels of anxiety. For example, there was no significant association between clinical anxiety ratings and amgydala volumes among children with GAD (De Bellis et al., 2000), but there was a significant relationship between STG volumes and child report on an anxiety measure among this same group of children (De Bellis, Keshavan, Shifflett, Iyengar, Dahl, et al., 2002). A related, yet relatively unaddressed, question relates to whether changes in anxiety may correspond with changes in brain structure. One study found that youth with OCD had significantly less gray matter in the right and left parietal lobes and less white matter in the right parietal lobe compared to matched controls (Lazaro et al., 2009). After successful treatment (with fluoxetine and cognitive-behavioral therapy [CBT]), however, structural differences between the groups were no longer significant. Similarly, Gilbert et al. (2000) found that despite differences at baseline, thalamic volumes of children with OCD were not significantly different from those of healthy controls after 12 weeks of treatment (with paroxetine). Although follow-up studies are needed, these data suggest that some structural abnormalities may be reversible with effective treatment.

In summary, MRI, PET, and CT technologies provide exciting possibilities for understanding the interplay of brain and emotion. However, the extant literature is small, fragmented, and inconclusive. More important, emerging data reveal that investigation of brain structure in the absence of an understanding of neurobiological function is unlikely to produce sufficient understanding of etiology. Thus, a second and related area of investigation includes differences in neurobiology. An increasing number of studies have examined neurobiological aspects of childhood anxiety disorders. For example, physiologic or pharmacologic challenge paradigms have commonly been used; children with anxiety disorders and their normal control counterparts are administered a substance believed to induce, or be related to, anxiety. As one example of a physiologic challenge, Pine et al. (2000) administered 5% carbon dioxide (CO_2) to children with anxiety disorders (separation anxiety disorder, GAD, panic disorder, or social phobia) and children with no psychiatric disorder. The objective was to determine whether breathing CO_2-enriched air would precipitate sensations of panic in children with anxiety disorders. The results indicated that 34% of children with an anxiety disorder met investigator-defined criteria for CO_2-induced panic compared to 2% of the control group. Panic ratings were based on specific questions posed to the children during the CO_2 administration, and raters were blind to the children's diagnosis. The results suggest that there is something different in the manner in which children with anxiety disorders respond to this aversive stimulus (similar to the finding of the "at-risk offspring" reported in this chapter).

An important consideration in interpreting these outcome data is that, in many physiologic challenge studies, the two groups often are different at baseline on a number of the crucial dependent variables. In this particular study, for example, the children with an anxiety disorder had significantly higher baseline self-report ratings of anxiety and panic symptoms (both of which went into the composite rating of panic). A close examination of the data indicated that both groups reported increases in panic symptoms when breathing the CO_2-enriched air, but because of their elevated baseline levels, more of the anxious children reached the panic criterion. In fact, it is not surprising that the anxious group was more likely to meet panic criteria as they started at an elevated anxiety level. This same phenomenon of baseline group differences was evident for the physiological variables of tidal volume and respiration rate, suggesting that their higher level of baseline arousal might be a factor in their higher likelihood to experience panic. Using covariance analyses to control for group differences would have allowed a stronger test of the hypotheses.

Pharmacological challenges also have been used to examine group differences in reactivity. In some instances, however, the responses of children with anxiety disorders have been found to differ from the responses of adults with this disorder, even when both groups are exposed to the same substance. For example, when administered clonidine, adults with anxiety disorders have a blunted growth hormone (GH) response (see Sallee, Sethuraman, Sine, & Liu, 2000, for a review of this literature). However, blunted GH responses are not characteristic of children with anxiety disorders (Sallee et al., 1998). Similarly, clonidine resulted in increased MHPG response in children with anxiety disorders (Pine et al., 1995, as cited in Sallee et al., 2000), whereas decreases in 3-Methoxy-4-hydroxyphenylglycol (MHPG) response are characteristic of adults with anxiety disorders. Why responses differ based on age is unclear, although several hypotheses have been proposed.

Yohimbine is another pharmacological substance that has been used in challenge studies. When compared to children without a disorder, the administration of yohimbine to children with panic disorder resulted in increases in self-rated anxiety, but no child panicked (Sallee et al., 2000). Anxiety was self-rated at various points during the challenge, and similar to the CO_2 challenge, the groups differed in anxiety levels even at the initiation of the challenge. Even though anxiety ratings decreased across the time of the challenge for the normal comparison group and increased for the anxious group, the time-by-group interaction was not significant. Therefore, like the CO_2 challenge, it is unclear that yohimbine alone was responsible for the group differences in self-reported anxiety because the groups were different prior to administration of the substance. With respect to the neurobiological (rather than emotional) reactivity, there was a group difference in GH response to yohimbine, with blunting characteristic of children with anxiety disorders in comparison to the normal control group. Unlike previous findings with other substances, in this instance yohimbine produced identical responses in children and adults with anxiety disorders (both groups experienced a blunted response).

More recent years have witnessed the proliferation of studies using fMRI technology to examine the underlying neural mechanisms of childhood anxiety disorders. Much of this work has built on research conducted in animals and adults. The dot-probe paradigm is a widely used task that, when coupled with fMRI data, allows for individual differences in anxiety and threat perception to be linked with specific areas of brain activation. In one of the most common versions of the dot-probe task, participants view pictures of different faces representing threatening (e.g., angry faces) or neutral stimuli. Among adolescents with GAD, greater activation in the right ventrolateral prefrontal cortex, but not the amygdala, was found in response to angry faces compared to children with no disorder (Monk et al., 2006). However, in another study including youth with GAD and controls, greater amygdala activation was found in response to the same threatening stimuli (Monk et al., 2008). In a study involving children with OCD, a symptom-provocation paradigm resulted in reduced activity in the insula and cortico-striatial-thalamic pathways compared to controls (Gilbert et al., 2009).

Although on the surface these findings appear somewhat inconsistent, other research has shown that specific cognitive processes, including attentional and appraisal biases, mediate these relationships. For example, McClure, Monk, Nelson, Parrish, Adler, Blair, et al. (2007) found enhanced amygdala activation in adolescents with GAD only when making threatening appraisals about angry or fearful faces. In the study by Monk et al. (2006), in which greater activation in the right ventrolateral prefrontal cortex was found in response to angry faces, adolescents with GAD demonstrated a significant bias away from angry faces. Accordingly, the authors found that as ventrolateral prefrontal cortex activation increased, severity of anxiety symptoms decreased. Similarly, when greater amygdala activation has been found, so has attentional bias toward angry faces among youth with GAD (Monk et al., 2008). Thus, while this body of experimental research is in its infancy, significant opportunity exists for developing a better understanding of how brain function and the processing of threat information interact to set the stage for childhood anxiety disorders. Of course, several critical methodological considerations also remain relatively unexamined, including the timing, intensity, and duration of threat stimuli used, rapid changes in cognitive maturation during childhood, and whether significant differences between anxious children and controls represent risk factors for as opposed to consequences of anxiety disorders.

In summary, in comparison to other aspects of childhood anxiety disorders, the number of studies addressing neuroanatomy and neurobiology is limited. One reason for the small number is that many investigators do not have access to MRI or PET technology. Also, there are ethical issues regarding the use of invasive assessment strategies such as PET, MRI, and CT scans in children for whom the procedures are not medically necessary. Similar concerns are raised regarding "challenge" strategies such as the administration of carbon dioxide or substances such as yohimbine in children. Pine et al. (2000) followed the children in the CO_2 challenge study for several years to determine any long-term effects of CO_2 administration (and found none). Many internal review boards (IRBs), however, prohibit the use of such invasive strategies when there is no specific therapeutic benefit to the individual child.

In addition to the ethical issues, the literature to date is fraught with many contradictions. Differences based on diagnosis have been discussed here. One striking issue is that the outcome for adult samples often is different from that found for children. In some cases, the findings are directly contradictory, and the most parsimonious conclusion would be that these outcomes are simply random findings. However, Sallee and March (2001) offer an alternative, and interesting, explanation for the disparate findings. In their review of the literature on stress and its effects on brain structure and functioning, they note that repeated stress, as well as severe or prolonged stress, can result, for example, in neuronal death, hippocampal atrophy, or decreased hippocampal volumes (see Sallee & March, 2001, for a detailed explanation of the effects of stress on brain functioning). In short, responses seen in childhood may be different in adulthood as a result of the chronic nature of untreated anxiety disorders (OCD, GAD, PTSD, or social anxiety disorder). Their continued presence could exert substantial psychological stress, which in turn results in changes in neuoranatomy and neuropsychiatric functioning and the differential resultant reactivity seen in children versus adults with the same disorder.

In summary, it seems clear that biology plays a role in the etiology of anxiety disorders but cannot serve as the entire explanation. In fact, biology may be more or less important in any one particular instance. As noted, psychological and environmental factors also play a role and sometimes may be even more influential than biology. For example, those who develop PTSD (see Chapter 13) do not always have a prior tendency toward anxiety. An adolescent who enjoyed driving might be involved in a serious car accident; after that, he or she may have continuing nightmares about the accident and begin to avoid driving in an effort to reduce the distress. In this instance, the etiological factors are primarily environmental and psychological.

Anxiety Proneness

If genetics, neuroanatomy, or neurobiology do not result in the development of a specific anxiety disorder, what role does biology play? The most likely mechanism through which biology contributes to the development of anxiety disorders is via the child's "personality or temperamental style." Individuals differ on traits such as fearlessness, nervousness, adventurousness, or inhibition (Caspi, Bem, & Elder, 1989), and these traits exist even in young children (Caspi & Silva, 1995).

Among researchers, commonly used terms include *trait anxiety, neuroticism, negative affect, behavioral inhibition* (BI), and *anxiety sensitivity*, all of which describe a tendency to respond in an overly emotional fashion to certain situations. In this chapter, use of the term *anxiety proneness* is designed to capture the meaning associated with all of these constructs and to describe this tendency.

Anxiety proneness is the potential to respond fearfully, become anxious, or feel threatened in situations that others find relatively harmless or, if found initially fearful, rapid habituation or loss of fear occurs. That is, when made fearful, some individuals adjust and adapt to the fearful stimuli, whereas others do not. Those high on anxiety proneness are more likely to become anxious in stressful situations, and they are less likely to habituate when they do become distressed. They also have more of the physical, cognitive (thinking), and behavioral characteristics of fear noted in Chapter 1. Also, the symptoms of fear occur more often in anxiety-prone children than in other children.

Among the very youngest children, the concept of anxiety proneness is usually termed *behavioral inhibition* (BI; Kagan, Reznick, Clarke, Snidman, & Garcia-Coll, 1984). One characteristic of children high in BI is their tendency to become uncomfortable in, and avoid, novel situations (Kagan et al., 1984). These children are often reluctant to engage in activities that might seem novel or adventurous, sometimes to the point of overt avoidance. When placed in these situations, they show high fear in laboratory episodes involving interaction with unfamiliar people and objects. In contrast, children who are not anxiety prone are less easily frightened, thrive on adventure, readily seek new experiences, and consider fewer situations dangerous. In a series of studies, Kagan and colleagues (Garcia-Coll, Kagan, & Reznick, 1984; Kagan et al., 1984; Kagan, Reznick, & Snidman, 1988; Kagan, Reznick, Snidman, Gibbons, & Johnson, 1988) identified a subset of children who demonstrated these characteristics of BI. In addition, when placed in unfamiliar situations, children with BI had higher heart rates and less heart rate variability. Across time, a number of the children with BI (those with high stable heart rates) were significantly less likely to speak spontaneously and were more likely to have anxiety symptoms. Other investigations have addressed the relationship of BI to anxiety disorders. For example, children with BI were more likely to have social anxiety disorder or avoidant disorder than children without BI (Biederman et al., 2001). The relationship between BI and social anxiety disorder appears specific inasmuch as other anxiety disorders were equally likely to occur among children who did not have BI.

Other investigators also have supported a specific relationship between BI in infant/toddlers and social anxiety disorder in adolescence

(Chronis-Tuscano et al., 2009; Hayward, Killen, Kraemer, & Taylor, 1998; Prior, Smart, Sanson, & Oberklaid, 2000; Schwartz, Snidman, & Kagan, 1999). For example, BI observed at ages 4–6 years was more predictive of social anxiety disorder during middle childhood than BI observed at age 21 months (Hirshfeld-Becker et al., 2007), and stable maternal reports of BI between the ages of 14 months and 7 years was associated with an almost four-fold increase in the risk for adolescent social anxiety disorder (Chronis-Tuscano et al., 2009). As noted, the same relationship does not exist between BI and other anxiety disorders, such as specific phobia or separation anxiety disorder, suggesting that there is something unique about the relationship between BI and social phobia. However, it is important to note that BI is not a necessary precursor for the development of social anxiety disorder (or any other anxiety disorder). Although persistently shy children were more likely than other children to have anxiety disorders when compared to children who were occasionally or never shy, 88% of children who had an anxiety disorder at ages 13–14 were not persistently shy as children (Prior et al., 2000).

Still, a number of individuals have hypothesized that BI might be a precursor to the development of anxiety disorders. In addition to the child/adolescent data presented, others have examined the presence of BI among the offspring of adults with an anxiety disorder. In general, rates of BI were higher among offspring of parents with panic disorder than among psychiatric controls (Battaglia et al., 1997; Manassis, Bradley, Goldberg, Hood, & Swinson, 1995; Rosenbaum et al., 1988, 2000). However, with respect to anxiety diagnoses in the offspring, it is important to note that few of the children had panic disorder even though their parents did. In fact, as noted, the disorder that was most common among children with BI was social anxiety disorder, although some children with BI also had other disorders, such as separation anxiety disorder or specific phobia. Thus, BI may represent a general state of anxious temperament but not necessarily predict the later onset of one particular anxiety disorder (see Turner, Beidel, & Wolff, 1996, for an extensive discussion of this issue). Briefly, although children who are high on the dimension of BI are *more likely* than others to develop anxiety, they are not necessarily *destined* to develop maladaptive fears. Thus, even though a child shows this temperamental style early in life, as noted, some children do become less inhibited as they mature. Currently, it is not possible to determine exactly which children will "outgrow" their inhibitions, although children who were more likely to remain behaviorally inhibited across a 6-year period were those who had high and extremely stable heart rates (Kagan, Reznick, & Snidman, 1988).

In addition to biological predisposition, several researchers have hypothesized that parents may play an important role in the stability of BI. Toddlers who display consistent inhibition across various environmental settings had mothers who were controlling and warm but not responsive to their children during interactions (Rubin, Hastings, Stewart, Henderson, & Chen, 1997). In contrast, when parents presented their shy and behaviorally inhibited children with opportunities for novelty, particularly novel social situations, they became more comfortable around others (Park, Belsky, Putnam, & Crnic, 1997). When these opportunities were combined with parental encouragement, fearful reactions to new situations (and perhaps the severity of the anxiety proneness itself) decreased (e.g., Asendorpf, 1990). In contrast, children whose parents did not encourage their children to socialize with other children, or whose parents did not provide the specific opportunities, did not appear to outgrow their BI. Outside specific social experiences and opportunities for social interaction, children with BI who had mothers with a permissive parenting style, characterized by a lack of follow through, ignoring misbehavior, and lack of self-confidence about parenting, also were more likely to have internalizing problems, including anxiety (Williams et al., 2009). Likewise, although there are not yet data in support of it, helping an anxiety-prone child determine what is dangerous and what is not could be useful in decreasing the severity of BI or anxiety proneness. Thus, although some children may have a biological predisposition to BI or anxiety proneness, environmental and psychological factors determine how this temperamental style, and therefore specific fears, develop.

SUMMARY

Overall, there is no single explanation for the etiology of anxiety disorders. Biological factors clearly play an important role, and genetic contribution has been estimated around 30%. However, specific genetic and neurobiological mechanisms remain to be identified for individual childhood anxiety disorders, and research has only just begun to understand how brain structure and circuitry interact to shape individual risk. Despite these considerable complexities, popular media explanations (and sometimes academic publications) often oversimplify an intricate process (e.g., the idea that anxiety results from an "imbalance in brain chemistry").

Psychological and environmental factors also play an important role in the etiology of anxiety disorders. These factors include direct associative conditioning experiences, observation, communication, parenting practices, and perhaps an environment marked by lack of control and predictability (i.e., an unstable environment). In some instances, these mechanisms work in tandem. For example, having a traumatic experience and watching someone else behave fearfully in the same situation could produce a severe fearful reaction. Also, anxiety disorders do not necessarily develop after a single conditioning event but can develop from multiple experiences over time. Therefore, an anxiety disorder that emerges after a particular event may not have been produced solely by that event but may be the cumulative result of many experiences. Similarly, an anxiety disorder need not develop simply because one experiences a traumatic event. Importantly, previous positive experiences with the same "traumatic" object or event may inoculate someone against the onset of a disorder in much the same way that a biological vaccine inoculates one against physical disease. Furthermore, as noted, not every child responds to the same object or event with the same emotions and behaviors. Situations that make some children reluctant, insecure, nervous, and apprehensive exert little influence on others. Some individuals thrive on danger and adventure; others do not. The facts suggest that some children are more anxiety prone than others. To date, however, there are no specific data that allow one to predict who will develop anxiety disorders. However, ongoing research may someday allow the ability to detect vulnerable individuals before the onset of the frank disorder. Indeed, a study from our laboratory (Turner et al., 2005) revealed that both diagnosed and nondiagnosed children of anxious parents had similar psychophysiological responses to various types of potentially fear-producing stimuli, responses that were significantly different from offspring of parents without a psychiatric disorder. A longitudinal study will be needed to determine if these variables have predictive value. Furthermore, the role of parenting is not yet fully understood. More specific data could help improve child-rearing practices and perhaps aid in developing prevention programs that "immunize" children against the development of fears.

At the beginning of this chapter, we noted that parents frequently worry that they may be genetically responsible for their children's fears. Family and family history studies indicate that there may indeed be a biological vulnerability that is transmitted from parents to children. However, at this time, there are no known interventions that can alter genetic makeup. Furthermore, it does not appear that biology alone guarantees or prevents the onset of a disorder. In fact, the most parsimonious explanation at this time is probably that of a diathesis-stress model; even if a child is anxiety prone, the onset of the disorder probably is triggered by the interaction of the biological predisposition with environmental/psychological factors. This chapter also discussed how some environmental factors might play a role in inoculating (preventing) a child against the onset of anxiety disorders. Again, environmental factors, particularly parents, can be a positive factor in the etiology or amelioration of anxiety disorders, regardless of a child's biological predisposition. Throughout the remaining chapters, factors relevant to the onset, maintenance, treatment, and prevention of specific fears and anxiety disorders are discussed.

CHAPTER 5

Sleep and Anxiety Disorders in Children

Malcolm is 8 years old. Every night, he insists that one of his parents stay with him when he sleeps. If his parents refuse, Malcolm becomes inconsolable, crying and screaming. He tells his parents that when they are not with him at night he is afraid that a burglar will break into the house and kill them all. Even with a parent present, Malcolm requires up to 60 minutes to fall asleep because he "keeps listening for strange noises." His parents find that it is easier to sleep with him in his bed than to try to get him to sleep independently. Malcolm often wakes up in the middle of the night to check that his parent is still with him. He worries about his sleep and feels "different" because his friends have sleepovers and go away to camp in the summer. As Malcolm puts it, they "just don't have these problems." Both Malcolm and his parents feel excessively tired during the daytime. Teachers have reported that Malcolm has difficulty completing his schoolwork and falls asleep in class at least once per week.

In addition to significant sleep disruption, Malcolm is likely suffering from an anxiety disorder. Like many anxious youth, Malcolm's fears are highly impairing during the nighttime, negatively affecting both his and his parents' sleep. Inadequate sleep is also interfering with his school performance, ability to socialize with friends, and family relationships. Malcolm's clinical presentation is not unusual. Up to 95% of children and adolescents with anxiety disorders experience some form of sleep disruption (Alfano, Beidel, Turner, & Lewin, 2006; Alfano, Ginsburg, & Kingery, 2007; Storch et al., 2008) and as a result obtain an insufficient amount of sleep for their age (Alfano, Pina, Zerr, & Villalta, 2010; Hudson, Gradisar, Gamble, Schniering, & Rebelo, 2009). Prior to embarking on a review and discussion of sleep in the context of childhood anxiety, however, it is necessary to understand the critical role of sleep during the early years of development.

SLEEP AND CHILD DEVELOPMENT

Although sleep problems may occur at any point during the life span, the role of sleep during childhood is most complex. Infancy and the preschool years are distinguished in part by the greatest need for sleep, which is apparent across almost all species. Sleep quantity, architecture, and timing continue to change from birth through adolescence, paralleling rates of brain maturation (Wolfson, 1996). Since this increased need for sleep early in life coincides with critical physical, cognitive, and emotional changes, the "cost" of sleep loss for children may be more severe than in adults (National Institutes of Health, 2003). For example, during the school-age years, in addition to steady increases in academic demands, children are expected to develop greater skills in monitoring and controlling their behavior and emotions. Insufficient sleep has been shown to directly interfere with these developmental tasks vis-à-vis impaired attention, poor impulse control, hyperactivity, decrements in working memory and reasoning abilities, and increased risk-taking behaviors (see McLaughlin-Crabtree & Witcher, 2008, for a review). The effects of inadequate sleep on physical health are similarly deleterious and include cardiovascular risks, compromised immune function, and metabolic changes such as insulin resistance (Amin et al., 2002; de la Eva, Baur, Donaghue, & Waters, 2002; Gozal & Kheirandish-Gozal, 2008). Evidence for a link between sleep and emotional functioning is equally abundant. Sleep problems are common across different forms of child psychopathology, and a majority of children presenting with a primary complaint of insomnia meet criteria for a psychiatric problem or disorder (Alfano & Gamble, 2009; Ivanenko, Barnes, Crabtree, & Gozal, 2004).

Despite the critical role of sleep early in life, assessment and treatment of sleep problems in children as compared to adults is a more challenging task that requires consideration of a number of unique factors. For example, normal developmental changes in sleep requirements, caregiver-dictated bedtime schedules and practices, and cultural norms surrounding sleep (at least partially) dictate the degree to which a child's sleep behavior may be considered problematic within the family. To better illustrate, a single mother working two jobs and living in a small apartment with her 12-year-old son might not consider his erratic sleep schedule and constant requests to cosleep as problematic, while a parent of a different cultural and socioeconomic background might seek professional help in eliminating the intermittent nighttime fears of his 6-year-old. Although discussion of all possible factors that have an impact on a child's sleep is beyond the scope of this chapter, it bears emphasizing that, unlike the individual sleep schedules, practices, and beliefs of different families, the biological sleep needs of children are relatively inflexible.

NIGHTTIME FEARS AND NIGHTMARES

Nighttime fears and nightmares are highly common in children, particularly in young children. For many, such fears are closely associated with separation from caregivers at night. Darkness, strange noises in the house, and poorer cognitive control related to tiredness also serve to increase anxiety and fearful thoughts during this period. Such fears are developmentally appropriate and occur in 65–75% of preschool and school-age children (Gordon, King, Gullone, Muris, & Ollendick, 2007; Muris, Merckelbach, Ollendick, King, & Bogie, 2001). Occasional nightmares or scary dreams occur in 80% of 4- to 12-year-olds, whereas approximately 15% of children experience frequent nightmares (at least once per month) (Hawkins & Williams, 1992; Muris et al., 2000). Dreams of monsters and imaginary creatures are prevalent during the preschool years, while personal failure and familial harm become more common themes with increasing age (Muris et al., 2000). Across development, a majority of youth with nighttime fears report one specific type of fear (Gordon et al., 2007). Also, consistent with research on general childhood fears, girls are more likely to report nighttime fears than boys (Gordon et al., 2007). Although most children overcome or outgrow their fears with age, these problems can result in transient or persistent sleep-related difficulties, such as refusal to sleep independently, delayed sleep onset, and middle-of-the-night awakenings.

Whereas transient nighttime difficulties are generally considered developmentally appropriate, a proportion of children experience persistent nighttime fears that interfere with sleep and family functioning on a more regular basis. For these children, fears may be indicative of an underlying anxiety disorder. For example, Muris and colleagues (2000) found severe nighttime fears to be associated with one or more anxiety disorders (as delineated by the *Diagnostic and Statistical Manual of Mental Disorders,* Fourth Edition [*DSM-IV,* APA 1994]) in 11% of a community sample of children ages 4–12 years. Separation anxiety disorder (SAD) and overanxious or generalized anxiety disorder (GAD) were most commonly found. A similar relationship has been reported between nightmares and trait anxiety. Mindell and Barrett (2002) found a significant positive relationship between levels of trait anxiety and frequency of nightmares in a community sample of children and adolescents. In addition, children who rated their nightmares as more distressing had higher trait anxiety scores. In a large longitudinal study, increased levels of child anxiety at age 3 were a stronger predictor of bad dreams at age 5 than demographic and parenting behaviors (Simard, Nielsen, Tremblay, Boivin, & Montplaisir, 2008), suggesting that sleep may be more vulnerable during different developmental periods.

Etiology of Nighttime Fears

Many researchers and theorists point out that we are "biologically prepared" to be more fearful at night since sleep, a state characterized by diminished environmental awareness, makes us more vulnerable to outside threats (Ellis, 1991; Seligman, 1971). This is particularly true of young children, who must rely on the awareness of caregivers in ensuring their safety needs. Indeed, it is not uncommon for young children to want to cosleep at night, even though they may not articulate fear as the underlying reason for this want. In fact, cosleeping represents the universal context in which human infant sleep has evolved since close proximity allows parents to detect and respond to a child's basic needs during a period of decreased arousal (McKenna & Gettler, 2008). In fact, it has been argued that the focus of Western society on independent sleep beginning in infancy underestimates the importance of close parent–child proximity at night and may be linked to the high prevalence of children's nighttime fears. Of course, this is an empirical question, and to date, evidence does not support this contention. For example, in a longitudinal study comparing independent sleepers and children who shared a bed with parents during the first years of life, no differences in emotional or behavioral problems were found during childhood and up to the age of 18 years (Okami, Weisner, & Olmstead, 2002).

A majority of research examining the etiology of nighttime fears in children suggests an interaction of biological and environmental factors (King, Hamilton, & Ollendick, 1988). Certainly, a significant relationship between increased levels of trait anxiety and nightmares in children may reflect the fact that increases in anxiety both result from and predispose a child to nighttime fears (Mindell & Barrett, 2002). Muris and colleagues (2000) examined the utility of Rachman's (1977) three-pathway theory in understanding the origins of children's nighttime fears by examining the extent to which classical conditioning (i.e., negative experiences), modeling (i.e., vicarious learning), and negative information transmission contributed to the acquisition of these fears. Results revealed that 62% of parents and 78% of children attributed nighttime fears to negative information transmission (mostly via television). These results differ from findings for the origins of other types of childhood fears, for which conditioning and modeling are more frequently endorsed (Muris, Merckelbach, & Collaris, 1997). The implications of these data are clear and include limiting children's exposure to electronic and other forms of media prior to bedtime. This may be particularly important among children with high levels of trait anxiety.

SLEEP IN CHILDREN WITH ANXIETY DISORDERS

Although *DSM-IV* (APA, 1994) specifically includes sleep disturbance as a possible diagnostic criterion for SAD, GAD, and posttraumatic stress disorder (PTSD), sleep disruption may co-occur with all types of childhood fears and anxieties. The presence of a sleep problem in children with anxiety disorders is associated with a more severe form of illness and unique impairments in functioning (Alfano et al., 2007; Storch et al., 2008). In the only study to date using objective measures of sleep among anxious youth, Forbes and colleagues (2008) used polysomnography, the gold standard for assessing sleep, to compare the sleep of 24 youth with different anxiety disorders to both depressed and healthy children. Anxious youth evidenced an increased number of nighttime arousals, increased sleep onset latencies, and decreases in slow-wave (deep) sleep compared to the other groups. Interestingly, however, anxious youth tended to underreport sleep problems in contrast to objective measures, raising the question of whether their perception of sleep difficulties may be somewhat inaccurate. Although research among community samples of children indicates that parents tend to underestimate their children's sleep problems (Gregory, Rijsdijk, & Eley, 2006; Schreck, Mulick, & Rojahn, 2005), this finding has not been replicated among anxious youth. Two separate studies found that a greater proportion of parents endorsed sleep difficulties as compared to their anxiety-disordered children (Alfano et al., 2010; Storch et al., 2008). Thus, several issues remain to be investigated, including the possibility that the presence of persistent sleep problems from a young age may result in poor awareness of sleep quality. Likewise, since many of the specific types of sleep problems experienced by anxious youth are also highly disruptive for parents (e.g., bedtime resistance, refusal to sleep alone, etc.), potential biases in parent reports require further study.

In another study, Hudson and colleagues (2009) used prospective, 1-week sleep diaries to examine the sleep patterns of 37 children with various anxiety disorders compared to healthy children. Sleep diaries revealed later bedtimes and significantly less sleep on weekdays among anxious youth; however, differences in sleep onset latencies and nighttime awakenings were nonsignificant. One methodological limitation of this study, as well as other studies (e.g., Forbes et al., 2008), is a lack of differentiation between youth with different anxiety disorders, with the a focus on primary anxiety diagnosis. Although child anxiety, in general, is closely linked with sleep problems, the presence of secondary (nonprimary) anxiety diagnoses is not associated with a significant increase in the likelihood of sleep problems (Alfano et al., 2010). Thus, sleep findings from studies that include anxiety-disordered children as one heterogeneous group may not generalize to all anxious youth. However, several studies have examined differences in rates and types of sleep problems based on individual anxiety diagnoses.

Sleep in Generalized Anxiety Disorder

Insomnia is the most prevalent sleep disorder among individuals with GAD. Up to 70% of adults with GAD report clinically significant (i.e., impairing) insomnia, and similarly high rates are emerging based on child research (Alfano & Mellman, 2010). In addition to hallmark symptoms of worry and avoidance (see Chapter 6), at least one of six possible physiologic symptoms is required for a *DSM-IV-TR* (APA, 2000) diagnosis of GAD in children. While "difficulty initiating and/or maintaining sleep" is one possible symptom, notably, two of the other physiologic symptoms listed (fatigue and irritability) are common consequences of sleep loss. Thus, the role of sleep may play a central role in the pathophysiology of GAD.

In one of the first studies to examine the sleep problems of anxiety-disordered children, Alfano, Beidel, Turner, and Lewin (2006) compared parent-reported sleep problems among children and adolescents with GAD versus other anxiety disorders. Among youth with GAD, 94% had at least one sleep-related problem compared to 74% in the other group. Nightmares, trouble sleeping, and daytime tiredness were most commonly reported. Using a larger sample, Alfano et al. (2007) compared the prevalence of parent- and clinician-reported sleep problems among anxious youth with and without a diagnosis of GAD. Children with GAD experienced significantly more sleep problems than children with social anxiety disorder (SOC) but not SAD. Confirming previous findings, nightmares, insomnia, and daytime tiredness were most common. Alfano and colleagues (2010) examined the sleep problems of children with primary GAD, SAD, SOC, and obsessive-compulsive disorder (OCD) based on both parent and child report. Although parents of all children reported similarly high rates of sleep problems, significant differences emerged based on child reports; 87% of youth with primary GAD reported difficulty sleeping and difficulty awakening in the morning (a proxy for insufficient sleep), a rate significantly higher than children with all other anxiety disorders. Insomnia therefore appears to occur early in the course of GAD and may very well persist for a majority of adults with the disorder.

Sleep in Separation Anxiety Disorder

In addition to refusing to separate from caregivers in public settings, it is not uncommon for children with SAD to have difficulty separating from their parents within the home, particularly at bedtime. Interestingly, while some early case reports referred to this particular problem as "sleep phobia" (Connell, Persley, & Sturgess, 1987), closer examination of clinical descriptions and case studies reveal a more pervasive problem with separation anxiety. In fact, refusal to sleep independently represents one of the most common reasons children with SAD are referred to anxiety specialty clinics (Eisen & Shaefer, 2005). Despite the prevalence of sleep-resistant behaviors in children with SAD, assessment and treatment research has paid surprisingly little attention to these problems.

In a study comparing the prevalence of sleep problems in youth with and without an SAD diagnosis based on parent and clinician report, sleep problems were significantly more common in youth with SAD than children with SOC, but not GAD (Alfano et al., 2007). Insomnia, refusal to sleep alone, and nightmares were most frequently endorsed by parents. Alfano et al. (2010) also found that parents of children with primary SAD reported significantly more parasomnias (e.g., sleepwalking, bed-wetting, night terrors) than parents of youth with primary SOC. Based on child report, 60% of children with primary SAD reported difficulty sleeping, and 70% reported difficulty awakening in the morning. In a study by Verduin and Kendall (2003), in which the occurrence of comorbid diagnoses was examined among children with SAD, GAD, and SOC, parasomnias were most likely to co-occur when a primary SAD diagnosis was present. Although reasons for the common presentation of parasomnias in this specific subgroup of anxious children remain speculative, children with separation difficulties may be most susceptible to heightened levels of stress and anxiety during the presleep period (i.e., leading up to a separation from caregivers). Presleep stress and anxiety, together with the negative effects of chronic sleep loss, may increase the likelihood that a parasomnia will occur (Mason & Pack, 2007).

Sleep in Posttraumatic Stress Disorder

Sleep disturbances represent *DSM-IV-TR* (APA, 2000) criteria and prominent reexperiencing and hyperarousal features of PTSD. In a review of the literature examining children's reactions to stressful events and traumas, Sadeh (1996) concluded that the sleep/wake system is among the most vulnerable systems to succumb to such events (p. 694).

Although evidence of sleep disruption is abundant among adults with PTSD (Alfano & Mellman, 2010), empirical data are comparatively limited in children. The limited research that is available has been conducted among trauma-exposed children more broadly. Further, most studies have used nonstructured rather than validated assessment tools. In one study using the PTSD Reaction Index, bad dreams were found to have strong diagnostic efficacy among a large sample of children and adolescents exposed to Hurricane Hugo (Lonigan, Phillips, & Richey, 2003). In another study of war-exposed refugee children from the Middle East, exploratory factor analysis of children's postwar symptomatology revealed only one clear factor: Sleep disturbance, including nightmares and difficulty falling or staying asleep, accounted for more than 10% of the overall variance in behavioral or emotional problems (Montgomery & Foldspang, 2006).

Two studies have used actigraphy (a small watch-like device worn during sleep that measures movement) to examine the sleep patterns of abused children. Glod, Teicher, Hartman, and Harakal (1997) found that children with a history of abuse demonstrated significantly longer sleep onset latencies than healthy controls and depressed youth. Further, both Glod et al. (1997) and Sadeh et al. (1995) found poorer sleep efficiencies among children with a history of physical compared to sexual abuse. Interestingly, however, abused children exhibited disrupted sleep regardless of whether a PTSD diagnosis was present. Thus, consistent with Sadeh's (1996) conclusions, the negative impact of early trauma on sleep may occur irrespective of other trauma-related symptomatology and a PTSD diagnosis.

Evidence for the negative effect of early trauma on sleep extends into adulthood. Using actigraphy, Bader and colleagues (2007) retrospectively examined associations between childhood traumatic events and sleep in adults with insomnia. Controlling for stress levels and depression, childhood trauma was the strongest predictor of sleep onset latency, sleep efficiency, and nocturnal activity in adulthood. Similarly, Noll, Trickett, Susman, and Putnam (2006) examined the sleep patterns of adult females reporting incidents of sexual abuse between the ages of 6 and 16 years. Sexually abused women reported significantly more sleep problems than a nonabused control group even after controlling for the presence of depressive symptoms. Since both studies examined adult sleep patterns in relation to earlier sexual abuse, it remains unclear when exactly sleep disturbances emerged and whether other types of childhood traumas (e.g., community violence, car accidents) may have a similar impact on sleep. Collectively, however, data suggest that early traumatic experiences lead to increased risk for enduring sleep difficulties.

Sleep in Obsessive-Compulsive Disorder

In one of the first studies to examine sleep in young OCD patients, Rapoport and colleagues (1981) used polysomnography to compare a small sample of adolescents (13–17 years) with OCD to healthy adolescents. Reduced total sleep time, poor sleep efficiency, and increased sleep onset latency were found among the OCD group. Adolescents with OCD required twice as long as control adolescents to initiate sleep and slept 1 hour less on average. Huntley and Alfano (2009) used actigraphy to examine the at-home sleep patterns of seven children between 7 and 11 years who had OCD. In addition to problems with sleep onset, actigraphy data revealed an average total sleep of 6.5 hours per night, a significantly reduced amount of sleep compared to recommended sleep allowances and published sleep norms (Iglowstein, Jenni, Molinari, & Largo, 2003; Owens, Spirito, & McGuinn, 2000). Further, more severe OCD symptoms were associated with significant increases in daytime tiredness. These results suggest the negative effects of sleep loss in children (e.g., on frontal lobe functions) may translate to poorer inhibitory control over obsessions and compulsions.

Among a sample of children referred for the treatment of OCD, Piacentini, Bergman, Keller, and McCracken (2003) found that more than 50% of parents reported that their child had trouble getting ready for bed and sleeping at night. Storch and colleagues (2008) also examined the presence of sleep problems among youth with primary OCD based on subjective reports. More than 90% experienced at least one type of sleep problem, including, most frequently, "trouble sleeping" and "daytime tiredness." In addition, while young children and females with OCD were more likely to experience sleep problems, overall sleep difficulties were associated with a more severe form of illness. Thus, in contrast to children with a history of abuse who are likely to exhibit sleep disruption irrespective of a PTSD diagnosis, the presence of sleep problems in youth with OCD may designate more severe levels of symptomatology and impairment.

SLEEP AND ANXIETY: A BIDIRECTIONAL RELATIONSHIP

As is evident from both clinical and empirical data, sleep disruption is a prominent feature of most anxiety disorders, reflective of the inherent incompatibility between anxious hyperarousal and sleep initiation and maintenance. Building on this conceptual framework, sleep and anxiety may be considered opposing processes in a larger system of arousal regulation (Dahl, 1996). Indeed, emergent evidence from several lines of research confirmed the presence of a reciprocal relationship. For example, experimental research in both humans and animals showed that even a modest amount of sleep loss results in poor emotional regulation generally and increases in anxiety and fear specifically (Dinges et al., 1997; Sagaspe et al., 2006; Silva et al., 2004). In anxiety-disordered adults, acute sleep deprivation has been observed to result in significant increases in anxiety and panic the next day (Roy-Byrne, Uhde, & Post, 1986).

Although experimental data in children are far more limited, longitudinal studies consistently showed early childhood sleep problems to be prognostic for the later development of anxiety disorders. For example, Gregory and colleagues (Gregory & O'Connor, 2002; Gregory, Eley, O'Connor, & Plomin, 2004) examined relationships between early sleep problems and the development of emotional or behavioral problems during childhood and midadolescence among two large community samples. The presence of sleep problems at age 4 significantly predicted elevated anxiety symptoms at ages 7 and 15. Johnson, Chilcoat, and Breslau (2000) also found parent-reported sleep problems at age 6 to predict increased levels of anxiety at age 11. Other research has focused on the rhythmicity (i.e., consistency of sleep habits and schedules) and level of motor activity associated with children's sleep as predictors for the development of internalizing disorders. In a 20-year follow-up study, low sleep rhythmicity predicted adolescent-onset anxiety disorders (Ong, Wickramaratne, Min, & Weissman, 2006). Finally, in another large epidemiological study, Gregory and colleagues (2005) reported that close to half (46%) of children with persistent sleep problems from ages 5 to 9 years developed an anxiety disorder by age 21. Childhood sleep problems predicted adult anxiety disorders even after accounting for anxiety symptoms during childhood.

Together, experimental and longitudinal findings highlight the close and complex associations among the regulation of sleep, arousal, and behavior. This collective literature suggests that (a) childhood anxiety disorders may give rise to or exacerbate persistent sleep problems; (b) insufficient or disturbed sleep from a young age may interfere with a child's ability to regulate arousal and emotion and lead to chronic problems with fear and anxiety; and (c) these problems may persist in a synergistic fashion for extended periods of time, impairing a child's functioning during both the day and nighttime. An important next step, therefore, is to better understand the specific biological and environmental factors that underlie these relationships toward the development of effective preventive and intervention methods. Although this body of research is only beginning to emerge, several important areas for future inquiry have been identified.

MECHANISMS OF SLEEP AND ANXIETY DISORDERS

Rapid-Eye-Movement Sleep

Compared to other sleep stages, rapid-eye-movement (REM) sleep bears the strongest relationship to emotional learning and memory. Experimental research has consistently demonstrated a link between deprivation of REM sleep and decrements in emotional memory. For example, Wagner, Gais, and Born (2001) found that REM sleep selectively favors the retention of affective as compared to neutral memories, and that these memory enhancements persist for several years (Wagner, Hallschmid, Rasch, & Born, 2006). Further, affective memories appear to be preferentially enhanced (consolidated) not only based on the quantity of REM sleep that follows the actual emotional experience but also the quality, including the speed of entry into REM sleep (i.e., REM latency) (Nishida, Pearsall, Buckner, & Walker, 2009). As described by Walker (2009), the reason affective memories are preferentially encoded involves the role of autonomic arousal at the time of the original experience (i.e., emotional memory). It is well established that emotionally charged experiences are consistently remembered better than neutral ones both in the laboratory and real-life settings. However, the fact that later recall of these experiences does not elicit the same level or degree of emotion, together with findings for the role of REM sleep in emotional memory consolidation, have led to the hypothesis that REM sleep specifically serves to detach emotional memories from their affective meaning. This overall model has aptly been described as "sleeping to forget" (Walker, 2009, p. 189).

While a REM sleep model of emotional memory processing has implications for understanding different anxious states, its implications for the development and course of PTSD in particular are remarkable. A hallmark feature of PTSD includes persistent symptoms of hyperarousal in the presence of cues or memories of the original trauma. This suggests that the heightened level of autonomic arousal experienced at the time of the actual trauma has not been adequately separated from memories of the event, indicating a failure of the REM mechanism to do its job. While sleep disturbance is a well-established symptom of the disorder, REM abnormalities in particular have consistently been found among individuals with both remitted (lifetime) and current PTSD. For example, nightmares, which occur during REM sleep, are common in the early aftermath of trauma, particularly among those who develop PTSD (Green, 1993; Mellman, David, Bustamante, Torres, & Fins, 2001). Other REM abnormalities include more frequent transitions from REM to Stage 1 sleep or wake (Breslau et al., 2004); shorter continuous periods of REM prior to stage shifts or arousals (Mellman, Bustamante, Fins, Pigeon & Nolan, 2002); "REM interruption" (Habukawa, Uchimura, Maeda, Kotorii, & Maeda, 2007); and increased sympathetic autonomic tone during REM sleep (Harvey, Jones, & Schmidt, 2003; Mellman & Hipolito, 2006). Although these findings have not been replicated in children with PTSD, available data indicate nightmares to be common posttraumatic symptoms of children who develop PTSD (Lonigan et al., 2003; Montgomery & Foldspang, 2006). Thus, future research investigating REM abnormalities in children with PTSD may assist in developing a better understanding of why the REM mechanism may fail in certain trauma-exposed individuals.

Neurobiological Factors

Experimental data also provide evidence of specific neuropsychological mechanisms linking sleep disruption and anxiety. For example, functional magnetic resonance imaging (fMRI) data have been used to examine the impact of sleep deprivation on the amygdala and medial prefrontal cortex (mPFC) areas of the brain. As discussed in Chapter 4, the amygdala plays a central role in the development and maintenance of fear and anxiety (LeDoux, 1996; Sweeney & Pine, 2004) and has both direct and indirect connections with the mPFC, which inhibits emotional responses and behaviors. Yoo, Gujar, Hu, Jolesz, and Walker (2007) randomized healthy adults to 35 hours of sleep deprivation or a normal sleep condition prior to fMRI scanning during which subjects were asked to classify 100 images ranging in emotional content from neutral to highly aversive. The sleep-deprived group showed 60% greater amygdala activity in response to negative images compared to controls. Further, increased amygdala activity was associated with a loss of functional connectivity with the mPFC in sleep-deprived subjects. These findings indicate that sleep deprivation both increases reactivity to aversive stimuli and reduces associated inhibitory responses. Since exposure to threat cues has been found to enhance inhibitory control among anxious youth (Hardin et al., 2009), these results suggest that sleep deprivation may increase anxiety by interfering with adaptive responses to (increased) perceived threat. Although more research is needed using children samples in particular, chronic partial sleep loss, which is common among anxious youth, may serve to exacerbate existing problems with anxious arousal and decreasing coping behaviors for managing threat.

The hypothalamic-pituitary-adrenal (HPA) axis is another important area of investigation in understanding the linkages underlying sleep and anxiety. The HPA axis is activated in response to stress and fear, resulting in increased secretion of the neurohormone cortisol. There is considerable evidence linking increased levels of cortisol with elevated risk for anxiety disorders in children (Goldsmith & Lemery, 2000; Kagan, Reznick, & Snidman, 1988; Schmidt et al., 1997; Warren et al., 2003). Similarly, because the HPA axis and cortisol play an important role in modulating arousal, dysfunction of this axis can also disrupt sleep (Buckley & Schatzberg, 2005). Two studies examining cortisol in anxiety-disordered children during the sleep period found altered patterns of nocturnal cortisol. In healthy individuals, sleep onset occurs concurrently with low levels of cortisol secretion, whereas sleep offset (arousal) is associated with steady rises in cortisol levels. However, Feder and colleagues (2004) reported a significantly reduced level of cortisol during the early morning hours among anxiety-disordered youth compared to depressed and healthy control children. Forbes and colleagues (2006) found increased levels of cortisol during the presleep period among anxiety-disordered youth compared to both depressed and control youth. Interestingly, however, follow-up analyses revealed increased cortisol among anxious children but not adolescents. The authors hypothesized that increases in presleep cortisol among the anxious children only may be reflective of adjustments in the HPA as a consequence of persistent anxiety. Although age at anxiety onset was not assessed in this study and these data cannot adequately address this question, some support for this hypothesis comes from other research in which persistent but not acute anxiety has been associated with morning cortisol levels in 10- to 12-year-old children (Greaves-Lord et al., 2007).

Environmental/Parenting Factors

Environmental factors account for a significant portion of the variance in childhood sleep problems and anxiety (Gregory et al., 2004; Gregory & O'Connor, 2002; van den Oord, Boomsma, & Verhulst, 2000). In a large twin study, longitudinal associations between sleep problems at age 3–4 and anxiety at age 7 were largely mediated by environmental factors (Gregory et al., 2004). In a separate investigation, both parental psychopathology and family disorganization (i.e., lack of structure or routine within the home) were highly correlated with childhood sleep problems and anxiety (Gregory et al., 2005). The specific nature of these associations, however, is less clear. One possibility includes the prospect that parents with psychiatric symptoms have greater difficulty imposing structure within the home in relation to both daytime and nighttime routines. Lack of structure or overly permissive parenting has been associated with both child anxiety and inadequate amounts of sleep

(Klackenberg, 1982; Meijer, Habekothe, & van den Wittenboer, 2001; Owens-Stively et al., 1997; Williams et al., 2009). For example, Meijer and colleagues (2001) found that lack of parental rules with respect to sleep (e.g., allowing children to decide their own bedtime) was associated with shorter sleep duration in children. Among children at risk for anxiety based on a behaviorally inhibited temperament, a permissive parenting style was associated with greater child internalizing problems, including anxiety (Williams et al., 2009).

Parental overcontrol also has been linked with both childhood anxiety and sleep problems. Overly involved, intrusive parenting that grants little autonomy has been identified among parents of anxiety-disordered children, who are less promoting of independence than parents of nonanxious children (Siqueland, Kendall, & Steinberg, 1996). Similar data also have emerged in relation to nighttime parenting behaviors. Since anxiety disorders run in families (Last et al., 1991; Turner et al., 1987), Warren and colleagues (2003) examined sleep-related parenting behaviors among nonanxious mothers and mothers with panic disorder. In-home assessments showed anxious parents were overly involved in the bedtime routines of their infants and young children compared to nonanxious parents. Parenting behaviors such as cosleeping and waiting until children fell asleep to put them to bed were associated with significantly higher rates of child sleep problems. These findings are consistent with data revealing high levels of anxiety among parents with anxiety disorders when physically separated from their children (Turner et al., 2003). Thus, nighttime may be as distressing for anxious parents. For children, however, delaying bedtimes, permitting cosleeping, or providing excessive reassurance may only serve to reinforce children's anxiety and ultimately interfere with the development of necessary self-regulatory skills (Dahl, 1996).

Similar findings have also been reported with respect to nonclinical levels of parental anxiety and child sleep behaviors. Level of maternal separation anxiety in particular has been the focus of increasing attention. In a community sample of 10-month-old infants and their mothers, maternal report of their own separation anxiety and perception of separation effects on their child were examined in relation to actigraphy-based sleep measures (Scher, 2008). High levels of maternal separation anxiety were associated with a greater number of infant night-waking episodes and less-efficient sleep even after controlling for infant temperament. However, perception of the child's separation distress was not associated with any sleep variables. The study also found significantly higher levels of separation anxiety among mothers who were actively involved in regulating their child's sleep (e.g., stroking, rocking, singing) compared to those who were uninvolved. Last, mothers who attributed their child's night-waking episodes to fear (as compared to physical discomfort such as hunger or having a wet diaper) reported higher levels of child separation anxiety. Findings from this study highlight several important linkages between infant sleep characteristics and caregiver behaviors. Even in the case of nonclinical levels of anxiety, specific parenting behaviors surrounding sleep may function first to serve parents' rather than children's immediate needs, and parents may project their own fears and anxiety onto infants. Although the impact of maternal anxiety and related nighttime behaviors remains to be investigated over the long term, one study found that while maternal separation anxiety was not associated with sleep patterns when infants were 3 months of age, it did predict increased night waking 6 months later (Scher, 1995). These data lend further support to the theory that parental separation anxiety serves as a modulator of children's sleep (Scher & Blumberg, 1999).

Cognitive Factors

Cognitive factors not only are a well-recognized feature of anxiety disorders in children and adults but also represent an important dimension of sleep disturbance (Gross & Borkovec, 1982; Harvey, 2002; Wicklow & Espie, 2000). Difficulty with excessive thought or worry prior to sleep onset is common among adults with both anxiety and sleep disorders (Harvey & Espie, 2004; Wicklow & Espie, 2000). Adult models of insomnia postulate that an individual's cognitive responses to initial sleep difficulties may serve to maintain or exacerbate sleep problems over time (Morin, 1993). In particular, insomnia is more likely to persist if sleep difficulties are perceived as harmful or a sign of loss of control. Among anxious children, similar cognitive biases, including interpretation biases (i.e., inaccurately perceiving situations or events as threatening) and judgment biases (i.e., negative estimations of one's ability to control outcomes or events) have been found and are hypothesized to contribute to the development of these disorders over time (Weems, Berman, Silverman, & Saavedra, 2001; Weems, Costa, Watts, Taylor, & Cannon, 2007).

Investigation of cognitive factors related to sleep disturbance in children is limited, but preliminary evidence exists for the presence of important relationships. Gregory and Eley (2005) found a significant association between a negative attributional style (i.e., internal, stable, global attributions for negative events) and sleep problems in a small community sample of children. Similarly, Alfano, Zakem, Costa, Taylor, and Weems (2009) found that adolescent sleep problems were significantly associated with interpretation biases in a community sample of youth. However, this association was fully mediated by the presence of anxiety and depression symptoms. In the first study to examine cognitive factors associated with the sleep problems of children with anxiety disorders, greater levels of presleep cognitive compared to somatic arousal were found, and presleep cognitive arousal was significantly associated with decreased total sleep duration and increased sleep problems (Alfano et al., 2010). Comparisons based on age revealed similar levels of presleep cognition among children 7–10 years and 11–14 years. While the specific content of anxious children's presleep thoughts remains to be empirically investigated, in clinical settings anxious children often report excessive nighttime worries that range in content from concrete fears (e.g., burglars) to more abstract worries (e.g., the potential impact of sleep loss on daytime performance). Taken together, clinical and research findings suggest cognitive factors play an important role in presleep arousal and associated sleep disruption among children as young as age 7 with anxiety disorders.

IMPACT OF ANXIETY TREATMENT ON CO-OCCURRING SLEEP PROBLEMS

Pharmacological Treatments

Although some pharmacological agents for anxiety, including selective serotonin reuptake inhibitors (SSRIs), are safe and effective for children, studies examining the effectiveness of these treatments have generally failed to consider changes in sleep when assessing treatment outcome. Alfano and colleagues (2007) found that fluvoxamine produced significantly greater reductions in parent- and clinician-reported sleep problems compared to placebo in youth with anxiety disorders after 8 weeks of treatment. Symptoms of insomnia and reluctance or refusal to sleep independently were significantly reduced, although more than 30% of youth continued to report at least mild levels of insomnia at posttreatment, and improvements in parent-reported nightmares were not observed. Although these data suggest some improvement in sleep difficulties following pharmacological treatment, it is important to note that systematic assessment of sleep was not included in the original treatment study (RUPP Anxiety Study Group, 2001), and that sleep data were retrospectively drawn from several sleep items included in other measures. In addition, because sleep problems such as insomnia are common side effects of treatment with SSRIs for childhood anxiety (e.g., Wagner et al., 2004), more research is ultimately needed to determine the impact and effectiveness of these interventions for anxious children with co-occurring sleep problems.

Behavioral Treatments

In general, cognitive-behavioral therapy (CBT) is highly efficacious for childhood anxiety disorders, with half to two thirds of treated youth showing significant reductions in anxious symptomatology following treatment (Silverman et al., 2008). Similar to pharmacologic treatment trials, however, this considerable body of research has not assessed potential changes in sleep as part of treatment outcome, despite the fact that co-occurring sleep problems may confer added risk for impairments in daytime functioning and reduce the effectiveness of treatment. For example, because sleep loss in children commonly manifests in the form of hyperactivity, inability to maintain attention, and a lack of motivation (Mindell, Owens, & Carskadon, 1999), insufficient sleep may undermine the effectiveness of CBT by interfering with central treatment components requiring children to learn new information, practice self-control techniques, and engage in behavioral exposures. With regard to the last, by which specific fears and anxieties are extinguished through repeated and controlled in-session tasks, experimental findings suggest that sleep loss may directly impede fear reduction. In particular, deprivation of REM sleep following a fear-conditioning task interferes with subsequent fear extinction in rodents (Graves, Heller, Pack, & Abel, 2003; Silvestri, 2005). In humans, adequate sleep promotes generalization from extinguished (those targeted during exposures) to unextinguished fears (those not directly targeted during exposures) (Pace-Schott et al., 2009).

    In the only study to date to examine changes in sleep following behavioral treatment, Storch and colleagues (2008) examined the impact of 14 weeks of CBT for pediatric OCD on children's co-occurring sleep problems. An overall significant decrease in parent-reported sleep problems, including nightmares and trouble sleeping, was reported, although a reduction in sleep problems based on child report was not found. The basis for this discrepancy is unclear but may be explained by a lack of structured, validated assessment of sleep. Moreover, certain types of sleep problems tend to be more problematic for parents compared to children (e.g., bedtime resistance and nighttime arousals), and a reduction in these specific behaviors may (erroneously) create the perception that the child's sleep quality has improved as well. In sum, it remains generally unknown whether sleep problems that commonly co-occur with childhood anxiety disorders improve along with reductions in anxiety and improvements in overall functioning or whether additional behavioral intervention may be required to produce optimal immediate and long-term treatment outcomes.

ASSESSMENT OF SLEEP IN CHILDREN

While elaborate discussion of different methodologies for evaluating sleep in children is not relevant to the primary aims of this chapter, several reliable and validated measures are commonly used in both practice and research settings.

Clinical Interviews

At present, there are no validated, structured interviews focused on sleep disorders in children. Part of the difficulty in developing such assessment tools relates to the many challenges inherent in determining what constitutes "disordered sleep" in children, including environmentally rather than biologically dictated sleep practices. Further, the proportion of children with insomnia without a comorbid psychiatric disorder appears to be low, and consensus for a definition of childhood insomnia is lacking (Glaze et al., 2002; Owens, 2005). While the interview of choice for the diagnosis of childhood anxiety disorders is the Anxiety Disorders Interview for Children for DSM-IV: Child and Parent Versions (ADIS-C/P; Silverman & Albano, 1996), only two types of sleep problems are included in the ADIS-C/P: enuresis and sleep terrors. However, as reviewed in this chapter, these specific problems do not appear to be the most sensitive indicators of sleep disruption in anxious youth.

Unstructured interviews for childhood sleep disorders generally include inquiries regarding a child's sleep history, current sleep schedule, behaviors and habits surrounding sleep, and the specific nature and duration of sleep difficulties. Although sleep-related impairments often mimic those seen in psychiatric disorders and can therefore be challenging to disentangle, some of the most robust indicators of insufficient sleep include excessive daytime tiredness (e.g., sleepiness in inappropriate settings such as school), inability to awaken in the morning, and increased sleep on weekends. The potential presence of environmental or familial factors that may cause or maintain sleep problems also should be assessed. Parental limit setting and responses to bedtime resistance, inconsistent household routines and bedtimes, cosleeping, and evening use of electronic media such as television and video games are common concomitants of ongoing sleep disruption.

Sleep Diaries

Children with a suspected sleep disorder should be asked to keep a 1- or 2-week sleep diary. Sleep diaries usually consist of a one-page, 24-hour

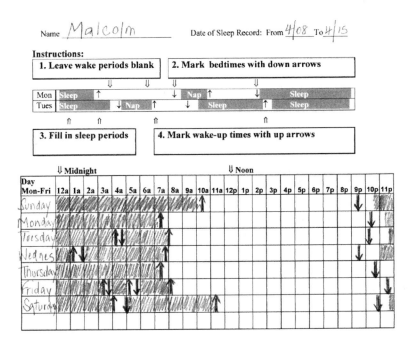

FIGURE 5.1   Malcolm's 1-week sleep log prior to treatment.

grid used to record sleep and wake periods on a prospective basis (see Figure 5.1). Information captured typically includes nightly bedtimes, time required to fall asleep, length and number of nighttime awakenings, morning wake times, and daytime naps. Most children need some parental assistance in completing sleep diaries with accuracy. Information collected can be used to calculate key sleep variables: average sleep-onset latency, variability in weekday and weekend sleep, sleep efficiency or the amount of time in bed actually spent sleeping, and awake periods after sleep onset. Benefits associated with the use of sleep diaries include a detailed, visual depiction of sleep behaviors and habits, minimization of biases associated with retrospective reporting of sleep, and ongoing assessment of sleep changes during treatment. Sleep diaries are also commonly used to confirm actigraphy-based sleep data.

Questionnaire Measures

There are several reliable and validated measures of children's sleep. The Children's Sleep Habits Questionnaire (CSHQ; Owens, Spirito, & McGuinn, 2000) is a comprehensive 33-item parent-report measure for children aged 4–12 years. The CSHQ yields a Total Sleep Problems score and eight subscale scores reflecting key sleep domains, including Bedtime Resistance, Sleep Onset Delay, Sleep Duration, Sleep Anxiety, Night Wakings, Parasomnias, Sleep-Disordered Breathing, and Daytime Sleepiness. The CSHQ also assesses average total sleep time and nightly bedtime. Similarly, the Sleep Disturbance Scale for Children (SDSC; Bruni et al., 1996) is a validated, 27-item parent-report questionnaire designed to assess the most common types of sleep disorders in childhood and adolescence (ages 3–18 years), including disorders of initiating and maintaining sleep, disorders of arousal or nightmares, sleep/wake transition disorders, and excessive sleepiness. The Sleep Self-Report (SSR; Owens, Spirito, McGuinn, & Nobile 2000) is a 26-item measure designed to be administered to or self-administered by school-aged children 7 to 12 years of age. The SSR assesses sleep domains corresponding to the CSHQ (parent version). For older adolescents, the School Sleep Habits Survey (SSHS; Wolfson & Carskadon, 1998) has been validated in comparison to both sleep diaries and actigraphy. The SSHS assesses adolescent sleep patterns and problems over the past 2 weeks, including variations in weekday and weekend sleep.

Actigraphy

Actigraphy has been used extensively in sleep research, including research with children of all ages. This small, watch-sized, device is worn on the nondominant hand 24 hours a day and measures movement. The unit collects and stores continuous movement data, typically in 1-minute epochs (i.e., activity level is sampled at 10-second intervals and summed across 1-minute intervals). Event markers provide specific information regarding sleep/wake times. Following use, data from the unit are downloaded onto a computer and scored by a computer-generated algorithm that has been shown to be reliable in identifying sleep and wake periods (Carskadon, Acebo, Richardson, Tate, & Seifer, 1997). Objective variables derived from actigraphy typically include total sleep time, sleep-onset latency, wake time after sleep onset, and sleep efficiency.

TREATMENT OF ANXIETY-
RELATED SLEEP PROBLEMS

Behavioral therapies for childhood anxiety disorders and sleep problems overlap to a large extent. Specifically, many of the same principles and strategies used to effectively manage children's daytime fears have been similarly effective at night. In fact, since little is known about the safety, tolerability, and efficacy of pharmacologic sleep agents for children, pediatric treatment guidelines designate behavioral interventions as treatments of choice for child sleep problems (Mindell & Owens, 2003).

Treatment of Nighttime Fears

In the case of transient nighttime fears, allowing children to sleep in a caregivers' bed may reduce fearful behaviors. However, this strategy has the potential to reinforce a child's fears, and the probability of this to ultimately lead to persistent sleep problems is high. The efficacy of other interventions based on cognitive-behavioral principles is, by comparison, well established. In one of the first controlled treatment trials to examine CBT for the treatment of severe nighttime fears, Graziano and Mooney (1980) randomized 6- to 12-year-old children to a 3-week treatment group that included weekly sessions and nightly practice of relaxation techniques, positive imagery and coping statements (e.g., "I am brave!"), or a wait-list control condition. Parents of children in the treatment group also provided "bravery tokens" for the successful completion of nightly practice and brave behaviors at night (i.e., contingency management). At the end of 3 weeks, children in the CBT group displayed significantly less nighttime fear, bedtime resistance, and time required to fall asleep compared to children in the wait-list group. Results were maintained more than 2 years later (Graziano & Mooney, 1982). Similar treatment packages have been used in other treatment studies; positive results were reported (Giebenhain & O'Dell, 1984; McMenamy & Katz, 1989).

One important methodological limitation of these studies, however, includes the inability to identify which specific treatment components are actually responsible for reducing children's nighttime fears. The potential role of nonspecific factors such as treatment expectancies and contact with a mental health professional is unknown. To address this issue, Friedman and Ollendick (1989) conducted a study using a multiple-baseline design to examine the efficacy of a treatment package, including relaxation, positive reinforcement, and self-statements, among six children with severe nighttime fears. The study specifically controlled for the potential effect of contact with a therapist by including placebo treatment sessions that did not introduce any specific treatment component. Although five of the six children showed reductions in disruptive bedtime behaviors following treatment, home monitoring revealed that behavioral improvements actually preceded the implementation of active treatment sessions. Thus, changes in behavior could not be attributed to active treatment. Other challenges involved in interpreting treatment outcome data for children's nighttime fears include a lack of diagnostic information for a majority of participants, small sample sizes, and lack of attention to changes in actual sleep patterns. Overall, while there is evidence to suggest that treatments utilizing some combination of relaxation, self-control strategies, and contingency management are efficacious for nighttime fears, an understanding of which specific strategies are actually effective is lacking.

Treatment of Nightmares

Although clinicians often stress the importance of providing reassurance and support to children who experience nightmares (e.g., Siegel & Bulkeley, 1998), controlled studies examining such approaches are actually unavailable. By comparison, imagery rehearsal therapy (IRT) has received considerable attention and empirical support in adults. In IRT, the individual is asked to modify the content of his or her most recent nightmare to include more positive images and experiences and then to rehearse the new dream while in a state of relaxation, either in session or at home prior to sleep. Numerous studies, including several randomized controlled trials, have shown IRT to reduce the frequency of nightmares as well as associated distress (Davis & Wright, 2005; Krakow, Kellner, Pathak, & Lambert, 1996; Neidhardt, Krakow, Kellner & Pathak, 1992). The effectiveness of IRT also has been demonstrated among adults with PTSD and posttraumatic nightmares (Forbes et al., 2003; Germain & Nielsen, 2003; Krakow et al., 1997).

In a 2001 study, Krakow and colleagues extended findings for the efficacy of IRT among a small sample of adolescent girls (ages 13–18 years) experiencing nightmares related to unwanted sexual experiences during childhood. St-Onge, Mercier, and De Koninck (2009) examined the applicability of IRT for children. Using a sample of children ages 9 to 11 years with persistent, moderate-to-severe nightmares (defined as one or more per week for 6 months), participants were randomized to either IRT or a wait-list condition. Any time children experienced a nightmare during the 8-week treatment period, they were asked to modify their nightmare the following evening and rehearse the newly scripted dream for at least 10 minutes before bedtime. Compared to the wait-list condition, IRT significantly reduced the frequency of children's nightmares at posttreatment, and results were maintained over a 9-month period. However, differences in self-ratings of distress associated with nightmares did not differ between groups, mainly because wait-list participants showed improvement on this measure in the absence of specific intervention. These results are comparable to those reported by Friedman and Ollendick (1989); reductions in children's disruptive bedtime behaviors were observed while families were simply awaiting treatment. Other important questions that remain to be addressed include whether criteria used to identify "persistent, moderate-to-severe nightmares" may have been overly sensitive and whether nightmares were linked with specific traumatic events.

TREATMENT OF SLEEP PROBLEMS IN A CHILD WITH GAD: A CASE EXAMPLE

As noted, Malcolm presented with a complex picture of sleep problems and anxiety. Even though he had always been an anxious child and a poor sleeper, the start of first grade last year was particularly difficult for him. He was up most of the night prior to the first day of school worrying about what his teacher would be like, whether he would be able to do the work, and whether he would make any friends. According to his parents, this marked the beginning of an extremely difficult period that had persisted for over a year.

INITIAL ASSESSMENT

Initial assessment included separate semistructured interviews using the ADIS-C/P (Silverman & Albano, 1996) with Malcolm and his parents, as well as the completion of several parent and child report questionnaires. During the assessment, Malcolm reported that he worries about numerous things in addition to his sleep, including his grades, natural disasters, his parents' health, and getting into a good college. He often feels different from his friends because they "don't seem to worry about stuff." His parents reported that he has always been a worrier, and that he seeks constant reassurance about things. In addition to difficulty sleeping alone, his parents reported that he is "always tired and irritable." Malcolm was given a primary diagnosis of GAD. In addition to his anxiety and worry, the family was asked about Malcolm's sleep problems during their interviews. Also, a sleep diary was mailed to the family to be completed during the 1-week period leading up the evaluation appointment. The sleep diary completed by Malcolm and his parents at baseline indicated several problems, including an irregular sleep/wake schedule, an excessive amount of time taken to fall sleep, and nightly awakenings (see Figure 5.1). Overall assessment revealed that Malcolm was receiving an inadequate amount of sleep for his age, as indicated by his inability to awaken in the morning, increased sleep on weekends, and excessive sleepiness in settings such as in school and watching TV.

MALCOLM'S TREATMENT PLAN

Behavioral intervention targeting Malcolm's unique problems included a focus on both daytime and nighttime anxiety and worry, which were related to a large extent.

PSYCHOEDUCATION

First, it was explained to Malcolm and his parents that it is helpful to think about "anxiety" in terms of three broad, but overlapping, symptom domains: physical symptoms and sensations (e.g., racing heart, sweaty palms); avoidant behaviors (e.g., refusing to go to school or to sleep alone, seeking constant reassurance); and negative thoughts or beliefs (e.g., "A burglar will break in," "I will never get into the college that I want"). It was explained that, to some extent, all of these symptoms serve to maintain anxiety and worry over time. In describing the model, Malcolm was asked to provide examples of common or typical symptoms he experienced when worried. Based on his age, Malcolm had some difficulty reflecting on his own feelings and thoughts, but his parents were able to help him remember how he commonly felt and acted in such situations. The family also learned about the role of sleep in relation to numerous aspects of functioning, including the management of anxiety: "When our brains and bodies are tired, they do a much poorer job of managing anxiety!" It was explained that falling asleep at night is not something we are born knowing how to do. Rather, we *learn* to fall asleep based on the presence of certain internal (e.g., fatigue and sleepiness) and external (e.g., dim light, our comfortable bed) cues. Sometimes, however, these cues or signals get "mixed up" and need to be reset. In Malcolm's case, bedtime signaled a time of stress, worry, and arousal rather than calm and quiescence. In addition, it was discussed with Malcolm's parents that, while intending to help him, they were actually reinforcing his nighttime anxious behavior and rumination by becoming a necessary "cue" for him to feel safe and initiate sleep.

PROGRESSIVE MUSCLE RELAXATION AND DEEP BREATHING

Malcolm was first taught to use and practice progressive muscle relaxation and deep breathing both when he became worried about something and before bed each night. While a more detailed description of these techniques is provided in Chapter 6, essentially progressive muscle relaxation is used to target high levels of general arousal. Based on Malcolm's young age, he was given two small squeezable balls to use (one for each hand) as a means of prompting and illustrating the concept of muscle tension and relaxation. In addition, the importance of using his breath to slow his heart rate and feel calmer was discussed. To make this exercise more fun and concrete, the therapist showed Malcolm how to breathe correctly by blowing bubbles through a small wand. Malcolm's parents were encouraged to provide him with his own small bottle of bubbles to practice deep breathing at home.

SLEEP HYGIENE

The concept of "sleep hygiene" was also explained to the family. To help Malcolm understand this idea in an age-appropriate way, sleep hygiene was compared with dental hygiene: "Just like dental hygiene keeping your teeth and gums clean and healthy, sleep hygiene helps you by keeping your mind and body rested and strong." In Malcolm's case, several new "sleep rules" were implemented, including (a) keeping a regular sleep schedule 7 days a week by going to bed and waking up at the same time every day; (b) avoiding daytime napping (which might interfere with his ability to fall asleep at the same time every night); (c) creating a sleep environment that is quiet, cool, and dimly lit; (d) avoiding caffeine; (e) using his bed for relaxation exercises and sleep *only* (i.e., not for homework or reading); and (f) developing a calm and relaxing presleep routine. It was decided that 60 minutes before bedtime Malcolm would take his bath, which he found relaxing. After his bath, he was responsible for brushing his teeth and putting on his pajamas independently, after which he would have reading time with a parent on the sofa under dim light. Following reading time, Malcolm would practice his relaxation and breathing exercises in his room independently before bedtime.

EXPOSURE

Both in vivo and imaginary exposures were used to target Malcolm's worry and anxiety. Since his sleep problems were of the greatest concern and interfered with the entire family's ability to sleep, worry about burglars was addressed first. During these exposure sessions, Malcolm was asked to sit in the therapy room by himself while the therapist made strange noises outside the room. Malcolm was given a "feeling thermometer," and the therapist would periodically ask for his distress level from outside the room. Malcolm habituated to this task (i.e., it no longer provoked anxiety) after only two sessions. Subsequent sessions included the same in vivo exposure task only with the lights in the therapy room turned off. He was successful in habituating quickly to this task as well and was offered small rewards for his success. Following each treatment session, Malcolm was also given a homework assignment. He was instructed to spend 20 minutes in his room by himself during the daytime engaged in a solitary activity with the door closed. Although Malcolm had great success in session, at-home assignments were more difficult. His parents reported that each time he attempted to stay in his room, he would inevitably leave the room, stating that he had to use the bathroom, that he had to ask his parents a question, or that he thought he heard "something weird." His parents were therefore coached in setting firm limits and offering attention and praise *only* after he successfully completed the assignment.

GRADUATED EXTINCTION PROCEDURE FOR SLEEPING ALONE

Since Malcolm was only marginally successful in completing at-home exposure assignments, a graduated extinction procedure was implemented to eliminate Malcolm's fear of sleeping in his room alone at night. Following a chosen quiet and independent presleep activity (e.g., reading), Malcolm's parents would tuck him in and then sit in a chair next to his bed (i.e., not sit on or lie in his bed). However, once in the chair they were instructed not to talk to or look at him. Once Malcolm fell asleep, they were to leave the room. Over successive nights, the chair was to be gradually moved away from the bed and closer to the door with the goal of not being in the room at bedtime after 1 week. Malcolm was told that as long as he remained quiet and in his bed, his parent would remain in the chair in his room. However, if he talked to his parent or got out of his bed, his parents were instructed to leave the room and not respond to Malcolm until he stopped crying, calling out to them, and the like and got back into bed. If he woke up in the middle of the night and went to his parents' bed, he was to be brought back to his own bed without discussion or fighting.

Treatment progress was tracked with weekly sleep logs and sticker charts. Specifically, for every night Malcolm followed his bedtime routine and slept in his bed alone, he earned a sticker. The number of stickers required to earn a reward was increased each week as he experienced greater success (i.e., contingency management). Malcolm was able to sleep in his room by himself without seeking or calling out to his parents at night after 2 weeks. His sleep logs simultaneously indicated a significant reduction in sleep onset latency (from 60 minutes to approximately 15 minutes) and an increase in total sleep time. As instructed, the family also created and maintained a consistent sleep schedule for Malcolm.

SUMMARY

Despite the documented high prevalence of sleep problems among anxious youth, surprisingly little is known about the role of sleep in the overall course of childhood anxiety disorders. Even less is known about specific mechanisms underlying this common overlap in symptoms, although neurobiological, cognitive, and environmental factors each may play an important role. Longitudinal data reveal that childhood sleep problems presage the later development of anxiety disorders, but it remains to be examined whether these problems represent early features of the same underlying pathophysiology or a distinct disorder that may give rise to broader problems with arousal dysregulation. As such, systematic examinations of sleep among anxious youth are needed and may provide critical insights into the mechanisms by which these disorders are caused and maintained. Data are beginning to emerge suggesting that although sleep disturbance may occur along with many forms of anxiety, rates and specific types of sleep problems vary based on individual child anxiety disorders. Youth with GAD, SAD, OCD, and PTSD appear to be at the greatest risk for persistent and impairing sleep problems, although objective sleep data are highly limited. Among these youth in particular, sleep should be considered as part of assessment procedures since unaddressed sleep problems during treatment may interfere with potential treatment gains. Systematic examination of sleep as part of treatment outcome research for childhood anxiety disorders is ultimately needed to better understand how sleep may (or may not) improve along with reductions in anxiety.

Anxiety Disorders
in Children

CHAPTER **6**

Excessive Worry and Generalized Anxiety Disorder

Melissa is 9 years old. Her mother brought her to the clinic because, several days earlier, Melissa told her mother that she was afraid she was going to die. She thinks that she might die from getting sick, and she would "lose everything." She also worries that she might have a heart attack when she's older but "not now." She worries that her mother might die, and that her father may get sick. She worries that her parents won't come back when they leave home because something may happen to them. She worries about burglars "a little but not as much as about dying." She also worries about vomiting and choking, and according to her mother, she has had two panic attacks.

Melissa has generalized anxiety disorder (GAD), a common, but poorly understood, childhood anxiety disorder. Interestingly, children with GAD often are regarded as well behaved, eager to please, perfectionistic, and overly mature (Ehrenreich & Gross, 2001). Melissa's worries certainly sound mature for her age. GAD is characterized by excessive anxiety and worry that is excessive, difficult to control, and associated with a variety of somatic complaints. Although somatic complaints and cognitive worry are the major components of GAD, they also exist independently and quite frequently in the general population. Thus, before discussing the clinical syndrome of GAD, it is necessary to examine the construct of childhood worry.

CHILDHOOD WORRY

Defined as a cognitive process, *worry* is characterized by negatively valenced thoughts or images related to potential threats or dangers

(Borkovec, 1985). In Vasey's (1993) seminal paper, childhood worry is defined as primarily anticipatory, catastrophic, and self-referential. Because it is cognitively based, consideration of worry in young children must first address the issue of basic cognitive development (see Alfano et al., 2002). To phrase it succinctly, some aspects of worry (e.g., the ability to consider the future and therefore to anticipate negative events) are dependent on basic cognitive maturation. Therefore, worry in children, or even the ability to worry, may be different from worry in adults.

At young ages, children's cognitive capacities are limited. Full capacity to imagine and anticipate future events appears to develop at age 7 or 8. Whereas 5- to 6-year-olds worry about threats to their physical well-being, among children age 8 and above, behavioral competence, social evaluation, and psychological well-being are more common (Vasey & Daleiden, 1994). Perhaps even more important, children older than age 8 endorsed a significantly greater number and variety of worries than 5- to 6-year-olds, reinforcing the notion that increased cognitive development leads to a greater capacity for worry (Henker, Whalen, & O'Neil, 1995; Vasey & Daleidin, 1994). As Melissa's case indicates, children as young as age 9 can worry about some future-oriented events, such as a heart attack "when I'm older." Nonetheless, the worry of an 8- or 9-year-old does not precisely resemble that of an adult. For example, the adult worry process involves greater attempts at problem solving (Szabo & Lovibond, 2002; Tallis & Eynsenck, 1994); more than half of adult worry is characterized by active problem solving compared to approximately 30% of children's worry processes (Szabo & Lovibond, 2002, 2004). Thus, this particular function of worry appears to still be developing between the ages of 8 and 12 and may not fully develop until the adolescent years. Szabo and Lovibond (2004) specifically compared the worry of 38 children with anxiety disorders (42% with primary GAD) and 51 control children and found that worry among the anxious children was associated with significantly fewer problem-solving attempts than controls. In addition, unlike control children, use of problem solving among anxiety-disordered youth did not improve with increasing age. Thus, it is both the controllability and the content of childhood worry that appear to distinguish clinically anxious and nonanxious youth.

Worry is common among children. In one of the earliest studies, more than 70% of primary school children endorsed 10 or more objects or events about which they worried (Orton, 1982). Among children in Grades 4 through 8, 88% reported at least one worry, and the average number of worries expressed by children was 3.9, most frequently encompassing academics as well as health and safety (Henker et al., 1995). In another nonclinical sample of preadolescent children (Silverman, La Greca, & Waserstein, 1995), more than 66% of the children reported at least one worry, most commonly health, school performance, and personal harm. Safety and personal injury were the most frequent worries.

Children classified as highly anxious based on self-report could be distinguished from the other children by a significantly greater number of specific worries and a greater number of areas of worry (Silverman et al., 1995). Furthermore, they worried more frequently. Similar results using a large sample of children and a comprehensive assessment strategy provide further support for this important distinction (Muris, Meesters, Merckelbach, Sermon, & Zwakhalen, 1998). Among nonselected school children aged 8–13, 69% reported that they worried "every now and then." Consistent with findings from other investigations (Silverman et al., 1995; Vasey & Daleidin, 1994), the most common worries were school performance, dying and health, and social contacts. For most children, the mean frequency of their worry was about 2–3 days per week. The level of interference and anxiety elicited by their worry was quite low (none to minimal interference or fear), but the children did note that their worries were difficult to stop. To summarize, while worry itself appears to be common among all children, frequency and intensity of worry may be what distinguishes children who have high anxiety from the "normal" worries of the general population. This conclusion, that frequency and impairment are the distinguishing factors, is consistent with data from comparative studies of children with and without anxiety disorders.

Even among children with psychiatric disorders, worry is not unique to children with anxiety disorders diagnoses. Perrin and Last (1997) assessed worry in children with anxiety disorders, attention deficit/ hyperactivity disorder, and never psychiatrically ill controls. Infrequent worrying was common among all of the children, including those who had never been diagnosed with an anxiety disorder. However, consistent with the study by Silverman et al. (1995), children with anxiety disorders reported more intense worrying than children in the other two groups but not more types of worries. Thus, based on the available evidence, it appears that what differentiates normal from pathological worry is not simply the existence of worry itself, but the extent and frequency of worry and its resultant impact on daily functioning. When worry does interfere with daily functioning or create somatic distress, intervention is usually necessary. Those interventions that have been successful in the treatment of childhood worry are presented here.

GENERALIZED ANXIETY DISORDER

As noted at the outset of this chapter, GAD is defined as excessive anxiety and worry that is difficult to control and is accompanied by various somatic complaints (*Diagnostic and Statistical Manual of Mental Disorders, Fourth Edition, Text Revision, DSM-IV-TR*; American Psychiatric Association [APA], 2000; see Table 6.1 for the specific diagnostic criteria). Prior to 1994, pervasive and substantive worry was the primary descriptor for overanxious disorder (OAD), listed in the "Disorders of Childhood" section of the third edition of the *DSM* (*DSM-III*; APA, 1980). However, there were numerous problems with this diagnostic category, including limited reliability, overdiagnosis, inappropriateness of the specific criteria, lack of distinctiveness from other childhood disorders, uncertain relationship to adult disorders, and lack of external validity (Werry, 1991). The most pertinent issues are discussed here.

Part of the problem with respect to the overdiagnosis of OAD stemmed from the vagueness of the diagnostic criteria. With respect to the specific content of worries, 31% of a sample of children without anxiety disorders worried about their competence, 23% sought excessive reassurance from their parents, 16% worried about their past behavior, 14.5% reported somatic complaints, and 9.8% reported excessive worrying (Bell-Dolan et al., 1990). Furthermore, 16% reported worrying that harm would befall an attachment figure, and 10% worried about self-harm. Concerning the issue of discriminant validity, Beidel (1991) compared children diagnosed with social phobia, OAD, or no disorder on a variety of clinical measures, including self-report inventories, daily diary data, and a psychophysiological assessment, determining skills and anxiety when taking a test or reading aloud. Children with social phobia could be distinguished from normal controls across a variety of measures (lower perceptions of competence, higher trait anxiety, higher anxiety during the behavioral assessment, and significant distress and impairment in daily functioning). In contrast, children with OAD differed from normal controls only by their higher scores on trait anxiety. Finally, with respect to functional impairment (Beidel, Silverman, & Hammond-Laurence, 1996), clinic-referred children with OAD were compared to a community sample who also met criteria for OAD on the presence of specific OAD symptoms, general measures of psychopathology, and family environment. The results indicated few differences between the two groups, and the differences that did exist represented ancillary, rather than core, features. Specifically, mothers of clinic-referred children endorsed a higher number of OAD symptoms, a higher frequency of mother-reported symptoms of being sick from

TABLE 6.1   *DSM-IV-TR* Diagnostic Criteria for Generalized Anxiety Disorder

---

A. Excessive anxiety and worry (apprehensive expectation), occurring more days than not for at least 6 months, about a number of events or activities (such as work or school performance).

B. The person finds it difficult to control the worry.

C. The anxiety and worry are associated with three (or more) of the following six symptoms (with at least some symptoms present for more days than not for the past 6 months). Note: Only one item is required in children.

    (1) restlessness or feeling keyed up or on edge

    (2) being easily fatigued

    (3) difficulty concentrating or mind going blank

    (4) irritability

    (5) muscle tension

    (6) sleep disturbance (difficulty falling or staying asleep or restless unsatisfying sleep)

D. The focus of the anxiety and worry is not confined to features of an Axis I disorder (e.g., the anxiety or worry is not about having a Panic Attack (as in Panic Disorder), being embarrassed in public (as in Social Phobia), being contaminated (as in Obsessive-Compulsive Disorder), being away from home or close relatives (as in Separation Anxiety Disorder), gaining weight (as in Anorexia Nervosa), having multiple physical complaints (as in Somatization Disorder) or having a serious illness (as in Hypochondriasis) and the anxiety and worry do not occur exclusively during Posttraumatic Stress Disorder.

E. The anxiety, worry, or physical symptoms cause clinically significant distress or impairment in social, occupational, or other important areas of functioning.

F. The disturbance is not due to the direct physiological effects of a substance (e.g., a drug of abuse, a medication) or a general medical condition (e.g., hyperthyroidism) and does not occur exclusively during a Mood Disorder, a Psychotic Disorder, or a Pervasive Developmental Disorder.

---

worrying and often being tense, and finally a higher number of comorbid diagnoses among the clinic sample. However, there were no group differences in functional impairment. Thus, the clinic-referred sample may present with more severe general psychopathology, but overall the results supported previous research, leading to the conclusion that OAD may not be a clinical syndrome but perhaps a prodromal state.

Based on these data as well as others, OAD was dropped as a separate diagnosis from the test revision of fourth edition of the *DSM* (APA, 2000) and subsumed under the diagnostic category of GAD. More recent studies have examined the validity and utility of GAD criteria in children. Pina, Silverman, Alfano, and Saavedra (2002) used parent and child reports to determine the relative contribution of specific *DSM-IV* criteria for diagnosing GAD. While some symptom differences emerged between child and parent reports, overall almost all *DSM-IV* symptoms were found to have high utility in diagnosing childhood GAD. Results from two other studies, however, indicated that only poor-to-fair parent–child agreement for the presence of the disorder (κ = .22 or .45) and poor agreement between parent and child with respect to the specific symptoms that comprise the disorder (κs range from .20 to .39) (Choudhury, Pimentel, & Kendall, 2003; Tracey, Chorpita, Douban, & Barlow, 1997). Only the OAD symptom of stomachaches had fair parent–child agreement (κ = .49). However, there was good agreement for the presence of clinical worry (actual κ not reported in the article), and all children with a *DSM-IV* diagnosis of GAD also met criteria for the *DSM-III-R* diagnosis of OAD. Thus, although the issue of reliability remains somewhat problematic for this diagnostic category, excessive, uncontrollable worry and somatic symptoms remain primary and useful clinical features. Nonetheless, because children who met diagnostic criteria for OAD also meet criteria for GAD and because both disorders include worry and accompanying somatic complaints as primary diagnostic features, data on clinical syndrome and treatment outcome for both diagnostic categories follow.

Clinical Features and Course

One of the major criticisms of the former OAD diagnostic category was that it often could not be distinguished as a distinct diagnosis. Tracey et al. (1997) reported that children with GAD had a significantly higher number of worries, GAD symptoms, and OAD symptoms than children with another anxiety disorder or children with no disorder. This would be expected inasmuch as the children would not have received the diagnosis without expressing worry and somatic complaints. However, children with GAD also had significantly higher scores on a measure of general anxiety (Revised Children's Manifest Anxiety Scale) and depression (Children's Depression Inventory). Thus, in addition to the specific presence of former OAD symptoms, children with GAD also have higher levels of general anxiety and depression when compared to children with other anxiety disorders, thus providing some validity for the diagnostic category.

Although OAD/GAD has received limited attention with respect to determining its prevalence and clinical features, the diagnosis is fairly prevalent, with rates as high as 15% in the general population (Costello, Egger, & Angold, 2005) and 10% in child psychiatric clinics (Tracey et al., 1997). The disorder also accounts for 38% and 59% of referrals to child anxiety clinics (Barrett, Dadds, & Rapee, 1996; Kendall et al., 1997), making it one of the most common anxiety disorders of childhood. However, fewer data exist with respect to the natural course of OAD/GAD. Early studies did not support the temporal stability of OAD. For example, Cantwell and Baker (1989) found that only 25% of youth retained the diagnosis at follow-up (4–5 years later); 25% were judged to no longer have the diagnosis, and 50% were diagnosed with a different disorder. These data underscore concerns raised with regard to the specificity and stability of DSM-III-R (APA, 1987) OAD.

More recently, research has focused on the developmental trajectories of children with OAD/GAD into adolescence and adulthood. Among a large clinic sample of adolescents, Pine, Cohen, Gurley, Brook, and Ma (1998) found that an OAD diagnosis during early adolescence significantly predicted social phobia, depression, panic disorder, and GAD in adulthood. Bittner and colleagues (2007) examined childhood anxiety disorders as predictors of adolescent psychiatric disorders. Because data were drawn from a large, ongoing longitudinal study, the predictive values of OAD and GAD were examined separately among over 900 youth. Whereas a childhood OAD diagnosis significantly predicted adolescent OAD, panic attacks, depression, and conduct disorder, childhood GAD predicted adolescent conduct disorder only. Thus, OAD was an overall better predictor of later anxiety disorders than GAD. In a follow-up study, many of the same investigators examined both child and adolescent anxiety disorders as predictors of adult psychopathology (Copeland, Shanahan, Costello, & Angold, 2009). Consistent with their previous results, adolescent OAD predicted adult GAD, panic disorder, and depression, whereas GAD predicted adult depression only. During childhood, OAD predicted adult panic disorder, whereas GAD predicted agoraphobia. Taken together, these authors argued that DSM-IV (1994) GAD criteria are insufficient for identifying youth with significant "generalized" anxiety and support the rehabilitation of OAD in the upcoming DSM-5. These conclusions are particularly striking in light of previous concerns raised with regard to former OAD criteria (Werry, 1991). Indeed, OAD may be a more robust predictor for later psychopathology than GAD; however this finding may well be related to the lack of specificity of the disorder rather than its sensitivity. Overall, neither diagnostic category is without its problems in that both have been linked with a number of subsequent diagnoses, and neither appears to have a specific or predictable course.

Although childhood anxiety disorders as a group have not been consistently associated with increased risk for later alcohol and substance abuse (e.g., Costello, Erkanli, Federman, & Angold, 1999), there is some evidence to suggest a specific link with GAD. One study found that children with significant generalized anxiety symptoms were at increased risk for alcohol use during the teenage years, even controlling for depressive symptoms (Kaplow, Curran, Angold, & Costello, 2001). By comparison, children with elevated symptoms of separation anxiety were at a reduced risk for adolescent alcohol use. Among a larger sample (N = 1,269) of youth and young adults (ages 12–28 years), Sartor, Lynskey, Heath, Jacob, and True (2007) examined specific psychiatric diagnoses associated with both initial alcohol use and the progression to alcohol dependence. Although GAD was not identified as a specific risk factor for initial use, a GAD diagnosis was associated with a nearly four-fold increase in the rate of progression from first use to the development of alcohol dependence.

Cognitive Symptoms

As noted in the section on worry, it is not content but rather frequency, intensity, and functional impairment that differentiated children with high levels of anxiety (as measured by a self-report inventory of anxiety) from those with low anxiety. A similar conclusion can be drawn with respect to worry among children with GAD. In the Muris et al. (1998) study on childhood worry, 69% of the children endorsed the presence of worry, but only 6.7% of the sample met diagnostic criteria for GAD or OAD. Children with GAD/OAD could be distinguished from the others on a number of worry variables. For example, those with GAD/OAD reported six specific areas of worry, whereas those without a disorder reported only one area of worry. In addition, those with GAD/OAD worried frequently, suffered more interference from daily activities as a result of their worry, had more anxiety linked to the worry, and had more difficulty controlling the worry.

In a similar investigation, children with GAD reported an average of 5.74 worries, spanning an average of 4.82 areas (Weems, Silverman, & La Greca, 2000). The most common areas included health, school, disasters, personal harm, and future events. Children's most intense worries were in the area of war, personal harm, disasters, school, and family, whereas the most frequent worries were in the areas of friends, classmates, school, health, and performance. Consistent with the data presented in Chapter 3 (e.g., Muris et al., 2002), children's most intense worries are not the worries that occur most frequently. Furthermore, developmental differences in worry are evident. Weems and colleagues (2000) found that older children (aged 12–16) reported more worries about performance, little things, and appearance than younger children (aged 6–8). Pina and colleagues (2002) found that adolescents with a GAD diagnosis were most likely to endorse worry about school, whereas children with GAD most commonly endorsed worry about the health of others. Also, based on a comparison of children with GAD versus specific phobia, there were few group differences in the frequency or content of worries; children with GAD reported more worries about the future and peer scapegoating, whereas children with specific phobias worried more about the health of others and about the family (Weems et al., 2000). There were significant group differences in the total number and intensity of their worries, however; in both cases, the children with GAD had the higher number of worries and more intense worries.

In addition to worry, a growing body of research has focused on the role of biased attention in youth with anxiety disorders, including GAD. This research has primarily been based on results from computerized Stroop or visual probe tasks. In one of the first studies to focus on attention processes in different anxiety diagnoses, Taghavi, Neshat-Doost, Moradi, Yule, and Dalgliesh (1999) compared the attentional biases of youth with GAD, youth with mixed anxiety and depressive disorders, and controls (ages 9 to 18 years) using a visual probe task that included threat, depression, and neutral words. The GAD group showed a significant bias toward threatening words compared to the other two groups. Monk and colleagues (2006) compared youth with GAD and controls based on a visual probe task that included emotional faces. In contrast to results for threatening words, GAD youth demonstrated a significant bias away from angry faces (i.e., they were avoided). In a second study by Monk et al. (2008) that presented emotional faces to subjects in a more rapid fashion, both groups showed attentional bias toward angry compared to happy and neutral faces. Finally, Waters, Mogg, Bradley, and Pine (2008) used a visual probe task, also utilizing emotional faces, albeit among a sample of younger children (7 to 12 years) with GAD and controls. Based on findings from the adult GAD literature, the GAD group was further divided (based on a median split) into groups with high and low anxiety severity. Results revealed significant differences between the high-anxiety and control groups only: Highly anxious children with GAD showed an attentional bias toward both angry and happy faces. Although the unique aspects of these individual samples and methodologies may account for some variability in results, overall it is difficult to reconcile these contrary findings, and the extent to which attentional biases may be present and function to maintain anxiety among youth with GAD remains unclear.

Physical Symptoms

> Melissa's physical symptoms sometimes occur in isolation and some-
> times combine in the form of a panic attack. She sometimes experi-
> ences heart palpitations, feels lightheaded, feels as if she were choking,
> and worries that she is going to "fall over and die." Melissa gets stom-
> achaches several times per week and headaches about once per week.
> She sometimes worries that she has phlegm in her throat; frequently,
> when this happens she feels that she is unable to breathe.

In addition to excessive worry and subjective anxiety, physical or "associated" symptoms (also called Criterion C; see Table 6.1) are characteristic
of GAD. In one sample of children and adolescents (Tracey et al., 1997),
restlessness was the associated symptom most frequently endorsed (74%
of the sample), followed by irritability (68%), concentration difficulties
(61%), sleep disturbance (58%), easy fatigue (52%), headaches (36%),
muscle tension (29%), and stomachaches (29%). Similar results were
reported by Pina and colleagues (2002); both adolescents and children
with GAD endorsed restlessness as the most frequent physical symptom
of their worry/anxiety. These data indicate that requiring the endorsement of one associated symptom as necessary for the diagnosis of GAD
maximizes sensitivity and specificity of the diagnosis.

In an interesting comparison that provides further validity for the
diagnosis of GAD (rather than OAD), Tracy, Chorpita, Douban, and
Barlow (1997) compared the rate of endorsement of OAD symptoms
versus GAD symptoms. Using a sample of children without a diagnosis,
only one child (5.5%) endorsed any GAD symptoms, whereas six children (33%) endorsed OAD symptoms. Although this sample of children
without a diagnosis was small ($n = 18$), the results suggest that the diagnostic criteria for GAD may result in a reduced frequency of false posi-
tives, one of the primary difficulties with the former diagnostic category
of OAD.

Compared to other studies that have found modest rates of muscle
tension (Pina et al., 2002; Tracey et al., 1997), two studies of Italian
children and adolescents with GAD (Masi, Mucci, Favilla, Romano, &
Poli, 1999; Masi et al., 2004) found feelings of tension were present
in 98–100% of youth. Interestingly, among adults with GAD, muscle
tension has been found to be the most sensitive (physical) predictor of
a GAD diagnosis. Findings based on both self-report and psychophysiological assessments during periods of rest and in response to laboratory
challenges confirmed increased muscle tension among adults with GAD
compared to both psychiatric and nonpsychiatric controls (Hazlett,
McLeod, & Hoehn-Saric, 1994; Hoehn-Saric, Harrison, & Clary, 1997;
Hoehn-Saric, McLeod, & Zimmerli, 1989; Joormann & Stober, 1999).

Unfortunately, to date, psychophysiological assessments of muscle tension among children with the disorder have not been conducted. Further, clinical assessment of this particular symptom is more challenging in youth for a number of reasons. First, child diagnosis often relies heavily on parent report of symptomatology, yet muscle tension is not easily identified by parents and outside observers compared to many other physical symptoms that tend to co-occur with worry or anxiety (e.g., irritability, sleep problems). In addition, our clinical experiences suggest that children differ considerably in their understanding of this symptom as it is diffuse, nonspecific, and difficult to detect.

Sociodemographic Influences

Although GAD can be diagnosed at any age, the average age of onset in children appears to be between 10.8 and 13.4 years (Last, Hersen, et al., 1987; Last, Strauss, et al., 1987; Masi et al., 2004). With respect to developmental differences, school-aged children with GAD generally report the same number and types of worries as their adolescent counterparts (Pina et al., 2002; Tracey et al., 1997). Rates of physical symptoms, apprehensive expectation, need for reassurance, and overall negative self-image also are highly similar across age groups (Masi et al., 1999, 2004). However, some differences based on age have been reported. Strauss et al. (1988) reported that older children had more symptoms than younger children, and Tracey et al. (1997) found a significant, but moderate, correlation between child report of the number of symptoms and increasing age. Also, with respect to the OAD symptoms of stomachaches and headaches, the latter were reported more often by adolescents.

There are few data on gender differences for children with GAD. Children between the ages of 9 and 13 appear to be equally affected by the disorder (Last, Hersen, Kazdin, Finkelstein, & Strauss, 1987). In contrast, during adolescence, many more girls than boys are diagnosed with GAD (Lewinsohn, Gotlib, Lewinsohn, et al., 1998). This difference appears to be due to a decrease in the number of boys with this disorder rather than an increase in the number of girls with this diagnosis (Velez, Johnson, & Cohen, 1989). In two separate studies, Masi et al. (1999, 2004) reported a lack of gender differences based on specific symptom profiles.

Comorbid and Differential Diagnosis

As noted by Silverman and Ginsburg (1995), differential diagnosis of GAD is complex because of the vagueness of the diagnostic criteria:

excessive worry more days than not for at least six months, about a number of events (APA, 2000). Among the earliest studies of comorbidity, 57% of a sample of children with a primary diagnosis of OAD had a secondary diagnosis of another anxiety disorder, and 18% received two or more additional anxiety diagnoses (Last, Hersen, et al., 1987). More recent data suggest rates of comorbidity above 90% for youth with GAD, with depression the most common secondary diagnosis (Masi et al., 1999, 2004).

Masi, Favilla, Mucci, and Millepiedi (2000) examined the clinical features of 108 children and adolescents with GAD, including youth with (51%) and without (49%) comorbid depression. Overall, there were no differences in comorbidity patterns based on age or gender. Whereas those with comorbid depression endorsed an average of 8.6 symptoms of GAD, those without depression reported an average of 7.8 symptoms, a difference that was significantly different, although probably not clinically meaningful inasmuch as both groups were endorsing a high number of symptoms. With respect to differences among the symptoms that comprise GAD, only complaints of irritability were significantly more frequent among children with GAD and depression. Finally, children with GAD and comorbid depression had significantly higher scores on the Children's Global Assessment Scale (CGAS), indicating a greater degree of functional impairment as a result of their comorbid status. In a similar study by Masi and colleagues (2004), youth with GAD without comorbid depression were significantly more likely to have a diagnosis of obsessive-compulsive disorder. Also, children with GAD but not depression had a significantly greater number of comorbid anxiety disorders.

Differences in rates of comorbidity also have been reported based on age. Masi et al. (1999) noted that 62% of their sample with primary GAD had a comorbid depressive disorder (58% of children and 64% of adolescents), whereas 53% (63% of children and 48% of adolescents) had a comorbid anxiety disorder; separation anxiety disorder (SAD; 21%), specific phobia (29%), or obsessive-compulsive disorder (10%). Comorbid externalizing disorders were rare (9%). Separation anxiety was significantly more frequent among children than adolescents, but there were no differences in the prevalence of comorbid disorders based on gender. In a separate study, children with primary dysthymic disorder with or without GAD (Masi, Mucci, Favilla, & Millipiedi, 2000) were examined on a number of clinical features. Although there was no group difference in the total number of depressive symptoms, suicidal ideation was higher in the comorbid group. Other internalizing disorders also were more frequent in the comorbid group, whereas externalizing disorders were more frequent in the group without comorbid GAD. Among the comorbid cases, the onset of GAD preceded the onset of dysthymia in 60% of the sample and followed dysthymia in the other 40% of the cases. In a later study, Masi and colleagues (2004) again found that children with GAD were significantly more likely to have a comorbid diagnosis of SAD compared to adolescents. Children with GAD were also more likely to meet criteria for an externalizing disorder. Rates of individual anxiety disorders were somewhat higher than found in their previous research: specific phobia (42%), SAD (31%), social phobia (28%), obsessive-compulsive disorder (20%), and panic disorder (17%).

Neurobiology of GAD

Although a growing body of literature addressing the neurobiology of GAD is available for adults (see Stein, 2009, for a review), fewer studies have examined these factors in children, and many were limited by high rates of comorbidity with other anxiety disorders and depression. Further, different methodologies and varying findings across studies as well as inconsistent results in comparison to adult GAD research make these cumulative data somewhat difficult to interpret.

Using magnetic resonance imaging (MRI), De Bellis, Keshavan, Shifflett, Iyengar, Dahl, Axelson, et al. (2002) examined amygdala volumes in 13 children with GAD compared to 98 healthy controls. The results indicated that there were no differences between specific brain regions (e.g., intracranial, temporal lobe, hippocampal, and basal ganglia regions) in children with and without GAD. However, those with GAD had significantly larger total white matter as well as gray and white matter superior temporal gyrus (STG) volumes. Furthermore, there was more pronounced right versus left asymmetry in total and white STG matter, leading the authors to suggest that this dysmorphometry may represent a vulnerability to GAD.

As described, Monk and colleagues (2006) examined 18 youth with GAD and 15 healthy controls in regard to a visual probe task using emotional faces. This study also used functional magnetic resonance imaging (fMRI) to examine specific regions of brain activation during the task. Children and adolescents with GAD showed greater activation in the right ventrolateral prefrontal cortex both in response to angry faces and when controlling for attentional differences between the groups. Contrary to the authors' hypotheses, no differences in amygdala activation were found. The potential impact of secondary diagnoses of depression or social anxiety disorder among GAD youth also was examined, with no significant differences found based on comorbidity. The authors suggested that the right ventrolateral prefrontal cortex may be involved in the manifestation of anxiety or represent a compensatory response designed to regulate abnormal function in other brain regions. In a follow-up study, in which emotional faces were presented in a more rapid fashion, greater amygdala activation in response to angry faces was found among children with GAD compared to controls (Monk et al., 2008). Further, while amygdala and right ventrolateral prefrontal cortex activation were negatively correlated among all youth, this relationship was significantly reduced in subjects with GAD. Thus, strength of amygdala activation appears to vary as a function of right ventrolateral prefrontal cortex activity, and this modulation process may be impaired in youth with GAD.

McClure and colleagues (2007) used a similar experimental methodology using emotional faces and fMRI among 15 adolescents with anxiety disorders (13 with confirmed GAD) and 20 healthy adolescents. In an attempt to address some of the limitations of previous research, the authors specifically examined changes in fMRI activation as a function of attentional focus. Anxious adolescents showed significantly greater activation in a "distributed fear circuit," including the amygdala, ventral prefrontal cortex, and anterior cingulate cortex, in response to fearful faces, but this occurred only when specifically focused on their own internal fear. These findings, which are similar to adult data, but somewhat contrary to other childhood findings (e.g., Monk et al., 2006), suggest that attentional processes modulate neural activity in GAD, and that changes in fear circuitry may occur as a result of the disorder (McClure et al., 2007).

Is GAD a Distinct Disorder?

One of the strongest arguments that GAD may not represent a unique disorder is that it rarely exists in isolation. Among one sample of children with GAD, only 13% (16% of children and 12% of adolescents) had GAD as their only diagnosis (Masi et al., 1999). Also, children with GAD did not have significantly higher scores on a general anxiety scale than children with other anxiety disorders (social phobia, specific phobia, or obsessive-compulsive disorder), as would be expected given that this disorder is one of the few characterized by general overall arousal (Tracey et al., 1997). Furthermore, the overlap is not merely concurrent with other anxiety or mood disorders. In some cases, GAD/OAD may exist as antecedent disorders. For example, the odds ratios for OAD and obsessive-compulsive disorder were significantly elevated for anorexia nervosa, whereas OAD and social phobia were significantly elevated for bulimia nervosa. The authors concluded that OAD (along with social phobia) may reflect underlying personality traits that may represent a general risk factor across various anxiety, affective, and eating disorders (Bulik, Sullivan, Fear, & Joyce, 1997).

Consistent with this hypothesis, some have suggested that GAD (like the construct of behavioral inhibition) actually may be the behavioral manifestation of a temperamental disposition such as neuroticism (Turner et al., 1996). Thus, GAD may be merely the temperamental basis through which interactions with environmental, sociodemographic, and cultural factors result in the development of psychopathology (Garrison & Earls, 1987). If this is the case, it would explain why the condition appears to exist so rarely in isolation and so commonly with depressive disorders. Along these lines, many have argued that GAD would be more appropriately classified as a mood disorder (Brown, DiNardo, et al., 2001; Watson, 2005), not only because the disorder appears genetically indistinguishable from depression (Mineka, Watson, & Clark, 1998) but also because factor analytic approaches often fail to distinguish GAD from depressive symptomatology (e.g., Lahey et al., 2008). However, data among children with GAD are far more limited than in adults, and the extent to which findings based on the adult disorder are applicable to the childhood years remains to be examined.

ETIOLOGY OF GAD

> Melissa's mother dated the onset of her daughter's worrying to a summer picnic when Melissa choked on a hot dog. Although she seemed "fine" for the rest of the summer, she began expressing worry about dying when she started school in the fall.

To date, there are no data specifically addressing the etiology of GAD in children. If, as previously noted, GAD represents an underlying vulnerability, then one might expect that it might be best conceptualized as a biological or constitutional predisposition. In such instances, as in the case of Melissa, the worry that appears to be the hallmark of GAD may represent an exacerbation of an underlying temperamental predisposition rather than the onset of a unique disorder. Thus, an anxious temperamental predisposition may make her more susceptible to a traumatic conditioning event. Also, as in Melissa's case, an event such as choking on a hot dog can in turn precipitate an increase in worry. In other words, Melissa's temperament might make her more vulnerable to the development of an anxiety disorder. Unlike children without this predisposition, the worry was not limited to choking and did not dissipate with time, as might be expected if no further events occurred. In Melissa's case, her fear exacerbated (perhaps due to the underlying trait anxiety) into a plethora of broader concerns about her own health and that of her family. In summary, the etiology of GAD is a severely understudied area, and the general etiological theories presented in Chapter 3 most likely apply to this disorder as it is currently conceptualized.

ASSESSMENT OF GAD

The same strategies used to assess other anxiety disorders also are useful in the assessment of GAD. Assessment should incorporate multiple methods using various informants and examining a variety of contexts (Morris, Hirshfeld-Becker, Henin, & Storch, 2004). Except among the very young, assessment must encompass more than parental report. As noted in Chapter 2, agreement on symptoms among parents and children may be only in the moderate range. There may be many different reasons for the low-to-moderate correlations (see Chapter 2); however, the important point is that assessment should include multiple methods and multiple informants.

Diagnostic Interviews

The importance of diagnostic interviews, both structured and semistructured formats, have been discussed. Furthermore, as previously stated, the reliability of the diagnosis of GAD is only in the moderate range. However, this should not negate the importance of conducting the interview. In fact, children who are described by their parents as "worrying" often describe a more circumscribed constellation of fears more consistent with SAD or social phobia as opposed to the broader pattern of worry that usually accompanies GAD. Thus, diagnostic interviews may function to clarify the symptom picture for the diagnostician as well as the parent and the child.

Self-Report

Prior to the third edition of the *DSM* (APA, 1980), children's anxiety was rarely considered in terms of specific disorders. Instead, anxiety was conceptualized along dimensions or in terms of cognitive and somatic symptoms. For example, the Children's Manifest Anxiety Scale–Revised (RCMAS; Reynolds & Richmond, 1978) assesses three factors: physiological arousal, worry/oversensitivity, and concentration. As noted by Strauss (1988), the scale has good psychometric properties and national normative data. Similarly, the State-Trait Anxiety Inventory for Children (STAIC; Spielberger, 1973) is often used to assess "general" anxiety in terms of state and trait dimensions. The STAIC has good psychometric properties and differentiates children with OAD from children without anxiety disorders (see Strauss, 1988). One limitation of these instruments is that they can differentiate children with anxiety from children without psychiatric disorders and children with anxiety disorders from those with externalizing disorders but not between children with anxiety disorders and children with affective disorders or among children with various types of anxiety disorders (Seligman, Ollendick, Langley, & Baldacci, 2004).

Newer measures of "general anxiety" have been introduced. Rather than addressing cognitive and physical symptoms or the state-trait dimension of anxiety, these measures focus on children's anxious complaints that mirror *DSM-IV* diagnostic categories. The Multidimensional Anxiety Scale for Children (MASC; March, 1997) assesses a range of anxiety symptoms. It allows the calculation of a total score as well as scores on various subscales (physical symptoms, harm avoidance, social anxiety, separation/panic). The scale has extensive normative data, excellent reliability, and a range of validity data, including factorial validity, discriminant validity, and concurrent validity. The Screen for Child Anxiety Related Emotional Disorders (SCARED; Birmaher et al., 1999) is a self-report instrument that has both parent and child versions. It assesses *DSM-IV* anxiety symptoms, has good psychometric properties in both clinical and community samples, and appears to be sensitive to treatment effects (RUPP Anxiety Study Group, 2001). Furthermore, the psychometric properties are consistent for African American and European American samples (Boyd, Ginsburg, Lambert, Cooley, & Campbell, 2003).

The most specific self-report measure of the cognitive component of GAD, worry, is a children's adaptation of the Penn State Worry Questionnaire (PSWQ-C; Chorpita, Tracey, Brown, Collica, & Barlow, 1997). This scale consists of 14 items that children rate on a 4-point Likert scale. Some of the items include "My worries really bother me; I always worry about something"; "Once I start worrying, I can't stop." The scale has good internal consistency, is unifactorial, and strongly and significantly correlates with the RCMAS Worry/Oversensitivity subscale and moderately and significantly correlates with the other RCMAS subscales. The PSWQ-C also has been shown to differentiate between normal and pathological worry in school-age children (Muris, Meesters, & Gobel, 2001) and to differentiate children with GAD from others with anxiety disorders (Chorpita, Tracey, et al., 1997).

Clinician Ratings

The Research Units on Pediatric Psychopharmacology (RUPP) Anxiety Study Group (2002) developed and validated the Pediatric Anxiety Rating Scale (PARS). The PARS was designed for clinicians to assess the severity of anxiety symptoms associated with common *DSM-IV* disorders, including social phobia, SAD, and GAD in children. Items were generated from the *DSM-IV* criteria and were reviewed by experts in the field until the pool was reduced to the final 50 items. Nine items assess social interactions or performance situations, 10 items deal with separation, 8 items address generalized anxiety, 4 items are allocated to specific phobia, 13 items assess physical signs and symptoms, and 6 items are included in a subscale called Other. Each item is scored as present or absent and then rated (using a 6-point scale) on seven dimensions: number of symptoms, frequency, severity of distress, severity of physical symptoms, avoidance, interference at home, and interference out of home. A total score also is calculated. Results of the studies to address the psychometric properties of the scale indicated no significant differences based on age or ethnicity (Caucasian vs. Hispanics). The PARS total score was moderately correlated with other clinician and parent-rated measures of anxiety. There were weaker correlations between the PARS and children's self-report measures of anxiety. Preliminary evidence indicated that the PARS total score is a sensitive measure of treatment outcome. As noted by the authors, the PARS fills a gap in the armamentarium for the assessment of children with anxiety disorders. Until the development of this measure, there was no clinician rating scale developed specifically for childhood anxiety disorders (other than for obsessive-compulsive disorder), and clinician assessment was based primarily on adult measures such as the Hamilton Anxiety Scale (HAMA; Hamilton, 1959) and the generic Clinical Global Impressions Scale (CGI; Guy, 1976).

Physiological Measures

Used almost exclusively in research settings, physiological measures such as heart rate may be useful in determining the severity of the child's distress. Beidel (1991) reported that children with OAD had higher resting pulse rates than children with social phobia. However, studies of the physiology of children with OAD/GAD are rare, perhaps in part because of the difficulty in finding children who have GAD without comorbid disorders. Nonetheless, physiologic data may provide greater understanding of the specific utility of certain GAD criteria for children given consistent findings of increased muscle tension among adults with the disorder.

Self-Monitoring

Perhaps the most useful assessment method for diagnostic and treatment planning purposes with respect to GAD is the use of self-monitoring/

daily diary methods. Although worry about a number of different situations/events is a hallmark characteristic of GAD in children, careful clarification could reveal a more specific pattern of fears. Melissa was asked to record her worries once per day using a simple recording sheet. One week's worth of monitoring revealed the following range and frequency of Melissa's specific worries and fears:

That I would choke on phlegm (3 of 7 days)
That I could not swallow (2 of 7 days)
That I would stop breathing (2 of 7 days)
That I would turn blind (1 of 7 days)
That I would throw up (5 of 7 days)
That the house would catch on fire (1 of 7 days)

As illustrated, Melissa's fears covered a range of situations. Daily diary ratings can be a valuable addition to the assessment of GAD. Although not without drawbacks (children's compliance with completing and returning the forms), they provide a useful day-to-day picture of the child's worries and are useful in designing and monitoring a comprehensive treatment plan.

TREATMENT OF GAD

To date, there are few pharmacological or psychosocial intervention trials specifically directed at the treatment of children with GAD. Rather, several large-scale intervention trials addressed the treatment of anxiety disorders in children and adolescents and included children with various anxiety disorders in the same sample. In some instances, the results were analyzed separately for those with OAD/GAD.

Pharmacological Treatment of GAD

In one of the first pharmacological trials, in an open, clinical trial Simeon and Ferguson (1987) examined the effects of alprazolam in children and adolescents with OAD or avoidant disorder. Fifty-eight percent of the children were significantly or moderately improved as a result of 4 weeks of alprazolam therapy, and these gains were maintained during a 4-week, drug-free follow-up. However, the results were not examined separately for children with OAD. In a randomized, placebo-controlled trial (Simeon et al., 1992), 30 children (mean age 12.6 years) with either OAD (n = 21) or avoidant disorder (n = 9) were treated with alprazolam

or matching placebo. Alprazolam appeared superior based on global ratings of anxiety after a 4-week period. However, superiority of alprazolam was not evident on posttreatment evaluator ratings using the
CGI scales. Furthermore, after drug tapering, there was a trend (albeit
nonsignificant) for patients treated with alprazolam to relapse, whereas
those treated with placebo continued to improve. Thus, the positive outcome of the open trial was not replicated in the controlled trial. These
negative results, as well as the serious side effects and dose-related complications associated with alprazolam, have led a number of researchers
to recommend that benzodiazepines should be considered only as a last
resort (Kratochvil, Kutcher, Reiter, & March, 1999; Pine & Grun, 1998;
Velosa & Riddle, 2000.

Selective serotonin reuptake inhibitors (SSRIs) are considered the
pharmacological treatment of choice for childhood anxiety disorders.
The safety and efficacy data indicate that these medications have high
tolerance levels, minimal side effects, and lack of the need for blood
level monitoring (Kratochvil et al., 1999; Pine & Grun, 1998; Velosa &
Riddle, 2000). In general, side effects are minimal and include headaches,
nausea, drowsiness, insomnia, jitteriness, and stomachaches (Velosa &
Riddle, 2000). In 2004, however, the Food and Drug Administration
released a black box warning label for antidepressant use in children and
adolescents, indicating an increased risk for suicidality. The warning was
updated in 2007 to include individuals up to 24 years of age. Although
these warnings have been met with significant declines in the prescription
of SSRIs to pediatric patients (Harman, Edlund, & Fortney, 2009; Libby,
Orton, & Valuck, 2009), a specific link between SSRIs and increased
suicidality in children remains controversial (Gibbons, Hur, Bhaumik,
& Mann, 2006; Leckman & King, 2007). Nonetheless, the use of SSRIs
for pediatric anxiety disorders is relatively well established. The SSRIs
include fluvoxamine (Luvox®), fluoxetine (Prozac®), sertraline (Zoloft®),
paroxetine (Paxil®), citalopram (Celexa®, and escitalopram (Lexapro®).

In an earlier retrospective study, the effects of fluoxetine (mean dose
25.7 mg/day) in 21 children age 11 to 17 years old who were diagnosed
with OAD, avoidant disorder, or social phobia were examined (Birmaher
et al., 1994). Based on chart review, 6–8 weeks of treatment resulted in
81% of the children being rated as markedly improved in anxiety symptoms. In another open trial treating children with various anxiety disorders, children considered nonresponsive to psychotherapy (aged 9–18
years) were administered fluoxetine (Fairbanks et al., 1997). Similar
to the results of Birmaher et al. (1994), improvement was apparent at
6–9 weeks, and those without comorbid disorders required lower doses
of medication. Because of the small sample size (n = 16), results were
not examined separately by diagnostic group, but overall 81% showed

moderate-to-marked improvement. However, 62.5% of the entire sample still met criteria for an anxiety disorder at posttreatment, suggesting that a longer trial or perhaps the addition of a psychosocial intervention might have enhanced treatment outcome.

In a 12-week trial (Birmaher et al., 2003), 74 youth with GAD, SAD, or social phobia were randomized to either fluoxetine or matching placebo. At posttreatment, 61% of the fluoxetine group and 35% of the placebo group were rated as much or very much improved according to the treating clinician's CGI ratings. Children with GAD treated with fluoxetine were significantly more likely to be rated as much or very much improved than those treated with placebo (67% vs. 36%, respectively). However, even though improved, at least 50% of the children were still symptomatic (defined by still having at least three symptoms of anxiety) at posttreatment. Furthermore, those children with GAD treated with fluoxetine did not have a significantly better functional outcome (defined as a rating of 70 or higher on the CGAS [scores range from 0 to 100]) than those children with GAD who were treated with placebo. Therefore, although anxiety symptoms were improved in the case of those with GAD, this reduction did not translate into enhanced functioning.

In the large, multicenter controlled trial known as the RUPP Anxiety Trial, 128 youth (aged 6–17 years) with SAD, social anxiety disorder, or GAD were randomly assigned to 8 weeks of either fluvoxamine or placebo (RUPP Anxiety Study Group, 2001). Both groups also received supportive psychotherapy. Fluvoxamine was superior to placebo based on children's scores on the PARS. Clinicians rated 76% of children treated with fluvoxamine as markedly improved in comparison to 29% treated with placebo. In fact, the fluvoxamine and placebo groups were significantly different at Week 3, with differences continuing to increase through Week 6, and then were maintained but with no further improvement. Treatment response was poorer for those with a diagnosis of social phobia versus those without such a diagnosis (RUPP Anxiety Study Group, 2002). Although not clearly presented, it would appear that, by inference, children with GAD had a better treatment response. However, among patients without social phobia, the placebo response rated was 40% (vs. 24% for those with social phobia). Therefore, those with GAD alone or SAD alone appeared to respond to placebo at a higher rate than other diagnostic groups. This casts some concern on the response rate reported for fluvoxamine if as many as 40% of children with these diagnoses respond to placebo alone. Importantly, however, 94% of those who initially responded to fluvoxamine maintained their improvement (Rupp Anxiety Study Group, 2002). One limitation of this double-blind study was that treating clinicians, not independent evaluators, rated both clinical outcome and adverse events. Thus, knowledge of side effects could have biased the clinician ratings of outcome. However, this was a large, well-controlled trial and provided important information on the efficacy of SSRIs for various childhood anxiety disorders, including GAD.

A multisite clinical trial compared sertraline, cognitive-behavioral therapy (CBT), their combination, and placebo (2:2:2:1 ratio) among 488 youth ages 7–17 years diagnosed with GAD, SAD, or social phobia (Walkup et al., 2008). Sertraline dosing was administered on fixed-flexible dose schedule starting at 25 mg/day and titrated up to 200 mg/day by Week 8, depending on treatment response and adverse events. Response rates based on clinician CGI ratings after 12 weeks of treatment were as follows: 54.9% for sertraline, 59.7% for CBT, 80.7% for their combination, and 23.7% for placebo. Thus, while all therapies were superior to placebo, the combination of sertraline and CBT was superior to both monotherapies. Measures of overall functioning (CGAS) and anxious symptomatology (PARS) produced similar results among the treatment groups. Of note, harm-related and suicidal adverse events were minimal and not reported more frequently among youth taking sertraline. Although follow-up studies will likely compare response rates for specific diagnostic groups, these data are unavailable at this time. However, 384 (79%) youth had GAD as either a primary or a secondary diagnosis.

One study examined the efficacy of an SSRI specifically for children with GAD. In a 9-week, randomized, placebo-controlled trial of sertraline in 22 children and adolescents with GAD (Rynn, Siqueland, & Rickels, 2001), children treated with sertraline had significantly lower scores on the Hamilton Rating Scale (total score, psychic factor score, somatic factor score) and the CGI Scale severity score than those receiving placebo. However, it is important to note that during the 2- to 3-week screening period, 18% of the children originally diagnosed with GAD no longer met the entry criteria. This finding that almost 1 of 5 children who meet diagnostic criteria at any one time did not do so 2–3 weeks later leads to questions about the validity of this diagnosis. Furthermore, it indicates the need to determine, prior to initiating treatment, that the symptoms are long standing and not merely a temporary reaction to some type of life event.

Two studies have examined the efficacy of extended-release venlafaxine (Effexor XR®), a serotonin-norepinephrine reuptake inhibitor (SNRI) for the treatment of GAD in children. Specifically, among a total sample of 323 children and adolescents (ages 6–17 years) with primary GAD, Rynn, Riddle, Yeung, and Kunz (2007) presented results from two randomized, double-blind, placebo-controlled trials conducted across 59 sites. Following a single-blind lead-in period of 4 to 10 days, children were randomized to one of the two treatment conditions for 8 weeks. Dosing of venlafaxine was started at 37.5 mg/day and increased to a maximum of 225 mg/day based on weight. The primary outcome measure included a composite score based on nine items from the GAD section of the Schedule for Affective Disorders and Schizophrenia for School-Aged Children (K-SADS) assessing severity and functional impairment. In the first study, children treated with venlafaxine evidenced a significant reduction in composite scores compared to placebo. However, this between-group difference failed to reach statistical significance in the second study ($p = .06$), primarily due to a lack of difference on items assessing GAD-related impairment. Children treated with venlafaxine in Study 1 demonstrated similar improvements over placebo on other measures as well, including the PARS, SCARED, HAMA, and CGI scales, whereas significant improvement was observed for children taking venlafaxine in Study 2 on CGI scales only. Although placebo response rates based on CGI Improvement scores were high across both studies (48% overall), they were particularly elevated in Study 2 (above 50%), which may have contributed to nonsignificant differences. Together with data from other trials (RUPP Anxiety Study Group, 2001), these findings suggest overall higher rates of placebo response among youth with GAD compared to other anxiety disorders.

In summary, SSRIs and SNRIs may be effective for many children with anxiety disorders, including those with GAD. However, it is unclear for which disorders they might be particularly or specifically efficacious inasmuch as, to date, sample sizes have been small and primarily of mixed diagnostic status. Further, a majority of the evidence for positive outcomes is based on a one-item clinician rating scale. Alternatively, and somewhat encouragingly, findings from a meta-analytic review comparing effect sizes for pharmacological treatments for GAD suggest that treatment in children and adolescents yields significantly higher effect sizes than in adults (Hidalgo, Tupler, & Davidson, 2007). Although this finding is based on a small number of studies and thus awaits replication, the authors propose that early diagnosis and treatment of the illness may improve the overall poor response rates seen among adults with GAD. Thus, long-term follow-up data also are needed, including assessments of overall functioning. Of course, some of these same issues pertain to the studies of psychosocial trials discussed next.

Psychosocial Treatment of GAD

In one of the earliest examinations of psychosocial treatment, Kane and Kendall (1989) examined a manualized CBT for four children with OAD. The CBT treatment, Coping Cat Program, encompassed 16–20 individualized treatment sessions with four components: recognizing somatic and cognitive reactions to anxiety, clarifying cognitions in anxiety-provoking situations, developing a coping plan (modifying self-talk, determining which coping activities might be successful), and self-evaluation and self-reinforcement. Behavioral training strategies such as modeling, exposure, role-play, relaxation training, and contingent reinforcement were used as part of the intervention. Using a single-case design, the intervention was effective for these four children.

This initial study formed the basis for a series of randomized controlled trials that have examined the efficacy of this intervention for children and adolescents with various anxiety disorders, including many children with diagnoses of OAD/GAD. In the first randomized trial (Kendall, 1994), children aged 9–13 (with diagnoses of SAD, OAD, or avoidant disorder) were randomized to either Coping Cat (CBT) program or a wait-list control group. At posttreatment, those treated with CBT showed significant improvement on self-report measures of anxiety, coping skills, negative cognitions, and depression when compared to those in the wait-list control group. Similar posttreatment differences were found for parent and teacher ratings as well as an overall score on a behavioral observation measure in which children were asked to speak for 5 minutes in front of a camera. Furthermore, at posttreatment, 64% of those in the CBT group no longer met diagnostic criteria at posttreatment, and treatment gains were maintained 3.35 years later (Kendall & Southam-Gerow, 1996).

A replication study using the same treatment design and the same anxiety diagnoses (Kendall et al., 1997) resulted in a similarly positive outcome for youth treated with CBT when compared to a wait-list control group. In addition, at posttreatment, 53% of those treated with CBT no longer met diagnostic criteria compared to 6% of the wait-list control group. Although specific data were not presented, outcome was reported as similar across the different diagnostic groups. Building on these initial successes, a more recent investigation examined administration of CBT (Coping Cat) in a group-versus-individual format for children with various anxiety disorders. Despite the manner of treatment implementation, children were significantly improved as a result of the intervention. The measurement strategy was similar to those used in prior investigations. The outcome did not reveal changes in children's social functioning, however (e.g., social anxiety, friendships, and social activities), which may suggest that this intervention is more appropriate for those children with GAD rather than for those with social phobia, for example. A 7.4-year follow-up (Kendall, Safford, Flannery-Schroeder, & Webb, 2004) indicated that 90.3% of the children/young adults no longer met the criteria of their primary diagnosis. However, because 50% of the follow-up sample received additional treatment (primarily outpatient therapy or medication), the long-term effectiveness of this specific intervention is difficult to determine.

Using Kendall's CBT intervention, the additive effects of a family intervention component (CBT + FAM) that included training in reinforcement/contingency management strategies, teaching parents coping techniques to deal with their own emotionality, and communication and problem-solving skills were examined (Barrett, Dadds, et al., 1996). Seventy-nine children with diagnoses of SAD, OAD, or social phobia were randomly assigned to one of three groups: CBT, CBT + FAM, and a wait-list control. Both active interventions (CBT and CBT + FAM) were provided on an individual basis and produced results significantly superior to those in the wait-list control group. Between the two active interventions, CBT + FAM was significantly superior to CBT alone. Specifically, 84% treated with CBT + FAM did not meet diagnostic criteria at posttreatment compared to 57% in the CBT group. Among children with OAD/GAD, 81% did not have a diagnosis 6 years later (Barrett, Duffy, Dadds, & Rapee, 2001). Another study (Barrett, 1998) compared the effectiveness of these same interventions but utilized a group format. In the total sample of 60 children, 30 had a diagnosis of GAD. The results indicated that group CBT (GCBT) and GCBT + FAM were significantly superior to wait list control. At posttreatment, 55.9% of the GCBT and 70.7% of the GCBT + FAM no longer met diagnostic criteria, and these results were maintained at 12-month follow-up. Unfortunately, the results were not reported separately by diagnostic groups; thus, the specificity of the treatment for those children with GAD is not clear, although overall it appears that the intervention was efficacious.

In an extension of this CBT intervention, Shortt, Barrett, and Fox (2001) developed the FRIENDS program, which combines traditional CBT interventions (exposure, cognitive strategies, relaxation, and contingency management); a family skills component (cognitive restructuring for parents, partner support training, and encouragement to build social networks); with an additional emphasis on the establishment of new friendships and specialized training for children in making internal attributions about their accomplishments. Again using a sample of children with one of several different anxiety disorders, including OAD/GAD, 69% of those treated with the FRIENDS program did not have a diagnosis at posttreatment, compared to 6% in the wait-list control group. Children in the FRIENDS condition demonstrated significant improvement on self-report measures of anxiety (RCMAS), and mothers reported a significant decrease in internalizing symptoms. Results were maintained 1 year later. The social validity of the FRIENDS program has been demonstrated in a series of studies examining its acceptability by parents and its utility for children of non-English-speaking background and for children who were former Yugoslavian refugees (Barrett, Moore, & Sonderegger, 2000; Barrett, Shortt, Fox, & Wescombe, 2001; Barrett, Sonderegger, & Sonderegger, 2001; Barrett, Sonderegger, & Xenos, 2003).

Silverman and her colleagues (Eisen & Silverman, 1993, 1998; Silverman, Kurtines, Ginsburg, Weems, Lumpkin, et al., 1999; Silverman, Kurtines, Ginsburg, Weems, Rabian, et al., 1999) also have examined CBT for children with anxiety disorders. In the initial trial (Eisen & Silverman, 1993), four children with OAD as defined in *DSM-III-R* (APA, 1987) were treated using a multiple-baseline design that consisted of six sessions of cognitive therapy, followed by six sessions of relaxation training, followed by six sessions of the combination treatment. Exposure also was consistently implemented across all 18 sessions. All children showed significant improvement from pre- to posttreatment, and gains were maintained at 6-month follow-up. The combined treatment appeared to result in greater improvement, although the greatest response appeared to occur when the intervention was matched to the child's particular symptom profile, for example, using cognitive therapy for a child with cognitive symptoms of worry, using relaxation therapy for a child who has a plethora of physical symptoms, and the combined intervention for those with both cognitive and physical symptoms. In a follow-up investigation (Eisen & Silverman, 1998), four children were randomized to receiving either a prescriptive treatment (cognitive treatment for cognitive symptoms, somatic treatment for physical symptoms) or nonprescriptive treatment (cognitive treatment for physical symptoms or somatic treatment for cognitive symptoms). Using a multiple-baseline design, each child received 10 individualized treatment sessions. Across a variety of treatment outcome measures, significantly greater improvement and high end-state functioning was evident when the children received the prescriptive treatments, although there also was improvement in symptoms not logically related to the intervention as well (cognitive interventions also produced decrements in the physical symptoms). As noted, even though children may meet criteria for a particular disorder, it does not necessarily mean that they endorse each particular symptom that is included in the diagnostic criteria. Thus, there is a need for careful assessment of a child's particular clinical presentation to ensure that the selected treatment strategy includes the appropriate interventions.

In a randomized controlled trial, Silverman and her colleagues (Silverman, Kurtines, Ginsburg, Weems, Lumpkin, et al., 1999) examined the utility of GCBT compared to a wait-list control group. The samples included children with social phobia, OAD, or GAD. GCBT included 12 weeks of gradual exposure, parent–child contingency management, and cognitive self-control training. At posttreatment, 64% of the GCBT group no longer met criteria for their primary diagnosis compared to 13% of controls. The superiority of GCBT also was confirmed by clinician ratings of severity, as well as parent and child report. Furthermore, treatment gains were maintained at 3-, 6-, and 12-month follow-up. In a reexamination of these outcome data (Pina, Silverman, Fuentes, Kurtines, & Weems, 2003), Hispanic/Latino and European American youth achieved equally positive treatment outcomes. Furthermore, long-term follow-up also was equally positive for both groups.

Ginsburg and Drake (2002b) adapted the GCBT treatment used by Silverman and her colleagues (Silverman, Kurtines, Ginsburg, Weems, Lumpkin, et al., 1999) to a school setting. Twelve African American children diagnosed with a variety of anxiety and mood disorders (GAD, social phobia, specific phobia, agoraphobia, major depressive disorder; most children had more than one disorder) who participated in a school-based program that included psychoeducation, relaxation training, cognitive restructuring, and graduated in vivo exposure. Children were randomly assigned to CBT or an attention support control. After 10 sessions, 75% of the CBT group no longer met criteria for their primary anxiety disorder at posttreatment as compared to 20% of those in the attention support group. Significant decrements in anxiety also were evident on self-report measures. Although the sample size was small, these results are encouraging and merit further study in a larger controlled trial.

Manassis et al. (2002) compared a group versus an individual CBT format for children with various anxiety disorders. Their intervention was adapted from Kendall's CBT program. Seventy-eight children (aged 8 to 12), 60.2% of whom had a diagnosis of GAD, were randomly assigned to either group or individual treatment, and both interventions included a parental component. Both interventions resulted in maternal reports of decreased anxiety and significantly improved global functioning when rated by a clinician unaware of group assignment. There were no treatment differences based on the intervention modality. However, the mother's actual scores of the child's anxiety at posttreatment were still elevated, and neither the father's ratings of the child's anxiety nor children's self-report ratings of anxiety changed as a result of the intervention.

In another trial of GCBT, 96 children (aged 7–16) with various anxiety disorders were randomized to either GCBT or a wait-list control group (Rapee, 2000). GCBT consisted of 9 sessions over 11 weeks and included the CBT strategies described in the previous paragraphs. At the same time, parents were trained in child management skills. The intervention resulted in significant improvement across a broad range of child and parent measures when compared to a wait-list control. Furthermore, clinicians unaware of group assignment rated 88.3% of those who received GCBT as moderately or markedly improved. This positive treatment outcome was maintained at 1-year follow-up, and a subset of children continued to improve during the follow-up period. Potential predictors of treatment outcome were examined, including child psychopathology and parental psychopathology. The only significant correlation with posttreatment outcome was father's level of anxiety; however, this correlation was low in strength ($r = .29$).

Consistent with the negative outcome regarding the additive effects of direct parental interventions to CBT treatment for children with anxiety, the use of a seven-session parental intervention did not enhance child treatment outcome (Nauta, Scholing, Emmelkamp, & Minderaa, 2001, 2003). Specifically, the use of teaching parents problem-solving skills and disputation of their own negative beliefs regarding their children's pathology did not increase treatment effects when compared to child treatment alone. Thus, perhaps because the role of parents in the etiology and maintenance of child anxiety disorders has not been adequately explored, adding interventions directed at parents with the intent of enhancing child treatment outcome may be premature.

In a small case series, Leger, Ladouceur, Dugas, and Freeston (2003) used a cognitive intervention to treat seven adolescents (ages 14–18 years) with a primary diagnosis of GAD. Treatment was based on a model of the disorder developed in adults (Dugas, Gagnon, Ladouceur, & Freeston, 1998), which outlines four problematic cognitive processes associated with GAD: intolerance of uncertainty, positive beliefs about worry, negative problem orientation, and cognitive avoidance. Although the appropriateness of this model for youth remains to be examined, treatment components in the adolescent study were similar to those used among adults, including awareness training, worry interventions, and relapse prevention. However, the authors defined treatment response as a 20% reduction in pretreatment scores on certain self-report measures, making results highly variable and difficult to interpret. Overall, of the six youth who completed treatment (duration of 13 weeks on average), three retained a GAD diagnosis, and three had considerable residual symptoms of GAD at posttreatment. As noted, a challenge of this specific treatment model is its unknown appropriateness for children and adolescents with GAD. For example, the problem-solving function of worry does not appear to fully develop until the adolescent years and may be further delayed for youth with pathological worry (Szabo & Lovibond, 2004). Thus, purely cognitive interventions, including problem solving, may have less utility in children than in adults. However, other components of the model may be more relevant for children. For example, we have begun to examine the construct of "intolerance of uncertainty" as part of our own research, and preliminary findings suggest that, in addition to specific worries and negative outcomes, children with GAD also commonly fear and avoid situations that are simply unfamiliar to them (i.e., involving uncertainty) without being able to explain exactly why the situation creates such distress.

CASE EXAMPLE: TREATMENT OF GAD

As noted, Melissa presented with myriad worries. Always a worrier, the incident at the summer picnic, when she choked on a hot dog, appeared to result in a significant exacerbation of her condition. However, her fears were not limited to choking on food. Rather, the pretreatment self-monitoring revealed that her worries covered myriad concerns (see Table 6.2).

MELISSA'S TREATMENT PLAN

RELAXATION TRAINING (DECREASE GENERAL AROUSAL)

Commonly used to treat adults with anxiety disorder, relaxation training also is used for children with high states of general arousal such as commonly found in GAD. When implementing relaxation training with children, there are several general recommendations. First, consider the developmental age of the child. Relaxation scripts for adults are usually 25–30 minutes long, which exceeds the attention span of young children. Therefore, relaxation instructions and the session itself should be shorter. Also, because young children sometimes have difficulty with instructions to tense and relax various muscle groups, scripts have been written for young children that cast the tension reduction cycle in terms of familiar objects. For example, rather than instructing children to tense and then relax their neck muscles, a script by Koppen (1974) instructs the child to imagine being a turtle and to "pull your head into your shell." Similarly, children are taught to tense and relax their arm and hand muscles: "Pretend you have a lemon in your left hand, and you want to make lemonade. Squeeze the lemon as hard as you can." This script and one for somewhat older children by Ollendick (1983) are useful for teaching deep muscle relaxation in children. In the case of Melissa, the Koppen (1974) script was used to provide instructions in relaxation training.

In addition, children will not successfully acquire these skills in just one training session. Relaxation is a skill and like other skills requires repetitive practice. Children should be encouraged to practice relaxation on a daily basis. To ensure that the child is practicing the skill correctly, the therapist should record the first training session and give the recording to the child to use at home. Since so many youth with GAD also have difficulty sleeping (see Chapter 5), the presleep period represents an ideal time for practicing relaxation skills. In some cases, parents might be encouraged to practice with children before bed to reinforce this behavior.

TABLE 6.2 Worries at Pretreatment, Posttreatment, and 6-Month Follow-Up

Pretreatment Week	Worry
Day 1	I would choke on phlegm; I would throw up.
Day 2	I could not swallow; I would choke on phlegm; I would throw up.
Day 3	I would stop breathing; I would throw up.
Day 4	I will go blind; I would throw up.
Day 5	I would choke on phlegm; I would stop breathing.
Day 6	My family will leave me.
Day 7	I will throw up; I would throw up.

Posttreatment Week

Although Melissa completed a week of self-monitoring forms, she only worried on 1 day.

Day 4	I might get stung by a bee.

Follow-Up Week

Again, Melissa completed a week of self-monitoring but only reported worry on 1 day.

Day 2	Moving to our new house.

Source: Reprinted from Beidel, D. C., & Turner, S. M. (2005). *Child Anxiety Disorders*. New York: Routledge. With permission.

COGNITIVE RESTRUCTURING

Using cognitive restructuring (Kendall, 1994), an attempt was made to teach Melissa how to examine her worries and substitute positive coping statements for her negative thoughts and worries. Although Melissa tried hard to accomplish this task, she was unable to do so. As noted by others (e.g., Spence, Donovan, & Brechman-Toussaint, 2000), younger children often have difficulty with the cognitive component of CBT. In Melissa's case, a decision was made to treat Melissa's fears with exposure.

EXPOSURE

Given the problems with cognitive restructuring and the difficulty engineering in vivo exposure to events such as vomiting or going blind, a decision was made to conduct exposure through the use of writing "scary" stories and reading them aloud. At each treatment session, Melissa was instructed to write a story about one of her worries. She would then read it to the therapist or the therapist would read it to her while monitoring her distress level using a 5-point subjective units of distress (SUDS) scale (see Chapter 3). The session was terminated when Melissa reported no anxiety while reading the story.

Following each treatment session, Melissa was given a homework assignment. She was instructed to spend 30 minutes per day reading the story at home to her mother. A 30-minute interval was selected because in-session data for Melissa indicated that 30 minutes was a sufficient time period for habituation. It has been our clinical experience that habituation intervals are often much shorter in children than in adults.

MELISSA'S EXPOSURE STORY

We went to the zoo today. We saw elephants and tigers and panda bears. My stomach felt funny. I said, "Mom, I think I am going to throw up." Mom said, "No you are not. You will be OK." And then I threw up right then and there on my mom. It was yellow, brown, white, and orange. It tasted yucky. It was all over my shirt and it smelled really really really really really bad. My mom and I ran to the bathroom. And while I was going to the bathroom I threw up again. But only this time I threw up in my own underwear. All the other people in the bathroom ran out because it smelled so bad. And after that we raced home. The End

Melissa was reluctant to write her first story, which is not unusual for people with anxiety disorders when asked to engage in exposure activities. She described it as "scary," as not wanting to think about throwing up, and needed substantial encouragement, in the form of stickers and praise, to begin the task. She rated her anxiety as a 5 (the highest) when she began. She also looked visibly anxious. Once she initiated the task, the anxiety quickly dissipated, and she began to laugh as she constructed, and later read aloud, the story. There were a total of six exposure sessions coupled with daily homework assignments. Each week, Melissa was asked to add a little more information to her story, but this did not increase her baseline level of anxiety or prevent habituation. At posttreatment, self-monitoring data indicated a significant decrease in the frequency of her worries and degree of distress associated with the worries that did occur. At 6-month follow-up, treatment gains were maintained (see Table 6.2 and Figure 6.1).

Prevention of Anxiety Symptoms/GAD in Children

In addition to developing interventions, researchers have directed their efforts toward prevention trials of anxiety symptoms in children. Delivered in a school setting and using a sample of 489 children (Barrett & Turner, 2001), the FRIENDS program, as administered by either a psychologist or a teacher, was compared to the standard

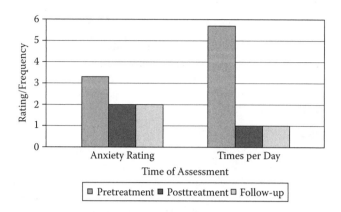

FIGURE 6.1 Anxiety rating and frequency of thoughts per week. (Reprinted from Beidel, D. C., & Turner, S. M. (2005). *Child Anxiety Disorders*. New York: Routledge. With permission.)

school curriculum. It should be noted that all children whose parents consented to their participation were included in the project. Thus, this was not a sample of children selected for the presence of anxiety symptoms. In addition to examining its efficacy on anxiety symptoms, the study examined if the intervention could be successfully implemented by teachers rather than mental health professionals. The results indicated that the FRIENDS program, whether conducted by a psychologist or teacher, resulted in a significant decrease in self-reported symptoms of anxiety. However, some of these differences, even though statistically significant, were quite small and would appear not to reflect clinically significant change. Although the authors attempted to examine the efficacy of the program for a subset of children with clinically significant anxiety, the sample size was too small to allow for adequate statistical power. In a second prevention trial, the efficacy of the FRIENDS program on both anxious and depressive symptomatology was examined (Lowry-Webster, Barrett, & Dadds, 2001). Similar to the first trial, the study also examined the efficacy of administration by teachers, and both groups were compared to a "standard curriculum" (no intervention). Again, the FRIENDS program decreased anxiety symptoms across all subjects. Depressive symptoms also decreased but only for children who had high anxiety symptoms prior to participating in the intervention. At 12-month follow-up, treatment gains were maintained. Furthermore, 85% of those treated with FRIENDS and originally considered "at risk" based on elevated anxiety and depression scores at pretreatment did not meet diagnostic criteria at follow-up. This compared to 31.2% of those in the wait-list group (Lowry-Webster, Barrett, & Lock, 2003). Furthermore, the program appeared effective for those in Grade 6 (children) and those in Grade 9 (adolescents; Barrett, Johnson, & Turner, in press).

These trials suggest that the FRIENDS program is effective in decreasing anxiety symptoms, and perhaps depressive symptoms, in children who are not necessarily selected because of their clinical status. In contrast, Ginsburg (2009) examined the efficacy of a preventive intervention specifically for children at risk for the development of anxiety based on having a parent with an anxiety disorder (either currently or during their lifetime). Forty children ages 7–12 years who did not meet criteria for an anxiety disorder (but could have subclinical anxiety symptoms) were randomized to either a family-based prevention program (Coping and Promoting Strength; CAPS) or a wait-list condition. The CAPS program included 6 to 8 weekly sessions and three monthly booster sessions and consisted of CBT components found to be effective for children with anxiety disorders (e.g., Silverman, Kurtines, Ginsburg, Weems, Lumpkin et al., 1999). Posttreatment assessments revealed that three of the children in the wait-list condition developed an anxiety disorder (all GAD) compared to none of the CAPS children. At 1-year follow-up, a total of six children in the wait-list group had developed an anxiety disorder (five GAD and one social phobia) compared to no children in CAPS. While these data are encouraging, a few points are noteworthy. First, although no child randomized to CAPS developed an anxiety disorder during the follow-up period, the child report of anxiety (based on the SCARED) was not significantly different between the groups at any time point. Also, although 30% of the wait-list sample developed an anxiety disorder within 1 year, examination of mean SCARED scores indicated that both parent and child report of anxiety actually decreased (albeit not significantly) over the 1-year period. The meaning of this particular finding is unclear. Last, the fact that almost all children who developed an anxiety disorder received a GAD diagnosis may relate to the validity of this diagnostic category for young children. Since excessive worry is the primary feature of GAD and children younger than age 7 or 8 do not typically experience (or report) the same worry process as adults, children who received a GAD diagnosis may have actually had clinically significant anxiety symptoms that did not fulfill diagnostic criteria at pretreatment. Of course, this would not explain why all of these children were in the wait-list condition rather than CAPS. Thus, longer-term follow-up among a large sample of children is needed and will allow the further determination of this program's efficacy in preventing anxiety disorders.

SUMMARY

Worry appears to be a common childhood experience, and its content covers a broad range of life areas. What appears to differentiate "pathological" from "normal" worry is not content per se, but frequency and intensity. When based simply on the presence of worry and physical symptoms such as headaches and stomachaches, the former diagnosis of OAD was unstable and highly prevalent in the general population. Based on the latest diagnostic revision in *DSM-IV*, requiring the inclusion of physical symptoms in addition to cognitive symptoms appears to increase the validity of the diagnostic category of GAD in children. However, other challenges remain, including the fact that GAD rarely exists in isolation and is genetically and phenomenologically similar to depression. Thus, despite increased diagnostic proficiency, it remains unclear if GAD represents a distinct diagnosis or merely a predispositional state from which more specific disorders emerge. In contrast to many other childhood anxiety disorders, there are few data on its etiology and natural course and even fewer data on the efficacy of pharmacological or psychosocial interventions specifically for those children with GAD. The majority of the studies reviewed here were comprised of mixed diagnostic groups even though a substantial number of children with GAD were included in the sample. However, based on the data currently available, both SSRIs and CBT demonstrate substantial treatment efficacy, but studies using samples consisting solely of children with GAD (rather than mixed diagnostic groups) are needed to further clarify the treatment outcome literature.

CHAPTER 7

Specific Phobia

Joshua is 10 years old. Referred by his mother, he has an extreme fear of injury and death. Currently, his behavior is characterized by hypervigilance and scanning of the environment. Joshua refuses to engage in any activity unless he is certain that he will not observe injury to himself or anyone else. He refuses to go to or participate in sporting events because someone might be injured. He refuses to go to the movies unless he knows the entire plot ahead of time because someone might get hurt. He also refuses to watch television, including those shows that he knows are "fake," such as cartoons, because there might be blood or injury. Although his mother reported that he was always a "sensitive" child, the frank onset of this disorder was triggered after watching the movie *Godzilla*.

Specific phobia (formerly known as simple phobia) is a marked and persistent fear that is excessive or unreasonable (American Psychiatric Association [APA], 2000). The fear is elicited by the presence or anticipation of a specific object or event that is not social in nature (social phobia) or is not marked by a pattern of avoidance that is based on the fear of having a panic attack (panic disorder with agoraphobia). In essence, a specific phobia can be related to virtually any other object, situation, or event (see Table 7.1 for the diagnostic criteria). There are several aspects of the diagnostic criteria that deserve comment. First, the formal diagnostic criteria contain qualifiers regarding the presentation of the disorder in children. Specifically, as noted in Chapter 3, children may express their anxiety by crying, tantrums, freezing, or clinging. A second qualifier pertaining to the diagnosis of specific phobia is that children need not recognize the unreasonableness of their fear. This was the situation with Joshua. He did not see his "need to know everything" ahead of time as unreasonable. For him, it was a protective behavior designed to prevent his distress. So, despite his parents' frustration, he considered his behavior as adaptive, not dysfunctional. Third, for children (i.e., those under the age of 18), the duration of the fear must be at least 6 months. This criterion acknowledges that, in childhood, many

TABLE 7.1   Diagnostic Criteria for Specific Phobia

A. Marked and persistent fear that is excessive or unreasonable, cued by the presence or anticipation of a specific object or situation (e.g., flying, heights, animals, receiving an injection, seeing blood).

B. Exposure to the phobic stimulus almost invariably provokes an immediate anxiety response, which may take the form of a situationally bound or situationally predisposed Panic Attack. *Note*: In children, the anxiety may be expressed by crying, tantrums, freezing, or clinging.

C. The person recognizes that the fear is excessive or unreasonable. *Note*: In children, this feature may be absent.

D. The phobic situation(s) is avoided or else is endured with intense anxiety or distress.

E. The avoidance, anxious anticipation, or distress in the feared situation(s) interferes significantly with the person's normal routine, occupational (or academic) functioning, or social activities or relationships or there is marked distress about having the phobia.

F. In individuals under age 18, the duration is at least 6 months.

G. The anxiety, Panic Attacks, or phobic avoidance associated with the specific object or situation are not better accounted for by another mental disorder, such as Obsessive-Compulsive Disorder (e.g., fear of dirt in someone with an obsession about contamination), Posttraumatic Stress Disorder (e.g., avoidance of stimuli associated with a severe stressor), Separation Anxiety Disorder (e.g., avoidance of school), Social Phobia (e.g., avoidance of social situations because of fear of embarrassment), Panic Disorder with Agoraphobia or Agoraphobia without History of Panic Disorder.

Specify Type

Animal Type: If the fear is cued by animals or insects. This subtype generally has a childhood onset.

Natural Environment Type: If the fear is cued by objects in the natural environment, such as storms, heights, or water. This subtype generally has a childhood onset.

Blood-Injection-Injury Type: If the fear is cued by seeing blood or an injury or by receiving an injection or other invasive medical procedure. This subtype is highly familial and is often characterized by a strong vasovagal response.

Situational Type: If the fear is cued by a specific situation such as public transportation, tunnels, bridges, elevators, flying, driving, or enclosed places. This subtype has a bimodal age-at-onset distribution, with one peak in childhood and another peak in the mid-20s. This subtype appears to be similar to Panic Disorder with Agoraphobia in its characteristic sex ratios, familial aggregation pattern, and age at onset.

TABLE 7.1   Diagnostic Criteria for Specific Phobia (Continued)

Other Type: If the fear is cued by other stimuli. These stimuli might include the fear or avoidance of situations that might lead to choking, vomiting, or contacting an illness; "space" phobia (i.e., the individual is afraid of falling down if away from walls or other means of physical support); and children's fears of loud sounds or costumed characters.

Source: Reprinted with permission from American Psychiatric Association, *Diagnostic and Statistical Manual of Mental Disorders* (4th ed., text revision). Washington, DC: Author. Copyright 2000. American Psychiatric Association.

fears can be transient. The duration of 6 months decreases the likelihood that treatment will be directed at something that might dissipate without intervention and, as illustrated in the treatment section of this chapter, children's fears appear to be reactive to nonspecific interventions. A fourth feature of the diagnostic criteria that merits comment is the fact that, for the first time, panic attacks are specifically included in the diagnostic criteria for specific phobia, again highlighting that these fears can be severe and may be accompanied by a high level of autonomic arousal.

Prior to the *Diagnostic and Statistical Manual of Mental Disorders, Fourth Edition* (*DSM-IV*; APA, 1994), specific phobia was known as simple phobia. However, careful study of this disorder made it clear that phobias often are not simple. Rather, they are complex phenomena that may have a significant impact on the daily functioning of the individual and sometimes of those around them.

Mallory is 12 years old and is an only child. She is terrified of being kidnapped by aliens during the night and refuses to sleep alone. In fact, Mallory has never slept alone. For her entire life, she has slept in the bed with her parents or, more recently, in a sleeping bag on the floor of their bedroom. She has resisted all of her parents' attempts to make her sleep in her own room. Mallory's parents have never had the privacy of their own bedroom.

Jamal is 15 years old. His brother needs a bone marrow transplant, and luckily, Jamal is a perfect match. Jamal really wants to help, but he is terrified of needles. Ever since he was a little boy, he became upset whenever he had to get a vaccination or tetanus shot and would have to be held down by the doctor, nurse, and his mother. His fear is so severe that he chooses to go without Novocain when he needs dental work, preferring the pain of the dentist's drill to the thought of the needle. He has not been able to sleep well ever since the bone marrow transplant procedures were explained to him.

CLINICAL FEATURES

Although the range of items that may engender fear can be infinite, the current diagnostic schema collapses specific phobias into five types: animal, natural environment, blood-injection-injury (BII), situational, and other (APA, 2000). These categories were developed based on data that suggested that there were categorical differences in age of onset, type of physiological response, and degree of familial aggregation. The characteristics of each type are described next along with a clinical case description.

Animal Type

The fear is cued by an animal or an insect, and the most common age of onset is childhood.

> Randy is 6 years old and has an extreme fear of bees. He has never been stung, but he saw his sister get stung one early autumn. Over the ensuing winter, he did not appear to have any problems, but the following spring, he became fearful of going outside. He needed a great deal of encouragement, and his mother noted that he would retreat to the house whenever possible ("I heard thunder," "I have to go to the bathroom"). By the beginning of summer, the symptoms had become much worse (he refused a trip to the zoo because bees might be there).

Natural Environment Type

In this category, the fear is cued by objects in the natural environment, including storms, heights, or water.

> Leslie is 13 years old and is afraid of the dark, "spooky things," and thunderstorms. Her parents report that she has been fearful for as long as they can remember. She refuses to enter dark places alone. She refuses to sleep alone, insisting that her much younger sister sleep in her room. She also is extremely afraid of thunderstorms and will hide in the closet until the storm is over. If the storm occurs at night, she will hide in the closet of her parents' bedroom. The family tries not to startle her.

Blood-Injection-Injury Type

BII type phobia is cued by objects or situations that involve blood, needles, or injury to the body. The onset is commonly in childhood, and there is a high familial aggregation.

> Bonnie is 17 years old. She reports a nearly lifelong problem of readily fainting at the sight or verbal report of an injury or blood, especially as it pertains to amputation of, or injury to, body parts. When she was 7 years old, she watched a magician "saw a woman in half." She fainted while watching the magic trick and has been sensitive to such sights ever since that time.

Unique to BII phobias is the individual's physiological reactivity on exposure to these objects or events (APA, 2000). As noted in Chapter 1, when in contact with the phobic stimulus, increased heart rate and blood pressure are common. However, the physiological response to BII phobias is different; it is biphasic in nature (see Figure 7.1). Specifically, when faced with the feared event (blood, needles, injury), the initial reaction for those with BII is increased heart rate and blood pressure. However, those

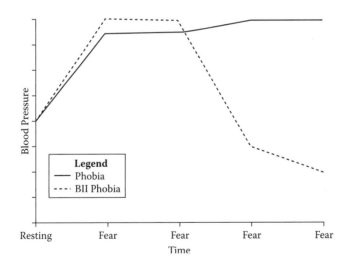

FIGURE 7.1 Blood pressure response on exposure to typical phobias and to blood-injection-illness phobia. (Reprinted from Beidel, D. C., & Turner, S. M. (2005). *Child Anxiety Disorders*. New York: Routledge. With permission.)

increases are followed by a sharp decrement in both blood pressure and pulse rate. In fact, in some cases, the decrease is so great that fainting is a distinct possibility. This unusual response makes BII unique and poses some special challenges for conventional treatments (see the section on treatment).

Situational Type

The situations that cue situational-type fears include public transportation, tunnels, bridges, elevators, flying, driving, or enclosed places (APA, 2000). Unlike the other types, the situational type has a bimodal age of onset. Childhood marks one peak age of onset, whereas the other peak occurs in the mid-20s. It has been suggested that this second subtype was similar to panic disorder with agoraphobia based on gender distribution, familial aggregation pattern, and age of onset (APA, 2000). This appears to be the case when the age of onset is in the mid-20s. However, children can suffer from the situational type as well.

> Patricia is 12 years old. She refuses to fly on an airplane. When she was 9 years old, Patricia was on an airplane that was caught in wind shear. The plane dropped several thousand feet before the pilot regained control. Ever since that time, she has been afraid to fly. She feels uncomfortable in an airport even if she is just going to greet her father after a business trip. Patricia's mother reported that Patricia also has a lifelong fear of heights.

Other Type

When fears are cued by "other" stimuli, they are classified as the other type. This includes fears of choking, vomiting, contracting an illness, or "space" phobias (afraid of falling because of loss of physical support). Phobias in this category can be particularly severe. In some instances, fears of vomiting or choking have been reported to result in weight loss that would meet the criteria for a diagnosis of anorexia nervosa, even when no other symptoms of an eating disorder are present or fear of vomiting or choking was the reason for the restricted eating behavior (Bailly & de Lenclave, 2005; Chorpita, Vitali, & Barlow, 1997; Manassis & Kalman, 1990).

> Edgar is 15. He refuses to go to school because he is afraid that he will vomit. He also avoids any social interactions because of his fear. When he was a toddler, he ingested a poisonous substance and was

given ipecac to induce vomiting. Always a "clingy" child, he started complaining of persistent stomachaches and fear of vomiting in the fourth grade.

An important issue to keep in mind is that sometimes individuals may present at clinics with what appears to be a specific phobia but instead may be an indication of a different anxiety disorder. For example, a "fear of knives" may be indicative of obsessive-compulsive disorder. Similarly, a "fear of tests" may indicate the presence of social phobia. Thus, a careful diagnostic evaluation is necessary to ensure that the child's fear is not representative of a different, or perhaps more pervasive, disorder.

EPIDEMIOLOGY

The prevalence rates for specific phobia range from 2.6% to 4.5% of the general population, with a mean of approximately 3.5% (Ollendick, King, & Muris, 2004; see Table 7.2 for available published prevalence rates). Consistent with data presented in Chapter 1, specific phobias (like fears in general) exist worldwide and affect a substantial percentage of the general population. Among treatment-seeking samples (i.e., children referred to anxiety disorders clinics for treatment), 15–36% met diagnostic criteria for a primary diagnosis of specific phobia (Last, Strauss, et al., 1987; Strauss & Last, 1993).

TABLE 7.2   Worldwide Prevalence Rates for Specific Phobia

Study	Country	Age Range (years)	Rate (%)
Anderson, Williams, McGee, & Silva (1987)	New Zealand	11	2.4
Bird et al. (1988)	Puerto Rico	4–16	2.6
Costello et al. (1993)	United States	12–18	3.6
Essau et al. (2000)	Germany	12–17	3.5
McGee et al. (1990)	New Zealand	15	3.6
Steinhausen, Metzke, Meier, & Kannenberg (1998)	Switzerland	7–16	2.6
Verhulst, van der Ende, Ferinand, & Kasius (1997)	Netherlands	12–18	4.5
Wittchen, Stein, & Kessler (1999)	Germany	14–24	2.3

Source: Reprinted from Beidel, D. C., & Turner, S. M. (2005). *Child Anxiety Disorders.* New York: Routledge. With permission.

Specific phobias appear to be relatively stable conditions when considered across assessment intervals ranging between 2- and 5-year follow-up (Ollendick et al., 2004). Depending on the specific time interval used, between 20% and 40% of children with a specific phobia at the initial assessment still meet criteria for the disorder at follow-up. In a long-term follow-up study, there was evidence for both the stability and the specificity of childhood phobic disorders into adulthood. In particular, a specific phobia diagnosis at age 32 was significantly associated with the same diagnosis, but not other anxiety disorders, during adolescence (Gregory et al., 2007). Moreover, other anxiety and mood disorders during adulthood were commonly preceded by specific phobias in childhood.

Among one sample of phobic children, specific phobias of the dark and school were most common, endorsed by 29% and 24% of the sample, respectively, followed by phobias of dogs (16%), other animals (8%), heights (8%), insects (8%), elevators (5%), closed places (3%), swimming (3%), needles (3%), drains (3%), and taxidermy (3%; Strauss & Last, 1993). As illustrated, the animal, natural environment, and situational type were most common. BII phobias were less common, as were phobias of closed places (claustrophobia), perhaps consistent with its much later age of onset. Among a large sample of German adolescents, in which 3.5% were found to meet criteria for specific phobia diagnosis, 31% had an animal phobia, 31% had natural environment phobias, 25% had situational phobias, 22% had BII phobia, and 11% had other phobias (Essau et al., 2000).

These subtypes were constructed based on data derived primarily from adult studies. However, data support the validity for these distinctions in children as well (Muris, Schmidt, & Merckelbach, 1999). Using a community sample, children rated their fearfulness with respect to 15 potentially fearful objects and situations drawn from the animal, BII, natural environment, and situational types. A factor analysis revealed that the 15 items loaded on three factors. Animal fears and BII fears loaded on separate, distinct factors. However, the natural environment and situational phobias loaded on the same factor, suggesting that those who report phobic symptoms of storms, the dark, and thunder also report phobic symptoms of flying and heights. Although the results did not perfectly replicate the *DSM-IV* typology, they do suggest some validity for the utility of distinct subtypes.

SOCIODEMOGRAPHIC INFLUENCES

Among a community sample of 1,000 children and adolescents, girls reported a higher level of specific phobia symptoms than did boys (Muris,

Schmidt et al., 1999), consistent with the data on fears in general. Among adolescents, more girls than boys were found to have specific phobias, although this overall gender difference was not statistically significant (Essau et al., 2000). Also, younger children (age ≤ 13) endorse a higher frequency of specific phobia symptoms than adolescents (age > 13) (Muris, Schmidt et al., 1999). When examined by specific phobia type, again girls and younger children were more likely than boys or older children to report animal, BII, and environmental-situational phobias. Thus, in the case of some phobias, age and gender may interact. For example, while some studies indicate that dental fears do not differ by age (Milgrom, Manci, King, & Weinstein, 1995; Townend, Dimigen, & Fung, 2000) or gender (Liddell & Murray, 1989; Milgrom et al., 1995; Ollendick & King, 1994), other data indicate increased dental fears in girls between the ages of 9 and 12 years (Murray, Liddell, & Donohue, 1989). As in the case of other childhood fears, it is unclear if this difference is real or represents a greater willingness among girls to express fear. Research on specific phobias across different ethnic groups is much more limited, although available findings based on the use of clinic samples suggest nonsignificant differences in the rate of specific phobias among European American, Latino, and African American children (Ginsburg & Silverman, 1996; Last & Perrin, 1993).

COMORBIDITY AND DIFFERENTIAL DIAGNOSIS

Throughout this volume, a recurring theme is that, among children, an anxiety disorder rarely exists alone. Rather, most children present with myriad symptoms, and many children appear to meet diagnostic criteria for more than one disorder. However, the data on comorbidity with respect to specific phobia appear mixed. Among one community sample, the comorbidity rate for the presence of a second disorder was lower when the *primary* diagnosis was a phobic disorder when compared to comorbidity rates for children who suffer from *primary* panic disorder or another anxiety disorder (Costello & Angold, 1995). However, when comorbidity rates among clinical samples are examined, 64% of children and adolescents with a primary phobic disorder were comorbid for a second disorder, most commonly another anxiety disorder (Last, Strauss, & Francis, 1987). In another sample of children with specific phobias, 61% were comorbid for a second disorder, most commonly separation anxiety disorder (SAD; Strauss & Last, 1993). In comparison to children with social phobia, those with specific phobia were less likely to have comorbid overanxious disorder or avoidant disorder. Somewhat consistent findings were reported by Verduin and Kendall (2003); children with a primary specific phobia diagnosis were most likely to have a secondary diagnosis of SAD (58%) or generalized anxiety disorder (GAD; 49%). In adolescents with a primary specific phobia diagnosis, approximately one third also met criteria for a depressive disorder (36.1%) or somatoform disorder (33.3%) (Essau et al., 2000). In terms of comorbid anxiety diagnoses, posttraumatic stress disorder (13.9%) was most common, followed by obsessive-compulsive disorder (11.1%). Ollendick et al. (2004) reported that approximately three quarters of children with a primary phobic disorder also had an additional disorder. Again, anxiety disorders were the most common comorbid diagnoses, followed by attention deficit/hyperactivity disorder and depressive disorders.

In general, specific phobias have an early age of onset. For example, in one study, children with specific phobia had an average age of onset of 7.8 years, compared to 12.3 years for social phobia, and were more likely to be prepubertal at the time they were referred for treatment, perhaps because of the earlier age of onset (Strauss & Last, 1993). School refusal was evident in both groups, although in differing proportions. Whereas 66% of the sample with social phobia expressed distress about school, only 24% of the group with specific phobia reported distress about attending school. In addition, some specific phobias may be more likely to occur at younger ages. In an early study, the average age of onset for BII phobias was 8.8 years, compared to 10.8 years for dental phobia and 11.9 years for thunderstorm phobia (Liddell & Lyons, 1978). Similarly, Öst (1987; Öst, Fellenius, & Sterner, 1991) found that dental phobia was most likely to develop around 12 years of age, BII phobia between 7 and 9 years of age, and animal phobias around 7 years of age. Situational phobias appear to have a much later age of onset, on average 21.8 years (Lipsitz, Barlow, Mannuzza, Hofmann, & Fyer, 2002).

ETIOLOGY OF SPECIFIC PHOBIA

Large twin studies examining genetic and environmental influences of specific phobias indicate that genetic, shared, and nonshared environmental factors significantly influence phobic disorders, with genetic factors contributing the largest amount of variance (Bolton et al., 2006; Eley et al., 2008). Family aggregation studies also highlight the heritability of specific phobias. For example, one study found that 31% of relatives of children with a specific phobia also had a specific phobia, compared to 11% of relatives of a normal control group (Fyer et al., 1990). However, some phobias may be more heritable than others. Using over 2,000 female twin pairs, Kendler and colleagues (1992b) found animal and situational phobias had the lowest rates of heritability among the phobic disorders, highlighting the role of environmental influences. BII phobia appears to have a strong familial component. In Bonnie's case, her father admitted feeling "queasy" around needles. Among those with BII phobia, approximately 67% have a relative with BII. This is among the highest rates for a familial relationship for an anxiety disorder, although again, it does not necessarily indicate a genetic vulnerability. Social learning or information transfer by a family member may contribute to the development of that fear in a child.

As noted, most specific phobias appear early in the life span. For example, the mean age of onset for animal phobias is age 7, and the mean age of onset for BII is age 9 (Öst, 1987). Notably, both fears are somewhat developmentally appropriate for this age group as both relate to safety and possible harm, so specific experiences that occur during this period may be highly influential in the development of these phobias. Indeed, phobias commonly develop through one of several learning mechanisms: direct conditioning, social learning (modeling), or information transfer. Direct conditioning appears to account for the largest percentage of phobic onsets. However, differences are apparent when examined by subtype (for an extensive review, see Merckelbach, de Jong, Muris, & van den Hout, 1996). Briefly, those with the animal or BII type more often attribute the etiology of their fear to social learning or negative information, whereas those with claustrophobia more often describe a situation consistent with a conditioning episode. Consistent with these data, modeling and information transfer are more often related to an earlier age of onset (Öst, 1987). For example, the role of parental modeling has been identified as the strongest influence in the acquisition of spider and dog phobias (King et al., 1997; Merckelbach, Muris, & Schouten, 1996), which commonly begin in childhood. Youth with dental fears commonly report knowing other dental phobics, suggesting information transfer as a possible mode of onset (Bedi, Sutcliffe, Donnan, & McConnachie, 1992). Townend et al. (2000), in a review of the literature, noted that many studies reported a consistent link between maternal trait anxiety and child dental fears, suggesting the presence of vicarious conditioning or information transfer.

The personality trait of disgust sensitivity has received some attention in the development of certain types of phobias, including animal phobias and BII. For example, in one study in which disgust sensitivity was examined among children with spider phobia before and after behavioral treatment, posttreatment reductions in spider fear corresponded with a reduction in disgust related to spiders (De Jong, Andrea, & Muris, 1997). In addition, similar to their phobic children, mothers also exhibited increased disgust sensitivity related to spiders, suggesting a possible genetic component. Despite these correlational findings, research has failed to establish the role of disgust sensitivity as causal. In fact, associations between disgust sensitivity and phobic disorders in children can be mainly accounted for by levels of trait anxiety (Muris, Merckelbach, Schmidt, & Tierney, 1999). Thus, the role of disgust sensitivity in the development of phobic symptoms does not appear etiological.

ASSESSMENT

Diagnostic interviews are discussed in Chapter 3 and discussion is not repeated here. Refer to Chapter 3 for an overview of diagnostic interviews and their use with children. The self-report instrument most commonly used (some might say universally used) to assess for specific phobias in children is the Fear Survey Schedule for Children–Revised (FSSC-R; Ollendick, 1983). As noted by Weems and colleagues (Weems, Silverman, Saavedra, Pina, & White-Lumpkin, 1999), the FSSC-R has an extensive body of psychometric data, including excellent reliability and validity, a well-validated factor structure, and extensive normative data. Furthermore, the instrument has been validated across a variety of cultures and countries (see Silverman & Hicks-Carmichael, 1999, and Weems et al., 1999, for extensive reviews). One aspect of the FSSC-R that has received less attention is its discriminative validity, particularly its ability to differentiate among children with different types of specific phobias. Examining the ability of the FSSC-R (both the child and parent versions) to differentiate among children with specific phobias of the dark, animals, shots/doctors, and social fears (Weems et al., 1999), a discriminant function analysis revealed that the children's scores on the FSSC-R were able to classify correctly 62% of the children. Specifically, 50% of those with animal phobias were correctly classified, as were 66.7% of those with phobias of the dark, 70% of those with fears of needles, and 55.9% of those with social phobia. Similarly, based on parental ratings, 63.6% of the children with animal phobias were correctly classified, as were 76.5% of those with phobias of the dark, 37.5% of those with needle phobias, and 81.5% of those with social phobias. The authors concluded that the FSSC-R could differentiate among children with various types of specific phobias; also parental ratings could differentiate those with social phobia from those with specific phobia. Thus, this well-validated instrument is, and should be, a staple in the assessment of childhood fears and phobias.

Whereas the FSSC-R assesses a range of different types of childhood fears, the newly developed Self-Efficacy Questionnaire for Specific

Phobias (SEQ-SP; Flatt & King, 2009) measures a child's perceived ability to cope with feared stimuli and phobic symptoms. Preliminary evidence for the reliability and validity of this 13-item measure has been reported, including two subscales: Cognitive/Physiological Efficacy and Behavioral Efficacy. Higher SEQ-SP scores also significantly correlated with lower scores on the Child Anxiety Sensitivity Index (CASI; Silverman, Fleisig, Rabian, & Peterson, 1991) and higher scores on a behavioral avoidance test (Flatt & King, 2009).

Behavioral assessments play a significant role in the history of the treatment of childhood phobias, although more recently this strategy appears to have fallen out of favor. For specific phobias, a behavioral approach test (BAT) allows the child to demonstrate his or her ability (or inability) to approach a feared object or situation. Unlike self-report data, BATs are less subject to social desirability. That is, unlike self-report data for which children are free to deny their degree of distress, asking a child who is afraid of heights to ride an escalator or a glass elevator will provide the therapist with a more valid assessment of the child's fear. BATs are simple to develop and are limited only by the therapist's creativity. For example, a BAT for fear of the dark might require asking the child to sit in a darkened room for as long as possible. Then, the number of seconds that the child can remain in the room is recorded. When assessing treatment outcome for fear of dogs, Bandura and colleagues (Bandura, Grusec, & Menlove, 1967) timed the number of minutes a formerly fearful child could remain in a pen with a dog. In other instances, the dependent measure is the distance between the individual and a feared object. For example, an individual afraid of snakes may be asked to approach a snake in a cage and to continue the approach until he or she becomes too anxious to approach any further. Then, the distance between the individual and the snake is assessed. At posttreatment, the test is repeated, and successful treatment outcome is judged by the individual's ability to get closer to the snake than he or she did at pretreatment (and it is hoped touch the snake). Although conducting a BAT requires more time and effort than simply giving a child a self-report inventory, the resultant data are less confounded by social desirability, expectations of treatment outcome, subject reactivity, or therapist demand.

TREATMENT

Interventions for children's fears are among the oldest established psychological treatments. The now-classic demonstration by Jones (1924) that counterconditioning (systematic exposure to the feared object in the presence of a response incompatible with fear) was effective in eliminating Peter's fear formed the basis for many subsequent studies of fear. Despite this early beginning, until recently information on the effectiveness of psychological interventions for children's fears consisted primarily of case descriptions. Controlled treatment studies of children's fears, particularly group comparison trials, are few. However, based on an extensive review (Ollendick & King, 1998), imaginal and in vivo desensitization, filmed and live modeling, and cognitive-behavioral interventions all appear efficacious for childhood phobias. Operant procedures, although backed by less literature, also appear probably efficacious. Controlled trials do not exist for other forms of psychosocial interventions. Pharmacological interventions are rarely, if ever, recommended for the treatment of specific phobia. Thus, this review is limited to the empirical data based on behavioral interventions.

Desensitization

In their review of the treatment literature, Ollendick and King (1998) detailed four controlled group outcome trials examining the efficacy of systematic desensitization for "stage fright" (Kondas, 1967), test anxiety (Barabasz, 1973; Mann & Rosenthal, 1969), and children with various phobic conditions (Miller, Barrett, Hampe, & Noble, 1972). Systematic desensitization is based on a classical conditioning model (Wolpe, 1958) and involves the pairing of a fear-producing stimulus (usually presented imaginally) with another stimulus or response that is incompatible with anxiety. The fearful stimuli are arranged hierarchically, from those that are least anxiety producing to most anxiety producing (see Table 7.3). In most cases, the incompatible response is relaxation, although with younger children food is sometimes used. In the studies cited, imaginal systematic desensitization was compared to various other active interventions, including relaxation training alone, presentation of the fear stimuli in a hierarchical fashion alone (no relaxation), vicarious individual desensitization, vicarious group desensitization, or traditional verbal or play therapy. Each study also included a wait-list control group. Across the four studies, systematic desensitization was more efficacious than the no treatment control condition, relaxation training alone, or presentation of the hierarchy alone. However, vicarious desensitization (group or individual) produced outcomes similar to systematic desensitization.

In fact, currently systematic desensitization is rarely used to treat children with phobic disorders. One reason might be that children's cognitive immaturity may not allow them to imagine the fearful stimuli in the fashion necessary for a successful desensitization outcome (see

TABLE 7.3   Randy's Hierarchy

Situation	SUDS Level
In-Session Tasks	
Looking at pictures of bees	1
Touching pictures of bees	2
Watching live bees on TV	2
Touching a dead bee	3
Sitting in a room with a live bee in a jar	3
Listening to bee sounds	3
Holding a jar with a live bee in it	4
Being outside when bees were present	5
At-Home Tasks	
Looking at pictures of bees	1
Conducting bee research on the computer	2
Watching live bees on TV	2
Listening to bee sounds	3
Carry a dead bee (encased in clear plastic) with him at all times	4
Keeping a dead bee in a jar in his room	4
Keeping a live bee in a jar in a room	5

Source: Reprinted from Beidel, D. C., & Turner, S. M. (2005). *Child Anxiety Disorders.* New York: Routledge. With permission.

Chapter 3). For example, in a comparison of imaginal and in vivo desensitization (Ultee, Griffioen, & Schellekens, 1982), water-phobic children aged 5–10 were assigned to either eight sessions of in vivo desensitization or four sessions of imaginal exposure plus four sessions of in vivo desensitization. Eight sessions of in vivo desensitization were superior, and according to the authors, one reason may have been that it facilitated familiarity in the water setting and the acquisition of skill, which would be an important component in ensuring fear reduction. However, an alternative explanation is that the young children were not able to successfully imagine the fearful situation, thus attenuating the efficacy of the intervention.

As noted, any response incompatible with anxiety can be used as part of a desensitization strategy, and competing responses other than relaxation have been successful. Kuroda (1969) randomized 58 Japanese children between the ages of 3 and 5 who were fearful of frogs or cats to either group in vivo desensitization or a no treatment control group.

Rather than relaxation, the children sang songs about frogs or cats, told stories about frogs or cats, and dramatized the movements of these animals. The results indicated that in vivo desensitization was superior to the no treatment control group.

Another variation of desensitization treatment is emotive imagery (Lazarus & Abramowitz, 1962). In this procedure, the relaxation component is replaced by instructions for the child to imagine an exciting story involving a superhero. Aspects of the fear hierarchy are woven into the story, for example, "Batman comes to you in the middle of the night. He needs your help on a very important mission. But you have to work with him in the dark so that the Riddler does not discover that you are aware of his evil plans." The rationale is that the positive emotion created by the exciting superhero story serves to counter the child's fear and inhibit the fearful response (Ollendick & King, 1998). However, as noted by these authors, there was only one controlled trial of emotive imagery (Cornwall, Spence, & Schotte, 1997). Twenty-four children aged 7–10 who were afraid of the dark were assigned to either emotive imagery or a wait-list control condition. Emotive imagery resulted in superior outcome on measures of self-report, parental report, and a BAT (a darkness tolerance test).

Modeling

Traditional desensitization and various forms of modeling (Mann & Rosenthal, 1969) were equivalent in terms of efficacy for the treatment of dog fears. Modeling (observational learning) has a long history in the treatment of children's phobias; it dates back to the seminal work of Bandura (1969), who proposed that extinction of fear would occur through observing a model behave nonfearfully in the presence of a feared stimulus. That is, a child with a dog phobia would observe a child who is not afraid of dogs playing happily with a dog. Also, Bandura hypothesized that learning would be enhanced as the child observed that the model did not experience aversive consequences. There are many variations in the manner in which modeling interventions are conducted. These include live or filmed modeling, observation or participant modeling, multiple modeling versus single modeling, or highly competent versus average competent models. Bandura and his colleagues (Bandura, Grusec, & Menlove, 1967; Bandura & Menlove, 1968) conducted several controlled, randomized trials examining different presentations of modeling and comparing them to no treatment groups for children with dog phobias. In the first study (Bandura et al., 1967), children were randomly assigned to modeling sessions during which the child observed

(a) the model behaving nonfearfully in the context of a birthday party, (b) the model behaving nonfearfully in a neutral context, and (c) the dog at the party but without the model. In the control condition, the child attended a party, but there was no dog or model present. Both modeling groups were efficacious, and equally efficacious, in comparison to the other two conditions, which did not differ from each other. A follow-up study compared the use of filmed modeling in two different modeling conditions: (a) one model interacting nonfearfully with one dog and (b) multiple models interacting nonfearfully with a variety of dogs. The control condition consisted of films without dogs. Both active treatment conditions were superior at posttreatment to the control group based on the posttreatment BAT (the length of time that the child could stay in a pen with a dog). Furthermore, those children who had observed various models and various dogs stayed in the pen with the dog for a significantly longer period of time than those exposed to the single model, thus suggesting some benefit for the use of multiple models and multiple variations of the fearful stimuli.

Bandura's results have been replicated by other researchers. Filmed modeling has been demonstrated to be effective in the treatment of preschool children who were fearful of dogs (Hill, Liebert, & Mott, 1968). In contrast, Lewis (1974) reported that filmed modeling alone was not as effective as either a participation condition (therapist encouraged and then assisted the child to engage in interactive activities at the swimming pool) or a combined filmed modeling/participation condition for children with water fears. In fact, filmed modeling alone did not result in any better outcome than did a control condition, whereas the combined condition exceeded even that of participation alone. It is unclear why filmed modeling alone was not effective in this case. However, it should be recalled that in vivo desensitization was superior to a combination of imaginal and in vivo desensitization for the treatment of children with fears of water (Ultee et al., 1982). Thus, using two different theoretical approaches, imaginal systematic desensitization or filmed modeling alone does not appear as efficacious as an in vivo approach. In the Ultee et al. (1982) study, the superiority of the all in vivo approach was attributed to allowing the children's acquisition of water skills. The same explanation may apply to the Hill et al. (1968) findings cited here. That is, for water phobias (like social phobia; see Chapter 10), the acquisition of skills may be a necessary component of fear reduction and positive treatment outcome.

Symbolic modeling (i.e., story characters behaving fearlessly in the face of fear) has been reported to be effective in the treatment of kindergarten children who were mildly to moderately fearful of the dark (Klingman, 1988). Modeling took the form of five 20-minute story group sessions during which single or multiple coping models dealt positively with the dark. Then, there was an unstructured group discussion during which children shared reactions and the therapist reinforced positive coping behavior. Both parental and child report indicated that symbolic modeling was significantly superior to a control condition in terms of decreasing fear and increasing coping statements. However, children with extreme fears of the dark were excluded from this study. Thus, the efficacy of this procedure has not been demonstrated in those who have the most severe fear.

Another variation of modeling is participant modeling, in which in addition to observing someone behaving fearlessly, the fearful child also engages with the model and the phobic object or situation. Several studies have confirmed that participant modeling is efficacious in the treatment of childhood phobias and in some cases actually may be more effective than simply live or filmed modeling. In one study, children (aged 5–11 years) who were fearful of snakes were randomized to live modeling, participant modeling, or a control group (Ritter, 1968). Both modeling conditions were judged superior to the control group; however, the participant modeling condition resulted in further significant improvement over live modeling alone. The superior outcome of participant modeling (over imaginal systematic desensitization, filmed modeling, and live modeling) was confirmed in a second study of snake-phobic adolescents and adults (Bandura, Blanchard, & Ritter, 1969) and another study of snake-phobic children (Murphy & Bootzin, 1973).

The importance of participant modeling and skill acquisition in the treatment of some childhood fears is reinforced by Jones and his colleagues in their work on fear of fire (Jones, Ollendick, McLaughlin, & Williams, 1989; Williams & Jones, 1989). Williams and Jones (1989) randomly assigned children aged 7.6 to 10.5 years to (a) a fire safety/fear reduction group, (b) a fire safety group, (c) an attention control condition, and (d) a wait-list control condition. The fire safety/fear reduction group included instructions in self-control statements. For example, children were taught that when faced with a fire situation, they should say, "I should relax and calm down. I can take care of myself because I know what to do." The therapist then modeled the use of self-control statements and stated the behavioral steps in a fire safety sequence (roll out of bed, get into a crawl position, crawl to the bedroom door, etc.). Children then verbally repeated each step. The fire safety group consisted of simple instructions to verbalize each fire safety skill. The children were not taught self-control statements. The attention control group consisted of discussing fire-related incidents, discussing fire-related stories, and drawing pictures of fire prevention activities. At posttreatment, both fire safety groups demonstrated significant gains in knowledge of fire safety skills.

However, at 3-month follow-up, the combined fire safety/fear reduction group had higher retention of skill knowledge. There was no significant difference across groups for reduction of fear. Although the use of self-instructional procedures was supposed to address fear reduction, the authors hypothesized that the manner in which the instructions were presented ("pretend you see a fire and 'really' experience the situation") may have served to exacerbate fear. The authors likened this situation to an exposure session, but because it was not implemented in a gradual fashion or for a sufficient period of time, it likely was ineffective.

Jones et al. (1989) compared the ability of two training procedures (behavior rehearsal and elaborative rehearsal) for the acquisition of fire safety skills and decrement in fear. In addition, a no treatment control group was included. Both groups were initially trained in the skills necessary to safely escape from a fire situation. For the process of behavior rehearsal, the therapist first modeled the sequence of skills, then the children performed each step. Errors or omissions were immediately corrected, and children rehearsed the responses again. Immediately after the behavior rehearsal, those assigned to the elaborative practice received additional training that included asking the children questions regarding the procedures they had learned, explaining correct responses to the questions and asking the child to repeat them, summarizing how correct responses would assist in safe evacuation, and providing the opportunity for children to ask questions regarding their training. Those who received behavioral rehearsal but no elaborative practice were given additional fire safety facts to equate for the therapist time. The results indicated that both groups acquired significant fire safety skills when compared to the control group, but there were no differences between the two active interventions. However, on a fear-of-fire inventory and on a general fear inventory, only the elaborative rehearsal group demonstrated significantly decreased fear. Furthermore, those in the elaborative group demonstrated greater understanding of the rationale. The authors concluded that although both methods resulted in improved skill acquisition, the elaborative rehearsal was superior in decreasing fear and long-term skill retention.

Contingency Management

Ollendick and King (1998) noted that contingency management procedures attempt to alter phobic behavior by manipulating its consequences. Their review concluded that reinforced practice, by which children are gradually exposed to the fearful stimulus, without benefit of counterconditioning strategies (such as relaxation) or modeling resulted in significant improvement in severe fears of dogs or riding a bus (Obler & Terwilliger, 1970), fears of the dark (Leitenberg & Callahan, 1973; Sheslow, Bondy, & Nelson, 1983), and fears of water (Menzies & Clarke, 1993). In each of these studies, reinforced practice was superior to no treatment control conditions. In a study of nighttime fears, graduated practice was compared to a combined condition consisting of graduated practice and training in verbal self-instruction to assist in handling fears of the dark (Sheslow et al., 1983). Another group received only verbal coping skills training. Both reinforced practice alone and the combination group were more efficacious than verbal coping skills training alone or the no treatment control group, again emphasizing the need for direct contact with the phobic stimulus. In another investigation, reinforced practice plus live modeling was superior to live modeling alone and a no treatment control group for children with water phobia (Menzies & Clarke, 1993). Furthermore, the combination group did not produce improvements over the reinforced practice condition alone. Again, the limitation of modeling alone for severe fears of water may be related to the need to develop specific skills (e.g., swimming skills) for fear to be diminished.

A recent, and controversial, variation to the treatment literature is the use of eye movement desensitization and reprocessing (EMDR) for the treatment of fears and anxiety. Shapiro (1995) hypothesized that EMDR reduced fear through the neural "reprocessing" of a traumatic event through the use of saccadic eye movements. Essentially in an imaginal exposure paradigm, patients are instructed to imagine the feared object or event and then "become aware" of the thoughts associated with that event. As the thoughts and images are reprocessed, fear is reduced. One of the purported advantages of EMDR is that it works quickly, sometimes in as little as one 90-minute session. EMDR is extremely controversial, and although studies exist either supporting or disputing the claims, there still is little reason to view this intervention as anything other than a form of exposure. EMDR was used to treat 22 girls (aged 9–14) with spider phobia (Muris, Meckelbach, Holdrinet, & Sijsenaar, 1998). This was an uncontrolled trial, although posttreatment outcome was compared to scores of nonphobic girls. Girls received 1.5 hours of EMDR and 1.5 hours of in vivo exposure. At posttreatment, scores on a spider phobia inventory were still elevated in comparison to those who were not phobic. There are several limitations to this investigation. First, this was not a controlled trial; thus, it is not possible to rule out the impact of nonspecific factors. Second, the use of both EMDR and in vivo exposure does not allow for a determination of the specific efficacy of EMDR. It is possible that the active intervention was in vivo exposure. Thus, although the contributions of this particular study to the overall treatment literature are limited, it does represent one of the first applications of EMDR to the treatment of childhood phobias.

Applied Tension

As noted, the physical response to BII phobias involves an initial increase in heart rate and blood pressure, followed by a rapid and sometimes dramatic decrease, possibly to the point of fainting. Thus, traditional exposure interventions may be contraindicated inasmuch as prolonged exposure to the phobic stimuli (e.g., a needle or blood) could result in fainting. Öst (e.g., Öst, Fellenius, & Sterner, 1991) developed a strategy to treat BII phobias that involves gradual exposure to the fearful objects or events while ensuring that the individual does not faint, thereby ensuring their participation in the exposure session. Applied tension teaches the individual to tense certain muscle groups (arms, hands, chest) when faced with the phobic object or situation. By tensing (rather than relaxing) these muscle groups, blood pressure increases, and fainting is prevented. Although the initial reaction of most clinicians would be that teaching a child to become tense in the presence of the phobic stimuli is inconsistent with the goal of an intervention designed to eliminate a phobia, it must be emphasized that the tensing procedure is not used to alleviate distress. Rather, its sole purpose is to increase blood pressure so that fainting and loss of consciousness do not occur, thus allowing the individual to participate in the exposure session. Although no controlled trials of applied tension exist in the child literature, the procedure has been used successfully with adults (Öst et al., 1991), and there are clinical reports of its successful use with children.

Cognitive-Behavioral Interventions

Cognitive-behavioral treatment (CBT) interventions have been used to treat childhood phobias. In one of the first investigations (Kanfer, Karoly, & Newman, 1975), children with severe fears of the dark were randomized to one of three conditions: competence ("I am brave and can take care of myself in the dark"), stimulus control ("The dark is a fun place to be"), and neutral (reciting nursery rhymes). At posttreatment, those in the competence group were significantly improved in comparison to the other groups. In another study, the utility of verbal self-instruction to treat severe nighttime fears also was examined (Graziano & Mooney, 1980). The intervention included relaxation training, imagining a pleasant scene, and reciting "brave" statements. In addition, parents were given instructions to provide children with verbal reinforcement and bravery tokens for appropriate behavior. When compared to the control group, those treated with the active intervention demonstrated significantly less nighttime fear, and the results were maintained up to 3 years later (Graziano & Mooney, 1982).

CBT also has been used to treat other types of fears. In a large controlled trial, Öst and his colleagues (Öst, Svensson, Hellstrom, & Lindwall, 2001) examined a one-session treatment (OST) for children with a variety of specific phobias, including animal, BII, natural environment, and the situation type. Children (aged 7–17) were randomly assigned to OST with the child alone, OST with the child and parent present, or a wait-list control group. The exposure session did not exceed 3 hours. The intervention, graduated in vivo exposure, was conceptualized as a series of behavioral tests from which the child could get new information. By accessing new information, the child could correct false beliefs held with respect to the phobic object or situation. Neither imaginal exposure nor cognitive therapy was part of the treatment. Rather, the therapists merely encouraged the children to examine and draw their own conclusions about their beliefs after the completed session. For those in the child-and-parent session, the intervention was identical to the child-only session. Depending on the therapist's judgment, some parents functioned solely as a support figure, whereas others were able to serve as a model if the child had initial difficulty engaging with the fearful object or situation. Both interventions were equally efficacious in reducing specific fears as well as decreasing self-report of general anxiety, anxiety sensitivity, and trait anxiety. Treatment gains were maintained at 1-year follow-up.

In one of the largest controlled trials (Silverman, Kurtines, Ginsburg, Weems, Rabian, et al., 1999), 81 children and their parents were randomized to self-control, contingency management, or wait list. In the self-control treatment, children were taught cognitive strategies such as self-observation, self-talk, self-evaluation, and self-reward, coupled with graduated exposure assignments. Contingency management was designed to facilitate graduated exposure. Parents were taught behavioral strategies, including positive reinforcement, shaping, extinction, and contingency contracting, which they implemented during the child's exposure sessions. In the educational support (ES) group, the therapist provided parent and child with information about phobias, including their nature and course, etiology, major theoretical approaches, and so on. No specific information was provided about any therapeutic strategy or how the interventions were implemented in practice. At posttreatment, all children, regardless of group, showed significant improvement on self-report measures of fear, general anxiety, depression, and negative cognitive errors. Furthermore, all children demonstrated clinically significant improvement, and all treatment gains were maintained at follow-up. This was a carefully designed and implemented randomized controlled trial, and the results are in contrast to a large body of literature suggesting that exposure is a key ingredient in fear reduction. It is unclear why the ES condition (conceptualized as a control for therapeutic support) was as efficacious as the two active interventions, although a similar ES group was efficacious for anxiety-based school refusal (see Chapter 8). This study was one of the few to include an active control condition rather than a wait list or no treatment control group; therefore, the outcome highlights an important omission in the current treatment literature. The vast majority of the current literature can be summed up by the statement "Doing something is better than doing nothing."

A multisite trial compared OST to ES (as well as a wait-list condition) among 196 youth (ages 7–16 years) with specific phobias (Ollendick et al., 2009). Participants had a variety of phobias, with the exception of BII phobia, based on results from Öst et al. (2001), suggesting that OST is less effective for this type of phobia. The OST condition was identical to the child-only treatment used in the work of Öst et al. (2001), while the active control condition was a modified version of ES as described by Silverman, Kurtines, Ginsburg, Weems, Rabian, et al. (1999). ES was similar in format to OST and included a child workbook that covered topics and activities related to how phobias are acquired, physical feelings associated with phobias, and how to manage "slips." However, no exposure or cognitive challenging tasks were included in ES. At posttreatment, children in the OST and ES conditions evidenced significant reductions in clinician-rated phobic severity and were less likely to receive a specific phobia diagnosis compared to the wait-list group. Further, OST was superior to ES on both of these outcome variables as well as child ratings of anxiety. At 6-month follow-up, children treated with OST continued to do better than children treated with ES. Interestingly, in both Ollendick et al.'s (2009) and Öst et al.'s (2001) studies, girls were more likely to respond to OST than boys. The nature of this finding remains unclear.

Based on the notion that computer-based CBT may have important advantages over traditionally delivered treatments, including greater availability and access, Dewis and colleagues (2001) compared the efficacy of computer-aided vicarious exposure (CAVE) to in vivo exposure and a wait-list condition for spider-phobic children ages 10 to 17 years. The CAVE program, which is based on social learning theory, instructs participants in vicarious exposure using a screen figure with the same phobia. Both active conditions consisted of three 45-minute sessions. Results indicated in vivo exposures were significantly more efficacious than CAVE as well as the wait-list condition, whereas the CAVE and wait-list groups did not differ on outcome measures. Thus, although pragmatically appealing, computer-aided exposure seems unlikely to produce a sufficient level of arousal, and in turn habituation, to be efficacious in reducing phobic disorders.

Pharmacological Treatment

Based on the high level of effectiveness of behavioral treatments as well as the prominent role of learning experiences in the development of fear, the use of pharmacological agents for the treatment of specific phobias, particularly in children, is uncommon. However, in treatment-refractory cases, when other comorbid anxiety disorders exist, or when significant complications or impairments are of concern, medication may be a treatment option. Banerjee, Bhandari, and Rosenberg (2005) provided case descriptions of the treatment of three children between the ages of 7 and 12 years, all with specific phobias of choking. In two cases, choking fears were clearly preceded by a specific conditioning event. All three youth were nonresponsive to prior psychological interventions and were severely limiting their food intake at the time of referral due to their fear. Treatment with 12.5 mg/day sertraline (liquid preparation) or 10–20 mg/day paroxetine was efficacious in reducing anxiety and increasing food consumption with no reported side effects. Thus, low dosages of selective serotonin reuptake inhibitors (SSRIs) may provide rapid improvement in children with severe and refractory phobias.

MEDIATING FACTORS IN THE TREATMENT OF CHILDHOOD PHOBIAS

To date, few studies have examined factors that might accentuate or attenuate the efficacy of these behavioral interventions. Combining two samples of children treated with exposure-based CBT (Berman et al., 2000), a variety of possible predictors (sociodemographics, diagnostic characteristics, treatment format, child- and parent-reported phobic symptoms, parental symptomatology, and marital distress) was examined. Higher pretreatment depression and trait anxiety were the strongest predictors of poor treatment outcome. Parental psychopathology, in the form of depression, hostility, and paranoia, also was associated with the child's poorer treatment outcome. When these predictors were examined by the child's age and whether the intervention was delivered in a group or individual format, the impact of parental psychopathology was weaker for older children or when the intervention was delivered in a group format. The finding that higher levels of depression and trait anxiety result in less-positive treatment outcome is consistent with findings from studies examining treatments for other anxiety disorders and suggests that intervention programs that are usually capped at 12 weeks of treatment may be insufficient for a subset of phobic children.

Another factor that merits careful consideration is the issue of treatment dropouts. As noted by others (Stanley & Turner, 1995), treatment outcome rates often are inflated because those who prematurely drop out are never considered when calculating treatment responders. Thus, it is important to examine the characteristics of those who leave treatment early. In a study of exposure-based CBT for children with anxiety disorders (Pina, Silverman, Weems, Kurtines, & Goldman, 2003), noncompleters received only an average of five treatment sessions. However, even though a variety of variables was examined (demographic characteristics, pretreatment scores on various self-report and parental report inventories), few significant group differences could be detected. The authors noted that their findings are consistent with previous studies, thus making it premature to offer recommendations about spotting "early terminators" or offering recommendations about how to promote compliance with the treatment protocol.

In an interesting report of children's perceptions of brief exposure treatment for specific phobias (Svensson, Larsson, & Öst, 2002), many of the children who participated in the Öst et al. (2001) brief exposure trial were interviewed. Children were questioned about several factors related to the treatment, including expectations prior to treatment; worry and cognitions before, during, and after treatment; perception of the therapeutic relationship; and outcome of and satisfaction with the intervention. Interestingly, 83.9% of the children stated that they wanted to participate in the treatment program; 8.9% did not, and 7.1% were doubtful. At pretreatment, only 55.4% thought the treatment would work, 25% were not sure, 17.9% did not think it would work, and 1.8% did not recall their expectations. After treatment, 58.2% described themselves as feeling very good and relaxed, 23.9% said that they were happy, and 7.5% admitted to feeling tired. With respect to final outcome, 82.1% reported being satisfied with the therapy outcome, 8.9% were disappointed, and 8.9% were unsure if they were satisfied or disappointed. A number of children felt that they needed more treatment sessions, and these were the children who demonstrated the least improvement from the single 3-hour session. This study is important because it represents some of the few available data on treatment satisfaction, particularly from the viewpoint of the child. The data indicate that, although many adults believe that exposure interventions are too intense for children, many children are eager to participate in treatment, understand the rationale, and do not suffer negative effects as a result of the intervention.

LIMITATIONS OF THE CURRENT
TREATMENT LITERATURE

One of the important limitations of the CBT literature is that, in many instances, the only comparison was to a wait-list control group. Although these data confirm that CBT is superior to doing nothing, as noted in Chapter 2, it remains unclear if these interventions are superior to "psychotherapy placebo" conditions. In addition to the Silverman, Kurtines, Ginsburg, Weems, Rabian, et al. (1999) and Ollendick et al. (2009) studies previously cited, other research suggests that children's phobias may be reactive simply to therapist attention and support. For example, six children (aged 7–10) with severe fears of the dark were treated with a combination of relaxation training, cognitive self-instruction, and positive reinforcement using a multiple-baseline design (Friedman & Ollendick, 1989). Children were instructed in positive self-statements such as, "I can take care of myself in the dark" and "I am brave and can take care of myself when I am alone." Reinforcers consisted of tokens that the children could earn for going to bed "with bravery." Tokens were later exchanged for a party. Although the intervention decreased nighttime fears, the authors noted that a careful examination of the multiple-baseline design indicated that changes occurred prior to the onset of the intervention (e.g., during the extended baseline and monitoring phase). Recall also that in Chapter 6, 18% of children diagnosed with GAD did not meet study criteria after the 2-week assessment phase (Rynn et al., 2001). As noted, many studies did not include an extended baseline; thus, changes in children's behavior attributed to the intervention may actually have been due to subject reactivity or demand characteristics. The Friedman and Ollendick (1989) baseline condition did include home monitoring of nighttime behaviors and some therapist expectations, such as the elimination of night lights, which may have served to affect behavior. However, because ethical considerations required that the children be treated, it remains unclear if the changes that occurred during baseline would have been maintained had no further intervention been available.

CASE EXAMPLES: TREATMENT FOR CHILDREN WITH SPECIFIC PHOBIAS

TREATMENT OF ANIMAL-TYPE PHOBIA

As previously described, Randy was 7 years old and had an extreme fear of bees. He was never stung by a bee but saw his sister get stung about 6 months ago. Over the ensuing winter, he did not appear to have any problems, but the following spring, he became fearful of going outside. He needed a great deal of encouragement, and his mother noted that he would retreat to the house whenever possible ("I heard thunder,"

"I have to go to the bathroom"). By summer, the symptoms had become much worse (he refused a trip to the zoo because bees might be there), and his mother sought treatment at our anxiety clinic.

The initial evaluation consisted of an interview with Randy and his mother. The interview did not reveal any other significant fears or other anxiety disorders. Because of Randy's age, he was not asked to complete self-report instruments independently; however, with his mother's help, he did complete the FSSC-R. Consistent with the interview, no other fears were rated in the severe range. Randy was aware that he was "too afraid" of bees. Prior to beginning treatment, self-monitoring procedures were instituted. Randy was asked to record his anxiety level whenever he went outside to go to school or when he got off the school bus in the afternoon. Because of his age, monitoring was made simple. Randy was given a series of five pictures of a child that illustrated various levels of distress (see Chapter 3). Prior to beginning self-monitoring, the scale was explained to Randy, and he was to be given several practice opportunities to ensure validity of the report. Randy's mother also provided monitoring data by recording the number of minutes each day that Randy played outside after school.

Graduated in vivo exposure was selected to address Randy's fear. Two hierarchies were constructed: one for in-session tasks and the second for homework assignments. To construct the hierarchy, items associated with Randy's fear were first generated by the therapist, Randy, and his mother. Then, the items were arranged hierarchically from least anxiety producing to most anxiety producing. Both hierarchies are presented in Table 7.3.

Implementing in vivo exposure requires contact with the feared object or situation for a time length of sufficient duration so that habituation (feeling comfortable) will occur. If ended prematurely, anxiety could be exacerbated. The session concludes when the child's distress is reduced by 50% from the highest rating reported during the session. This is commonly referred to as *within-session habituation* (see Figure 7.2). As depicted, anxiety initially is high but decreases over time (x-axis). The vertical axis is labeled SUDS (subjective units of distress), a Likert rating scale used by the child to indicate subjective distress. In Figure 7.2, a 7-point SUDS scale is used, ranging from 0 (no distress) to 7 (extreme distress), although with younger children, a simpler scale (perhaps 5 points) might be used.

In addition to within-session habituation (which should occur at each session), the ultimate goal of exposure is the achievement of between-session habituation. That is, across exposure sessions, peak distress should progressively decrease, and the time to return to baseline should progressively shorten. An example of between-session habituation is depicted in Figure 7.3.

Implementing exposure interventions with children requires another important consideration. Whereas adults and older adolescents usually understand that the only way to get over a fear is to

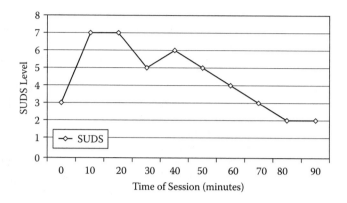

FIGURE 7.2 Change in self-report of anxiety during a single-exposure session is known as within-session habituation. (Reprinted from Beidel, D. C., & Turner, S. M. (2005). *Child Anxiety Disorders*. New York: Routledge. With permission.)

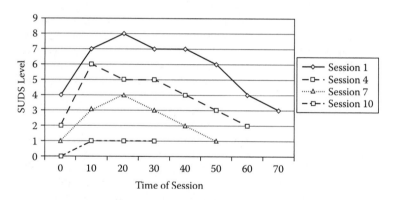

FIGURE 7.3 Change in self-report of anxiety across multiple-exposure sessions is known as between-session habituation. (Reprinted from Beidel, D. C., & Turner, S. M. (2005). *Child Anxiety Disorders*. New York: Routledge. With permission.)

face it, younger children do not always understand the logic behind exposure. Taking the time to carefully explain the rationale to parents and children is important. This allows parents to encourage and reinforce the child's participation in the therapeutic process. In addition, because children are often reluctant to participate in treatment, external reinforcers to encourage engagement in the in vivo situations may be necessary. Small activities or prizes that can serve as rewards for participation should be available.

In Randy's case, items initially were presented in clinic treatment sessions. No homework was assigned until that item (or a similar item) did not elicit any distress when presented in the clinic. Consistent with a habituation paradigm, items were presented without the use of any competing response that would serve to minimize the child's distress. Rather, because a graduated hierarchy was used, each item elicited only a minimal degree of distress when it was presented.

When implementing the exposure session, Randy's attention was directed toward the phobic stimulus. Thus, when touching a dead bee, for example, Randy was encouraged to describe how the bee looked and felt. In that way, the therapist could be assured that his attention remained focused on the phobic stimulus. Every 10 minutes, Randy was asked to report his level of distress using a 5-point SUDS scale, and the session was terminated when, in the therapist's judgment, he appeared relaxed and when he reported two ratings of a "1," indicating no distress. When in-session items no longer elicited distress, the item was assigned to Randy for homework.

A total of seven once-weekly, in vivo sessions coupled with homework assignments resulted in significant decreases in Randy's avoidance of bees, as indicated by the self-monitoring data depicted in Figure 7.4. Results were maintained at 3-month follow-up.

TREATMENT OF NATURAL ENVIRONMENT-TYPE PHOBIA

Leslie was 13 years old and afraid of the dark, "spooky things," and thunderstorms. Her parents reported that she was fearful for as long

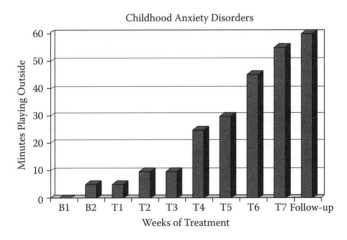

FIGURE 7.4   Number of minutes Randy played outside during baseline (B1 and B2) and during treatment (T1–T7) and follow-up. (Reprinted from Beidel, D. C., & Turner, S. M. (2005). *Child Anxiety Disorders.* New York: Routledge. With permission.)

as they could remember. She would not enter dark places alone or sleep alone, insisting that her much younger sister sleep in her room. She also was extremely afraid of thunderstorms and would hide in the closet until the storm was over. If the storm occurred at night, she would hide in the closet of her parents' bedroom. The family tried not to startle her.

In addition to these specific phobias, the diagnostic evaluation revealed the existence of some symptoms characteristic of GAD. Specifically, although Leslie did not report specific categories of worry or a significant amount of worry, both she and her mother reported heightened physiological arousal; she was easily startled, complained of headaches or stomachaches at least once per week, and often appeared unable to sit still. Therefore, although she did not meet diagnostic criteria for GAD, she exhibited a high level of general anxiety. Leslie did not meet diagnostic criteria for any other *DSM-IV* disorder. To determine a baseline level of functioning, Leslie was asked to monitor the frequency of stomachaches and headaches she experienced each day (see Figure 7.5). In addition, part of Leslie's home exposure involved the number of minutes she was able to remain in the dark (see Figure 7.6).

Leslie's case is typical of many children with specific phobias in that there often is the existence of several specific phobias. Thus, the challenge for clinicians is to consider whether the specific phobias should be treated in a combined or sequential fashion. In the case of Leslie, a decision was made to combine the two situations into one graded hierarchy to be used in the clinic. In addition, a home exposure hierarchy was created (see Table 7.4 for both hierarchies). In vivo exposure was

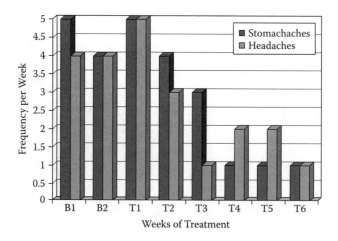

FIGURE 7.5 Frequency of Leslie's stomachaches and headaches during baseline (B1 and B2) and treatment (T1–T6). (Reprinted from Beidel, D. C., & Turner, S. M. (2005). *Child Anxiety Disorders*. New York: Routledge. With permission.)

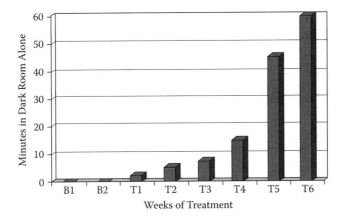

FIGURE 7.6   Length of time that Leslie was able to stay alone in the dark during baseline (B1 and B2) and treatment (T1–T6). (Reprinted from Beidel, D. C., & Turner, S. M. (2005). *Child Anxiety Disorders.* New York: Routledge. With permission.)

initiated in the clinic. Leslie was required to remain in the situation until she did not report or display any anxiety. She was not introduced to the next step until the previous item did not elicit any distress, even on initial presentation (i.e., between-session habituation was achieved for the individual item). As illustrated in the hierarchy, Leslie was exposed to increasing levels of darkness for an increasing period of time. As was the case with Randy, home exposure was not instituted until Leslie was comfortable in the dark in the clinic. As illustrated in Figures 7.5 and 7.6, the intervention resulted in a significant decrease in distress, and within 3 weeks, Leslie slept in her own bed for an entire night; by the end of Week 6, she had slept in her own bed for an entire week. In addition, she was able to stay in her room during a thunderstorm. The frequency of stomachaches and headaches decreased in intensity, although they did not disappear entirely. Because Leslie continued to demonstrate general tension and headaches, relaxation training was implemented to teach her to deal with her general distress (see Chapter 6 for the treatment of GAD).

TREATMENT OF BII-TYPE PHOBIA

Bonnie is 17 years old and faints at the sight of, or even the verbal report of, blood or injury. Following what appeared to be a conditioning event, in which a magician "sawed a woman in half," she faints whenever she observes an injury or blood or even when someone is describing these types of events. She avoids using a knife and any other activity in which knives or injury scenes were depicted or described (cooking, movies, TV shows, removing herself from friends who may be discussing an injury).

TABLE 7.4   Leslie's In-Clinic and Home Exposure Hierarchies

In-Clinic Hierarchy	SUDS
Sit in a room alone with only one desk lamp providing lighting	2
Sit in a room alone without lights but with the door open (thus providing minimal illumination)	3
Sit in a room alone with no lighting at all	4
Sit in a room alone, in the dark, with thunderstorm sounds (on audiotape)	5
Sit in a room alone, in the dark, with "spooky" sounds (on audiotape)	6
Sit in a room alone, in the dark, with thunderstorm and "spooky" sounds (on audiotape)	7

Home Hierarchy

First night: Sit in the dark for 5 minutes. Each night stay 3 minutes longer until you can sit in the dark with no anxiety for 30 minutes.

After completing the above, lie in bed for 30 minutes with the light off. Increase by 5 minutes each night.

Rewards for Home Hierarchy Compliance

For every night that Leslie is able to complete her homework, she earns 5 minutes of extra telephone time (on the weekend). The first night she is able to sleep in her bed for the entire night, she earns an extra video rental. When she can sleep in her bed for the entire night for an entire week, she earns a sleepover party with up to five friends.

Source: Reprinted from Beidel, D. C., & Turner, S. M. (2005). *Child Anxiety Disorders*. New York: Routledge. With permission.

The pretreatment assessment did not reveal the presence of any other anxiety disorder, although Bonnie reported that her mother often told her that she "worried too much." However, she did not endorse the presence of any other symptoms consistent with a diagnosis of GAD. Self-monitoring data (see Figure 7.7) indicated daily avoidance of activities involving knives and two fainting episodes.

Because Bonnie fainted easily (and often), she was taught to use Öst's applied tension procedure to prevent fainting during the exposure episodes. Bonnie's age suggested that imaginal exposure might be a useful first step. Also, given the need to be extremely careful about direct contact with blood-borne pathogens, imaginal exposure eliminates this risk. The imaginal flooding scene is presented in Table 7.5.

As noted, Bonnie was instructed that during imaginal exposure, she should use the applied tension procedure if she began to feel faint. Fifteen imaginal flooding sessions were needed to achieve between-session habituation. Home exposure also is presented in Table 7.5. After 15 weeks of treatment, Bonnie had stopped avoiding knives and situations

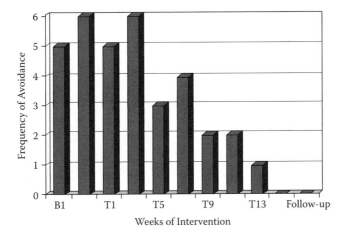

FIGURE 7.7 Frequency of Bonnie's avoidance of situations related to blood-injection-injury situations during baseline (B1), treatment (T1–T13), and follow-up. (Reprinted from Beidel, D. C., & Turner, S. M. (2005). *Child Anxiety Disorders*. New York: Routledge. With permission.)

that involved sight or descriptions of blood or injury. Treatment gains were maintained at 6-month follow-up (see Figure 7.7).

TREATMENT OF SITUATIONAL-TYPE PHOBIA

Twelve-year-old Patricia refuses to fly on an airplane. When Patricia was 9 years old, she had been on an airplane that was caught in a wind shear. Since that time, she is uncomfortable in an airport even if there is no expectation that she will fly (e.g., going with her mother to pick up her father after a business trip). She also has a lifelong fear of heights.

An interview with Patricia and her mother did not indicate the presence of any other psychiatric disorders. Although Patricia did not like being fearful of airplanes, she was unhappy and embarrassed about having to come to the clinic. Given that her fear was precipitated only when she was at an airport, daily self-monitoring data were not collected. Rather, the outcome of successful treatment was defined as Patricia's ability to fly to Disney World for a family vacation that was scheduled for approximately 4 months from intake. Patricia's hierarchy is presented in Table 7.6. Clinic treatment sessions occurred once per week for 12 weeks. Patricia was able to take the flight to Disney World, although she complained of a headache during that initial flight. However, she did not express any somatic symptoms on the return flight and subsequently has not been reluctant to fly.

It should be noted that Patricia was treated prior to September 11, 2001, and the airline was lenient about allowing unticketed individuals to pass through security, thus allowing the items on the hierarchy

TABLE 7.5 Bonnie's Imaginal Scene

It is early on Sunday morning. You and your friends are driving to the ski resort for a day of skiing. You are all sleepy and feel as if you are moving in slow motion. You pull into a fast food restaurant for breakfast. You park the car, and everyone gets out. Just as your friend hits the electronic locks and locks the door, you hear your friend Sue screaming. You know it is bad and serious. As you rush over, you see Sue has tears in her eyes, and she looks very scared. The door is not fully shut, and Sue's hand is stuck in the door. You yell, "Open the door!" Someone finally unlocks the door, and Sue's hand is free, but the blood begins to rush out. She is crying, and you are getting very nauseous. You take Sue to the bathroom in the fast food restaurant to wash off the blood. After about 30 seconds, Sue passes out on the floor. She hits her head, and now blood is gushing from her head and her hand. You yell for help, and another friend calls for an ambulance. There is a lot of blood all around Sue. You can see her fingers. The fleshy part of the index finger has been crushed, and the nail is hanging off. The middle joint bone of her middle finger is broken backward so that the tip is pointed sideways at about a 35-degree angle. Another nail is all crushed to pieces. There is blood everywhere. You feel dizzy and nauseous as if you are about to faint. You are lightheaded and sweaty, but you cannot run away. Your friend needs you. She wants you to hold her injured hand. It is all you can do to keep from vomiting as you hold her crushed, bloodied hand in your hands.

Home Exposure

Every day:

    Week 1 & 2 Handle a butter knife until any anxiety that is elicited dissipates

    Week 3 & 4 Handle a steak knife until any anxiety that is elicited dissipates

    Week 5 & 6 Handle a carving knife until any anxiety that it elicited dissipates

    Week 7 & 8 Use a paring knife; cut up vegetables (celery, carrots, radishes) until any anxiety that is elicited dissipates

    Week 9 & 10 Watch a TV show such as *ER* every day

    Week 11 & 12 Watch younger sister cut up vegetables

    Week 13–15 Observe father shaving

Source: Reprinted from Beidel, D. C., & Turner, S. M. (2005). *Child Anxiety Disorders*. New York: Routledge. With permission.

to be completed in vivo. Given current security restrictions at public airports in the United States, different items (or an imaginal approach) may be necessary, although it still might be possible to implement this hierarchy at a private airport facility.

TREATMENT OF OTHER-TYPE PHOBIA

Edgar (aged 15) refused to go to school because he was afraid that he would vomit. He also avoided any social interactions because of his fear.

TABLE 7.6   Patricia's Hierarchy

Clinic Hierarchy	SUDS
Riding the elevators alone	2
At the airport but only in the boarding area	3
In the airplane jetway	4
Sitting on the plane, no motor running	5
Sitting on the plane, motor running	6
Flying in the day, ground visible	7
Flying at night	8
Flying in the day, cloudy weather conditions	9

Homework Exposure

Ride escalators for at least 15 minutes at least four times per week. Patricia is to ride alone, although for safety's sake, parent should be present and observing the exposure.

Source: Reprinted from Beidel, D. C., & Turner, S. M. (2005). *Child Anxiety Disorders.* New York: Routledge. With permission.

When he was a toddler, he ingested a poisonous substance and was given ipecac to induce vomiting. Always a "clingy" child, he started complaining of persistent stomachaches and fear of vomiting in the fourth grade. Because of his concerns, he had two endoscopic procedures, which did not reveal any physical cause for his fear. He avoids eating before social events, avoids eating certain foods (milk, cheese, yogurt, and spicy foods); avoids situations (such as school) from which escape might be difficult if he becomes nauseous; and avoids "hanging out" with his friends. He also had occasional panic attacks at bedtime.

Thus, Edgar also met criteria for panic disorder and SAD. Self-monitoring data included recording the frequency of nighttime panic attacks, stomachaches, number of times that he engaged in "sleepovers" with his friends.

For this complicated case (see Roberson-Nay & Turner, 2002, for an extended case presentation), intervention included interoceptive exposure (direct exposure to the cues of vomiting) and in vivo exposure. Specifically, the in vivo exposure consisted of a tongue depressor that was used to stimulate gagging and nausea- or vomiting-related sensations. Edgar was asked to place the tongue depressor in the back of his mouth to stimulate the gag reflex. For each session, Edgar had to continue eliciting the gag reflex until he could gag without experiencing any distress. Between-session habituation was judged not only by decreases in SUDS across sessions but also by increases in the number of times that he voluntarily elicited the gagging reflex during the exposure session (see Figures 7.8 and 7.9). As depicted in Figure 7.9, Edgar's ability to voluntarily make himself gag was low during Session 1,

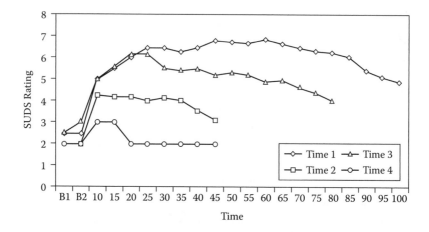

FIGURE 7.8 Within-session and between-session habituation for Edgar's in vivo exposure to gagging. (Reprinted from Beidel, D. C., & Turner, S. M. (2005). *Child Anxiety Disorders*. New York: Routledge. With permission.)

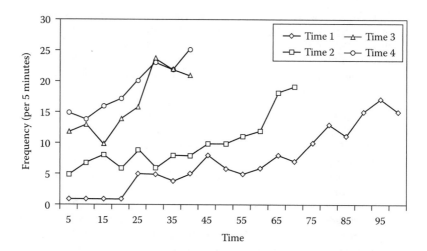

FIGURE 7.9 Frequency of gagging response voluntarily produced by Edgar during exposure sessions. (Reprinted from Beidel, D. C., & Turner, S. M. (2005). *Child Anxiety Disorders*. New York: Routledge. With permission.)

during which initially he refused to attempt to elicit the gag reflex. However, by the fourth session, he was able to voluntarily elicit the gag reflex 25 times in a 5-minute period, indicating decreased anxiety with the idea that he would gag and vomit.

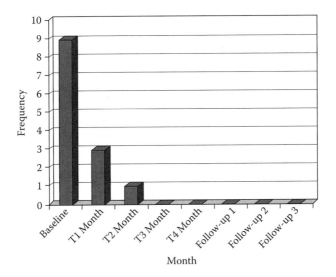

FIGURE 7.10   Frequency of Edgar's panic attacks during baseline, treatment, and follow-up. (Reprinted from Beidel, D. C., & Turner, S. M. (2005). *Child Anxiety Disorders*. New York: Routledge. With permission.)

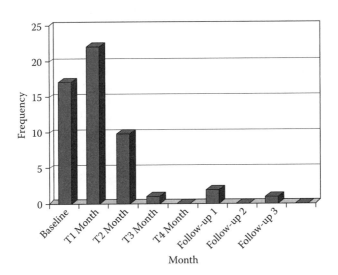

FIGURE 7.11   Frequency of Edgar's stomachaches during baseline, treatment, and follow-up. (Reprinted from Beidel, D. C., & Turner, S. M. (2005). *Child Anxiety Disorders*. New York: Routledge. With permission.)

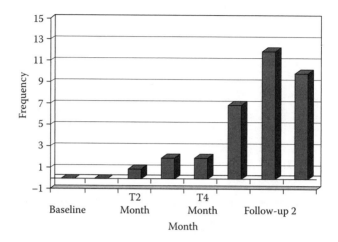

FIGURE 7.12 Frequency of sleeping over at a friend's house as a result of reduced fear of vomiting. (Reprinted from Beidel, D. C., & Turner, S. M. (2005). *Child Anxiety Disorders*. New York: Routledge. With permission.)

A total of five exposure sessions were necessary to achieve between-session habituation. In addition to these in-clinic sessions, Edgar had homework assignments that consisted of the following: leaving the house once per day for at least 30 minutes and once per day eating one previously "avoided" food, such as milk, cheese, yogurt, or a spicy food. Finally, a hierarchy was developed to facilitate reentry into school (see Chapter 8 for treatment of school refusal). Self-monitoring data indicated substantial improvement across all categories of behavior (see Figures 7.10 to 7.12). At follow-up, Edgar was consistently attending school, was spending a great deal of time away from home, stayed at home for 4 days without his parents but with an older sibling, and was gaining weight as a result of eating previously avoided foods.

SUMMARY

To summarize, it is evident that behavioral interventions based on exposure paradigms are successful in treating children with a variety of specific phobias. As noted, the literature indicates that the best successes are achieved when the child has the opportunity to come directly into contact with the feared stimulus. Thus, even if a clinician uses one of the other intervention strategies described in this chapter, in vivo exposure (at least in the form of homework assignments) should be included in the overall intervention strategy. Furthermore, given the highly specific nature of these phobias, it is clear that standardized self-report inventories that would be useful for treatment planning or determining treatment outcome do not exist. Thus, clinicians will need to use self-monitoring strategies that identify problematic behaviors and measure changes in those behaviors as a result of the intervention.

CHAPTER 8

School Refusal

Mark is 15 years old. He wants to go to school but has not done so consistently for the past 2 years. According to his mother, he misses about 2 days of school per week, and on the other days, he is late about 50% of the time, sometimes not arriving until noon. Mark is oppositional and has been verbally abusive and physically intimidating toward his mother, but only when she tries to make him go to school. On some days, he describes feeling anxious and panicky. On other days, he reports being "just too tired." When he stays home, he cannot watch television or play with his computer or video games. He is allowed to play with his hamsters and guinea pig, which Mark claims are more interesting than the privileges that are taken away. The situation has become so severe that Mark's mother has quit her job to be home with him.

ISSUES OF DEFINITION REGARDING SCHOOL REFUSAL

As a working definition, school refusal can be either (a) refusal to attend or (b) difficulty remaining in school for an entire day (Kearney & Silverman, 1990). School refusal is a complicated behavior because children refuse to go to school for many different reasons. Most important, school refusal must be differentiated from truancy. This distinction was initially discussed during the 1930s and 1940s (see Kearney, Eisen, & Silverman, 1995), when school absenteeism was defined as a "clinical behavior" and distinguished from truancy. Truancy, a disruptive behavior, was considered to be an aspect of juvenile delinquency, whereas school refusal described children who desired to go to school but nevertheless were uncomfortable about attendance. In the 1940s, the term *school phobia* (Johnson, Falstein, Szurek, & Svendsen, 1941) was used to describe a constellation of behaviors: the presence of child anxiety, maternal anxiety, and an enmeshed mother–child relationship. Specifically, psychoanalytic theory implied that a close symbiotic relationship between mother and child led to overdependence, which resulted in the child's reluctance to attend school. Later, behavioral theory postulated school refusal as a learned reaction to a specific event or situation associated with the school environment (see section on etiology for an extended description of these theories).

Others have forgone linking the refusal behavior to a particular etiological theory and described school refusal as one of two subtypes: neurotic or characterological (Coolidge, Hahn, & Peck, 1957). In 1965, Kennedy published a seminal paper on school phobia (school refusal) based on two categories of presenting symptoms. Type 1 was a "neurotic crisis," whereas Type 2 was a "way-of-life" phobia. Both types shared common features: (a) fears associated with school attendance; (b) frequent somatic complaints; (c) a symbiotic relationship with mother, resulting in fears of separation and anxiety about many different things; and (d) conflict between parents and school administration. Despite these similarities, there are a number of important differences that are depicted in Table 8.1. As discussed in the section on treatment, these two subtypes show dramatically different treatment outcomes.

TABLE 8.1   Type 1 and Type 2 School Phobia

Type 1	Type 2
1. Present illness is first episode	1. Second, third, or fourth episode
2. Monday onset, following an illness on the previous Thursday or Friday	2. Monday onset but a minor illness not a prevalent antecedent
3. An acute onset	3. Incipient onset
4. Lower grades most prevalent	4. Upper grades most prevalent
5. Expressed concern about death	5. Death theme not present
6. Mother's physical health in question; she is ill or child thinks so	6. Mother's health not an issue
7. Good communication between parents	7. Poor communication between parents
8. Mother and father well adjusted in most areas	8. Mother shows neurotic behavior; father has a character disorder
9. Father competitive with mother in household management	9. Father shows little interest in household or children
10. Parents achieve understanding of dynamics easily	10. Working with parents is difficult

Source: Reprinted from Beidel, D. C., & Turner, S. M. (2005). *Child Anxiety Disorders.* New York: Routledge. With permission.

Despite the reconceptualization of school refusal by focusing on symptoms instead of potential etiological factors, there remained difficulty with the use of the term *school phobia*. Specifically, children's self-report often was not consistent with the idea of a phobia. For example, some children may be absent from school as a result of being bullied or threatened, creating a desire to avoid school as a result of concerns about physical safety (Dube & Orpinas, 2009). Other children refusing to go to school rated "having to go to school" as "somewhat fearful," not "excessively fearful," as might be expected given their behavioral avoidance (Kearney et al., 1995). In addition, these children rated fears of nonschool items as high as and sometimes higher than their fear of school. Consistent with these data, only 39% of another sample of children with problematic school attendance reported "a lot" of fear of having to go to school (Barton, Kearney, Eisen, & Silverman, 1993). Other investigators have reported that between 0% and 52.4% of their school-refusing samples met diagnostic criteria for a primary or secondary social or simple (specific) phobia that could be related to school avoidance (Bernstein & Garfinkel, 1986, 1988; Last & Strauss, 1990). Additional data indicate that negative affectivity (a concept that encompasses both anxiety and depression) also may be characteristic of at least some children with poor school attendance (see Kearney et al., 1995). Overall, these data suggest that although fear may drive school refusal behavior in some children, the terms *school phobia* and *school refusal* are not synonymous.

Rather than relying on diagnostic criteria, modern conceptualizations of school refusal propose that it results from one of four different motivations: (a) avoidance of stimuli that precipitate negative affectivity (e.g., anxiety or depression); (b) escape from aversive social or evaluative situations (e.g., peer relationships, oral presentations); (c) attention (e.g., disruptive behavior to stay home with one's parents); and (d) positive tangible reinforcement (e.g., finding it more rewarding to be at home than at school; Kearney, 1995; Kearney & Silverman, 1990). Whereas the first two types are considered to be motivated by negative reinforcement, the second two describe school refusal motivated by positive reinforcement (Kearney, 1995, 2007). Conceptualizing school refusal in terms of a functional model allows for a prescriptive approach to treatment planning; a diagnosis describes the child's difficulty but does not necessarily indicate a strategy for remediation (Kearney, 2007). The functional (or prescriptive) approach allows for identification of the factors that maintain the problematic behavior and thus indicates avenues for appropriate treatment planning.

To reiterate, *truancy* refers to youth who do not attend school because of lack of interest or defiance of adult authority, whereas *school refusal* (formerly school phobia) describes youth who desire, but do not attend, school because of emotional distress such as fear, anxiety, or depression. Thus, school refusal is not a clinical syndrome but a descriptive term that may indicate the presence of a variety of emotional disorders. In some instances, no discernible disorder may be present. The focus of this chapter is on youth who refuse to attend school because of fear or anxiety.

CLINICAL ISSUES

The characteristic presentation of children with anxiety-based school refusal includes both physical and behavioral symptoms. On awakening, children often express somatic complaints such as headaches, stomachaches, or sore throats. Somatic complaints, particularly symptoms related to the autonomic and gastrointestinal systems, also were common among adolescents who refused to attend school (Bernstein et al., 1997). Typically, these physical complaints are more frequent on schooldays than on weekends or during summer vacations. Sleep difficulties also exist among children with anxiety-based school refusal. In one epidemiological sample of school-refusing children (Egger, Costello, & Angold, 2003), 18% of the children reported night terrors, 14% reported nightmares, 32% reported trouble falling or staying asleep, 12% reported fatigue, 8% were reluctant to sleep alone, and 26% got out of bed in the middle of the night to check on family members. Morning tantrums also were common (King & Bernstein, 2001), particularly among younger children, whereas adolescents, like Mark, were more likely to "stall" or delay personal hygiene rituals or simply refuse to get out of bed. Finally, others go to school but cannot stay the entire day.

> Stephanie is 7 years old. She attended first grade without any difficulties. Now in second grade, she is having extreme difficulty with school attendance. She refuses to ride the bus but will allow her mother to drive her to school and escort her to her classroom. Approximately an hour after her mother leaves, Stephanie becomes agitated and fearful. She cries inconsolably. The school feels they cannot handle her behavior, and they call her mother to come to take her home. This has happened every day for the last month. Her mother is seeking treatment for Stephanie because having to leave work every day to pick up her daughter at school is resulting in negative feedback from her employer.

Whereas some children beg parents or caregivers to allow them to stay home, others, like Stephanie, will go to school but then disrupt the school environment, causing the school to request the child's removal.

Refusal to attend school has long been related to academic achieve-ment (Chazan, 1962). In one study, learning disabilities and language impairments were significantly more common among an inpatient sam-ple of depressed adolescents who refused school when compared to a matched group of psychiatric controls (Naylor, Staskowski, Kenney, & King, 1994). Furthermore, test anxiety, which may impair academic per-formance, has been reported to be a common precursor to school refusal (Kearney et al., 1995). Of course, all these data are correlational and do not allow conclusions to be reached regarding etiology. Specifically, it appears that school refusal may be a cause, an effect, or simply a cor-relate of academic underachievement.

The school environment provides opportunity for more than cogni-tive achievement. Schools provide an opportunity for social development and the establishment of friendships. Children who refuse to attend school miss important opportunities for social development. Among children with anxiety-based school refusal (Egger et al., 2003), 28.2% reported shyness with peers, 28.9% reported fears of being bullied or teased, 18.9% reported difficulty making friends because of social with-drawal, 17.5% reported difficulty making friends because of aggression, and 27% reported conflictual peer relationships. Because these children had a pattern of school refusal at the time of the study, it is unclear if these peer problems were the cause or the result of their avoidance behaviors. A prospective design would be necessary to tease out the nature of these relationships. However, it is clear that a percentage of children who refuse to attend school have difficulties in the area of peer interactions.

Strained or poor family relationships also may present as part of the symptom picture (Last & Strauss, 1990). In one sample, two familial factors, single-parent households and a biological or nonbio-logical parent being treated for a mental health problem, were asso-ciated with anxiety-based school refusal (Egger et al., 2003). Other investigators have examined patterns of family functioning rather than family structure among children who refuse school (Bernstein, Svingen, & Garfinkel, 1990). Among four groups of school refusers (depressive disorder only, anxiety disorder only, anxiety and depres-sive disorder, no anxiety or depressive disorder), family dysfunction was evident among all groups except when school refusal was based solely on an anxiety disorder, but dysfunction did exist when chil-dren were comorbid for anxiety and depressive disorders (see sec-tion on comorbidity). However, correlational studies do not allow for a determination of whether the dysfunctional patterns preceded or followed the school refusal. In Mark's case, marital discord was a result of his school refusal. Therefore, a careful assessment of familial functioning and marital relationships should be a standard part of the assessment battery as they may play a role in the maintenance or treatment of the behavior.

Parent's occupational functioning can be impacted by the child's school refusal. In some cases, as was true for Stephanie's mother, parents are at risk of losing their jobs because of the need to leave work to pick up the child at school. In other instances, such as Mark's, his mother quit her job to deal with his refusal. In these instances, school refusal affected not only the child's functioning but also family functioning as well as potentially disrupting the home environment.

School refusal is associated with later adult maladaptive behaviors, including agoraphobia, job difficulties, social avoidance, poor school adaptation, and constricted personality development (Burke & Silverman, 1987). A controlled long-term follow-up investigation of Swedish children indicated that those with school refusal suffered long-term social maladjustment (Flakierska, Lindstrom, & Gillberg, 1988; Flakierska-Praquin, Lindstrom, & Gillberg, 1997). At the 20- to 29-year follow-up interval (participants were at least 30 years old), adults who refused school as children had more psychiatric consultations, were more likely to be residing with their parents, and had fewer children than the general population, suggesting that school refusal has the ability to have an impact on long-term outcome even when school attendance is no longer mandated.

DIAGNOSTIC ISSUES

School refusal describes behavior but does not indicate the presence of a particular syndrome. Among children with school refusal treated by private practitioners, the desire to stay at home with parents and desire to avoid aversive social situations were equally common reasons for school refusal (26.1% and 25%, respectively; Kearney & Beasley, 1994). Less-frequent reasons included difficulty with homework or curriculum (12.2%), aversive evaluative situations, including tests (10%); fear of specific situations in or related to the school setting (10%); positive tangible rewards (7.8%); and other (6.9%). Thus, even when restricted to anxiety-based school refusal, there are still different anxiety disorders associated with this behavior, including separation anxiety disorder, social phobia, panic disorder and agoraphobia, and perhaps posttraumatic stress disorder (PTSD). The relationship of these disorders and school refusal is discussed. For an extensive discussion of each disorder, see the individual chapters in this book.

Separation Fears

An early theory regarding school refusal focused on an enmeshed mother–child relationship. Although this particular conceptualization is no longer the most popular explanation, separation from a caregiver remains one potential factor. Among a clinical sample of 63 children aged 7–17 years with school refusal, 38% had a primary diagnosis of separation anxiety disorder, a diagnosis most commonly found in younger children (Kearney et al., 1995). Using an epidemiological sample of children with anxiety-based school refusal, 18% reported worry about calamitous separation from parents, 17% reported fear of what might happen at home while at school, and 5% reported worry about leaving home for school (Egger et al., 2003). One might conclude from these numbers that separation from caregivers was characteristic of only a small percentage of school-refusing children. However, other results from this epidemiological survey indicated that maladaptive sleep behaviors were present (8% were reluctant to sleep alone, and 26% got out of bed in the middle of the night to check on family members). These complaints could be indications of separation anxiety among a subset of children with school refusal, suggesting that the percentage of children who refuse to go to school because of separation fears may be higher than some data might indicate.

Social Fears

Jessica is 16 years old, and she loves school. However, she has not been able to go in the last few weeks. She fears being called on in class and giving the wrong answer, causing herself great embarrassment. Now, her anticipation of that possibility is so intense that she wakes up nauseated every morning. When asked about her refusal, she said, "I would love to go to school, but I cannot stop vomiting long enough to get on the bus." Her mother agrees, noting that every morning Jessica gets up and gets dressed in an attempt to go to school. However, as the time to leave for the school bus approaches, she runs to the bathroom and begins to vomit.

In the clinical sample described (Last & Strauss, 1990), 30.2% of school refusers had a primary diagnosis of social phobia. Early investigations (Partridge, 1939; Warren, 1948) described children who did not attend school as poorly socially adjusted or timid and sensitive. More recent investigations confirmed that social phobia may be a factor in some cases of school refusal (Last, Francis, Hersen, Kazdin, & Strauss,

1987; Miller et al., 1972; Ollendick, King, & Frary, 1989). For example, school absenteeism peaks when children encounter a new school setting (elementary school, middle school, or high school; Granell de Aldaz, Feldman, Vivas, & Gelfand, 1987), perhaps as a result of a fear of getting lost and appearing incompetent in front of others (Kearney et al., 1995). Other potentially distressing school situations include giving oral reports, writing on the blackboard, taking tests, or being reprimanded by a teacher or principal. Having to interact with other children at recess or around group projects also will evoke anxiety among children with social phobia. A less-common, although still significant and functionally impairing social phobia, is that of vomiting in front of others (and being embarrassed by it).

Specific Fears

Among one clinical sample (Last & Strauss, 1990), 22% of school refusers met criteria for a primary diagnosis of specific phobia. Specific phobias may include fear of riding the school bus, physical education classes, fire, or other types of events. In comparison to children with separation anxiety disorder, children with social or specific phobias had a later age of onset, had a more severe pattern of school refusal, and were less likely to have mothers with a history of school refusal (Last & Strauss, 1990).

Other Anxiety Disorders

Panic disorder, generalized anxiety disorder (formerly overanxious disorder), PTSD, and obsessive-compulsive disorder also may lead to school refusal behavior, although these disorders are less commonly reported in the school refusal literature.

> Susan is 12 years old. She is very fearful of contamination and getting cancer. She is afraid to touch anything that might have been touched by someone who has cancer. There are several children at her school who have been treated for cancer, one of whom is in her class. Susan refuses to go to school because she is afraid that she will touch something that has been touched by one of the children with cancer. Despite repeated explanations by her parents and her pediatrician that she cannot get cancer by touching something belonging to, or being touched by, a cancer patient, Susan remains anxious and fearful and refuses to attend school.

As illustrated in our clinical example, panic disorder also may lead to school refusal behavior.

Mark's school refusal appeared to be related to several underlying conditions. A core feature appeared to be concern with unfamiliarity both with situations and with people. For example, although he would go to malls with which he was familiar, he refused to go to "new malls" and stated that he gets "wobbly kneed" in new situations. He also became uncomfortable in and avoided church. He reportedly became overwhelmed in crowds and could document panic attacks on at least three occasions: at the mall, at a barber shop, and in a movie theater, with symptoms consisting of weakness in his knees, shortness of breath, and a strong desire to escape the situation. Social fears also appeared to play a role. For example, he left a family reunion, and it was his mother's impression that he was overwhelmed by all of the unfamiliar people, describing heart palpitations, feeling flushed, and feeling weak kneed. At school, he has several friends but had difficulty in gym class when the students had to "pair up." He did not have any friends in the class, became uncomfortable (heart palpitations and feeling flushed), and refused to participate.

Thus, although the prevalence is lower than for other anxiety disorders among children, panic disorder may be a precipitating cause for school refusal. However, Mark also presented with some degree of social phobia, although the severity of this diagnosis was secondary to his panic and depression.

In summary, the prevalence of generalized anxiety disorder, obsessive-compulsive disorder, panic disorder, and PTSD among children who refuse to go to school is much lower than for separation anxiety disorder, social phobia, and specific phobia. Because of their lower prevalence, much less information is available on the relationship of these disorders and school-refusing behavior. However, it is clear from the case examples that the disorders can be just as impairing as those more commonly associated with school refusal.

Sociodemographic Influences

In a review (King & Bernstein, 2001), approximately 5% of all children manifested school refusal behavior, although rates appeared to be higher in urban populations. In a longitudinal study of the development of psychiatric disorders in an epidemiological sample of 1,422 children aged 9 through 16 (Great Smoky Mountain Study; Egger et al., 2003), the

3-month prevalence of anxious school refusal was 2.0%, whereas the rate of truancy was 6.2%. In a study of clinician referral and practice characteristics (Kearney & Beasley, 1994), 6% of children referred for treatment presented with school refusal behavior. Thus, although not an extremely common disorder, children with school refusal behavior exist among the caseloads of private practitioners.

School refusal is equally common in boys and girls (Granell de Aldaz et al., 1987; Kearney & Beasley, 1994; Kennedy, 1965; King & Ollendick, 1989) and cuts across socioeconomic status (King & Bernstein, 2001). Among outpatient samples (Kearney & Beasley, 1994), children with school refusal ranged from age 5 to 17, with the highest prevalence rate among 7- to 9-year-olds (31.5%) and the lowest rates among 5- to 6-year-olds (11.2%) and 16- to 17-year-olds (15.2%). In a specialty anxiety clinic, the ages of children with school refusal also ranged from 7 to 17 years, with the most frequent age being 13–15 years, followed by age 10 (Last & Strauss, 1990). However, by the time some children are brought to the clinic for treatment, school refusal may be present for several years. Thus, the implied etiological age of onset for a clinic-seeking sample (Last & Strauss, 1990) is consistent with suggestions by others (e.g., Ollendick & Mayer, 1984) that school refusal appears to have certain peak ages, particularly between 5–6 years and 10–11 years. At the younger age, separation anxiety disorder is probably the more common etiological factor, whereas social phobia is more common at older ages (Last, Francis, et al., 1987). Thus, these peaks may represent the common clinical conditions found at those ages (i.e., separation anxiety disorder and social phobia).

Another age-related difference is the mode of onset for school refusal. Among younger children, an acute onset is more common, whereas an "insidious development" occurs more frequently among older children and adolescents (King & Ollendick, 1989). Among school-refusing samples, adolescents usually present with more severe and chronic disturbance and thus are less responsive to treatment (Burke & Silverman, 1987; also see the treatment section of this chapter).

Several sociodemographic variables, along with clinical and family variables, appear to be related to the severity of school refusal. Higher rates of absenteeism were associated with older age, less fear (measured by a self-report inventory), and family environments that place less emphasis on out-of-home recreational activities (Hansen, Sanders, Massaro, & Last, 1998). Less fear among those with the highest rates of absenteeism may seem contradictory, although several factors may have influenced this finding. First, reduced fear may result from more consistent avoidance of the phobic stimulus, in this case, the school (Hansen et al., 1998). That is, if the child succeeds in avoiding the feared situation, the child may report only minimal fear. However, a second consideration has to do with the fact that, in general, older children have lower scores on fear inventories than younger children (see Chapter 1). Thus, lower fear scores among children with higher rates of absenteeism may simply reflect the fact that older children (who also have higher rates of absenteeism) tend to score lower on self-report measures of anxiety than younger children. Future investigations will need to control for the participant's age when examining the relationship between fear and avoidance.

COMORBID AND DIFFERENTIAL DIAGNOSIS

In addition to his anxiety symptoms, Mark reported difficulty sleeping, with both sleep-onset and sleep-continuity problems. He endorsed being depressed, lethargic, and irritable, and during the initial evaluation, he was tearful, and his affect was blunted. Furthermore, his parents reported oppositional behaviors, such as being defiant and deliberately testing limits. These behaviors occurred primarily around school attendance but also in other public places, such as church. Thus, on admission, Mark met diagnostic criteria for panic disorder and major depression. His oppositional behaviors were viewed as originally secondary to his fears, although they recently had increased in scope such that a diagnosis of oppositional defiant disorder was warranted.

In addition to youth who refuse school due to the presence of an anxiety disorder, there is a subset of children and adolescents who present with symptoms of both anxiety and depression. There also are youth with school refusal who appear to suffer only from depression, but that group is not discussed here except for comparative purposes (see Kearney, 1993, for a review of depression and school refusal). Among school refusers with anxiety disorders only, anxiety and depressive disorders, depression only, or disruptive behavioral disorders, youth comorbid for both anxiety and depressive disorders had significantly higher scores on both mood dimensions (anxiety and depression) than groups with one disorder alone, thus suggesting a more severe symptom picture for this diagnostic group (Bernstein, 1991). Furthermore, in comparison to children with anxiety disorders alone, children with comorbid anxiety and depression and their mothers reported decreased abilities to solve problems and respond to crises, less definition and integration of family roles, maladaptive communication styles, and limited agreement about (a) components of the family's value system and (b) the family's adherence to a particular culture (Bernstein et al., 1990). In another study (Bernstein, Warren, Massie, & Thuras, 1999), 63% of school-refusing adolescents with both anxiety and depression and 52% of their parents viewed their families as low on family cohesion (i.e., they reported high disengagement). Also, 52% of adolescents and 38% of their parents viewed their families as low on adaptability (i.e., they were quite rigid). Interestingly, their ideal families were conceptualized as more cohesive and flexible than their real family. Of course, this study did not allow one to determine if these factors preceded or followed the onset of the school refusal behavior, and it did not include a control group. Furthermore, it is unclear if these family factors played a role in treatment outcome.

ETIOLOGY

Even when school refusal samples are limited to those with anxiety-related disorders, there still are many potential etiological factors. Family history may contribute to its onset, although the data are equivocal. One study (Berg, Butler, & Pritchard, 1974) did not find a higher incidence of overall psychiatric illness in the mothers of school-phobic adolescents, whereas others suggested that children who refuse school also had mothers with a history of school refusal (Berg, Marks, McGuire, & Lipsedge, 1974; Last & Strauss, 1990). In one investigation that examined parent–child concordance with respect to the specific disorder that precipitated the school refusal (Martin, Cabrol, Bouvard, Lepine, & Mouren-Simeoni, 1999), children with separation anxiety disorder had parents with increased prevalence of panic disorder or panic disorder with agoraphobia. In contrast, parents of children who refuse to attend school because of phobic disorders had an increased prevalence of specific or social phobias. Of course, a family history does not necessarily mean that these disorders are genetically or biologically determined. Learning theory also can account for increased prevalence of specific disorders within families. However, it again suggests that (a) school refusal does not result from one unique etiology, and (b) anxiety disorders are familial.

Certain life events have been associated with the development of school refusal. These include death or illness in a parent or close relative, change of class or school, traumatic events at school, and prolonged absence from school because of personal illness (King & Ollendick, 1989). Although it is unclear how often these events precipitate episodes of school refusal, they appear to be most consistent with children who have Type 1 school refusal.

Classical conditioning, vicarious conditioning, and operant conditioning theories all provide possible explanations for the onset of anxiety-based school refusal. Events such as being embarrassed by a teacher, getting up in front of the class and being unable to speak, or being teased by peers have been related to subsequent school refusal (via classical conditioning). Similarly, if a child observes these events happening to another child who then displays distress, the observing child may develop a fear vicariously. Finally, a child who complains of somatic symptoms and is allowed to stay home, thereby escaping from an aversive situation (i.e., negative reinforcement), will develop school refusal as a result of operant procedures.

In summary, then, even when school refusal is anxiety based, its etiology is still multifaceted. Some children may be predisposed to the development of anxiety or depressive disorders and develop school refusal secondary to the disorder. For other children, school refusal may develop after a traumatic event, resulting in the child's refusal to return to the school environment. It is clear that identifying the basis for the disorder is necessary for effective treatment implementation.

ASSESSMENT

Because school refusal may indicate the presence of any number of different anxiety disorders or a combination of anxiety and depression (as well as no disorder), the assessment strategy should be broad and inclusive not only for anxiety but also for depression and externalizing disorders. Instruments useful for assessing conditions or factors responsible for school refusal are presented next.

Interviews

The Anxiety Disorders Interview Schedule for DSM-IV: Child and Parent Versions (ADIS-C/P; Silverman & Albano, 1996) is a general diagnostic interview and contains a specific section to assess for the presence of school refusal. This interview is administered separately to parents and children, and the section on school refusal may provide some preliminary data on the reason for the refusal. Reliability and validity data for the ADIS-C/P are presented in Chapter 3.

Self-, Parental, or Teacher Report

Although many self-report instruments are available for assessing specific anxiety disorders, they are reviewed in the chapters addressing each of these disorders. Here, self-report instruments designed specifically for school refusal are reviewed.

The School Refusal Assessment Scale (SRAS; Kearney & Silverman, 1990, 1999) and its revision, the School Refusal Assessment Scale–Revised (SRAS-R; Kearney, 2002), consists of 24 items assessing four motivating factors: (a) avoidance of stimuli that provoke negative affectivity, (b) escape from aversive social or evaluative situations, (c) attention-getting behavior or traditional separation anxiety, and (d) positive tangible rewards. Six questions assess each factor. The scale has good test–retest reliability and good concurrent and construct validity (Kearney, 2002), and different anxiety disorder diagnoses were associated with different motivations for school refusal (Kearney & Albano, 2004). Specifically, anxiety-related diagnoses were more often associated with negative reinforcement, separation anxiety disorder was more often associated with attention-seeking behavior, and tangible reinforcement was most often associated with oppositional defiant disorder and conduct disorder. As noted, a specific advantage of this scale is that the data can be used prescriptively by the therapist to design an individualized behavioral treatment plan.

The Self-Efficacy Questionnaire for School Situations (SEQ-SS; Heyne et al., 1998) assesses the child's perceptions regarding ability to cope with potentially anxiety-producing school situations. These situations include doing schoolwork, handling questions about absence from school, and being separated from parents or caregivers. Factor analysis revealed two factors: separation/discipline stress and academic/social stress. Although the scale has good reliability, further explication of the validity of the scale would be beneficial.

Another self-report instrument designed to assess anxiety in school-refusing children is the Visual Analogue Scale for Anxiety–Revised (VASA-R; Bernstein & Garfinkel, 1992). Similar to the other instruments, the VASA-R has three factors: anticipatory/separation anxiety, performance anxiety, and affective response to anxiety. The VASA-R has good internal consistency and test-retest reliability over a 1-week period and good concurrent validity.

Commonalities cutting across all instruments include the acknowledgment that many factors may lead to school refusal. Thus, all of these instruments assess for different anxiety disorders and, in the case of the SRAS-R, nonanxiety conditions. These scales allow the clinician to better understand the disorder that results in school refusal and to provide a more targeted treatment plan.

Behavioral Assessment

Daily diaries, completed by parents and children, often provide a valuable source of information necessary for treatment planning. Depending on the child's particular difficulty, a self-monitoring plan may include the child's thoughts as well as behaviors and should include the parent's responses to the child's behaviors as well. Mark's daily diary is presented in Figure 8.1.

In Mark's case, the assessment battery included a diagnostic interview with the ADIS-C/P, the SRAS, and other self-report measures of anxiety and depression. In addition, both Mark and his mother completed 2 weeks of self-monitoring data regarding his school attendance. Finally, a behavioral assessment conducted in the clinic assessed physical symptoms associated with his panic attacks.

The results of the SRAS indicated that one of the primary motivating factors behind Mark's school refusal was avoidance of situations related to negative affectivity. Consistently, the behavioral assessment indicated that the primary panic symptoms included dizziness, increased heart rate, shortness of breath, and feeling weak in his knees. Furthermore, self-monitoring data revealed parenting practices that allowed Mark to manipulate the family environment to his advantage.

TREATMENT

The American Academy of Child and Adolescent Psychiatry (AACAP) recommends a multimodal strategy for the treatment of children with anxiety-based school refusal. Specifically, the AACAP recommends consideration of the following components: education and consultation, behavioral or cognitive-behavioral strategies, family intervention, and medication, if warranted (King & Bernstein, 2001). Empirical data in support of these interventions are examined here.

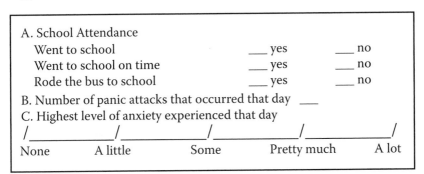

FIGURE 8.1 Mark's self-monitoring (daily diary) form. (Reprinted from Beidel, D. C., & Turner, S. M. (2005). *Child Anxiety Disorders*. New York: Routledge. With permission.)

Pharmacological Intervention

A landmark study on the pharmacological treatment of "school phobia" (Gittelman-Klein & Klein, 1971) randomized children refusing to attend school to either imipramine or pill placebo. At the end of the 6-week treatment, 81% of children in the imipramine group had returned to school compared to 47% of the placebo group, indicating superiority for imipramine. One limitation of this study was that the sample of school-phobic children probably contained children with a variety of diagnostic disorders, such as anxiety or depression. Thus, the utility of these findings for a sample of children with solely anxiety-based school refusal is unclear. However, a follow-up study of the use of imipramine for the treatment of children with separation anxiety disorder did not show any superiority for imipramine over placebo (Klein, Koplewicz, & Kanner, 1992). Imipramine is no longer considered a "first-line" pharmacological intervention, having been replaced by the newer selective serotonin reuptake inhibitors (SSRIs) with their more benign side-effect profile (see concerns about the SSRI black box warning in Chapter 10).

In an open trial (Bernstein, Garfinkel, & Borchardt, 1990), 17 children (aged 9.5 to 17.0 years; 11 with comorbid depressive and anxiety disorders, 4 with depressive disorder only, and 2 with an anxiety disorder only) were prescribed either alprazolam or imipramine. Each child also received a school reentry program and psychotherapy. After 8 weeks, 67% of children treated with alprazolam were rated as moderately or markedly improved in anxiety or depressive symptoms, and 55% had returned to school. Similarly, 67% of those treated with imipramine were rated as moderately or markedly improved, and 50% had returned to school. The small sample size precluded analyses separately by diagnosis. However, these promising findings led to a double-blind, placebo-controlled trial of these two pharmacological agents (Bernstein, Garfinkel & Borchardt, 1990). Twenty-four children (mean age 14.1 years) with school refusal behavior were randomly assigned to alprazolam, imipramine, or placebo. Ten children had a depressive disorder only, 4 had an anxiety disorder only, and 10 had comorbid anxiety and depressive disorders. In addition to medication, the intervention included a school reentry component that consisted of gradually increasing the number of days that the child went to school, providing a school support person, and attending a classroom for emotionally and behaviorally disturbed students. In addition, a psychotherapy component consisted of weekly sessions with a child psychologist or a child psychiatry resident. Thus, this treatment might be better considered a multimodal intervention. After 8 weeks of treatment, scores on rating scales suggested that those treated with alprazolam showed the most improvement, with the imipramine group showing moderate improvement, and the placebo group the least improvement. However, baseline scores were substantially different for these three groups, and when the pretreatment score was used as a covariate, there were no significant group differences in change scores for anxiety and depression. Similarly, among those for whom school attendance data were available, all subjects in the alprazolam and imipramine groups ($n = 6$ in each group) returned to school with improved attendance (although this term was not fully operationalized). However, five of six children in the placebo group returned to school with improved attendance. Thus, these data are unclear with respect to the additive specific effects of imipramine and alprazolam on school refusal over psychosocial treatment alone. In fact, the few data that are available indicate that medication alone is not a well-established intervention for school refusal. Furthermore, as we will present, even when medication or multimodal treatment results in statistically significant decreases on measures of anxiety or depression, this does not always translate into improved school attendance.

As noted, recommendations by the AACAP consider medication to be part of a multimodal treatment plan for those with anxiety disorders and are not meant to be prescribed alone (King & Bernstein, 2001). Using a multimodal strategy (Bernstein, Borchardt, Perwien, Crosby, Kushner, Thuras, et al., 2000), 8 weeks of imipramine plus cognitive-behavioral treatment (CBT) were compared to 8 weeks of placebo plus CBT for 63 adolescents comorbid for anxiety and depression who were refusing school. Anxiety and depressive symptoms improved for both groups, although depression improved faster for those treated with imipramine. Using a criterion of 75% school attendance, 54.2% of the imipramine group met this criterion, as opposed to 16.7% of the placebo group. Thus, although a number of adolescents were improved, particularly those in the imipramine group, many still were not able to go to school on a regular basis. Furthermore, a naturalistic follow-up (Bernstein et al., 2001) indicated that 1 year later, 64.1% met criteria for at least one anxiety disorder, and 33.3% met criteria for dysthymia or major depression, with no differences between those treated with imipramine or placebo. In addition, 67.5% received at least one pharmacological trial during the follow-up period, and 75% received additional outpatient therapy. Rates of school attendance were not available, but most children were reported to be attending school.

In summary, available data indicate that, in most instances, active pharmacological agents are only minimally superior to placebo. Rates of school attendance after pharmacological treatment remain variable and sometimes depend on study-specific criteria. In some cases, 75% attendance is considered successful, whereas more stringent criteria are used in other studies. Furthermore, most studies combined pharmacological with behavioral interventions, as reviewed here. Thus, it remains unclear whether medication really is efficacious for the treatment of this behavior.

Psychosocial Interventions

Similar to the literature for childhood anxiety disorders in general, much of the early literature on the treatment of school refusal was based on case studies and reports. Among clinicians in private practice (Kearney & Beasley, 1994), parent training/contingency management is the most common intervention (40.3%), followed by cognitive restructuring (14.4%), contingency contracting (12.2%), forced school attendance (11.6%), imaginal or in vivo desensitization (8.3%), modeling and role-play (6.6%), play therapy (6.1%), and pharmacotherapy (0.6%). As reviewed here, some of these interventions are more effective than others.

Kennedy's (1961) seminal publication on the behavioral treatment of school refusal examined rapid intervention for children with Type 1 school refusal. Recall that Type 1 has an acute onset and occurs more commonly in younger ages and in intact families in which both parents play a role in parenting (see clinical presentation section for a more complete description). Kennedy's intervention was based on behavioral procedures that blocked the child's escape from the feared situation (school) and prevented the establishment of secondary gains. In addition, the child was reinforced for attending school without complaint. The specific elements included establishing good professional relationships, avoiding attending to somatic complaints, forcing school attendance, and educating parents. This last component had several subcomponents, including portraying optimism, emphasizing success, and presenting the treatment plan, which consisted of the following: (a) no discussion of school attendance on the weekend; (b) getting the child ready to go to school on Monday escorted by the father in a matter-of-fact fashion (without questions or comments about school); (c) reinforcing the child on Monday evening for going to school despite somatic complaints or fears; and (d) repeating the procedure for Tuesday and Wednesday. By Wednesday, it was expected that the child's fear would be virtually eliminated. The intervention was successful with 50 children, and there was no remission at follow-up (Kennedy, 1965). As noted by the author, evaluation was based solely on self-report and school attendance data. Diagnostic interviews were not part of the investigation. Furthermore, no control group was available for comparison. Thus, it is not possible to determine if some of the children would have returned to school without intervention. In addition, the program's success in treating Type 2 (rather than the Type 1) cases was less impressive. Despite these limitations, this study has been considered the landmark study for the behavioral treatment of school refusal. Furthermore, the approach, based on sound behavioral principles, is still used in treating many children with anxiety-based school refusal.

An initial group trial (Blagg & Yule, 1984) compared behavioral intervention to inpatient hospitalization to a homebound instruction and psychotherapy group for children with school refusal. The behavioral condition included (a) stimulus desensitization through humor and emotive imagery; (b) blocking the avoidance response through forced school attendance; (c) positive reinforcement both at school and at home for school attendance; and (d) extinction of negative behaviors (somatic complaints, fearful expressions). It should be noted that children were not randomized to these conditions. Rather, preexisting data were analyzed. Thirty children were treated with the behavioral treatment approach (BTA), 16 were treated with inpatient hospitalization (HU), and 20 received home instruction and psychotherapy (HT). Most were between the ages of 11 and 16, and there were no differences on sociodemographic variables. Using the Type 1 or Type 2 classification system, about 50% of those treated with BTA, 75% of the HU group, and 25% of the HT group were classified as having Type 2 school refusal. After a year of treatment, 93% of those in the BTA group were judged as treatment successes compared to 37% of the HU group and 10% of the HT group. When school attendance rates (defined as school attendance on 80% of the days) were examined, 83% of the BTA group met this criterion compared to 37% of the HU group and 10% of the HT group. Furthermore, not only was the BTA intervention more effective, but also it was more efficient. The average treatment length was 2.5 weeks for the BTA group compared with 45.3 weeks for the HU group and 72.1 weeks for the HT group. These results are impressive, although limitations include the lack of a control group and the lack of randomization to the treatment assignments. One might expect that requiring inpatient hospitalization represented more severe psychopathology. However, the study was crucial in promoting the use of behavioral procedures for this disorder in terms of both treatment efficacy and cost-effectiveness.

King and his colleagues (King, Tonge, Heyne, Pritchard, Rollings, Young, et al., 1998) randomized 34 children aged 5–17 with school refusal behavior to either a 4-week CBT intervention or a wait-list control group. The majority of the children met diagnostic criteria for an anxiety or phobic disorder. CBT consisted of coping skills, exposure, and contingency management. In comparison to the wait-list control, those treated with CBT exhibited significant improvement, and 88% achieved at least 90% school attendance. Only 29% of the wait-list control group met this criterion. CBT also increased children's confidence in coping skills and decreased their anxiety. At 3- to 5-year follow-up, 13 of the 16 treated with CBT (and who could be contacted) were attending school regularly and had not had any further school refusal incidents. Among the three children who relapsed, two had been having problems academically, and one was expelled for "uncontrollable behavior." One limitation of this study was the small sample size and the lack of an extensive clinical interview at follow-up (which might have detected the presence of other clinical conditions). Despite this limitation, the 4-week CBT intervention appeared to have remarkable long-term effects for a majority of the children.

In one of the few studies to compare CBT to an attention-placebo control group (Last, Hansen, & Franco, 1998), 56 children with anxiety-based school refusal were randomly assigned to 12 weeks of CBT or an educational support group. CBT included graduated in vivo exposure, cognitive restructuring, and coping self-statement training, whereas educational support included educational presentations, supportive psychotherapy, and a daily diary of thoughts and fears. There was no encouragement for "facing your fears" in the educational control group. Although the educational support group was designed as a placebo control, the results indicated that both groups demonstrated marked improvement in school attendance, anxiety, and depression and global improvement. Similarly, at posttreatment, 65% of those treated with CBT and 50% of those in educational support no longer met criteria for an anxiety disorder. Treatment gains were maintained at 4-week follow-up. Nevertheless, not all children benefited from 12 weeks of CBT. Thirty-five percent of the children assigned to CBT did not achieve 95% school attendance, and 60% had difficulty attending school during the next year. These data are important inasmuch as they indicate that perhaps a more extensive intervention or an additional treatment strategy may be necessary at least for a subsample of the population.

Kearney and Silverman (e.g., Kearney & Silverman, 1990) have been at the forefront in promoting a functional model of treatment for school refusal. Based on their studies of psychopathology and the identification of four patterns of school refusal behavior, their treatment approach tailors the intervention strategy not only to the school refusal itself but also to the particular behaviors and clinical symptoms that maintain this behavior. In the initial investigation (Kearney & Silverman, 1990), seven children and adolescents with difficulty attending school were treated with "prescriptive" behavioral treatment (developed specifically for their particular fears). Thus, some children received (a) modeling and cognitive instruction (for social fears category), (b) systematic desensitization and relaxation training (for specific fears category), (c) shaping and differential reinforcement of other behaviors (inappropriate attention seeking from parents), or (d) contingency contracting (tangible rewards category). At posttreatment, six of seven children had returned to school on a full-time basis (the seventh decided not to return to school but began work with parental permission), and at 6-month follow-up, five of the six continued to attend school regularly. The results of this preliminary trial are limited by the lack of a control group (either a wait-list control or children who were randomly assigned to treatment rather than matched based on their specific clinical profile). However, like the earlier studies (e.g., Blagg & Yule, 1984), this report provides the initial impetus for further investigation in this area, particularly for more tightly controlled clinical trials.

A randomized controlled trial (Heyne et al., 2002) examined the efficacy of individualized cognitive-behavioral therapy (ICBT), parent and teacher training (PTT), or ICBT plus PTT for 65 children ages 7–14 years who were refusing to go to school. At posttreatment, all three groups showed significant improvement on mood and anxiety ratings, and the two groups that included PTT resulted in better school attendance than ICBT alone. At the 2-week follow-up, all treatment gains were maintained, with no differences across groups, even in school attendance.

In summary, the psychosocial treatment outcome literature is in much the same status as the pharmacological treatment data. There have been only a few controlled trials, and although uncontrolled trials indicate substantial treatment success for behavioral interventions, a large randomized controlled trial did not indicate that the behavioral intervention was superior to an attention-placebo control condition. In a review of the literature (Pina, Zerr, Gonzales, & Ortiz, 2009), treatment outcome for both single-case designs and randomized controlled trials of behavioral and cognitive-behavioral interventions was examined using effect sizes. When examined in this fashion, both school attendance and mood and anxiety symptoms improved significantly with behavioral treatments and CBT. Positive outcome was achieved whether the intervention was directed specifically at the child, specifically at the parent and teacher, or at all three participants. However, not everyone had a positive response, indicating a need to examine factors that might moderate or mediate treatment outcome (Pina et al., 2009).

Predictions of Treatment Success

Several factors appear to be related to positive treatment outcome, including younger age (Last et al., 1998), higher levels of school attendance at baseline (Last et al., 1998; Layne, Bernstein, Egan, & Kushner, 2003), and combining CBT with medication (Layne et al., 2003). Interestingly, in this same study, negative treatment response was predicted by the presence of comorbid separation anxiety disorder or former avoidant disorder. In combination, these four variables accounted for 51% of the treatment outcome variance. However, the small number of patients included in this sample precludes drawing broad conclusions from these analyses.

One important message for parents and clinicians is the importance of treating children with school refusal as quickly as possible (Kennedy, 1965; Last et al., 1998). Unlike other fears in children for which parents might be advised to wait 6 months to see if the child might "outgrow" his or her distress, when the clinical syndrome includes school refusal, intervening quickly appears to be the empirically supported approach. When comorbid conditions exist, the intervention may need to be broadened to specifically address the comorbid conditions.

School Personnel Participation

As noted by Kearney (1995), the atmosphere surrounding cases of school refusal is often stressful, sometimes reaching "crisis-like" dimensions. Thus, as the treatment plan is implemented, daily (or near-daily) contact with parents, child, and the school is necessary. Much of the implementation of the behavioral program will occur at the school setting. At least initially, daily contact with the school allows for "troubleshooting" and gives school personnel the reassurance that the therapist is available for assistance. This is particularly important when children's distress in school has in the past resulted in removal from the school setting. Therapists should initially meet with school personnel to present and discuss the treatment plan. Furthermore, the therapist's physical presence at school on the first day of the child's return enhances assurance that the program is implemented by the school in the manner in which it was designed by the therapist. The investment of a few hours of clinical time on the first day often eliminates the need for "backtracking" at a later date when it become apparent that the program was misunderstood or not implemented correctly.

Obstacles to Treatment Success

Although in certain instances there may be a need for a graduated approach to treatment, rapid treatment has gained widespread acceptance among researchers and clinicians (King & Ollendick, 1989). Rapid treatment minimizes the possibility of "secondary treatment gain," one of the major impediments to successful outcome. Basic learning principles explain secondary gain. Specifically, if the child experiences fear in anticipation of school attendance and is therefore allowed to remain at home, the child's fear dissipates (i.e., avoidance is negatively reinforced). Thus, staying home eliminates distress. In addition, at home the child often is allowed (at least initially) to watch television, play computer games, or engage in other pleasant activities. So, positive reinforcement also plays a role in secondary gain. Staying home results in engagement in enjoyable activities rather than attending school, which may be less enjoyable. Therefore, the more quickly the child returns (or is returned) to school, the less likely that secondary gain will complicate the intervention strategy.

In a cogent review of the treatment for school refusal (Kearney, 1995), some potential obstacles to successful outcome were noted, including poor clinic attendance, hostility from a family member, noncompliance with treatment procedures, comorbid disorders, and psychopathology in the parents. Some of these factors are impediments for the successful treatment outcome for any disorder, not just school refusers. However, one often-overlooked impediment to treatment is simply the inability to attend clinic sessions. Among families in which there is a child who refuses to attend school, approximately 25–40% of families do not arrive for their initial visit, and the rate of "no shows" increases as the school year progresses (Kearney, 1995). One factor may be the high spontaneous remission rate associated with school refusal. Another factor may be that the parent is not able to bring the child in for the evaluation session. This is consistent with the parents' inability to make the child go to school. Overcoming this last obstacle often is a matter of parent training, and it is possible that initial sessions may need to be conducted without the child present.

Other obstacles not often addressed in the empirical literature but faced every day by clinicians treating school refusal behavior include the child's reluctance to attend school due to having fallen behind academically. Children also often express reluctance to return to school because they do not know how to explain their absence to their classmates. Children's concerns about these issues appear to increase as a function of the length of the absence, again emphasizing the advantage of early intervention. Although there is no single strategy to deal with these anxieties, there are several guidelines that we have found useful. With respect to the academic issue, tutoring or sending schoolwork to the home might allow most children to maintain their academic status (see also the section on homebound instruction). With respect to the issue of explaining their absence to peers, social skills training could be useful (King & Ollendick, 1989).

Relapse prevention is crucial for successful treatment of school refusal. Minor relapses may occur following long weekends or extended vacations (Kearney, 1995). Returning to school after summer vacation represents another crucial period for relapse. Booster sessions may be needed at these times to consolidate treatment gains.

The Issue of Homebound Instruction

A major hurdle for the treatment of school refusal is homebound instruction. As noted, children who have refused school for a number of weeks tend to fall behind academically. This in turn places additional pressure on the child with respect to returning to school. Not only is the child faced with questions from peers regarding the absence, but also the child is faced with "making up" all of the missed schoolwork. Conversely, engaging a homebound instructor for the child, even for the time during which behavioral intervention occurs, can lead to decreased motivation to return to school. There is no universal way to handle this issue, and decisions must be made on an individual basis. Our practice has been to base our decisions on the length of the child's absence. If it has been several weeks, we rely on assignments being sent home by the teacher to allow the child to maintain academic progress. If school absence has been more extensive and it is our opinion that one aspect of the child's concern regarding returning to school is the issue of academics, we negotiate with parent and child regarding a brief period of homebound instruction. That is, we support the request for homebound instruction provided it (a) is only for a limited (usually 1-month) period of time and (b) it does not interfere with other aspects of the treatment plan.

CASE EXAMPLE: TREATMENT OF SCHOOL REFUSAL

As noted, Mark's clinical presentation was complicated. In addition to panic attacks and social anxiety, Mark was depressed, oppositional, and disrespectful of his mother's authority. Thus, the treatment plan (presented in Table 8.2) addressed the various aspects of his clinical presentation, including school refusal/oppositionality, depression, and anxiety/panic. Specific strategies were developed to deal with each of these issues. In this chapter, only the portion of the plan addressing school refusal is presented.

SCHOOL ATTENDANCE PLAN

The treatment goal was to increase the time in school such that Mark achieved full-time attendance in 6 weeks. Mark and his mother were given specific instructions and contingencies for certain behaviors, and

TABLE 8.2   Mark's Treatment Plan

Problem Area	Intervention
School refusal/oppositionality	1. Parent management training 2. Transfer responsibility for school attendance to Mark (a) Reward successes (b) End morning negotiations (c) Strict bedtime rules
Depression	1. Medication 2. Increase pleasant events
Anxiety/panic	1. Social effectiveness therapy for children 2. Interoceptive exposure

Source: Reprinted from Beidel, D. C., & Turner, S. M. (2005). *Child Anxiety Disorders.* New York: Routledge. With permission.

rewards were established. To provide ongoing assessment and reward intermediate achievements, both short-term and long-term goals were established. The long-term goal was to own a dog, something that Mark had wanted for some time, but that his parents were unwilling to provide given Mark's baseline behavior. However, they were willing to agree to a dog given the contingencies set forth in the contract.

At baseline, Mark was attending school 3 days a week, arriving at about 11:00 a.m. This was chosen as the target goal for the first week. This provided the opportunity to "troubleshoot" the contract and to allow Mark and his mother to become familiar with earning and providing rewards without adding in the need to increase his school attendance in the first week of the program. The specific school contract is depicted in Table 8.3.

School attendance was monitored on a daily basis, and three specific data points were collected: (1) number of days per week that Mark adhered to the contract, (2) number of days per week that he went to school but arrived late, and (3) number of days that he did not go at all. As depicted, Mark initially had trouble adhering to the contract. In addition, although there was an opportunity for Mark to complete the contract and earn the dog within a 7-week time period, the length of the contract had to be extended for an additional 6 weeks because of his oppositional behaviors. That is, when Mark was disrespectful or physically intimidating to his mother, additional days were added to the length of the contract. Mark was aware of this contingency before it was implemented, but of course, simple awareness does not ensure compliance.

The basic rules of contingency management would dictate that required behaviors and rewards should be one to one. That is, if Mark went to school at the appropriate time, he should receive the reward. However, in this case, part of the contract included leaving for school in an appropriate, respectful fashion. In other words, it was not acceptable

TABLE 8.3   Mark's Weekly School Contract

Overall Guidelines

1. For each day that Mark meets the school attendance goal for the week, his mother will spend up to an hour accompanying him to get a video game or movie. (Mark can use the video game or movie once his nightly homework is completed.)

2. Each week that Mark meets his weekly goal, the calendar will be marked with a point at the end of the week. In addition, at the end of 7 weeks if Mark has stuck to the plan (attends school on time, stays in school for the entire day for 3 weeks at Weeks 5, 6, and 7), then Mark will earn a pet dog.

3. Mark will have to earn all 7 points to get the dog. Keeping the dog will depend on Mark taking care of the pet (cleaning up after it, walking it when not in school) and staying in school full time. If Mark does not stay in school, the dog will be taken away.

4. For each day that Mark is disrespectful to his mother or father (e.g., saying "shut up," grabbing, shoving, banging the wall, cussing, calling his mom an idiot, or anything else that his mom considers disrespectful), an extra day will be added to the final 3 weeks of full-time school attendance before Mark can have his dog.

Week 1

Goal for the week: Mark gets himself to school by 11 a.m. on 3 days.

To accomplish this

1. Mark will be responsible for waking himself at _____. He will get ready for school on his own. Mom can make breakfast for Mark, and it will be ready at _____. If Mark is not ready to eat, the breakfast can remain there but cannot be heated up by Mom. Mark can do it himself if he desires. Mark will be ready to leave for school at _____ to be there by 11 a.m.

2. If Mark does not go to school at all or goes late, he will not be allowed to play with his pets, watch TV, listen to the radio, play video games, use the computer, play with friends, or interact with his parents during school hours. After school hours, his parents can interact with him as usual. However, there will be no discussion about school or attendance.

3. If Mark goes above and beyond the expectation of the week (extra day of school attendance at or before the time selected on point days), he will get an additional rental from the video store.

Week 2

Goal for the week: Mark gets himself to school by 10 a.m. on 3 days.

The contingencies for Week 1 are still in effect.

TABLE 8.3   Mark's Weekly School Contract (Continued)

Week 3

Goal for the week: Mark gets himself to school by 9 a.m. on 3 days. The contingencies for Week 1 are still in effect.

Week 4

Goal for the week: Mark gets himself to school by 8 a.m. on 4 days. The contingencies for Week 1 are still in effect.

Weeks 5, 6, 7

Goal for the week: Mark gets himself to school by 8 a.m. on 5 days.

Ultimate Goal

After full-time attendance all week for 3 weeks (Weeks 5–7), then he will have earned the dog. If Mark does not stay in school full time, he will not be able to keep the dog. Also, if Mark does not care for the dog, it will be taken away.

Mark's Signature Date	Mother's Signature Date	Father's Signature Date

for him to curse at or physically intimidate his mother, even if he still got to school on time. Thus, the required behavior was not simply school attendance; it was going to school in a behaviorally appropriate manner.

Several aspects of the weekly contract deserve comment. First, a behavioral assessment of the morning interactions between Mark and his mother indicated two areas of conflict. First, although Mark would set his alarm, he would not get out of bed. Mark's mother would make numerous trips to his room in an attempt to encourage him to get out of bed. This attention by the mother was viewed as reinforcing Mark's refusal to get out of bed inasmuch as staying in bed elicited substantial attention from his mother. Thus, the contract made Mark solely responsible for getting out of bed in the morning. The second area of contention involved breakfast. Specifically, Mark would ask his mother to make breakfast for him, but then by the time that he would get to the kitchen, the breakfast was cold, and he would demand that it be heated again, illustrating his disrespectful behavior. Therefore, in the weekly contract, the time that breakfast would be ready was noted, allowing Mark to plan his morning routine appropriately. If he was late, he had the option of reheating his own breakfast. In addition, Mark craved his parents' attention, and when he did not go to school, he talked to his mother all day. Clearly, even if his anxiety was important in the etiology of his school refusal, tangible reinforcement obviously was playing a role in maintaining the behavior. In addition to the usual reinforcers (TV, video games), tangible reinforcement in this case included interaction with his mother. Therefore, all of these tangible reinforcers were eliminated during school hours. Other parts of Mark's program included interoceptive conditioning (see Chapter 12) and social effectiveness therapy for children (see Chapter 10).

SUMMARY

School refusal is a complicated behavior. Many disorders and conditions may result in school absence, and the first action on the part of parents or therapists is to develop a clear understanding of the underlying motivation. Even when the avoidance appears to be anxiety based, there are still many possibilities potentially responsible for eliciting this behavior. Diagnostic assessments, self-report measures, and self-monitoring data all may assist in establishing the proper diagnosis and suggesting the appropriate intervention strategy. It is important to note that, as in Mark's case, school refusal may result from one disorder and yet be maintained by additional factors. Thus, refusal may be precipitated by anxiety but yet maintained by other factors such as depression. Furthermore, oppositional behaviors may play a role either as a result of parental attempts to force the child to go to school or as part of a more general pattern of oppositionality. In either case, parent management training often is a necessary component of a comprehensive intervention program.

With respect to specific strategies, both pharmacological and psychosocial interventions have been described in the literature. Pharmacological interventions have been the subject of several controlled trials, and although results sometimes have been positive, the AACAP recommends the use of pharmacological agents as part of a multimodel treatment strategy. There is some evidence that the combination may be helpful, although further controlled trials are needed. With respect to psychosocial interventions, there is a rich clinical history suggesting the efficacy of behavioral interventions. Starting with the initial work of Kennedy (1965), a rapid response to initial school refusal appears advantageous.

Although there are many instances when behavioral interventions appear to be efficacious, some of the recent controlled trials have been disappointing, suggesting that they may be no more effective than attention-placebo controls. The reasons are unclear, although it may be that the intervention programs have not taken advantage of the relevant research on the psychopathology of this disorder. Specifically, if not classified according to types or diagnostic criteria, "one-size treatment" may not fit all. Given the data presented by numerous authors, and most recently by Kearney and his colleagues, closer attention needs to be paid to the factors behind the school-refusing behavior and the specific intervention. Thus, future investigations will need to attend to functional analyses and matching symptom presentation to a specific intervention strategy.

CHAPTER 9

Separation Anxiety Disorder

Leslie is 10 years old. For the past 6 months, she has refused to go anywhere but school unless accompanied by one of her parents. She was fearful in "unfamiliar places" (her words), including soccer practice, playing at her friend's house, or even taking out the garbage at night. Leslie has no prior history of separation anxiety disorder. In fact, she is quite distressed by her fear and embarrassed by her inability to be away from her parents. Furthermore, she does not like to have to go to therapy and wishes that she was in school instead.

Separation anxiety disorder (SAD) is a severe and unreasonable fear of separation from a parent or caregiver (hereafter called caregiver). Most prevalent among young children (aged 5–7), the disorder can occur at any age during childhood or adolescence. Children with SAD are extremely worried that, when apart from a caregiver (sometimes called an attachment figure), harm will occur to that person or to themselves. The anxiety can be so intense that children refuse to separate from their caregiver, in many cases, refusing to go to school. In the most severe cases, the children may be reluctant to be separated, even in their own home. This sometimes results in children sleeping with the caregiver well beyond the accepted age.

The construct of SAD is rooted in concepts of psychoanalytic theory and attachment theory (Bowlby, 1973). Attachment was defined as a bond between mother and infant that was selective, warm, and biologically motivated and expressed in infant behavior such as maintaining physical contact and proximity. The predisposition to become attached is considered a survival mechanism, and protest results when separation from the survival figure occurs. Although on the surface there are apparent similarities between the separation protests of attachment theory and the protests exhibited by children with SAD, many questions remain regarding the relationship between these concepts. A full exploration of these issues is beyond the scope of this chapter, but one relevant question is the relationship of these biologically based (and therefore theoretically universal traits among children) and the relatively few children who go on to develop SAD. To date, there has been little empirical data to address this issue.

It is important to distinguish between "normal" separation anxiety and SAD. As noted in Chapter 1, "stranger anxiety," common among children between 1 and 2 years of age, is characterized by expressions of distress (usually crying or turning away) whenever anyone other than the child's parents (or primary caregiver) attempt to hold or engage the child in some type of social activity. Although much has been hypothesized about why children behave in this fashion, empirical data regarding the basis for the fear are rare. In fact, because stranger anxiety is considered a typical developmental stage, there has been little research into motivations behind this particular fear reaction. However, SAD is distinguishable from "stranger fear" on many dimensions, including age of onset, degree of emotional distress, and degree of functional impairment. The remainder of this chapter addresses SAD, first introduced into the diagnostic nomenclature in 1980 with the third edition of the *Diagnostic and Statistical Manual of Mental Disorders* (*DSM-III*; American Psychiatric Association [APA], 1980). As currently defined in the text revision of the fourth edition of the *DSM* (*DSM-IV-TR*; APA, 2000), SAD is a severe and excessive fear of separation from an attachment figure (caregiver) that results in significant distress and substantially impairs daily functioning. See Table 9.1 for the *DSM-IV-TR* diagnostic criteria for SAD.

CLINICAL FEATURES

SAD is considered a common childhood disorder (Silverman & Dick-Niederhauser, 2004). However, there are few carefully controlled trials examining the psychopathology of SAD. Perhaps one limiting factor is that for many years, the terms *school phobia* and *separation anxiety disorder* were used interchangeably. In many instances, reviews and empirical investigations purporting to examine the psychopathology of SAD used samples of children who refused to go to school. As discussed in the chapter on school refusal, children who refuse to go to school suffer from many different psychiatric disorders; therefore, the terms *school phobia/refusal* and *SAD*, and their related literatures, are not interchangeable.

With that caveat in mind, school refusal is common among children with SAD. Particularly at earlier ages, school is one place where children are traditionally expected to separate from their parents and where attendance is mandatory. Among one sample of children with SAD, 73% presented to the clinic with school refusal (Last, Francis, et al., 1987). Thus, although a high percentage of children with SAD will avoid

TABLE 9.1   Diagnostic Criteria for Separation Anxiety Disorder

1. Developmentally inappropriate and excessive anxiety concerning separation from home or from those to whom the individual is attached, as evidenced by three (or more) of the following:

   a. Recurrent excessive distress when separation from home or from major attachment figures occurs or is anticipated

   b. Persistent and excessive worry about losing, or about possible harm befalling, major attachment figures

   c. Persistent and excessive worry that an untoward event will lead to separation from a major attachment figure (e.g., getting lost or being kidnapped)

   d. Persistent reluctance or refusal to go to school or elsewhere because of fear of separation

   e. Persistently and excessively fearful or reluctant to be alone or without major attachment figures at home or without significant adults in other settings

   f. Persistent reluctance or refusal to go to sleep without being near a major attachment figure or to sleep away from home

   g. Repeated nightmares involving the theme of separation

   h. Repeated complaints of physical symptoms (such as headaches, stomachaches, nausea, or vomiting) when separation from major attachment figures occurs or is anticipated

2. The duration of the disturbance is at least 4 weeks.

3. The onset is before age 18 years.

4. The disturbance causes clinically significant distress or impairment in social, academic (occupational), or other important areas of functioning.

5. The disturbance does not occur exclusively during the course of a Pervasive Developmental Disorder, Schizophrenia, or other Psychotic Disorder and, in adolescents and adults, is not better accounted for by Panic Disorder With Agoraphobia.

Specify if:

Early Onset: if onset occurs before age 6 years

Source: Reprinted with permission from American Psychiatric Association, *Diagnostic and Statistical Manual of Mental Disorders* (4th ed., text revision). Washington, DC: Author. Copyright 2000. American Psychiatric Association.

school, as illustrated by Leslie, not all children with SAD will refuse to go to school (see also Silverman & Dick-Niederhauser, 2004, for a discussion of this issue).

An interesting paradox is that although 3–5% of the population may be diagnosed with SAD, it is among the least stable of the anxiety disorders. In one of the first longitudinal investigations examining the stability of psychiatric disorders in children (including anxiety disorders; Cantwell & Baker, 1989), only 11% of nine children initially diagnosed with SAD still had the disorder at follow-up. Another 44% had a different disorder. The other children (45%) did not have any disorder at follow-up. When compared to the other diagnostic categories, SAD had one of the highest recovery rates. Overall, SAD was one of the least stable diagnostic categories, and that presents some constraints for treatment outcome investigations (see section on treatment).

Among epidemiological samples, only 20–36.1% of SAD diagnoses are still present at a later date (Foley, Pickles, Maes, Silberg, & Eaves, 2004; Shear, Jin, Ruscio, Walters, & Kessler, 2006). Among a sample of 8- to 17-year-old twins (Foley, Pickles, et al., 2004), 80% of youth with a diagnosis of SAD at Time 1 had remitted an average of 18 months later. Children with persistent SAD (present at Time 1 and Time 2) had significantly more symptoms of oppositional defiant disorder and more impairment associated with symptoms of attention deficit/hyperactivity disorder. Among adolescents, more symptoms of SAD at Time 1 were associated with the persistence of SAD at follow-up. In addition, 59% of the youth who had SAD at Time 1 had no psychiatric diagnosis at follow-up, whereas 26% had a different diagnosis at follow-up, which was not present at Time 1. Overanxious disorder was the most common "new" disorder (43%), followed by minor or major depression (33%), attention deficit/hyperactivity disorder (14%), conduct disorder (10%), and phobia (10%).

High recovery rates were also characteristic of a clinical sample of children with SAD (Last et al., 1996); 96% of those initially diagnosed with SAD had recovered by 3–4 years later. Similar to earlier studies (e.g., Cantwell & Baker, 1989), among children who no longer met SAD diagnostic criteria, 25% were diagnosed with a new psychiatric disorder. Diagnostic instability also was reported in a longitudinal study of children diagnosed with SAD at age 3 (9 with SAD and 18 with subclinical SAD; Kearney, Sims, Pursell, & Tillotson, 2003). After 3.5 years, among the 9 children originally diagnosed with SAD, only 2 children still met diagnostic criteria, 5 had subclinical SAD, and 2 had no disorder. Among the 18 originally categorized as having subclinical SAD, 1 was diagnosed with SAD at follow-up, 4 had subclinical SAD, and 13 had no disorder. These data suggest that SAD may not be a stable disorder. A subset of children may develop other disorders at a later date, and many will have no diagnosis.

A challenge for researchers and clinicians is determining the difference between separation fears and SAD. Particular attention should be paid to strictly enforcing the functional impairment criterion. As discussed in the chapter on generalized anxiety disorder (see Chapter 6), "normal" worries may be overinterpreted as a true disorder. Some degree of concern about a parent's well-being is probably normal, particularly for young children. Severity and impairment are what distinguish "typical" from "pathological" fear. Also, it may be that the current diagnostic criteria are not sufficiently stringent or perhaps are incorrect. Another possibility is that what has been termed separation anxiety may be a transient condition under the control of changing environmental factors. Clearly, this instability creates difficulty for treatment outcome studies, and one retrospective study of adults who reported a childhood history of SAD indicated that only 21.8% of the sample had ever received treatment during childhood or adolescence (Shear et al., 2006). Without proper control groups, inaccurate conclusions about the efficacy of the intervention may result.

SAD may be an important risk factor for the later development of other anxiety disorders. Using data from the Oregon Adolescent Depression project (Lewinsohn, Holm-Denoma, Small, Seeley, & Joiner, 2008), 78.6% of the sample with a childhood diagnosis of SAD met diagnostic criteria for another disorder during young adulthood (defined as ages 19–30). The most common disorders were panic disorder or major depression, and the likelihood of developing these disorders was increased for females. Furthermore, these individuals were significantly more likely to develop panic disorder when compared to adults who had (a) a different anxiety disorder as a child or (b) a disorder other than anxiety as a child or had no disorder as a child.

It is important to note, however, that among the subgroup that does have a chronic course, the long-term impact of SAD can be significant. A 20- to 29-year follow-up investigation compared 35 individuals with SAD treated for school refusal at ages 7 to 12 years with 35 psychiatric patients without school refusal and 35 children from the general population (Flakierska-Praquin et al., 1997). Children with SAD had more psychiatric consultations, were more likely to live with their parents, and had fewer children than both of the comparison groups. Thus, SAD, particularly when coupled with school refusal, can have an impact on long-term social development. It may be that those with school refusal behavior represent the most severe cases of SAD, and that this is the group that, without treatment, may continue to suffer from the disorder, even in adulthood.

RELATIONSHIP TO ADULT PANIC DISORDER

Since the 1970s, there has been continued controversy about the relationship of childhood SAD to adult panic disorder. Klein (1964) was the first to examine this relationship, noting that severe separation anxiety was prominent in the histories of patients with panic disorder, and that panic attacks often started after a major personal loss (Klein, 1995). Klein (1964) proposed that "spontaneous panic attacks" could be a sign of the "protest-despair" response to separation, and that SAD in childhood may be a developmentally immature form of panic disorder/agoraphobia in adulthood. With respect to this linkage, there are three lines of research that address this issue: (1) similar drug treatment response, (2) family concordance for SAD and panic disorder, and (3) history of childhood SAD in adults with panic disorder/agoraphobia. Each is discussed here.

Initially, pharmacological interventions for panic disorder and school phobia (presumed to be precipitated by SAD) found that imipramine was efficacious for both disorders (see Gittelman & Klein, 1984, for a review of this literature). However, a later investigation using a sample of children with a primary diagnosis of SAD (rather than school phobia) did not find imipramine to be more effective than placebo (Klein, Koplewicz, et al., 1992; see the treatment section for discussion of this issue). Thus, data on equivalent pharmacological treatment response for panic disorder and SAD are equivocal.

The second line of data relates to family history. In the initial publication (Klein, 1964), 50% of patients with panic described an early history of SAD. However, other data are more conflictual. Weissman and colleagues (1984) reported a higher prevalence of SAD among offspring of parents who were comorbid for depression and panic disorder. However, when these same children reached adulthood and were reinterviewed directly, no relationship was found (Mufson, Weissman, & Warner, 1992). Again, no definitive conclusions can be drawn.

The third line of evidence examines the history of SAD in adults with panic disorder. With respect to one of Klein's (1964) initial observations that spontaneous panic attacks could be a sign of the protest-despair response to separation, several investigations examined the prevalence of separation/trauma in the childhood histories of adult patients with panic disorder.

Interestingly, a history of traumatic separation events is not more common in the childhood histories of adults with agoraphobia when compared to adults with specific phobia (Thyer, Nesse, Cameron, & Curtis, 1985). Similarly, there was no difference in the number of separation-related events between youth with SAD alone and youth with SAD and comorbid panic disorder (Doerfler, Toscano, & Connor, 2008).

Furthermore, some retrospective data suggest that a history of SAD is significantly more common among female, but not male, patients with

agoraphobia with panic (when compared to patients with social phobia or specific phobia; Zitrin & Ross, 1988). SAD was more common
among patients with panic disorder when compared to a group of medi-
cal/surgical patients (Battaglia et al., 1995) but not when compared to
the childhood histories of patients with other types of anxiety disorders
(Lipsitz et al., 1994). Interestingly, a childhood history of SAD was more
common among patients with two or more anxiety disorders as adults
(regardless of the type) than those who had only a single disorder. This
suggests that SAD may indicate the presence of severe anxiety (as indicated by the presence of multiple anxiety disorders) rather than predict
the presence of one particular anxiety disorder (Lipsitz et al., 1994).
Again, the data remain conflictual and inconclusive.

   Four longitudinal studies have examined the relationship of SAD
in children and panic disorder/agoraphobia in adults. Two investigations did not find a higher prevalence of adult panic disorder among
children previously diagnosed with SAD when compared to children
with other anxiety disorders (Aschenbrand, Kendall, Webb, Safford, &
Flannery-Schroeder, 2003; Craske, Poulton, Tsao, & Plotkin, 2001). A
third study found that a childhood history of SAD did predict the later
onset of panic disorder, but the relationship was not unique (Lewinsohn
et al., 2008). Childhood SAD also predicted the onset of major depression in adulthood. A fourth study (Klein, 1995) examined the prevalence of anxiety disorders among adults who previously were treated
as children for SAD. The probands with a prior history of SAD were
compared to a normal comparison sample. The results indicated that
adult panic disorder was the only anxiety disorder that distinguished
the two groups. However, the prevalence of panic disorder among the
SAD probands was only 7% (compared to 0% among the comparison group). Given the other findings reported, the lack of a psychiatric
control comparison group limits the conclusions that should be drawn
from this investigation.

   There have been research efforts to examine the continuity of
SAD in childhood/adolescence and SAD in adulthood. Clinical evaluations and self-report data indicate that some adults report symptoms
consistent with *DSM-IV-TR* (APA, 2000)-derived criteria for SAD
(Manicavasagar & Silove, 1997; Manicavasagar, Silove, & Curtis, 1997;
Manicavasager, Silove, Curtis, & Wagner, 2000), and adults retrospectively endorsed the presence of these symptoms as children. As noted by
Silverman and Dick-Niederhauser (2004), although intriguing, these data
are based on retrospective reports and self-report instruments with only
limited psychometric properties. A more recent investigation still used
retrospective data, but diagnostic decisions were based on structured
interviews (Shear et al., 2006). These data suggest that approximately

36.1% of adults with a diagnosis of SAD in childhood continue to manifest this disorder in adults. However, a number of individuals appear to develop the disorder in adulthood, and about 40% of adults suffering from this disorder report severe impairment, most common in their social or personal functioning. Thus, although all these data are suggestive, the validity of a relationship between child/adolescent SAD and adult SAD remains inconclusive, as does the relationship between childhood SAD and adult panic disorder.

EPIDEMIOLOGY

Among all of the childhood anxiety disorders, SAD is one of the most common. However, an important consideration is that even when past the "typical age" for developmentally appropriate fears, as suggested in this chapter, many children endorse thoughts of separation. In fact, when functional impairment is not considered, up to 50% of 8-year-old children express separation fears (Kashani & Orvaschel, 1990). Thus, as discussed in Chapter 6, many children express thoughts associated with anxiety disorders. However, for most children, these concerns do not impair their daily functioning or their social or academic development; therefore, they would not be considered to have a disorder. This issue is raised as a consideration for clinicians and parents when attempting to determine the severity of a child's fear. A simple expression of fear does not necessarily mean that a disorder is present. Fear plus impairment are necessary to substantiate the presence of an anxiety disorder.

SAD is considered to be a common psychiatric disorder, and prevalence rates in the general population range from 3% to 5% (Lewinsohn et al., 2008; Shear et al., 2006; see also Silverman & Dick-Niederhauser, 2004, for a review), with a "peak" age of onset between the ages of 7 and 9 (Suveg, Aschenbrand, & Kendall, 2005). The prevalence rate among the general adolescent population is slightly lower (2.4%; Bowen, Offord, & Boyle, 1990). The disorder is more prevalent in children than adolescents and more prevalent among younger, than older, adolescents (Suveg et al., 2005). Among children referred to a general outpatient psychiatric clinic, 9.9% had SAD, and an additional 2.8% were comorbid for both SAD and overanxious disorder (Westenberg, Siebelink, Warmenhoven, & Treffers, 1999). Few data are available for specialty clinic samples, although one study reported that 33% of children referred to a childhood anxiety clinic had a primary diagnosis of SAD (Last, Francis, et al., 1987).

SOCIODEMOGRAPHIC INFLUENCES

With respect to sex, some studies report that SAD is more common among girls than boys (Anderson et al., 1987; Bowen et al., 1990; Last, Francis, et al., 1987; March et al., 1997; Shear et al., 2006), whereas others report equal prevalence (Bird, Gould, Yager, Staghezza, & Canino, 1989; Francis, Last, & Strauss, 1987; Last et al., 1996). Among boys and girls diagnosed with SAD, specific symptoms do not differ based on sex (Francis et al., 1987).

As suggested, the peak age of onset is between 7 and 9 years (Bird et al., 1989; Last, Perrin, Hersen, & Kazdin, 1992; Pruis et al., 1990), although SAD also may develop during adolescence (Bowen et al., 1990; Last et al., 1992) or even adulthood (Shear et al., 2006). However, SAD is more common among children than adolescents (Breton et al., 1999; Kashani & Orvaschel, 1988, 1990; McGee et al., 1990). In addition to differences in prevalence, age differences occur in SAD symptom expression (Francis et al., 1987). Young children (5–8 years old) with SAD were significantly more likely than older children (9–12 years old) and adolescents to endorse nightmares about separation. Excessive distress on separation was common among the younger and older children but not among adolescents. Interestingly, physical complaints were endorsed by 100% of the adolescents, but only among 58% of the younger children and 69% of the older children. Thus, age appears to be an important consideration in the symptomatic expression of SAD.

Several studies have reported that 50–75% of children with SAD are from the lower socioeconomic strata (Last et al., 1992; Last, Francis, et al., 1987; Velez et al., 1989), although the reasons are unclear. Within the United States, rates of SAD are similar for European American, African American, and Hispanic children (Ginsburg & Silverman, 1996; Last & Perrin, 1993). An interesting cross-cultural study compared Japanese and U.S. preschoolers (4–5 years old) and their mothers on measures of security, sensitivity, and separation (Mizuta, Zahn-Waxler, Cole, & Hiruma, 1996). After settling the child, the mother left the playroom and returned 60–90 minutes later. Mother and child behaviors surrounding separation and reunion were coded for anxiety, physical proximity, and affection. The results indicated that there were no group differences in overall levels of security or sensitivity on separation or reunion. However, on reunion, Japanese children displayed more desire for bodily closeness with their mother (a Japanese concept known as *amae*). Although amae was positively correlated with internalizing symptoms among U.S. children, there was no correlation among Japanese children, suggesting the importance of considering culture when assessing behavior. In this case, physical contact with mother may be a signal of separation distress and anxiety for children raised in the United States, but the behavior does not have the same meaning for their Japanese counterparts.

COMORBIDITY AND DIFFERENTIAL DIAGNOSIS

As with the other anxiety disorders, children with SAD are likely to present with a variety of comorbid diagnoses, primarily other anxiety disorders. Among one sample of youth with primary SAD, 92% had a concurrent anxiety or affective disorder (Last, Francis, et al., 1987). Fifty percent had a comorbid anxiety disorder (primarily overanxious disorder or school phobia), and 33% had a comorbid affective disorder. Illustrating the influence of age, the percentage of youth with SAD and a comorbid diagnosis drops to 35% when the sample is restricted to adolescents (Bowen et al., 1990).

We noted the relationship between childhood anxiety disorder and adult panic disorder, but among one clinical population, 33% of youth with SAD were comorbid for panic disorder (Doerfler et al., 2008). Both groups also had other comorbid conditions, including other anxiety disorders, depressive disorders, and externalizing disorders, and the groups were not different on the number or type of comorbid diagnoses. When compared to the youth who had SAD but not panic disorder, youth with comorbid panic disorder had a later age of onset of SAD (4.7 years vs. 6.9 years), but the groups did not differ on severity of SAD symptoms. However, they were rated by psychiatrists as having a more severe illness and having significantly more functional impairment. Consistently, parents also rated the comorbid group as more anxious/depressed on the subscale of the Child Behavior Checklist (CBCL) and on the delinquent and aggressive subscales. Although the two groups did not differ on the broad-band Internalizing scale, the group with comorbid conditions had significantly higher scores on the broad-band Externalizing scale. These data suggest that even though the onset of SAD occurs 2 years later on average, children with SAD and panic disorder may have increased risk of illness severity and functional impairment than youth with the comorbid panic disorder.

Depression also is a common comorbid condition (Keller et al., 1992; Kovacs, Gatsonis, Paulauskas, & Richards, 1989; Last et al., 1987; Ryan et al., 1987) and in most cases appears after the onset of SAD. In some instances, the prevalence of depression may depend on the complexity of the child's anxiety disorder. In a sample of adolescents with SAD plus overanxious disorder, the prevalence of depression with or without an externalizing disorder was 63% (50% had depression alone, and 13% had depression plus at least one externalizing disorder; Bowen et al., 1990). However, among adolescents with SAD alone, only 13% had comorbid depression (9% had depression alone, and 4% had depression plus an externalizing disorder). These data again illustrate that it may be the prevalence of a more complex anxiety state, rather than any one particular disorder, that increases the likelihood of co-occurring nonanxiety disorders.

ETIOLOGY

Although there are many theories, there are few empirical data addressing the etiology of SAD. With respect to biology, twin data (Eaves et al., 1997; Topolski et al., 1997) did not find a genetic component for this disorder. In fact, the heredity estimate for SAD was only 4%, whereas the shared environment estimate, particularly family factors, was 40%. Other data have suggested that the biologically based concept of behavioral inhibition (BI; see Chapter 4) might be a risk factor for the development of SAD. However, all available data indicate that although some children with BI may be diagnosed with SAD at a later date, by far BI is more specifically related to social phobia than to any other anxiety disorder, including SAD (Biederman et al., 1993).

Among parents of children with SAD, 68–83% of mothers had a lifetime anxiety disorder, and 47% had a current anxiety disorder (Last, Francis, et al., 1987; Last, Hersen, et al., 1987). Among parents with panic disorder or panic disorder plus depression, offspring are 3 to 10 times more likely to have SAD when compared to offspring of parents with depression alone or parents with no psychiatric disorder (Leckman et al., 1985; Weissman et al., 1984). It is important to emphasize that even though anxiety disorders run in families, it is not always the same disorder in parent and child. Also, familial relationships need not imply biological (genetic) transmission. Psychological and environmental factors may play a role.

Among groups of children with different types of anxiety disorders, factors such as parental overcontrol and less autonomy granting have sometimes been associated with the presence of these disorders. However, the diagnostic categories are rarely examined separately, and appropriate psychiatric control groups are not usually included in the design. Therefore, it is unclear if these parental behaviors are associated with a specific disorder, anxiety disorders in general, or psychological disorders in general. It may be that constructs such as overcontrol or less autonomy are too broad to allow for investigation of specific relationships. One investigation examined the relationship between parental intrusiveness and SAD (Wood, 2006). In this investigation, parental intrusiveness was defined as the tendency of parents to take over tasks that children are capable of performing independently and imposing an immature level of functioning on the children, thereby restricting autonomy. The model suggests that when separated from parents, children who have intrusive parents may experience anxiety when faced with a novel or ambiguous task, which they must now resolve on their own. They may see this novel or ambiguous situation as threatening and react with fear of separation. An empirical test of this hypothesis found some support for the specific relationships between parent intrusiveness and SAD. Based on separation anxiety scores derived from a semistructured diagnostic interview and a parental report, parental intrusiveness was significantly correlated with SAD, whereas there was no correlation between parental intrusiveness and either social phobia or generalized anxiety disorder.

ASSESSMENT

The assessment of SAD has not been the subject of much investigation. Some data (Foley, Rutter, et al., 2004) suggest that there is only poor agreement between parents and children on the presence of SAD in children, again raising concerns about diagnostic validity. However, these data were from a large community sample of twins. It is likely that there may be higher symptom agreement when a clinic or treatment-seeking sample is used. In general, the assessment strategies used with other anxiety disorders are also relevant for SAD. The Anxiety Disorders Interview Schedule for DSM-IV: Child and Parent Versions (ADIS-C/P; Silverman & Albano, 1996) is perhaps the most relevant and valid of the diagnostic interviews. Its psychometric properties are reviewed in Chapter 3. There are no self-report instruments specifically designed to assess the symptoms of SAD, although the Multidimensional Anxiety Scale for Children (MASC; March, 1997) and the Screen for Anxiety Related Emotional Disorders (SCARED; Birmaher, Brent, Chiappetta, Bridge, Monga, & Baugher, 1999) both contain subscales for SAD. Both instruments have established validity for the assessment of SAD (Birmaher et al., 1999; March, 1997). In controlled trials, behavioral assessment is rarely used. In the case example in this chapter, the use of a behavioral assessment to gauge treatment outcome is presented.

TREATMENT

In 1997, the American Academy for Child and Adolescent Psychiatry recommended psychological interventions as the first-line treatments for childhood anxiety disorders. Pharmacological interventions are conceptualized as adjunctive treatments for "treatment-resistant" cases, a recommendation reiterated in 2001 (Masi, Mucci, & Millepiedi, 2001). In fact, there are few randomized controlled trials specifically examining pharmacological or psychological interventions for children with SAD. In the majority of instances, children with SAD have been included among larger samples of children with various types of anxiety disorders. The available literature on treatment of SAD is reviewed next.

Overall, psychological interventions in the form of behavioral and cognitive-behavioral interventions appear to be successful in the treatment of children with anxiety disorders (Barrett, Dadds, et al., 1996; Flannery-Schroeder & Kendall, 2000; Kendall, 1994; Kendall et al., 1997; Silverman, Kurtines, Ginsburg, Weems, Lumpkin, et al., 1999; Silverman, Kurtines, Ginsburg, Weems, Rabian, et al., 1999). These interventions, which include exposure, cognitive restructuring, contingency management, self-statement training, and parent training, among others, were reviewed in detail in Chapter 6 and are not reviewed again here. It is important to note, however, that none of these investigations found a differential treatment effect for children with SAD in comparison to children with other anxiety disorders. In some studies, treatment outcome based on diagnosis was not examined. In other instances, no difference in outcome based on diagnosis was noted. Thus, in these studies, the positive improvement reported for the entire group appears to reflect the outcome for SAD. As noted (Silverman & Dick-Niederhauser, 2004), one conclusion that can be drawn from these outcome data is that perhaps a specific intervention for SAD is not necessary. However, given the high spontaneous remission rate for SAD, more carefully controlled, randomized trials using solely SAD patients and including sufficient long-term follow-up are necessary to definitively address the outcome of behavior therapy and cognitive-behavior therapy (CBT) for SAD.

In addition to directing treatment at the child or adolescent, some of the interventions cited incorporate parents into psychoeducational components or some of the other treatment sessions. Parents have been more fully integrated into treatment for youth with SAD recently. Parent–child interaction training, an empirically supported treatment for young children with oppositional behaviors, was reported to be successful for three children with SAD (Choate, Pincus, Eyberg, & Barlow, 2005). Using a different approach, parent training teaches parents how to work with their children, teaching skills such as progressive muscle relaxation, construction of a hierarchy, and principles of contingency management (Eisen, Raleigh, & Neuhoff, 2008). Parents are also instructed how to conduct imaginal or in vivo exposure sessions, and tips for relapse prevention are provided. Using a multiple-baseline design, five of the six children whose parents participated in parent training were judged as achieving high end-state functioning. Interestingly, clinically significant improvement appeared to be related to improvement in parental process factors, including enhanced efficacy or satisfaction and reduced stress. The one child who did not improve differed from the others on several variables; the parent had higher scores on self-reported anxiety and stress, the child was the only participant who had several severe comorbid disorders, and the child was the youngest in the sample (age 7). With respect to the child's age, the authors suggested that she may have had difficulty learning cognitive self-control strategies (Eisen et al., 2008).

With respect to pharmacological treatment, the data also are sparse. There are few randomized, controlled trials examining pharmacological interventions, specifically examining their efficacy for children with SAD. In one of the few randomized trials, imipramine was administered to 21 children with SAD (Klein, Koplewicz, & Kanner, 1992) in an attempt to replicate an earlier successful outcome for imipramine treatment of school refusal (see Chapter 8). Unfortunately, the earlier positive findings could not be replicated in this new sample, although the reason for the negative outcome was unclear. It should be noted, however, that the sample in this study also was nonresponsive to a behavioral intervention and thus may represent a particularly refractory group.

With respect to the selective serotonin reuptake inhibitors (SSRIs), there have been no interventions that used a sample consisting solely of children with SAD. Several investigations examined the use of fluoxetine and fluvoxamine for children with anxiety disorders (Birmaher et al., 1994; RUPP Anxiety Study Group, 2001), and children with SAD were included in these samples. In each of these investigations, the outcome for children treated with medication was superior to placebo. However, the results were not examined separately for children with SAD.

Two investigations (Birmaher et al., 2003; Fairbanks et al., 1997) examined the use of fluoxetine for children with anxiety disorders and examined its efficacy for SAD specifically. In an open trial (Fairbanks et al., 1997), 16 children nonresponsive to psychotherapy (defined as 4 weeks of behaviorally oriented psychotherapy and supportive therapy) were treated with fluoxetine. At the end of the 9-week trial, all 10 children with a diagnosis of SAD were rated as clinically improved (4 were rated as improved, and 6 were rated as much improved). These data are promising; however, this was an open trial with no control group. A more recent investigation (Birmaher et al., 2003) consisted of a 12-week, randomized, controlled trial. Thirteen patients with SAD were randomized to fluoxetine, and 22 patients were randomized to placebo. Outcome was based on blinded clinician ratings and revealed that the clinical response for those children with SAD was not significantly different for those treated with fluoxetine (54% improved) versus those treated with placebo (41%). Thus, as noted throughout this volume, initial positive results from open treatment are often not confirmed by follow-up controlled trials. In this particular trial, placebo was just as effective as fluoxetine for the treatment of SAD, and it is noteworthy that only slightly more than half of the sample treated with fluoxetine had a positive treatment response.

A clinical trial compared sertraline, CBT, their combination, and placebo (2:2:2:1 ratio) among 488 youth ages 7–17 years with SAD, generalized anxiety disorder, or social phobia (Walkup et al., 2008; see Chapter 6 for a full discussion of this trial). After 12 weeks of treatment, blinded clinician ratings indicated that 54.9% of youth treated with sertraline, 59.7% treated with CBT, 80.7% treated with their combination, and 23.7% treated with placebo had a positive treatment outcome. All three active treatments were superior to placebo, and the combination of sertraline and CBT was superior to either of the individual therapies. However, outcome by specific diagnostic group was not reported.

In an investigation of the use of antianxiety agents, 11 children completed a double-blind placebo crossover trial consisting of 4 weeks of clonazepam and 4 weeks of placebo (Graae, Milner, Rizzotto, & Klein, 1994). At the end of the 8-week trial, 50% of the children no longer met criteria for an anxiety disorder, but there was no order effect, meaning that positive treatment response was equally likely to occur with placebo as with clonazepam. Furthermore, there were no differences between clonazepam and placebo on clinician ratings when rates of improvement were compared to baseline. Although the sample size was small, as noted by the authors, the crossover design should have allowed for the detection of a beneficial medication effect, thus leading the authors to conclude that clonazepam (in doses up to 2 mg/day) is not effective for the treatment of anxiety disorders (specifically SAD) in children and adolescents.

To summarize the treatment literature on SAD, data on the psychopathology and assessment of this disorder are so limited that judgments of improvement are based primarily on self-report of anxiety or clinical evaluations of global improvement. Thus, whether these interventions target and alleviate the specific concerns of children with SAD or only result in a better sense of general well-being remains unclear. Furthermore, the natural history data discussed previously in this chapter indicate that SAD often remits without intervention; thus, appropriate study designs with appropriate control groups and long-term follow-up data are needed before the effectiveness of psychological and pharmacological interventions for SAD can be appropriately determined.

CASE EXAMPLE: TREATMENT FOR SEPARATION ANXIETY DISORDER

As presented at the beginning of this chapter, Leslie is a 10-year-old girl who came to the clinic with her mother because of a 6-month history of separation fears.

ASSESSMENT

A diagnostic interview with Leslie and her mother revealed that Leslie had significant separation fears. The primary worry was that something "bad" would happen to Leslie if she was away from her parents. According to Leslie, she defined *unfamiliar places* as any place other than school where she was not accompanied by her parents. An important element of Leslie's clinical presentation was that the onset of her fears was much later than is typical for SAD. Thus, examining environmental factors that could have been associated with onset was considered paramount. The diagnostic interview revealed that the onset of her fears coincided with a medical illness. Specifically, Leslie developed stomach ulcers approximately 3 months ago. Although now under control, she was subsequently diagnosed with asthma, which was currently being treated by oral medication and inhalers. She was under good control with only minimal need for emergency inhalers. However, neither her parents nor her physician had explained her medical condition to her. Another important element of her clinical presentation was that, because Leslie was highly embarrassed by her fear, she was motivated to participate in (and end) treatment. In many instances, children do not understand the negative impact of their disorder, and much time is spent engaging their cooperation in the treatment program. This was not an issue in Leslie's case.

As noted, there are no self-report measures developed specifically and solely for SAD. However, her score on the MASC separation anxiety subscale was in the clinically significant range. Because there are so few specific separation anxiety measures, we conducted a simple behavioral test to assess the severity of her condition and to establish baseline values by which to determine treatment efficacy. This assessment was conducted outside the office. Specifically, while her mother stood at the entrance to the building, Leslie and the therapist began to walk away from her mother. Leslie was instructed to continue walking until her anxiety was a 5 (severe) on a 5-point scale of subjective units of distress (SUDS). She also was instructed not to turn around and look at her mother as she was walking away. Leslie was able to walk only a short distance (50 yards) before she indicated that her distress level was at the maximum rating of 5. Furthermore, she stopped and looked back at her mother eight times as she was walking that distance.

TREATMENT PROGRAM

In determining Leslie's treatment plan, both in vivo and imaginal exposure options were considered. However, given Leslie's age, imaginal exposure was not considered to be a viable option. Therefore, the treatment program consisted of education, graduated exposure, and parent training in the implementation of a home-based treatment program. Leslie's parents were firmly committed to helping their daughter, and her mother in particular was enthusiastic and available to assist in the treatment program. Thus, this was an instance when using a parent to participate in the intervention represented a positive factor.

With respect to education, the onset of Leslie's fears coincided with her illness and subsequent asthma diagnosis. Given her lack of prior anxiety disorders or even lack of a history of substantial fears, it appeared that this illness played a major role in the onset of her SAD. However, no one had talked to Leslie about her asthmatic condition and its actual impact on her daily functioning. Thus, providing her with a full explanation of her medical condition constituted the first phase of the treatment program. Leslie's parents were asked to contact her pediatrician, who met with Leslie, talked to her about asthma, answered her questions, and practiced the use of her inhalers with her. Leslie had several questions for the pediatrician about her health and the likelihood that she would die from an asthma attack and whether adults other than her parents could help her if an attack occurred. Clearly, her separation fears were related to her misunderstanding of her medical condition. Following the pediatrician consultation, Leslie demonstrated good understanding of her asthma and how to control it through the use of inhalers. However, a repeat of the behavioral assessment demonstrated no increase in her ability to leave her mother, a phenomenon characteristic of anxiety disorders. Specifically, knowledge and insight alone do not eliminate the fear. Thus, it was necessary to proceed with the behavioral intervention.

As the family lived several hours away from the clinic, massed therapist-assisted exposure sessions were not possible. Therefore, it was clear that a large part of the exposure program would have to be conducted by her parents. Prior to initiating a home in vivo exposure program, the second phase of the treatment program trained Leslie's mother in the proper implementation of the graduated exposure program. The elements of the parental training sessions are depicted in Table 9.2.

TABLE 9.2   Elements Included in the Parental Training Session

1. Mother trained in use of SUDS rating scale.
2. Mother presents exposure task to Leslie in positive fashion.
3. Mother encourages Leslie's attempts at the task.
4. Mother ignores Leslie's complaints.
5. Mother reinforces Leslie's completion of the task.
6. Mother instructed to call the clinic when Leslie completes the task three times without distress.

Source: Reprinted from Beidel, D. C., & Turner, S. M. (2005). *Child Anxiety Disorders.* New York: Routledge. With permission.

The graduated exposure program (Phase 3) consisted of both home and clinic in vivo exposure sessions. At the clinic, treatment sessions also focused on separation of Leslie from her mother. Specifically, Leslie's mother was instructed to drop her off at the clinic and then leave without telling Leslie how long she would be away (5 minutes, 20 minutes, 1 hour) or where she was going. During that time, Leslie engaged in activities in which children might engage in at home (do homework, play computer games, watch television). The object of the sessions was for Leslie to be in an unfamiliar environment (the clinic) without the presence of her mother. Allowing Leslie to engage in typical child activities simulated what many children would do if they were home (appropriately supervised) and parents were away running errands, for example. Her SUDS level was assessed every 10 minutes, and she was not allowed to know that her mother had returned to the clinic until her anxiety habituated. Her at-home hierarchy is presented in Table 9.3. Each item had to be successfully completed three times with a rating of 0 distress prior to moving to the next item. Thus, Leslie was receiving exposure sessions at the clinic and at home.

It took approximately 2 months to complete all of the hierarchy items with no distress. On completion, a posttreatment behavioral assessment, identical to the pretreatment assessment, was conducted. In contrast to pretreatment, when Leslie was able to walk only 50 yards away and looked at her mother eight times, at posttreatment she was able to walk 500 yards (including turning a corner so that she could no longer see her mother) and never attempted to look back. In fact, because Leslie turned the corner, meaning that visual contact with the therapist was lost, the therapist had to pursue her and halt the assessment at 500 yards. Seven years later, Leslie contacted the clinic to tell her therapist that she had not had any further episodes and had just been accepted to a very prestigious Ivy League university 3,000 miles from home.

TABLE 9.3   Leslie's At-Home Hierarchy

Activity	SUDS Level
Take out the trash at night	1.5
Go to a friend's house in the daytime	2.0
Ride bike—every day increase the distance from home	2.5
Go into a store alone	2.5
Eat in a restaurant with friends	3.0
Go to a birthday party	3.5
Go to afterschool activity without a parent	4.0
Sleep over at a friend's house	4.5
Go on overnight camping trips without parents	5.0

Source: Reprinted from Beidel, D. C., & Turner, S. M. (2005). *Child Anxiety Disorders.* New York: Routledge. With permission.

SUMMARY

SAD is a prevalent anxiety disorder that can exert substantial interference with academic and social development and have a significant impact on many aspects of parental and family functioning. For some youth, SAD can continue to affect their lives as adults. For other children and adolescents, the form of the disorder may change—meaning that children no longer express fears of separation, but they may continue to suffer from anxiety or mood disorders. The disorder will sometimes remit without intervention, although at this time, it is impossible to determine which children will outgrow the disorder. Because the disorder is not stable in a majority of children, it presents a challenge for evaluating the efficacy of pharmacological and psychological interventions. One of the most pressing needs at this time is to examine the natural course of SAD, particularly over the short term. Until that happens, the most conservative treatment recommendation is that children with SAD should receive treatment, particularly if there is functional interference in the form of school refusal. To date, behavioral and cognitive-behavioral interventions and SSRIs appear to have the most empirical support, although it should be pointed out that in no case has there been a treatment trial examining these interventions with a specific and sufficient sample of children with SAD. Perhaps such trials will be forthcoming.

CHAPTER 10

Social Anxiety Disorder and Selective Mutism

Jessica is 9 years old. She refuses to read aloud in class, and during recess she stands on the sideline watching the other children play games. Outside school, she interacts only with her immediate family, her cousins, and one friend. When people, even her grandparents, come to the house to visit, Jessica hides in her room. She will go to dancing lessons but refuses to perform on stage in the year-end dance recital. She also refuses to go to birthday parties or join the neighborhood soccer team.

Nick is 17 years old. He was accompanied to the evaluation by his parents, but they were late because Nick tried to stall and keep the family from the appointment. His parents note that he has always been shy, and it has affected his academic achievement. Their motivation to seek treatment at this time is that Nick will leave for college next year. His parents are afraid that Nick's social anxiety will interfere with his college success.

Jessica and Nick are just two examples of the many children and adolescents who suffer from social anxiety disorder (SOC), one of the most common childhood anxiety disorders. Previously, those who were anxious in social interactions were considered "just a little shy." However, data are now emerging to suggest that SOC, although related to shyness, is a much more severe and disabling condition (Heiser, Turner, & Beidel, 2003).

SOCIABILITY AND SHYNESS

The term *shyness* describes behaviors that are commonly recognized by most individuals. Although definitions of shyness have evolved into descriptions of low-level anxiety states that precipitate social avoidance, shyness initially described withdrawal from social encounters regardless of the motivating factors. It is important to distinguish shyness from *sociability*, which is a preference for affiliation and companionship rather than solitude (Buss & Plomin, 1984). In fact, these two constructs might be considered orthogonal. Some children are low on the dimension of sociability; they choose not to interact with others but show (or feel) little emotional distress when forced to do so. To the contrary, most children desire social contact, and among this group, most feel comfortable during social interactions. However, there is a subset of children who strongly desire social interaction but become distressed when engaged in these encounters (e.g., Coplan, Prakash, O'Neil, & Armer, 2004). In the child developmental literature, these children are described as shy.

Empirically, shyness can be detected at an early age and appears to be stable across periods of developmental change (Bromberg, Lamb, & Hwang, 1990; Kagan et al., 1984). In the United States, childhood shyness among elementary school children is associated with higher levels of trait anxiety and loneliness and lower levels of global self-worth (Fordham & Stevenson-Hinde, 1999; Rubin & Asendorpf, 1993). Shy children are described by their teachers as less prosocial and more behaviorally withdrawn and, on behavioral observation, display more reticent behavior and more parallel (rather than interactive) play (Coplan et al., 2004). In addition, early shyness may lead to long-term social consequences. Longitudinal studies suggested that persistently shy children are more likely to have anxiety disorders in adolescence (Prior et al., 2000), generalized social anxiety in particular (Schwartz et al., 1999). However, most shy children did not develop an anxiety disorder, and most adolescents with anxiety disorders were not especially shy as children (Prior et al., 2000). Thus, there may be a relationship between shyness and SOC, but it is one that is complicated.

The developmental literature on shyness is extensive, and a complete review is beyond the scope of this volume. This discussion is meant simply to illustrate the overlap between the constructs of shyness and SOC and to caution readers that these conditions do not exist along a continuum. Although the data on childhood shyness might prove instructive in some cases, it is important to remember that there are many children who are described as shy. In contrast, SOC (characterized by extreme fear and by functional impairment) affects a smaller proportion of the population, and it is to this disorder that we now turn our attention.

SOCIAL ANXIETY DISORDER

SOC (also called social phobia) is characterized by pervasive social inhibition and timidity. Descriptions of the disorder have existed since the time of Hippocrates (Marks, 1985). Modern portrayals of SOC were discussed by Marks (1970) and appeared in the American psychiatric nomenclature with the third edition of the *Diagnostic and Statistical Manual of Mental Disorders* (*DSM-III*; American Psychiatric Association [APA], 1980). SOC, particularly among children, initially was understudied, in part because of the belief that shy children subsequently "outgrow" this condition (e.g., Bruch, Giordano, & Pearl, 1986). In addition, until *DSM-IV* (APA, 1994), children fearful of social interaction could be diagnosed not only with SOC but also with other disorders. Specifically, descriptions of overanxious disorder in the revised third edition of the *DSM* (*DSM-III-R*; APA, 1987) also included social-evaluative concerns as part of the diagnostic criteria, and avoidant disorder of childhood described children who withdrew from others. Only since the early 1990s (Beidel, 1991; Beidel & Turner, 1988; Francis, Last, & Strauss, 1992; Strauss & Last, 1993) has childhood SOC been studied as a distinct diagnostic entity.

Clinical Features

The *DSM-IV* diagnostic criteria for SOC are depicted in Table 10.1, several aspects of which deserve further mention. First, a child with SOC must have the capacity for age-appropriate social interactions, thereby differentiating this disorder from autism or Asberger's disorder, for which there is often a preference for social avoidance. Second, the physiological reactions and behavioral signs of distress in children with SOC differ from those of adults. Children may express their distress by crying, tantrums, freezing, or shrinking from social encounters. Clinically, parents of children with this disorder will report that if a stranger comes to the house, the child will run and hide. Third, as noted elsewhere, because of limited cognitive abilities, children need not necessarily recognize that their fear is excessive or unreasonable. Fourth, the fears must exist for at least a 6-month period to avoid temporary distress as a result of adjustment to a new neighborhood or a new school.

As depicted in Table 10.2, SOC can result in distress across a broad range of interpersonal encounters (Beidel et al., 1999; Rao et al., 2007; Strauss & Last, 1993), and the extent of the distress increases with age. Children and adolescents endorse distress when engaged in performance situations (speaking or reading in front of a group, writing or eating in front of others) or in more informal social encounters (speaking to other children, talking on the telephone, talking informally to adults). In a number of situations, significantly more adolescents endorsed distress in these situations than did their younger counterparts (Rao et al., 2007). For those with SOC, distressful events occur approximately every other day, significantly more frequently than for children without a psychiatric

TABLE 10.1   Diagnostic Criteria for Social Anxiety Disorder

1. A marked and persistent fear of one or more social or performance situations in which the person is exposed to unfamiliar people or to possible scrutiny by others. The individual fears that he or she will act in a way (or show anxiety symptoms) that will be humiliating or embarrassing. *Note*: In children, there must be evidence of the capacity for age-appropriate social relationships with familiar people and the anxiety must occur in peer settings, not just in interactions with adults.

2. Exposure to the feared social situation almost invariably provokes anxiety, which may take the form of a situationally bound or situationally predisposed panic attack. *Note*: In children, the anxiety may be expressed by crying, tantrums, freezing, or shrinking from social situations with unfamiliar people.

3. The person recognizes that the fear is excessive or unreasonable. *Note*: In children, this feature may be absent.

4. The feared social or performance situations are avoided or else are endured with intense anxiety or distress.

5. The avoidance, anxious anticipation, or distress in the feared social or performance situation(s) interferes significantly with the person's normal routine, occupational (academic) functioning, or social activities or relationships, or there is marked distress about having the phobia.

6. In individuals under age 18 years, the duration is at least 6 months.

7. The fear or avoidance is not due to the direct physiological effects of a substance (e.g., a drug of abuse, a medication) or a general medical condition and is not better accounted for by another mental disorder (e.g., Panic Disorder With or Without Agoraphobia, Separation Anxiety Disorder, Body Dysmorphic Disorder, a Pervasive Developmental Disorder, or Schizoid Personality Disorder).

8. If a general medical condition or another mental disorder is present, the fear is unrelated to it, e.g., the fear is not of stuttering, trembling in Parkinson's disease, or exhibiting abnormal eating behavior in Anorexia Nervosa or Bulimia Nervosa.

Specify if:

Generalized: if the fears include most social situations (also consider the additional diagnosis of Avoidant Personality Disorder)

Source: Reprinted with permission from American Psychiatric Association, *Diagnostic and Statistical Manual of Mental Disorders* (4th ed., text revision). Washington, DC: Author. Copyright 2000. American Psychiatric Association.

TABLE 10.2   Percentage of Children and Adolescents With Social Anxiety Disorder Who Express at Least Moderate Fear in Common Social Situations

	Children ($n = 74$) (%)	Adolescents ($n = 76$) (%)
ADIS-C/P Situations		
Answering questions in class	68	75
Reading aloud	82	88
Asking a teacher a question	70	87**
Taking a test	39	51
Writing on the chalkboard	50	67*
Working/playing with others in a group	45	62*
Gym class	26	53***
Walking in the hallway	14	44***
Starting or joining a conversation	82	91
Using public bathrooms	18	30
Eating in public	16	34**
Group or team meetings	45	62
Answering or talking on the telephone	34	53*
Musical or athletic performance	82	82
Inviting a friend to get together	42	63**
Speaking to adults	81	83
Speaking to new people	88	90
Attending dances or parties	58	82**
Having your picture taken	27	41
Dating	8	47***

Source: Modified from Beidel, D. C., & Turner, S. M. (2005). *Child Anxiety Disorders.* New York: Routledge. With permission. From Rao, P. A., Beidel, D. C., Turner, S. M., Ammerman, R. T., Crosby, L. E., & Sallee, F. R., *Behaviour Research and Therapy, 45,* 1181–1191, 2007.
$*p < .05.$ $**p < .01.$ $***p < .001.$

disorder (Beidel, 1991). School is a commonly feared social situation (Beidel et al., 1999; Strauss & Last, 1993), and when in that setting, unstructured peer interactions (e.g., having to talk to another child) were most frequently endorsed (Beidel et al., 1999; Rao et al. 2007). Other common anxiety-provoking situations included taking tests, performing in front of others, and reading aloud. Consistent with the data for pre-adolescent children, informal speaking/interaction tasks were the most frequently occurring fear-provoking situations for adolescents with SOC (Hofman et al., 1999; Rao et al., 2007). Therefore, even though public speaking is the most universally feared social situation, interpersonal conversations are the most frequently occurring feared situation. When in a distressing situation, both children and adolescents respond with negative coping behaviors, such as physical complaints, crying, or oppositionality and behavioral avoidance (Beidel, 1991; Essau, Conradt, & Petermann, 1999a).

> Matt was 10 years old. When asked if he knew why he was at the clinic, he looked the interviewer straight in the eye and said, "Dr. Beidel, all I want in the world is to have one friend."

Although a diagnosis of SOC can be assigned without evidence of functional interference in life areas such as academic or social development, the disorder often does result in immediate and long-term consequences, including depression (Perrin & Last, 1993), school impairment, and school refusal (Essau et al., 1999; Last et al., 1991a).

> Nick's IQ test indicated above-average intelligence. However, his grades were Cs, Ds, and Fs, primarily because he would never ask the teacher for help, and he avoided turning in his homework if it involved the need to interact with his teachers.

SOC also results in social isolation and loneliness (Beidel et al., 1999; Essau et al., 1999a).

> Suzanne was 12 years old. As her mother related during the interview, "Suzanne is the kind of child that 1 year later, none of the other children even remember that she was in their class."

Interestingly, cultural differences may mediate the consequences of SOC. Chinese children labeled as shy-inhibited were more likely to be accepted by peers than "average" children and were more likely to be considered by their peers for honorship and leadership positions (Chen, Rubin, & Li, 1995). Furthermore, they were rated by their teachers as the most competent in school. Thus, the consequences of SOC encompass many different areas of life functioning but may vary depending on the cultural context.

Although there are no prospective investigations of the long-term outcome of SOC, a retrospective study using an epidemiological sample reported that about 50% of those with SOC later "recovered" from the disorder (DeWit, Ogborne, Offord, & MacDonald, 1999). The strongest predictor of recovery was a later age of onset of social fears. That is, those whose symptoms occurred after 13 years of age were 8.59 times more likely to recover from the disorder than those who reported the onset prior to the age of 7 (DeWit, Ogborne, Offord, & MacDonald, 1999). Similarly, Davidson (1993) reported that an age of onset prior to age 11 predicted nonrecovery from SOC in adulthood. With respect to other potential long-term consequences, longitudinal studies of shy and behaviorally inhibited children are instructive (Caspi, Elder, & Bem, 1988; Kerr, Lambert, & Bem, 1996). Shy boys marry and become parents later than do nonshy boys, whereas shy girls are less likely to attend college than are nonshy girls. Similarly, as adults, behaviorally inhibited children had a less-positive and less-active social life and were less likely to move away from their family of origin (Gest, 1997). In summary, although some children with SOC may outgrow their disorder, this is most unlikely for those with an early age of onset. Furthermore, in addition to the immediate consequences of SOC, there are data suggestive of possible long-term consequences.

Physical Symptoms

> Jeremy blushed profusely whenever he had to interact with, or perform in front of, others. As he stated in his interview, "The only time I was ever able to be in a school play was when we all wore masks because then no one would see me blush."

Among adults with SOC, physical symptoms associated with the β-adrenergic system (heart palpitations, sweating, trembling, and blushing) are the most commonly experienced (Gorman & Gorman, 1987). Few data are available for socially phobic children and adolescents, but those that do exist indicate that heart palpitations (70.8% of the sample), shaking (66.7%), flushes/chills (62.5%), sweating (54.2%), and nausea (54.2%) are most frequently endorsed (Beidel, Christ, et al., 1991).

Cognitive Symptoms

People with SOC worry that others will perceive their behavior as "dumb" or "stupid," and that they will be embarrassed or humiliated. When examining cognitions in children with SOC, it is necessary to distinguish between cognitive content and cognitive process. With respect to cognitive content, the issue is whether children with SOC have cognitions that differ in type or frequency from children with no disorder. That determination sometimes depends on the particular assessment method. Thus, children with SOC reported significantly greater frequency of negative cognitions than children with no disorder (Alfano et al., 2002) based on the cognitive items on the Social Phobia and Anxiety Inventory for Children (SPAI-C; Beidel et al., 1995). However, when negative cognitions are assessed during actual social interactions (rather than a global paper-and-pencil measure), group differences have not been consistently documented (Alfano, Beidel, & Turner, 2006; Beidel, 1991; Bogels & Zigterman, 2000; Treadwell & Kendall, 1996). For example, children with SOC had fewer total thoughts during a social interaction than normal control children, but they were significantly more likely to report the presence of negative cognitions (Spence, Donovan, & Brechman-Toussaint, 1999). However, the actual average number of negative thoughts reported by children with SOC or children with no disorder was 4.33 and 3.56, respectively. Therefore, although the difference was statistically significant, the clinical significance remains unclear. Similarly, after a role-play task children with SOC reported an average of 1.39 negative and neutral thoughts compared to an average of 1.91 thoughts for children with no disorder (Alfano, Beidel, & Turner, 2006). The presence of negative and neutral thoughts appears to increase among adolescents with SOC. During the same role-play task, adolescents with SOC reported an average of 2.35 thoughts, compared to 1.90 thoughts for adolescents with no disorder. These mean averages were not significantly different.

One hypothesis for the low frequency of reported thoughts and the often-cited lack of significant group differences is that when youth are engaged in these social interactions, they are so overcome by anxiety that they cannot think. Later, they may report worries or anticipatory anxiety when asked to retrospectively recall their thoughts. To summarize, when differences in cognitive content between children with SOC/ anxiety disorders and those with no disorder are reported they tend to occur (a) prior to the onset of a specific task rather than during the task itself or (b) when children use paper-and-pencil inventories rather than when using thought listing or video-mediated recall procedures (see Alfano et al., 2002; Alfano, Beidel, & Turner, 2006).

With respect to cognitive processes, children with SOC expect their performance to be less successful than children with no disorder during social and performance situations (Alfano, Beidel, & Turner, 2006; Spence et al., 1999). After the interaction, youth with SOC evaluate their performance as even worse than their initial expectation (Alfano, Beidel, & Turner, 2006). These expectations appear accurate, however; blinded observers rate their interactions with a same-age peer as less effective than children and adolescents with no disorder (Alfano, Beidel, & Turner, 2006). Furthermore, children, particularly preadolescent children, often confuse emotion with cognition. Using video-mediated recall procedures to assess cognitions during an anxiety-provoking task, preliminary data from our clinic suggest that younger children frequently report emotional feelings when asked about specific thought content. For example, a child is asked, "What were you thinking when you were reading aloud?" The child responds, "I was very nervous." In fact, the ability to think about thinking requires metacognitive skill, a cognitive ability not present in young children (see Alfano et al., 2002). In certain instances, the pattern of "negative thoughts" reported by children with SOC is not thoughts at all, but the presence of negative emotional states. In summary, research on the cognitive aspects of childhood anxiety has produced confusing and divergent findings, and this statement is applicable for the even smaller body of literature on childhood SOC.

In the attempt to modify adult theories of this disorder, some investigators have paid scant attention to basic developmental factors that may inhibit a child's ability to perform complex cognitive functions. In a study of the effects of negative self-imagery among adolescents (Alfano, Beidel, & Turner, 2008), the presence of negative self-imagery (induced among a sample of adolescents without social phobia) did not result in significantly higher levels of self-reported anxiety or observer anxiety when engaged in a social interaction task. Furthermore, even while engaging in this negative self-imagery, their social performance was no different from a control group who did not engage in negative thoughts about their behavior. In summary, although the role of negative cognitions in childhood SOC cannot be discounted completely at this time, further work is needed to establish their presence and their potential role in its psychopathology.

Behavioral Symptoms

> Suzanne sought to minimize her anxiety around others by refusing to make eye contact. As she told the therapist, "The only way that I recognize the other children in my class is by their shoes. I've never looked at their faces, but I associate their voices with their shoes."

Avoidant behaviors are characteristic of children with SOC (Beidel et al., 1999). Furthermore, the effects of this disorder often extend to greater reluctance to engage in typical social activities, such as conversing with others, attending social events, and participating in class, than children without social anxiety (Ferrell, Beidel, & Turner, 2001), a group difference that becomes more pronounced after age 10 (Rao et al., 2007).

A controversy in the literature concerns the presence of social skills deficits in those with SOC. Although clinical lore suggests that at least some children with SOC possess good social skills, empirical data indicate that social skills deficits do exist among this population (Beidel et al., 1999; Rao et al., 2007; Spence et al., 1999). Behavioral raters blind to diagnostic status rated children and adolescents with SOC as displaying significantly poorer social skills and significantly more anxiety in both social interactions and public performance situations when compared to age-matched, nonanxious peers (Beidel et al., 1999; Beidel, Turner, Young, Ammerman, & Sallee, 2007). Coupled with the fact that interpersonal encounters are the most frequently occurring distressful situation, the presence of these deficits indicates that treatment of SOC should include attention to acquiring appropriate social skill as well as decreasing social anxiety and distress.

Social environment awareness is an aspect of social skill often only implicitly addressed in most studies of social skill deficits. For social interactions to be successful, children must be able to recognize cues that the interpersonal partner is interested in a social interaction. Therefore, correctly recognizing facial affect is an important, but often overlooked, social skill. Among socially phobic children and adolescents, two studies suggest that those with SOC are less accurate in recognition of facial affect. Children and adolescents with SOC according to *DSM-IV* were less accurate in the identification of adult facial affect, particularly expressions of happiness, anxiety, sadness, and disgust (Simonian, Beidel, Turner, Berkes, & Long, 2001). Those with SOC also reported more anxiety during the facial affect recognition task. Similarly, a community sample of Italian children identified as highly socially anxious had lower rates of accuracy when asked to identify various facial affects of boys and girls (Battaglia et al., 2004). Both boys and girls were most likely to misidentify anger as disgust. Furthermore, girls' neutral expressions were often misclassified as sadness. Although certainly more studies are necessary, these studies suggest that attention to facial affect must be an important part of social skills training for children with SOC.

Subtypes of Social Anxiety Disorder

Among adults with SOC, about 70% have the generalized subtype, a term used to describe individuals who experience social anxiety across a range of interpersonal situations (Turner, Beidel, & Jacob, 1994). Among samples in the United States, 89% of children (Beidel et al., 1999) and 45.5–92% of adolescents were assigned the generalized subtype (Beidel, Turner, Young, Ammerman, & Sallee, 2007; Hofmann et al., 1999). Among German adolescents (aged 14–17), 33% were assigned the generalized subtype (Wittchen et al., 1999). However, in that study, test anxiety was included as a trait of SOC, a situation inconsistent with the *DSM-IV* (APA, 1994) criteria. A large number of adolescents in that study had only testing fears and therefore were classified as nongeneralized social phobics. This subtyping strategy differs from the other studies, and that may account for the lowered prevalence of that sample for the generalized subtype.

Although among youth the generalized/nongeneralized distinction remains controversial, several studies have examined group differences based on subtype. Overall, the generalized subtype is characterized by more severe symptomatology. Adolescents with the generalized subtype had an earlier overall age of onset, higher rates of comorbid diagnoses (depression, specific phobia, posttraumatic stress disorder), higher overall symptoms, and particularly more severe fear of humiliation (Wittchen et al., 1999). However, a higher rate of comorbid diagnoses among the generalized subtype was not reported in another sample (Hofmann et al., 1999); thus, the controversy remains.

Comorbid and Differential Diagnosis

Similar to the situation for other anxiety disorders, many youth with primary SOC present with comorbid conditions. Among preadolescent children (Beidel et al., 1999), 60% had a comorbid disorder, including generalized anxiety disorder (GAD; 10%), specific phobia (10%), selective mutism (SM; 8%), separation anxiety disorder (6%), obsessive-compulsive disorder (6%), attention deficit/hyperactivity disorder (10%), depression (6%), panic disorder (2%), and adjustment disorder with anxious and depressed mood (2%). Among adolescent clinic samples, 57.1% had an Axis I comorbid diagnosis, the majority of which (74.1%) had GAD (Beidel, Turner, Young, Ammerman, Sallee, & Crosby, 2007). Other diagnoses included specific phobia, obsessive-compulsive disorder, separation anxiety disorder, and SM. Mood disorders were present in 11.1% of the sample. When these samples are compared, preadolescent children have more comorbid disorders and a broader range of associated conditions (Rao et al., 2007). Adolescents have a more restricted range of comorbid disorders (depression, GAD, and substance abuse), a pattern more consistent with the primary comorbid disorders found among adults. Among an epidemiological sample of German adolescents, 41.2% were reported to have a somatoform disorder, 29.4% had a depressive disorder, and 23.5% had a substance abuse disorder (Essau et al., 1999a). Conduct and oppositional behavioral problems, as well as substance abuse or dependence, also exist among some adolescents with SOC (Clark, 1993; DeWit, MacDonald, et al., 1999; Essau et al., 1999a). It is important to note that sometimes the presence of oppositional behaviors does not indicate the presence of a distinct disorder but rather a symptom of severe anxiety and distress. For example, when teachers attempted to force Nick to talk in front of the class or to engage in social interactions with peers, he often would get angry and "storm" out of the classroom. He would seek out his guidance counselor, with whom he had good rapport, and ask her to intercede with his teachers to stop making those demands on him. Thus, comorbidity is common, but there is a need to use a broad perspective to avoid assuming that every behavior necessarily represents a distinct comorbid condition when in fact they may be part of the primary disorder (in this case, SOC).

Neurobiology

With advances in assessment technologies such as positron emission tomography (PET), magnetic resonance imaging (MRI), and functional MRI (fMRI), investigators have begun to examine the neurobiology of SOC, including neurological structure and function and the neuroendocrine systems. However, to date there is no evidence for a clear neurobiological abnormality in adults with this disorder (Bell, Malizia, & Nutt, 1999). With respect to children, there are even fewer studies; the work has been preliminary and exploratory, and neuroendocrine studies have used chemical challenges more typically used when examining those with panic disorder (Argyropoulos, Bell, & Nutt, 2001). Based on what does exist, there do not appear to be any neurological structural abnormalities associated with SOC (Argyropoulos et al., 2001; Potts, Davidson, Krishnan, & Doraiswamy, 1994). Functional abnormalities show that those with panic disorder can be reliably differentiated from those with SOC (Argyropoulos et al., 2001; Coupland, 2001), but it is unclear how often people with SOC can be differentiated from those with other anxiety disorders or normal controls. As suggested (Stein, 1998), what may be necessary to finally determine neurological abnormalities is the use of neuroimaging to study neurobiological functioning while the patient is engaged in "disorder-relevant neuropsychologic tasks" such as processing facial affect. Although it is possible that such data may prove more informative on the potential role of neurobiology in SOC, at this time there is no evidence that neurobiology plays a distinctive role in this disorder.

Sociodemographic Influences

As discussed elsewhere (Beidel, Morris, & Turner, 2004) prior to *DSM-IV* (APA, 1994), the reported prevalence of SOC was about 1% of the general child population (Anderson et al., 1987; Kashani & Orvaschel, 1990), but this figure likely is an underestimate. Prior to *DSM-IV*, children with social fears were diagnosed with social phobia, avoidant disorder of childhood, or overanxious disorder. For example, using *DSM-III-R* (APA, 1987) criteria, 8% of a clinic sample of children with anxiety disorders was diagnosed with social phobia, but when *DSM-IV* criteria were applied, 40% met criteria (Kendall & Warman, 1996). With the *DSM-IV* revisions (APA, 1994), all children with social fears now are assigned a diagnosis of SOC, raising its prevalence to approximately 3% of the general child and adolescent population (Beidel & Turner, 1998). Among German adolescents, prevalence ranges between 1.6% and 4% of the general population (Essau et al., 1999a; Wittchen et al., 1999) and increases with increasing age (Essau et al., 1999a; Kashani & Orvaschel, 1990; Wittchen et al., 1999).

Based on child and adolescent samples, the average age of onset for SOC ranges from 11.3 to 12.7 years (DeWit, Ogborne, et al., 1999; Last et al., 1992; Strauss & Last, 1993), but the disorder is common even in children as young as age 8 (Beidel & Turner, 1988; Schneier, Johnson, Hornig, Liebowitz, & Weissman, 1992). Sex distribution is approximately equal among preadolescent children (Beidel et al., 1999) but becomes increasingly more female among adolescents (5.5% vs. 2.7%, respectively), with respect to overall rate (Essau et al., 1999a; Wittchen et al., 1999) and distribution based on subtype (Wittchen et al., 1999). Both Caucasian and African American children have similar clinical presentations (Beidel et al., 1999) and similar rates of positive treatment outcome, although sample sizes are small (Ferrell, Beidel, & Turner, 2004).

Etiology

Among the etiological pathways to SOC, direct conditioning experiences account for 44–58% of adults with this diagnosis (Öst, 1985; Stemberger, Turner, Beidel, & Calhoun, 1995). When examined by subtype, traumatic conditioning events were reported by 40% and 56% of those with the generalized and specific (nongeneralized) subtypes, respectively, whereas 20% of adults without SOC also reported past events consistent with traumatic conditioning. These data are important for several reasons. First, about 50–60% of adults with SOC cannot recall a specific conditioning event. Second, some individuals experience traumatic social events yet never develop the disorder. Therefore, conditioning experiences occur but are not necessary or sufficient for the onset of SOC.

Social learning also has been hypothesized as an etiological factor in the development of this disorder. Adults with SOC describe childhood family environments in which at least one parent was shy or avoidant (Bruch, Heimberg, Berger, & Collins, 1989). Socially reticent parents also are characteristic of children with social anxiety (Bogels, van Oosten, Muris, & Smulders, 2001) and SM (Brown & Lloyd, 1975). Other family studies, assessing the presence of SOC among relatives of someone with a disorder, often are used as evidence of a genetic or biological predisposition. Those studies are presented in the section on biological etiology, although it should be noted that social learning theory, in addition to genetics, also may account for higher rates of disorders among the relatives of someone with a disorder.

Information transfer has been associated with the onset of SOC in a limited number of cases. Three percent of adults with SOC reported that their fears were acquired through this modality (Öst, 1985). Although limited by the retrospective research design, adults with SOC sometimes describe family communication patterns emphasizing shame, social isolation, and concern about the opinion of others (Bruch & Heimberg, 1994; Bruch et al., 1989). Of course, retrospective data are subject to the veracity of recall that may be affected by passage of time or perceptions of an individual with a disorder.

Parental characteristics such as parental overprotection and parental rejection also have been reported to be associated with SOC in children, adolescents, and young adults (Bogels et al., 2001; Caster, Inderbitzen, & Hope, 1999; Lieb et al., 2000). Among children in Grades 7 though 11, there was a positive relationship between high levels of child social anxiety and perceptions of parents as restricting their children's social interactions (i.e., they were more socially isolating of their children), less socially active themselves, more concerned about others' opinions, and more concerned about the child's social anxiety and poor performance (Caster et al., 1999). However, the relationship of these parenting practices to social distress may not be specific to parents with SOC. Rather, the association between parental rejection and adolescent SOC is significant irrespective of the specific type of parental psychopathology. A limitation of many family investigations is that the data are based on self-report, which may be colored by the presence of a diagnosis.

In one of the few observational studies in the area of family interactions among children with SOC (Hummel & Gross, 2001), parent–child interactions were observed when the parents and children (mean age 11.8 years) worked on solving a jigsaw puzzle. This study is remarkable for assessing father–child interaction, mother–child interaction, and mother–father–child interaction. The results indicated that parents of children with no disorder used significantly more explanations and suggestions and significantly less negative feedback than parents of children with SOC, again suggesting a certain degree of negative parental interaction when the child has SOC. Overall, parents of socially anxious children engaged in significantly fewer verbal exchanges with their children. Interestingly, the analysis of child verbal interactions indicated that socially anxious children used significantly fewer explanations, less positive feedback, and fewer questions when compared to the nonanxious peers. Furthermore, they were significantly more likely to use negative feedback and commands than their nonanxious peers, suggesting that these familial communication patterns are reciprocal among parents and children. However, it is not clear if (a) these behaviors preceded the onset of the disorder and (b) the behaviors are specific to SOC or characteristic of children with any type of disorder.

Biological factors also play a role in the etiology of SOC, although what appears to be inherited is an anxious temperament or disposition, also known as "anxiety proneness," and not a specific disorder. For example, the familial aggregation of agoraphobia, SOC, situational phobia, and specific phobia was consistent with "phobia proneness," but the conclusion was that the genetic contribution was "by no means overwhelming in the etiology of phobias" (Kendler et al., 1992b, p. 279). More recent investigations support the interplay between genetics and environment. Among a sample of 5,440 twin pairs who were part of the Australian Twin Registry, odds ratios for both twins having SOC was calculated for monozygotic (MZ) and dizygotic (DZ) twin pairs (Mosing et al., 2009). Odds ratio for a MZ co-twin having SOC given the presence of SOC in the proband was 11.9. In contrast, an odds ratio of 1.3 was reported as the likelihood of the DZ co-twin having SOC when this disorder was present in the proband. There was no evidence for the influence of shared genetic factors, suggesting that although genetics played a moderate role, the largest proportion of the variance in liability was explained by nonshared environmental factors. In another twin study (Eley et al., 2008), the data indicated that nonshared environment was the largest significant influence on the development of SOC (79%), with smaller and nonsignificant influences of genes (14%) and shared environment (10%). Finally, a twin study that examined low extraversion and high neuroticism as indicies of genetic and environmental risk factors for SOC (Bienvenu, Hettema, Neale, Prescott, & Kendler, 2007) found moderate and negative correlations between extraversion and SOC. In addition, there was a high and positive correlation between neuroticism and SOC. Furthermore, all of the genetic risk factors for SOC were shared with the factors that influenced neuroticism and extraversion, indicating that the genetic factors that account for variation in neuroticism and extraversion account entirely for the genetic liability for SOC. These data suggest that although genetics may play a role in the onset of SOC, it is not the most significant factor. What appears to be inherited is not a specific disorder but temperamental factors, such as neuroticism and extraversion, which may predispose the individual to be more vulnerable to the impact of environmental factors.

Initial family and family history studies suggest that SOC was significantly more prevalent among the first-degree relatives of probands when compared to normal controls (Bogels et al., 2001; Mancini et al., 1996) but not more prevalent than among parents of children with attention deficit/hyperactivity disorder (Last et al., 1991). More recent investigations are conflictual with respect to these familial relationships. For example, whereas 2.1% of offspring (aged 14–24) of parents with no disorder had SOC, the rate increased to 9.6% if their parents also had SOC (Lieb et al., 2000). This rate was significantly higher than the 2.1% for the normal control group. However, significantly higher rates of SOC also existed in the adolescent offspring of parents with other anxiety disorders, depression, or alcohol use disorders. These findings suggest that elevated SOC in adolescent offspring is not specific to parents with SOC but exists across various diagnostic groups.

Behavioral inhibition is another predispositional construct that is related to SOC. Among behaviorally inhibited young children, the rate of SOC (defined here as the presence of either a diagnosis of SOC or avoidant disorder) was 17%, significantly higher than the 5% rate found among uninhibited children (Biederman et al., 2001). Furthermore, as noted in Chapter 3, behavioral inhibition in early childhood may be a precursor of later anxiety disorders, particularly SOC. Childhood behavioral inhibition (social avoidance) was significantly associated with adolescent generalized social anxiety (Schwartz et al., 1999) and adolescent SOC (Hayward, Killen, Kraemer, & Taylor, 1998). No such relationship was found for behavioral inhibition and specific fears, separation anxiety disorder, or performance anxiety (Schwartz et al., 1999). At this time, there are sufficient data to conclude that preschool children who display severe and persistent behavioral inhibition are at elevated risk for the development of SOC and perhaps additional anxiety disorders (Hirshfeld-Becker et al., 2008).

It is likely that no one single factor leads to the development of SOC, and in one of the prospective studies (Hayward et al., 2008), a number of risk factors previously identified as related to the etiology of SOC were examined. Potential factors in the child included negative affect, shyness, separation anxiety disorder, and chronic illness. Parent potential factors included major depression, panic disorder, and agoraphobia. Adolescents were assessed yearly for 4 years. Using recursive partitioning, the risk of having high adolescent social anxiety based on childhood shyness alone was 1.8 times more likely than adolescents who did not have a history of childhood shyness. In contrast, those with the combination of childhood shyness and childhood chronic illness were four times more likely to have high social anxiety as children with neither of these factors. None of the other factors was associated with any heightened risk. Why a history of childhood chronic illness should impart specific risk for adolescent social anxiety is unclear. The authors suggest that parents may behave more cautiously or be overprotective with these children, leading to a general pattern of reinforcing cautious or avoidant behavior. Further, early chronic medical illness along with frequent medical appointments may result in considerable missed opportunities for social interaction and development as well as questions from peers and, in turn, may serve to increase levels of social anxiety. Although this study does not provide the definitive answer to the etiology of SOC, it illustrates a model for approaching what is clearly a multifactorial and complex etiology.

Assessment

As with other disorders discussed throughout this volume, assessment of SOC should be multidimensional and developmentally sensitive (Morris et al., 2004). Assessment instruments and strategies used for adults or older adolescents need to be modified for use with younger children. For example, when designing behavioral assessment paradigms, impromptu speeches, often used to assess social fears in adults, are not appropriate with young children because this is not a situation that they commonly encounter. A developmentally appropriate alternative would be reading aloud in front of a group, something that children do regularly in a school setting. Methods for the assessment of childhood SOC are reviewed next.

Diagnostic Interviews

As recommended in other chapters, the most appropriate semistructured diagnostic interview for the assessment of childhood SOC is the Anxiety Disorders Interview Schedule for DSM-IV: Child and Parent Versions (ADIS-C/P; Silverman & Albano, 1996). The ADIS-C/P is reviewed in Chapter 3 and provides its psychometric properties.

Self-Report

There are two commonly used self-report inventories for children and adolescents with SOC. The Social Anxiety Scale for Children–Revised (SASC-R; La Greca & Stone, 1993) consists of 22 items rated on a

5-point Likert scale (1, not at all; 2, hardly ever; 3, sometimes; 4, most of the time; 5, all of the time). The SASC-R has three subscales: Fear of Negative Evaluation, Social Avoidance and Distress with new or unfamiliar people (SAD-New), and generalized Social Avoidance and Distress (SAD-General). Along with a similar scale for adolescents (SASC-A), the SASC-R has been demonstrated to have good reliability and validity (Morris et al., 2004) for the assessment of social anxiety.

Another self-report inventory, the SPAI-C (Beidel et al., 1995) assesses social anxiety across a range of interpersonal and performance situations using a 3-point Likert scale (1, never or rarely; 2, sometimes; 3, most of the time or always). The scale also assesses the presence of physiological symptoms and negative cognitions that sometimes accompany this disorder. In addition, some of the items assess distress with three different interpersonal partners—adults, boys, or girls that I know, boys or girls that I don't know. The SPAI-C was designed for clinical as well as research purposes. Clinically, the SPAI-C can be useful in treatment planning by assisting in determining the specific situations that can be used to develop graduated exposure programs. The SPAI-C has excellent psychometric properties, including high reliability (Beidel et al., 1995), excellent concurrent validity (Beidel, Turner, & Morris, 1998) as well as good external and discriminant validity (Beidel, Turner, Hamlin, & Morris, 2000). The factor structure of the SPAI-C has been examined by a number of different investigators and across different cultural groups (Aune, Stiles, & Svarva, 2008; Gauer, Picon, Vasconcellos, Turner, & Beidel, 2005; Storch, Masia-Warner, Dent, Roberti, & Fisher, 2004) and appears fairly consistent; variations in the total number of factors derived (usually three or five) are usually explained by the particular characteristics of the sample. The SPAI-C is appropriate for children aged 8–14. Above that age, the adult Social Phobia and Anxiety Inventory (Turner, Beidel, Dancu, & Stanley, 1989) is recommended. Although less thoroughly investigated, the parent version (SPAI-C-PV) has good internal consistency and concurrent validity and a three-factor solution, consistent with the factor structure found in the SPAI-C (Higa, Fernandez, Nakamura, Chorpita, & Daleiden, 2006).

Clinician Ratings

The Liebowitz Social Anxiety Scale for Children and Adolescents (LSAS-CA; Masia, Hofmann, Klein, & Liebowitz, 1999) uses a 4-point Likert rating system and consists of two subscales: social and performance situations. Each item is rated by a trained clinician for fear and avoidance. The scale has good psychometric properties, including good reliability and convergent validity with self-report measures and judgments of the presence or absence of an anxiety disorder (Masia-Warner,

Storch, Pincus, Klein, Heimberg, & Liebowitz, 2001). The scale is sensitive to treatment effects (Masia, Klein, Storch, & Corda, 2001).

Behavioral Assessment

Behavioral assessments for childhood SOC usually involve one or both of the following tasks: role-play with an interpersonal partner or performance in front of a group (reading aloud or giving a short speech). The tasks are usually videotaped and ratings of skill or anxiety are obtained by raters blind to group assignment. Behavioral assessments provide important data on the social skills and anxiety of children with SOC. Although they are powerful assessment tools, they are underutilized, often in favor of easier-to-administer self-report measures.

Self-Monitoring

Like behavioral assessment, self-monitoring (behavioral diaries; Beidel, Neal, et al., 1991) can provide important information on children's daily social functioning. The caveats for self-monitoring presented in the chapter on obsessive-compulsive disorder also are relevant here. Specifically, the form should be easy to complete in terms of the data collected and the time it takes for completion. For children with SOC, for example, a simple form might include a daily distress rating, the number of times that a child found himself or herself in an anxiety-producing event that day, and the child's response to that event (avoidance, physical ailment, etc.).

Treatment

The literature on efficacious treatment for childhood SOC is limited when compared to that for adults with this disorder. An important trend is that both pharmacological and psychosocial trials are moving away from including children with SOC among larger samples of children with various types of anxiety disorders and toward samples composed entirely of children with primary SOC. Furthermore, there are now two comparative trials (psychosocial vs. pharmacological interventions) that provide information on the comparative and combination effects of these interventions. The empirical evidence for both pharmacological and psychosocial interventions for children with SOC is examined next.

Pharmacological Treatment

The majority of published pharmacological trials have evaluated selective serotonin reuptake inhibitors (SSRIs), considered first-line agents because of their high tolerance levels, minimal side effects, and the lack of need for blood level monitoring (Kratochvil et al., 1999; Pine & Grun,

1998; Velosa & Riddle, 2000). SSRIs include fluvoxamine (Luvox®), flu-oxetine (Prozac®), sertraline (Zoloft®), paroxetine (Paxil®), citalopram (Celexa®), and escitalopram (Lexapro®). Initially, minimal side effects such as headaches, nausea, drowsiness, insomnia, jitteriness, and stom-achaches have been reported (Velosa & Riddle, 2000). However, con-cerns exist about the number of children treated with SSRIs who may have increased suicidal ideation when compared to those on placebo. Although to date suicidal ideation has been documented only among children and adolescents with depression, in 2004 the United States Food and Drug Administration (FDA) ordered a "black box" warning be placed on these medications. The warning was expanded in 2007 to include individuals up to 24 years of age. There have been significant declines in the prescription of SSRIs to pediatric patients (Harman et al., 2009; Libby et al., 2009), but the relationship between use of SSRIs and increased suicidality remains controversial (Gibbons et al., 2006; Leckman & King, 2007). It should be noted that children with SOC were not included in the analysis conducted by the FDA (Khalid-Khan, Santibanez, McMicken, & Rynn, 2007). Nonetheless, SSRIs continue to be prescribed for youth with anxiety disorders.

Initial reports of the efficacy of fluoxetine, based on retrospective chart data, indicated that 81% of children with SOC, overanxious dis-order, and separation anxiety disorder exhibited marked improvement (based on clinician ratings) after 6–8 weeks of treatment (Birmaher et al., 1994). In an open prospective trial (Fairbanks et al., 1997), 16 chil-dren (aged 9–18 years) with various anxiety disorders considered non-responsive to psychotherapy were treated with fluoxetine. Outcome was rated by parental and clinician report. Similar to the retrospective report (Birmaher et al., 1994), treatment gains occurred after 6–9 weeks, and lower doses were efficacious for children who had a single anxiety disor-der. Eighty percent of youth with SOC (8 of 10) were clinically improved, similar to the improvement rates for the other diagnostic groups. Even though improved, 62.5% of the entire sample still met criteria for an anxiety disorder at posttreatment, suggesting continued impairment.

In the multicenter Research Units on Pediatric Psychopharmacology (RUPP) Anxiety Trial, 128 children with separation anxiety disorder, SOC, or GAD (aged 6–17 years) were randomly assigned to either 8 weeks of fluvoxamine or placebo accompanied by supportive psychotherapy (RUPP Anxiety Study Group, 2001). Using the Pediatric Anxiety Rating Scale (PARS), fluvoxamine was superior to placebo in reducing anxiety symptoms. In addition, 76% of the fluvoxamine group and 29% of the placebo group showed marked clinical improvement as measured by the Clinical Global Impressions Scale (CGI). Significant between-group dif-ferences were detected by Week 3 and increased through Week 6. At that point, group differences were maintained, but no further improvement occurred. Improvements were maintained at 6-month follow-up (RUPP Anxiety Study Group, 2002).

Examination of potential moderators and mediators of treatment outcome revealed a significant interaction effect for SOC and type of treatment (RUPP Anxiety Study Group, 2003). There were no response rate differences for fluvoxamine in children with a primary or secondary diagnosis of SOC versus children without a diagnosis of SOC (79% vs. 71%, respectively). In contrast, the placebo response rate was 25% for children with any diagnosis of SOC versus 40% for children without this diagnosis; children with SOC were less likely to respond to placebo. Although the number of children with SOC as a primary diagnosis was small, these results suggest that fluvoxamine may be efficacious for SOC, although it is unclear how the presence of other comorbid disorders may affect treatment response. Furthermore, the results indicate that youth with SOC may be less responsive to placebo than children with other anxiety disorders. An important limitation of the RUPP trial was that although this was a double-blind study, treating clinicians (not independent evaluators) rated both clinical outcome and adverse events. Thus, knowledge of side effects may have created bias regarding clinician judgment of outcome. Further, because children with primary SOC were not examined separately, the specific effect of fluvoxamine for this disorder is unknown.

In a randomized, placebo-controlled trial of fluoxetine for 74 children and adolescents (aged 7–17) with GAD, separation anxiety disorder, or SOC (Birmaher et al., 2003), 76% of children with SOC treated with fluoxetine were rated as much or very much improved on the CGI Improvement Scale in comparison to 21% who were placebo responders. Furthermore, 45.5% of youth with SOC treated with fluoxetine achieved a positive functional outcome, defined as a score of 70 or higher on the Children's Global Assessment Scale (scores range from 0 to 100) compared to 10% in the placebo group. Despite these improvements, at least 50% of the total sample remained symptomatic (defined as still having at least three symptoms of anxiety at posttreatment). In effect, the assessment strategies used in pharmacological trials lead to a judgment of improvement but can be misleading inasmuch as many children, although improved, remain symptomatic.

Following four 1-hour sessions of cognitive-behavior therapy (CBT) that did not result in significant improvement, sertraline was administered to youth with SOC (Compton et al., 2001). Treatment outcome included (a) CGI Severity and Improvement ratings assigned by an independent evaluator, (b) scores on the SPAI-C (see assessment section), and (c) ratings of distress when youth participated in two behavioral tasks (an 8-minute speech and a conversation with a confederate). After 8 weeks, 36% of youth were treatment responders, and 29% were partial responders. SPAI-C scores improved significantly from pre- to posttreatment, and posttreatment scores fell in the range reported by children without a diagnosis. Ratings of distress on the behavioral tasks likewise showed significant improvement. Side effects (nausea, headache, trouble sleeping, restlessness) were characterized as mild or moderate, and all were controlled by decreasing the dosage. The results of this trial are promising, although as noted by the authors, the study was limited by the small number of patients (n = 14), the lack of a placebo control group, no randomization, and the possible carryover effects of the brief CBT trial. At the debriefing, several patients attributed their improvement to the combination of the two interventions rather than to either one alone. Despite these limitations, follow-up using a double-blind, placebo-controlled design is worthy of investigation.

In a multicenter, randomized, double-blind, placebo-controlled investigation, 322 youth with SOC were randomized to either paroxetine or placebo (Wagner et al., 2004). After 16 weeks, 77.6% of youth treated with paroxetine (vs. 38.4% treated with placebo) were rated as much improved or very much improved based on the CGI Improvement Scale. Youth treated with paroxetine had a significantly greater reduction on the LSAS-CA than the placebo group. However, only 34.6% of those treated with paroxetine (and 8% in the placebo group) met remission criteria, and these percentages did not differ by age. Thus, although paroxetine was statistically significantly superior to placebo on these measures, the study had two significant limitations. First, all of the outcome measures were based on clinician ratings rather than using multidimensional assessment strategy. In addition, the percentage of children in each group who no longer met diagnostic criteria was not reported. Second, even though youth treated with placebo had poorer outcomes, few children treated with paroxetine met remission criteria, indicating that these children were still suffering from SOC.

A new medication, mirtazapine, is a presynaptic α_2-antagonist that acts by increasing noradrenergic and serotonergic neurotransmission. In an open-label trial of youth with SOC, 56% were classified as treatment responders, and of that group, 17% achieved full remission after the 8-week protocol (Mrakotsky et al., 2008). However, 61% of the participants did not complete the 8-week trial, 22% due to adverse side effects, 28% due to study burden, 6% for insufficient response, and 6% who pursued herbal treatment. Clearly, randomized controlled trials are necessary before drawing any conclusions about the efficacy of this medication, and the high rate of discontinuation is a cause for concern.

A meta-analysis examining CBTs or pharmacological treatments for childhood SOC indicated that SSRIs had large effect sizes (ESs) (ES = 1.30 for reduction in social anxiety and 2.29 for reduction in social impairment; Segool & Carlson, 2008). In contrast, there were moderate-to-large effect sizes for CBT (ES = 0.86 and 1.56, respectively). It should be noted that a strictly behavioral treatment for SOC, Social Effectiveness Therapy for Children (SET-C; Beidel, Turner, & Morris, 2000) was not included in this analysis. These large effect sizes are promising.

In summary, SSRIs are effective for the treatment of childhood anxiety disorders, but the data are limited by the use of a single rating scale to assess improvement. There has been scant attention to the issue of remission, which should be the ultimate goal of treatment. Furthermore, pretreatment attrition is a threat to external validity that is rarely discussed, although the only study to address this factor reported that reluctance toward medication treatment accounted for 44.7% of treatment refusals, a percentage far higher than other reasons for declining participation in a treatment trial (Young et al., 2006). Furthermore, reluctance to take medication was disproportionately more common among ethnic minority families. Another limitation of the SSRI literature is that long-term follow-up data are not available, and in most cases, studies have not assessed outcome in terms of specific social functioning. Of course, some of these same issues pertain to the studies of psychosocial trials as discussed here.

Psychosocial Treatment

The psychosocial treatment literature for youth with SOC is ahead of its pharmacological counterpart. Following initial studies in which children with this disorder were included among a larger group with various anxiety disorders (Barrett, Dadds, et al., 1996; Barrett, 1998; Flannery-Schroeder & Kendall, 2000; Kendall, 1994; Kendall et al., 1997; Manassis et al., 2002; Rapee, 2000; Shortt et al., 2001; Silverman, Kurtines, Ginsburg, Weems, Lumpkin, et al., 1999; Silverman, Kurtines, Ginsburg, Weems, Rabian, et al., 1999), there now are several randomized, controlled studies using samples consisting solely of youth with SOC. Studies using multiple diagnostic groups are reviewed in Chapter 6 and are not repeated here.

The first intervention designed specifically for adolescents with SOC (Albano, Marten, Holt, Heimberg, & Barlow, 1995) was Group Cognitive-Behavioral Treatment for Adolescents (GCBT-A), which consisted of psychoeducation, skill building (such as social skills, problem solving, and assertiveness training), cognitive restructuring, behavioral exposure, and parental involvement. In the initial investigation, five adolescents (aged 13–17) with SOC were treated with GCBT-A using a single-case design. At posttreatment, SOC symptoms had decreased to subclinical levels in 80% of the adolescents. The results of this investigation were promising, and larger, controlled trials followed.

A later comparison of CBGT-A with or without family involvement revealed that both interventions were significantly efficacious (70% did not meet diagnostic criteria at posttreatment) when compared to a wait list, but family involvement did not enhance treatment efficacy (Tracey et al., 1998). Another trial (Hayward, Varady, Albano, Thienemann, Henderson, & Schatzberg, 2000) randomized 35 female adolescents with SOC to CBGT-A (without parental involvement) or a no treatment control group. After treatment, 45% of the CBGT-A group no longer met diagnostic criteria for SOC compared to 4% of the no-treatment group. Despite improvement, residual symptoms remained at posttreatment, and at 1-year follow-up, there were no significant group differences in frequency of diagnosis or self-report of social anxiety severity. It is unclear why these follow-up results were less favorable than for adult populations utilizing a similar treatment protocol (Heimberg et al., 1990) or the initial single-case design study (Albano et al., 1995). However, some of the adolescents in this trial had comorbid depressive symptoms, and this may have attenuated treatment outcome or promoted relapse.

In one of the few attempts to look specifically at whether one form of CBT (Coping Cat; Kendall, 1994) had specific efficacy, outcome for children with primary SOC was compared to children with a primary diagnosis of GAD or primary separation anxiety disorder (Crawley, Beidas, Benjamin, Martin, & Kendall, 2008). The comparison indicated that significantly fewer children with SOC were classified as treatment responders when compared to the other two groups. A further analysis suggested that this lower treatment effect might be the result of comorbid affective disorder among some of the children with SOC. However, the absolute frequency or rate of response for the groups was not presented, thus making interpretation difficult. Therefore, the most parsimonious conclusion is that when treated with interventions designed for several different anxiety disorders, the specific efficacy for SOC remains unknown.

Whereas CBGT includes cognitive interventions as well as some social skills training, the multicomponent behavioral treatment, SET-C consists of 12 weeks of group social skills training, peer-generalization experiences, and individual in vivo exposure (see Beidel, Turner, & Morris, 2000). SET-C does not include a cognitive component because, as noted, currently there is insufficient evidence that negative cognitions play a major role in the clinical presentation of childhood SOC (Alfano et al., 2002), particularly in preadolescent children. In an initial trial (Beidel, Turner, & Morris, 2000), SET-C was compared to an active, nonspecific intervention, Testbusters, which is a behavioral program designed to reduce test anxiety.

At posttreatment, 67% of the SET-C group no longer met criteria for SOC, compared to 5% in Testbusters. Across various outcome measures, children treated with SET-C were less anxious, less avoidant of social situations, more skillful in their social interactions, and more engaged in social discourse based on child and parent report as well as independent evaluator ratings. A 5-year follow-up study indicated that all treatment gains were maintained; 81% of the sample did not meet diagnostic criteria for SOC, and the relapse rate was less than 10% (Beidel, Turner, & Young, 2006).

Other investigators have examined the efficacy of SET-C, sometimes using modified versions of the protocol. In a transcultural treatment study (Olivares, Garcia-Lopez, Beidel, et al., 2002; Olivares, Garcia-Lopez, Turner, et al., 2002), a version of SET-C for adolescents was equally effective as a psychosocial intervention that included distinct elements of traditional cognitive therapy (therapy for adolescents with generalized social phobia; Olivares, Garcia-Lopez, Beidel, et al., 2002) and CBGT-A. All were superior to a wait-list control group in decreasing social anxiety symptoms, improving social skills, and enhancing self-esteem. Although only 15 adolescents were randomized to each group, these results are promising and suggest that SET-C and CBGT-A are effective across cultures. Another version of SET-C was modified for implementation in a school environment (Masia-Warner et al., 2005). The results of a randomized controlled trial revealed that 67% of the participants treated with the modified SET-C protocol no longer met diagnostic criteria at posttreatment compared to 6% of the wait-list participants.

Using a different group CBT program (social skills training, relaxation techniques, social problem solving, positive self-instruction, cognitive challenging, and exposure) children with SOC ages 7 to 14 were randomly assigned to either group CBT with parental involvement (CBT-PI), group CBT with no parental involvement (CBT-PNI), or a wait-list control group (Spence, Donovan, & Brechman-Toussaint, 2000). Parental involvement focused on teaching proper modeling and reinforcement of children's newly acquired social skills and encouragement of participation in outside social activities. Following treatment, 87.5% of the CBT-PI group and 58% of the CBT-PNI group no longer met diagnostic criteria for SOC compared to 7% of the wait-list control. Although both groups had significantly higher outcome rates than the wait-list group, outcome for the two groups was not significantly different. The interventions did not appear to affect peer interactions, parental report of competence with peers, or independent observer ratings of assertiveness during behavioral observation. Treatment effects were maintained at 6- and 12-month follow-up, and both active treatment conditions were associated with improved social skills from pretreatment to 12-month follow-up (based on parent report).

Combination and Comparative Treatments

Clinical trials using comparative and combination treatment designs are emerging. One such trial combined psychoeducation and citalopram for 12 youth (aged 8–17) with generalized SOC (Chavira & Stein, 2002). Over the 12-week trial, children and parents attended eight 15- to 20-minute psychoeducational sessions consisting of basic psychoeducation and instruction in construction of anxiety hierarchies, graduated exposure tasks, basic social skills and cognitive challenges, and relapse prevention. At posttreatment, 83.3% of the sample were judged as improved, 41.7% as much improved, and 41.7% as very much improved. Significant improvement also was found on self-report measures of social anxiety and depression and parent ratings of social skill. However, even though scores were significantly decreased at posttreatment, the children remained somewhat impaired according to the SPAI-C scores (Beidel et al., 1995). These results are promising, but as with other open-label trials using small sample sizes, they require replication with a larger sample and a randomized, placebo-controlled design.

A clinical trial compared sertraline, CBT, their combination, and placebo (2:2:2:1 ratio) among 488 youth ages 7–17 years with GAD, separation anxiety disorder, or SOC (Walkup et al., 2008). Sertraline dosing was administered on a fixed-flexible dose schedule starting at 25 mg/day and titrated up to 200 mg/day by Week 8 depending on treatment response and adverse events. Response rates based on clinician CGI ratings after 12 weeks of treatment were as follows: 54.9% for sertraline, 59.7% for CBT, 80.7% for their combination, and 23.7% for placebo. Thus, while all therapies were superior to placebo, the combination of sertraline and CBT was superior to both monotherapies. Measures of overall functioning (Children's Global Assessment Scale, CGAS) and anxious symptomatology (PARS) produced similar results among the treatment groups. Of note, harm-related and suicidal adverse events were minimal and not reported more frequently among youth taking sertraline. Although follow-up studies will likely compare response rates for specific diagnostic groups, these data are unavailable at this time.

A second completed two-site trial compared fluoxetine, SET-C, and pill placebo for youth (aged 7–17) with SOC (Beidel et al., 2007). Both fluoxetine and SET-C were more efficacious than placebo in reducing distress in social situations and decreasing behavioral avoidance. Both active treatments were also superior in improving overall global functioning. However, youth treated with SET-C were significantly more improved than the fluoxetine groups on each of these measures, and SET-C was the only intervention to significantly improve social skills, decrease anxiety in specific social interactions, and enhance ratings of self-competence.

On the CGI Improvement scale, 79% of the SET-C group were judged as treatment responders (53% no longer had a diagnosis of SOC), compared to 36.4% treatment responders in the fluoxetine group (21% without a diagnosis), and 6.3% treatment responders in the pill placebo group (3.1% without a diagnosis). All treatment gains were maintained 1 year later. An interesting differential timing-of-treatment effect was evident. Whereas fluoxetine appeared to reach its optimal level of treatment efficacy at Week 8, youth in the SET-C group continued to make treatment gains throughout Week 12. An examination of potential moderators and mediators of treatment outcome indicated that loneliness scores and social effectiveness during a role-play task predicted changes in social anxiety and overall functioning at posttreatment (Alfano, Pina, et al., 2009). Furthermore, changes in social anxiety were mediated by child-reported loneliness. In contrast to CBT (Crawley, Beidas, Benjamin, Martin, & Kendall, 2008), neither age nor depressive symptoms moderated treatment outcome.

CASE EXAMPLE: TREATMENT OF SOCIAL ANXIETY DISORDER

Prior to presenting the specifics of Jessica's treatment, there are a few general treatment recommendations to consider. First, as with other disorders, children often need encouragement to participate in the treatment. In the case of SOC, children often realize that because of their fears, they are missing out on "fun" things, and that they do not have friends like other children. So, most children have some motivation to participate in treatment. However, they are going to be asked to do things that create significant distress, and their attempts at facing their fears should be acknowledged and rewarded. Second, the program requires homework, and compliance with assignments will often require parental cooperation. Parents must be willing to take children to places necessary for them to complete their homework and assume responsibility for homework completion, particularly for preadolescent children. Thus, homework assignments must be devised so that compliance is maximized.

Following a comprehensive assessment, Jessica was assigned to SET-C (Beidel, Turner, & Morris, 2000). She participated in both group social skills training and peer generalization sessions as well as individual exposure sessions. In addition to the standard verbal content that is part of the SET-C social skills training, Jessica's individual skill deficits (depicted in Table 10.3) were targeted for remediation during the group sessions. For example, while learning to initiate a conversation, the group leaders attended to the need for Jessica to make proper eye contact while using the appropriate verbal content. Of course, all children need to make eye contact. However, in Jessica's case, she needed constant reminders for several weeks to keep her head

TABLE 10.3   Jessica's Social Skills Deficits

One-word answers
Barely audible voice volume
Flat tone
Minimal eye contact
Tearful in interactions

Source: Reprinted from Beidel, D. C., & Turner, S. M. (2005). *Child Anxiety Disorders*. New York: Routledge. With permission.

TABLE 10.4   Range of Jessica's Fears and Associated Exposure Tasks

Fear	Clinic Exposure Task	Homework Assignment
Reading aloud	Read aloud in front of others	Read aloud to family every night
Speaking to adults	Ask questions of store clerks	Answer the telephone at home
Joining in with a group	Ask children at arcade to join in a video game	Invite two children to "sleep over"
Performing in public	Play her flute in a public setting	Go to Sunday school and participate
Ordering food in a restaurant	Order food in fast food restaurants	Order food for family at restaurants
Writing on the blackboard	Take a test in public using an easel pad	Play drawing game with friends

Source: Reprinted from Beidel, D. C., & Turner, S. M. (2005). *Child Anxiety Disorders*. New York: Routledge. With permission.

up and to look at the other person. Similarly, to increase her voice volume, Jessica was required to repeat her responses until she was able to speak loudly enough to be detected by a decibel meter set at 60 dB. Other children in the group had similar individualized treatment plans that were implemented within the group social skills context.

Table 10.4 depicts the tasks used for Jessica's individual exposure sessions and, if possible, the corresponding homework assignments. Homework is always assigned, and when an appropriate corresponding homework assignment cannot be developed for a particular in vivo task, other homework assignments, such as "say hello to 10 people per day" may be used. Homework assignments are an important part of the generalization process and should never be overlooked. In Jessica's case, small external reinforcers (costume jewelry, stickers) were used to increase compliance with both clinic exposure sessions and homework assignments.

At posttreatment, Jessica no longer met criteria for SOC, and her SPAI-C score was 16.9, below the cutoff usually considered indicative of SOC, although still reflecting some level of social distress. This is not uncommon for intensive, but short-term, interventions such as SET-C. Often, children continue to improve for several months following treatment if they continue to practice the skills they acquired during the treatment program. At 3-year follow-up, Jessica had maintained her treatment gains.

SELECTIVE MUTISM

Charlie is 6 years old. When he was 3 years old, he did not want to go to preschool. His mother forced him to go. At the end of the first week, his teacher told his mother that Charlie had not spoken a word for the entire week. His mother became upset and begged Charlie to talk at school. Charlie refused and since that time has not spoken to anyone except his parents.

Selective mutism (SM) was first described as "aphasia voluntaria" (Kussamaul, 1897, as cited in Dummit et al., 1997). The term was later changed to "elective mutism" (Tramer, 1934) to describe a boy who, despite speaking at home, would not speak at school. In most instances, children with SM will speak freely at home, but less so to their family when they are in public, and hardly at all, if ever, to unfamiliar adults and children. However, it is an error to assume, as some people do, that children with SM are noncommunicative. Such is not the case. Although they do not speak, children with SM will communicate with gestures, nodding, pulling, or pushing (Krysanski, 2003) or even by e-mail.

Clinical Features

The *DSM-IV-TR* (APA, 2000) criteria for SM are depicted in Table 10.5. Rates of speaking to different individuals vary by child, but in general, children with SM are more likely to speak to peers than to teachers or other adults at school (Bergman, Piacentini, & McCracken, 2002; Steinhausen & Juzi, 1996). Children with SM have significantly higher rates of psychopathology, especially social anxiety, when compared to children with no disorder (Andersson & Thomsen, 1998; Elizur & Perednik, 2003; Steinhausen & Juzi, 1996; Yeganeh, Beidel, Turner, Pina, & Silverman, 2003). Among one sample, the course of the disorder

TABLE 10.5   *DSM-IV-TR* Criteria for Selective Mutism

A. Consistent failure to speak in specific social situations (in which there is an expectation for speaking, e.g., at school) despite speaking in other situations.
B. The disturbance interferes with educational or occupational achievement or with social communication.
C. The duration of the disturbance is at least 1 month (not limited to the first month of school).
D. The failure to speak is not due to a lack of knowledge of, or comfort with, the spoken language required in the social situation.
E. The disturbance is not better accounted for by a communication disorder (e.g., stuttering) and does not occur exclusively during the course of a pervasive developmental disorder, schizophrenia, or other psychotic disorder.

Source: Reprinted with permission from American Psychiatric Association, *Diagnostic and Statistical Manual of Mental Disorders* (4th ed., text revision). Washington, DC: Author. Copyright 2000. American Psychiatric Association.

was chronic for 53% of the children, whereas symptoms decreased for 35% of children and fluctuated for the final 8% (Steinhausen & Juzi, 1996). In a review of the SM literature (Freeman, Garcia, Miller, Dow, & Leonard, 2004), it appears that the majority of children with SM may outgrow the disorder, but it is not clear whether some degree of social fears remains. As noted, however, the disorder often persists for several years prior to remission; thus, interventions may be useful in shortening its course.

Comorbid and Differential Diagnosis

Although the full extent of its relationship is not yet clear, most children with SM also meet diagnostic criteria for SOC (Black & Uhde, 1994; Dummit, Klein, Tancer, Asche, & Martin, 1996; Sharp, Sherman & Gross, 2007). Furthermore, children have additional comorbid disorders, including separation anxiety disorder (26%), overanxious disorder (14%), and simple phobia (34%; Dummit et al., 1997). Other samples have reported high comorbidity with developmental disorders or delays, ranging from 18% to 68.5% across various samples (Kristensen, 2000; Steinhausen & Juzi, 1996). Depression appears to be less common, as is hyperactivity (Steinhausen & Juzi, 1996).

One controversial issue with respect to SM is whether children with this disorder have speech, language, and learning disabilities.

One etiological theory of SM is that mutism results from the presence of articulation and expressive language disorders that result in the child's reluctance to speak. However, the actual prevalence of these disorders in children with SM is variable, ranging from 11% to 50% of various samples (Andersson & Thomsen, 1998; Dummit et al., 1997; Kristensen, 2000; Steinhausen & Juzi, 1996). Interestingly, in one study that used a comparison group (Andersson & Thomsen, 1998), 27.2% of children without a psychiatric disorder also had delayed speech development, suggesting that these types of disorders are common among children. In another comparative study, children with SM and comorbid for SOC scored significantly lower on discrimination of speech sounds than those with SOC alone (Manassis et al., 2003). However, there were no differences on five other measures of language, and thus the clinical significance of this one statistically significant finding is unclear. Therefore, although children with SM may have speech and language difficulties, so do a substantial number of children with no psychiatric disorder, and it is not clear if the rate is significantly higher than is found in the general population. At this time, even if the deficits exist, there is little evidence to suggest that they are etiological in nature.

> Sasha is 11 years old. In the clinic waiting room, he talks loudly to his mother and his sister. The minute that he sees the therapist approach, he makes eye contact with the therapist, stops talking, presses his lips together, and folds his arms across his chest.

A controversial area in the SM literature are the clinical reports suggesting that at least a subset of children with SM display oppositional behavior (Beidel & Turner, 1998), and data suggest that children with SM may display elements of oppositionality. For example, in comparison to normal controls, children with SM were rated by their parents as more "stubborn, sullen, or irritable" (Elizur & Perednik, 2003). The actual rates of opposition-defiance/aggressive behavior was 21% in one sample of children with SM (Steinhausen & Juzi, 1996). In a different sample, children with SM plus SOC had significantly higher scores on the Delinquency subscale of the Child Behavior Checklist than children with SOC alone (Yeganeh et al., 2003), although the scores were not in the clinically significant range. In an interesting comparison (Andersson & Thomsen, 1998), 27% of a selectively mute sample was described as aggressive, sulky, and stubborn at school, whereas 67.5% were noted to exhibit these same behaviors when they were at home. However, other investigations (Cunningham, McHolm, & Boyle, 2006; Vecchio & Kearney, 2005) did not find a significantly higher rate of externalizing disorders or externalizing symptoms among children with SM when compared to children with SOC alone or community controls.

These data suggest that oppositional behaviors may be present in at least a subset of children with SM, but it is often subtle. Furthermore, oppositionality may function as an avoidance strategy to deal with social distress rather than as a separate disorder. Like SM itself, oppositional behaviors may be cued by specific environmental factors or internal triggers, such as severe social anxiety. Another important consideration is the observation that oppositional behaviors are more likely to be found among samples of children with SM who are older and clinically referred as opposed to younger, epidemiological samples (Elizur & Perednik, 2003). A number of individuals and self-help groups who promote SM as simply the most severe form of social anxiety or SOC do not want these children to be portrayed as having externalizing disorders such as oppositional defiant disorder. What fails to be understood by these groups, however, is that oppositional behavior is not the same as an oppositional disorder. As noted in the beginning of this chapter, children with SOC may express fear by freezing or having a tantrum. Thus, oppositional behaviors may be a result of fears and not a deliberate attempt simply to defy a parent or other authority figure.

An alternative hypothesis related to our discussion of oppositionality is that SM develops in those with high social anxiety through operant mechanisms. That is, these children learn that they can control their environments by not speaking. Indeed, in our experience, parental behavior clearly functions to maintain the disorder. This is not to say that parents are responsible for the disorder. Yet, in many instances, they reinforce the child by attending to the child's refusal to speak or speaking for the child.

These data suggest that not every child who presents with SM is suffering from the same disorder. Several different types of SM may exist. Using a latent profile analysis of 130 children with SM (Cohan et al., 2008), three groups were identified: an anxious-mildly oppositional group (44.6% of the sample), an anxious-communication-delayed group (43.1% of the sample), and an exclusively anxious group (12.3% of the sample). What is most significant among these data is that the behaviors exhibited by the anxious-mildly oppositional group were just that—mild. They did not rise to the level of clinical significance or meet diagnostic criteria for an externalizing disorder. Thus, as noted for some time (e.g., Beidel & Turner, 1998), the oppositional behavior seen among these children probably reflects their significant degree of anxiety and is not the result of a separate, comorbid disorder. Similarly, the language problems identified in the anxious-communication-delayed group were not sufficiently severe to meet *DSM-IV-TR* (APA, 2000) diagnostic criteria. Furthermore, although the groups could be distinguished by aspects of the clinical syndrome, across all three groups the unifying factor was severe anxious distress.

Sociodemographic Influences

Epidemiological data indicate that although SM is not an extremely rare disorder, it is still uncommon, with worldwide epidemiological rates ranging from 0.18% to 0.76% of the general population (Bergman et al., 2002; Elizur & Perednik, 2003; Kopp & Gillberg, 1997). Among a sample of kindergarten through second graders diagnosed with SM (Bergman et al., 2002), 58% were in kindergarten, 17% were in first grade, and 25% were in second grade. Six months later, children with SM showed significantly decreased anxious symptomatology, even though impairment was still evident when compared to the control group. Children who were female and in kindergarten made the most improvement. In the case of kindergarten, it is the first structured educational experience for many children, and some children (perhaps those with milder fears) may overcome their mutism once the novelty of the situation lessens.

> Becky is 6 years old. Her mother reports that she appeared to have had anxiety at 6 months of age. Even at that age, whenever someone tried to make eye contact with Becky, she would avert her eyes.

SM is a disorder that occurs early, with the reported mean age of onset ranging from 3.4 to 5 years (Dummit et al., 1997; Steinhausen & Juzi, 1996). In cases like Becky, the onset appears insidious, but when it starts abruptly, as was the case with Charlie, the mean age of onset is 6.3 years (Andersson & Thomsen, 1998). Girls are more likely to present with SM than boys (see Dow, Sonies, Scheib, Moss, & Leonard, 1995, for a review), although boys tend to exhibit the pathology at an earlier age (Steinhausen & Juzi, 1996).

In several investigations, children whose families had immigrated to another country had higher rates of SM when compared to overall epidemiological data (Elizur & Perednik, 2003; Steinhausen & Juzi, 1996). The rates among immigrant families remained significantly higher even when the children themselves were born in the adopted country (Elizur & Perednik, 2003). However, the particular reasons for and implications of these findings remain unclear.

Etiology

> Becky is in first grade. During the course of the interview, Becky's mother confided that she understood how Becky felt because she, herself, was selectively mute until she was in third grade.

There are numerous etiological explanations for SM, including unresolved family conflicts, negatively reinforced patterns of learning, SOC among family members, faulty family relationships, or a reaction to traumatic events (Krysanski, 2003). With respect to traumatic events, although 36.4% of one sample reported a history of a patient or family trauma (Andersson & Thomsen, 1998), there are few empirical data suggesting that SM results from traumatic events (Black & Uhde, 1994; Steinhausen & Juzi, 1996). Importantly, when trauma does result in mutism, it is not specific to certain social situations but occurs universally across all settings. It is important to emphasize the nonrelationship between SM and trauma because there have been instances when evaluation of children with SM by mental health workers and school systems has resulted in accusations of parental abuse (Freeman, Garcia, Miller, Dow, & Leonard, 2004). Thus, it cannot be overemphasized that despite an occasional report of SM caused by hospitalization or trauma, data from controlled investigations do not indicate that SM is a reaction to, or result of, trauma.

There are now substantial data that children with SM suffer from significant social anxiety (see reviews by Sharp et al., 2007; Viana, Beidel, & Rabian, 2009). Refusing to speak is an avoidance behavior designed to decrease distress in social situations, in much the same way that refusal to enter high places prevents distress associated with height phobia. An interesting and key question is why some children with SOC continue to speak and others do not. If SM is the result of extreme social distress, then these children should be at the extreme end of the SOC continuum, with the highest scores on measures of social anxiety. Only recently have several investigations directly compared children with SM and SOC and children with SOC but no SM on various measures of psychopathology to test this hypothesis (Manassis et al., 2003; Yeganeh et al., 2003). The results indicated that children with both disorders or SOC only are not significantly different on self-report measures of social anxiety or general anxiety (Manassis et al., 2003; Yeganeh et al., 2003), suggesting that children with SM and SOC did not report higher levels of social distress than children with SOC alone. Mean scores for both groups were in the moderate range. Similarly, children with SM did not differ from children with any anxiety disorder on parental measures of internalizing disorders (Vecchio & Kearney, 2005).

Interestingly, clinician ratings of social distress were significantly higher for children with SM and SOC than children with SOC alone (Yeganeh et al., 2003). However, this may have been due to the fact that children with SM and SOC did not respond to the interviewer's questions; thus, clinicians were not blinded to group assignment. Similarly, children with SM refused to speak during the behavioral assessment of social skill and anxiety. Therefore, children with both disorders were rated as having significantly fewer social skills and significantly higher social distress during both role-play social interactions and reading aloud in front of a group (Yeganeh et al., 2003), probably because of their nonresponse. Interestingly, consistent with their SPAI-C scores, children's self-ratings of distress during these behavioral interactions did not differ between groups; again, mean scores for both groups were in the moderate range. In essence, although clinicians and behavioral raters judged the group with SM and SOC as significantly more impaired, the children themselves did not report heightened distress. In summary, although children with SM exhibit social anxiety, extant self-report data do not indicate that their self-reported level of distress is different from children with SOC alone. Clinician and behavioral observer ratings did differ between the groups, but it is difficult to discount the fact that the children's mutism may have influenced the severity ratings.

Assessment

The specific origin of SM remains unclear; therefore, careful assessment is necessary to rule out other causes for lack of speech. Behaviors not characteristic of SM (e.g., not talking to immediate family, absence of speech in any environment) may indicate the presence of a different disorder (aphasia, autism; Dow et al., 1995). Other atypical language problems could indicate Asperger's disorder or any number of neurological problems or learning disabilities. Speech and language difficulties should be specifically queried, and if parents report abnormalities, a speech and language assessment may be necessary. Although difficult to accomplish in person, speech and language clinics sometimes can glean important information about children's conversational skills by watching videotapes of children with SM engaged in conversation with family. Furthermore, nonverbal tests of receptive language abilities can be administered (see Dow et al., 1995, for a review of this literature).

As noted, children with SM are not necessarily totally noncommunicative, and children will often respond to an interviewer with nods, gestures, and pointing. Using questions that require a simple nod "yes" or "no" and allowing the child to use a visual scale to indicate level of distress allows clinical information to be gathered. It allows the child to communicate directly with the therapist and begins to break the pattern of always having someone else communicate for the child. It also allows the therapist to set expectations for the therapeutic relationship.

Self-Report

There are few self-report measures of SM, and it is probably one of the few conditions for which clarification of the disorder by behavioral observation rather than self-report is easy to achieve. The Selective Mutism Questionnaire (SMQ) is available to assess severity, scope, and functional impairment (Bergman, Keller, Wood, Piacentini, & McCracken, 2001). The SMQ is designed for use in clinical and research settings and has three subscales: school, home/with family, and public (nonschool) items. The scale has good psychometric properties and can discriminate children with SM from children with other anxiety disorders (Bergman, Keller, Piacentini, & Bergman, 2008; Letamendi et al., 2008).

Behavioral Assessment

Because operant factors appear to be an important component of SM, assessment should include observation of parent–child interactions designed to elucidate behaviors that might reinforce mutism. For example, parent and child might be asked to work on a word puzzle and then have a stranger come in and try to engage the child in conversation. Observation of the parent during this interaction may reveal important behaviors that serve to maintain the child's mutism.

Treatment

Psychodynamic, family systems, behavior therapy, and pharmacotherapy have been used to treat SM (Cohan, Chavira, & Stein, 2006). The literature on psychodynamic and family systems therapy is descriptive and retrospective, making it difficult to evaluate treatment outcome (Anstendig, 1998). With respect to family systems approaches discussed, SM no longer is conceptualized as resulting from family pathology (Dow et al., 1995) except that certain family members' behaviors may serve to maintain the disorder. Thus, family therapy no longer is the treatment of choice for SM even though in many cases families still need to be integrally involved in the treatment plan.

Behavior therapy is the most commonly reported intervention and has the strongest empirical database. Furthermore, multimodal behavioral approaches appear more efficacious than a single behavioral intervention (Anstendig, 1998). Pharmacological interventions are more recent, with mixed outcomes reported. A review of pharmacological and behavioral treatments follows.

Pharmacological Treatment

Two trials (one open and one double blind) have examined the use of fluoxetine with children with SM. In an open trial (Dummit et al., 1996), 78% of children (mean age 8.2 years) with SM (also comorbid for either avoidant disorder of childhood or SOC) had decreased anxiety and increased speech at posttreatment. Using a double-blind, placebo-controlled design (Black & Uhde, 1994), SM children (aged 6–12 years) comorbid for either SOC or avoidant disorder were significantly improved over the placebo group according to the parental CGI rating. However, there were no group differences using clinician or teacher ratings. Furthermore, overall treatment effects were viewed as modest, and most fluoxetine patients were still symptomatic at posttreatment. Thus, in contrast to the open clinical trial, this placebo-controlled trial resulted in only moderate support for fluoxetine. Currently, there are no controlled trials of combined pharmacological and behavioral interventions in the literature, but we agree with others who recommend that combination treatments may be appropriate for children with SM who are older or treatment refractory (Freeman et al., 2004).

Psychosocial Interventions

Data on psychological treatments for SM are restricted primarily to case descriptions or single-case designs. Behavioral procedures that have been reported to be successful include positive reinforcement, stimulus fading, shaping, and contingency management (i.e., operant strategies; Krysanski, 2003; Sharkey, Mc Nicholas, Barry, Begley, & Ahern, 2008). In many of these investigations, outcome was based on behavioral data collected through observational strategies; therefore, the data are not comparable either across other psychosocial intervention investigations or to the results of pharmacological trials. In a review of 33 individual case or uncontrolled group investigations (Cunningham, Cataldo, Mallion, & Keyes, 1983), reinforcement procedures were most successful when a minimal level of speech already existed. When there was no baseline speech, stimulus-fading procedures were most effective. Response cost contingencies improved the efficacy of both of these interventions, and longer interventions resulted in more positive treatment outcome. Across follow-up intervals, only one child showed deterioration of speech at the time of the follow-up assessments.

Many of the behavioral procedures just discussed are addressed in other chapters in this book, but a brief explanation of stimulus fading is included here. Stimulus fading is the "transfer of stimulus control through the attenuation of the discriminative stimulus" (Krysanski, 2003, p. 35). In the case of children with SM, this involves the gradual introduction of people into an environment in which the child already speaks. For example, in the clinic setting, the child may be placed in a room with the parent alone, where is it likely that the child may talk. Then, a stranger may be gradually faded into the room using a fear hierarchy such as those discussed in other chapters in this book. Such a hierarchy may include the stranger (a) standing in the doorway to the room and wearing earmuffs, (b) standing in the doorway without earmuffs, (c) standing just inside the room, not wearing earmuffs but also not looking directly at the child (perhaps reading a book), and so on. Therapy would progress up the hierarchy, adding more people until the child is speaking comfortably in a variety of situations. For another example of a treatment hierarchy, see the case example for Charlie in this chapter.

In a randomized controlled trial (Calhoun & Koenig, 1973), eight children with SM were randomly assigned to either a treatment or a control group. Outcome was determined by the number of words spoken in a 30-minute interval. Treatment consisted of teacher and peer contingent reinforcement for verbal behavior by the SM child. At posttreatment (5 weeks later), children in the treatment group had significantly more vocalizations than the control condition, but group differences disappeared at 1-year follow-up.

Using an alternating single-case design (Vecchio & Kearney, 2009), the efficacy of child-focused, exposure-based therapy was compared to parent-focused contingency management. The number of treatment sessions varied from 8 to 32, and outcome was based on a variety of ratings and the number of words spoken at school/in public per day. At posttreatment, eight of the nine children no longer met diagnostic criteria for SM, and the results showed greater efficacy for exposure in comparison to contingency management. However, given the parental behaviors described, it is likely that the combination of these procedures would produce the optimal effect.

Although not yet the subject of a randomized controlled trial, a clinical report described the use of the Internet-based version of CBT (Fung, Manassis, Kenny, & Fiksenbaum, 2002). The format included eight sessions of skills training and six sessions of practice and application; the child recorded short messages on the computer that were replayed by the therapist during the treatment session. Playing back the recording in the presence of the therapist allowed desensitization of social fears. In other words, it allowed the opportunity for others to hear the child speak without the child actually producing speech in front of the audience. Such desensitization procedures often are used by behavior therapists when treating children with SM (although the use of a computer is a novel, and perhaps extremely engaging, variation on this strategy). Pre- and posttreatment ratings of anxiety by the child, parent, and teacher indicated some improvement, as did the SMQ. The results of this case description are interesting and, given the refractory nature of SM, suggest that larger-scale clinical trials are important.

CASE EXAMPLE: TREATMENT OF SELECTIVE MUTISM

Returning to Charlie, the behavioral assessment identified several factors that were important for his treatment plan. First, his mother reinforced his mutism by speaking for him or laughing or smiling when he would not respond. Thus, his mother was instructed in principles of reinforcement and given practice in ignoring Charlie for mute behaviors. Second, with respect to the construction of the exposure hierarchy, consideration included the following factors: (a) Charlie had two friends (David and Sarah) in whose presence he would speak, even though he would not speak to them directly; (b) school and dealing with teachers were the hardest situations for him; (c) Charlie was interested in mechanical toys and electronic equipment. The in vivo exposure program was developed with these factors in mind (see Charlie's exposure hierarchy in Table 10.6).

Because of the presence of oppositional behaviors and the need to teach his mother to reinforce positive attempts at speaking rather than attending to mute behaviors, a formal contingency contract was established between Charlie and his parents (see Table 10.7). Charlie was assigned each item to do at home. He continued to practice that item until it was completed with only minimal anxiety (no more than a rating of 1 on a rating scale of 0–4). The outcome measure selected to assess improvement and monitored daily by his parents was the number of "new" people to whom Charlie spoke each day. For display, data are collapsed by week. Because of his age, his parents were in charge of monitoring his level of subjective units of distress (SUDS) and counting the number of new people to whom he spoke (see Figure 10.1 for an illustration of the outcome data). As depicted, the program was successful, and at Week 14–15, Charlie was speaking to a wide variety of people across various settings.

TABLE 10.6   Charlie's Exposure Hierarchy

Item	SUDS
Whisper aloud to Mom and Dad so that David or Sarah can hear	0
Talk aloud to Mom and Dad so that David or Sarah can hear	1
Whisper directly to David	2
Talk aloud to David	3
Talk aloud to David and Sarah together	3
With Mom and Dad present, say one word to an unfamiliar adult	4
With Mom and Dad present, say one sentence to an unfamiliar adult	5
Say "Hello" to next-door neighbor outside of the presence of Mom and Dad	5
Say "Hello" to teacher at school	6
Say "Hi" to a classmate	6
Using the walkie-talkie, stand in a different room and talk to the teacher and class (so they can hear your voice)	7
Talk to teacher without the walkie-talkie	8

Source: Reprinted from Beidel, D. C., & Turner, S. M. (2005). *Child Anxiety Disorders.* New York: Routledge. With permission.

TABLE 10.7   Charlie's Contract

I will try my best to do each step. If I try, I will get either

- a sticker that smells
- a popcorn snack

If I complete the step, I will get

- a small plastic dinosaur
- 15 minutes of cartoon watching
- an "extra" dessert

After I complete three items, I will get to play miniature golf.
After I complete three more items, I will get a walkie-talkie set.
After I complete three more items, I will get a day at the water park.
After all the items are completed, I will get an erector set of my choice.

Source: Reprinted from Beidel, D. C., & Turner, S. M. (2005). *Child Anxiety Disorders.* New York: Routledge. With permission.

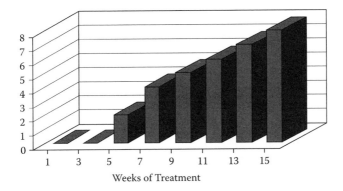

FIGURE 10.1   Number of new people spoken to each week. (Reprinted from Beidel, D. C., & Turner, S. M. (2005). *Child Anxiety Disorders.* New York: Routledge. With permission.)

SUMMARY

SOC is a prevalent and serious disorder with immediate and long-term implications for academic, social, and emotional functioning. The recognition that this disorder can result in serious lifetime impairment has spurred the development of both pharmacological and psychosocial interventions to remediate it. Parents whose children were receiving treatment in a primary care setting indicated favorable attitudes toward psychological treatment for children with social anxiety, whereas attitudes toward pharmacological treatment were "neutral" (Chavira, Stein, Bailey, & Stein, 2003). Despite these favorable attitudes, the literature on efficacious pharmacological and psychosocial treatments specifically for children with SOC is still limited. With respect to medication, two pharmacological trials indicated that improvement on SSRIs appears to be superior to placebo conditions. On the psychosocial side, there is accumulating evidence that behavioral interventions, in the form of exposure, social skills training, and perhaps cognitive restructuring, are efficacious, although in the vast majority of published trials outcome for youth with SOC has not been examined separately. Demonstrating that these pharmacological and psychosocial interventions are efficacious (and superior to placebo) for children with SOC as a distinct diagnostic entity (rather than examining efficacy across diagnostically different groups of children) represents a continuing challenge for outcome researchers. For example, the few data that are available suggest that, in comparison to disorders such as GAD, SOC may be one of the few conditions for which SSRIs actually may be significantly superior to placebo (Birmaher et al., 2003; RUPP Anxiety Study Group, 2002). Similarly, although CBT interventions appear to be effective in reducing general anxiety, they may not be as effective in addressing the specific deficits of children with SOC. Furthermore, even though current treatment outcomes indicate statistically significant improvement at posttreatment, many of these trials noted that clinically significant symptoms remain at posttreatment and follow-up. Therefore, the question that remains is whether additional treatment sessions would produce an even more positive outcome, an alternative treatment strategy is necessary, or initial incomplete improvement results in complete remission over time.

Another area in need of further investigation is the relative contribution of specific treatment components in allowing greater efficiency in the delivery of these services. Currently, we do not know which components are necessary or sufficient, although based on meta-analyses conducted with adult outcome studies, exposure in some form would appear to be the key ingredient. Finally, there has been little attention given to the interplay of developmental considerations and the utility of specific psychosocial treatment components. Most studies included youth between the ages of 7 and 17, with few attempts to address developmental issues that could affect intervention or assessment of treatment outcome. Given the major developmental changes that occur across this age range, future studies may need to focus on restricted age ranges or to examine outcomes separately for different developmental subgroups. Finally, long-term outcome data for psychosocial treatment are beginning to emerge, and additional studies are under way. Pharmacological treatment trials lag behind in this regard, but it is hoped that such data will be forthcoming.

CHAPTER **11**

Obsessive-Compulsive Disorder and Trichotillomania

Anthony is a 16-year-old teen referred for evaluation of compulsive behaviors that include excessive hand washing, the need to enter a certain room in a specific fashion, and the need to touch objects that he feels compelled to carry with him at all times. Although he had previous episodes of compulsive behaviors (showering for 45 minutes at a time), the current compulsions began about 2 years ago when his family moved from Maine to the southeast. At the time of the evaluation, he has intrusive thoughts that harm might come to him or his family. Most of the time, the thoughts are uncontrollable, and repetitive behaviors designed to relieve them bring only temporary relief. The behaviors cause disruption in his schoolwork, family interactions, and peer socialization.

Angela is 9 years old. She has been anxious "her whole life," but her fears have increased in the past year. She has myriad negative thoughts and images, all with the underlying theme of harm or death to herself. Her fears include enclosed places, eating food without washing her hands, tornadoes, house fires, her house sinking into the ground, and her heart stopping. In response to these obsessions, Angela engages in numerous rituals and avoidance behaviors, including reassurance seeking, hand washing (three times per hour with dishwasher detergent), and refusing to eat certain foods or refusing to eat without washing her hands first. As her fears have increased, her grades at school have decreased, and there is increased family tension. Angela has been treated in the past, unsuccessfully, for specific phobias.

OBSESSIVE-COMPULSIVE DISORDER

Anthony and Angela have obsessive-compulsive disorder (OCD), one of the most severe and disabling of the anxiety disorders. Pediatric OCD was identified at the turn of the 20th century (Janet, 1903), but only since the 1990s has there been extensive study of this condition. Children with OCD suffer from intrusive, unwanted thoughts or feelings that create significant distress. To decrease that distress, children, like their adult counterparts, feel compelled to engage in rituals that appear to counteract their concerns and temporarily alleviate their anxiety. Children with OCD are at risk for impairment in their academic, social, and familial functioning (Adams, Waas, March, & Smith, 1994). Particularly challenging for clinicians is that the children often are not able to conceptualize or communicate their exact concerns, often stating that they feel compelled to do something until it "feels right." Furthermore, not all children with OCD feel that their behavior is unusual or dysfunctional, presenting further significant challenges for treatment compliance. The *Diagnostic and Statistical Manual of Mental Disorders, Fourth Edition, Text Revision* (*DSM-IV-TR*; American Psychiatric Association [APA], 2000; see Table 11.1 for the diagnostic criteria) indicates that children need not have insight into their disorder to be given a diagnosis of OCD (Foa & Kozak, 1995; Geller et al., 1998).

> Michael had obsessional thoughts about dirt, germs, and contracting a disease. His mother did not wash his clothes to his satisfaction, so Michael did his own laundry. He washed his clothes approximately 16 hours per day. In fact, he wore out three washing machines in 1 year, forcing his parents to replace each worn-out machine with a new one. Michael did not see this as a problem. He sincerely believed that his parents should just keep replacing the washing machines.

As with other disorders, children can suffer for many years before treatment is initiated (Last & Strauss, 1989b; Thomsen, 1995). Like adults with OCD who often perform their rituals in secret, children also hide their rituals from their parents, sometimes for many months prior to parental awareness (Swedo, Rapoport, Leonard, Lenane, & Cheslow, 1989). Among a large epidemiological sample (Rapoport et al., 2000), 91% of OCD cases were diagnosed based on child report alone. In fact, only 16% of children with OCD had parents who had any awareness of their child's symptoms. These data are important for two reasons. First, it indicates that children can be secretive regarding their symptoms (as is often the case with adults), allowing the disorder to become firmly entrenched. Second, it suggests that epidemiological data based on parental report alone may severely underestimate the prevalence of this disorder.

TABLE 11.1 *DSM-IV-TR* Diagnostic Criteria for Obsessive-Compulsive Disorder

A. Either obsessions or compulsions:

Obsessions are defined as:

1. Recurrent and persistent thoughts, impulses, or images that are experienced, at some time during the disturbance, as intrusive and inappropriate and that cause marked anxiety or distress.
2. The thoughts, impulses, or images are not simply excessive worries about real-life problems.
3. The person attempts to ignore or suppress such thoughts, impulses, or images, or to neutralize them with some other thought or action.
4. The person recognizes that the obsessional thoughts, impulses, or images are a product of his or her own mind (not imposed from without as in thought insertion).

Compulsions are defined as:

1. Repetitive behaviors (e.g., hand washing, ordering, checking) or mental acts (e.g., praying, counting, repeating words silently) that the person feels driven to perform in response to an obsession, or according to rules that must be applied rigidly.
2. The behaviors or mental acts are aimed at preventing or reducing distress or preventing some dreaded event or situation; however, these behaviors or mental acts either are not connected in a realistic way with what they are designed to neutralize or prevent or are clearly excessive.

B. At some point during the course of the disorder, the person has recognized that the obsessions or compulsions are excessive or unreasonable. *Note:* This does not apply to children.

C. The obsessions or compulsions cause marked distress, are time consuming (take more than 1 hour a day), or significantly interfere with the person's normal routine, occupational (or academic) functioning, or usual social activities or relationships.

D. If another Axis I disorder is present, the content of the obsessions or compulsions is not restricted to it.

E. The disturbance is not due to the direct physiological effects of a substance (e.g., a drug of abuse, a medication) or a general medical condition.

Source: Reprinted with permission from American Psychiatric Association, *Diagnostic and Statistical Manual of Mental Disorders* (4th ed., text revision). Washington, DC: Author. Copyright 2000. American Psychiatric Association.

Clinical Features and Course

In general, symptoms of OCD extend along a continuum. Among high school students, for example, 19% reported behaviors consistent with subclinical OCD (Valleni-Basile et al., 1994). *Subclinical* was defined as (a) having obsessive-compulsive (OC) symptoms insufficient for a diagnosis or (b) having symptoms sufficient for a diagnosis but without functional impairment. In fact, whereas 10% of youth endorsed the presence of significant OC symptoms, only 4.1% endorsed significant interference as a result of their symptoms (Thomsen, 1993). Among general outpatient clinic samples, 5% of children under 18 years of age had OC symptoms (Honjo, Hirano, Murase, & Kaneko, 1989), although they did not meet full diagnostic criteria. What differentiates those with OCD from individuals with these subsyndromal conditions are the content, frequency, and severity of the behaviors (Leonard, Goldberger, Rapoport, Cheslow, & Swedo, 1990).

The current diagnostic criteria indicate that individuals with OCD may have either obsessions or compulsions. However, such a clinical presentation (i.e., only obsessions or compulsions) is usually the exception rather than the rule (Flament et al., 1988; Geller et al., 1998; Hanna, 1995; Last & Strauss, 1989b; Riddle, Scahill, et al., 1990). When only one component is present, children, in comparison to adolescents, are more likely to present with compulsions only (Geller et al., 1998; Last & Strauss, 1989b), although obsessions without rituals have been reported as well (Flament et al., 1988). In general, however, a majority of children with OCD report one predominant type of obsession and related compulsion at any given time (Masi et al., 2005). Each component of the clinical presentation of OCD is reviewed next.

Cognitive Symptoms

The hallmark cognitive symptoms of OCD are obsessional thoughts. However, obsessions can be in the form of thoughts, impulses, or images.

> Anthony had intrusive thoughts that something "bad" would happen to himself or his family (primarily become ill or be in an accident) if he did not engage in certain behaviors. Angela had intrusive images of her house sinking into the ground or a hurricane blowing her house away.

With respect to content, the most common obsessions include contamination fears and concerns about illness and disease (Barrett & Healy-Farrell, 2003; Flament et al., 1988; Hanna, 1995; Last & Strauss, 1989b; Riddle, Scahill, et al., 1990; Swedo et al., 1989). Despite their prevalence, primary contamination fears may be associated with less impairment than other types of obsessions and compulsions (Masi et al., 2005). Also common but somewhat less frequently reported by children with OCD are thoughts of aggression (inflicting harm on self or others), symmetry/exactness, religion, sex, and somatization. Specific obsessional thoughts are more common among adolescents than younger children. For example, whereas 74% of adolescents with OCD reported the presence of specific obsessions (Valleni-Basile et al., 1994), among children, the most frequent reason for why they had to perform certain behavioral acts was that they "had no idea" (Swedo et al., 1989). Overall, it remains somewhat unclear whether the lower incidence of specific obsessions among children compared to adolescents with OCD may relate to a greater reliance on parent report among young children (i.e., parents are more likely to observe and thus be aware of compulsive behaviors as opposed to obsessive thoughts) or the fact that younger children simply have a more difficult time identifying and articulating specific obsessions.

Overt Behaviors

Rituals or compulsive behaviors are the overt manifestations of the distress experienced by a child with OCD. In most instances, rituals have some topographical relationship to the child's obsessional thoughts. Thus, washing and cleaning rituals are most often related to fears of contamination, and concern about harm to self or others is usually related to checking behaviors. However, compulsions can also be nonsensical and unrelated to any specific thought, such as the need to use a certain number or words or having to do things in a certain order. Children often explain such compulsions as simply "feeling right."

> Anthony engaged in a variety of behaviors designed to decrease his distress. These included washing his hands, carrying a rabbit's foot with him at all times and constantly checking to make sure it was there, checking that he did not harm himself or others, checking that he did not make a mistake, touching objects until it "feels right," and having to first turn around in a circle before entering a certain room in his home.

It is important to note that ritualistic behaviors alone do not automatically indicate the presence of OCD. For example, children with Crohn's disease and ulcerative colitis endorsed the presence of ritualistic behaviors, but these behaviors appeared secondary to the demands of their illnesses (Burke, Meyer, Kocoshis, Orenstein, Chandrea, & Sauer, et al., 1989). Similarly, children with autism spectrum disorders (ASDs) commonly engage in rituals and stereotyped behaviors. In fact, because ritualized behaviors are a central feature of ASDs, *DSM-IV-TR*

(APA, 2000) specifies that an OCD diagnosis not be given when an ASD is present. Although the diagnostic boundaries between these disorders remain somewhat controversial (Cath, Ran, Smit, van Balkom, & Comijs, 2008; Klin, Pauls, Schultz, & Volkmar, 2005), in general ritualized or stereotyped behaviors performed by children with ASD are often more acceptable (i.e., not distressing) to the child; are not linked to a specific, identifiable obsession; and may be used as a form of self-stimulation.

Also, repetitive behavior among unselected samples of young children actually is common (Evans et al., 1997; Zohar & Felz, 2001). For example, children between the ages of 2 and 4 years (mean age 39 months) exhibited approximately 10 ritualistic behaviors at any one time (e.g., preparing for bedtime by engaging in a certain routine, liking to eat food in a particular way, arranging objects or performing certain behaviors until they seem just right, collecting or storing objects; Zohar & Felz, 2001). However, over 98% of mothers denied worry about the behaviors. Thus, repetitive behaviors are common, at least among young children, and as discussed in Chapter 1, developmental considerations are important when determining behavioral abnormalities. An important distinction in determining whether repetitive behaviors actually are OCD rituals is the motivating factor. Unlike "normal" rituals, compulsions develop at a later age, frequently persist into adulthood, and are incapacitating and distressing and interfere with normal development (King, Ollendick, & Montgomery, 1995).

The most prevalent rituals include checking, hand washing, and cleaning (Barrett & Healy-Farrell, 2003; Flament et al., 1988; Hanna, 1995; Last & Strauss, 1989b; Riddle, Scahill, et al., 1990; Swedo et al., 1989). Other common rituals include repeating, ordering/arranging, touching, counting, and hoarding/saving. Although less frequent than other types of compulsions seen in children with OCD (Masi et al., 2005), hoarding behaviors have been associated with poor insight, magical thinking, ordering and arranging compulsions, and higher levels of anxiety, aggression, somatic complaints, and overall externalizing and internalizing symptoms (Storch et al., 2007).

> Henry was unable to throw away anything that he felt belonged to him—this included magazines, school papers, clothing that no longer fit him, and 2-year-old school lunches. Often when walking down the street, he would feel compelled to pick something up and bring it home. His room was overflowing with items and, because of the rotting food, had a terrible odor. By the time his parents sought treatment for Henry, they had been forced to rent a unit at the local self-storage facility because their house was no longer able to contain Henry's hoarded belongings.

Among Danish children hospitalized for OCD, repeating was the most commonly reported ritual, although those with washing rituals were the most severely affected (Thomsen, 1995). Some children are able to control their ritualistic behaviors temporarily when in public settings. In addition to rituals, some children attempt to control their anxiety through behavioral avoidance (Swedo et al., 1989), and many children exhibit a combination of ritualistic and avoidant behaviors.

> When meeting Saundra, the first thing that one noticed was that she wore a pair of athletic socks on each hand. This was to prevent her hands from contamination. Saundra also refused to go to school because of potential contamination. If she accidentally came into contact with a contaminated object, an elaborate 4-hour bathing ritual ensued.

As illustrated by Anthony, the specific pattern of obsessions and compulsions often changes, with 90–100% of children changing ritualistic behaviors across time (Rettew, Swedo, Leonard, Lenane, & Rapoport, 1992; Swedo et al., 1989). However, it is important to note that even though specific symptoms may change, and the disorder intensity may wax and wane, the disorder itself rarely remits without intervention.

Physical Symptoms

Although rarely discussed, children with OCD can present with the same constellation of symptoms that exist for children with other anxiety disorders. In fact, for some children, persistent physical symptoms of anxiety can lead to obsessions concerning the child's overall health and wellness. Furthermore, children, like adults, may experience panic attacks when faced with a feared object or situation (such as accidentally touching a contaminated object).

> When the intrusive thoughts occur, Anthony reported that his stomach "churns," and he suddenly becomes very warm. When Saundra was confronted by an object that she felt was contaminated, her hands sweated profusely. The reaction was so severe, it appeared that her hands were "raining" perspiration.

Clinical Course

As noted, OCD is a complex and chronic disorder. Long-term outcome studies are somewhat mixed, however, with some suggesting that a majority of children with OCD continue to have considerable symptoms into adulthood, and others indicating high rates of adult remission. For example, one study reported that among adults treated for OCD as children, only 28% had no symptoms at follow-up (Thomsen & Mikkelsen,

1993), whereas 26% had "subclinical" OCD symptoms, 21% had phasic OCD (sometimes meeting diagnostic criteria and sometimes falling to subclinical levels), and 26% had a chronic, disabling course. There was no difference in outcome based on gender. In contrast, a meta-analysis of longitudinal studies indicated that as many as 40% to 59% of cases of pediatric-onset OCD remit by adulthood (Stewart et al., 2004). However, several points should be made with regard to the studies included in this meta-analysis. First, many of these data were not based on reliable and validated diagnostic measures of OCD; thus, the number of subjects who may have had subthreshold OCD is unclear. Also, follow-up intervals in a majority of studies ranged only from 1 to 5 years, suggesting limited ability to assess adult outcomes.

Bloch and colleagues (2009) also examined adult outcomes among 45 children with OCD an average of 9 years after the onset of the disorder, in early adulthood. Primary outcome measures included a structured, clinician-rated, OCD symptom severity scale (Children's Yale-Brown Obsessive Compulsive Scale) and structured diagnostic interviews. Follow-up data revealed that 20 patients (44%) had minimal OCD symptoms (classified as having experienced remission), 14 patients (31%) had mild OCD, 6 patients (13%) had moderate OCD, and 5 patients (11%) had severe OCD. Thus, a significant proportion of children experienced remission by early adulthood. It may be worth noting that children in this study had an average age of OCD onset reported to be somewhat younger than in other studies (Leckman et al., 1994; Leonard et al., 1993).

Sociodemographic Influences

Based on one epidemiological sample, the 1-year incidence rate for OCD among young adolescents was 0.7% (Valleni-Basile et al., 1996). With respect to prevalence, rates range from 1.9% to 4% of the general population (Flament et al., 1988; Geller et al., 1998; Valleni-Basile et al., 1994) and are consistent across samples collected in the United States and internationally. However, rates calculated via the use of symptom inventories are often higher than those based on a diagnostic interview. When diagnoses of OCD are determined by clinical interview rather than self-report, the prevalence rate is much lower, averaging 2.2% of the general population (Geller et al., 1998).

The average age of onset for OCD among children is approximately 10 years but has been reported to range from 5 to 18 years (Flament et al., 1988; Geller et al., 1998; Last & Strauss, 1989b; Leckman et al., 1994; Leonard et al., 1993; Masi et al., 2005; Riddle, Scahill, et al., 1990; Swedo et al., 1989; Thomsen, 1995). We have even seen frank OCD in a 3-year-old child who was the son of a patient in our clinic. Research among children with an onset of OCD prior to age 10 is relatively rare, however.

Unlike adults, children with OCD are predominantly male (3:2 male–female ratio; Geller et al., 1988; Last & Strauss, 1989b; Masi et al., 2005), and boys have an earlier age of onset (Geller et al., 1998). However, gender disparity disappears as samples become older (Swedo et al., 1989; Valleni-Basile et al., 1994). In addition to an earlier age of onset, boys are more likely to have a family member with OCD or Tourette's syndrome (TS; March, Franklin, Leonard, & Foa, 2004). With respect to race or ethnicity, few studies have examined similarities and differences in the clinical presentation of OCD. One study from Australia (Barrett, Healy-Farrell, & March, 2004) indicated that washing and cleaning rituals were the most common among Australian children and adolescents with OCD, as they are in the United States.

Comorbid and Differential Diagnosis

The majority of children with OCD, perhaps as many as 74%, present with comorbid conditions (Flament et al., 1988; Last & Strauss, 1989b; Masi et al., 2005; Swedo et al., 1989). Other anxiety disorders are most common (Flament et al., 1990; Last & Strauss, 1989b; Riddle, Scahill, et al., 1990; Swedo et al., 1989), and sometimes it is difficult to determine the primary condition. As presented in this chapter, Angela had been diagnosed previously with multiple specific phobias. Treatment directed toward her specific fears had been unsuccessful as the elimination of each specific fear was replaced by another concern. Treatment was successful only after her concerns were reconceptualized as an obsession about dying and behavioral interventions targeted that concern. In many instances, the primary disorder is the one that creates the greatest functional impairment, and in most instances, particularly with respect to anxiety disorders, that would be OCD.

The incidence of comorbid depression among children with OCD is more controversial. Some samples found a very low incidence of comorbid depression (Last & Strauss, 1989b; Riddle, Scahill, et al., 1990), whereas others reported high rates of comorbidity (Flament et al., 1988; Masi et al., 2005; Swedo et al., 1989; Valleni-Basile et al., 1994). It should be noted that in the latter study, children were screened initially for the presence of depression (rather than OCD); thus, one would expect rates of depression to be higher than in a sample of those with primary OCD. Therefore, some of the differences in comorbidity rates might be due to different sampling strategies.

Disruptive behavior disorders also exist in children with OCD; again, the reported rates are variable. Whereas Flament et al. (1990) reported that only 8% of their follow-up sample had a lifetime diagnosis of conduct disorder, Geller et al. (1998) reported that 70% of children referred to a specialized OCD clinic had a disruptive disorder, including attention deficit/hyperactivity disorder (ADHD) and oppositional defiant disorder. The specific rate of comorbid ADHD among one population of children with OCD was 30%. In a separate sample of 121 children with primary ADHD (Geller et al., 2002), 55% were diagnosed with comorbid OCD based on diagnostic interview. The age of onset for ADHD (4 years) was earlier than the age of onset of OCD (6.4 years), and ADHD preceded the onset of OCD in 82% of the comorbid cases. There were no differences in ADHD symptomatology between children comorbid for OCD and those with ADHD alone. However, the study did not describe the type of obsessions or compulsions or compare the comorbid group to a group with OCD alone. Thus, it is unclear whether the clinical symptoms of OCD in the comorbid group were consistent with those usually characteristic of OCD. One major difficulty clinicians often face in determining whether a comorbid ADHD diagnosis is appropriate among children with OCD relates to the fact that, at least to some extent, inattention tends to be a resultant symptom of the disorder. That is, although children with OCD are able to pay close attention to or fixate on one particular thought or idea, this often translates to an inability to attend to or focus on other cues or factors within their environment. Thus, firm determinations regarding a comorbid diagnosis of ADHD sometimes require adequate treatment of OCD.

Other disorders comorbid with OCD include tics and TS, although the strength of the relationship depends on the manner in which the sample is recruited or the specific types of OCD symptoms present. Specifically, rates of comorbid TS are low when the sample consists of those with primary OCD (Flament et al., 1990; Last et al., 1989; Riddle, Scahill, et al., 1990; Swedo et al., 1989), whereas rates of OCD or OCD symptoms are high when the sample consists of individuals initially evaluated for TS (e.g., Grad, Pelcovitz, Olson, Matthews, & Grad, 1987). Among children with confirmed OCD, those with primary contamination fears or hoarding behaviors were less likely to have a comorbid tic disorder than children with aggressive, sexual, and religious thoughts or ordering and symmetry compulsions (Masi et al., 2005). Interestingly, in a 2- to 7-year follow-up study of children with OCD (Leonard et al., 1992), 11% of children (all males) initially diagnosed with OCD had developed TS at follow-up. However, other than an earlier age of onset, there were no differences in the clinical presentation of those children who later developed TS versus those who did not. Prior to determining that comorbid OCD exists among children with TS, it is important to carefully examine the behaviors that are termed ritualistic. In many instances, the behaviors of those with TS or tics are characterized by small muscle movements, often appearing nonpurposive. In contrast, the ritualistic behaviors of those with OCD are more complex, voluntary, and directly related to the nature of the obsessions. Hence, it is not clear that the behaviors referred to in some studies meet the usual criteria for compulsions. Trichotillomania (TTM), another repetitive behavior, also has been noted among children with OCD (March et al., 2004), and this disorder is discussed in a separate section of this chapter.

Etiology of OCD

For 33–50% of adults with OCD, onset occurred during childhood (Rasmussen & Eisen, 1990). For some children, symptom onset can be gradual, with no identifiable environmental stressors (Flament et al., 1988), but 55% of children hospitalized for OCD reported that onset occurred in conjunction with a precipitating event, such as death or illness of the parents or a child's impending operation (Thomsen, 1995). Various theories regarding the etiology of OCD are reviewed here.

From a neurobiological perspective, Leonard and Rapoport (1989) hypothesized that OCD resulted from a basal ganglia dysfunction, which in turn resulted in the manifestation of thoughts and behaviors without the usual sensory triggers. Evidence for the hypothesis included an increased incidence of OCD in neurological illnesses of the basal ganglia (TS, postencephalitic Parkinson's disease, and Sydenham's chorea) as well as possible frontal lobe/basal ganglia dysfunction. Of course, the previous caveats regarding the need to examine the form and content of the repetitive behaviors and their relationship to obsessions are important to consider. In fact, many of these early investigations were conducted on adult patients, and their relevance to childhood OCD is unclear.

Several additional lines of evidence suggest a neurobiological basis for OCD (March et al., 2004). First, family studies found that the odds of having OCD are 11 times greater in first-degree relatives of pediatric OCD patients (Hanna, Himle, Curtis, Gillepsie, 2005). Among children with OCD, 17–25% have a parent with OCD, either at the time of the assessment or at some point during their lifetime (Lenane et al., 1990; Riddle, Scahill, et al., 1990; Swedo et al., 1989; Thomsen, 1995). Fathers were almost three times more likely than mothers to be diagnosed with OCD or obsessive-compulsive personality disorder (Lenane et al., 1990). Furthermore, up to 52% of parents may have "subclinical" OCD (Riddle, Hardin, King, Scahill, & Woolston, 1990). Increased degree of familiality of OCD symptoms appears to be correlated with an earlier age of onset in the proband (Pauls, Alsobrook, Goodman, Rasmussen, & Leckman, 1995).

In addition to parental psychopathology, OCD behaviors sometimes exist in siblings of children with OCD. The rate of OCD in siblings is approximately 5% (Pauls et al., 1995; Thomsen, 1995). In addition, a child with OCD can have an impact on sibling emotional status and behavior even when the sibling does not have OCD (Barrett, Rasmussen, & Healy, 2001). Specifically, when a child has OCD, siblings report higher rates of anxiety and depression when compared to a control group. Furthermore, they often accommodate to the child's disorder by providing reassurance and helping with rituals /or avoidance behaviors. Finally, sibling relationships are negatively impacted as a result of a child's OCD. Encouragingly, as children with OCD respond positively to cognitive-behavioral treatment (CBT), the quality of the sibling relationship improves, as does the sibling's level of anxiety and depression (Barrett et al., 2001).

Family studies also have examined the specific relationship between OCD and TS. Several investigations (Pauls et al., 1995; Pauls, Towbin, Leckman, Zahner, & Cohen, 1986) documented that first-degree relatives of individuals with tics or TS have a higher rate of both tic disorders and OCD. Similarly, there is an increased prevalence of tics and TS in relatives of those with OCD (Leonard et al., 1992), although the previous caveats regarding diagnosis remain a consideration. To reiterate, these relationships are highly dependent on specific sample characteristics, and the overt behaviors exhibited by those with TS often differ in form and content from the ritualistic behaviors of the child with OCD.

The second line of evidence for the neurobiological hypothesis is based on neuropsychological and neuroimaging studies that implicate abnormalities in the basal ganglia, the cortex, and the connecting pathways (Rosenberg, MacMillan, & Moore, 2001). Several investigations have documented neurological abnormalities that may be related to learning disabilities. For example, neuropsychological evaluation of one sample suggested that over 80% of children with OCD had results indicative of underlying frontal lobe basal ganglia dysfunction (e.g., Denkla, 1989). Childhood OCD has been conceptualized as a reversible glutamatergically mediated thalamo-cortical-striatal dysfunction (Rosenberg et al., 2001). A full discussion of this issue is beyond the scope of this chapter; refer to the work of Rosenberg et al. (2001) for further information. One aspect of this hypothesis deserves mention here, however. Unlike other theories that would suggest that these morphological characteristics are inflexible (e.g., increased thalamic volumes are fixed characteristics of those with the disorder), Rosenberg et al. (2001) hypothesized that identified structural abnormalities may be malleable to some forms of intervention. For example, thalamic volumes of treatment-naïve children with OCD were significantly larger than healthy controls prior to treatment but decreased significantly in size after 12 weeks of successful treatment with paroxetine and in fact were no longer different in size from controls (Gilbert et al., 2000). However, in a follow-up investigation, there was no significant decrease in thalamic volume when children with OCD were treated with CBT (Rosenberg, Benazon, Gilbert, & Sullivan, 2000). Furthermore, there was no decrease in glutamatergic neural activity in the caudate nucleus following successful treatment with CBT (Benazon, Moore, & Rosenberg, 2003), although decreased activity had been previously reported following successful treatment with selective serotonin reuptake inhibitors (SSRIs) (Rosenberg et al., 2000). These results suggest that pharmacological and behavioral interventions may each work differently but achieve the same effect. An alternative hypothesis is that these morphological changes are side effects of the drug treatment and not causally related to treatment outcome. Furthermore, based on extant data, it appears that changes in anatomical structure and function are not necessary for successful treatment outcome. Finally, even if these neuroanatomical differences exist and can be changed by treatment, it is still necessary to emphasize that any initial group differences found in treatment-naïve children could be a result, rather than a cause, of OCD.

It also bears mentioning that the role of basic neural development is likely to be highly salient in understanding the neurobiological basis of OCD. Results from one study seem to illustrate this point well. Specifically, a symptom-provocation paradigm was used among 18 children with OCD and 18 controls to examine abnormalities in specific neural pathways associated with OCD symptoms (Gilbert et al., 2009). Participants viewed pictures of common obsessions and compulsions (e.g., contamination/washing symptoms) and neutral pictures while undergoing functional magnetic resonance imaging (fMRI) scans. Viewing OCD-related pictures was associated with greater subjective distress in the OCD group as well as reduced activity of the insula and cortico-striatial-thalamic pathways. Research among adults with OCD has found abnormalities in the same brain regions, yet the direction of the abnormality in the child study was reversed. These data suggest neurobiological differences in pediatric versus adult OCD that may be partly mediated by basic neurodevelopmental processes. For example, a steady decrease in gray matter of the frontal lobe is a normal part of development beginning around 10 years of age and continuing into early adulthood (Giedd et al., 1999, 2009; Sowell, Thompson, Tessner, & Toga, 2001). In the study by Gilbert et al. (2009), reductions in gray matter of the dorsolateral prefrontal cortex were found in all youth but were greater in OCD children than controls (despite no differences in age or gender). Although more data are needed, Rosenberg and Keshavan (1998) have suggested that alterations in cortical volumes among children with OCD may result from delayed or inefficient pruning of neurons during early development.

Other studies have identified changes in gray matter volumes in relation to treatment for OCD. Based on fMRI scans, Lazaro et al. (2009) compared 15 youth with OCD and 15 healthy controls. OCD youth were evaluated both before and after 6 months of treatment with fluoxetine (20–60 mg/day) and CBT consisting of psychoeducation and exposure with response prevention. At baseline, patients with OCD showed significantly less gray and white matter volume in the parietal lobes compared to controls. After 6 months of treatment, however, differences between patients with OCD and controls in parietal lobe gray and white matter volumes were no longer statistically significant. Although these findings await replication, data suggest the possible reversibility of structural brain abnormalities with clinical improvement of OCD symptoms.

The third area identified by March et al. (2004) are neurotransmitter and neuroendocrine abnormalities in childhood-onset OCD. Among one sample, boys with OCD were significantly shorter and thinner than a matched group of psychiatric controls and those with no disorder (Hamburger, Swedo, Whitaker, Davies, & Rapoport, 1989). Furthermore, their growth curves, although within the 95% confidence interval, were flatter than for the general male population. These differences suggest perhaps some subtle differences in neuroendocrine functioning, but again, the difference could be a result of the disorder rather than its cause. In a study examining levels of the neurohormone cortisol, Gustafsson, Gustafsson, Ivarsson, and Nelson (2008) compared 23 children and adolescents with OCD to a large group of healthy youth. Youth with OCD displayed higher early-morning cortisol levels compared to controls. Also, cortisol levels in the OCD group diminished in response to a psychological stressor, whereas cortisol levels in the control group increased (as would be expected), suggesting the presence of hypothalamic-pituitary-adrenal (HPA) axis dysfunction in OCD. In another study, a 20% decrease in the pituitary gland (responsible for cortisol secretion) volumes of boys with OCD compared to healthy male control children was found (MacMaster et al., 2006). In contrast, however, Flament, Rapoport, Murphy, Berg, and Lake (1987) reported no neurotramsmitter abnormalities as assessed by platelet serotonin and monoamine oxidase activity, plasma epinephrine, or norepinephrine concentrations. Thus, in most areas, data are only beginning to emerge, and many findings require replication. Overall, it remains unclear which findings may represent etiological factors and which may be features and consequences of OCD.

Pediatric Autoimmune Neuropsychiatric Disorder Associated With Streptococcal Infection

Over the last decade, there has been great interest in and attention to a subset of children who appear to have a sudden onset or acute exacerbation of OCD symptoms that follows a β-hemolytic streptococcal infection. This acute exacerbation is known as pediatric autoimmune neuropsychiatric disorder associated with streptococcal infection (PANDAS; Leonard & Swedo, 2001). Diagnostic criteria for PANDAS include (a) presence of OCD or tics with a prepubertal onset; (b) abrupt onset or episodic course of symptom severity; (c) exacerbations associated with streptococcal infections; and (d) exacerbations associated with neurologic abnormalities, such as hyperactivity or choreiform movements (Swedo et al., 1998). This autoimmune theory of OCD is based on three primary research findings, including evidence of β-hemolytic streptococcal infections associated with OCD symptom exacerbation, high rates of OCD behaviors in children with Sydenham's chorea (which is a variant of rheumatic fever triggered by antistreptococcal antibodies and results in an autoimmune inflammation of the basal ganglia, also a potential site of OCD), and the presence of putative pathogenic antibrain antibodies (see Shulman, 2009, for a review). Collectively, these data form the basis of a biological model for OCD (Swedo et al., 1998), postulating that antineuronal antibodies formed after a strep infection cross-react with tissue in the caudate nucleus and initiate OC symptoms (March et al., 2004).

An autoimmune theory of OCD is beset with numerous challenges, however. First, evidence that specific antineuronal antibodies react against cortical or basal ganglia tissue in children with OCD, which would provide strong indication of autoimmune involvement, is mixed (Dale, Heyman, Giovannoni, & Church, 2005; Gause et al., 2009; Morer et al., 2008). In addition, titer elevations commonly found in cross-sectional studies of children with OCD do not prove recent streptococcal infection. Similar to children with rheumatic fever, some children who have OCD may have persistent immune activation to strep, leading to titer elevations lasting 6 months to a year without clear evidence of preceding streptococcal infection (Murphy et al., 2004). Further, in a prospective, blinded-cohort, multicenter study of 40 matched pairs of OCD and control children, researchers found that the vast majority of children who met PANDAS criteria represented a subgroup with chronic tic disorder or OCD who experienced some strep-related exacerbations, but that strep infections were not the sole or even the most common antecedent of symptom exacerbation (Kurlan, Johnson, Kaplan, & Tourette Syndrome Study Group, 2008). In fact, strep infection accounted for only 5 of the 40 exacerbations that were observed in a group of 40 patients over 2 years. Another major challenge for an autoimmune theory of OCD includes the fact that many pediatric-onset neuropsychiatric disorders, including ADHD and depression, are also related to prior streptococcal infections (Douglas et al., 2008), and it remains unclear whether this may be the result of a nonspecific stress response or secondary to immune system activation. Therefore, even if autoimmune processes do play an etiological role in some cases of pediatric-onset OCD, the validity of PANDAS as a nosological category is unclear at this time.

An Etiological Role for Environmental Factors in OCD?

In addition to genetic and neurobiological factors, some research has suggested that shared environmental factors, including parenting and family environment, may play a role in the etiology of OCD. However, much of this research is fraught with methodological limitations that do not allow for adequate assessment of causality. For example, in a large sample of 7-, 10-, and 12-year-old twins, Hudziak et al. (2004) found that shared environmental influences accounted for 16% of the variance in pediatric OCD symptoms, but beginning only at 12 years of age. However, because this study examined genetic and environmental contributions of OCD symptoms rather than the actual disorder, firm conclusions cannot be drawn. Wilcox et al. (2008) used data drawn from two large genetic studies to examine associations between parenting factors (maternal and paternal overprotection and warmth prior to the age of 16) and a lifetime diagnosis of OCD. Accounting for genetic contributions, results showed that maternal and paternal overprotection were positively associated with OCD in offspring. However, after stratifying the data based on parental OCD status, significant associations were observed only among OCD offspring for whom neither parent was affected with OCD. The fact that overprotection and warmth were not associated with OCD when at least one parent had OCD suggests that these parenting factors may pose additional risk for some but not other (i.e., at genetic high risk) children. It also is important to point out that data were based retrospective reports and only focused on a limited number of environmental/parenting factors. Thus, overall, there is limited evidence for the role of environmental factors in the etiology of OCD, and documented associations may be largely moderated by the presence of other factors, including level of genetic risk.

Behavioral and Cognitive Theories

Behavioral theories of fear acquisition also may account for the etiology of OCD. These models are presented in Chapter 4, which provides extensive discussion. However, the issue of familial transmission also deserves mention when considering behavioral etiologies. Specifically, there is a higher prevalence of OCD among first-degree relatives of a patient with OCD when compared to controls, but the pattern of rituals often is not the same for adults and their offspring (Lenane et al., 1990). Recall that, in children, ritualistic behaviors change across time; therefore, depending on the time of the assessment, parent and child rituals may or may not match. Although some have indicated that lack of concordance with respect to ritualistic behavior argues against a simple modeling hypothesis (Lenane et al., 1990), it also argues against simple biological transmission. In fact, the data still are consistent with modeling strategies if one conceptualizes the modeled behavior as a general pattern of dealing with anxious distress (Henin & Kendall, 1997). Thus, what may be modeled is not a specific ritual but a pattern of behavioral rigidity or behavioral responses to anxious events.

There has been interest in a cognitive theory of the etiology of OCD based on the notion that obsessions represent the extreme end of a continuum of normal, unwanted, intrusive cognitions (Parkinson & Rachman, 1981; Rachman & de Silva, 1978; Salkovskis & Harrison, 1984). Among adult samples, the form and content of "obsessional" thoughts do not differ between adults with OCD and those with no disorder. The difference is in terms of their frequency and the resultant interpretation (e.g., horrific, catastrophic). According to this model, for an intrusive thought to turn into a clinical obsession, the person must first have dysfunctional beliefs that involve blame or responsibility for harm occurring to self or others (Salkovskis, 1989). Rachman (1993) used the term thought-action fusion (TAF) to describe the cognitive process by which thoughts of harm are equated with actually doing harm and those with OCD feel equally responsible for either thinking or acting on these thoughts. There are two specific TAF cognitive biases. First, there is a likelihood bias by which thinking of an aversive event increases the likelihood that it will occur. Second, thoughts concerning immoral behavior are equal to acting immorally.

Although the distortions identified by these cognitive theories (inflated sense of responsibility, overestimates of harm probability and severity, self-doubt and lack of cognitive control, TAF) are sometimes detected in adults with OCD, they have not been demonstrated to be etiological in nature or unique to individuals with OCD. Furthermore, it is not clear how these "dysfunctional beliefs" differ from the primary characteristics of OCD or whether they exist independently of those who would meet clinical criteria for the disorder. In fact, the description of these cognitive factors appears to be nothing more than a description of the cognitive component of OCD. In other words, it has yet to be determined that these "cognitive processes" are independent of the disorder and therefore etiological in nature. Indeed, if they are etiological in nature, they should exist in children with OCD as well.

Along these lines, Barrett and Healy (2003) examined the role of responsibility in pediatric OCD based on experimental manipulation. These researchers manipulated levels of perceived responsibility among 43 youth with OCD during in-home behavioral assessment tasks and examined resultant effects on perceptions of harm, severity of harm, distress, avoidance, and compulsive behaviors. Findings showed that inflated perceptions of responsibility during the behavioral assessment tasks did not result in increases in perceived probability or severity of harm, distress, avoidance, or compulsive behaviors. Results were similar for both children and adolescents with OCD, suggesting, overall, that perceived responsibility is not critical to the presentation of the disorder during childhood.

An additional challenge for cognitive theories includes the fact that to be viable as an etiological theory, it would be necessary to demonstrate that these factors are unique to OCD rather than a reflection of general psychopathology. To examine this issue, children with OCD, those with other anxiety disorders, and those with no disorder were compared on the following variables: veracity of an obsessional statement (e.g., "If I think that I have germs on my hands and don't wash over and over, I will get really sick"), severity of the negative outcome, probability that the negative event would occur, and responsibility for the negative outcome. Self-doubt and cognitive control also were assessed (Barrett & Healy, 2003). Although there were significant differences on all six variables when those with OCD were compared to normal controls, only the variables of veracity and cognitive control differentiated children with OCD from those with other anxiety disorders. These results present serious difficulties for cognitive etiological theories. Specifically, it suggests that many of the hypothesized cognitive elements may not be unique to children with OCD but exist across children with various types of anxiety disorders. In summary, these data also do not support a cognitive etiological model for OCD. Rather, they suggest that these "cognitive factors" are merely elements of the disorder (i.e., epiphenomenon), not separate cognitive processes that lead to its development.

Impact of OCD on Family Functioning

In addition to family influences on etiology, family interaction patterns are affected when a child has OCD. In laboratory settings, parents exhibit higher levels of criticism or overinvolvement than parents of
children without a disorder (Hibbs et al., 1991). Similarly, adolescents
with OCD describe their family environment as significantly less warm,
less emotionally supportive, and more emotionally distant than children
with no disorder (Valleni-Basile et al., 1995). Note, however, that it has
not been demonstrated that these behaviors exist prior to the onset of
OCD. Hence, they could be reactions to OCD rather than etiological
factors. Only one study has demonstrated that some family characteristics are specific to children with OCD (Barrett, Shortt, & Healy, 2002).
In comparison to parents of children with another anxiety disorder, an
externalizing disorder, or no disorder, mothers and fathers of children
with OCD were less confident in their child's ability to solve problems,
less rewarding of independence, and less likely to use positive problem-
solving strategies with their children. Similarly, children with OCD
showed significantly less-positive problem solving, had less confidence
in their ability to solve problems, and were less warm in their social
interactions than the other groups. However, because these children
already had a disorder, these data do not address etiology. Nevertheless,
the study highlights concerns about "lumping" all children with anxiety
disorders into a single group for the purposes of studying psychopathology or treatment outcome. Children with various anxiety disorders
have different symptoms and associated clinical parameters, and treatment outcome must be examined separately for the various diagnostic
groups.

Storch et al. (2007) examined the relations among family accommodation, symptom severity, functional impairment, and child behaviors among a clinic sample of 57 youth ages 7 to 17 years with OCD.
Overall, parents reported high rates of accommodation of their child's
symptoms, most commonly in the form of providing reassurance about
obsessions or fears or by participating in rituals. Parents also commonly reported that their children became upset or angry when accommodation was withheld; 16% indicated that these emotional displays
occurred nearly every day. Importantly, family accommodation also
was found to mediate the relationship between OCD symptom severity
and parent-rated functional impairment, indicating that accommodation accounts for a portion of this relationship. Thus, an important
issue for clinicians is the role of the family in the perpetuation of rituals. Parents (perhaps as many as 70%) become intimately involved in

ritualistic behavior, particularly the form of checking known as reassurance seeking (Allsopp & Verduyn, 1990; Geller et al., 1998). A smaller percentage of parents respond to rituals in a hostile fashion (Allsopp & Verduyn, 1990).

> Saundra's parents were extremely conflicted regarding her compulsions. They complained loudly and were verbally abusive toward her when she would engage in cleaning behaviors—telling her that if she only read the Bible more she could just "stop this nonsense." On the other hand, they assisted in her rituals, buying the "special soap" needed for washing and showering and photocopying material sent home from school so Saundra would not have to touch "contaminated" school papers.

Assessment

In clinical settings, assessment strategies should be thorough but applied in a clinically sensitive and developmentally appropriate manner. Therefore, depending on the child's age, diagnostic and clinical interviews might be conducted privately with adolescents but in the presence of parents for younger children. Self-monitoring strategies also should be tailored to age and developmental status. Various strategies for the assessment of OCD in children and adolescents are reviewed here.

Diagnostic Interviews

As noted in other chapters, assessment should always begin with a thorough diagnostic interview, such as the Anxiety Disorders Interview Schedule for DSM-IV: Child and Parent Versions (Silverman & Albano, 1996). A description of this interview as well as its psychometric properties are presented in Chapter 3.

Self-Report

The original Leyton Obsessional Inventory–Child Version was a 44-item assessment strategy that used a card-sort method to allow children to indicate the presence or absence of obsessions and compulsions (Berg, Rapoport, & Flament, 1986). A shorter, 20-item, paper-and-pencil version now is commonly used. Obsessions and compulsions are rated using a 4-point Likert scale. Items load onto four factors: general-obsessive, dirt-contamination, numbers-luck, and school (Berg, Whitaker, Davies, Flament, & Rapoport, 1988). The scale has good psychometric properties (Berg et al., 1988; Roussos et al., 2003). A shorter 11-item screening version with three subscales (compulsions, obsessions/completeness, and cleanliness) has been developed. It appears to have good reliability and the ability to discriminate those with OCD from normal controls and those with depression (Bamber, Tamplin, Park, Kyte, & Goodyer, 2002).

Compared to symptom domains and severity, assessment of specific functional impairments associated with pediatric OCD has received less attention. The Child Obsessive Compulsive Impact Scale–Revised (COIS-R; Piacentini, Peris, Bergman, Chang, & Jaffer, 2007) was developed for this purpose. The original pool of COIS items was generated from a series of focus groups and individual interviews with children with OCD and their parents, clinic chart reviews, and the existing clinical and empirical literature. Parallel parent and child report versions of the measure are completed using a 4-point Likert scale. The parent version yields four distinct areas of impairment (daily living skills, family, social, and school), while the youth version yields three areas (school, social, and activities). Both measures appear to have good internal consistency, concurrent validity, and test-retest reliability. The measure also has been shown to be sensitive to the effects of both medication (Geller et al., 2001; Liebowitz et al., 2002) and CBT (Martin & Thienemann, 2005; Valderhaug, Larsson, Gotestam, & Piacentini, 2007) in alleviating impairment associated with OCD.

Clinician Ratings

The Children's Yale-Brown Obsessive-Compulsive Scale (CY-BOCS; Scahill et al., 1997) is a clinician-administered interview assessing a broad range of obsessions and compulsions as well as severity, interference, and ability to control or resist obsessions and compulsions. Scores range from 0 to 40; scores of 20 or higher indicate at least moderate severity, whereas scores of 10 or below indicate subclinical OCD. Few data on the reliability and validity of the CY-BOCS are available, although clinically it is a useful interview for case conceptualization and treatment planning, and it has become a mainstay of pharmacological research trials.

The National Institute of Mental Health (NIMH) Global Scale is a 15-point, one-item clinician scale that rates OCD severity and impairment. Scores of 7 or greater are indicative of clinically significant OCD (Insel et al., 1983). The scale often is used in pharmacological studies of OCD treatment.

Behavioral Assessment

Behavioral avoidance tests (BATs) are commonly used, at least among behavior therapists, to provide an objective assessment of OCD symptoms. BATs have moderate convergent validity with self-report measures of OCD and are sensitive to the effects of treatment (Barrett,

Healy, & March, 2003). Most BATs ask the child to approach and, it is hoped, to touch the "feared object" (e.g., contaminated object) and then measure the distance that the child is able to cover. In addition, rituals performed during the BAT are assessed (see Barrett, Healy, et al., 2003, for a detailed description of how to conduct a BAT for OCD). BATs provide a much more objective assessment of psychopathology than self-report or clinician ratings. Even so, demand characteristics play a role as children may feel pressure to do more than they normally would because of the assessment environment. An additional limitation is that BATs are most appropriate for obsessions and rituals involving contamination (washing) and, in some cases, future events (checking). It is more difficult to construct BATs for covert behaviors (such as cognitive rituals).

Self-Monitoring

Self-monitoring can provide information on the daily frequency of obsessions and compulsions as well as daily information on emotional distress. A key issue for self-monitoring, particularly with children, is increasing compliance with the monitoring task. First, it is important that parents do not attempt to force compliance. Given that familial relationships already are under some strain as a result of the child's disorder, creating more conflict by asking parents to enforce self-monitoring contingencies often is ill-advised. Instead, clinicians can increase compliance by constructing self-monitoring forms that are simple to use and require no more than 5 minutes a day to complete. Thus, asking for a daily rating of distress as well as for an estimate of the time spent carrying out obsessions and compulsions will provide needed information by which to gauge treatment success while not being overly burdensome to the child. In addition, small, developmentally appropriate reinforcers will increase compliance with self-monitoring procedures (Beidel, Neal, et al., 1991).

Treatment

Like assessment, treatment for OCD must be developmentally sensitive. Of course, medication dosages are different depending on the age and weight of the child. Similarly, psychosocial interventions also must be adapted to the child's age (March et al., 2004). Thus, the goal of treatment is always the same, even if the manner in which that goal is achieved differs. By addressing developmental issues, children with OCD as young as age 5 can be treated with behavioral interventions (March et al., 2004).

Pharmacological Treatments

Several pharmacological agents are used to treat childhood OCD. Initial investigations focused on clomipramine (Anafranil; DeVeaugh-Geiss, et al., 1992; Flament et al., 1985; Leonard et al., 1989). Flament et al. (1985) reported that treatment with clomipramine was superior to placebo, with 75% having moderate-to-marked improvement. Treatment outcome was positively correlated with high concentrations of platelet serotonin ($r = .73$) at pretreatment and a greater decrease in serotonin concentration during treatment ($r = .78$; Flament et al., 1987). However, 16% of those treated with clomipramine were unchanged, and even those judged as responders still had significant residual symptoms. In a double-blind crossover design (Leonard et al., 1989), clomipramine was superior to desipramine for 48 children and adolescents with OCD. In a multicenter trial (DeVeaugh-Geiss et al., 1992), 60% of the clomipramine group were rated as much or very much improved. Mean reduction in CY-BOCS score was 37% for the clomipramine group and 8% for the placebo group. However, at posttreatment, the CY-BOCS score for the clomipramine group was 17.1, still indicative of mild-to-moderate OCD. In summary, although clomipramine appears effective in reducing (but not eliminating) OCD symptoms in children and adolescents, its side effects are more severe than those of the SSRIs (as reviewed next) (see DeVeaugh-Geiss et al., 1992; Flament et al., 1985; Leonard et al., 1989). As a result, despite its apparent efficacy, clomipramine is not considered a first-line pharmacological treatment for children with OCD.

In contrast, the SSRIs (fluoxetine, fluvoxamine, sertraline) are considered the pharmacological treatment of choice. In an open trial (Riddle, Hardin, et al., 1990), 50% of the children were fluoxetine responders. Subsequent double-blind, placebo-controlled trials (Geller et al., 2001; Liebowitz et al., 2002) have yielded similar outcomes. Geller et al. (2001) reported that children treated with fluoxetine were significantly improved when compared to those on placebo (based on their final CY-BOCS score), a difference first evident at Week 7. At posttreatment, CY-BOCS had decreased 9.5 points with fluoxetine (in comparison to 5.2 points with placebo), but children still reported mild-to-moderate OCD. Improvement rates were 55% for fluoxetine and 18.8% for placebo. Liebowitz et al. (2002) reported a similar outcome. After 16 weeks of treatment, 57% were responders to fluoxetine treatment compared to 27% placebo responders. Group differences were not detected until after 8 weeks of active treatment, suggesting that the effect of the drug might take longer than 8 weeks to be apparent. Consistent with Geller et al. (2001), fluoxetine resulted in a 10-point decrement in CY-BOCS scores at posttreatment.

In a large multicenter randomized controlled trial (March, Biederman, et al., 1998), 156 children and adolescents were treated with 12 weeks of either sertraline or placebo. The sertraline group had significantly greater reductions on the CY-BOCS and the NIMH OC scale. Between-group differences were evident at Week 3 and were maintained throughout the trial. At posttreatment, 42% of sertraline patients and 26% of placebo patients were rated as much or very much improved. Unfortunately, the data were presented only as change scores. The actual scores for the various instruments were not presented. Thus, it is impossible to determine what level of OCD severity remained at the end of the 12-week treatment trial.

The same conclusion can be drawn for a randomized, multicenter trial of paroxetine (Geller et al., 2004). After 10 weeks of treatment, CY-BOCS scores had decreased by 8.78 points for the paroxetine group compared to 5.34 points for the placebo group, a difference that was statistically significant. There also was a statistically significant group difference in the number of children who were judged to be treatment responders based on a greater than 25% reduction in CY-BOCS scores (64.9% for paroxetine vs. 41.8% for placebo). However, actual posttreatment scores on CY-BOCS were not provided; therefore, it is not possible to determine the children's final clinical status. Finally, responders based on Clinical Global Impressions (CGI) improvement scores were not significantly different by group (46.9% vs. 33.3%). This last percentage suggests that fewer than 50% responded to paroxetine, whereas one third responded to placebo.

In a naturalistic study of 94 youth with primary OCD (ages 7–18 years) referred to a pediatric psychopharmacology clinic, Masi and colleagues (2005) examined treatment response rates associated with different classes of psychotropic medications, including SSRIs, mood stabilizers, and antipsychotics. Prescription practices were based in part on treatment responsiveness or refractoriness or the presence of comorbid diagnoses. Approximately one half of patients did not respond satisfactorily to SSRI monotherapy and required adjunctive treatment. Overall, 67% of the 94 patients were judged to be treatment responders based on a CGI Improvement score of 1 or 2. Although results from this investigation are informative for clinicians, it is important to note that youth in this study were specifically referred to a pharmacological treatment center and thus may represent a more impaired subsample of children with OCD.

Until recent years, SSRIs were presumed to have a good safety profile. Few changes in blood pressure, pulse, weight, or electrocardiogram (EKG) were reported (e.g., Liebowitz et al., 2002; Riddle, Hardin, et al., 1990). Among children treated with fluoxetine or sertraline, the more common side effects when compared to placebo include behavioral agitation, insomnia, nausea, heart palpitations, weight loss, drowsiness, tremors, nightmares, and muscle aches (Liebowitz et al., 2002; March et al., 1998; Riddle, Hardin, et al., 1990). Currently, many of the SSRIs carry a "black box warning" because of an association with suicidal ideation (see Chapter 6).

These findings highlight important issues regarding pharmacological treatment for OCD. First, beneficial effects begin at 2–3 weeks and usually reach their peak by 3 months (March, Biederman, et al., 2004). Unlike older antidepressants, SSRIs do not have the potential for cardiac toxicity. A meta-analysis (Abramowitz, Whiteside, & Deacon, 2005) indicated that children treated with SSRIs reported reduced symptoms but in many instances still had obsessions and compulsions severe enough to meet entrance criteria for most clinical trials, a finding also noted by March et al. (2004). In addition, about 33% of patients failed to benefit from single pharmacotherapy. We agree with the conclusion of the meta-analysis that augmenting drug treatment with behavior therapy is a better option than augmenting with a second pharmacological treatment. Actually, we would go one step further, agreeing with King et al. (1998) that behavior therapy should be the first line of treatment and medications used only in specific instances.

Psychosocial Treatment

It is generally agreed that psychoanalytic treatment is not effective for the treatment of OCD (Esman, 1989), whereas behavior therapy (exposure and response prevention, ERP) is the treatment of choice for children and adolescents (Expert Consensus Guidelines; March et al., 1997). Initial uncontrolled treatment trials of behavior therapy using small samples (March, Mulle, & Herbel, 1994; Franklin, Kozak, Cashman, Rheingold, & Foa, 1998) were promising, with 50–72% reduction in CY-BOCS scores at posttreatment and follow-up. Using a larger sample of children ($n = 42$; mean age 11.8 years), in vivo and imaginal exposure, response prevention, and cognitive restructuring (March & Mulle, 1998) resulted in a treatment response rate of 79% (Piacentini, Bergman, Jacobs, McCracken, & Kretchman, 2002). Fifty-two percent of the children were on psychotropic medication during their participation in this trial. There were no significant differences in response rate between the children who were treated with CBT only (85%) and those who also received medication (73%).

A group adaptation of the March and Mulle's (1998) CBT program implemented with 18 adolescents with OCD (Thienemann, Martin, Cregger, Thompson, & Dyer-Friedman, 2001) resulted in statistically significant changes on the CY-BOCS and on a global rating of OCD severity. However, the degree of improvement was substantially less than that reported for other CBT trials. Specifically, only 50% of patients achieved a 25% or greater improvement in symptoms. Although the 6.2 decrement in the average CY-BOCS score was statistically significant, the posttreatment mean score of 18.6 would still qualify a child for entry into clinical trials. It may be that group treatment dilutes the amount of time required for efficacious exposure treatment, thereby attenuating treatment outcome.

Family members may play a role in treatment outcome, depending on the type of family involvement (Waters & Barrett, 2000). For example, parents who participate in their child's rituals need instruction to cease any assistance and to provide encouragement for compliance with the treatment program. Parents who are hostile toward their children require education regarding the nature of OCD, what the child should be expected to be able to do and not do at various treatment phases, and how the parents can be active, positive participants in the treatment process. The need to formally address these issues has led some investigators to the development of behavioral treatments that include a family component, although given the diversity of family responses to a child's OCD, it is unclear that one intervention would work for all families. In an initial open trial (Waters, Barrett, & March, 2001), a parent skills training component was added to psychoeducation, anxiety management and cognitive training, and graduated exposure with response prevention. The parent skills training consisted of educating parents about OCD and its treatment, reducing parental involvement in the child's symptoms, encouraging family support of home-based ERP, and increasing family problem-solving skills. Children reported significant improvement in OCD symptoms, and there was significant decrease in family accommodation behaviors. However, contrary to expectations, there was no change in parental functioning as a result of the intervention.

A follow-up controlled trial compared individual cognitive-behavioral family treatment (CBFT), group CBFT, and a 6-week wait-list control (Barrett et al., 2004). Again, significant improvement in OCD symptoms was evident for both active treatment conditions, and treatment gains were maintained at 6-month follow-up. There was a 65% reduction in CY-BOCS scores for those treated individually, and 61% reduction for those treated in a group. At follow-up, 65% of those in the individual treatment and 87% of those in the group treatment did not meet criteria for a diagnosis. Sibling level of accommodation and depression also decreased across both treated groups. However, as with the pilot data, there was no significant change in parental functioning or parental distress, and families scored in the unhealthy range of functioning at both pre- and posttreatment. Thus, the intervention was efficacious for childhood OCD, and in this case, group and individual interventions were equally efficacious. However, the family component did not affect family dysfunction; thus, its necessity as a treatment component for childhood OCD remains unclear, although it may be important for preventing relapse. In a 1-year follow-up study, Barrett, Farrell, Dadds, and Boulter (2005) examined the durability of individual and group treatments among 48 youth (90% of the original sample). Treatment gains were largely maintained, with 70% of patients treated with CBFT and 84% treated with group CBFT free of an OCD diagnosis at follow-up, respectively. This between-group difference was not statistically significant.

To examine whether intensive treatment might produce better outcomes than standard once-a-week sessions for pediatric OCD, Storch et al. (2007) compared the efficacy of 14 CBT sessions delivered daily over a 3-week period to weekly sessions held over 14 weeks. Participants were 40 children and adolescents with primary OCD (ages 7–17 years) randomized to one of the two treatment conditions. Both treatments were based on a manualized protocol developed by Lewin et al. (2005) that includes family psychoeducation, ERP, cognitive coping strategies, and parental coaching for at-home exposures. All treatment sessions were 90 minutes long. At posttreatment, 75% of the intensive treatment group and 50% of the weekly treatment group reached remission status (based on CY-BOCS scores of below 10). Further, 90% of youth in the intensive group and 65% in the weekly group were deemed treatment responders based on CGI Improvement scores at posttreatment. Although neither group difference was statistically significant, effect sizes for intensive and weekly treatment were 2.62 and 1.73, respectively. Also, a significant difference was detected for level of family accommodation at posttreatment, with the intensive group showing a greater reduction in the degree to which family members accommodated the child's OCD symptoms. At the 3-month follow-up assessment, however, outcomes for both groups were largely similar due primarily to a slight decrease in treatment effectiveness among the intensive group. These data suggest both treatments were efficacious, but that all youth may require some level of additional care, at least during the initial follow-up period. Also, although combined pharmacotherapy and CBT are often considered the treatment of choice for pediatric OCD, Storch et al. (2007) found that children in their study ($n = 24$) taking psychotropic medications (mostly SSRIs) did not differ in outcome from those not taking medication.

Combination and Comparison Treatment

In an earlier combination treatment trial (Wever & Rey, 1997), 57 children with OCD received medication and ERP (2 weeks of medication followed by the addition of daily ERP). The combination resulted in a 68% remission rate and a 60% mean reduction in OCD symptoms. A 12-week comparative trial examined the effect of ERP versus clomipramine in 22 children with OCD (de Haan, Hoogduin, Buitelaar, & Keisjers, 1998). Both treatments resulted in significant improvement, but rates for ERP were significantly higher; 67% of those who received ERP were judged as treatment responders, compared to 50% of those treated with clomipramine. Similarly, reduction in symptom severity was 60% for those treated with ERP and 33% for those treated with clomipramine.

Asbahr et al. (2005) compared group CBT (GCBT; based on an adaptation of the work of March & Mulle, 1998) to sertraline in a study of 40 youth with OCD (9 to 17 years) randomized to one of the two treatments. Youth in both groups evidenced significant improvements on the CY-BOCS and measures of anxiety and depression at posttreatment, with no difference reported between treatment groups. At 9-month follow-up, however, youth treated with GCBT reported significantly lower rates of OCD symptoms, indicating long-term durability of GCBT over sertraline.

In the first randomized, placebo-controlled comparison trial (The Pediatric OCD Treatment Study [POTS], 2004), CBT, sertraline, their combination, and pill placebo were compared among 112 youth with OCD ages 7–17 years. Participants were seen weekly over a 12-week period. Sertraline dosing began at 25 mg/day and was increased to a maximum dose of 200 mg/day by Week 6. The manualized 12-week CBT protocol was adapted from the work of March and Mulle (1998) and included psychoeducation, cognitive training, symptom tracking, and ERP. Three parent sessions were also conducted as part of the 12-week treatment. At posttreatment, CY-BOCS scores indicated significant improvement among all active treatment conditions compared to placebo, although children in the combination condition showed significantly greater symptom reductions on the CY-BOCS compared to those treated with sertraline or CBT. However, when clinical remission rates were examined (defined as posttreatment CY-BOCS score below 10), 53.6% of the combination group, 39% of the CBT group, 21% of the sertraline group, and 3% taking placebo reached remission status. Statistically, the difference between combined treatment and CBT was not significant, although combination treatment was superior to sertraline alone. Also, while combination treatment and CBT were superior to placebo, sertraline did not differ from placebo based on remission rates. Effect sizes for combined treatment, CBT alone, and sertraline were 1.4, 0.97, and 0.67, respectively. Clearly, these data suggest a significant advantage of treatment with CBT, leading the study team to conclude that treatment should begin with CBT alone or the combination of CBT and an SSRI.

Summary of Treatment Outcome

Overall, CBT that includes ERP is the most empirically supported intervention and the treatment of choice for childhood OCD (Expert Consensus Guidelines; March et al., 1997), just as it is for adults (Stanley & Turner, 1995). This conclusion was confirmed by data from a meta-analysis examining pharmacological and psychosocial interventions (Abramowitz et al., 2005) and from the first multisite comparison treatment trial for pediatric OCD (POTS Team, 2004). Effect sizes from the meta-analysis were 0.88 for SSRIs, 0.84 for clomipramine, and 1.60 for ERP, which was significantly more effective than either pharmacotherapy or placebo ($p < .01$), but pharmacotherapy (all types of medications combined) was not more effective than placebo ($p < .10$). However, when considered alone, SSRIs were more effective than placebo ($p < .05$). In terms of clinical significance, at posttreatment children treated with pharmacotherapy scored at the lower end of the moderate range of symptoms. In contrast, those treated with ERP scored in the mild range; those in the placebo group were still in the moderate range. As with the effect size analysis, the CY-BOCS scores of those treated with ERP were significantly lower than those treated with pharmacotherapy or placebo, and the two pill conditions were not significantly different. Results from the POTS study were somewhat consistent with these results. That is, while treatment with an SSRI and CBT produced similar remission rates to CBT alone, the combination treatment was superior to an SSRI alone. One distinct possibility for differences in outcome between the meta-analysis and the POTS study includes the specific behavioral treatment used. That is, although the CBT protocol in the POTS study included ERP, the inclusion of several other CBT components suggests that children did not receive 12 weeks of actual ERP. Collectively, outcome data suggest that ERP should be the focus of behavioral interventions for OCD and that ERP be used as the first line of treatment.

Predictors of Treatment Outcome

Among adults with OCD, those with washing and cleaning rituals are considered to have the best prognosis, whereas cognitive rituals are considered the most difficult to address. Among children, however, consistent data are lacking with respect to any specific predictors of treatment outcome. Poorer treatment outcome has been associated with oppositionality and aggression (Wever & Rey, 1997), poorer initial response to medication, lifetime history of tics, a psychiatric disorder in the parent (Leonard et al., 1993), more severe obsessions and greater academic impairment (Barrett, Farrell, Dadds, & Boulter, 2005; Piacentini et al., 2002), and greater levels of family dysfunction (Barrett, Farrell, Dadds,

& Boulter, 2005). In a larger examination of potential predictors of treatment outcome (Abramowitz et al., 2005), neither sample characteristics (age, gender, severity of illness, symptom duration, or comorbidity) nor treatment characteristics (treatment duration, number of treatment sessions, or number of sessions per week) were predictive of treatment outcome. In contrast, among a sample of 45 treated children with OCD followed for an average of 9 years, Bloch and colleagues (2009) reported that decreased OCD severity during childhood, presence of a comorbid tic disorder, and absence of hoarding symptoms were associated with higher remission rates in adulthood. However, while the majority of subjects were taking SSRIs or other medications at both assessment points and those with remitted versus nonremitted OCD did not significantly differ in medication use at either the baseline (childhood) or follow-up (early adulthood) evaluation, history and potential impact of behavioral interventions were not examined or reported.

In a naturalistic treatment study by Masi et al. (2005) including 94 youth with OCD (ages 7–18 years), patients with more treatment-resistant OCD were older on average, had more frequent inpatient hospitalizations, were more severely impaired at baseline, and had longer follow-up care. Also, children with primary hoarding symptoms were less likely to respond to treatment, and those with primary contamination fears and rituals tended to respond best to SSRI monotherapy. Among a sample of 96 youth with OCD (range 7–19 years) treated with CBT, Storch and colleagues (2007) found that number of comorbid conditions was negatively related to treatment outcome. Also, comorbid major depressive disorder and disruptive behavior disorders, including ADHD, were related to lower CBT response rates.

CASE EXAMPLES: TREATMENT OF OCD

Following are two examples of the behavioral treatment for children with OCD. Prior to presenting the specific treatment plans, a few general caveats are in order. First, among all of the anxiety disorders, OCD is the one that is most likely to create significant familial distress, a clinical impression confirmed by empirical data (e.g., Waters & Barrett, 2000). Therefore, it is necessary first to carefully consider the parent's role, if any, in the treatment program. In many instances, parents will need to actively participate by taking the child to places or situations necessary for homework completion. However, particularly with respect to response prevention, many parents might need to play a secondary role. That is, aspects of the response prevention program sometimes are contentious, at least initially (i.e., the child is not supposed to engage in activities that formerly reduced anxiety, therefore they are anxious and likely somewhat irritable). The role of the parent should be to remind the child that the response prevention program exists, but not try to be the therapist, to police the child, or to badger the child into compliance. Rather, parental participation should be in the form of positive support. In fact, rather than focusing on the child's pathology, parents should positively reinforce the child for compliance with the treatment program.

As discussed in previous chapters, use of contingency contracting to complete homework assignments is particularly relevant for the treatment of children with OCD. Children often do not understand the need for the intervention and are not always willing, at least initially, to comply with the program. Acknowledging that the program is difficult, can be stressful, and takes time away from other activities is an important part of therapeutic engagement. Furthermore, offering rewards as an acknowledgment of the time and effort needed to participate in the program increases compliance, particularly among young children. In other words, a sound background in behavioral theory is necessary to implement behavioral programs effectively.

ANTHONY'S TREATMENT PLAN

The initial diagnostic interview confirmed the presence of OCD but did not indicate the presence of any other disorder. Further information on Anthony's specific pattern of obsessions and compulsions was collected with the CY-BOCS. Intrusive thoughts occurred 1–3 hours per day, were disturbing, resulted in moderate interference with social and school activities, and were only sometimes able to be controlled. Rituals also occupied 1–3 hours per day and, although they could be delayed, could not be prevented. As with the obsessions, the rituals had an impact on his academic and family functioning. Consistent with the diagnostic interview, scores on Anthony's self-report inventories indicated the lack of psychopathology other than OCD. His baseline self-monitoring data (see Figures 11.1 and 11.2) depicted the presence of moderate distress and a significant number of intrusive thoughts per day.

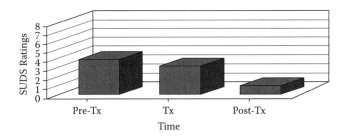

FIGURE 11.1   Anthony's distress experienced by obsessional thoughts. Tx, treatment. (Reprinted from Beidel, D. C., & Turner, S. M. (2005). *Child Anxiety Disorders*. New York: Routledge. With permission.)

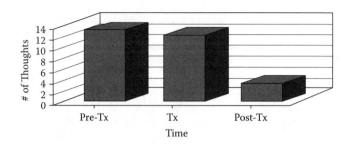

FIGURE 11.2 Anthony's number of obsessional thoughts per day. Tx, treatment. (Reprinted from Beidel & Turner, 2005. Permission granted by Routledge.)

His treatment plan included imaginal and in vivo exposure as well as response prevention. Imaginal sessions were conducted in the office (see Table 11.2), whereas the in vivo ERP program occurred outside the clinic sessions. Anthony was given a detailed response prevention program (see Table 11.3) to ensure that the instructions were implemented correctly. Treatment consisted of 11 clinic sessions and the accompanying homework assignments. At the end of the treatment, rituals were decreased to less than 5 minutes per day and obsessions to less than 10 minutes per day.

TABLE 11.2 Anthony's Imaginal Exposure Scene

I want you to imagine that you are at home with your younger sister alone. Your parents have gone out for the evening, and you expect them to be arriving home sometime soon. It begins to get later and later, and you are beginning to wonder where they are. They are now about an hour late, and they have not called. More time passes, and you begin to get concerned. You think, "What if something has happened to them?" As the thought comes into your mind, you begin to feel uncomfortable, your stomach churns, and you feel yourself becoming warm. These feelings grow more intense as it gets later and later. Suddenly, the phone rings. You go to answer, expecting it to be your parents. However, it is a doctor calling to tell you that your father has been hospitalized. He tells you that your father is in the hospital ill, and that someone will be sent to pick you up. When you get to the hospital, you find that your mother is there and that your father is seriously ill. He is in great pain, and they do not know what is wrong with him or whether he will live or die. When you see him and how bad he is, you panic, and thoughts go through your head so fast you can't keep up with them. Your heart is pounding, you feel sick and overcome with fear.

Source: Reprinted from Beidel, D. C., & Turner, S. M. (2005). *Child Anxiety Disorders*. New York: Routledge. With permission.

TABLE 11.3   Anthony's Exposure and Response Prevention Program (Self-Delivered)

1. Put the box with the rabbit's foot in a room away from you for 3 hours each day. Do not check on the box, touch it, or do anything with the rabbit's foot during that time.

2. Practice coming down the stairs and going into the kitchen through the family room without turning around. *Do this 10 times each evening.* Do not touch the box or its contents after having done this. Also, do not carry out the ritual (entering the kitchen by doing the turning behavior) after you have carried out the assignment.

3. When getting up in the A.M., do not touch the box or the rabbit's foot. Go downstairs, enter the kitchen through the family room. Do not execute the turning behavior. Do not touch the box or the rabbit's foot after completing this.

4. When preparing to leave your house, you are allowed to touch the box and the rabbit's foot only once for a period not to exceed 15 seconds. Then leave the room and do not return.

Source: Reprinted from Beidel, D. C., & Turner, S. M. (2005). *Child Anxiety Disorders.* New York: Routledge. With permission.

ANGELA'S TREATMENT PLAN

For Angela, the standard clinical interview did not reveal any psychiatric disorder other than OCD. A detailed analysis of her clinical presentation indicated that contact with specific situations or images triggered thoughts of harm to herself. These situations included enclosed places, heights, airplanes, eating food without washing her hands, tornadoes, house fires, her house sinking into the ground, vampires, death, her heart stopping, dirt, or germs. Rituals performed in response to the obsessions included reassurance seeking from her parents, monitoring weather reports for hurricanes or tornadoes, washing hands three times per hour with dishwasher detergent, and refusal to eat (even a small snack such as a cookie) without washing her hands.

The decision was made to treat Angela with a combination of in vivo exposure and response prevention. In addition, a variant of imaginal exposure was incorporated to address her fear of dying. Prior to initiating treatment, Angela's obsessional thoughts were arranged in the hierarchy shown in Table 11.4. Each item was presented until Angela reported a subjective units of distress (SUDS) rating of 0. Also, the response prevention program in Table 11.5 was implemented by Angela and her parents.

Figure 11.3 depicts the within-session and between-session habituation data for the task "eating without washing hands." For this task, Angela was presented with several of her favorite cookies and was asked to eat the cookies without first washing her hands. She had to remain in the situation (slowly eating cookies) until her anxiety regarding eating dissipated. As depicted in Figure 11.3, she habituated to this task over four sessions.

TABLE 11.4   Angela's Exposure Hierarchy

Fear	SUDS Rating
Eating without washing hands	3
Riding in an elevator	4
Fire drills at school	5
Heights	6
Tornadoes or hurricanes	7
Heart stopping	8

Source: Reprinted from Beidel, D. C., & Turner, S. M. (2005). *Child Anxiety Disorders.* New York: Routledge. With permission.

TABLE 11.5   Angela's Response Prevention Program

1. You may wash your hands for 30 seconds with nonantiseptic hand soap only after using the bathroom or 30 minutes before you eat.
2. No washing your hands immediately before eating.
3. Have a snack before bedtime—something you must eat with your fingers. You may not wash your hands first.
4. You cannot watch the weather report or the weather channel or read the weather report in the newspaper.
5. If you feel an urge to do any of these things, get someone to distract you until the urge goes away.

Source: Reprinted from Beidel, D. C., & Turner, S. M. (2005). *Child Anxiety Disorders.* New York: Routledge. With permission.

Although several of the items on Angela's hierarchy were able to be presented in vivo, it obviously is not possible to overtly replicate items such as tornadoes or a child's heart stopping. With adolescents and adults, imaginal exposure would be the most appropriate intervention. Table 11.6 depicts Angela's imaginal scene. However, given Angela's age, typical imaginal flooding was not considered appropriate. As an alternative, Angela was asked to write out her obsessions in the form of stories. Standard exposure procedures were used. That is, she would write out the story and continue to write or read it aloud until her anxiety habituated. In this way, it was not necessary for Angela to try to continuously imagine a scene, something that often is difficult for young children. However, by having to read the story over and over, she remained constantly engaged with the critical stimuli. Within- and between-session habituation data are presented in Figure 11.4. As depicted, use of this writing exposure task produced within- and between-session habituation

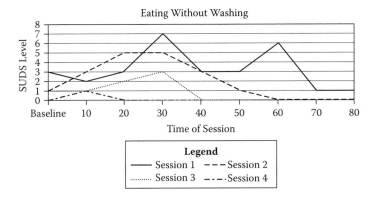

FIGURE 11.3   Angela's level of distress during in vivo exposure sessions. (Reprinted from Beidel, D. C., & Turner, S. M. (2005). *Child Anxiety Disorders*. New York: Routledge. With permission.)

TABLE 11.6   Angela's Imaginal Exposure Story

All Nine-Year-Old Girls Go to Heaven

I am in the doctor's office. I had to wait 20 minutes. When the doctor came in, he says, "Angela, there is something wrong with your heart. Not enough blood is being pumped." I say, "Can you fix it?" He says, "Yes but you will be in the hospital." I say, "No way, how am I supposed to make up all that work?" He shakes his head. We go home, and I start on my homework. I notice my heart is beating slower and slower. I put my hand on my heart, and it has stopped. I know that you only have 5 minutes before you don't get any oxygen to your brain. I am very scared. And I wonder if I will die before I go to the hospital. I call for my mom and tell her, "My heart has stopped." My mom calls 911. And that is when I die. Everything just goes black. It is like I was shooting at warp speed back in time. I can hear my parents crying. But I can't do anything. I am dead.

Source: Reprinted from Beidel, D. C., & Turner, S. M. (2005). *Child Anxiety Disorders*. New York: Routledge. With permission.

consistent with other forms of imaginal and in vivo exposure. There were a total of 20 clinic sessions with response prevention implemented as homework. Treatment outcome was successful, with obsessions and rituals reduced to less than 5 minutes per day at posttreatment.

TRICHOTILLOMANIA

Trichotillomania (TTM), or compulsive hair pulling, was first identified by Hallopeau, a French dermatologist, in 1889 (Vitulano, King,

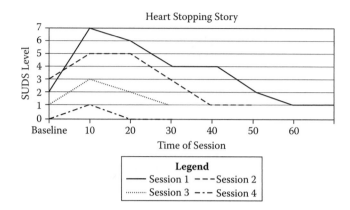

FIGURE 11.4 Angela's level of distress during imaginal exposure sessions. (Reprinted from Beidel, D. C., & Turner, S. M. (2005). *Child Anxiety Disorders*. New York: Routledge. With permission.)

Scahill, & Cohen, 1992). TTM is a frustrating condition both for the child who suffers from it and for the therapist who attempts to treat it. The repetitive nature of the pulling, the family history of OCD among many of those with TTM, as well as higher-than-expected rates of TTM among the relatives of patients with OCD, the secretive nature of the behavior, and the response of pharmacological treatments have led many to suggest that this disorder is related to OCD (Bienvenu et al., 2000; Jaspers, 1996; Swedo & Rapoport, 1991). However, there also are some clear differences between OCD and TTM (King, Ollendick, et al., 1995), and the treatment of this disorder is only rarely discussed in the literature. Thus, a brief discussion of the disorder and its treatment are included here.

Epidemiological data are scarce, but perhaps up to 8 million Americans suffer from TTM (Swedo & Rapoport, 1991). Although data on children are even more limited, a lifetime prevalence rate of approximately 0.6% has been found in two separate studies (APA, 2000; Christenson, Pyle, & Mitchell, 1991; Duke, Bodzin, Tavares, Geffken, & Storch, 2009), primarily including adults. The hair pulling often occurs in conjunction with (a) negative emotions such as stress, irritation, or doubt; (b) when the individual is sitting alone, perhaps doing homework, watching television, or reading; or (c) after significant life events (starting school, moving to a new city, an automobile accident; Chang, Lee, Chiang, & Lu, 1991; Christenson, Ristvedt, & Mackenzie, 1993; Hanna, 1997; Reeve, Bernstein, & Christenson, 1992). Hair may be pulled from the head, eyebrows, eyelashes, or pubic area. A survey study among 133 youth ages 10 to 17 years with TTM found the most common sites of hair pulling are the scalp (86%), eyelashes (52%), eyebrows

(38%), pubic region (27%), legs (18%), and arms (9%) (Franklin et al., 2008). Hair selected to be pulled is described as feeling different in some way (too kinky or straight, too short or long, or just odd in some way). In some instances, hairs are pulled only from areas where it is easy to cover the bald spot; in other cases, the baldness may be so extensive that concealment is not possible. Some children eat the hair or at least the root, and in certain instances, hair pulling is related to thumb sucking (Walsh & McDougle, 2001).

In one of the first studies to examine differences in clinical and phenomenological characteristics between OCD and TTM, Flessner, Berman, Garcia, Freeman, and Leonard (2009) compared 154 children with OCD alone and 48 with OCD and comorbid TTM or skin picking (SP). Results indicated that children with comorbid TTM or SP reported more obsessions and compulsions than those with OCD alone based on the CY-BOCS, although the groups were equivalent in overall symptom severity. Further, children presenting with both disorders more commonly reported contamination, aggressive, sexual, somatic, and religious obsessions and washing/cleaning, checking, repeating, and counting compulsions. No differences were found with respect to age at OCD onset, course of OCD, or the presence of mood or other anxiety symptoms. However, parents of children with both OCD and TTM more commonly reported that their child experienced tactile/sensory sensitivity than those in the OCD alone group.

As with anxiety disorders in general, some children have TTM alone, whereas for others, a broader pattern of psychopathology is present (Hanna, 1997; Reeve et al., 1992; Swedo & Rapoport, 1991). Despite some similarities, the relationship of TTM and OCD remains unclear. In one study of 10 children with TTM, none had associated obsessions and compulsions (Reeve et al., 1992). Other studies indicated up to 19% of children with TTM meet criteria for OCD (Christenson, Mackenzie, Mitchell, & Callies, 1991; Christenson, Pyle, et al., 1991; Cohen et al., 1995; King, Scahill, et al., 1995; Stewart, Jenike, & Keuthen, 2005). Tolin, Franklin, Diefenbach, Anderson, and Meunier (2007) found the prevalence of OCD in a clinical sample of children with TTM to be 6.6%. However, other comorbidities appear to be common as well. For example, 13–20% also met criteria for an affective disorder (King, Scahill, et al., 1995; Reeve et al., 1992). Reeve et al. (1992) reported that 60% of their sample of children with overanxious disorder and King, Scahill, et al. (1995) reported that 90% of their sample met criteria for a disruptive behavior disorder, suggesting that the relationship of OCD to TTM is not unique.

The mean age of onset of some TTM samples is early to midadolescence (Duke et al., 2009; King, Scahill, et al., 1995; Swedo & Leonard, 1992). However, in other samples, approximately one third of children with TTM had an onset prior to age 10, and 14% had an onset prior to age 7 (Muller, 1987; Walsh & McDougle, 2001). Among a sample of Chinese patients with TTM, the most prominent time of onset was during elementary school (Chang et al., 1991), and in a U.S. sample, the mean age was 8.5 years, with a range of 2 to 13.5 years (Hanna, 1997). TTM sometimes remits spontaneously or with minimal intervention in the form of explanation, reassurance, and emotional support (Chang et al., 1991). However, adults may present with a childhood or adolescent age of onset, thus indicating a chronic or waxing-and-waning course for others (Chang et al., 1991; Cohen et al., 1995).

TTM can also occur at very young ages. In one sample of infants and children (Swedo & Leonard, 1992), age at onset ranged from 11 to 54 months of age. Approximately 50% pulled hair while sleeping, 30% pulled while sucking their thumb, and 60% pulled while watching television. Other situations were associated with pulling but to lesser degrees. Among this very young sample, pulling was episodic in nature, with approximately one to three periods of remission per year. Two cases (20%) had relapses that occurred following streptococcal infections, although consistent with previous discussion of the PANDAS literature, the specific association between strep infections and childhood neuropsychiatric disorders remains unclear. Since hair pulling in preschool children is often accompanied by other habit disorders, such as scratching, SP, and thumb sucking and commonly occurs around sleep, TTM at an early age may represent a separate entity with a distinct natural course compared with TTM in older children and adults (Bruce, Barwick, & Wright, 2005).

The lack of controlled treatment trials in children with TTM coupled with the typical secrecy associated with the disorder present major challenges for clinicians. While a few controlled trials of pharmacological treatment for TTM have been conducted in adults, its applicability to children is currently unknown. Clomipramine, fluoxetine, and lithium have been used in children, but their utility remains unclear (Pomnoppadol & Todd, 1999; Vitulano et al., 1992), and data on the long-term efficacy of these medications suggest a high rate of relapse with discontinuation (see Walsh & McDougle, 2001). In a review of available case studies for children with TTM, Bruce et al. (2005) concluded that behavioral treatments have the greatest support. Nonetheless, there also are few data examining the utility of behavioral treatments. When pulling behavior occurs in conjunction with thumb sucking, elimination of thumb sucking often eliminates TTM (e.g., Watson & Allen, 1993). In addition, traditional behavioral interventions such as self-monitoring, progressive muscle relaxation, habit interruption, prevention training and competing reaction training, overcorrection, awareness training, annoyance review, and reinforcement and differential reinforcement of other behaviors have been reported as successful (e.g., Blum, Barone, & Friman, 1993; Vitulano et al., 1992). Some of these procedures (self-monitoring, progressive muscle relaxation, reinforcement) have been discussed in previous chapters and are not repeated here. With respect to the other procedures, habit interruption, prevention training, and competing response training refer to teaching engagement in an alternative, opposite movement when the child becomes aware of pulling or experiences an urge to pull. An easy opposite movement is clenching the fists when experiencing the urge to pull. Overcorrection usually has aversive connotations (Foxx & Bechtel, 1982) but in the case of children with TTM has been used as positive practice by having the children comb or brush their hair after a hair-pulling session (Vitulano et al., 1992). Annoyance review simply refers to having the children acknowledge the problematic nature of hair pulling and their reasons for wanting to stop; this is probably most effective for preadolescents and adolescents rather than younger children. Differential reinforcement of other behavior means giving the child attention when pulling behavior is absent.

Obviously, the selection of the specific treatment components will be dependent on the child's age. Several challenges to treating children and adolescents with TTM have been identified (Vitulano et al., 1992). First are potential problems with compliance and motivation. Children sometimes find it difficult to adhere to self-monitoring procedures and can be embarrassed to collect their hairs and bring them to the therapist. As noted elsewhere, compliance with self-monitoring is a challenge faced by those who do behavioral interventions. Particularly with children and adolescents, who are often reluctant to participate in treatment, two factors seem to increase the likelihood of compliance: (a) keeping the self-monitoring as simple as possible (no more than one page per day) and (b) small rewards for completion of self-monitoring or behavioral assignments.

A second challenge when treating children with TTM also has been mentioned with respect to children with OCD: Family conflict and parental frustration often confound treatment outcome (Vitulano et al., 1992). As noted, helping the parents distance themselves from the treatment program and from the child's behavior may be necessary to reduce family conflict and enhance treatment compliance and outcome.

CASE EXAMPLE: TREATMENT OF TTM

Erica is 3.5 years old. Her mother requested treatment for chronic hair pulling. At the time of the initial evaluation, Erica had pulled out all of the hair on her head. This behavior began about 12 months ago and was continuous since that time. Her mother sought treatment from Erica's pediatrician, who prescribed clomipramine and then fluoxetine, both of which were unsuccessful. Currently, the pediatrician was recommending a trial of Haldol®, but Erica's mother wanted to investigate behavioral treatment first.

Obviously, in this case, all of the information had to be collected from Erica's mother. At the time of the initial evaluation, Erica's family situation was chaotic and no doubt contributed to her emotional distress. Her older sister had a debilitating physical illness, and there was a newborn infant in the family. Her parents were under some financial stress due to extensive medical bills. Finally, her grandmother had OCD.

In addition to these family influences, several operant factors were identified that played a role in the maintenance of Erica's hair pulling. Specifically, her parents and grandparents, distressed by her hair pulling, spent much time trying to talk to Erica about why she should stop. Thus, there was substantial attention from both her parents and her grandmother for pulling her hair. In fact, Erica would seek attention from family friends and strangers by running up to them and saying, "I pull my hair." Finally, her mother indicated that, like other children with TTM, at night Erica tended to suck her thumb and pull her hair.

Traditional interventions for TTM determine the outcome of treatment by counting the number of hairs daily. However, given Erica's age and the fact that parental attention appeared to be a maintaining factor for the behavior, a decision was made to use the number of hairs pulled at night as an indication of treatment outcome. Each morning, Erica's mother collected the hair on the pillow, and each week, her mother brought the hairs to the clinic, where they were counted and the total number graphed (see Figure 11.5).

The initial treatment program consisted of eliminating attention for hair pulling. The parents were instructed to ignore Erica when she pulled her hair and to provide positive attention when she was not

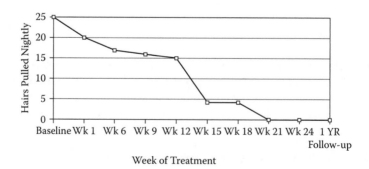

FIGURE 11.5 Erica's hair-pulling behavior. (Reprinted from Beidel, D. C., & Turner, S. M. (2005). *Child Anxiety Disorders*. New York: Routledge. With permission.)

pulling her hair. Furthermore, an hourly sticker program was implemented. Specifically, at the top of every hour, if Erica's hands were not near her face or head, she earned a sticker. After 5 weeks, there was a slight, but not substantial, decrease in nightly hair pulling (see Figure 11.5). One reason was that Erica's mother was not able to comply with the sticker program. Therefore, at Week 6, relaxation training was added to the treatment plan to reduce Erica's stress level. The child relaxation script by Koppen (1974) was used but was modified for Erica's age. In addition, both her mother and Erica were taught the relaxation exercises and were instructed to do it at home together. Surprisingly, even given her young age, Erica participated fully in the relaxation exercises and by the third week had actually memorized parts of the script. This phase of the intervention led to a further decrease in Erica's hair puling, and by her mother's report, daytime hair pulling was eliminated. However, she was still pulling her hair at night when she sucked her thumb (see Figure 11.5), and substances applied to her thumb to prevent sucking were ineffective.

To deal with the nighttime hair pulling, a decision was made to attempt to prevent Erica from sucking her thumb and pulling her hair in her sleep. The treatment program involved pink mittens and cherry ice cream. See Table 11.7 for the details of the contingency contract. As depicted in Figure 11.5, this contract was successful in eliminating the remaining hair-pulling behavior. Implementation of the contract was only necessary for a 5-week period. After that, Erica's newly growing hair and her pride in her new appearance negated the need for her "ice cream breakfast."

There are several reasons why this plan was successful. First, Erica lived in the southeastern United States and rarely had opportunities to wear mittens. Erica viewed wearing her mittens at bedtime as exciting,

TABLE 11.7   Pink Mittens and Cherry Ice Cream
(Erica's Treatment Program)

A. Erica had a pair of pink mittens that she liked to wear.

B. Erica's favorite food was cherry ice cream.

C. If Erica wore her mittens all night (i.e., they were still on when she woke up in the morning), she could have cherry ice cream for breakfast.

D. Erica had no access to cherry ice cream or her pink mittens at any other time.

E. Erica got ice cream for breakfast no matter what else she might have done wrong (ice cream could not be withdrawn as a punishment).

Source: Reprinted from Beidel, D. C., & Turner, S. M. (2005). *Child Anxiety Disorders.* New York: Routledge. With permission.

not as a punishment. Second, it was imperative that Erica understand the contract contingencies. To help her remember, the contract was put to a tune of a child's song so that Erica could sing the words and remember the contract. Third, if a contract is to be effective, it must be implemented correctly. A major compliance concern would be whether Erica took her mittens off to pull her hair and then put her mittens back on in the morning. However, given her age, Erica was unable to put her mittens on correctly without help (she could not get her thumb correctly in the thumb "hole"). Therefore, it was easy for her mother to determine whether she kept her mittens on all night. In summary, self-monitoring data were useful in determining the efficacy of the program and making alterations when the data indicated that ongoing strategies had reached maximal effectiveness.

SUMMARY

OCD is a chronic and disabling disorder that presents significant challenges for children and clinicians alike. Studies of psychopathology have clarified important aspects of the psychopathology of this disorder, although its etiology remains unclear. ERP is clearly the treatment of choice for childhood OCD and results in positive treatment outcomes for a majority of patients. However, exactly which patients are most likely to benefit from ERP is still unknown, and still more data are necessary on its long-term outcome. Similarly, TTM is a perplexing disorder, and few data are available on effective treatments. In short, both OCD and TTM will continue to challenge researchers and clinicians for the foreseeable future.

CHAPTER 12

Panic Disorder

Angela is 17 years old. She has a history of anxiety since childhood and panic attacks since the age of 14. Her physical symptoms include breaking into a cold sweat, being chilled to the bone, feeling jittery, having a racing heart, and feeling like she wants to run away but does not know where to run. She has continued to go to school but often must go to the nurse's office to lie down because of the anxiety she experiences. She is reluctant to go places alone and has discontinued her social interactions and afterschool activities. She is seeking treatment now because she wants to attend an out-of-state college next year and is concerned that when the time comes, she will not be able to leave home.

PANIC ATTACKS

Panic attacks are discrete episodes of fear and anxiety sometimes experienced by youth with different anxiety disorders. Unlike other anxiety disorders, however, one cannot meet criteria for panic disorder unless a panic attack has occurred. A *panic attack* is an acute episode of anxiety that consists of somatic and sometimes cognitive symptoms. The somatic symptoms include heart palpitations, chest pain, tingling sensations, chills or hot flushes, dizziness, feelings of choking, nausea, sweating, trembling, or shaking. Cognitive symptoms include fear of losing control or going crazy, feelings of unreality or detachment, and fear of dying. The symptoms usually peak in intensity within 5–10 minutes of onset and subside approximately 15–30 minutes later (*Diagnostic and Statistical Manual of Mental Disorders, Fourth Edition, Text Revision* [*DSM-IV-TR*], American Psychiatric Association [APA], 2000). When the symptoms occur unexpectedly, there may be concern about the onset of future attacks, the possibility of an illness, or the possibility of death.

The most recent *Diagnostic and Statistical Manual of Mental Disorders* (*DSM-IV-TR*; APA, 2000) defines a *panic attack* as the simultaneous presence of at least four of the symptoms mentioned in the preceding paragraph (see Table 12.1). Limited-symptom attacks are events

TABLE 12.1   *DSM-IV-TR* Criteria for Panic Attack and Panic Disorder Without Agoraphobia

Panic Attack

A discrete period of intense fear or discomfort, in which four (or more) of the following symptoms developed abruptly and reached a peak within 10 minutes:
- palpitations, pounding heart, or accelerated heart rate
- sweating
- trembling or shaking
- sensations of shortness of breath or smothering
- feeling of choking
- chest pain or discomfort
- nausea or abdominal distress
- feeling dizzy, unsteady, lightheaded, or faint
- derealization (feelings of unreality) or depersonalization (being detached from oneself)
- fear of losing control or going crazy
- fear of dying
- paresthesias (numbing or tingling sensations)
- chills or hot flushes

Panic Disorder

A. Both (1) and (2):

1. Recurrent unexpected Panic Attacks

2. At least one of the attacks followed by 1 month (or more) of one (or more) of the following: persistent concern about having additional attacks, worry about the implications of the attack or its consequences (e.g., losing control, having a heart attack, "going crazy"), or a significant change in behavior related to the attacks

B. Absence of Agoraphobia

C. The Panic Attacks are not due to the direct physiological effects of a substance (e.g., a drug of abuse, a medication) or a general medical condition (e.g., hyperthyroidism).

D. The Panic Attacks are not better accounted for by another mental disorder, such as Social Phobia (e.g., occurring on exposure to feared social situations), Specific Phobia (e.g., on exposure to a specific phobic situation), Obsessive-Compulsive Disorder (e.g., on exposure to dirt in someone with an obsession about contamination), Posttraumatic Stress Disorder (e.g., in response to stimuli associated with a severe stressor), or Separation Anxiety Disorder (e.g., in response to being away from home or close relatives).

that otherwise meet the criteria for a panic attack but consist of fewer than four symptoms. In addition, panic attacks are categorized as one of three types: (1) uncued, (2) situationally bound, and (3) situationally predisposed. Uncued attacks occur unexpectedly or are perceived to come out of the blue. Situationally bound attacks occur in the context of, or in anticipation of, a specific feared object, situation, or event. Situationally predisposed attacks fall somewhere between these two extremes; although triggered by specific events, situation, or objects, situationally predisposed attacks do not always occur when in contact with the feared event.

The term *panic attack* is part of everyday language and often is used to describe feelings of distress that might not meet the actual diagnostic criteria. Self-report of the presence and frequency of panic reveal that many individuals describe an anxiety response as "having had a panic attack." However, even when restricted to its actual *DSM-IV* definition (APA, 1994), panic attacks are common among children and adolescents. In one survey, 60–63% of 13- to 18-year-olds reported having at least one panic attack (Macaulay & Kleinknecht, 1989; Warren & Zgourides, 1988). Among African American adolescents, 26% reported panic attack symptoms (Ginsburg & Drake, 2002a). A close examination of adolescent self-report data (Warren & Zgourides, 1988) indicated that 28.1% of adolescents appeared to have experienced a panic attack consistent with diagnostic criteria, and among those, 17.5% described uncued panic attacks, but only 1.5% had uncued attacks alone. In contrast to unselected samples, 47% of those with clinically diagnosed panic attacks reported that the attack was uncued (Essau et al., 1999b).

Rather than self-report surveys, structured diagnostic interviews conducted among unselected samples of school students revealed a prevalence of 5.3% for panic attacks among sixth and seventh graders (Hayward et al., 1992), whereas the prevalence was 8.7–11.6% among high school students (Hayward, Killen, & Taylor, 1989; Hayward, Wilson, Lagle, Killen, & Taylor, 2004). In each investigation, prevalence was based on the documented presence of at least one four-symptom attack. Interestingly, an additional 3.2% of ninth graders endorsed the presence of limited-symptom attacks (Hayward et al., 1989). Thus, panic attacks occur with some frequency, although the overall prevalence decreases substantially when trained interviewers and structured diagnostic interviews are used. Another important consideration is that developmentally, prevalence appears to increase with increasing age (see sociodemographic section).

PANIC DISORDER

Approximately 18% of adults with panic disorder endorsed the onset of panic attacks prior to the age of 10 (von Korff, Eaton, & Keyl, 1985). This would suggest that the incidence of panic disorder (as opposed to panic attacks) in young children is rare. In one investigation, the clinical narratives that accompanied structured diagnostic interviews of 903 adults were examined for the presence of uncued panic during the participant's childhood (Klein, Mannuzza, Chapman, & Fyer, 1992). The patients consisted of 343 consecutive admissions to an anxiety disorders clinic and 560 first-degree relatives of clinic patients. Among the entire group, only 1% (nine individuals: six patients and three first-degree relatives) reported spontaneous panic attacks prior to the age of 13. In only one case, however, was there convincing evidence of early-onset panic disorder. In the other instances, the "spontaneous panic" was determined not to be spontaneous but occurred in the context of other anxiety disorders, such as separation anxiety disorder, social phobia, or specific phobia.

Of course, these data are limited by all of the pitfalls of retrospective recollection even though the diagnostic interviews were conducted by, and diagnoses were assigned by, acknowledged experts in the area of anxiety disorders. These data illustrate the difficulty in determining the presence of panic attacks and panic disorder in young children. Self-report data are especially suspect as they appear to overinflate the incidence of panic attacks and spontaneous panic attacks. Even when structured diagnostic interviews are conducted by trained experts, a subsequent careful examination of the case history often indicates that the attacks were not out of the blue even if perceived that way by the respondent. Rather, just as is the case for adults, panic attacks many occur within the context of another disorder or during the time of stressful life events (e.g., Faravelli & Pallanti, 1989; see section on etiology).

CLINICAL FEATURES

As noted, panic attacks consist of a variety of physical and cognitive symptoms that occur with sudden intensity. The physical symptoms most commonly reported by children and adolescents include heart palpitations, trembling and shaking, dizziness, sweating, hot or cold flushes, and shortness of breath (Biederman et al., 1997; Bradley & Hood, 1993; Doerfler, Connor, Volungis, & Toscano, 2007; Essau et al., 1999b; Kearney, Albano, Eisen, Allan, & Barlow, 1997; Masi et al., 2000; Vitiello, Behar, Wolfson, & McLeer, 1990). It is important to distinguish between symptoms endorsed most frequently and symptoms reported as most severe (Kearney et al., 1997). Whereas the most frequently reported symptoms included rapid heartbeat, nausea, hot and cold flashes, and shaking/jitteriness, the symptoms reported as most severe included shortness of breath, feeling faint, rapid heartbeat, and choking. Thus, the physical symptoms of panic attacks in youth appear to be similar to those experienced by adults.

As presented in Chapter 3, there is a long-standing controversy regarding the existence of panic disorder in children. The cognitive model of panic is predicated on the premise that physiological symptoms such as heart palpitations, dizziness, and shortness of breath are misinterpreted as physically dangerous, and that this misinterpretation increases anxiety and leads to more physical sensations and more panic attacks (Clark, 1986). An early review (Nelles & Barlow, 1988) argued that although children experience the physiological symptoms of panic, because of their limited cognitive abilities, they are not capable of making the catastrophic interpretations of "going crazy" or dying. This argument is reviewed in depth in Chapter 3 and is not repeated here. It should be noted, however, that the cognitive symptoms are not necessary for one to meet the diagnostic criteria for panic attacks or panic disorder (Ollendick, Mattis, & King, 1994). Thus, even if children are incapable of making the cognitive attributions, they may still experience panic attacks.

Even if the cognitive symptoms are not necessary for a diagnosis of panic disorder, the data regarding the existence of panic disorder in children are mixed. Some studies report low frequency rates for cognitive symptoms (Biederman et al., 1997; Bradley & Hood, 1993; Kearney et al., 1997), whereas others suggest that these symptoms are frequent among child and adolescent populations (Last & Strauss, 1989; Vitiello et al., 1990). Across all studies, physiological symptoms are more frequently endorsed than cognitive symptoms. Furthermore, cognitive symptoms are more common among adolescents than children (Doerfler et al., 2007). Of course, prior to determining whether panic attacks in children include cognitive symptoms, the first question is whether children have the capacity to formulate catastrophic internal attributions. In one of the few empirical studies to address this issue, children in the third, sixth, and ninth grade were assessed regarding their ability to conceptualize the causes of illness (in this case, panic symptoms; Mattis & Ollendick, 1997). Children in third grade were significantly less likely than those in the sixth or ninth grade to attribute somatic symptoms of panic to psychophysiological causes. However, there was no difference between the last two groups. Over 90% of these children attributed panic symptoms to psychophysiological causes, suggesting that at least by age 12, most children/adolescents are capable of the cognitions included in the diagnostic criteria for panic attacks.

This investigation (Mattis & Ollendick, 1997) also examined children's attributions regarding the onset of the panic attack. Attributions were classified as one of four types: external/noncatastrophic ("I'd think there were germs around that I had been exposed to"), external/catastrophic ("I'd think something or someone was trying to kill me"), internal/noncatastrophic ("I'd think I was worried about something"), internal/catastrophic ("I'd think that I must be dying"). Using guided imagery, children listened to an audiotape describing a panic attack and then completed the attribution checklist. Across all three grades, both boys and girls endorsed more internal than external attributions; thus, there was no main effect for age. However, contrary to what would be expected from cognitive models of panic, irrespective of grade level and gender, children endorsed more noncatastrophic than catastrophic attributions. These results indicated that children were able to make internal attributions, but they were of a noncatastrophic nature ("I'd think I was worried about something"), but across the age span (ages 8 through 14), there was no developmental progression of cognitive functioning. Although a few children at each age did respond with catastrophic interpretations, the majority of children were more likely to attribute the somatic arousal to noncatastrophic situations, such as being sick, worried, or scared rather than to dying, With respect to the onset of this disorder in youth, these data call into question the theory that panic disorder develops as a result of somatic symptoms that are catastrophically interpreted. One important caveat is that the sample did not include children who were diagnosed with panic disorder, and results with a clinical sample might differ. However, these results suggest that the symptoms characteristic of panic disorder do not automatically result in cognitive misinterpretations. Thus, other etiological explanations must be considered. Indeed, one hypothesis is that these cognitive variables are metaphenomena and are merely secondary with no causal role, a hypothesis we fully support.

Similar to the behavioral avoidance exhibited by children with other disorders, youth with panic attacks avoid many situations due to concern about the onset of a panic attack. Among high school students with a history of panic attacks, social situations (parties, speeches, conflict with parents or friends, games/sports competitions, restaurants, public restrooms, and classes) were avoided by 44% of the sample (Warren & Zgourides, 1988). Agoraphobic situations (crowded places, being alone, and movie theaters) were avoided by 37% of the sample. Fifteen percent avoided blood/injury situations (hospital, funeral, dentists), whereas avoidance of physically dangerous situations (icy roads, crossing highways) were endorsed by 5% of the sample. In a small sample of children and adolescents with clinically diagnosed panic disorder (Kearney et al., 1997), "typical" situations associated with agoraphobia such as restaurants (35%), crowds (30%), small rooms (25%), auditoriums, elevators, parks, grocery stores, shopping malls, homes, and theaters (each 20%) were most commonly avoided. As indicated, the percentage of youth who avoid situations is often less than 50% (Doerfler et al., 2007), suggesting that behavioral avoidance is not always present among children and adolescents with panic disorder.

Among youth in clinic or hospital settings who are diagnosed with panic attacks, school refusal, aggression, depression, and somatic complaints often are the precipitating factors that lead parents to seek treatment for their children (Alessi & Magen, 1988; Vitiello et al., 1990). When compared to children with a primary diagnosis of generalized anxiety disorder or depressive disorder, children with primary panic disorder were more severely impaired (Masi et al., 2000). In summary, physical symptoms of panic attacks/panic disorder include a variety of somatic complaints but most commonly heart palpitations, trembling and shaking, dizziness, and sweating. Behavioral avoidance is common but not characteristic of every child. With respect to cognitions, a subset of children as young as Grade 3 may have the capacity for catastrophic thinking, but the majority of children and adolescents do not react to the physical symptoms of panic with these types of thoughts (Doerfler et al., 2007). Thus, although cognitions may be reported by a subset of children, the disorder is more likely characterized as consisting primarily of physical symptoms.

HYPERVENTILATION SYNDROME

As we discussed in Chapter 6, the presence of physical distress in children usually leads parents to seek treatment from traditional medical professionals. Just as worry in children often is associated with gastrointestinal symptoms and a medical diagnosis of recurrent abdominal pain, in the past children with panic attacks or panic disorder received a medical diagnosis of "hyperventilation syndrome" (Herman, Stickler, & Lucas 1981; Joorabchi, 1977). In an early study (Enzer & Walker, 1967), 44 cases of childhood hyperventilation syndrome were identified among pediatric hospital records. The children were free of cardiac and respiratory disease, and 70% of the sample was female. The children ranged in age from 5 to 16 years, although most were 12 years and older. The most common symptoms included respiratory complaints, dizziness, paresthesias, and headaches. All of the children and their parents described an episodic nature of attacks, and children endorsed being anxious during the attacks. There also were a number of related fears, such as fear of dying, worry about school, and concern about the possible death of parents or friends. Clearly, these cases of hyperventilation syndrome in pediatric clinics are highly similar to the psychiatric symptoms of panic. However, patients and parents are not always willing to see the relationship between physical symptoms and emotional distress. For example, reviewing all cases referred to one child psychiatric consultation service, four cases of panic disorder (one child, three adolescents) were identified (Garland & Smith, 1990). In three of these cases, referral to a psychiatry consultation service occurred only after months of medical tests and procedures. In some instances, the parents resented the implication of a psychiatric diagnosis, believing that it invalidated the severity of the child's physical distress. If such practices are still common in pediatric respiratory clinics, current prevalence rates for panic disorder may be an underestimate. However, rates of hyperventilation syndrome also appear to be low, such that overall rates probably increase only slightly with the addition of those children.

EPIDEMIOLOGY

There is significant controversy regarding the presence of panic disorder among prepubescent children. Among a sample of school-age adolescents, no child age 12 or 13 met diagnostic criteria for panic disorder, although 0.9% of 14- to 15-year-olds and 0.7% of 16- to 17-year-olds did so (Essau et al., 1999b). Other authors, however, described single cases of panic disorder among prepubertal children (Ballenger, Carek, Steele, & Cornish-McTighe, 1989; Last & Strauss, 1989; Vitiello et al., 1990). Among unselected samples of high school students (Hayward et al., 1992; Warren & Zgourides, 1988), 4.7–5.3% met criteria for panic disorder (according to their self-report). When diagnostic interviews conducted by mental health professionals were used, the lifetime prevalence among adolescents ages 14–17 years dropped to 0.6% (Whitaker et al., 1990). When the sample was further limited to those seeking treatment for psychiatric and behavioral problems, prevalence ranged from 0.6% to 10.5% (Alessi & Magen, 1988; Biederman et al., 1997; Last & Strauss, 1989; Masi et al., 2000; Suveg et al., 2005; Vitiello et al., 1990). The difference in prevalence can be explained at least in part by the nature of the sample. In some instances, the sample was composed entirely of patients with anxiety. In other instances, the presenting problems were more mixed.

Among one sample of children and adolescents referred to a pediatric psychopharmacology clinic, 13% had a diagnosis of panic disorder (Doerfler et al., 2007). Even among youth diagnosed according to *DSM-IV* with panic disorder, the frequency of panic attacks was variable. Forty-one percent of the children and adolescents had panic attacks that were more frequent than once per week, 15% had panic attacks more than once per month (but less often than once per week), and 44% had panic attacks less than once per month (Bradley & Hood, 1993). Thus, similar to the adult literature, the rate and frequency of panic attacks probably is a function of many different variables, but physical and cognitive development likely play a role. Also, some cases of panic may be misdiagnosed, as presented further in this chapter.

SOCIODEMOGRAPHIC INFLUENCES

Among samples of adolescents, the age of onset for the first panic attack was 11.6–12.0 years of age (Bradley & Hood, 1993; Warren & Zgourides, 1988), whereas the age of onset for prepubescent children ranged from 5 to 11 years. Children with the earliest age of onset had the most severe functional impairments (Vitiello et al., 1990).

Among a sample of high school students (Hayward et al., 1992), there was a strong association between panic attacks and sexual maturity; none of their identified cases was a prepubescent child. In contrast, 8% of the girls who completed puberty had a history of at least one panic attack, and between 11 and 13 years of age, a history of panic attacks was more common in those who were more sexually mature. As the authors noted, this study documented an intriguing association between panic attacks and pubertal stage but did not illuminate the stage of the physical maturity process when panic attacks are more likely to occur. Furthermore, the study used only a restricted age range (sixth and seventh graders), only one gender, and could not rule out the contribution of hormonal or psychosocial factors. Furthermore, important advances in cognitive development also take place during this time. In conclusion, the data from this study are interesting, but many explanations other than simple changes in hormonal status may play a role in the onset of panic attacks.

Several investigations have reported that panic disorder appears to be more common among females (Bradley & Hood, 1993; Essau et al., 1999; Last & Strauss, 1989; Suveg et al., 2005), although in one investigation, 61% of those diagnosed with panic disorder were male (Masi et al., 2000). Similarly, in one study, boys reported a greater frequency of panic attacks than did girls (Bradley & Hood, 1993), whereas in other investigations, there were no differences in prevalence of panic disorder based on gender (Essau et al., 1999b; Hayward, Killen, Kraemer, & Taylor, 2000; King et al., 1993), or the attacks were more common among girls (Ginsburg & Drake, 2002). In summary, there are sufficient data to suggest that panic disorder is more common among adolescents than prepubertal children. The role of gender is less clear and may depend on the specific sample characteristics.

The number of physical symptoms reported by youth with panic disorder averages 6.3 symptoms per attack (Masi et al., 2000). Age and gender also may play a role in the severity of the symptom picture. Panic attacks in adolescents (age 13 and older) averaged 6.6 specific panic symptoms versus 6.0 panic symptoms in children (ages 12 and younger). With respect to group differences across individual symptoms, only chills or hot flushes differentiated the two groups, with a significantly greater frequency of children more likely to report this symptom when compared to adolescents (80% vs. 23%; Masi et al., 2000). Also, panic symptoms appear to be more severe among females (Hayward et al., 1989; Hayward, Killen, et al., 2000; Macaulay & Kleinknecht, 1989), although it is important to note, as we do throughout this book, that girls always endorse more frequent and more severe symptomatology when compared to boys. Thus, it is unclear if the greater severity reported by females is valid or merely reflects the tendency of males to underreport anxiety symptoms.

As noted, children in various countries endorse the presence of panic attacks and panic disorder (although the majority of the data to date are based on Caucasian samples). In addition to the rates established for samples in the United States, the prevalence of panic attacks is similar when reported for Australian children (42.9%; King et al., 1993) and German adolescents (18% of an epidemiological sample; Essau et al., 1999b). In contrast, the prevalence of panic disorder among children in the United States or Germany (Essau et al., 1999b) ranges from 0.6% to 5.3%, which is lower than among Italian children (10.4%; Masi et al., 2000).

COMORBIDITY AND DIFFERENTIAL DIAGNOSIS

Consistent with other anxiety disorders in youth, comorbidity is a common occurrence among children with panic attacks or panic disorder, with 50% to 90% of youth suffering from a comorbid condition (Suveg et al., 2005). With respect to children with panic attacks, the comorbid condition is an anxiety or mood disorder. Ninth graders with panic attacks had significantly higher scores on a self-report measure of depression when compared to the group without a panic attack (Hayward et al., 1989). The score for the panic attack group was in the mild-to-moderate range on the inventory, suggesting that those with panic attacks might be experiencing a moderate level of dysphoria but not necessarily severe depression.

Separation anxiety disorder, generalized anxiety disorder (or over-anxious disorder according to the revised third edition of the *DSM* [*DSM-III-R*]; APA, 1987), and depressive disorders appear to be the most common comorbid conditions among children and adolescents with panic disorder, with no difference in prevalence rate based on pubertal status. Among samples of children clinically diagnosed with panic disorder, 48–86% had comorbid separation anxiety disorder or a history of separation anxiety disorder (Alessi & Magen, 1988; Biederman et al., 1997; Masi et al., 2000; Vitiello et al., 1990). Similarly, 62–74% had comorbid generalized anxiety disorder (Biederman et al., 1997; Masi et al., 2000), and 43–80% had a depressive disorder, either major depression or dysthymic disorder (Alessi & Magen, 1988; Biederman et al., 1997; Essau et al., 1999b; Masi et al., 2000). One hundred percent of a small sample of six children and adolescents with panic disorder had a history of depressive disorders (Black & Robbins, 1990). Based on a sample of 20 children and adolescents with panic disorder (with or without ago-raphobia), 30% had a *DSM-IV* diagnosis of major depressive disorder/ dysthymia, a significantly higher frequency (5%) of comorbid depressive diagnoses than that found in a group of matched patients with anxiety disorder who did not have panic disorder (Kearney et al., 1997).

Comorbid externalizing disorders such as attention deficit/hyperac-tivity disorder and oppositional defiant disorder are high among treat-ment-seeking samples (Suveg et al., 2005). In the sample drawn from the pediatric psychopharmacology clinic, the rate of comorbid external-izing disorders was 90% (Doerfler et al., 2007). In summary, although the data on comorbidity are not extensive, those that do exist suggest that comorbidity is common. However, it is not yet clear what role the comorbid condition plays in the clinical presentation of the disorder or if it affects treatment efficacy.

ETIOLOGY OF PANIC DISORDER

As noted (Klein, Mannuzza, et al., 1992), diagnostic interviews con-ducted by highly experienced clinicians found that a number of adults retrospectively reported the existence of panic attacks prior to the age of 13, but only one had clearly documented panic disorder as a child. However, at least five others in this study reported panic in the context of other disorders diagnosed in childhood (separation anxiety disorder, social phobia, or specific phobia) and went on to develop panic disorder as adults (Klein, Mannuzza, et al., 1992).

> Angela reported that as a young child she was "scared of so many things," including wars, earthquakes, being separated from her parents, and the dark. Even at age 17, she still slept with the lamp on her nightstand turned on. Although she never actually experienced an event such as a war or an earthquake, she was exposed to them via the television and newspaper. For a period of time, she stopped watching the news and reading the newspaper.

Thus, early childhood anxiety, and perhaps the presence of situationally bound or predisposed panic attacks, may be predispositional factors for the development of panic disorder. However, it is not established that the presence of a childhood anxiety disorder is either necessary or sufficient for the development of panic disorder.

Specific life events sometimes are associated with the first onset of panic attacks in children and adolescents (Bradley & Hood, 1993). Interpersonal conflicts (with parents, friends, and teachers) were commonly reported (Warren & Zgourides, 1988), as were loss-related events (loss of someone cared about, parents separated or divorced, or moved to a different house or town; Hayward et al., 1989; Warren & Zgourides, 1988); academic difficulties (Warren & Zgourides, 1988); and physical events (such as medical illness or reaction to alcohol or drugs; Warren & Zgourides, 1988). One limitation of this last study was that it was based solely on the adolescent's recall of events occurring 1 week to 6 months prior to the first panic attack. Six months prior to the attack is a long time frame, and it is unclear if distress occurring that long ago could continue to influence emotional behavior 6 months later. Furthermore, it was unclear if the items endorsed represented a singular event or a continuous source of conflict. However, the data represent an important reminder that panic attacks, even when perceived to occur out of the blue, most often occur within an environmental context.

> In Angela's case, her parents were undergoing a period of marital distress. There were frequent verbal shouting matches, and Angela witnessed many of these arguments. She stated that she began to get thoughts such as, "I don't want to be here," and she felt restricted and confined. One day when she was having these thoughts, she began to sweat, feel jittery, experience heart palpitations, and wanted to run away. She did leave and go to a friend's house.

Family history also may represent an etiological factor in the onset of panic disorder in children. Among the studies that assessed family psychopathology, 53–100% of children with panic disorder had a family history of panic disorder or panic attacks severe enough to cause emotional distress or impairment (Bradley & Hood, 1993; Vitiello et al.,

1990). In other samples, 68–90% of the children had at least one parent with an anxiety disorder (Bradley & Hood, 1993; Masi et al., 2000). However, the presence of panic disorder in the parent alone may not be the best sole predictor of the presence of panic disorder in the offspring (Biederman et al., 2005). When the presence of panic disorder among the offspring of parents with panic disorder was examined, what differentiated the offspring who had panic disorder versus offspring who did not was the presence of comorbid (lifetime) separation anxiety disorder, social phobia, obsessive-compulsive disorder, and bipolar disorder in the parent or spouse. The risk of a child having panic disorder was particularly high if both parents had a history of social phobia. The impact of these other disorders, even if they were not currently present, suggests that it may be the lifetime presence of anxiety disorder, not necessarily a particular disorder, that enhances the likelihood of an anxiety disorder, in this case panic disorder, in the offspring.

Three factors appear to be predictive of the onset of panic in 58% of one sample of adolescents affected with panic disorder (Hayward et al., 2004). Parental history of panic attacks was the highest risk factor, identifying 24% of the adolescents with panic attacks. Among those without a positive family history, two other risk factors were identified: high childhood negative affect (14%) and a history of separation anxiety disorder (20%). Interestingly, when adolescents were assessed, childhood separation anxiety disorder was not a risk factor for panic disorder. Although negative affectivity was identified, it was not specific to panic disorder; it was also a risk factor for major depression. The only factor that appeared to be a specific risk for panic onset and that predicted the presence of four symptoms of panic was anxiety sensitivity.

To summarize, there are few data examining the etiology of panic disorder in youth, probably due in part to its low prevalence in children and adolescents. Studies of etiology require large samples and thus are extremely difficult to conduct. A multicenter study, which is costly, probably is necessary to understand the factors that contribute to the development of this disorder in youth.

ASSESSMENT

Consistent with the limited data on psychopathology, the formalized assessment of panic disorder in youth lags far behind what is available for other disorders. Several well-validated self-report inventories to assess the physiological, cognitive, and behavioral aspects of panic disorder and agoraphobia exist for adults, but they have not been validated with children. The Revised Child Anxiety and Depression Scale (RCADS;

Chorpita, Yim, Moffitt, Umemoto, & Francis, 2000) is a 47-item self-report measure that assesses symptoms of several anxiety disorders in youth, including panic disorder, based on *DSM-IV-TR* (APA, 2000) criteria. Items are scored as 1 "never," 2 "sometimes," 3 "often," or 4 "always." Chorpita et al. (2000) examined the factorial validity of the measure in a large school sample of children and adolescents, as well as its reliability and validity. Results indicated an item set and factors consistent with *DSM-IV-TR* anxiety disorders (and depression). The RCADS also demonstrates convergent validity with existing measures of childhood anxiety. A parent version of the measure is also available.

Other generalized measures of fears and anxiety, such as the Fear Survey Schedule for Children–Revised (FSSC-R; Ollendick, 1983; see Chapter 7) also may help identify places or situations associated with panic attacks, which in turn will assist in the development of an exposure hierarchy. The FSSC-R does not, however, identify symptoms or frequency of panic attacks. Rather, assessment of the frequency, severity, and situations surrounding the onset of panic is most easily accomplished through self-monitoring, such as a daily diary. Although there is no specific format necessary to adequately collect data, one form that we have found useful is presented in Figure 12.1.

TREATMENT

In one of the earliest investigations addressing how high school students cope with panic (Warren & Zgourides, 1988), adolescents used a variety

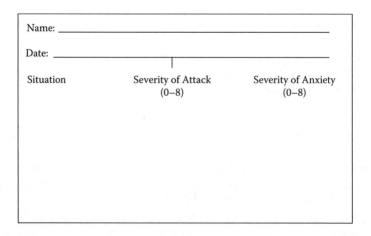

FIGURE 12.1 Panic attack daily diary.

of strategies to manage their panic attacks. Avoidance tactics (just forgot about it, forced self not to think about it, avoided situations where panic might occur, and used alcohol or drugs to reduce anxiety) were the most common method, endorsed by 98% of the sample. However, within this specific group of behaviors, only 13% specifically endorsed the use of drugs or alcohol to reduce anxiety. Talking to a friend was endorsed by 30% of the sample, whereas 26% reported that they talked to a professional (doctor, counselor, teacher, hospital emergency room staffer, or pastor/rabbi). Finally, 3% of the sample sought information or education about panic attacks.

The literature on the pharmacological treatment of panic disorder in children is limited. Ballenger and colleagues (1989) described the treatment of three children (ages 8, 11, and 13) with panic disorder with agoraphobia. Two children were treated with imipramine and the third with alprazolam and imipramine. Two children were able to be withdrawn from their medications after a period of time without recurrence of their symptoms. Panic attacks for the third child were controlled with medication but recurred whenever the medication was withdrawn. Selective serotonin reuptake inhibitors (SSRIs) are commonly prescribed clinically, but controlled clinical trials specifically for this disorder are not available.

The literature on the psychosocial treatment of panic disorder is similarly sparse. The data that do exist support the use of behavioral and cognitive-behavioral treatment. The low prevalence of this disorder limits the collection of a sufficient sample for an adequately powered controlled trial. In a review of panic disorder in children and adolescents (Ollendick, Birmaher, & Mattis, 2004), the primary cognitive-behavioral model was panic control treatment (PCT; Barlow, 2002), a model that has been adapted for children and adolescents (Mattis & Ollendick, 2002). Two single-case studies have been published (Barlow & Seidner, 1983; Ollendick, 1995), and there is one controlled trial (Pincus, May, Whitton, Mattis, & Barlow, 2010). In the initial publication (Barlow & Seidner, 1983), three adolescents diagnosed with agoraphobia were treated with an early version of PCT that consisted of 10 group sessions. Treatment included panic management procedures, cognitive restructuring, and in vivo exposure that was assigned as homework. Mothers were included in the intervention to assist in the exposure sessions, and parents were educated about the nature of agoraphobia and procedures for dealing with their child's anxiety. Two of the three adolescents showed marked improvement at the end of the 10-week intervention, whereas the third did not show any treatment response. The authors attributed the lack of improvement in the third adolescent to a conflictual parent–child relationship.

In the second study (Ollendick, 1995), four adolescents (aged 13–17) diagnosed with panic disorder with agoraphobia were treated with an adapted version of PCT. The average age of onset was 4 years prior to the decision to seek treatment, indicating a fair degree of chronicity for this sample. The treatment package consisted of psychoeducation, relaxation training and breathing retraining, cognitive restructuring, interoceptive exposure, participant modeling, in vivo exposure, and positive reinforcement. Treatment consisted of between 10 and 12 individual sessions, and parents again participated in the program. All four adolescents benefited from the intervention, which eliminated panic attacks, reduced behavioral avoidance, decreased negative mood, and enhanced confidence in their abilities to handle future anxiety symptoms. Results were maintained at 6-month follow-up, suggesting some promise for this particular intervention.

A controlled trial of a developmentally appropriate adaptation of PCT for adolescents with panic disorder and agoraphobia, called PCT-A, was completed (Mattis et al., 2006). PCT-A consists of 11 individual treatment sessions that utilize seven treatment elements: psychoeducation, situational exposures, breathing retraining, cognitive restructuring, interoceptive exposure, hypothesis testing, and naturalistic interoceptive exposure. The intervention is based on a cognitive model that postulates that catastrophic misinterpretation of typical physiological reactions results in panic attacks (Clark, 1988). The results indicated that PCT-A was superior to a wait-list condition on self-report measures of anxiety and clinician ratings of improvement of panic. These results are promising, but further controlled trials with larger samples and comparisons to placebo conditions and other active interventions are necessary.

CASE EXAMPLE: TREATMENT OF PANIC DISORDER

Angela was interviewed with the Anxiety Disorders Interview Schedule for DSM-IV: Child Version (ADIS-C; Silverman & Albano, 1996) and met diagnostic criteria for panic disorder with agoraphobia and generalized anxiety disorder. A battery of self-report instruments (the State-Trait Anxiety Inventory for Children, the Fear Survey Schedule for Children, and the Children's Depression Inventory) indicated high state anxiety, trait anxiety, a plethora of specific fears, and mild dysphoria. Thus, scores on the self-report inventories were consistent with her responses on the diagnostic interview. The self-monitoring data indicated an average of four panic attacks per week. In addition, she was avoiding approximately five activities per week.

To address her panic attacks and associated avoidance, a treatment program of interoceptive exposure and in vivo exposure was developed. Interoceptive exposure (Barlow, 2002) is a procedure whose purpose is to disrupt or weaken associations between specific bodily cues and panic reactions. The full theoretical rationale underlying this procedure is beyond the scope of this chapter (see Barlow, 2002, for a full discussion) but is consistent with other forms of exposure (i.e., imaginal and in vivo). Specifically, to overcome a fear, there must be exposure to the object that elicits the fear response. In the case of panic attacks, the basis of the fear is the physical symptoms that comprise the attack. Thus, interoceptive exposure involves contact with the panic symptoms. Because panic attacks sometimes occur unexpectedly, the challenge for therapy is to elicit the physical symptoms so that the child has the opportunity to habituate to the fear associated with them (as happens in other forms of exposure). When conducting interoceptive exposure, the child engages in exercises designed to produce panic-like physical sensations. Such exercises may include running up a flight of stairs (to increase heart rate), spinning in a chair (to elicit feelings of dizziness), or breathing through a straw (to mimic sensations of shortness of breath).

The following case material does not provide all of the instructions necessary for PCT or interoceptive exposure to be implemented effectively. Rather, it is intended to provide a sense of how the interventions are conducted. Clinicians interested in conducting interoceptive exposure should consult the work of Barlow (2002).

Interoceptive exposure involves a structured assessment of somatic symptoms through a series of exercises. The elicited sensations are rated by the patient for symptom intensity, anxiety intensity, and panic similarity. The results of Angela's interoceptive exposure assessment are presented in Table 12.2.

Items rated as moderately stressful or higher are arranged in a hierarchy (see Table 12.3), and the patient engages in the appropriate

TABLE 12.2   Angela's Interoceptive Exposure Assessment Results

Task	Severity of Sensation	Severity of Anxiety	Similarity to Panic
Shake head	6	2	0
Lifting head	3	2	0
Run in place for 1 minute	7	7	7
Spin in chair	8	8	0
Straw breathing	6	6	7
Hold a push-up for 1 minute	3	5	5
Hyperventilate for 1 minute	5	6	5

Source: Reprinted from Beidel, D. C., & Turner, S. M. (2005). *Child Anxiety Disorders*. New York: Routledge. With permission.

exercise to elicit the symptom. Presentation of the symptom is repeated until its elicitation results in no distress or only mild distress (fear rating of 0, 1, or 2 on a 9-point scale) but never more than five times in one session. On habituation, the next item on the hierarchy is presented. In the case of adults, interoceptive exposure is coupled with cognitive restructuring procedures. However, as has been noted in this chapter, cognitions often are not part of the clinical presentation of panic disorder in youth, and this was the case for Angela as well. Thus, her exposure plan did not include cognitive restructuring.

As noted, Angela avoided numerous situations because of concern that if a panic attack occurred, she might not be able to escape the situation. Angela avoided crowded situations such as shopping malls, buses, and movie theaters as well as small places such as elevators. Clinician-assisted in vivo exposure sessions included having Angela ride crowded buses and walk around a crowded shopping mall. Each exposure session was conducted for at least 90 minutes, longer if necessary for Angela to report her anxiety as a subjective units of distress (SUDS) rating of 2 or less. In addition, Angela was given homework exposure assignments that were to be carried out three times per week for 90 minutes each time. Angela's exposure to homework is presented in Table 12.4.

TABLE 12.3   Interoceptive Exposure Hierarchy

Item	SUDS Rating
Hold a push-up for 1 minute	3
Hyperventilate for 1 minute	5
Run in place for 1 minute	7
Breathe through a straw for 1 minute	7

Source: Reprinted from Beidel, D. C., & Turner, S. M. (2005). *Child Anxiety Disorders.* New York: Routledge. With permission.

TABLE 12.4   Angela's Homework Exposure Hierarchy

Walk around the neighborhood
Go to the park
Go to the shopping mall
Go to a restaurant
Go to a movie theater
Go to church

Source: Reprinted from Beidel, D. C., & Turner, S. M. (2005). *Child Anxiety Disorders.* New York: Routledge. With permission.

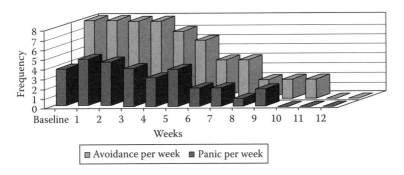

FIGURE 12.2   Angela's self-monitoring data.

Throughout treatment, Angela continued to monitor the number of panic attacks that she experienced and the number of situations that she avoided. Her progress is presented in Figure 12.2. At 1-year follow-up, Angela's treatment gains were maintained, and she was attending a small out-of-state college.

SUMMARY

In 1992, Kearney and Silverman reviewed existing studies of panic disorder, noting that the majority used small inpatient samples and nonstandardized assessment procedures, evaluated few sources of information, and did not assess panic severity or differentiate between cued and uncued panic. Although some of these criticisms have been answered by more recent empirical studies, others remain relevant. It is clear that children and adolescents suffer from panic disorder. Prevalence rates are fairly consistent, but it is clear that the type of assessment has a substantial effect on estimated prevalence. Also, there now are substantial findings that adolescents more often suffer from panic disorder than preadolescent children, and that the physical symptoms expressed by children and adolescents are consistent with those found in adults. Children and adolescents do avoid situations typically associated with panic disorder and agoraphobia. However, children and adolescents rarely report the cognitive symptoms listed in the *DSM-IV* diagnostic criteria for panic disorder. As is the case with other disorders, cognitive symptoms may not emerge until children develop basic cognitive/metacognitive skills.

Although the years since 2000 have illuminated at least some aspects of the psychopathology of panic disorder in children, the etiology of this disorder remains unclear. There are few studies addressing the development of panic disorder in children and adolescents, although potential factors appear to be similar to those found for other disorders. Perhaps because of the limited number of children and adolescents with this disorder, assessment instruments and treatment data lag far behind the literature established for other conditions. Much work is needed to construct reliable, valid, and usable assessment instruments and to determine efficacious and effective intervention strategies. Given the chronic nature of these disorders, these efforts are sorely needed.

CHAPTER 13

Posttraumatic Stress Disorder

Marla is 17 years old. Her parents own a local tourist company, and the family trains horses for carriage rides. Marla helps train the horses after school and on the weekends. Her career goals include going to college, becoming a veterinarian's assistant, and returning to help run the family business. Last year, she was training a new horse that became frightened and suddenly bolted, severely injuring Marla. In addition to ongoing physical sequelae (headaches, blackouts, and stuttering), she has a high level of general arousal, sleep disturbance, startle reactions whenever she sees a horse or enters the training area, and intrusive thoughts and nightmares regarding the accident. In addition, she has withdrawn socially and refuses to go back to training the horses.

Marla is suffering from posttraumatic stress disorder (PTSD), one of the most scientifically understudied anxiety disorders among children and adolescents. Although having many similarities to other anxiety disorders, PTSD differs in a number of respects. For example, unlike other anxiety disorders, the onset of PTSD always begins with an identifiable traumatic event (Koverola, 1995). However, the factors that determine who then goes on to develop PTSD are yet to be completely elucidated. In fact, in comparison to every other anxiety disorder, there are few empirical data available for any aspect of PTSD, even though there is voluminous clinical literature. Furthermore, even within the small body of empirical literature, few studies have used standardized diagnostic instruments when examining PTSD in children, although a number have used other types of structured procedures to assess PTSD symptoms (Lonigan et al., 2003). Thus, in this chapter, available data are presented with a caveat that this is an anxiety disorder with a poorly developed scientific base.

STRESSFUL AND TRAUMATIC EVENTS

Events that could precipitate stress reactions in children appear to be common in the general population. For example, stabbings, shootings, and murder were witnessed by 35%, 39%, and 25%, respectively, of one sample of adolescents (Jenkins & Bell, 1994). Another large study found that 68% of children in the United States have experienced a traumatic event, and half of these children have experienced multiple traumas (Copeland, Keeler, Angold, & Costello, 2007). As would be expected, young children are less likely to experience a traumatic event, with occurrence rates prior to age 6 around 1% (Storr, Ialongo, Anthony, & Breslau, 2007). Regardless of age, however, natural disasters (hurricanes, floods, lightning strikes), man-made disasters (airline disasters, boat sinkings), and events such as terrorism and war all may result in increased stress among those who are its victims. However, the mere experience of an event that has the potential to produce stress does not guarantee the subsequent emergence of PTSD.

Work on loss and trauma illustrates this assertion well. Whereas 50–60% of the U.S. population is exposed to a traumatic event at some point in their lives, approximately only 5–10% develop PTSD (Helzer, Robins, & McEvoy, 1987; Kessler, Chiu, Demler, Merikangas, & Walters, 2005; Ozer, Best, Lipsey, & Weiss, 2003). These data illustrate the substantial empirical literature demonstrating that although many individuals exposed to traumatic events may show brief PTSD or subclinical stress, these reactions most commonly dissipate after a few months. Despite the often-made clinical predictions, relatively few individuals develop symptomatology severe enough actually to meet criteria for PTSD. In fact, in the face of traumatic events such as the September 11, 2001, terrorist attacks, the Oklahoma City bombing, or the Los Angeles riots, most individuals show *recovery* (threshold or subthreshold psychopathology for a few months followed by a return to pretrauma levels of functioning) or *resilience* (those who maintain a stable equilibrium in the face of the traumatic event rather than experiencing the symptomatology of PTSD; Bonanno, 2004). As illustrated throughout this chapter, despite all of the clinical suppositions and clinical descriptions that attempt to pathologize the behavior of all individuals exposed to a traumatic event, the empirical data clearly indicate that recovery and resilience, not PTSD, are more common behavioral responses (Bonanno, 2004).

Initially, as with anxiety disorders in general, there was skepticism that children could suffer from PTSD (American Academy of Child and Adolescent Psychiatry [AACAP], 1998). However, studies of children traumatized by events such as the Chowchilla school bus kidnapping

(Terr, 1979), the Buffalo Creek dam collapse (Green et al., 1991), and sniper attacks on the schoolyard (Pynoos et al., 1987) soon illustrated that certain events could produce traumatic stress in children. Traumatic events that might precipitate onset of PTSD have been conceptually and usefully divided into two distinct subgroups (Terr, 1991). Type I traumas are those that are unpredictable and sudden and represent a single-incident event (that may be repeated). Type II traumas are chronic, expected, and repeated stressors, commonly childhood physical or sexual abuse. This classification delineates the different literatures and different treatment approaches (McKnight, Compton, & March, 2004). Although the Type II trauma literature is voluminous, far more clinical and descriptive reports are available rather than empirical data. Further, the seemingly ubiquitous examination of "posttraumatic stress symptoms" rather than PTSD has produced an array of findings with unclear implications for children with the actual disorder. Thus, we discuss the research on Type II traumas only briefly.

Type II Traumas

Exposure to repeated or cumulative stressors has been proposed to result in a complex form of PTSD that, in addition to *DSM-IV* (*Diagnostic and Statistical Manual of Mental Disorders, Fourth Edition*; American Psychiatric Association [APA], 1994) criteria, may include disturbances in interpersonal functioning and attachment, self-regulatory skills, anger management, impulse control and aggression, dissociative symptoms, or socially avoidant behaviors (Herman, 1992; Pynoos et al., 2009). Although not a formal diagnosis, the proposed syndrome "complex PTSD" has been the subject of increasing clinical dialogue based on the fact that existing criteria do not adequately capture the broad range of symptoms seen among children exposed to Type II traumas (Cloitre et al., 2009; Cook et al., 2005). Although this may certainly be the case, complex PTSD as a specific syndrome has not been subject to adequate empirical examination. Further, as described in available case reports and studies, adverse events thought to result in complex PTSD range considerably, including physical and sexual abuse, emotional abuse, neglect, maltreatment, witnessing domestic violence, child removal from the home, foster placement, child exploitation, wartime exposure, imprisonment, loss of a parent, having a psychiatrically ill parent, medical illness (in the child or a family member), repeated medical procedures, or exposure to community or school violence, to name only some. The likelihood that each of these diverse experiences may lead to the same clinical syndrome, be it complex PTSD or any other, is less than clinically intuitive, particularly when one considers the wide range of variation in duration, intensity, and level of threat involved. In addition, in many cases children remain in a stressful or traumatic situation (e.g., domestic violence, foster placement, medical illness) for extended periods of time, including the time at which assessment occurs. Thus, by definition, the child has not yet reached the "posttrauma" stage since the threat to safety or harm is still very much present.

Beyond inherent conceptual challenges, establishment of any nosological category requires adequate construct validity. Compared to a handful of studies involving children who have experienced Type I traumas (e.g., Anthony, Lonigan & Hecht, 1999; Lonigan et al., 2003), data examining the construct validity of PTSD (or complex PTSD) in children who have suffered repeated traumas are unavailable. In one study that included 311 refugee children (3–15 years) from the Middle East with a history of exposure to war conditions, organized violence, or human rights violations, the validity of some PTSD criteria were assessed in relation to 34 specific types of traumatic (although not mutually exclusive) events (Montgomery & Foldspang, 2006). Overall, children's behavioral and emotional symptoms did not cluster in any consistent pattern, and only 2 of the 34 events examined (mother being tortured and father having disappeared) were associated with PTSD symptoms specifically. Thus, beyond a lack of validity for existing *DSM-IV* criteria for PTSD, results from this study do not support the utility of any one set of diagnostic criteria in this sample. Of course, the extent to which the impact of war-related traumas compares to that of other traumatic events is unclear and highlights a significant gap in this literature. In sum, several critical issues remain to be adequately addressed with regard to Type II traumas and PTSD, including the considerable diversity present among most samples of children, lack of operational definition for what constitutes a Type II trauma, and examination of a broad array of symptoms rather than a specific set of diagnostic criteria.

Acute Stress Disorder

Theoretically related to PTSD is the more recently introduced acute stress disorder (ASD) diagnostic category (APA, 1994). ASD may last for a minimum of 2 days and a maximum of 4 weeks following exposure to a trauma. Thus, like PTSD, ASD is precipitated by exposure to a traumatic event and is accompanied by or followed by dissociative symptoms that include three of the following: (a) a subjective sense of numbing or detachment, (b) a reaction in awareness of surroundings,

(c) derealization, (d) depersonalization, and (e) dissociative amnesia (APA, 1994). Other PTSD symptom clusters (reexperiencing, avoidance, and hyperarousal) also are required for a diagnosis, although ASD is unique in its requirement of three or more dissociative symptoms. Although ASD is presumed to be a predictor of future psychopathology, including PTSD, the disorder has received little attention with respect to its incidence in children except perhaps as a "first stage" of PTSD (McKnight et al., 2004). However, available longitudinal data examining this first-stage hypothesis provided mixed support.

For example, after automobile accidents in which injuries requiring hospitalization were sustained, 8% of children met criteria for ASD, and 14% met criteria for subsyndromal ASD (Kassam-Adams & Winston, 2004). However, only 14% of those with ASD went on to develop PTSD, whereas 60% of those who developed PTSD did not have any earlier symptoms of ASD. Meiser-Stedman and colleagues (Meiser-Stedman, Smith, Glucksman, Yule, & Dalgleish, 2007; Meiser-Stedman, Yule, Smith, Glucksman, & Dalgleish, 2005) examined the utility of ASD in predicting PTSD in two separate studies. One study included youth between the ages of 10 and 16 following an assault or motor vehicle accident (Meiser-Stedman et al., 2007). Although child report of ASD following the trauma was significantly associated with a PTSD diagnosis 6 months later, parent report of ASD was unrelated to later PTSD. Further, overall parent–child agreement for an ASD diagnosis was notably poor (Cohen's κ = -.04). In a similar study including youth assessed within 4 weeks of an assault or motor vehicle accident and again 6 months later, ASD was found to be a good predictor of PTSD, correctly classifying 82.8% of PTSD cases (Meiser-Stedman et al., 2005).

Dalgleish et al. (2008) also found that presence of ASD following a motor vehicle accident correlated significantly with a PTSD diagnosis 6 months later among children and adolescents. However, an important limitation of this multisite study included the use of different assessment instruments across sites, including various structured interviews and questionnaires.

Thus, data supporting the theoretical notion that ASD is a precursor of PTSD among children are limited. Also of concern, criteria delineated for this syndrome appear to have poor empirical support. For example, although the alleged rationale behind the requirement of three or more dissociative symptoms was that dissociation in the acute phase of trauma can identify those at risk of later PTSD, research has found dissociation to account for little variance in predicting PTSD in adults as well as children (Dalgleish et al., 2008; Harvey & Bryant, 1998). Indeed, in our view, this is a poorly supported diagnostic category as currently defined.

POSTTRAUMATIC STRESS DISORDER

Even when restricted to Type I events, the extant data are further limited by the lack of a standardized, or even consistent, system by which to determine the presence of a PTSD diagnosis. Criteria established by the text revision of the fourth edition of the *DSM* (*DSM-IV-TR*; APA, 2000) have become the diagnostic standard. The *DSM-IV-TR* criteria are presented in Table 13.1.

As illustrated, there are four criteria necessary for a diagnosis of PTSD. First, of course, there must be exposure to a traumatic event and the perception that death or serious physical injury could result. As noted, a broad range of events, such as natural disasters, man-made disasters, medical illnesses, war and combat, and personal injury, could serve as a qualifying event for a diagnosis of PTSD. Since the introduction of the diagnostic category in 1980 (third edition of the *DSM* [*DSM-III*]; APA, 1980), the definition of a triggering traumatic event has changed dramatically. In *DSM-III*, the event was defined as something outside the range of normal human experience (the classic notion regarding stimuli capable of producing PTSD). The fourth edition revision evolved from perceptions that certain events precipitating the development of PTSD (rape, child abuse, domestic violence, community violence, war) were not necessarily rare. Instead, under *DSM-IV-TR* (APA, 2000), the traumatic event must be considered "extreme." This has led to a broadening of the class of traumatic events as well as their definition: It must involve experiencing, witnessing, or confronting an event capable of causing death, injury, or threat to physical integrity to self or another person. The more subjective nature of the diagnostic criteria now allow the clinician to judge whether a particular stress is extreme, creating potential for great variability in judging qualifying events and thus a diagnosis of PTSD. This, in effect, introduces two levels of subjectivity into the diagnostic process: that of the patient and that of the clinician. Overall, in our view, the diagnostic category likely is too broad to be scientifically or clinically meaningful. Much work is needed to restore the clinical and scientific integrity of this diagnostic category and remove it from its political and economic arena.

As for other anxiety disorders, PTSD diagnostic criteria include developmental descriptors to increase its appropriateness for children. For example, among children, "recurrent and intrusive distressing recollections" may be repetitive play that may incorporate themes of the trauma. Similarly, for "recurrent distressing dreams of the event," frightening dreams with no recognizable content are considered a developmentally appropriate equivalent. Finally, instead of having the experience of

TABLE 13.1 *DSM-IV-TR* Criteria for Posttraumatic Stress Disorder

A. The person has been exposed to a traumatic event in which both of the following were present:

(1) The person experienced, witnessed, or was confronted with an event or events that involved actual or threatened death or serious injury, or a threat to the physical integrity of self or others.

(2) The person's response involved intense fear, helplessness, or horror. *Note*: In children, this may be expressed instead by disorganized or agitated behavior.

B. The traumatic event is persistently reexperienced in one (or more) of the following ways:

(1) Recurrent and intrusive distressing recollections of the event, including images, thoughts, or perceptions. *Note*: In young children, repetitive play may occur in which themes or aspects of the trauma are expressed.

(2) Recurrent distressing dreams of the event. *Note*: In children, there may be frightening dreams without recognizable content.

(3) Acting or feeling as if the traumatic event were recurring (includes a sense of reliving the experience, illusions, hallucinations, and dissociative flashback episodes, including those that occur on awakening or when intoxicated). *Note*: In young children, trauma-specific reenactment may occur.

(4) Intense psychological distress at exposure to internal or external cues that symbolize or resemble an aspect of the traumatic event.

(5) Physiological reactivity on exposure to internal or external cues that symbolize or resemble an aspect of the traumatic event.

C. Persistent avoidance of stimuli associated with the trauma and numbing of general responsiveness (not present before the trauma), as indicated by three (or more) of the following:

(1) efforts to avoid thoughts, feelings, or conversations associated with the trauma

(2) efforts to avoid activities, places, or people that arouse recollections of the trauma

(3) inability to recall an important aspect of the trauma

(4) markedly diminished interest or participation in significant activities

(5) feeling of detachment or estrangement from others

(6) restricted range of affect (e.g., unable to have loving feelings)

(7) sense of a foreshortened future (e.g., does not expect to have a career, marriage, children, or a normal life span)

D. Persistent symptoms of increased arousal (not present before the trauma), as indicated by two (or more) of the following:

(1) difficulty falling or staying asleep

(2) irritability or outbursts of anger

(Continued)

TABLE 13.1   *DSM-IV-TR* Criteria for Posttraumatic Stress
Disorder   (Continued)

(3) difficulty concentrating

(4) hypervigilance

(5) exaggerated startle response

E. Duration of the disturbance (symptoms in Criteria B, C, and D) is more
than 1 month.

F. The disturbance causes clinically significant distress or impairment in
social, occupational, or other important areas of functioning.

Specify if:

• Acute: if duration of symptoms is less than 3 months

• Chronic: if duration of symptoms is 3 months or more

Specify if:

• With Delayed Onset: if onset of symptoms is at least 6 months after the
stressor

Source: Reprinted with permission from American Psychiatric Association,
Diagnostic and Statistical Manual of Mental Disorders (4th ed., text
revision). Washington, DC: Author. Copyright 2000. American
Psychiatric Association.

acting or feeling as if the event were recurring (sense of reliving the experience, illusions, hallucinations, or flashbacks), trauma-specific reenactment may be present. Despite these developmental descriptors, a number
of researchers argued that the current set of criteria may not be sensitive enough for preschool-aged children. Based on results from several
studies (Levendosky, Huth-Bocks, Semel, & Shapiro, 2002; Ohmi et
al., 2002; Scheeringa, Peebles, Cook, & Zeanah, 2001; Scheeringa &
Zeanah, 2008; Scheeringa, Zeana, Drell, & Larrieu, 1995; Scheeringa,
Zeanah, Myers, & Putnam, 2003), it has been suggested that a developmentally sensitive, alternative algorithm (PTSD-AA) may better capture
the disorder as experienced by preschoolers (Scheeringa et al., 2003).

In addition to some modifications in the wording of certain criteria,
the major proposed change is to lower the requirement of Criterion C,
which requires at least three of seven possible symptoms of numbing and
avoidance, to just one. Specifically, because most of these symptoms represent primarily internalized phenomena (e.g., avoiding thoughts related
to the trauma, inability to recall important aspects of the trauma, sense
of foreshortened future), they are either developmentally impossible in
young children or difficult to detect (Scheeringa et al., 2003).

Certainly, many of the current diagnostic criteria rely on verbal
descriptions that exceed the abilities of preverbal children (Gurwitch,
Kees, & Becker, 2002). However, rather than immediately concluding

that prevalence rates among young children are underestimated, it also is important to remember that basic cognitive abilities, like verbal abilities, also are underdeveloped in very young children. Therefore, it is necessary to consider whether young children have the cognitive capacity to interpret the significance of certain traumatic events prior to determining that they have been negatively affected by them but are not able to verbally express their symptomatology and distress. A good example comes from research examining the responses of children under the age of 5 living in close proximity to ground zero on September 11, 2001. In addition to some fearful and distressed reactions, many children were described by their parents as calm and cooperative (Klein, Devoe, Miranda-Julian, & Linas, 2009). Thus, to some extent, young children may derive protection from their failure to comprehend situation-based levels of threat and harm, even though this possibility remains largely unexamined.

Two studies have actually compared the utility of *DSM-IV* criteria and PTSD-AA criteria among trauma-exposed preschool children. Among preschoolers who had been involved in motor vehicle accidents, the prevalence of PTSD based on *DSM-IV* criteria was 1.7% compared to 10% using PTSD-AA criteria (Meiser-Stedman, Smith, Glucksman, Yule, & Dalgleish, 2008). Among children affected by Hurricane Katrina, the rate of *DSM-IV* PTSD was 15.7%, while the rate of PTSD-AA was 50% (Scheeringa & Zeanah, 2008). Although there is only one published community study of PTSD in preschool-age children and *DSM-III-R* (revised third edition of the *DSM*; APA, 1987) criteria were used, the prevalence of PTSD in this study was 0.1% (Lavigne et al., 1996). Again, since available research indicated that the vast majority of individuals exposed to a traumatic event do not develop PTSD, these findings suggest that alternative criteria for PTSD in preschoolers only adds to existing problems of poor diagnostic specificity.

Clinical Features and Course

In addition to exposure to a traumatic event, *DSM-IV* criteria require the presence of symptoms from each of three symptom clusters. Each cluster is discussed in detail next.

> As the horse reared up, Marla felt helpless and thought that she was going to die. Every night, she dreams of that moment and wakes up in a cold sweat.

Reexperiencing of the traumatic event in some fashion is a hallmark feature of PTSD. Reexperiencing may occur in the form of intrusive thoughts, dreams, or flashbacks, although the last appear to be less common among children and adolescents (McKnight et al., 2004). By comparison, bad dreams or nightmares are more commonly seen (Lonigan et al., 2003), although not necessarily depicting the previous trauma. Similar to obsessive-compulsive disorder (OCD), the intrusive thoughts associated with PTSD can occur spontaneously or in response to environmental events; sights, sounds, smells, people, or places that are associated with or are reminiscent of the traumatic event. In addition, among young children, reexperiencing also may take the form of traumatic play (reenactment; McKnight et al., 2004). It is important, however, not to automatically interpret any behavior as indicative of trauma reenactment. For example, Gurwitch et al. (2002) noted that after the Oklahoma City bombing, children built and destroyed buildings made of blocks. However, many children who have never been victims of bombings will build block buildings or sandcastles and then delight in knocking them down. Without clear understanding of typical child play and the ability to compare behaviors of those with PTSD to developmentally appropriate and normative data, the possibility exists that certain behaviors will be misinterpreted as indicative of PTSD. Thus, it is critical not to erroneously attribute every behavior as indicative of PTSD, even among those exposed to a traumatic event. To do so creates confusion in the empirical literature and delays the accumulation of scientific knowledge necessary to develop efficacious interventions.

Avoidance and numbing are another cluster of symptoms necessary for a diagnosis of PTSD. A child with PTSD may attempt to avoid situations, places, or people that precipitate the reexperiencing phenomena previously described.

> Despite all of her parents' efforts, Marla refused to go back to the stable where she was injured.

Thus, children may refuse to go to school if a violent event occurred there previously. Previous enjoyable activities now may be refused because of their association with a traumatic event. Some children may show behaviors typical of an earlier stage of development, such as enuresis and thumb sucking (McKnight et al., 2004). Among young children, avoidance behaviors may also manifest in the form of increased clinginess or refusal to separate from caregivers (Gurwitch, Sullivan, & Long, 1998).

> Theresa was seriously injured in an automobile accident in which her two best friends were killed. Their automobile was struck by a drunk driver in a blue sedan. Now, whenever she sees a blue sedan, Theresa's heart races, she sweats, and she begins to cry.

The third cluster of behaviors (and the fourth necessary criterion for PTSD) are those that represent hyperarousal. Specific symptoms include difficulty initiating or maintaining sleep, difficulty concentrating, irritability, exaggerated startle responses, and hypervigilance (McKnight et al., 2004). Children may appear tense, scanning the environment for other potential threats or traumas. In addition to a general tonic increase in arousal, children and adolescents may experience panic attacks if they encounter stimuli that are associated with the traumatic event.

As described, it has been suggested that the symptomatic expression of PTSD may differ depending on the type of trauma (Type I vs. Type II). Sleep disturbances, autonomic hyperarousal, and reexperiencing have been hypothesized to occur more frequently among those who experienced a Type I traumatic event, whereas dissociation, restricted affect, aggression and externalizing problems, sadness, and detachment are more characteristic of Type II traumas (Cooley-Quille, Turner, & Beidel, 1995; Famularo, Fenton, Kinscherff, & Augustyn, 1996; Terr, 1991). Thus, repeated traumas appear to result in a much broader range of symptoms and problem behaviors, and at least one study has reported a significantly positive relationship between number of childhood traumas and symptom complexity (Cloitre et al., 2009). Within Type I trauma, the symptoms with the highest degree of diagnostic efficacy (e.g., identifying children with PTSD after exposure to Hurricane Hugo) were behavioral avoidance, bad dreams, emotional avoidance, and repetitive thoughts (Lonigan et al., 2003). Similarly, after Hurricane Andrew, symptoms of reexperiencing were more frequent than those of avoidance and hyperarousal (Vernberg, La Greca, Silverman, & Prinstein, 1996).

Symptoms of PTSD can negatively affect school functioning. After Hurricane Hugo, for example, the average decrease in school performance for children who met criteria for posttraumatic stress syndrome (not necessarily PTSD) was more than three times the decrease for children who did not meet full criteria for the syndrome (Shannon, Lonigan, Finch, & Taylor, 1994). Among a sample of several thousand children displaced by Hurricane Katrina, Osofsky, Osofsky, Kronenberg, Brennan, and Hansel (2009) reported that children were forced to attend an average of two schools during the 2005–2006 school year, with some children attending up to five schools. Thus, the long-term sequelae of trauma and PTSD can be extensive and complicated. Even though the actual event may last for only a short period of time, the resultant disruption in everyday functioning often persists and continues to exert significant distress on those affected. For example, even 7 months after Hurricane Andrew, 27% of the children in a sample initially affected by the hurricane (but not necessarily meeting PTSD criteria) reported that most of the damage to their home was not yet fixed, and 23% were still living in alternative housing. Forty-four percent were still experiencing two or more disaster-related sequelae (housing disruption, parent out of work). Among youth affected by Hurricane Katrina, children lived in an average of 3 different places in the year following the storm, with a range of 1 to 10 different placements (Osofsky et al., 2009). By the following year, well over half of the children surveyed still had not returned to their prestorm homes. Clearly, such ongoing stress may function to maintain or exacerbate PTSD symptomatology, although to date, empirical data examining this relationship are limited.

Sociodemographic Influences

As noted (McKnight et al., 2004), although events that might precipitate PTSD appear to be common among the general population, there are few actual epidemiological data. The few data that do exist suggest that its lifetime prevalence ranges from 1% to 14% (APA, 1994). However, it is difficult to calculate trends in prevalence rates because the defining event has been substantially expanded; often, cases are included that do not meet the full criteria.

Among children experiencing a documented Type I traumatic event, rates of the development of PTSD range from 5.2% to 100% (see Table 13.2 for specific PTSD rates for different traumatic events). Furthermore, the absence of data make it difficult to determine the natural course of the disorder. However, the long-term follow-up of young adults who as adolescents survived the sinking of the cruise ship *Jupiter* are instructive (Yule et al., 2000). Across the 5- to 8-year follow-up period, 51.7% of survivors developed PTSD at some point during follow-up, and 17.5% were still affected 5–8 years later. In 90% of the PTSD cases, onset occurred within the first 6 months postdisaster, and for 30% of those affected, duration was less than 1 year. However, 34% of those with PTSD (as noted, 17.5% of the entire sample) still met criteria 5–8 years later. It is unclear whether recovery occurred as a result of therapeutic intervention or was a naturally occurring process. Furthermore, determining which variables may function to hasten or retard recovery has yet to be done.

The role of gender in PTSD is unclear. Some investigations confirmed the greater likelihood for the development of PTSD symptoms and PTSD among females (Green et al., 1991; Gurwitch, Lefwich, Pfefferbaum, & Pynoos, 2000, cited in Gurwitch et al., 2002; Hensley & Varela, 2008; Lonigan, Shannon, Taylor, Finch, & Sallee, 1994; Udwin, Boyle, Yule, Bolton, & Oryan, 2000; Weems, Pina, et al., 2007). Even when exposed to the same trauma (i.e., sinking of the cruise ship *Jupiter*), 56.6% of

TABLE 13.2 Rates of PTSD Among Children Subject to Different Type I Traumatic Events

Study	Nature of Disaster	PTSD Rate
Aaron et al. (1999)	Pediatric injury and hospitalization	23%
Daviss et al. (2000)	Pediatric injury and hospitalization	12.5%
Goenjian et al. (1995)	Spitak, Armenia, earthquake (18 months later)	
	Epicenter	95%
	20 miles away	76%
	47 miles away	26%
Green et al. (1991)	Buffalo Creek Dam disaster	
	2 years later (probable PTSD)	37%
	17 years later (definite PTSD)	7%
Kassam-Adams & Winston (2004)	Motor vehicle accident	6%
La Greca, Silverman, Vernberg, & Prinstein (1996)	Hurricane Andrew	
	After 3 months	39.1%
	After 7 months	24.0%
	After 10 months	18.1%
McFarlane (1987)	Australian bush fire	
	After 8 months	29.5%
	After 26 months	26.3%
Pynoos et al. (1987)	School playground sniper attack	
	Overall prevalence	60.4%
	On the playground during shooting	77%
	In the school during shooting	67%
	Already left school for the day	26%
	Absent from school that day	17%
Shannon et al. (1994)	Hurricane Hugo	5.2%
Terr (1983)	School bus hijacking (4 years later)	100%
Udwin et al. (2000)	Sinking of the cruise ship *Jupiter*	51.5%
Yule et al. (2000)	Sinking of the *Jupiter* (5–8 years later)	34%

Source: Reprinted from Beidel, D. C., & Turner, S. M. (2005). *Child Anxiety Disorders.* New York: Routledge. With permission.

the females and 32.6% of the males developed PTSD (Yule et al., 2000). Differences in specific type of PTSD symptoms also have been reported. Among adolescents exposed to a supercyclone that hit the east coast of India, males were more likely to report bad dreams about the disaster, strong memories of the event, and greater cognitive avoidance than females, whereas girls reported stronger startle reactions (Kar & Bastia, 2006). However, other investigations did not report gender differences in rates or types of PTSD symptoms or the disorder (Kassam-Adams & Winston, 2004; Nader, Pynoos, Fairbanks, & Frederick, 1990; Pynoos et al., 1987). The potential for gender bias following certain types of traumatic events also should be considered. For example, among a sample of youth reported to child protective services for alleged sexual abuse, gender-based comparisons did not reveal any differences in objective measures of abuse severity or posttraumatic stress symptoms, yet caseworkers rated girls significantly higher on levels of associated harm (Maikovich, Koenen, & Jaffee, 2009).

Age also may play a role in the presentation some specific PTSD symptoms (see Lonigan et al., 2003). In a review summarizing the earlier literature (Fremont, 2004), younger children (aged 5 and under) were more likely to exhibit behaviors such as bed-wetting, thumb sucking, or fear of the dark, as well as increased difficulties separating from parents following a trauma. Notably, these symptoms and behaviors were not specifically included in *DSM-IV* criteria. Latency age children were more likely to exhibit attentional problems, impaired school performance, school avoidance, somatic complaints, irrational fears, sleep problems, nightmares, irritability, and anger outbursts. Adolescents were more likely to express intrusive thoughts, hypervigilance, emotional numbing, nightmares, sleep disturbances, and avoidance, thereby indicating a relatively consistent pattern of symptoms from middle childhood through adolescence (Lonigan et al., 2003). Thus, as children mature, their symptomatology becomes more similar to that found for adults with PTSD.

Younger children also are more likely to report posttraumatic stress syndrome than early or late adolescents (9.2%, 4.2%, and 3.1%, respectively; Shannon et al., 1994). Repetitive thoughts and getting upset by the thoughts, bad dreams, fear of reoccurrence, anhedonia, emotional isolation, sleep difficulties, behavioral avoidance, upset at reminders of Hurricane Hugo, and reckless behaviors all were endorsed more frequently by children than adolescents (Shannon et al., 1994). In contrast, younger children were less likely to report amnesia for part of the trauma and less likely to have avoidance or numbing symptoms or visual flashbacks, and because of their limited cognitive capabilities, may be less likely to perceive or understand the idea of a foreshortened future (see AACAP, 1998, for a review of this literature).

An important consideration when examining the role of age and gender is to carefully consider the assessment method used to determine the presence of the syndrome. When data are based solely on self-report, there is a need to interpret these data carefully as overall, younger children and females tend to score higher on self-report measures of anxiety and fears. Thus, the finding that younger children and females reported higher levels of hurricane damage to their homes (Shannon et al., 1994) might be an artifact of reporting inasmuch as there is no rational reason why physical hurricane damage would vary by the age or gender of a child. Therefore, significantly higher rates of PTSD for females than males (6.9% vs. 3.8% for Hurricane Hugo victims; Shannon et al., 1994) also must be considered in light of the propensity for females to endorse a greater number of anxiety symptoms than males, as are younger children in comparison to older children or adolescents.

After Hurricane Andrew, African American and Hispanic children reported more traumatic distress than White children (La Greca et al., 1996), but it remains unclear whether rates of PTSD differ among children of different racial and ethnic groups (see AACAP, 1998, for a review). In certain natural disasters (such as hurricanes), socioeconomic factors may be related to the extensiveness of the physical damage that may result. For example, children from lower socioeconomic groups are more likely to live in housing more easily damaged from hurricane-force winds. Thus, reported group differences based on racial or ethnic minority status need to be considered in terms of socioeconomic factors. Several studies examining PTSD symptoms among families affected by Hurricane Katrina are now available; however, because even before the hurricane struck, families from the Gulf Coast were among the poorest and most underserved in the United States (U.S. Department of Health and Human Services, 2005), examination of PTSD rates based solely on racial and ethnic characteristics is difficult. However, Pina et al. (2008) did not find any differences in PTSD symptoms between Caucasian and African American children assessed 6 months post-Katrina even though a higher percentage of African American children reported losing their homes (19.4% compared to 66.7%, respectively). In another investigation that did control for other demographic and exposure factors (Shannon et al., 1994), African American children still reported more symptoms of PTSD than non-African American children after exposure to Hurricane Hugo, although there was no group difference in the percentage of children from each group who met criteria for the full PTSD stress syndrome (6.3% vs. 5.1%; Shannon et al., 1994). Other investigations also concluded that group differences in rates of PTSD were inconsistent and need to be more concerned with controlling socioeconomic status (see Lonigan et al., 2003, for a review).

Comorbid and Differential Diagnosis

In addition to her frank PTSD symptoms, Marla is severely depressed.

A majority of children with PTSD also suffer from other comorbid conditions. In fact, high rates of comorbidity among most children with PTSD contribute to concerns regarding the diagnostic specificity and sensitivity of *DSM-IV* (1994) and *IV-TR* (2000) criteria. For example, PTSD criteria overlap considerably with criteria for major depressive disorder (i.e., decreased interest in activities, sleep disturbance, restricted affect, and decreased concentration) as well as generalized anxiety disorder (GAD; i.e., sleep disturbance, irritability, and decreased concentration). Some researchers have argued that this extensive overlap has resulted in a large number of traumatized children, particularly those experiencing Type II traumas, not receiving a PTSD diagnosis (van der Kolk, 2005). To date, however, there are no empirical data to support this claim.

Another concern that warrants mention relates to the temporal associations between PTSD and comorbid disorders. Although it is often assumed clinically that comorbid conditions develop after PTSD, in fact most child studies have generally failed to specifically inquire about timing of onset. Available data suggest that, in some instances, these comorbid disorders existed prior to the onset of PTSD (see section on etiology), whereas in others, the onset of the comorbid disorder follows the diagnosis of PTSD. In these latter cases, depressive disorders appear to be the most common comorbid condition (AACAP, 1998; Brent et al., 1995; Goenjian et al., 1995; McKnight et al., 2004, Yule & Canterbury, 1994), although substance abuse, GAD, agoraphobia, and separation anxiety disorder also have been reported (see AACAP, 1998). Adolescents with PTSD are at an increased risk for the later development of cannabis dependence and abuse (Cornelius et al., 2010), while preschool-age children with PTSD commonly develop separation anxiety disorder and oppositional defiant disorder (Scheeringa et al., 2003; Scheeringa & Zeanah, 2008). Further, children and adolescents with PTSD are 25 times more likely than youth without PTSD to have another anxiety disorder 12–18 months later (Cortes et al., 2005).

Among children with PTSD, 41% developed a comorbid major depressive disorder by the time they were 18 years old (Giaconia et al., 1995). In contrast, only 8% of children without PTSD developed major depression by age 18. Rates of social phobia (33%), specific phobia (29%), and alcohol and drug dependence (46% and 25%, respectively) also were higher among children with PTSD, in most cases with onset occurring after PTSD. Other investigations also have reported higher rates of self-reported anxiety, depression, and misconduct when compared to children with specific phobia or no psychiatric disorder (Saigh, 1989; Yule, Udwin, & Murdoch, 1990), but no differences from children with other anxiety disorders. These differences were evident not only immediately after the event but also 5 months later (Yule et al., 1990). Comorbidity rates have also been compared among abused children (i.e., experiencing Type II traumas) with and without PTSD (Linning & Kearney, 2004). Children meeting PTSD criteria had significantly more comorbid diagnoses overall, and dysthymia and major depressive disorder accounted most for this group difference. GAD, panic disorder, and specific phobias also were more common in the PTSD group.

Neurobiology of PTSD

In recent years, the relationship between certain brain structures and traumatic events has been the subject of an increasing number of investigations. The brain regions most vulnerable to and influenced by stress and trauma include the hippocampus, corpus callosum, and prefrontal cortex (De Bellis, 2001; Teicher et al., 1997). The hippocampus is a structure of the limbic system involved in explicit and working memory for episodic events. Despite consistent findings of reduced hippocampal volumes among adults with the disorder, the majority of a limited number of studies have not provided compelling evidence for this structural deficit in children with PTSD (Carrion et al., 2001; De Bellis et al., 1999; De Bellis, Keshavan, Shifflett, et al., 2002; De Bellis, Hall, Boring, Frustaci, & Moritz, 2001). In fact, in one study, increased hippocampal volumes were found among children with PTSD compared with healthy controls (Tupler & De Bellis, 2006). However, Carrion and colleagues (2007) provided evidence of developing hippocampal volume deficits 12–18 months after a sample of children with PTSD were initially assessed. Together with existing data, this finding suggests that structural changes to the hippocampus may be a consequence rather than a risk factor for PTSD. Carrion et al. (2007) also found baseline-level cortisol levels predicted hippocampal reductions 12–18 months later. Since the stress response involves secretion of several neurohormones, including cortisol, this finding may reflect the neurotoxic effects of prolonged cortisol release on this brain structure. Other studies also have found elevated cortisol levels in children with PTSD as well as subclinical PTSD (Carrion et al., 2002; De Bellis et al., 1999). However, collective evidence suggests that after initial increases in cortisol following a traumatic event, the hypothalamic-pituitary-adrenal (HPA) axis may be altered such that decreased cortisol levels (hypocortisolism) are observed with the passage of time (e.g., Goenjian et al., 1996).

Other research has focused on the corpus callosum (the main tract of nerve fibers controlling communication between the two hemispheres of the brain) and PTSD. Three separate studies have reported differences in medial and posterior corpus callosum areas in children with PTSD compared to healthy controls (De Bellis et al., 1999; De Bellis, Keshavan, Shifflett, et al., 2002; Jackowski et al., 2008). Significant reductions in total or subregional corpus callosum areas were not detected in another study, however (Carrion et al., 2009). Reduction in the corpus callosum has also been found in psychiatric inpatients with a history of childhood maltreatment compared to both psychiatric and healthy controls without a history of trauma exposure (Teicher et al., 2004). Although it has been hypothesized that corpus callosum abnormalities in children with PTSD reflect a neurodevelopmental deficit resulting from traumatic experiences (De Bellis et al., 1999), the nature of these findings remains unclear.

Abnormality of the prefrontal cortex is another area of burgeoning interest in pediatric PTSD. Carrion et al. (2001) found an attenuation of frontal lobe asymmetry in children with abuse-related PTSD compared to controls. These investigators reported prefrontal morphological differences between these groups, including increased gray matter volume in superior and inferior prefrontal regions and increased gray matter density in ventral prefrontal regions associated with PTSD (Carrion et al., 2009). Thus, it has been proposed that functional deficits in the frontal lobe may lead to a failure to regulate key areas of the limbic system, such as the amygdala and hippocampus. Consistent with a hypothesis of prefrontal dysfunction, other research has demonstrated that children with PTSD perform poorly on subtests assessing executive function (e.g., Beers & De Bellis, 2002).

Overall, available data suggest important neurobiological and neurophysiological differences between children with and without PTSD. However, these studies are not without methodological limitations, and many variables remain to be considered in future imaging studies. For example, age at the time of trauma exposure may be critical to consider since childhood is marked by rapid changes in normal brain development and emotion regulation. Thus, trauma exposure may have a different impact on brain structure and physiology at different stages of development. In addition, a majority of research to date on the neurobiology of pediatric PTSD has been conducted among youth exposed to Type II traumas such as abuse and maltreatment. The potential implications of these findings for possible morphological changes associated with one-time, unexpected events are unclear at this time.

Etiology

Behavioral perspectives form the basis of the majority of explanations for the development of PTSD, and its etiology is in some ways simple, yet in other ways complex. The simple part is that all instances of PTSD start with exposure to a traumatic event, although the definition of this event has changed in recent years. From there, the pathway to the disorder can become complex, and not everyone who experiences a traumatic event develops PTSD. Overall, a conceptual model for predicting children who are most likely to develop posttraumatic stress or PTSD has been proposed (Green et al., 1991) and modified by La Greca et al. (1996). Factors hypothesized to influence the development of posttraumatic reactions include (a) characteristics of the stressor (e.g., severity, loss of life or property); (b) characteristics of the child (e.g., demographic characteristics and predisaster functioning); (c) characteristics of the postdisaster environment (e.g., social support and occurrence of major life stressors); (d) the child's efforts to process and cope with the disaster; and (e) intervening stressful life events. Evidence for these factors in the development of PTSD in children and adolescents are reviewed here.

Considered most important for the development of PTSD are concurrent disaster-related factors that may include physical proximity to the event (Pynoos et al., 1987); actual injury or observation of injuries (Udwin et al., 2000); having to flee from the disaster site (Udwin et al., 2000); actual or perceived severity of the event (Green et al., 1991; Fremont, 2004; Lonigan et al., 1994; Fairbank, 2008); fears of dying, not being able to escape, or becoming panicked; and feeling scared or alone (Lonigan et al., 1994; Udwin et al., 2000), all of which have predicted the onset of PTSD. Among all of the concurrent variables, data from the most well-controlled investigations (Goenjian et al., 1995; La Greca et al., 1996; Udwin et al., 2000) indicate that primacy of exposure to the traumatic experience (direct injury or threat of injury as well as direct exposure to the sights and sounds of the event) is the factor most likely to predict the onset of PTSD. Other investigators have described this variable as proximity to the traumatic event (Pynoos et al., 1987). Higher rates of PTSD appear to occur among children within closest proximity to the event (Goenjian et al., 1995; Pynoos et al., 1987). Even 18 months later, 95% of a sample of children at the epicenter of the devastating Spivak, Armenia, earthquake (where the majority of buildings were destroyed, and up to 50% of children in their schools were killed) still met criteria for PTSD, compared to 71% of the children who lived in a city 20 miles away (where approximately 50% of the buildings were destroyed) and 26% of children who lived in a city 47 miles away (where there was only minimal damage and no loss of life; Goenjian et al., 1995). Rates of concurrent depression and separation anxiety disorder also covaried with respect to the distance from the epicenter of the earthquake.

Predisaster factors associated with increasing the likelihood of developing PTSD included being female (Green et al., 1991; La Greca et al., 1996; Udwin et al., 2000); mental health difficulties prior to the traumatic event (Daviss et al., 2000; Udwin et al., 2000); higher levels of premorbid trait anxiety (La Greca et al., 1996; Lonigan et al., 1994; Pfefferbaum et al., 1999); lower family income (Spell et al., 2008); and prior violence in the home (Udwin et al., 2000). By far, premorbid history was the most empirically supported factor. For example, Storr and colleagues (2007) found that high levels of depression and anxiety in the first grade were associated with a 1.5-fold increase in the likelihood of later developing PTSD. Similarly, La Greca et al. (1996) found anxiety level 15 months prior to Hurricane Andrew predicted higher levels of posttraumatic symptoms (PTSs) 3 and 7 months after the hurricane. Whereas inattention levels 15 months prior to the hurricane predicted higher PTS levels at 3 months but not 7 months later, preexisting conduct problems did not predict higher symptomatology at either time. These data suggest that it is preexisting levels of anxiety, and not psychopathology in general, that predict onset of PTS after a traumatic event. Furthermore, these data suggest, as with other anxiety disorders, that those with what we have previously termed anxiety proneness (Turner et al., 1996) are more likely to develop PTSD. Thus, personal attributes likely contribute as much as the particular stimulus to the development of PTSD.

Postdisaster factors associated with the onset of PTSD include significant amnesia, feelings of guilt and intense fear (Udwin et al., 2000), high scores on self-report of psychopathology 5 months postdisaster (Udwin et al., 2000), increased numbers of subsequent major life events (La Greca et al., 1996), and extent of loss of family members (Goenjian et al., 1995; McLaughlin et al., 2009). Damage to the home, displacement from home, and parental loss of job also are associated with a greater risk for PTSD (Lonigan et al., 1994; McLaughlin et al., 2009). For example, in New Orleans, where the effects of Hurricane Katrina were most profound, children were more likely to experience property loss, housing displacement, and death of a loved compared to children from other affected areas. In other areas, physical adversity (e.g., difficulty obtaining food or clothing) was more commonly reported. However, both death of a family member among New Orleans children and physical adversity among children from other areas were associated with the highest rates of PTSD symptoms in affected families (McLaughlin et al., 2009). Thus, postdisaster factors also may interact in ways that serve to increase (or decrease) the likelihood of posttraumatic symptomatology.

Social support also has been related to level of posttraumatic stress, although not to the extent of the first three factors. Higher support from parents, classmates, and community members is associated with lower levels of PTSD symptoms (AACAP, 1998; La Greca et al., 1996; Pina et al., 2008). Pina et al. (2008) found that perceived helpfulness of community members, including teachers and friends, as well as perceived helpfulness from professional support services such as public health agencies were associated with decreased PTSD symptoms in children following Hurricane Katrina. Related to the construct of social support, the potential role of discrimination in the aftermath of trauma also was examined in this study. Results showed that African American families experienced significantly more discrimination than Caucasian families, but that discrimination was only marginally associated with PTSD symptoms. As noted, the preexisting racial and economic composition of the Gulf region prior to the storm render such comparisons a challenge, yet given the association between perceived discrimination and mental health outcomes (Brody et al., 2006; Taylor & Turner, 2002), a greater focus on these relationships is needed in future research.

Consistent with receiving help and social support, a number of investigations have reported that family relationships and family pathology exert a significant impact on the development of PTSD. After exposure to the Australian bush fires, posttraumatic stress was more likely to occur among children whose parents had a negative response to the disaster (McFarlane, 1987). Other investigations (Daviss et al., 2000; Green et al., 1991; see also review by Fremont, 2004) also supported the notion that parental distress, depression, and negative responses increased the likelihood of PTSD among offspring, whereas strong family relationships were protective even for children exposed to Type II stressors such as the Pol Pot regime (American Academy of Child and Adolescent Psychiatry, 1988). Among families exposed to Hurricane Katrina, maternal PTSD predicted child internalizing symptoms even after controlling for level of hurricane exposure and other sociodemographic variables (Spell et al., 2008). Finally, with respect to specific coping variables, higher levels of blame/anger and social withdrawal were associated with more severe PTSD symptoms (La Greca et al., 1996), with blame/anger showing the strongest effect.

Long-term follow-up data are more limited, and comparisons over time are often difficult based on the use of different measurement tools. In one study of the chronicity and severity of PTSD (Udwin et al., 2000), survivors of the cruise ship *Jupiter* disaster who had a premorbid history of poor social relationships, learning disabilities, and postdisaster depression were the most likely to have PTSD that lasted 2 years or more. With respect to PTSD severity, retrospectively assigned premorbid diagnoses of separation anxiety and postdisaster depression were associated with more severe PTSD, whereas children who received help and social support in the aftermath of the disaster had fewer PTSD symptoms (see also Fremont, 2004). This study illustrated the interplay of the various factors and the complexity involved in predicting the onset, chronicity, and severity of the disorder. Long-term follow-up data of youth exposed to Hurricane Katrina indicated "serious emotional disturbance" (including PTSD symptoms) among roughly 15% of children 18–27 months after the storm (McLaughlin et al., 2009). Weems and colleagues (2010) also examined the presence of PTSD symptoms 24 and 30 months after Hurricane Katrina. In addition to high rates of posttrauma symptoms at the 24-month assessment, the authors reported disturbingly high rates of symptom stability; 41% of children reported the same degree of symptoms, and 29% had increased PTSD symptom severity at 30 months. Thus, in this study 70% of youth continued to display considerable PTSD symptoms 2.5 years later. These data are in stark contrast to those reported for youth exposed to other natural disasters, such as the 2004 tsunami in Southeast Asia, where a significant decrease in PTSD symptoms was observed 2.5 years later (Jensen, Dyb, & Nygaard, 2009). Of course, the extent of community devastation and loss associated with Hurricane Katrina was unprecedented, and it is unclear how well these data may generalize to other types of traumas.

Assessment

Diagnostic Interviews

As noted, one of the unique aspects of PTSD is that there are both semistructured diagnostic interviews that include a PTSD module and distinct PTSD interviews. The latter group has been the most commonly used, and although assessing the same symptoms, they do not always map directly on the current PTSD diagnostic criteria. Furthermore, these PTSD-only interviews do not allow for ruling out other diagnostic conditions, thus making it more difficult to interpret the resultant data.

As noted numerous times throughout this volume, the semistructured interview of choice for the diagnosis of anxiety disorders is the Anxiety Disorders Interview Schedule for DSM-IV: Child and Parent Versions (Silverman & Albano, 1996). This interview not only allows for a thorough assessment of PTSD symptomatology but also assesses for the presence of other disorders that, as noted, can sometimes coexist with PTSD.

Among specific PTSD interview schedules, a child version of a well-known adult PTSD diagnostic interview has been developed. The child version, the Clinician-Administered PTSD Scale–Child and Adolescent Version (CAPS-CA; Nader, Blake, Kriegler, & Pynoos, 1994) combines a quantifiable, dimensional approach to the assessment of PTSD and allows the assignation of both current and lifetime PTSD diagnoses. The scale has been described as detailed and allowing for reliable and valid diagnoses of PTSD, although it may be a bit extensive for everyday clinical use (McKnight et al., 2004).

The Children's PTSD Inventory (Saigh et al., 2000) is keyed to *DSM-IV* criteria and was developed for use with children ages 7 to 18. The scale includes assessment of potential exposure to traumatic events, reaction to the events, an inventory of potential PTSD symptoms, and questions regarding impairment in various areas of functioning. As noted (Lonigan et al., 2003), it is the most comprehensive diagnostic interview and has high internal consistency, good interrater and test-retest reliability, good convergent validity, and adequate sensitivity and specificity for the diagnosis of PTSD.

Although structured assessment serves to increase the reliability of a PTSD diagnosis, parent–child agreement is commonly discordant. For example, Scheeringa, Wright, Hunt, and Zeanah (2006) assessed 62 children and parents 2 months after hospitalization at a Level I trauma center due to serious injuries (e.g., car accidents, gunshot wounds, burns). According to structured interviews, 8.3% of children met criteria for a PTSD diagnosis based on child report compared to 4.2% for parent report. Meanwhile, Meiser-Stedman et al. (2007) found that of 51 youth assessed 6 months after an assault or motor vehicle accident, 11.9% met criteria for PTSD based on child report compared 13% based on parent report. However, agreement for a PTSD diagnosis was only fair (Cohen's κ = .21). Levels of agreement for the different PTSD symptom clusters also were examined. The strongest levels of agreement were found for hyperarousal (Cohen's κ = .45) and avoidance (Cohen's κ =.38) symptoms, followed by dissociation and impairment in functioning (both .22). Thus, data suggest that both child and parent reports are necessary for increasing the likelihood of accurate diagnosis.

Clinician Ratings

With respect to PTSD-specific instruments, one of the most commonly used measures is the Posttraumatic Stress Reaction Index (PTS-RI; Pynoos et al., 1987). This widely used instrument does have moderate empirical support despite the fact that it was not designed as a diagnostic tool (McKnight et al., 2004). The measure consists of 20 items composing three factors: intrusiveness/numbing/avoidance, fear/anxiety, and disturbances in sleep and concentration. Symptomatic cutoffs have been recommended to delineate children who are suffering from mild,

moderate, severe, and very severe stress, and its psychometric properties are good (Lonigan et al., 2003), with the exception of discriminant
validity and specificity as an indicator of PTSD. Although the PTS-RI
was originally intended for use as an interview, in fact it is more often
used as a self-report measure and only assesses reactions to a specific
traumatic event (Hawkins & Radcliffe, 2006).

Self-Report

In epidemiological investigations assessing a broad variety of potentially
traumatic events, the Child and Adolescent Trauma Survey (CATS;
March, 1999), the Child PTSD Symptom Scale (CPSS; Foa, Johnson,
Feeny, & Treadwell, 2001), and the UCLA PTSD Reaction Index for
DSM-IV (CPTS-RI; Pynoos, Rodriguez, Steinberg, Stauber, & Frederick,
1998) have been most commonly used. The CATS specifically assesses
for the presence of *DSM-IV* diagnostic criteria. Normative data are
available, the instrument is sensitive to change (March, Amaya-Jackson,
Murray, & Schulte, 1998), and it includes stable indices of non-PTSD
events and qualifying stressors (see McKnight, Compton, & March,
2004, for additional information on the CATS). The CPSS uses a 5-point
Likert scale (not at all to five times a week) to assess how often the child
is affected by each of the 17 *DSM-IV* symptoms. In addition, it assesses
current functioning at school, with family, and with friends. The scale
has good test-retest reliability as well as good convergent and divergent
validity. The CPTS-RI is a newer version of the PTS-RI that has been
through several revisions. The newest version of the CPTS-RI includes
child, adolescent, and parent versions aimed to provide preliminary
PTSD diagnoses using *DSM-IV* criteria. All measures contain approximately 20 questions designed to increase the sensitivity of screening for
trauma exposure that meets *DSM-IV* A1 and A2 criteria. Its validity and
reliability are well established (Steinberg, Brymer, Decker, & Pynoos,
2004), and it has been used extensively across a variety of traumas, age
ranges, settings, and cultures (Steinberg et al., 2004).

Behavioral Assessment

Constructing behavioral avoidance tests (BATs) often is considered difficult to impossible to do for cases of PTSD inasmuch as it does not seem
feasible to replicate hurricanes or automobile accidents in vivo. Such an
assertion is incorrect; it ignores the fact that when conditioning occurs,
it encompasses many specific stimuli (characteristics of the place where
the event occurred, other people who were present, etc.). Thus, while it
may not be possible to replicate the 140-mile-per-hour winds of a hurricane, it is still possible to construct BATs to the associated stimuli, for
example, assessing approach/avoidance to objects (e.g., automobiles) or

situations (place where the individual was standing when the dam broke/ tornado touched down). Not only do BATs allow for an objective assessment of the ability to approach (or avoid) these objects or situations, but also subjective distress or overt physiological response can be determined. For example, a BAT constructed to assess treatment outcome for a 14-year-old boy previously abducted by the Lebanese militia for 48 hours consisted of a 10-minute walk where the teen "left his home, walked to the area where the abduction occurred, entered a shop, made a purchase, and returned by an alternate route" (Saigh, 1987, p. 148). The teen reported his progress (how far he was able to walk) and was unobtrusively observed by research assistants. Although not reported in this study, it would also be possible to rate subjective level of distress when attempting these tasks. With respect to assessing physiological response to stimuli associated with the trauma, sound effect records, movies, videos, or virtual reality programs may be used to create feared situations such as hurricanes or automobile accidents. Patients could be asked to rate their level of distress while listening to or engaging in these tasks, and overt physiological responses such as blood pressure, heart rate, or skin conductance could be assessed.

Self-Monitoring

Data collection through self-monitoring could include number of times that the child attempts to approach or avoid a feared object or situation. Depending on the child's clinical presentation, other behaviors such as sleep difficulties, intrusive thoughts, flashbacks, or general level of distress also might be monitored. As noted in other chapters, the keys to self-monitoring are simplicity and ease of completion.

Treatment

Despite some efforts to reduce rates of PTSD or other long-term psychological problems by intervening in the immediate aftermath of a traumatic event (e.g., critical incident debriefing), currently there is no evidence that such interventions are effective for reducing short- or long-term distress in youth (La Greca, 2008). Thus, a majority of treatments focus on the short- and long-term recovery phases of traumatic exposure. Prior to conducting any intervention, however, it is necessary to emphasize the importance of careful screening to distinguish normal, developmentally appropriate reactions to trauma from abnormal reactions (Fremont, 2004) that might require intervention.

Suggested essential components for the treatment for children with PTSD include direct exploration of the trauma, stress management techniques, cognitive interventions to correct inaccurate attributions regarding the trauma, and the need to include parents in treatment (AACAP, 1998). However, as noted (McKnight et al., 2004), the empirical database for the treatment of childhood PTSD is sparse, and the same issues that plague the overall trauma literature (e.g., Type I versus Type II traumas) are highly relevant for interpreting the results of available treatment studies. For example, despite broad etiological differences and symptom presentations associated with different forms of trauma (e.g., natural disaster, motor vehicle accidents, physical abuse by a parent, sexual assault by a stranger, etc.), these differences are inadequately integrated into most treatment packages.

Results from one meta-analysis examining the effectiveness of 25 different psychosocial treatments for child maltreatment (including physical abuse, sexual abuse, physical neglect, and general maltreatment) illustrated the extent of heterogeneity present. An average treatment effect size of .54 was found across all studies, yet outcomes varied widely according to a number of variables, including informant type, type of maltreatment, study design, treatment orientation, and self-referred versus court-mandated treatment (Skowron & Reinemann, 2005). Also, larger effects were found based on child (.44) and parent reports (.42) than for behavioral observations (.21). In addition, the three nonbehavioral interventions included in the analysis yielded larger effects than did behavioral treatments (.87 and .40, respectively), yet because duration of nonbehavioral interventions averaged 1 year as compared to 3 months for behavioral interventions, results may be largely related to the amount of treatment received. Most problematic of all, the specific targets of these interventions varied considerably, and in many cases, PTSD was not the main focus. Thus, despite attempts to synthesize and compare treatment outcomes among maltreated children, available findings create more questions than answers.

Treatment of Type II Traumas

Among treatments specifically aimed at repeated traumas, trauma-focused cognitive-behavioral therapy (TF-CBT; Cohen, Mannarino, & Deblinger, 2006) is the only treatment that meets well-established treatment criteria for children and adolescents (Chambless et al., 1996; Chambless & Hollon, 1998). More specifically, TF-CBT has been found to be statistically significantly superior to psychosocial placebo or another treatment in at least two group design experiments conducted in at least two independent research settings and by two independent investigatory teams. TF-CBT (which has occasionally been referred to by slightly different names) includes working with the child individually using cognitive-behavioral procedures that include exposure tasks via narratives, drawings, or imaginal methods. In some cases, treatment may include parents in either individual meetings or joint child-parent sessions.

In one of the first studies of TF-CBT, Deblinger, Lippman, and Steer (1996) compared the relative efficacy of four treatments among a sample of 100 sexually abused children and adolescents randomized to one of four treatment conditions: child-only TF-CBT, child-plus-parent TF-CBT, standard therapeutic care, and a parent-only intervention. The two TF-CBT conditions were identical in content except for the inclusion of a 45-minute session of parent training and joint session lasting 30 minutes. Posttreatment comparisons showed significantly greater reductions in posttraumatic stress symptoms (based on the PTSs scale of the Schedule for Affective Disorders and Schizophrenia for School-Aged Children; K-SADS) among youth treated with either form of TF-CBT. Similar results have been reported for TF-CBT among sexually abused preschool-aged children (Cohen & Mannarino, 1996), with positive gains maintained 6 and 12 months later (Cohen & Mannarino, 1997).

Cohen, Deblinger, Mannarino, and Steer (2004) compared TF-CBT and child-centered therapy among a larger sample ($N = 229$) of sexually abused children and adolescents. In 3 of the 12 TF-CBT sessions, therapists met together with the child and parent to discuss the writings and illustrations of the youth and to train parents in effective communication with their child. Child-centered therapy involved the use of listening skills, reflection, and empathy. Posttreatment comparisons revealed statistically significant improvements for both treatment groups; however, the TF-CBT group showed significantly greater improvement on the PTSS scale of the K-SADS, as well as the Children's Depression Inventory and Child Behavior Checklist.

Similarly, Cohen, Mannarino, and Knudsen (2005) compared TF-CBT and nondirective supportive therapy among 82 sexually abused children and adolescents using a TF-CBT program similar in content and duration to the treatment used in the work of Cohen et al. (2004). The nondirective supportive therapy condition served to control for the nonspecific aspects of therapy. Overall results showed significant improvement for both groups, but the TF-CBT group evidenced significantly greater improvements on most outcome measures. In addition, 6- and 12-month follow-up assessments showed continued improvements in terms of anxiety, depression, and PTSD symptoms.

Despite its status as a well-established treatment for childhood trauma, the vast majority of outcome research for TF-CBT has been conducted among sexually abused children and adolescents (Cohen et al., 2004, 2005; Cohen & Mannarino, 1996a; Deblinger et al., 1996; Jaberghaderi, Greenwald, Rubin, Zand, & Dolatabadi, 2004; King et al., 2000). As such, the applicability of the treatments to other trauma-exposed populations, including exposure to Type I traumas, remains to be examined.

Treatment of PTSD Associated With Type I Traumas

Unfortunately, few randomized, controlled treatment studies have focused on youth exposed to Type I traumas. However, a useful conceptual model that incorporates both prevention and intervention (triage, coping responses for anticipated grief and trauma responses, treating the development of PTSD if it occurs and other disorders if they also occur) has been recommended by the AACAP (1998). With respect to specific modes of intervention, cognitive-behavioral treatment (CBT) has been recommended as the treatment of choice (Cohen, Berliner, & March, 2000). In an early study using CBT, March, Amaya-Jackson and coworkers (1998) reported that an intervention for PTSD delivered in a school setting was efficacious for children who had been exposed to a single-incident stressor. The intervention, multimodal trauma treatment (MMTT) is 18 weeks in length and combines psychoeducation, anxiety management training, anger coping, cognitive training, and exposure. Findings indicated significant improvements in clinician-rated PTSD, and results were maintained at 6-month follow-up. Of the 14 treatment completers, 8 (57%) no longer met PTSD criteria at posttreatment, and 12 (86%) no longer met criteria at 6-month follow-up. In a follow-up open trial (Amaya-Jackson et al., 2003), 57% of the children no longer met criteria for PTSD at posttreatment, and 86% were diagnosis free at 6-month follow-up. Symptoms were reduced by 40% at posttreatment and another 40% at follow-up, and similar improvements were evident for measures of anxiety, depression, and anger. In follow-up investigations using 14, rather than 18, sessions, outcome was consistent with the initial trial for both elementary and high school students (Amaya-Jackson et al., 2003).

In another treatment study of children with PTSD based on a single traumatic event, Smith and colleagues (2007) compared 10-week CBT to a wait-list control condition among 24 youth exposed to a motor vehicle accident, assault, or violence. Treatment consisted of 10 individual child sessions and 10 individual parent sessions, with joint parent-child sessions as needed. As described by the authors, the CBT intervention included psychoeducation, activity scheduling/reclaiming life, imaginal reliving (e.g., writing and drawing techniques), cognitive restructuring and integration of restructuring into reliving, revisiting the site of the trauma, stimulus discrimination with respect to traumatic reminders, direct work with nightmares, image transformation techniques, behavioral experiments, and work with parents. At posttreatment, significant improvements for the CBT but not for the wait-list group were observed for self-reports of PTSs, depression, and anxiety. Further, 11/12 (92%)

youth in the CBT group were free of a PTSD diagnosis posttreatment compared to 5/12 (42%) youth in the wait-list group at the end of the waiting period. Six-month follow-up data showed treatment gains were maintained, with all 12 youth treated with CBT free of a PTSD diagnosis. Although the authors noted that the intervention specifically focused on targeting cognitive factors, considerable use of imaginal and in vivo exposures also is apparent (e.g., imaginal reliving, revisiting the site of the trauma). Thus, because the treatment included a large number of therapeutic components and techniques, follow-up studies examining the specific contribution of each will be informative.

Catani and colleagues (2009) compared six sessions of narrative exposure therapy (NET) and six sessions of meditation-relaxation among 31 children with PTSD approximately 1 month after a tsunami in northeast Sri Lanka. Children were randomized to one of the two treatment conditions, and interventions were conducted by trained local counselors. *DSM-IV* diagnosis and severity of PTSD were assessed using the UCLA PTSD Index for *DSM-IV*. The NET condition included having children construct a detailed chronological account of their own biography, including experiences related to the tsunami. The autobiography was filled with greater details during each subsequent session, during which the child was asked about physiological, cognitive, and behavioral reactions. The meditation-relaxation condition included psychoeducation, discussion of the child's current problems, breathing exercises, and different forms of relaxation training. The two groups showed similar reductions in PTSD symptoms 1 month following treatment, with 75% of the children treated with NET and 66.6% of those treated with meditation-relaxation free of a PTSD diagnosis. Six months later, 81% of the NET group and 71% of the meditation–relaxation group did not receive a PTSD diagnosis. Between-group differences were nonsignificant at both time points. These results are highly encouraging, particularly in light of the fact that these were short-term interventions delivered by trained community professionals.

An interesting variation in the delivery of treatment for children with PTSD is the concept of "pulsed" intervention. Following the initial intervention designed to help the child cope with the immediate aftermath of the traumatic event, treatment is suspended (or pulsed) until clinical issues dictate that continued intervention is necessary. This necessity may take the form of developmental transitions (transition to middle school, leaving for college) or clinical issues such as increases in anxiety or depression. The idea behind pulsed, rather than continuous, intervention is to minimize feelings of ongoing helplessness in the child by minimizing dependence on the therapist (McKnight et al., 2004). To date, there are no data suggesting that pulsed interventions are more efficacious than standard treatment; in effect, it is counter to behavioral theories of exposure intervention, which demonstrate that recovery of fear will occur if therapy is discontinued prior to achievement of habituation.

Cohen and colleagues (2009) described Project Fleur de Lis™ (PFDL), established to provide a tiered approach to triage and treatment of children experiencing trauma symptoms in the greater New Orleans region. PFDL, which was initiated 15 months after Hurricane Katrina struck, is funded by a number of corporations, foundations, individuals, and nonprofit agencies. The overall aims of the project are to (a) implement school-based intervention for children exposed to traumatic events; (b) better identify children with mental health and psychoeducational needs beyond what can be addressed in the school setting; (c) provide increased access to mental health care and effective treatments for children with PTSD symptoms; and (d) provide empirical evidence that effective treatments for childhood trauma can be delivered in both school and community-based settings. The project will examine the effectiveness of three treatment programs with established efficacy: TF-CBT (Cohen et al., 2006), Cognitive Behavioral Intervention for Trauma in Schools (CBITS; Jaycox, 2003; Stein et al., 2003), and a classroom-based intervention (CBI; Macy, Macy, Gross, & Brighton, 2006) implemented in many schools in New Orleans. In line with a tiered approach, CBI serves as universal intervention, CBITS as a selected intervention for those with lingering symptoms following CBI, and TF-CBT is for children with PTSD who do not respond to either school-based intervention. Although data collection from PFDL is ongoing, initial case reports of treated children are encouraging (Cohen et al., 2009).

Pharmacological Treatment

In 1998, the Practice Parameters for the Assessment and Treatment of Children and Adolescents with Posttraumatic Stress Disorder concluded that, despite prescribing practices, there was inadequate empirical support for the use of any particular medication to treat childhood PTSD (AACAP, 1998). Thus, although selective serotonin reuptake inhibitor (SSRI) medications are often effective for the treatment of other childhood anxiety disorders, there are no placebo-controlled trials available confirming the efficacy of these medications for PTSD. In one of the few published studies, Cohen, Mannarino, Perel, and Staron (2007) examined the potential benefit of adding sertraline (an SSRI) versus a pill placebo to TF-CBT in a double-blind treatment study. Sexually abused children between the ages of 10 and 17 meeting criteria for *DSM-IV* PTSD based on the K-SADS were randomized to one of the two groups. TF-CBT was provided over the course of 12 weeks, and children were seen for medication checks at Weeks 1, 3, 5, 8, and 12. Medication was started at 25 mg/day, and dosages were titrated on a fixed-flexible schedule up to a maximum of 200 mg/day, with a mean maximum dose for the TF-CBT plus sertraline group of 150 mg/day. There were no significant differences between the groups with regard to remission of PTSD or other clinical symptomatology at posttreatment, suggesting that sertraline offered no benefits above CBT alone.

CASE EXAMPLE: TREATMENT OF PTSD

Following Marla's initial assessment, several behaviors (general arousal, frequency of intrusive thoughts, and distance from the stable where the accident occurred) were selected as indicators of treatment efficacy. These variables were monitored for 1 week prior to treatment, during treatment, and for 1 week at 6-month follow-up (see Figures 13.1–13.3). Because Marla was 17 years old, imaginal exposure was selected for use. The imaginal scene is presented in Table 13.3. Treatment was conducted twice per week for the first 3 weeks and then once per week for an additional 8 weeks for a total of 14 sessions. During the first 3 weeks, two sessions per week were conducted in an effort to quickly decrease general levels of distress, begin to improve sleep hygiene, and to closely monitor Marla's clinical condition. Other aspects of treatment implementation were conducted using the guidelines presented in Chapter 11 on OCD. Homework assignments included grooming other horses in the outdoor training area, cleaning bridles, and sitting in the empty tourist carriages. Treatment outcome is presented in Figures 13.1–13.3. As depicted, the treatment was effective in decreasing general arousal and intrusive thoughts, improving stuttering (not monitored on a daily basis), and allowing Marla to return to the stable and to resume her training activities.

SUMMARY

PTSD in children is an understudied disorder, and little is known about its clinical presentation, etiology, or efficacious treatment strategies. To date, the research has been hampered by changing and subjective diagnostic criteria and myriad events that might be considered as "traumatic" but do not meet the classic definition of a traumatic event.

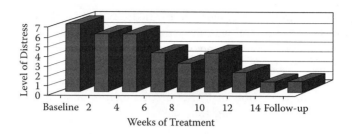

FIGURE 13.1   Marla's daily level of general arousal. (Reprinted from Beidel, D. C., & Turner, S. M. (2005). *Child Anxiety Disorders*. New York: Routledge. With permission.)

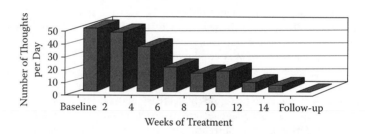

FIGURE 13.2   Marla's frequency of intrusive thoughts. (Reprinted from Beidel, D. C., & Turner, S. M. (2005). *Child Anxiety Disorders*. New York: Routledge. With permission.)

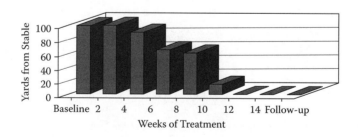

FIGURE 13.3   Distance Marla is able to comfortably stand and look at the stable. (Reprinted from Beidel, D. C., & Turner, S. M. (2005). *Child Anxiety Disorders*. New York: Routledge. With permission.)

TABLE 13.3   Marla's Imaginal Scene

I want you to imagine that you are in the stable. It is quiet, and you are getting the new horse, Lucky, ready for his training session. Lucky is high spirited, but you and your dad have had some success in training him so far. As you begin to lead Lucky out to the training grounds, a mouse runs across the stable floor. You jump, and Lucky is startled. This scares you, and you think, "I do not know this horse very well. What if he spooks in the stable?" You know this is dangerous because the stable is tight, and there is little room to maneuver. As you try to calm Lucky, he begins to bolt even more, and you are knocked to the ground. Your heart is racing, you feel dizzy, and as you look up, you see Lucky's front hooves coming toward you. You move your head, but Lucky's front hoof grazes the side of your head. You are very frightened, and you think, "I am going to die." Your heart is racing, you can't breathe, and you can't move. Lucky continues to be out of control, and when the hooves come crashing down again, they hit your arm and hand. Lucky rears up again, and you realize that there is no room to escape. The horse is out of control, and you cannot do anything about the situation. No one else is here to help you. You are in such pain that you cannot move out of the way. Lucky's hooves come toward you again, and you think, "This is it. Now I am going to die." Then, all you see is a blinding white light, and you feel excruciating pain.

Source: Reprinted from Beidel, D. C., & Turner, S. M. (2005). *Child Anxiety Disorders.* New York: Routledge. With permission.

Furthermore, most of the available data have centered on child sexual abuse. There has been little attempt to merge this literature with findings from other types of traumatic events. Indeed, the separation of these types of abuse into Type I and Type II events and the resultant differing clinical presentations suggest that these indeed may be very different conditions, thereby questioning the validity of the Type I versus Type II classification. With respect to Type I events, factors that may contribute to the onset of PTSD are beginning to be elucidated. Furthermore, assessment measures are becoming more sophisticated; this in turn should allow for the empirical assessment of pharmacological and psychosocial interventions. Currently, behavioral and cognitive-behavioral interventions appear to have the most (albeit still extremely limited) outcome data. The use of behavioral interventions theoretically makes sense inasmuch as PTSD can be conceptualized as a disorder that is acquired as a result of a traumatic conditioning event. One potential impediment to the implementation of behavioral treatment programs is the belief that those with PTSD are "too fragile" to handle exposure interventions. Of course, there are no data to support this assumption, but this view may hinder consideration of the efficacy of these interventions. To the contrary, what data we have show the opposite to be true. When conducted by qualified professionals using appropriate clinical guidelines, there is no reason to assert that behavioral interventions, so efficacious for other anxiety disorders, would be any less so for children and adolescents with PTSD.

References

Aaron, J., Zagul, H., & Emery, R. E. (1999). Posttraumatic stress in children following acute physical injury. *Journal of Pediatric Psychology, 24*, 335–343.

Abramowitz, J. S., Whiteside, S. P., & Deacon, B. J. (2005). Treatment of pediatric obsessive-compulsive disorder: A comprehensive meta-analysis of the outcome research. *Behavior Therapy, 36,* 55–63.

Achenbach, T. M. (1985). Assessment of anxiety in children. In A. H. Tuma & J. D. Maser (Eds.), *Anxiety and the anxiety disorders* (pp. 707–734). Hillsdale, NJ: Erlbaum.

Adams, G. B., Waas, G. A., March, J. S., & Smith, M. C. (1994). Obsessive compulsive disorder in children and adolescents: The role of the school psychologist in identification, assessment, and treatment. *School Psychology Quarterly, 9,* 274–294.

Agras, W. S., Chapin, H. N., & Oliveau, D. (1972). The natural history of phobias: Course and prognosis. *Archives of General Psychiatry, 26,* 315–317.

Agras, W. S., Sylvester, D., & Oliveau, D. (1969). The epidemiology of common fears and phobias. *Comprehensive Psychiatry, 10,* 151–156.

Albano, A. M., Marten, P. A., Holt, C. S., Heimberg, R. G., & Barlow, D. H. (1995). Cognitive-behavioral group treatment for social phobia in adolescents: A preliminary study. *Journal of Nervous and Mental Disease, 183,* 649–656.

Alessi, N. E., & Magen, J. (1988). Panic disorder in psychiatrically hospitalized children. *American Journal of Psychiatry, 145,* 1450–1452.

Alfano, C. A., Beidel, D. C., & Turner, S. M. (2002). Considering cognition in childhood anxiety disorders: Conceptual, methodological and developmental considerations. *Clinical Psychology Review, 22,* 1209–1238.

Alfano, C. A., Beidel, D. C., & Turner, S. M. (2006). Cognitive correlates of social phobia among children and adolescents. *Journal of Abnormal Child Psychology, 34,* 189–201.

Alfano, C. A., Beidel, D. C., & Turner, S. M. (2008). Negative self-imagery among adolescents with social phobia: A test of and adult model of the disorder. *Journal of Clinical Child and Adolescent Psychology, 37*, 327–336.

Alfano, C. A., Beidel, D. C., Turner, S. M., & Lewin, D. S. (2006). Preliminary evidence for sleep complaints among children referred for anxiety. *Sleep Medicine, 7*, 467–473.

Alfano, C. A., & Gamble, A. (2009). The role of sleep in childhood psychiatric disorders. *Child and Youth Care Forum, 38*, 327–340.

Alfano, C. A., Ginsburg, G. S., & Kingery, J. (2007). Sleep-related problems among children and adolescents with anxiety disorders. *Journal of the American Academy of Child and Adolescent Psychiatry, 46*, 224–232.

Alfano, C. A., & Mellman, T. (2010). Sleep in anxiety disorders. In J. W. Winkelman & D. T. Plante (Eds.), *Foundations of psychiatric sleep medicine*. London: Cambridge University Press.

Alfano, C. A., Pina, A. A., Villalta, I. K., Beidel, D. C., Ammerman, R. T., & Crosby, L. E. (2009). Mediators and moderators of outcome in the behavioral treatment of childhood social phobia. *Journal of the American Academy of Child and Adolescent Psychiatry, 48*, 945–953.

Alfano, C. A., Pina, A. A., Zerr, A. G., & Villalta, I. K. (2010). Pre-sleep arousal and sleep problems of anxiety-disordered youth. *Child Psychiatry and Human Development, 41*, 156–167.

Alfano, C. A., Zakem, I. H., Costa, N. M., Taylor, L. K., & Weems, C. F. (2009). Sleep problems and their relation to cognitive factors, anxiety and depressive symptoms in children and adolescents. *Depression and Anxiety, 26*, 503–512.

Allsopp, M., & Verduyn, C. (1990). Adolescents with obsessive-compulsive disorder: A case note review of consecutive patients referred to a provincial regional adolescent psychiatry unit. *Journal of Adolescence, 13*, 157–169.

Amaya-Jackson, L., Reynolds, V., Murray, M. C., McCarthy, G., Nelson, A., Cherney, M. S., et al. (2003). Cognitive-behavioral treatment for pediatric posttraumatic stress disorder: Protocol and application in school and community settings. *Cognitive and Behavioral Practice, 10*, 204–213.

American Academy of Child and Adolescent Psychiatry. (1998). Practice parameters for the assessment and treatment of children and adolescents with posttraumatic stress disorder. *Journal of the American Academy of Child and Adolescent Psychiatry, 37*(Suppl.), 4S–26S.

American Academy of Pediatrics (2001). Children, adolescents and television. *Pediatrics, 107*, 423–426.

American Psychiatric Association. (1980). *Diagnostic and statistical manual of mental disorders* (3rd edition). Washington, DC: Author.

American Psychiatric Association. (1987). *Diagnostic and statistical manual of mental disorders* (3rd edition, revised). Washington, DC: Author.

American Psychiatric Association. (1994). *Diagnostic and statistical manual of mental disorders* (4th edition). Washington, DC: Author.

American Psychiatric Association. (2000). *Diagnostic and statistical manual of mental disorders* (4th edition, text revision). Washington, DC: Author.

Amin, R. S., Kimball, T. R., Bean, J. A., Jeffries, J. L., Willging, J. P., Cotton, R. T., et al. (2002). Left ventricular hypertrophy and abnormal ventricular geometry in children and adolescents with obstructive sleep apnea. *American Journal of Respiratory and Critical Care Medicine, 165,* 1395–1399.

Anderson, J. C., Williams, S., McGee, R., & Silva, P. A. (1987). DSM-III disorders in preadolescent children: Prevalence in a large sample from the general population. *Archives of General Psychiatry, 44,* 69–77.

Andersson, C. B., & Thomsen, P. H. (1998). Electively mute children: An analysis of 37 Danish cases. *Norwegian Journal of Psychiatry, 52,* 231–238.

Andrews, G., Stewart, G., Allen, R., & Henderson, A. S. (1990). The genetics of six neurotic disorders: A twin study. *Journal of Affective Disorders, 19,* 23–29.

Angelino, H., Dollins, J., & Mech, E. V. (1956). Trends in the "fears and worries" of school children as related to socioeconomic status and age. *Journal of Genetic Psychology, 89,* 263–276.

Anstendig, K. (1998). Selective mutism: A review of the treatment literature by modality from 1980–1996. *Psychotherapy: Theory, Research, Practice, Training, 35,* 381–391.

Anthony, J. L., Lonigan, C. J., & Hecht, S. A. (1999). Dimensionality of posttraumatic stress disorder symptoms in children exposed to disaster: Results from confirmatory factor analyses. *Journal of Abnormal Psychology, 108,* 326–336.

Argyropoulos, S. V., Bell, C. J., & Nutt, D. J. (2001). Brain function in social anxiety disorder. *The Psychiatric Clinics of North America, 4,* 707–722.

Asbahr, F. R., Castillo, A. R., Ito, L. M., Latorre, M. R., Moreira, M. N., & Lotufo-Neto, F. (2005). Group cognitive-behavioral therapy versus sertraline for the treatment of children and adolescents with obsessive-compulsive disorder. *Journal of the American Academy of Child and Adolescent Psychiatry, 44,* 1128–1136.

Aschenbrand, S. G., Kendall, P. C., Alicia Webb, A., Safford, S. M., & Flannery-Schroeder, E. (2003). Is childhood separation anxiety disorder a predictor of adult panic disorder and agoraphobia? A seven-year longitudinal study. *Journal of the American Academy of Child and Adolescent Psychiatry, 42*, 1478–1485.

Asendorpf, J. S. (1990). Development of inhibition during childhood: Evidence for situational specificity and a two-factor model. *Developmental Psychology, 26*, 721–730.

Aune, T., Stiles, T. C., Svarva, K. (2008). Psychometric properties of the Social Phobia and Anxiety Inventory for Children using a non-American population-based sample. *Journal of Anxiety Disorders, 22*, 1075–1086.

Bader, K., Schafer, V., Schenkel, M., Nissen, L., Kuhl, H. C., & Schwander, J. (2007). Increased nocturnal activity associated with adverse childhood experiences in patients with primary insomnia. *Journal of Nervous and Mental Disease, 195*, 588–595.

Bailly, D., & de Lenclave, M. (2005). Choking phobia in children and adolescents: Rarely described but worth studying. In P. I. Swain (Ed.), *Adolescent eating disorders* (pp. 163–188). Hauppauge, NY: Nova Biomedical Books.

Ballenger, J. C., Carek, D. J., Steele, J. J., & Cornish-McTighe, D. (1989). Three cases of panic disorder with agoraphobia in children. *American Journal of Psychiatry, 146*, 922–924.

Bamber, D., Tamplin, A., Park, R. J., Kyte, Z. A., & Goodyer, I. M. (2002). Development of a short Leyton Obsessional Inventory for Children and Adolescents. *Journal of the American Academy of Child and Adolescent Psychiatry, 41*, 1246–1252.

Bandura, A. (1969). *Principles of behavior modification*. New York: Holt, Rinehart, & Winston.

Bandura, A., Blanchard, E. B., & Ritter, B. (1969). Relative efficacy of desensitization and modeling approaches for inducing behavioral, affective, and attitudinal changes. *Journal of Personality and Social Psychology, 13*, 173–199.

Bandura, A., Grusec, J. E., & Menlove, F. L. (1967). Vicarious extinction of avoidance behavior. *Journal of Personality and Social Psychology, 5*, 16–23.

Bandura, A., & Menlove, F. L. (1968). Factors determining vicarious extinction of avoidance behavior. *Journal of Personality and Social Psychology, 3*, 99–108.

Banerjee, S. P., Bhandari, R. P., & Rosenberg, D. R. (2005). Use of low-dose selective serotonin reuptake inhibitors for severe, refractory choking phobia in childhood. *Journal of Developmental and Behavioral Pediatrics, 26*, 123–127.

Barabasz, A. F. (1973). Group desensitization of test anxiety in elementary school. *The Journal of Psychology, 83*, 295–301.

Bar-Haim, Y., Lamy, D., Pergamin, L., Bakermans-Kranenburg, M. J., & van IJzendoorn, M. H. (2007). Threat-related attentional bias in anxious and nonanxious individuals: A meta-analytic study. *Psychological Bulletin, 133*, 1–24.

Barlow, D. H. (2002). *Anxiety and its disorders: The nature and treatment of anxiety and panic* (2nd ed.). New York: Guilford Press.

Barlow, D. H., & Seidner, A. L. (1983). Treatment of adolescent agoraphobics: Effects on parent-adolescent relations. *Behaviour Research and Therapy, 21*, 519–526.

Barrett, P. M. (1998). Evaluation of cognitive-behavioral group treatments for childhood anxiety disorders. *Journal of Clinical Child Psychology, 27*, 459–468.

Barrett, P. M., Dadds, M. R., & Rapee, R. M. (1996). Family treatment of childhood anxiety: A controlled trial. *Journal of Consulting and Clinical Psychology, 64*, 333–342.

Barrett, P. M., Duffy, A. L., Dadds, M. R., & Rapee, R. M. (2001). Cognitive-behavioral treatment of anxiety disorders in children: Long-term (6 year) follow-up. *Journal of Consulting and Clinical Psychology, 69*, 135–141.

Barrett, P., Farrell, L., Dadds, M., & Boulter, N. (2005). Cognitive-behavioral family treatment of childhood obsessive-compulsive disorder: Long-term follow-up and predictors of outcome. *Journal of the American Academy of Child and Adolescent Psychiatry, 44*, 1005–1014.

Barrett, P. M., Fox, T., & Farrell, L. J. (2005). Parent-child interactions with anxious children with their siblings: An observational study. *Behaviour Change, 22*, 220–235.

Barrett, P. M., & Healy, L. J. (2003). An examination of the cognitive processes involved in childhood obsessive-compulsive disorder. *Behaviour Research and Therapy, 41*, 285–299.

Barrett, P., & Healy-Farrell, L. (2003). Perceived responsibility in juvenile obsessive-compulsive disorder: An experimental manipulation. *Journal of Clinical Child and Adolescent Psychology, 32*, 430–441.

Barrett, P., Healy, L., & March, J. S. (2003). Behavioral avoidance test for childhood obsessive-compulsive disorder. *American Journal of Psychotherapy, 57*, 80–100.

Barrett, P., Healy-Farrell, L., & March, J. S. (2004). Cognitive-behavioral family treatment of childhood obsessive-compulsive disorder: A controlled trial. *Journal of the American Academy of Child and Adolescent Psychiatry, 43*, 46–62.

Barrett, P. M., Johnson, S., & Turner, C. (2005). Developmental differences in universal preventive intervention for child anxiety. *Clinical Child Psychology and Psychiatry, 10*, 539–555.

Barrett, P. M., Moore, A. M., & Sonderegger, R. (2000). The FRIENDS program for young former-Yugoslavian refugees in Australia: A pilot study. *Behaviour Change, 17*, 124–133.

Barrett, P. M., Rasmussen, P., & Healy, L. (2001). The effects of childhood obsessive compulsive disorder on sibling relationships in late childhood and early adolescence: Preliminary findings. *The Australian Educational and Developmental Psychologist, 17*, 82–102.

Barrett, P. M., Rapee, R. M., Dadds, M. R., & Ryan, S. M. (1996). Family enhancement of cognitive style in anxious and aggressive children: Threat bias and the FEAR effect. *Journal of Abnormal Child Psychology, 24*, 187–203.

Barrett, P. M., Shortt, A. L., Fox, T. L., & Wescombe, K. (2001). Examining the social validity of the FRIENDS treatment program for anxious children. *Behaviour Change, 18*, 63–77.

Barrett, P. M., Shortt, A., & Healy, L. (2002). Do parent and child behaviours differentiate families whose children have obsessive-compulsive disorder from other clinic and non-clinic families? *Journal of Child Psychology and Psychiatry, 43*, 597–607.

Barrett, P. M., Sonderegger, R., & Sonderegger, N. L. (2001). Evaluation of an anxiety-prevention and positive coping programs (FRIENDS) for children and adolescents of non-English speaking background. *Behaviour Change, 18*, 78–91.

Barrett, P. M., Sonderegger, R., & Xenos, S. (2003). Using FRIENDS to combat anxiety and adjustment problems among young migrants to Australia: A national trial. *Clinical Child Psychology and Psychiatry, 8*, 241–260.

Barrett, P., & Turner, C. (2001). Prevention of anxiety symptoms in primary school children: preliminary results from a universal school-based trial. *British Journal of Clinical Psychology, 40*, 399–410.

Barrios, B. A., Hartmann, D. B., & Shigetomi, C. (1981). Fears and anxieties in children. In E. J. Mash & L. G. Terdal (Eds.), *Behavioral assessment of childhood disorders* (pp. 259–304). New York: Guilford Press.

Barton, L., Kearney, C. A., Eisen, A. R., & Silverman, W. K. (1993, April). *The relationship of school phobia to school refusal behavior: Not separate but not equal.* Symposium presented at the meeting of the Western Psychological Association, Phoenix, AZ.

Battaglia, M., Bajo, S., Strambi, L. F., Brambilla, F., Castronovo, C., Vanni, G., et al. (1997). Physiological and behavioral responses to minor stressors in offspring of patients with panic disorder. *Journal of Psychiatric Research, 31*, 365–376.

Battaglia, M., Bertella, S., Politi, E., Bernardeschi, L., Perna, G., Gabriele, A., et al. (1995). Age at onset of panic disorder: Influence of familial liability to the disease and of childhood separation anxiety disorder. *American Journal of Psychiatry, 152*, 1362–1364.

Battaglia, M., Ogliari, A., Zanoni, A., Villa, F., Citterio, A., Binaghi, F., et al. (2004). Children's discrimination of expressions of emotions: Relationship with indices of social anxiety and shyness. *Journal of the American Academy of Child and Adolescent Psychiatry, 43*, 358–365.

Baxter, L. R., Jr. (1992). Neuroimaging studies of obsessive compulsive disorder. *Psychiatric Clinics of North America, 15*, 718–725.

Beck, A. T. (1988). Cognitive approaches to panic disorder: Theory and therapy. In S. Rachman and J. D. Maser (Eds.), *Panic: Psychological perspectives* (pp. 91–109). Hillsdale, NJ: Erlbaum.

Bedi, R., Sutcliffe, P., Donnan, P. T., & McConnachie, J. (1992). The prevalence of dental anxiety in a group of 13- and 14-year old Scottish children. *International Journal of Paediatric Dentistry, 2*, 17–24.

Beers, S. R., & De Bellis, M. D. (2002). Neuropsychological function in children with maltreatment-related posttraumatic stress disorder. *American Journal of Psychiatry, 159*, 483–486.

Beesdo, K., Knappe, S., & Pine, D. (2009). Anxiety and anxiety disorders in children and adolescents: developmental issues and implications for DSM-V. *The Psychiatric Clinics of North America, 32*(3), 483–524.

Beidel, D. C. (1988) Psychophysiological assessment of anxious emotional states in children. *Journal of Abnormal Child Psychology, 97*, 80–82.

Beidel, D. C. (1991). Social phobia and overanxious disorder in school-aged children. *Journal of the American Academy of Child and Adolescent Psychiatry, 30*, 54–552.

Beidel, D. C., Christ, M. A. G., & Long, P. J. (1991). Somatic complaints in anxious children. *Journal of Abnormal Child Psychology, 19*, 659–670.

Beidel, D. C., Morris, T. L., & Turner, M. W. (2004). Social phobia. In T. L. Morris and J. S. March (Eds.), *Anxiety disorders in children and adolescents* (2nd ed., pp. 141–163). New York: Guilford Press.

Beidel, D. C., Neal, A. M., & Lederer, A. S. (1991). The feasibility and validity of a daily diary for the assessment of anxiety in children. *Behavior Therapy, 22*, 505–517.

Beidel, D. C., Silverman, W. K., & Hammond-Laurence, K. (1996). Overanxious disorder: Subsyndromal state or specific disorder? *Journal of Clinical Child Psychology, 25,* 25–32.

Beidel, D. C., & Stanley, M. A. (1993). Developmental issues in the measurement of anxiety. In C. G. Last (Ed.), *Anxiety across the lifespan: A developmental perspective* (pp. 167–203). New York: Springer.

Beidel, D. C., & Turner, S. M. (1988). Comorbidity of test anxiety and other anxiety disorders in children. *Journal of Abnormal Child Psychology, 16,* 275–287.

Beidel, D. C., & Turner, S. M. (1997). At risk for anxiety: I. Psychopathology in the offspring of anxious parents. *Journal of the American Academy of Child and Adolescent Psychiatry, 36,* 918–925.

Beidel, D. C., & Turner, S. M. (1998). *Shy children, phobic adults: The nature and treatment of social phobia.* Washington, DC: American Psychological Association.

Beidel, D. C., & Turner, S. M. (2005). *Child Anxiety Disorders.* New York: Routledge.

Beidel, D. C., Turner, S. M., Hamlin, K., & Morris, T. L. (2000). The Social Phobia and Anxiety Inventory for Children (SPAI-C): External and discriminative validity. *Behavior Therapy, 31,* 75–87.

Beidel, D. C., Turner, S. M., & Morris, T. L. (1995). A new inventory to assess childhood social anxiety and phobia: The Social Phobia and Anxiety Inventory for Children. *Psychological Assessment, 7,* 73–79.

Beidel, D. C., Turner, S. M., & Morris, T. L. (1998). *Social Phobia and Anxiety Inventory for Children.* North Tonawanda, NY: Multi-Health Systems.

Beidel, D. C., Turner, S. M., & Morris T. L. (1999). Psychopathology of childhood social phobia. *Journal of the American Academy of Child and Adolescent Psychiatry, 38,* 643–650.

Beidel, D. C., Turner, S. M., & Morris, T. L. (2000). Behavioral treatment of childhood social phobia. *Journal of Consulting and Clinical Psychology, 68,* 1072–1080.

Beidel, D. C., Turner, S. M., & Young, B. (2006). Social Effectiveness Therapy for Children: Five years later. *Behavior Therapy, 37,* 416–425.

Beidel, D. C., Turner, S. M., Young, B., & Paulson, A. (in press). Social effectiveness therapy for children: Three year follow-up. *Journal of Consulting and Clinical Psychology.*

Beidel, D. C., Turner, S. M., Young, B., Ammerman, R. A., & Sallee, F. R. (2007). Psychopathology of adolescent social phobia. *Journal of Psychopathology and Behavioral Assessment, 29,* 47–54.

Beidel, D. C., Turner, S. M., Sallee, F. R., Ammerman, R. T., Crosby, L. A., & Pathak, S. (2007). SET-C versus fluoxetine in the treatment of childhood social phobia. *Journal of the American Academy of Child and Adolescent Psychiatry, 46,* 1622–1632.

Bell, C., Malizia, A., & Nutt, D. (1999). The neurobiology of social phobia. *European Archives of Psychiatry and Clinical Neuroscience, 249*(Suppl. 1), S11–S18.

Bell-Dolan, D. J., Last, C. G., & Strauss, C. C. (1990). Symptoms of anxiety disorders in normal children. *Journal of the American Academy of Child and Adolescent Psychiatry, 29,* 759–765.

Benazon, N. R., Moore, G. J., & Rosenberg, D. R. (2003). Neurochemical analyses in pediatric obsessive-compulsive disorder in patients treated with cognitive-behavioral therapy. *Journal of the American Academy of Child and Adolescent Psychiatry, 42,* 1279–1285.

Berg, C. J., Rapoport, J. L., & Flament, M. (1986). The Leyton Obsessional Inventory–Child Version. *Journal of the American Academy of Child Psychiatry, 25,* 84–91.

Berg, C. Z., Whitaker, A., Davies, M., Flament, M. F., & Rapoport, J. L. (1988). The survey form of the Leyton Obsessional Inventory— Child Version: Norms from an epidemiological study. *Journal of the American Academy of Child and Adolescent Psychiatry, 27,* 759–763.

Berg, I., Butler, A., & Pritchard, J. (1974). Psychiatric illness in the mothers of school-phobic adolescents. *British Journal of Psychiatry, 125,* 466–467.

Berg, I., Marks, I., McGuire, R., & Lipsedge, M. (1974). School phobia and agoraphobia. *Psychological Medicine, 4,* 428–434.

Bergman, R. L., Keller, M., Wood, J., Piacentini, J., & McCracken, J. (2001, October). *Selective Mutism Questionnaire (SMQ): Development and findings.* Presented at the annual meeting of the American Academy of Child and Adolescent Psychiatry, Honolulu.

Bergman, R. L., Piacentini, J., & McCracken, J. T. (2002). Prevalence and description of selective mutism in a school-based sample. *Journal of the American Academy of Child and Adolescent Psychiatry, 41,* 938–946.

Bergman, R. L., Keller, M. L., Piacentini, J., & Bergman, A. J. (2008). The development and psychometric properties of the selective mutism questionnaire. *Journal of Clinical Child and Adolescent Psychology, 32,* 456–464.

Berman, S. I., Weems, C. F., Silverman, W. K., & Kurtines, W. M. (2000). Predictors of outcome in exposure-based cognitive and behavioral treatments for phobic and anxiety disorders in children. *Behavior Therapy, 31,* 713–731.

Bernstein, G. A. (1991). Comorbidity and severity of anxiety and depressive disorders in a clinic sample. *Journal of the American Academy of Child and Adolescent Psychiatry, 30*, 43–50.

Bernstein, G. A., Borchardt, C. M., Perwien, A. R., Crosby, R. D., Kushner, M. G., Thuras, P. D., et al. (2000). Imipramine plus cognitive–behavioral therapy in the treatment of school refusal. *Journal of the American Academy of Child and Adolescent Psychiatry, 39*, 276–283.

Bernstein, G. A., & Garfinkel, B. D. (1986). School phobia: The overlap of affective and anxiety disorders. *Journal of the American Academy of Child and Adolescent Psychiatry, 25*, 235–241.

Bernstein, G. A., & Garfinkel, B. D. (1988). Pedigrees, functioning, and psychopathology in families of school phobic children. *American Journal of Psychiatry, 145*, 70–74.

Bernstein, G. A., & Garfinkel, B. D. (1992). The visual analogue scale for anxiety revisited: Psychometric properties. *Journal of Anxiety Disorders, 6*, 223–239.

Bernstein, G. A., Garfinkel, B. D., & Borchardt, C. M. (1990). Comparative studies of pharmacotherapy for school refusal. *Journal of the American Academy of Child and Adolescent Psychiatry, 29*, 773–781.

Bernstein, G. A., Hektner, J. M., Borchardt, C. M., & McMillan, M. H. (2001). Treatment of school refusal: One year follow-up. *Journal of the American Academy of Child and Adolescent Psychiatry, 40*, 206–213.

Bernstein, G. A., Massie, E. D., Thuras, P. D., Perwein, A. R. Borchardt, C. M., & Crosby, R. D. (1997). Somatic symptoms in anxious-depressed school refusers. *Journal of the American Academy of Child and Adolescent Psychiatry, 36*, 661–668.

Bernstein, G. A., Svingen, P. H., & Garfinkel, B. D. (1990). School phobia: Patterns of family functioning. *Journal of the American Academy of Child and Adolescent Psychiatry, 29*, 24–30.

Bernstein, G. A., Warren, S. L., Massie, E. D., & Thuras, P. D. (1999). Family dimensions in anxious-depressed school refusers. *Journal of Anxiety Disorders, 5*, 515–528.

Biederman, J., Farone, S. V., Marrs, A., Moore, P., Farcia, J., Ablon, S., et al. (1997). Panic disorder and agoraphobia in consecutively referred children and adolescents. *Journal of the American Academy of Child and Adolescent Psychiatry, 36*, 214–223.

Biederman, J., Hirshfeld-Becker, D. R., Rosenbaum, J. F., Friedman, D., Snidman, N., Kagan, J., et al. (2001). Further evidence of association between behavioral inhibition and social anxiety in children. *American Journal of Psychiatry, 158*, 1673–1679.

Biederman, J., Petty, C., Faraone, S., Hirshfeld-Becker, D., Henin, A., Dougherty, M., et al. (2005). Parental predictors of pediatric panic disorder/agoraphobia: A controlled study in high-risk offspring. *Depression and Anxiety, 22*(3), 114–120.

Biederman, J., Rosenbaum, J. F., Bolduc-Murphy, E. A., Faraone, S. V., Charloff, J., Hirshfeld, D. R., et al. (1993). A 3-year follow-up of children with and without behavioral inhibition. *Journal of the American Academy of Child and Adolescent Psychiatry, 32*, 847–850.

Bienvenu, O. J., Hettema, J. M., Neale, M. C., Prescott, C. A., & Kendler, K. S. (2007). Low extraversion and high neuroticism an indices of genetic and environmental risk for social phobia, agoraphobia, and animal phobia. *The American Journal of Psychiatry, 164*, 1714–1721.

Bienvenu, O. J., Samuels, J. F., Riddle, M. A., Hoehn-Saric, R., Liang, K. Y., Cullen, B. A. M., et al. (2000). The relationship of obsessive-compulsive disorder to possible spectrum disorders: Results from a family study. *Biological Psychiatry, 48*, 287–293.

Bird, H. R., Canino, G., Rubio-Stipec, M., Gould, M. S., Ribera, J., Sesman, M., et al. (1988). Estimates of the prevalence of childhood maladjustment in a community survey in Puerto Rico. *Archives of General Psychiatry, 45*, 1120–1126.

Bird, H. R., Gould, M. S., Yager, T., Staghezza, B., & Canino, G. (1989). Risk factors for maladjustment in Puerto Rican children. *Journal of the American Academy of Child and Adolescent Psychiatry, 28*, 847–850.

Birmaher, B., Axelson, D. A., Monk, K., Kalas, C., Clark, D. B., Ehmann, M., et al. (2003). Fluoxetine for the treatment of childhood anxiety disorders. *Journal of the American Academy of Child and Adolescent Psychiatry, 42*, 415–423.

Birmaher, B., Brent, D. A., Chiappetta, L., Bridge, J., Monga, S., & Baugher, M. (1999). Psychometric properties of the Screen for Childhood Anxiety Related Emotional Disorders (SCARED): A replication study. *Journal of the American Academy of Child and Adolescent Psychiatry, 38*, 1230–1236.

Birmaher, B., Waterman, G. S., Ryan, N., Cully, M., Balach, L., Ingram, J., et al. (1994). Fluoxetine for childhood anxiety disorders. *Journal of the American Academy of Child and Adolescent Psychiatry, 33*, 993–998.

Bittner, A., Egger, H., Erkanli, A., Costello, E., Foley, D., & Angold, A. (2007). What do childhood anxiety disorders predict? *Journal of Child Psychology and Psychiatry, 48*, 1174–1183.

Black, B., & Robbins, D. R. (1990). Panic disorder in children and adolescents. *Journal of the American Academy of Child and Adolescent Psychiatry, 29*, 36–44.

Black, B., & Uhde, T. W. (1994). Treatment of elective mutism with fluoxetine: A double-blind placebo-controlled study. *Journal of the American Academy of Child and Adolescent Psychiatry, 33,* 1000–1006.

Blagg, N. R., & Yule, W. (1984). The behavioural treatment of school refusal: A comparative study. *Behaviour Research and Therapy, 22,* 119–127.

Blakely, K. S. (1994). Parents' conceptions of social dangers to children in the urban environment. *Children's Environments, 11,* 16–25.

Bloch, M. H., Craiglow, B. G., Landeros-Weisenberger, A., Dombrowski, P. A., Panza, K. E., Peterson, B. S., et al. (2009). Predictors of early adult outcomes in pediatric-onset obsessive-compulsive disorder. *Pediatrics, 124,* 1085–1093.

Blum, N. J., Barone, V. J., & Friman, P. C. (1993). A simplified behavioral treatment for trichotillomania: Report of two cases. *Pediatrics, 91,* 993–995.

Bodden, D., Dirksen, C., & Bögels, S. (2008). Societal burden of clinically anxious youth referred for treatment: A cost-of-illness study. *Journal of Abnormal Child Psychology, 36,* 487–497.

Bogels, S. M., van Oosten, A., Muris, P., & Smulders, D. (2001). Familial correlates of social anxiety in children and adolescents. *Behaviour Research and Therapy, 39,* 273–287.

Bogels, S. M., & Zigterman, D. (2000). Dysfunctional cognitions in children with social phobia, separation anxiety disorder, and generalized anxiety disorder. *Journal of Abnormal Child Psychology, 28,* 205–211.

Bolton, D., Eley, T. C., O'Connor, T. G., Perrin, S., Rabe-Hesketh, S., Rijsdijk, F., et al. (2006). Prevalence and genetic and environmental influences on anxiety disorders in 6-year-old twins. *Psychological Medicine, 36,* 335–344.

Bonanno, G. A. (2004). Loss, trauma, and human resilience. *American Psychologist, 59,* 20–28.

Bondy, A., Sheslow, D., & Garcia, L. T. (1985). An investigation of children's fears and their mother's fears. *Journal of Psychopathology and Behavioral Assessment, 7,* 1–12.

Borkovec, T. D. (1985). Worry: A potentially valuable concept. *Behaviour Research and Therapy, 23,* 481–482.

Bowen, R. C., Offord, D. R., & Boyle, M. H. (1990). The prevalence of overanxious disorder and separation anxiety disorder: Results from the Ontario Child Health Study. *Journal of the American Academy of Child and Adolescent Psychiatry, 29,* 753–758.

Bowlby, J. (1973). *Attachment and loss: Vol. 2. Separation anxiety and anger.* New York: Basic Books.

Boyd, R. C., Ginsburg, G. A., Lambert, S. F., Cooley, M. R., & Campbell, K. D. M. (2003). Screen for Child Anxiety Related Emotional Disorders (SCARED): Psychometric properties in an African-American parochial high school sample. *Journal of the American Academy of Child and Adolescent Psychiatry, 42,* 1188–1196.

Bradley, S. J., & Hood, J. (1993). Psychiatrically referred adolescents with panic attacks: Presenting symptoms, stressors and comorbidity. *Journal of the American Academy of Child and Adolescent Psychiatry, 32,* 826–829.

Brady, E. U., & Kendall, P. C. (1992). Co-morbidity of anxiety and depression in children and adolescents. *Psychological Bulletin, 111,* 244–255.

Brent, D. A., Perper, J. A., Moritz, G., Liotus, L., Richardson, D., Canobbio, R., et al. (1995). Posttraumatic stress disorder in peers of adolescent suicide victims: Predisposing factors and phenomenology. *Journal of the American Academy of Child and Adolescent Psychiatry, 34,* 209–215.

Breslau, N., Roth, T., Burduvali, E., Kapke, A., Schultz, L., & Roehrs, T. (2004). Sleep in lifetime posttraumatic stress disorder: A community-based polysomnographic study. *Archives of General Psychiatry, 61,* 508–516.

Bretherton, I., Fritz, J., Zahn-Waxler, C., & Ridgeway, D. (1986). Learning to talk about emotions: A functionalist perspective. *Child Development, 57,* 529–548.

Breton, J. J., Bergeron, L., Valla, J. P., Bertiaume, C., Gauder, N., Lambert, J., et al. (1999). Quebec child mental health survey: Prevalence of DSM-III-R mental health disorders. *Journal of Child Psychology and Psychiatry, 40,* 375–384.

Brody, G. H., Chen, Y., Murry, V. M., Ge, X., Simons, R. L., Gibbons, F. X., et al. (2006). Perceived discrimination and the adjustment of African American youths: A five-year longitudinal analysis with contextual moderation effects. *Child Development, 77,* 1170–1189.

Bromberg, A., Lamb, M. E., & Hwang, P. (1990). Inhibition: Its stability and correlates in sixteen to forty month old children. *Child Development, 61,* 1153–1163.

Brown, A., Deacon, B., Abramowitz, J., Dammann, J., & Whiteside, S. (2007). Parents' perceptions of pharmacological and cognitive-behavioral treatments for childhood anxiety disorders. *Behaviour Research and Therapy, 45*(4), 819–828.

Brown, J. B., & Lloyd, H. (1975). A controlled study of children not speaking at school. *Journal of the Association of Workers for Maladjusted Children, 3,* 49–63.

Brown, T. A., Di Nardo, P. A., Lehman, C. L., & Campbell, L. A. (2001). Reliability of DSM-IV and mood disorders. *Journal of Abnormal Psychology, 110*, 49–58.

Bruce, T. O., Barwick, L. W., & Wright, H. H. (2005). Diagnosis and management of trichotillomania in children and adolescents. *Pediatric Drugs, 7*, 365–376.

Bruch, M. A., & Heimberg, R. G. (1994). Differences in perceptions of parental and personal characteristics between generalized and nongeneralized social phobics. *Journal of Anxiety Disorders, 8*, 155–168.

Bruch, M. A. Giordano, S., & Pearl, L. (1986). Differences between fearful and self-conscious shy types in background and current adjustment. *Journal of Research in Personality, 20*, 172–186.

Bruch, M. A., Heimberg, R. G., Berger, P., & Collins, T. M. (1989). Social phobia and perceptions of early parental and personal characteristics. *Anxiety Research, 2*, 57–63.

Bruni, O., Ottaviano, S., Guidetti, V., Romoli, M., Innocenzi, M., Cortesi, F., et al. (1996). The Sleep Disturbance Scale for Children (SDSC) construction and validation of an instrument to evaluate sleep disturbances in childhood and adolescence. *Journal of Sleep Research, 5*, 251–261.

Buckley, T. M., & Schatzberg, A. F. (2005). Review: On the interactions of the hypothalamic pituitary-adrenal (HPA) axis and sleep: Normal HPA axis activity and circadian rhythm, exemplary sleep disorders. *The Journal of Clinical Endocrinology and Metabolism, 90*, 3106–3114.

Bulik, C. M., Sullivan, P. F., Fear, J. L., & Joyce, P. R. (1997). Eating disorders and antecedent anxiety disorders: A controlled study. *Acta Psychiatrica Scandinavia, 96*, 101–107.

Burke, A. E., & Silverman, W. K. (1987). The prescriptive treatment of school refusal. *Clinical Psychology Review, 7*, 353–362.

Burke, P., Meyer, V., Kocoshis, S., Orenstein, D. M., Chandrea, R., Nord, D. J., et al. (1989). Depression and anxiety in pediatric inflammatory bowel disease and cystic fibrosis. *Journal of the American Academy of Child and Adolescent Psychiatry, 28*, 948–951.

Burke, P., Meyer, V., Kocoshis, S., Orenstein, D. M., Chandrea, R., & Sauer, J. (1989). Obsessive-compulsive symptoms in childhood inflammatory bowel disease and cystic fibrosis. *Journal of the American Academy of Child and Adolescent Psychiatry, 28*, 525–527.

Burnham, J. J. (2005). Fears of children in the United States: An examination of the American Fear Survey Schedule with 20 new contemporary fear items. *Measurement and Evaluation in Counseling and Development, 38*, 78–91.

Burnham, J. J. (2007). Children's fears: A pre-9/11 and post-9/11 comparison using the American Fear Survey Schedule for Children. *Journal of Counseling and Development, 85,* 461–466.

Burnham, J. J. (2009). Contemporary fears of children and adolescents: Coping and resiliency in the 21st century. *Journal of Counseling and Development, 87,* 28–35.

Burnham, J. J., & Hooper, L. M. (2008). Fears of American children following terrorism. *Journal of Loss and Trauma, 13,* 319–329.

Buss, A. H., & Plomin, R. (1984). *Temperament: Early developing personality traits.* Hillsdale, NJ: Erlbaum.

Calhoun, J., & Koenig, K. P. (1973). Classroom modification of elective mutism. *Behavior Therapy, 4,* 700–702.

Campbell, S. B. (1986). Developmental issues. In R. G. Gittleman (Ed.), *Anxiety disorders of childhood.* New York: Guilford.

Campos, J. J., Emde, R. N., Gaensbauer, T., & Henderson, C. (1975). Cardiac and behavioral interrelationships in the reaction of infants to strangers. *Developmental Psychology, 11,* 589–601.

Cantor, J., & Nathanson, A. I. (1996). Children's fright reactions to television news. *Journal of Communication, 46,* 139–152.

Cantwell, D. P., & Baker, L. (1989). Stability and natural history of DSM-III childhood diagnoses. *Journal of the American Academy of Child and Adolescent Psychiatry, 28,* 691–700.

Carrion, V. G., Weems, C. F., Eliez, S., Patwardhan, A., Brown, W., Ray, R. D., et al. (2001). Attenuation of frontal asymmetry in pediatric posttraumatic stress disorder. *Biological Psychiatry, 50,* 943–951.

Carrion, V. G., Weems, C. F., Ray, R. D., Glaser, B., Hessl, D., & Reiss, A. L. (2002). Diurnal salivary cortisol in pediatric posttraumatic stress disorder. *Biological Psychiatry, 51,* 575–582.

Carrion, V. G., Weems, C. F., & Reiss, A. L. (2007). Stress predicts brain changes in children: A pilot longitudinal study on youth stress, posttraumatic stress disorder, and the hippocampus. *Pediatrics, 119,* 509–516.

Carrion, V. G., Weems, C. F., Watson, C., Eliez, S., Menon, V., & Reiss, A. L. (2009). Converging evidence for abnormalities of the prefrontal cortex and evaluation of midsagittal structures in pediatric posttraumatic stress disorder: An MRI study. *Psychiatry Research: Neuroimaging, 172,* 226–234.

Carskadon, M. A., Acebo, C., Richardson, G. S., Tate, B. A., & Seifer, R. (1997). An approach to studying circadian rhythms of adolescent humans. *Journal of Biological Rhythms, 12,* 278–289.

Caspi, A., Bem, D. J., & Elder, G. H. (1989). Continuities and consequences of interactional styles across the life course. *Journal of Personality, 57,* 375–406.

Caspi, A., Elder, G. H., & Bem, D. J. (1988). Moving away from the world: Life-course patterns of shy children. *Developmental Psychology, 24,* 824–831.

Caspi, A., & Silva, P. A. (1995). Temperamental qualities at age 3 predict personality traits in young adulthood: Longitudinal evidence from a birth cohort. *Child Development, 66,* 486–498.

Caster, J., Inderbitzen, H., & Hope, D. (1999). Relationship between youth and parent perceptions of family environment and social anxiety. *Journal of Anxiety Disorders, 13,* 237–251.

Catani, C., Kohiladevy, M., Ruf, M., Schauer, E., Elbert, T., & Neuner, F. (2009). Treating children traumatized by war and tsunami: A comparison between exposure therapy and meditation-relaxation in North-East Sri Lanka. *BMC Psychiatry, 9,* 22–32.

Cath, D. C., Ran, N., Smit, J. H., van Balkom, A. J. L. M., & Comijs, H. C. (2008). Symptom overlap between autism spectrum disorder, generalized social anxiety disorder, and obsessive-compulsive disorder in adults: A preliminary case-controlled study. *Psychopathology, 41,* 101–110.

Chambless, D. L., & Hollon, S. D. (1998). Defining empirically supported therapies. *Journal of Consulting and Clinical Psychology, 66,* 7–18.

Chambless, D. L., Sanderson, W. C., Shoham, V., Bennett Johnson, S., Pope, K. S., Crits-Christoph, P., et al. (1996). An update on empirically validated therapies. *The Clinical Psychologist, 49,* 5–18.

Chang, C. H., Lee, M. B., Chiang, Y. C., & Lu, Y. C. (1991). Trichotillomania: A clinical study of 36 patients. *Journal of the Formosan Medical Association, 90,* 176–180.

Chavira, D. A., & Stein, M. B. (2002). Combined psychoeducation and treatment with selective serotonin reuptake inhibitors for youth with generalized social anxiety disorder. *Journal of Child and Adolescent Child Psychopharmacology, 12,* 47–54.

Chavira, D. A., Stein, M. B., Bailey, K., & Stein, M. T. (2003). Parental opinions regarding treatment for social anxiety disorder in youth. *Journal of Developmental and Behavioral Pediatrics, 24,* 315–322.

Chazan, M. (1962). School phobia. *British Journal of Educational Psychology, 32,* 209–217.

Chen, X., Rubin, K. H., & Li, B. (1995). Social and school adjustment of shy and aggressive children in China. *Development and Psychopathology, 7,* 337–349.

Choate, M. L., Pincus, D. B., Eyberg, S. M., & Barlow, D. H. (2005). Parent-child interaction therapy for treatment of separation anxiety disorder in young children: A pilot study. *Cognitive and Behavioral Practice, 12,* 126–135.

Chorpita, B. F., Albano, A. M., & Barlow, D. H. (1996). Cognitive processing in children: Relation to anxiety and family influences. *Journal of Clinical Child Psychology, 25*, 170–176.

Chorpita, B. F., Tracey, S. A., Brown, T. A., Collica, T. J., & Barlow, D. H. (1997). Assessment of worry in children and adolescents: An adaptation of the Penn State Worry Questionnaire. *Behaviour Research and Therapy, 35*, 569–581.

Chorpita, B. F., Vitali, A. E., & Barlow, D. H. (1997). Behavioral treatment of choking phobia in an adolescent: An experimental analysis. *Journal of Behavior Therapy and Experimental Psychiatry, 28*, 307–315.

Chorpita, B. F., Yim, L. M., Moffitt, C. E., Umemoto, L. A., & Francis, S. E. (2000). Assessment symptoms of DSM-IV anxiety and depression in children. *Behavior Research and Therapy, 38*, 835–855.

Choudhury, M. S., Pimentel, S. S., & Kendall, P. C. (2003). Childhood anxiety disorders: Parent-child (dis)agreement using a structured interview for the DSM-IV. *Journal of the American Academy of Child and Adolescent Psychiatry, 42*, 957–964.

Christenson, G. A., Mackenzie, T. B., Mitchell, J. E., & Callies, A. L. (1991). A placebo-controlled, double-blind crossover study of fluoxetine in trichotillomania. *American Journal of Psychiatry, 148*, 1566–1571.

Christenson, G. A., Pyle, R. L., & Mitchell, J. E. (1991). Estimated lifetime prevalence of trichotillomania in college students. *Journal of Clinical Psychiatry, 52*, 415–417.

Christenson, G. A., Ristvedt, S. L., & Mackenzie, T. B. (1993). Identification of trichotillomania cue profiles. *Behaviour Research and Therapy, 31*, 315–320.

Chronis-Tuscano, A., Degnan, K. A., Pine, D. S., Perezedgar, K., Henderson, H., Diaz, Y., et al. (2009). Stable early maternal report of behavioral inhibition predicts lifetime social anxiety disorder in adolescence. *Journal of the American Academy of Child and Adolescent Psychiatry, 48*, 928–935.

Clark, D. B. (1993, March). *Assessment of social anxiety in adolescents.* Paper presented at the Anxiety Disorders Association of America Annual Convention, Charleston, SC.

Clark, D. M. (1986). A cognitive approach to panic. *Behaviour Research and Therapy, 24*, 461–470.

Clark, D. M. (1988). A cognitive model of panic attacks. In S. Rachman & J. D. Maser (Eds.), *Panic: Psychological perspectives* (pp. 71–89). Hillside, NJ: Erlbaum.

Cloitre, M., Stolbach, B. C., Herman, J. L., van der Kolk, B., Pynoos, R., Wang, J., et al. (2009). A developmental approach to complex PTSD: Childhood and adult cumulative trauma as predictors of symptom complexity. *Journal of Traumatic Stress, 22*, 399–408.

Cohan, S. L., Chavira, D. A., Shipon-Bun, E., Hitchcock, C., Roesch, S., & Stein, M. B. (2008). Refining the classification of children with selective mutism: A latent profile analysis. *Journal of Clinical Child and Adolescent Psychology, 37,* 770–784.

Cohan, S. L., Chavira, D. A., & Stein, M. B. (2006). Practitioner review: Psychosocial interventions for children with selective mutism: A critical evaluation of the literature from 1990–2005. *Journal of Child Psychology and Psychiatry, 47,* 1085–1097.

Cohen, J. A., Berliner, L., & March, J. (2000). Treatment of children and adolescents. In E. B. Foa, T. M. Keane, & M. J. Friedman (Eds.), *Effective treatments for PTSD* (pp. 106–138). New York: Guilford Press.

Cohen, J. A., Deblinger, E., Mannarino, A. P., & Steer, R. (2004). A multisite, randomized controlled trial for children with abuse-related PTSD symptoms. *Journal of the American Academy of Child and Adolescent Psychiatry, 43,* 393–402.

Cohen, J. A., Jaycox, L. H., Walker, D. W., Mannarino, A. P., Langley, A. K., & DuClos, J. L. (2009). Treating traumatized children after Hurricane Katrina: Project Fleur-de Lis. *Clinical Child and Family Psychology Review, 12,* 55–64.

Cohen, J. A., & Mannarino, A. P. (1996). A treatment outcome study for sexually abused preschool children: Initial findings. *Journal of the American Academy of Child and Adolescent Psychiatry, 35,* 42–50.

Cohen, J. A., & Mannarino, A. P. (1997). A treatment outcome study for sexually abused preschool children: Outcome during a one-year follow-up. *Journal of the American Academy of Child and Adolescent Psychiatry, 36,* 1228–1235.

Cohen, J. A., Mannarino, A. P., & Deblinger, E. (2006). *Treating trauma and traumatic grief in children and adolescents.* New York: Guilford Press.

Cohen, J. A., Mannarino, A. P., & Knudson, K. (2005). Treating sexually abused children: 1 year follow-up of a randomized controlled trial. *Child Abuse and Neglect, 29,* 135–145.

Cohen, J. A., Mannarino, A. P., Perel, J. M., & Staron, V. (2007). A pilot randomized controlled trial of combined trauma-focused CBT and sertraline for childhood PTSD symptoms. *Journal of the American Academy of Child and Adolescent Psychiatry, 46,* 811–819.

Cohen, L. J., Stein, D. B., Simeon, D., Spadaccini, E., Rosen, J., Aronowitz, B., et al. (1995). Clinical profile, comorbidity, and treatment history in 123 hair pullers: A survey study. *Journal of Clinical Psychiatry, 56,* 319–326.

Cohen, P., Cohen, J., & Brook, J. (1993). An epidemiological study of disorders in late childhood and adolescence. II: Persistence of disorders. *Journal of Child Psychology and Psychiatry, 34,* 869–877.

Compton, S. C., Grant, P. J., Chrisman, A. K., Gammon, P. J., Brown, V. L. O., & March, J. S. (2001). Sertraline in children and adolescents with social anxiety disorder: An open trial. *Journal of the American Academy of Child and Adolescent Psychiatry, 40,* 564–571.

Compton, S. N., March, J. S., Brent, D, Albano, A. M., Weersing, R., & Curry, J. (2004). Cognitive-behavioral psychotherapy for anxiety and depressive disorders in children and adolescents: An evidence-based medicine review. *Journal of the American Academy of Child and Adolescent Psychiatry, 43,* 930–959.

Connell, H. M., Persley, G. V., & Sturgess, J. L. (1987). Sleep phobia in middle childhood—A review of six cases. *Journal of the American Academy of Child and Adolescent Psychiatry, 26,* 449–452.

Cook, M., & Mineka, S. (1989). Observational conditioning of fear to fear-relevant versus fear-irrelevant stimuli in rhesus monkeys. *Journal of Abnormal Psychology, 98,* 448–459.

Cook, M., & Mineka, S. (1991). Selective associations in the origins of phobic fears and their implications for behavior therapy. In P. Martin (Ed.), *Handbook of behavior therapy and psychological science: An integrative approach* (pp. 413–434). Elmsford, NY: Pergamon Press.

Cook, A., Spinazzola, J., Ford, J., Lanktree, C., Blaustein, M., Cloitre, M., et al. (2005). Complex trauma in children and adolescents, *Psychiatric Annals, 35,* 390–398.

Cooley-Quille, M. R., Turner, S. M., & Beidel, D . C. (1995). Emotional impact of children's exposure to community violence: A preliminary study. *Journal of the American Academy of Child and Adolescent Psychiatry, 34,* 1362–1368.

Coolidge, J. C., Hahn, P. B., & Peck, A. L. (1957). School phobia: Neurotic crisis or way of life. *American Journal of Orthopsychiatry, 27,* 296–306.

Cooper, P. J., Fearn, V., Willetts, L., Seabrook, H., & Parkinson, M. (2006). Affective disorder in the parents of a clinic sample of children with anxiety disorders. *Journal of Affective Disorders, 93,* 205–512.

Copeland, W. E., Keeler, G., Angold, A., & Costello, E. J. (2007). Traumatic events and posttraumatic stress in childhood. *Archives of General Psychiatry, 64,* 577–584.

Copeland, W. E., Shanahan, L., Costello, J., & Angold, A. (2009). Childhood and adolescent psychiatric disorders as predictors of young adult disorders. *Archives of General Psychiatry, 66,* 764–772.

Coplan, R. J., Prakash, K., O'Neil, K., & Armer, M. (2004). Do you "want" to play? Distinguishing between conflicted shyness and social disinterest in early childhood. *Developmental Psychology, 40,* 244–258.

Cornelius, J. R., Kirisci, L., Reynolds, M., Clark, D. B., Hayes, J., & Tarter, R. (2010). PTSD contributes to teen and young adult cannabis use disorders. *Addictive Behaviors, 35,* 91–94.

Cornwall, E., Spence, S. H., & Schotte, D. (1997). The effectiveness of emotive imagery in the treatment of darkness phobia in children. *Behaviour Change, 13,* 223–229.

Cortes, A. M., Saltzman, K. M., Weems, C. F., Regnault, H. P., Reiss, A. L., & Carrion, V. G. (2005). Development of anxiety disorders in a traumatized pediatric population: A preliminary longitudinal evaluation. *Child Abuse and Neglect, 29,* 905–914.

Costello, E. J., & Angold, A. (1995). Epidemiology. In J. S. March (Ed.), *Anxiety disorders in children and adolescents* (pp. 109–124). New York: Guilford Press.

Costello, E. J., Costello, A. J., Edelbrock, C., & Burns, B. J. (1988). Psychiatric disorders in pediatric primary care: Prevalence and risk factors. *Archives of General Psychiatry, 45,* 1107–1116.

Costello, A. J., Edelbrock, C., Kalas, R., Kessler, M., & Klaric, S. A. (1982). *Diagnostic Interview Schedule for Children (DISC).* Written under contract to the National Institute of Mental Health.

Costello, E., Egger, H., & Angold, A. (2005). The developmental epidemiology of anxiety disorders: phenomenology, prevalence, and comorbidity. *Child and Adolescent Psychiatric Clinics of North America, 14,* 631–648.

Costello, E. J., Erkanli, A., Federman, E., & Angold, A. (1999). Development of psychiatric comorbidity with substance abuse in adolescents: Effects of timing and sex. *Journal of Clinical Child Psychology, 28,* 298–311.

Costello, E. J., Stoudhamer-Loeber, M., & DeRosier, M. (1993). *Continuity and change in psychopathology from childhood to adolescence.* Paper presented at the annual meeting of the Society for Research in Child and Adolescent Psychopathology, Santa Fe, New Mexico.

Coupland, N. J. (2001). Social phobia: Etiology, neurobiology, and treatment. *Journal of Clinical Psychiatry, 62*(Suppl. 1), 25–35.

Craske, M. G., Poulton, R., Tsao, J. C. I., & Plotkin, D. (2001). Paths to panic disorder/agoraphobia: An exploratory analysis from age 3 to 21 in an unselected birth cohort. *Journal of the American Academy of Child and Adolescent Psychiatry, 40,* 556–563.

Crawley, S. A., Beidas, R. S., Benjamin, C. L., Martin, E., & Kendall, P. C. (2008). Treating socially phobic youth with CBT: Differential outcomes and treatment considerations. *Behavioural and Cognitive Psychotherapy, 36,* 379–389.

Croake, J. W., & Knox, F. H. (1973). The changing nature of children's fears. *Child Study Journal, 3,* 91–105.

Crowe, R. R., Noyes, R., Persico, T., Wilson, A. F., & Elston, R. C. (1988). Genetic studies of panic disorder and related conditions. In D. L. Dunnel, E. S. Gershon, & J. E. Barrett (Eds.), *Relatives at risk for mental disorders* (pp. 73–85). New York: Raven Press.

Cunningham, C. E., Cataldo, M. F., Mallion, C., & Keyes, J. B. (1983). A review and controlled single case evaluation of behavioral approaches to the management of elective mutism. *Child and Family Behavior Therapy, 5,* 25–49.

Cunningham, C. E., McHolm, A. E., & Boyle, M. H. (2006). Social phobia, anxiety, oppositional behavior, social skills, and self-concept in children with specific selective mutism, generalized selective mutism, and community controls. *European Child and Adolescent Psychiatry, 15,* 245–255.

Dahl, R. E. (1996). The regulation of sleep and arousal: Development and psychopathology. *Development and Psychopathology, 8,* 3–27.

Dale, R. C., Heyman, I., Giovannoni, G., & Church, A. W. J. (2005). Incidence of anti-brain antibodies in children and adolescents with obsessive-compulsive disorder. *The British Journal of Psychiatry, 187,* 314–319.

Dalgleish, T., Meiser-Stedman, R., Kassam-Adams, N., Ehlers, A., Winston, F., Smith, P., et al. (2008). Is acute stress disorder the optimal means to identify child and adolescent trauma survivors at risk for later PTSD? *British Journal of Psychiatry, 192,* 392–393.

Davidson, J. (1993, March). *Childhood histories of adult social phobics.* Paper presented at the Anxiety Disorders Association of America Annual Convention, Charleston, SC.

Davis, J. L., & Wright, D. C. (2005). Case series utilizing exposure, relaxation, and rescripting therapy: Impact on nightmares, sleep quality, and psychological distress. *Behavioral Sleep Medicine, 3,* 151–157.

Daviss, W. B., Mooney, D., Racusin, R., Ford, J. D., Fleischer, A., & McHugo, G. J. (2000). Predicting posttraumatic stress after hospitalization for pediatric injury. *Journal of the American Academy of Child and Adolescent Psychiatry, 39,* 576–583.

De Bellis, M. D. (2001). Developmental traumatology: The psychobio-logical development of maltreated children and its implications for research, treatment, and policy. *Development and Psychopathology, 13,* 539–564.

De Bellis, M. D., Casey, B. J., Dahl, R. E., Birmaher, B., Williamson, D. E., Thomas, K. M., et al. (2000). A pilot study of amygdala volumes in pediatric generalized anxiety disorder. *Biological Psychiatry, 48,* 51–57.

De Bellis, M. D., Hall, J., Boring, A. M., Frustaci, K., & Moritz, G. (2001). A pilot longitudinal study of hippocampal volumes in pedi-atric maltreatment-related posttraumatic stress disorder. *Biological Psychiatry, 50,* 305–309.

De Bellis, M. D., Keshavan, M., Clark, D. B., Casey, B. J., Giedd, J., Boring, A. M., et al. (1999). A. E. Bennett Research Award. Developmental traumatology. Part II: Brain development. *Biological Psychiatry, 45,* 1271–1284.

De Bellis, M. J. D., Keshavan, M., Frustaci, K., Shifflett, H., Iyengar, S. L., Beers, S. R., et al. (2002). Superior temporal gyrus volumes in mal-treated children and adolescents with PTSD. *Biological Psychiatry, 51,* 544–552.

De Bellis, M. D., Keshavan, M. S., Shifflett, H., Iyengar, S., Beers, S. R., Hall, J., et al. (2002). Brain structures in pediatric maltreatment-related posttraumatic stress disorder: A sociodemographically matched study. *Biological Psychiatry, 52,* 1066–1078.

De Bellis, M. D., Keshavan, M. S., Shifflett, H., Iyengar, S., Dahl, R. E., Axelson, D. A., et al. (2002). Superior temporal gyrus volumes in pedi-atric generalized anxiety disorder. *Biological Psychiatry, 51,* 553–562.

Deblinger, E., Lippman, J., & Steer, R. (1996). Sexually abused children suffering posttraumatic stress symptoms: Initial treatment outcome. *Child Maltreatment, 1,* 310–321.

De Haan, E., Hoogduin, K., Buitelaar, J., & Keisjers, G. (1998). Behavior therapy versus clomipramine for the treatment of obsessive-compulsive disorder. *Journal of the American Academy of Child and Adolescent Psychiatry, 37,* 1022–1029.

De Jong, P. J., Andrea, H., & Muris, P. (1997). Spider phobia in children: disgust and fear before and after treatment. *Behaviour Research and Therapy, 35,* 559–562.

De la Eva, R., Baur, L., Donaghue, K., & Waters K. (2002). Metabolic correlates with obstructive sleep apnea in obese subjects. *Journal of Pediatrics, 140,* 654–659.

Delprato, D. J., & McGlynn, F. D. (1984). Behavioral theories of anxiety disorders. In S. M. Turner (Ed.), *Behavioral theories and treatment of anxiety* (pp. 1–49). New York: Plenum Press.

Denkla, M. B. (1989). The neuropsychological examination. In J. L. Rapoport (Ed.), *Obsessive-compulsive disorder in children and adolescents* (pp. 107–118). Washington, DC: American Psychiatric Press.

DeVeaugh-Geiss, J., Moroz, G., Biederman, J., Cantwell, D., Fontaine, R., Greist, J. H., et al. (1992). Clomipramine hydrochloride in childhood obsessive-compulsive disorder. *Journal of the American Academy of Child and Adolescent Psychiatry, 31,* 45–49.

Dewis, L. M., Kirkby, K. C., Martin, F., Daniels, B. A., Gilroy, L. J., & Menzies, R. G. (2001). Computer-aided vicarious exposure versus live graded exposure for spider phobia in children. *Journal of Behavior Therapy and Experimental Psychiatry, 32,* 17–27.

DeWit, D. J., MacDonald, K., & Offord, D. R. (1999). Childhood stress and symptoms of drug dependence in adolescence and early adulthood. *American Journal of Orthopsychiatry, 69,* 61–72.

DeWit, D. J., Ogborne, A., Offord, D. R., & MacDonald, K. (1999). Antecedents of the risk of recovery from DSM-III-R social phobia. *Psychological Medicine, 29,* 569–582.

DiNardo, P. A., Guzy, L. T., Jenkins, J. A., Bak, R. M., Tomasi, S. F., & Copland, M. (1988). Etiology and maintenance of dog fears. *Behaviour Research and Therapy, 26,* 241–244.

Dinges, D. F., Pack, F., Williams, K., Gillen, K. A., Powell, J. W., Ott, G. E., et al. (1997). Cumulative sleepiness, mood disturbance, and psychomotor vigilance performance decrements during a week of sleep restricted to 4–5 hours per night. *Sleep, 20,* 267–277.

Doerfler, L., Connor, D., Volungis, A., & Toscano, P. (2007). Panic disorder in clinically referred children and adolescents. *Child Psychiatry and Human Development, 38*(1), 57–71.

Doerfler, L., Toscano, P., & Connor, D. (2008). Separation anxiety and panic disorder in clinically referred youth. *Journal of Anxiety Disorders, 22,* 602–611.

Dong, Q., Yang, B., & Ollendick, T.H. (1994). Fears in Chinese children and adolescents and their relations to anxiety and depression. *Journal of Child Psychology and Psychiatry, 35,* 351–363.

Doogan, S., & Thomas, G. V. (1992). Origins of fear of dogs in adults and children: The role of conditioning processes and prior familiarity with dogs. *Behaviour Research and Therapy, 30,* 387–394.

Douglas, L., Kozma, L., Martin, A., Landeros, A., Katsovich, L., King, R. A., & Leckman, J. F. (2008). Neuropsychiatric disorders associated with streptococcal infection: A case-control study among privately insured children. *Journal of the American Academy of Child and Adolescent Psychiatry, 47*, 1166–1172.

Dow, S. P., Sonies, B. C., Scheib, D., Moss, S., & Leonard, H. L. (1995). Practical guidelines for the assessment and treatment of selective mutism. *Journal of the American Academy of Child and Adolescent Psychiatry, 34*, 836–845.

Dube, S., & Orpinas, P. (2009). Understanding excessive school absenteeism as school refusal behavior. *Children and Schools, 31*(2), 87–95.

Dubi, K., & Schneider, S. (2009). The Picture Anxiety Test (PAT): A new pictorial assessment of anxiety symptoms in young children. *Journal of Anxiety Disorders, 23*, 1148–1157.

Dugas, M. J., Gagnon, F., Ladouceur, R., & Freeston, M. H. (1998). Generalized anxiety disorder: A preliminary test of a conceptual model. *Behaviours Research and Therapy, 36*, 215–226.

Duke, D. C., Bodzin, D. K., Tavares, P., Geffken, G. R., & Storch, E. A. (2009). The phenomenology of hairpulling in a community sample. *Journal of Anxiety Disorders, 23*, 1118–1125.

Dummit, E. S., Klein, R. G., Tancer, N. K., Asche, B., & Martin, J. (1996). Fluoxetine treatment of children with selective mutism: An open trial. *Journal of the American Academy of Child and Adolescent Psychiatry, 35*, 615–621.

Dummit, E. S., Klein, R. G., Tancer, N. K., Asche, B., Martin, J., & Fairbanks, J. A. (1997). Systematic assessment of 50 children with selective mutism. *Journal of the American Academy of Child and Adolescent Psychiatry, 36*, 653–660.

Eaves, L. J., Silberg, J. L., Meyer, J. M., Maes, H. H., Simonoff, E., Pickles, A., et al. (1997). Genetics and developmental psychopathology: 2. The main effects of genes and environment on behavioral problems in the Virginia Twin Study of Adolescent Behavioral Development. *Journal of Child Psychology and Psychiatry, 38*, 965–980.

Egger, H., & Angold, A. (2006). Common emotional and behavioral disorders in preschool children: Presentation, nosology, and epidemiology. *Journal of Child Psychology and Psychiatry, 47*, 313–337.

Egger, H. L. Costello, E. J., & Angold, A. (2003). School refusal and psychiatric disorders: A community study. *Journal of the American Academy of Child and Adolescent Psychiatry, 42*, 797–807.

Ehrenreich, J. T., & Gross, A. M. (2001). Treatment of childhood generalized anxiety disorder/overanxious disorder. In H. Orvaschel & J. Faust, *Handbook of conceptualization and treatment of child psychopathology* (pp. 211–238). Amsterdam, Netherlands: Elsevier Science.

Eisen, A., Raleigh, H., & Neuhoff, C. (2008). The unique impact of parent training for separation anxiety disorder in children. *Behavior Therapy, 39,* 195–206.

Eisen, A. R., & Shaefer, C. E. (2005). *Separation anxiety in children and adolescents.* New York: Guilford Press.

Eisen, A. R., & Silverman, W. K. (1993). Should I relax or change my thoughts? *Journal of Cognitive Psychotherapy, 7,* 265–279.

Eisen, A. R., & Silverman, W. K. (1998). Prescriptive treatment for generalized anxiety disorder in children. *Behavior Therapy, 29,* 105–121.

Ekman, P., Roper, G., & Hager, J. C. (1980). Deliberate facial movement. *Child Development, 51,* 886–891.

Eley, T. C., Rijsdijk, F. V., Perrin, S., O'Connor, T. G., & Bolton, D. (2008). A multivariate genetic analysis of specific phobias early in childhood. *Journal of Abnormal Child Psychology, 36,* 839–848.

Elizur, Y., & Perednik, R. (2003). Prevalence and description of selective mutism in immigrant and native families: A controlled study. *Journal of the American Academy of Child and Adolescent Psychiatry, 42,* 1451–1459.

Ellis, E. M. (1991). Watchers in the night: An anthropological look at sleep disorders. *American Journal of Psychotherapy, 45,* 211–220.

Eme, R., & Schmidt, D. (1978). The stability of children's fears. *Child Development, 49,* 1277–1279.

Enzer, N. B., & Walker, P. A. (1967). Hyperventilation syndrome in childhood: A review of 44 cases. *Journal of Pediatrics, 70,* 521–532.

Esman, A. (1989). Psychoanalysis in general psychiatry: Obsessive-compulsive disorder as a paradigm. *Journal of the American Academy of Child and Adolescent Psychiatry, 37,* 319–336.

Essau, C. A. (2000). Frequency, comorbidity and psychosocial impairment of anxiety disorders in German adolescents. *Journal of Anxiety Disorders, 14,* 263–279.

Essau, C. A., Conradt, J., & Petermann, F. (1999a). Frequency and comorbidity of social phobia and social fears in adolescents. *Behaviour Research and Therapy, 37,* 831–843.

Essau, C. A., Conradt, J., & Petermann, F. (1999b). Frequency of panic attacks and panic disorder in adolescents. *Depression and Anxiety, 9*, 10–26.

Essau, C. A., Conradt, J., & Petermann, F. (2000). Frequency, comorbidity, and psychosocial impairment of specific phobia in adolescents. *Journal of Clinical Child Psychology, 29*, 221–231.

Evans, D. W., Leckman, J. F., Carter, A., Reznick, J. S., Henshaw, D., King, R. A., et al. (1997). Ritual, habit and perfectionism: The prevalence and development of compulsive behavior in normal young children. *Child Development, 68*, 58–68.

Eysenck, H. J. (1979). The conditioning model of neurosis. *Behaviour and Brain Sciences, 2*, 155–199.

Fairbank, J. A. (2008). Epidemiology of trauma and trauma related disorders in children and youth. *PTSD Research Quarterly, 19*, 1–7.

Fairbanks, J. M., Pine, D. S., Tancer, N. K., Dummit, E. S., Kentgen, L. M., Martin, J., et al. (1997). Open fluoxetine treatment of mixed anxiety disorder in children and adolescents. *Journal of Child and Adolescent Psychopharmacology, 7*, 17–29.

Famularo, R., Fenton, T., Kinscherff, R., & Augustyn, M. (1996). Psychiatric comorbidity in childhood posttraumatic stress disorder. *Child Abuse and Neglect, 20*, 953–961.

Faravelli, C., & Pallanti, S. (1989). Recent life events and panic disorder. *American Journal of Psychiatry, 146*, 622–626.

Feder, A., Coplan, J. D., Goetz, R. R., Mathew, S. J., Pine, D. S., Dahl, R. E., et al. (2004). Twenty-four-hour cortisol secretion patterns in prepubertal children with anxiety or depressive disorders. *Biological Psychiatry, 56*, 198–204.

Feehan, M., McGee, R., & Williams, S. M. (1993). Mental health disorders from age 15 to 18 years. *Journal of the American Academy of Child and Adolescent Psychiatry, 32*, 1118–1126.

Fergusson, D. M., Horwood, L. J., & Lynsky, M. T. (1993). Prevalence and comorbidity of DSM-III-R diagnoses in a birth cohort of 15 year olds. *Journal of the American Academy of Child and Adolescent Psychiatry, 31*, 243–263.

Ferrell, C., Beidel, D. C., & Turner, S. M. (2001). A scale to determine the effectiveness of treatment for childhood social phobia. Unpublished manuscript, University of Maryland-College Park.

Ferrell, C., Beidel, D. C., & Turner, S. M. (2004). Assessment and treatment of socially phobic children: A cross cultural comparison. *Journal of Clinical Child and Adolescent Psychology, 33*, 260–268.

Field, A. P, Hamilton, S. J., Knowles, K. A., & Plews, E. L. (2003). Fear information and social phobic beliefs in children: A prospective paradigm and preliminary results. *Behaviour Research and Therapy*, *41*, 113–123.

Field, A. P., & Lawson, J. (2003). Fear information and the development of fears during childhood: effects on implicit fear responses and behavioural avoidance. *Behaviour Research and Therapy*, *41*, 1277–1293.

Flakierska, N., Lindstrom, M., & Gillberg, C. (1988). School refusal: A 15–20 year follow-up study of 35 Swedish children. *British Journal of Psychiatry*, *152*, 834–837.

Flakierska-Praquin, N., Lindstrom, M., & Gillberg, C. (1997). School phobia with separation anxiety disorder: A comparative 20 to 29–year follow-up study of 35 school refusers. *Comprehensive Psychiatry*, *38*, 17–22.

Flament, M. F., Koby, E., Rapoport, J. L., Berg, C. J., Zahn, T., Cox, C., et al. (1990). Childhood obsessive-compulsive disorder: A prospective follow-up study. *Journal of Child Psychology and Psychiatry*, *31*, 363–380.

Flament, M. F., Rapoport, J. L., Berg, C. J., Sceery, W., Kilts, C., Mellstrom, et al. (1985). Clomipramine treatment of childhood obsessive-compulsive disorder: A double blind controlled study. *Archives of General Psychiatry*, *42*, 977–983.

Flament, M. F., Rapoport, J. L., Murphy, D. L., Berg, C. J., & Lake, R. (1987). Biochemical changes during clomipramine treatment of childhood obsessive-compulsive disorder. *Archives of General Psychiatry*, *44*, 219–225.

Flament, M. F., Whitaker, A., Rapoport, J. L., Davies, M., Zaremba Berg, C., Kalikow, K., Sceery, W., & Shaffer, D. (1988). Obsessive compulsive disorder in adolescence: An epidemiological study. *Journal of the American Academy of Child and Adolescent Psychiatry*, *27*, 764–771.

Flannery-Schroeder, E. C., & Kendall, P. C. (2000). Group and individual cognitive-behavioral treatments for youth with anxiety disorders: A randomized clinical trial. *Cognitive Therapy and Research*, *24*, 251–278.

Flatt, N., & King, N. (2009). The Self-Efficacy Questionnaire for Phobic Situations (SEQ-SP): Development and psychometric evaluation. *Behaviour Change*, *26*, 141–152.

Flavell, J. H., Flavell, E. R., & Green, F. L. (2001). Developments of children's understanding of connections between thinking and feeling. *Psychological Science*, *12*, 430–432.

Flavell, J. H., Green, F. L., Flavell, E. R., & Grossman, J. B. (1997). The development of children's knowledge about inner speech. *Child Development, 68,* 39–47.

Flessner, C. A., Berman, N., Garcia, A., Freeman, J. B., & Leonard, H. L. (2009). Symptom profiles in pediatric obsessive-compulsive disorder (OCD): The effects of comorbid grooming conditions. *Journal of Anxiety Disorders, 23,* 753–759.

Foa, E. B., Johnson, K. M., Feeny, N. C., & Treadwell, K. R. H. (2001). The child PTSD Symptom Scale: A preliminary examination of its psychometric properties. *Journal of Clinical Child Psychology, 30,* 376–384.

Foa, E. B., & Kozak, M. J. (1995). DSM-IV field trial: Obsessive-compulsive disorder. *American Journal of Psychiatry, 152,* 90–96.

Foley, D. L., Pickles, A., Maes, H. M., Silberg, J. L., & Eaves, L. J. (2004). Course and short-term outcomes of separation anxiety disorder in a community sample of twins. *Journal of the American Academy of Child and Adolescent Psychiatry, 43,* 1107–1114.

Foley, D., Rutter, M., Pickles, A., Angold, A., Maes, H., Silberg, J., & Eaves, L. (2004). Informant disagreement for separation anxiety disorder. *Journal of the American Academy of Child and Adolescent Psychiatry, 43,* 452–460.

Fonseca, A. C., & Perrin, S. (2001). Clinical phenomenology, classification, and assessment of anxiety disorders in children and adolescents. In W. K. Silverman and P. D. A. Treffers (Eds.), *Anxiety disorders in children and adolescents* (pp. 126–158). Cambridge, UK: Cambridge University Press.

Fonseca, A. C., Yule, W., & Erol, N. (1994). Cross-cultural issues. In T. H. Ollendick, N. J. King, & W. Yule (Eds.), *International handbook of phobic and anxiety disorders in children and adolescents* (pp. 67–84). New York: Plenum Press.

Forbes, D., Phelps, A. J., McHugh, A. F., Debenham, P., Hopwood, M., & Creamer, M. (2003). Imagery rehearsal in the treatment of post-traumatic nightmares in Australian veterans with chronic combat-related PTSD: 12-month follow-up data. *Journal of Traumatic Stress, 16,* 509–513.

Forbes, E. E., Bertocci, M. A., Gregory, A. M., Ryan, N. D., Axelson, D. A., Birmaher, B., et al. (2008). Objective sleep in pediatric anxiety disorders and major depressive disorder. *Journal of the American Academy of Child and Adolescent Psychiatry, 47,* 148–155.

Forbes, E. E., Williamson, D. E., Ryan, N. D., Birmaher, B., Axelson, D. A., & Dahl, R. E. (2006). Peri-sleep-onset cortisol levels in children and adolescents with affective disorders. *Biological Psychiatry, 59,* 24–30.

Fordham, K., & Stevenson-Hinde, J. (1999). Shyness, friendship quality and adjustment during middle childhood. *Journal of Child Psychology and Psychiatry, 40,* 757–768.

Foxx, R. M., & Bechtel, D. R. (1982). Overcorrection. *Progress in Behavioral Modification, 13,* 227–281.

Francis, G., Last, C. G., & Strauss, C. C. (1987). Expression of separation anxiety disorder: The roles of age and gender. *Child Psychiatry and Human Development, 18,* 82–89.

Francis, G., Last, C. G., & Strauss, C. C. (1992). Avoidant disorder and social phobia in children and adolescents. *Journal of the American Academy of Child and Adolescent Psychiatry, 31,* 1086–1089.

Franklin, M. E., Flessner, C. A., Woods, D. W., Keuthen, N. J., Piacentini, J. C., Moore, P., et al. (2008). The child and adolescent trichotillomania impact project: Descriptive psychopathology, comorbidity, functional impairment, and treatment utilization. *Journal of Developmental and Behavioral Pediatrics, 29,* 493–500.

Franklin, M. E., Kozak, M. J., Cashman, L. A., Coles, M. E., Rheingold, A. A., & Foa, E. B., (1998). Cognitive-behavioral treatment of pediatric obsessive-compulsive disorder—An open clinical trial. *Journal of the American Academy of Child and Adolescent Psychiatry, 37,* 412–419.

Freeman, J. B., Garcia, A. M., Miller, L. M., Dow, S. P., & Leonard, H. L. (2004). Selective mutism. In T. L. Morris & J. S. March (Eds.), *Anxiety disorders in children and adolescents* (2nd ed., pp. 280–301). New York: Guilford Press.

Fremont, W. P. (2004). Childhood reactions to terrorism-induced trauma: A review of the past 10 years. *Journal of the American Academy of Child and Adolescent Psychiatry, 43,* 381–392.

Freud, S. (1975). Analysis of a phobia in a five-year-old boy. In *The standard edition of the complete works of Sigmund Freud* (7th ed., Vol. 10, pp. 5–149). London: Hogarth Press and the Institute of Psychoanalysis. (Original work published 1909)

Friedman, A. G., Latham, S. A., & Dahlquist, L. M. (1998). Childhood cancer. In T. H. Ollendick, & M. Hersen (Eds.), *Handbook of child psychopathology* (3rd ed., pp. 435–461). New York: Plenum Press.

Friedman, A. G., & Ollendick, T. H. (1989). Treatment programs for severe night-time fears: A methodological note. *Journal of Behavior Therapy and Experimental Psychiatry, 20,* 171–178.

Fung, D. S. S., Manassis, K., Kenny, A., & Fiksenbaum, L. (2002). Web based CBT for selective mutism. *Journal of the American Academy of Child and Adolescent Psychiatry, 39,* 721–726.

Fyer, A. J., Mannuzza, S., Chapman, T. F., Martin, L. Y., & Klein, D. F. (1995). Specificity in familial aggregation of phobic disorders. *Archives of General Psychiatry, 52,* 564–573.

Fyer, A. J., Mannuzza, S., Gallops, M. S., Martin, L. Y., Aaronson, C., Gorman, J. M., et al. (1990). Familial transmission of simple phobias and fears. *Archives of General Psychiatry, 47,* 252–256.

Garcia-Coll, C., Kagan, J., & Reznick, J. S.(1984). Behavioral inhibition in young children. *Child Development, 55,* 1005–1019.

Garcia-Lopez, L. J., Ingles, C. J., & Garcia-Fernandez, J. M. (2008). Exploring the relevance of gender and age differences in the assessment of social fears in adolescence. *Social Behavior and Personality, 36,* 385–390.

Garland, E. J., & Smith, D. H. (1990). Panic disorder in a child psychiatric consultation service. *Journal of the American Academy of Child and Adolescent Psychiatry, 29,* 785–788.

Garrison, W. T., & Earls, F. J. (1987). *Temperamental and child psychopathology.* Newbury Park, CA: Sage.

Gauer, G. J. C., Picon, P., Vasconcellos, S. J. L., Turner, S. M., & Beidel, D. B. (2005). Validation of the Social Phobia and Anxiety Inventory for Children (SPAI-C) in a sample of Brazilian children. *Brazilian Journal of Medical and Biological Research, 38,* 795–800.

Gause, C., Morris, C., Vernekar, S., Pardo-Villamizar, C., Grados, M. A., & Singer, H. S. (2009). Antineuronal antibodies in OCD: Comparisons in children with OCD-only, OCD + chronic tics and OCD + PANDAS. *Journal of Neuroimmunology, 29,* 118–124.

Geller, D. A., Biederman, J., Faraone, S. V., Cradock, K., Hagermoser, L., Aman, N., et al. (2002). Attention-deficit/hyperactivity disorder in children and adolescents with obsessive-compulsive disorder: Fact or artifact? *Journal of the American Academy of Child and Adolescent Psychiatry, 41,* 52–58.

Geller, D., Biederman, J., Jones, J., Park, K., Schwartz, S., Shapiro, S., et al. (1998). Is juvenile obsessive-compulsive disorder a developmental subtype of the disorder? *Journal of the American Academy of Child and Adolescent Psychiatry, 37,* 420–427.

Geller, D. A., Hoog, S. L., Heiligenstein, J. H., Riadi, R. K., Tamura, R., Kluszynski, S., et al. (2001). Fluoxetine treatment for obsessive-compulsive disorder in children and adolescents: A placebo-controlled clinical trial. *Journal of the American Academy of Child and Adolescent Psychiatry, 40,* 773–779.

Geller, D. A., Wagner, K. D., Emslie, G., Murphy, T., Carpenter, D. J., Wetherhold, E., et al. (2004). Paroxetine treatment in children and adolescents with obsessive-compulsive disorder: A randomized, multi-center, double-blind, placebo-controlled trial. *Journal of the American Academy of Child and Adolescent Psychiatry, 43,* 1387–1396.

Germain, A., & Nielsen, T. (2003). Impact of imagery rehearsal treatment on distressing dreams, psychological distress, and sleep parameters in nightmare patients. *Behavioral Sleep Medicine, 1,* 140–154.

Gerull, F. C., & Rapee, R. M. (2002). Mother knows best: Effects of maternal modeling on the acquisition of fear and avoidance behaviour in toddlers. *Behaviour Research and Therapy, 40,* 279–287.

Gest, S. D. (1997). Behavioral inhibition: Stability and association with adaptation from childhood to early adulthood. *Journal of Personality and Social Psychology, 72,* 467–475.

Giaconia, R. M., Reinherz, H. Z., Silverman, A. B., Pakiz, B., Frost, A. K., & Cohen, E. (1995). Traumas and posttraumatic stress disorder in a community population of older adolescents. *Journal of the American Academy of Child and Adolescent Psychiatry, 34,* 1369–1380.

Gibbons, R. D., Hur, K., Bhaumik, D. K., & Mann, J. J. (2006). The relationship between antidepressant prescription rates and early adolescent suicide. *American Journal of Psychiatry, 163,* 1898–1904.

Giebenhain, J. E., & O'Dell, S. L. (1984). Evaluation of a parent-training manual for reducing children's fear of the dark. *Journal of Applied Behavior Analysis, 17,* 121–125.

Giedd, J. N., Blumenthal, J., Jeffries, N. O., Castellanos, F. X., Liu, H., Zijdenbos, A., et al. (1999). Brain development during childhood and adolescence: A longitudinal MRI study. *Nature Neuroscience, 2,* 861–863.

Giedd, J. N., Lalonde, F. M., Celano, M. J., White, S. L., Wallace, G. L., Lee, N. R., et al. (2009). Anatomical brain magnetic resonance imaging of typically developing children and adolescents. *Journal of the American Academy of Child and Adolescent Psychiatry, 48,* 465–470.

Gilbert, A. R., Akkal, D., Almeida, J. R. C., Mataix-Cols, D., Kalas, C., Devlin, B., et al. (2009). Neural correlates of symptom dimensions in pediatric obsessive-compulsive disorder: A functional magnetic resonance imaging study. *Journal of the American Academy of Child and Adolescent Psychiatry, 48,* 936–944.

Gilbert, A. R., Moore, G. J., Keshavan, M. S., Paulson, L. A. D., Narula, V., MacMaster, F. P., et al. (2000). Decrease in thalamic volumes of pediatric patients with obsessive-compulsive disorder who are taking paroxetine. *Archives of General Psychiatry, 57,* 449–456.

Ginsburg, G. S. (2009). The child anxiety prevention study: Intervention model and primary outcomes. *Journal of Consulting and Clinical Psychology, 77,* 580–587.

Ginsburg, G. S., & Drake, K. L. (2002a). Anxiety sensitivity and panic attack symptomatology among low-income African-American adolescents. *Journal of Anxiety Disorders, 16,* 83–96.

Ginsburg, G. S., & Drake, K. L. (2002b). School-based treatment for anxious African-American adolescents: A controlled pilot study. *Journal of the American Academy of Child and Adolescent Psychiatry, 41,* 768–775.

Ginsburg, G., Riddle, M., & Davies, M. (2006). Somatic symptoms in children and adolescents with anxiety disorders. *Journal of the American Academy of Child and Adolescent Psychiatry, 45,* 1179–1187.

Ginsburg, G . S., & Silverman, W. K. (1996). Phobic and anxiety disorders in Hispanic and Caucasian youth. *Journal of Anxiety Disorders, 10,* 517–528.

Gittleman-Klein, R., & Klein, D. F. (1971). School phobia: Controlled imipramine treatment. *California Medicine, 115*(3), 42.

Gittelman, R., & Klein, D. F. (1984). Relationship between separation anxiety and panic and agoraphobic disorders. *Psychopathology, 17*(Suppl. 1), 56–65.

Glaze, D. G., Rosen, C. L., & Owens, J. A. (2002). Toward a practical definition of pediatric insomnia. *Current Therapeutic Research, 63,* B4–B17.

Glod, C. A., Teicher, M. H., Hartman, C. R., & Harakal, B. S. (1997). Increased nocturnal activity and impaired sleep maintenance in abused children. *Journal of the American Academy of Child and Adolescent Psychiatry, 36,* 1236–1243.

Goenjian, A. K., Pynoos, R. S., Steinberg, A. M., Najarian, L. M., Asarnow, J. R., Karaya, I., et al. (1995). Psychiatric comorbidity in children after the 1988 earthquake in Armenia. *Journal of the American Academy of Child and Adolescent Psychiatry, 34,* 1174–1184.

Goenjian, A. K., Yehuda, R., Pynoos, R. S., Steinberg, A. M., Tashjian, M., Yang, R. K., et al. (1996). Basal cortisol, dexamethasone suppression of cortisol, and MHPG in adolescents after the 1988 earthquake in Armenia. *American Journal of Psychiatry, 153,* 929–934.

Goldsmith, H. H., & Lemery, K. S. (2000). Linking temperamental fearfulness and anxiety symptoms: A behavior-genetic perspective. *Biological Psychiatry, 48,* 1199–1209.

Gordon, J. A., & Hen, R. (2004). Genetic approaches to the study of anxiety. *Annual Review of Neuroscience, 27,* 193–222.

Gordon, J., King, N. J., Gullone, E., Muris, P., & Ollendick, T. H. (2007). Treatment of children's nighttime fears: The need for a modern randomised controlled trial. *Clinical Psychology Review, 27,* 98–113.

Gorman, J. M., & Gorman, L. F. (1987). Drug treatment of social phobia. *Journal of Affective Disorders, 13,* 183–192.

Gozal, D., & Kheirandish-Gozal, L. (2008). The multiple challenges of obstructive sleep apnea in children: Morbidity and treatment. *Current Opinion in Pediatrics, 20,* 654–658.

Graae, F., Milner, J., Rizzotto, L., & Klein, R. G. (1994). Clonazepam in childhood anxiety disorders. *Journal of the American Academy of Child and Adolescent Psychiatry, 33,* 372–376.

Grad, L. R., Pelcovitz, D., Olson, M., Matthews, M., & Grad, G. J. (1987). Obsessive-compulsive symptomatology in children with Tourette's Syndrome. *Journal of the American Academy of Child and Adolescent Psychiatry, 26,* 69–73.

Graham, J., & Gaffan, E. A. (1997). Fear of water in children and adults: Etiology and familial effects. *Behavior Research and Therapy, 35,* 91–108.

Granell de Aldaz, E., Feldman, L., Vivas, E., & Gelfand, D. M. (1987). Characteristics of Venezualan school refusers: Toward the development of a high risk profile. *Journal of Nervous and Mental Disease, 175,* 401–407.

Graves, L. A., Heller, E. A., Pack, A. I., & Abel, T. (2003). Sleep deprivation selectively impairs memory consolidation for contextual fear conditioning. *Learning and Memory, 10,* 168–176.

Graziano, A. M., DeGiovanni, I. S., & Garcia, K. A. (1979). Behavioral treatment of children's fears: A review. *Psychological Bulletin, 86,* 804–830.

Graziano, A. M., & Mooney, K. C. (1980). Family self-control instruction for children's nighttime fear reduction. *Journal of Consulting and Clinical Psychology, 48,* 206–213.

Graziano, A. M., & Mooney, K. C. (1982). Behavioral treatment of "Nightfears" in children: Maintenance of improvement at 2½-3-year follow-up. *Journal of Consulting and Clinical Psychology, 50,* 598–599.

Greaves-Lord, K., Ferdinand, R. F., Oldehinkel, A. J., Sondeijker, F. E., Ormel, J., & Verhulst, F. C. C. (2007). Higher cortisol awakening response in young adolescents with persistent anxiety problems. *Acta Psychiatrica Scandinavia, 116,* 137–144.

Greco, L. A., & Morris, T. L. (2002). Parental child-rearing style and child social anxiety: Investigation of child perceptions and actual father behavior. *Journal of Psychopathology and Behavioral Assessment, 24,* 259–267.

Green, B. L. (1993). Disasters and posttraumatic stress disorder. In J. R. T. Davidson, & E. B. Foa (Eds.), *Posttraumatic stress disorder DSM-IV and beyond* (pp. 75–97). Washington, DC: American Psychiatric Press.

Green, B. L., Korol, M., Grace, M. C., Vary, M. G., Leonard, A. C., Gleser, G. C., et al. (1991). Children and disaster: Age, gender, and parental effects on PTSD symptoms. *Journal of the American Academy of Child and Adolescent Psychiatry, 30,* 945–951.

Gregory, A. M., Caspi, A., Moffitt, T. E., Koenen, K., Eley, T. C., & Poulton, R. (2007). Juvenile mental health histories of adults with anxiety disorders. *American Journal of Psychiatry, 164,* 301–308.

Gregory, A. M., Caspi, A., Eley, T. C., Moffitt, T. E., O'Connor, T. G., & Poulton, R. (2005). Prospective longitudinal associations between persistent sleep problems in childhood and anxiety and depressive disorders in adulthood. *Journal of Abnormal Child Psychology, 33,* 157–163.

Gregory A. M., & Eley, T. C. (2005). Sleep problems, anxiety and cognitive style in school-aged children. *Infant and Child Development, 14,* 435–444.

Gregory, A. M., Eley, T. C., O'Connor, T. G., & Plomin, R. (2004). Etiologies of associations between childhood sleep and behavioral problems in a large twin sample. *Journal of the American Academy of Child Adolescent Psychiatry, 43,* 744–751.

Gregory, A. M., & O'Connor, T. G. (2002). Sleep problems in childhood: A longitudinal study of developmental change and association with behavioral problems. *Journal of the American Academy of Child Psychiatry, 41,* 964–971.

Gregory, A. M., Rijsdijk, F. V., & Eley, T. C. (2006). A twin-study of sleep difficulties in school aged children. *Child Development, 77,* 1668–1679.

Grillon, C., Dierker, L., & Merikangas, K. R. (1997). Startle modulation in children at risk for anxiety disorders and/or alcoholism. *Journal of the American Academy of Child and Adolescent Psychiatry, 36,* 925–932.

Grillon, C., Dierker, L., & Merikangas, K. R. (1998). Fear-potentiated startle in adolescent offspring of parents with anxiety disorders. *Biological Psychiatry, 44,* 990–997.

Grills, A. E., & Ollendick, T. (2002). Issues in parent-child agreement: The case of structured diagnostic interviews. *Clinical Child and Family Psychology Review, 5,* 57–83.

Grills, A. E., & Ollendick, T. H. (2003). Multiple informant agreement and the Anxiety Disorders Interview Schedule for Parents and Children. *Journal of the American Academy of Child and Adolescent Psychiatry, 42,* 30–40.

Gross, R. T., & Borkovec, T. D. (1982). Effects of a cognitive intrusion manipulation on the sleep-onset latency of good sleepers. *Behavior Therapy, 13,* 112–116.

Gullone, E. (2000). The development of normal fear: A century of research. *Clinical Psychology Review, 20,* 429–451.

Gullone, E., & King, N. J. (1992). Psychometric evaluation of a revised fear survey schedule for children and adolescents. *Journal of Child Psychology and Psychiatry and Allied Disciplines, 33,* 987–998.

Gullone, E., & King, N. J. (1993). The fears of youth in the 1990s: Contemporary normative data. *Journal of Genetic Psychology, 154,* 137–153.

Gullone, E., & King, N. J. (2001). Self-reported anxiety in children and adolescents: A three year follow-up study. *Journal of Genetic Psychology, 162,* 5–20.

Gurwitch, R. H., Kees, M., & Becker, S. M. (2002). In the face of tragedy: Placing children's reactions to trauma in a new context. *Cognitive and Behavioral Practice, 9,* 286–295.

Gurwitch, R. H., Sullivan, M. A., & Long, P. J. (1998). The impact of trauma and disaster on young children. *Child and Adolescent Clinics of North America, 7,* 19–32.

Gustafsson, P. E., Gustafsson, P. A., Ivarsson, T., & Nelson, N. (2008). Diurnal cortisol levels and cortisol response in youths with obsessive-compulsive disorder. *Neuropsychobiology, 57,* 14–21.

Guy, W. (1976). *ECDEU assessment manual for psychopharmacology.* Washington, DC: DHEW.

Habukawa, M., Uchimura, N., Maeda, M., Kotorii, N., & Maeda, H. (2007). Sleep findings in young adult patients with posttraumatic stress disorder. *Biological Psychiatry, 62,* 1179–1182.

Hamburger, S. D., Swedo, S., Whitaker, A., Davies, M., & Rapoport, J. L. (1989). Growth rate in adolescents with obsessive-compulsive disorder. *American Journal of Psychiatry, 146,* 652–655.

Hamilton, M. (1959). The assessment of anxiety states by rating. *British Journal of Medical Psychology, 32,* 50–55.

Hanna, G. L. (1995). Demographic and clinical features of obsessive-compulsive disorder in children and adolescents. *Journal of the American Academy of Child and Adolescent Psychiatry, 34,* 19–27.

Hanna, G. L. (1997). Trichotillomania and related disorders in children and adolescents. *Child Psychiatry and Human Development, 27,* 255–268.

Hanna, G. L., Himle, J. A., Curtis, G. C., & Gillepsie, B. W. (2005). A family study of obsessive-compulsive disorder with pediatric probands. *American Journal of Medical Genetics Part B: Neuropsychiatric Genetics, 134B,* 13–19.

Hansen, C., Sanders, S. L., Massaro, S., & Last, C. G. (1998). Predictors of severity of absenteeism in children with anxiety-based school refusal. *Journal of Clinical Child Psychology, 27,* 246–254.

Hardin, M. G., Mandell, D., Mueller, S. C., Dahl, R. E., Pine, D. S., & Ernst, M. (2009). Inhibitory control in anxious and healthy adolescents is modulated by incentive and incidental affective stimuli. *Journal of Child Psychology and Psychiatry, 50,* 1550–1558.

Harman, J. S., Edlund, M. J., & Fortney, J. C. (2009). Trends in antidepressant utilization from 2001–2004. *Psychiatric Services, 60,* 611–616.

Harter, S. (1990). Issues in the assessment of the self-concept of children and adolescents. In A. M. LaGreca (Ed.), *Through the eyes of the child: Obtaining self-reports from children and adolescents* (pp. 292–325). Boston: Allyn & Bacon.

Harvey, A. G. (2002). Pre-sleep cognitive activity in insomnia: A comparison of sleep-onset insomniacs and good sleepers. *British Journal of Clinical Psychology, 39,* 275–286.

Harvey, A. G., Jones, J., & Schmidt, D. A. (2003). Sleep and posttraumatic stress disorder: A review. *Clinical Psychology Review, 23,* 377–407.

Harvey, K. J., & Espie, C. A. (2004). Development and preliminary validation of the Glasgow Content of Thoughts Inventory (GCTI): A new measure for the assessment of pre-sleep cognitive activity. *British Journal of Clinical Psychology, 43,* 409–420.

Harvey, R. A., & Bryant, A. G. (1998). Relationship between acute stress disorder and posttraumatic stress disorder following mild traumatic brain injury. *American Journal of Psychiatry, 155,* 625–629.

Hawkins, C., & Williams, T. I. (1992). Nightmares, life events, and behavior problems in preschool children. *Child: Care, Health and Development, 18,* 117–128.

Hawkins, S. S., & Radcliffe, J. (2006). Current measures of PTSD for children and adolescents. *Journal of Pediatric Psychology, 31,* 420–430.

Hayward, C., Killen, J. D., Hammer, L. D., Litt, I. F., Wilson, D., Simonds, B., et al. (1992). Pubertal stage and panic attack history in sixth- and seventh-grade girls. *American Journal of Psychiatry, 149,* 1239–1243.

Hayward, C., Killen, J. D., Kraemer, H. C., & Taylor, C. B. (1998). Linking self-reported childhood behavioral inhibition to adolescent social phobia. *Journal of the American Academy of Child and Adolescent Psychiatry, 37,* 1308–1315.

Hayward, C., Killen, J. D., Kraemer, H. C., & Taylor, C. B. (2000). Predictors of panic attacks in adolescents. *Journal of the American Academy of Child and Adolescent Psychiatry, 39,* 207–214.

Hayward, C., Killen, J. D., & Taylor, C. B. (1989). Panic attacks in young adolescents. *American Journal of Psychiatry, 146,* 1061–1063.

Hayward, C., Varady, S., Albano, A. M., Thienemann, M., Henderson, L., & Schatzberg, A. F. (2000). Cognitive-behavioral group therapy for social phobia in female adolescents: Results of a pilot study. *Journal of the American Academy of Child and Adolescent Psychiatry, 39,* 721–726.

Hayward, C., Wilson, K. A., Lagle, K., Killen, J. D., & Taylor, C. B. (2004). Parent-reported predictors of adolescent panic attacks. *Journal of the American Academy of Child and Adolescent Psychiatry, 43,* 613–620.

Hayward, C., Wilson, K. A., Lagle, K., Kraemer, H. C., Killen, J. D., & Taylor, C. B. (2008). The developmental psychopathology of social anxiety in adolescents. *Depression and Anxiety, 25,* 200–206.

Hazlett, R. L., McLeod, D. R., & Hoehn-Saric, R. (1994). Muscle tension in generalized anxiety disorder: elevated muscle tonus or agitated movement? *Psychophysiology, 31,* 189–195.

Heimberg, R. G., Dodge, C. S., Hope, D. A., Kennedy, C. R., Zollo, R., & Becker, R. E. (1990). Cognitive-behavioral group treatment for social phobia: Comparison to a credible placebo control. *Cognitive Therapy and Research, 14,* 1–23.

Heiser, N. A., Turner, S. M., & Beidel, D. C. (2003). Shyness: Relationship to social phobia and other psychiatric disorders. *Behaviour Research and Therapy, 41,* 209–221.

Helzer, J. E., Robins, L. N., & McEvoy, L. (1987). Post-traumatic stress disorder in the general population: Findings of the Epidemiologic Catchment Area Survey. *New England Journal of Medicine, 317,* 1630–1634.

Henin, A., & Kendall, P. C. (1997). Obsessive-compulsive disorder in childhood and adolescence. *Advances in Clinical Child Psychology, 19,* 75–131.

Henker, B., Whalen, C. K., & O'Neil, R. (1995). Worldly and workaday worries: Contemporary concerns of children and young adolescents. *Journal of Abnormal Child Psychology, 23,* 685–702.

Hensley, L., & Varela, R. E. (2008). PTSD symptoms and somatic complaints following Hurricane Katrina: The roles of trait anxiety and anxiety sensitivity. *Journal of Clinical Child and Adolescent Psychology, 37,* 542–552.

Herman, J. L. (1992). Complex PTSD: A syndrome in survivors of prolonged and repeated trauma. *Journal of Traumatic Stress, 5,* 377–391.

Herman, S. P., Stickler, G. B., & Lucas, A. R. (1981). Hyperventilation syndrome in children and adolescents: Long-term follow-up. *Pediatrics, 67,* 183–187.

Hettema, J. M., Annas, P., Neale, M. C., Kendler, K. S., & Fredrikson, M. (2003). A twin study of genetics of fear conditioning. *Archives of General Psychiatry, 60,* 702–708.

Heyne, D., King, N. J., Tonge, B., Rollings, S., Pritchard, M., Young, D., et al. (1998). The Self-Efficacy Questionnaire for School Situations: Development and psychometric evaluation. *Behaviour Change, 15,* 31–40.

Heyne, D., King, N., Tonge, B., Rollings, S., Young, D., Pritchard, M., et al. (2002). Evaluation of child therapy and caregiver training in the treatment of school refusal. *Journal of the American Academy of Child and Adolescent Psychiatry, 41,* 687–695.

Hibbs, E. D., Hamburger, S. D., Lenane, M., Rapoport, J. L., Kruesi, M. J. P., Keysor, C. S., et al. (1991). Determinants of expressed emotion in families of disturbed and normal children. *Journal of Child Psychology and Psychiatry, 32,* 757–770.

Hidalgo, R. B., Tupler, L. A., & Davidson, J. R. T. (2007). An effect-size analysis of pharmacologic treatments for generalized anxiety disorder. *Journal of Psychopharmacology, 21,* 864–872.

Higa, C. K., Fernandez, S. N., Nakamura, B. J., Chorpita, B. F., & Daleiden, E. L. (2006). Parental assessment of childhood social phobia: Psychometric properties of the Social Phobia and Anxiety Inventory for Children-parent report. *Journal of Clinical Child and Adolescent Psychology, 35,* 590–597.

Hill, J. H., Liebert, R. M., & Mott, D. E. W. (1968). Vicarious extinction of avoidance behavior through films: An initial test. *Psychological Reports, 22,* 192.

Hirshfeld, D. R., Biederman, J., Brody, L., Faraone, S. V., & Rosenbaum, J. F. (1997). Expressed emotion toward children with behavioral inhibition: Associations with maternal anxiety disorder. *Journal of the American Academy of Child and Adolescent Psychiatry, 36,* 910–917.

Hirshfeld-Becker, D. R., Biederman, J., Henin, A., Faraone, S. V., Davis, S., Harrington, K., et al. (2007). Behavioral inhibition in preschool children at risk is a specific predictor of middle school social anxiety: A five-year follow-up. *Journal of Developmental and Behavioral Pediatrics, 28,* 225–233.

Hirshfeld-Becker, D. R., Micco, J., Henin, A., Bloomfield, A., Biederman, J., & Rosenbaum, J. (2008). Behavioral inhibition. *Depression and Anxiety, 25,* 357–367.

Hoehn-Saric, R., Harrison, W., & Clary, C. (1997). Obsessive-compulsive disorder with comorbid major depression: A comparison of sertraline and desipramine treatment. *European Neuropsychopharmacology, 7,* 180–181.

Hoehn-Saric, R., McLeod, D., & Zimmerli, W. D. (1989). Somatic manifestations in women with generalized anxiety disorder: Psychophysical responses to psychological stress. *Archives of General Psychiatry, 46*, 1113–1119.

Hofmann, S. G., Albano, A. M., Heimberg, R. G., Tracey, S., Chorpita, B. F., & Barlow, D. H. (1999). Subtypes of social phobia in adolescents. *Depression and Anxiety, 9*, 15–18.

Honjo, S., Hirano, C., Murase, S., & Kaneko, T.(1989). Obsessive-compulsive symptoms in childhood and adolescence. *Acta Psychiatrica Scandinavia, 80*, 83–91.

Hudson, J. L., Gradisar, M., Gamble, A., Schniering, C. A., & Rebelo, I. (2009). The sleep patterns and problems of clinically-anxious children. *Behaviour Research and Therapy 37*, 339–344.

Hudson, J. L., & Rapee, R. M. (2001). Parent-child interactions and anxiety disorders: An observational study. *Behaviour Research and Therapy, 39*, 1411–1427.

Hudson, K. L., & Rapee, R. M. (2002). Parent child interactions in clinically anxious children and their siblings. *Journal of Clinical Child and Adolescent Psychology, 31*, 548–555.

Hudziak, J. J., van Beijsterveldt, C. E. M., Althoff, R. R., Stanger, C., Rettew, D. C., Nelson. E. C., et al. (2004). Genetic and environmental contributions to the Child Behavior Checklist obsessive-compulsive scale. *Archives of General Psychiatry, 61*, 608–616.

Hummel, R. M., & Gross, A. M. (2001). Socially anxious children: An observational study of parent-child interaction. *Child and Family Behavior Therapy, 23*, 19–41.

Huntley, E., & Alfano, C. A. (2009). *Actigraphy-based assessment of sleep in pediatric obsessive compulsive disorder.* Poster presented at the annual meeting of the Associated Professional Sleep Societies, Seattle, WA. March.

Iglowstein, I., Jenni, O. G., Molinari, L., & Largo, R. H. (2003). Sleep duration from infancy through adolescence: Reference values and generational trends. *Pediatrics, 11*, 302–307.

Ingman, K. A., Ollendick, T. H., & Akande, A. (1999). Cross-cultural aspects of fears in African children and adolescents. *Behaviour Research and Therapy, 37*, 337–345.

Insel, T., Murphy, D., Cohen, R., Alterman, I. L., Kilts, C., & Linnoila, M. (1983). Obsessive-compulsive disorder in five U.S. communities. *Archives of General Psychiatry, 40*, 605–612.

Ivanenko, A., Barnes, M., Crabtree, V., & Gozal, D. (2004). Psychiatric symptoms in children with insomnia referred to a pediatric sleep medicine center. *Sleep Medicine, 5*, 253–259.

Izard, C. (1994). Intersystem connections. In P. Ekman & R. Davidson (Eds.), *The nature of emotion: Fundamental questions* (pp. 345–375). New York: Oxford University.

Jaberghaderi, N., Greenwald, R., Rubin, A., Zand, S. O., & Dolatabadi, S. (2004). A comparison of CBT and EMDR for sexually-abused Iranian girls. *Clinical Psychology and Psychotherapy, 11,* 358–368.

Jackowski, A. P., Douglas-Palumberi, H., Jackowski, M., Win, L., Schultz, R. T., Staib, L. W., et al. (2008). Corpus callosum in maltreated children with posttraumatic stress disorder: A diffusion tensor imaging study. *Psychiatry Research: Neuroimaging, 162,* 256–261.

Janet, P. (1903). *Les obsessions et la psychiasthenie.* Paris: Felix Arcan.

Jaspers, J. P. (1996). The diagnosis and psychopharmacological treatment of trichotillomania: A review. *Pharmacopsychiatry, 29,* 115–120.

Jay, S. M., Ozolins, M., Elliott, C. H., & Caldwell, S. (1983). Assessment of children's distress during painful medical procedures. *Health Psychology, 2,* 133–147.

Jaycox, L. H. (2003). *Cognitive behavioral interventions for trauma in schools (CBITS).* Longmont, CO: Sopris West Educational Services.

Jenkins, E. J., & Bell, C. C. (1994). Violence among inner city high school students and posttraumatic stress disorder. In S. Friedman (Ed.), *Anxiety disorders in African Americans* (pp. 76–88). New York: Springer.

Jensen, T. K., Dyb, G., & Nygaard, E. (2009). A longitudinal study of post-traumatic stress reactions in Norwegian children and adolescents exposed to the 2004 tsunami. *Archives of Pediatric and Adolescent Medicine, 163,* 856–861.

Jersild, A. T., & Holmes, F. B. (1935). Methods of overcoming children's fears. *Journal of Psychology, 1,* 75–104.

Johnson, A. M., Falstein, E. I., Szurek, S. A., & Svendsen, M. (1941). School phobia. *American Journal of Orthopsychiatry, 11,* 702–711.

Johnson, E. O., Chilcoat, H. D., & Breslau, N. (2000). Trouble sleeping and anxiety/depression in childhood. *Psychiatry Research, 94,* 93–102.

Johnson, S. B., & Melamed, B. G. (1979). The assessment and treatment of children's fear. In B. B. Lahey & A. E. Kazdin (Eds.), *Advances in clinical child psychology* (Vol. 2, pp. 107–139). New York: Plenum Press.

Jones, M. C. (1924). The elimination of children's fears. *Journal of Experimental Psychology, 7,* 382–390.

Jones, R. T., Ollendick, T. H., McLaughlin, K. J., & Williams, C. E. (1989). Elaborative and behavioral rehearsal in the acquisition of fire emergency skills and the reduction of fear of fire. *Behavior Therapy, 20,* 93–101.

Joorabchi, B. (1977). Expressions of the hyperventilation syndrome in childhood. *Clinical Pediatrics, 16,* 1110–1115.

Joormann, J., & Stober, J. (1999). Somatic symptoms of generalized anxiety disorder from the DSM-IV: Associations with pathological worry and depression symptoms in a nonclinical sample. *Journal of Anxiety Disorders, 13,* 491–503.

Kagan, J., Reznick, J. S., Clarke, C., Snidman, N., & Garcia-Coll, C. (1984). Behavioral inhibition to the unfamiliar. *Child Development, 55,* 2212–2225.

Kagan, J., Reznick, J. S., & Snidman, N. (1988). Biological bases of childhood shyness. *Science, 240,* 167–171.

Kagan, J., Reznick, J. S., Snidman, N., Gibbons, J., & Johnson, M. O. (1988). Childhood derivatives of inhibition and lack of inhibition to the unfamiliar. *Child Development, 59,* 1580–1589.

Kane, M. T., & Kendall, P. C. (1989). Anxiety disorders in children: A multiple-baseline evaluation of a cognitive-behavioral treatment. *Behavior Therapy, 20,* 499–508.

Kanfer, F. H., Karoly, P., & Newman, A. (1975). Reduction of children's fear of the dark by competence-related and situational threat-related verbal cues. *Journal of Consulting and Clinical Psychology, 43,* 251–258.

Kaplow, J. B., Curran, P. J., Angold, A., & Costello, E. J. (2001). The prospective relation between dimensions of anxiety and the initiation of adolescent alcohol use. *Journal of Clinical Child Psychology, 30,* 316–326.

Kar, N., & Bastia, B. K. (2006). Post-traumatic stress disorder, depression and generalised anxiety disorder in adolescents after a natural disaster: A study of comorbidity. *Clinical Practice and Epidemiology in Mental Health, 2,* 17–23.

Kashani, J. H., Beck, N. C., Hoeper, E. W., Fallahi, C., Corcoran, C. M., McAllister, J. A., et al. R (1987). Psychiatric disorders in a community sample of adolescents. *American Journal of Psychiatry, 144,* 584–589.

Kashani, J. H., & Orvaschel, H. (1988). Anxiety disorders in mid-adolescence: A community sample. *American Journal of Psychiatry, 145,* 960–964.

Kashani, J. H., & Orvaschel, H. (1990). A community study of anxiety in children and adolescents. *American Journal of Psychiatry, 147,* 313–318.

Kassam-Adams, N., & Winston, F. K. (2004). Predicting child PTSD: The relationship between acute stress disorder and PTSD in injured children. *Journal of the American Academy of Child and Adolescent Psychiatry, 43,* 403–411.

Katz, E. R., Kellerman, J., & Siegel, S. E. (1980). Behavioral distress in children with cancer undergoing medical procedures: Developmental considerations. *Journal of Consulting and Clinical Psychology, 48,* 356–365.

Kearney, C. A. (1993). Depression and school refusal behavior: A review with comments on classification and treatment. *Journal of School Psychology, 31,* 267–279.

Kearney, C. A. (1995). School refusal behavior. In A. R. Eisen, C. A. Kearney, & C. E. Shaeffer (Eds.), *Clinical handbook for treating fear and anxiety in children and adolescents* (pp. 19–52). Northvale, NJ: Aronson.

Kearney, C. A. (2002). Identifying the function of school refusal behavior: A revision of the School Refusal Assessment Scale. *Journal of Psychopathology and Behavioral Assessment, 24,* 235–245.

Kearney, C. (2007). Forms and functions of school refusal behavior in youth: An empirical analysis of absenteeism severity. *Journal of Child Psychology and Psychiatry, and Allied Disciplines, 48,* 53–61.

Kearney, C. A., & Albano, A. M. (2004). The functional profiles of school refusal behavior. *Behavior Modification, 28,* 147–162.

Kearney, C. A., Albano, A. M., Eisen, A. R., Allan, W. D., & Barlow, D. H. (1997). The phenomenology of panic disorder in youngsters: An empirical study of a clinical sample. *Journal of Anxiety Disorders, 11,* 49–62.

Kearney, C. A., & Beasley, J. F. (1994). The clinical treatment of school refusal behavior: A survey of referral and practice characteristics. *Psychology in the Schools, 31,* 128–132.

Kearney, C. A., Eisen, A. R., & Silverman, W. K. (1995). The legend and myth of school phobia. *School Psychology Quarterly, 10,* 65–85.

Kearney, C. A., & Silverman, W. K. (1990). A preliminary analysis of a functional model of assessment and treatment for school refusal behavior. *Behavior Modification, 14,* 344–360.

Kearney, C. A., & Silverman, W. K. (1999). Functionally-based prescriptive and nonprescriptive treatment for children and adolescents with school refusal behavior. *Behavior Therapy, 30,* 673–695.

Kearney, C. A., Sims, K. E., Pursell, C. R., & Tillotson, C. A. (2003). Separation anxiety disorder in young children: A longitudinal and family analysis. *Journal of Clinical Child and Adolescent Psychology, 32,* 593–598.

Keller, M. B., Lavori, P. W., Wunder, J., Beardslee, W. R., Schwartz, C. E., & Roth, J. (1992). Chronic course of anxiety disorders in children and adolescents. *Journal of the American Academy of Child and Adolescent Psychiatry, 31,* 595–599.

Kendall, P. C. (1994). Treating anxiety disorders in children: Results of a randomized clinical trial. *Journal of Consulting and Clinical Psychology, 62,* 100–110.

Kendall, P. C., Brady, E. U., & Verduin, T. L. (2001). Comorbidity in childhood anxiety disorders and treatment outcome. *Journal of the American Academy of Child and Adolescent Psychiatry, 40,* 787–794.

Kendall, P. C., & Chansky, T. E. (1991). Considering cognition in anxiety-disordered children. *Journal of Anxiety Disorders, 5,* 167–185.

Kendall, P. C., Compton, S. N., Walkup, J. T., Birmaher, B., Albano, A. M., Sherrill, J., et al. (2010). Clinical characteristics of anxiety disordered youth. *Journal of Anxiety Disorders, 24,* 360–365.

Kendall, P. C., Flannery-Schroeder, E., Panichelli-Mindel, S., Southam-Grow, M., Henin, A., & Warman, M. (1997). Therapy for youths with anxiety disorders: A second randomized clinical trial. *Journal of Consulting and Clinical Psychology, 65,* 366–380.

Kendall, P. C., Safford, S., Flannery-Schroeder, E., & Webb, A. (2004). Child anxiety treatment: Outcomes in adolescence and impact on substance use and depression at 7.4-year follow-up. *Journal of Consulting and Clinical Psychology, 72,* 276–287.

Kendall, P. C., & Southam-Gerow, M. A. (1996). Long-term follow-up of a cognitive-behavioral therapy for anxious youth. *Journal of Consulting and Clinical Psychology, 62,* 724–730.

Kendall, P. C., & Warman, M. J. (1996). Anxiety disorders in youth: Diagnostic consistency across DSM-III-R and DSM-IV. *Journal of Anxiety Disorders, 10,* 453–463.

Kendler, K. S., Neale, M. C., Kessler, R. C., Heath, A. C., & Eaves, L. J. (1992a). Generalized anxiety disorder in women: A population-based twin study. *Archives of General Psychiatry, 49,* 262–272.

Kendler, K. S., Neale, M. C., Kessler, R. C., Heath, A. C., & Eaves, L. J. (1992b). The genetic epidemiology of phobias in women: The interrelationship of agoraphobia, social phobia, situational phobia, and simple phobia. *Archives of General Psychiatry, 49,* 273–281.

Kendler, K. S., Neale, M. C., Kessler, R. C., Heath, A. C., & Eaves, L. J. (1993). Major depression and phobias: The genetic and environmental sources of comorbidity. *Psychological Medicine, 23*, 361–371.

Kendler, K. S., Walters, E. E., Neale, M. C., Kessler, R. C., Heath, A. C., & Eaves, L. J. (1995). The structure of the genetic and environmental risk factors for six major psychiatric disorders in women. *Archives of General Psychiatry, 52*, 374–383.

Kennedy, W. A. (1965). School phobia: Rapid treatment of fifty cases. *Journal of Abnormal Psychology, 70*, 285–289.

Kerr, M., Lambert, W., & Bem, D. J. (1996). Life course sequelae of childhood shyness in Sweden: Comparison with the United States. *Developmental Psychology, 32*, 1100–1105.

Kessler, R. C., Avenevoli, S., Green, J., Gruber, M. J., Guyer, M., He, Y., et al. (2009). National comorbidity survey replication—adolescent supplement (NCS-A): III. Concordance of DSM-IV/CIDI diagnoses with clinical reassessments. *Journal of the American Academy of Child and Adolescent Psychiatry, 48*, 386–399.

Kessler, R. C., Chiu, W. T., Demler, O., Merikangas, K. R., & Walters, E. E. (2005). Prevalence, severity, and comorbidity of 12-month DSM-IV disorders in the National Comorbidity Survey Replication. *Archives of General Psychiatry, 62*, 617–627.

Khalid-Khan, S., Santibanez, M. P., McMicken, C., & Rynn, M. A. (2007). Social anxiety in children and adolescents: Epidemiology, diagnosis, and treatment. *Pediatric Drugs, 9*, 227–237.

King, N. J., & Bernstein, G. A. (2001). School refusal in children and adolescents: A review of the past 10 years. *Journal of the American Academy of Child and Adolescent Psychiatry, 40*, 197–205.

King, N. J., Clowes-Hollins, V., & Ollendick, T. H. (1997). The etiology of childhood dog phobia. *Behaviour Research and Therapy, 35*, 77.

King, N. J., Eleonora, G., & Ollendick, T. H. (1998). Etiology of childhood phobias: Current status of Rachman's three pathways theory. *Behaviour Research and Therapy, 36*, 297–309.

King, N. J., & Gullone, E. (1990). Fear of AIDS: Self-reports of Australian children and adolescents. *Psychological Reports, 66*, 245–246.

King, N. J., Gullone, E., Tonge, B. J., & Ollendick, T. H. (1993). Self-reports of panic attacks and manifest anxiety in adolescents. *Behaviour Research and Therapy, 31*, 111–116.

King, N. J., Hamilton, D. I., & Ollendick, T. H. (1988). *Children's fears and phobias: A behavioral perspective.* Chichester, UK: Wiley.

King, N. J., & Ollendick, T. H. (1989). School refusal: Graduated and rapid behavioral treatment strategies. *Australian and New Zealand Journal of Psychiatry, 23*, 213–233.

King, N. J., Ollendick, T. H., & Montgomery, I. M. (1995). Obsessive-compulsive disorder in children and adolescents. *Behaviour Change, 12,* 51–58.

King, N. J., Tonge, B. J., Heyne, D., Pritchard, M. Rollings, S., Young, D., Myerson, N., & Ollendick, T. H. (1998). Cognitive-behavioral treatment of school refusing children: A controlled evaluation. *Journal of the American Academy of Child and Adolescent Psychiatry, 37,* 395–403.

King, N. J., Tonge, B. J., Heyne, D., Turner, S., Pritchard, M. K., Young, D., et al. (2001). Cognitive-behavioural treatment of school-refusing children: Maintenance of improvement at 3- to 5-year follow-up. *Scandinavian Journal of Behavior Therapy, 30,* 85–89.

King, N. J., Tonge, B. J., Mullen, P., Myerson, N. M., Heyne, D., Rollings, S., et al. (2000). Treating sexually abused children with posttraumatic stress symptoms: A randomized clinical trial. *Journal of the American Academy of Child and Adolescent Psychiatry, 39,* 1347–1355.

King, R., Leonard, H., & March, J. (1998). Practice parameters for the assessment and treatment of children and adolescents with obsessive compulsive disorder. *Journal of the American Academy of Child and Adolescent Psychiatry, 37,* 27–45.

King, R. A., Scahill, L., Vituano, L. A., Schwab-Stone, M., Tercyak, K. P., & Riddle, M. A. (1995). Childhood trichotillomania: Clinical phenomenology, comorbidity, and family genetics. *Journal of the American Academy of Child and Adolescent Psychiatry, 34,* 1451–1459.

Klackenberg, G. (1982). Sleep behaviour studied longitudinally. Data from 4–16 years on duration, night-awakening and bed-sharing. *Acta Pediatrica Scandinavica, 71,* 501–506.

Klein, D. (1964). Delineation of two drug-responsive anxiety syndromes. *Psychopharmacologia, 5,* 397–408.

Klein, D. F., Mannuzza, S., Chapman, T., & Fyer, A. J. (1992). Child panic revisited. *Journal of the American Academy of Child and Adolescent Psychiatry, 31,* 112–116.

Klein, R. G. (1995). Is panic disorder associated with childhood separation anxiety disorder? *Clinical Neuropharmacology, 18*(Suppl. 2), S7–S14.

Klein, R. G., Koplewicz, H., & Kanner, A. (1992). Imipramine treatment of children with separation anxiety disorder. *Journal of the American Academy of Child and Adolescent Psychiatry, 31,* 21–28.

Klein, T. P., Devoe, E. R., Miranda-Julian, C. M., & Linas, K. (2009). Children's responses to September 11th: The New York City experience. *Infant Mental Health Journal, 30,* 1–22.

Klin, A., Pauls, D., Schultz, R., & Volkmar, F. (2005). Three diagnostic approaches to Asperger syndrome: Implications for research. *Journal of Autism and Developmental Disorders, 35,* 221–234.

Klingman, A. (1988). Biblioguidance with kindergartners: Evaluation of a primary prevention program to reduce fear of the dark. *Journal of Clinical Child Psychology, 17,* 237–241.

Kondas, O. (1967). Reduction of examination anxiety and "stage fright" by group desensitization and relaxation. *Behaviour Research and Therapy, 5,* 275–281.

Kopp, S., & Gillberg, C. (1997). Selective mutism: A population-based study: A research note. *Journal of Child Psychology and Psychiatry, 38,* 257–262.

Koppen, A. S. (1974). Relaxation training for children. *Elementary School Guidance and Counseling, 9,* 14–21.

Korhonen, P., & Lahikainen, A. R. (2008). Recent trends in children's television-induced fears in Finland. *Journal of Children and Media, 2,* 147.

Korte, S. M. (2001). Corticosteriods in relation to fear, anxiety and psychopathology. *Neuroscience and Biobehavioral Research, 25,* 117–142.

Kovacs, M. J. (1998). Internalizing disorders in childhood. *Journal of Child Psychology and Psychiatry, 39,* 47–63.

Kovacs, M., Gatsonis, C., Paulauskas, S. L., & Richards, C. (1989). Depressive disorders in childhood: 4. A longitudinal study of comorbidity with and risk for anxiety disorders. *Archives of General Psychiatry, 46,* 776–782.

Koverola, C. (1995). Posttraumatic stress disorder. In R. T. Ammerman & M. Hersen (Eds.), *Handbook of child behavior therapy in the psychiatric setting* (pp. 389–408). Oxford, UK: Wiley.

Krakow, B., Kellner, R., Pathak, D., & Lambert, L. (1996). Long-term reduction of nightmares with imagery rehearsal treatment. *Behavioural and Cognitive Psychotherapy, 24,* 135–148.

Krakow, B., Sandoval, D., Schrader, R., Kuehne, B., McBride, B. S., Yaw, C. L., & Tandeberg, D. (2001). Treatment of chronic nightmares in adjudicated adolescent girls in a residential facility. *Journal of Adolescent Health, 29,* 94–100.

Krakow, B., Tandberg, D., Cutchen, L., McBride, L., Hollifield, M., Lauriello, J., et al. (1997). Imagery rehearsal treatment of chronic nightmares in PTSD: A controlled study. *Sleep Research, 26,* 245.

Kratochvil, C., Kutcher, S., Reiter, S., & March, J. S. (1999). Pharmacotherapy of pediatric anxiety disorders. In S. W. Russ & T. Ollendick (Eds.), *Handbook of psychotherapies with children and families* (pp. 345–366). New York: Kluwer Academic.

Kristensen, H. (2000). Selective mutism and comorbidity with developmental disorder/delay, anxiety disorder, and elimination disorder. *Journal of the American Academy of Child and Adolescent Psychiatry, 39*, 249–256.

Krysanski, V. L. (2003). A brief review of the selective mutism literature. *The Journal of Psychology, 137*, 29–40.

Kurlan, R., Johnson, D., Kaplan, E., & Tourette Syndrome Study Group. (2008). Streptococcal infection and exacerbations of childhood tics and obsessive-compulsive symptoms: A prospective blinded cohort study. *Pediatrics, 121*, 1188–1197.

Kuroda, J. (1969). Elimination of children's fears of animals by the method of experimental desensitization: An application of learning theory to child psychology. *Psychologia, 12*, 161–165.

La Greca, A. M. (2008). Interventions for posttraumatic stress in children and adolescents following natural disasters and acts of terrorism. In R. G. Steele, T. D. Elkins, & M. C. Roberts (Eds.), *Handbook of evidence-based therapies for children and adolescents: Bridging science and practice. Issues in clinical child psychology* (pp. 121–141). New York: Springer.

La Greca, A. M., Silverman, W. K., Vernberg, E. M., & Prinstein, M. J. (1996). Symptoms of posttraumatic stress in children after Hurricane Andrew: A prospective study. *Journal of Consulting and Clinical Psychology, 64*, 712–723.

La Greca, A. M., & Stone, W. L. (1993). Social Anxiety Scale for Children–Revised: Factor structure and concurrent validity. *Journal of Clinical Child Psychology, 22*, 17–27.

Lahey, B. B., Rathouz, P. J., Van Hulle, C., Urbano, R. C., Krueger, R. F., Applegate, B., et al. G., & (2008). Testing structural models of DSM-IV symptoms of common forms of child and adolescent psychopathology. *Journal of Abnormal Child Psychology, 36*, 187–206.

Lang, P. J. (1968). Fear reduction and fear behavior: Problems in treating a construct. In J. M. Shlien (Ed.), *The structure of emotion* (pp. 18–30). Seattle, WA: Hogrefe & Huber.

Langley, A. K., Bergman, R. L., & Piacentini, J. C. (2002). Assessment of childhood anxiety. *International Review of Psychiatry, 14*, 102–113.

Lapouse, R., & Monk, N. (1959). Fears and worries in a representative sample of children. *American Journal of Orthopsychiatry, 29*, 803–818.

Last, C. G. (1991). Somatic complaints in anxiety disordered children. *Journal of Anxiety Disorders, 5*, 125–138.

Last, C. G., Francis, G., Hersen, M., Kazdin, A. E., & Strauss, C. C. (1987). Separation anxiety and school phobia: A comparison using DSM-III criteria. *American Journal of Psychiatry, 144*, 653–657.

Last, C. G., Hansen, C., & Franco, N. (1998). Cognitive-behavioral treatment of school phobia. *Journal of the American Academy of Child and Adolescent Psychiatry, 37*, 404–411.

Last, C. G., Hersen, M., Kazdin, A. E., Finkelstein, R., & Strauss, C. C. (1987). Comparison of DSM-III separation anxiety and generalized anxiety disorders: Demographic characteristics and patterns of comorbidity. *Journal of the American Academy of Child and Adolescent Psychiatry, 26*, 527–531.

Last, C. G., Hersen, M., Kazdin, A., Orvaschel, H., & Perrin, S. (1991). Anxiety disorders in children and their families. *Archives of General Psychiatry, 49*, 928–934.

Last, C. G., & Perrin, S. (1993). Anxiety disorders in African-American and white children. *Journal of Abnormal Child Psychology, 21*, 153–164.

Last, C. G., Perrin, S., Hersen, M., & Kazdin, A. E. (1992). DSM-III-R anxiety disorders in children: Sociodemographic and clinical characteristics. *Journal of the American Academy of Child and Adolescent Psychiatry, 31*, 1070–1076.

Last, C. G., Perrin, S., Hersen, M., & Kazdin, A. E. (1996). A prospective study of childhood anxiety disorders. *Journal of the American Academy of Child and Adolescent Psychiatry, 35*, 1502–1510.

Last, C. G., & Strauss, C. C. (1989a). Panic disorder in children and adolescents. *Journal of Anxiety Disorders, 3*, 87–95.

Last, C. G., & Strauss, C. C. (1989b). Obsessive-compulsive disorder in childhood. *Journal of Anxiety Disorders, 3*, 295–302.

Last, C. G., & Strauss, C. C. (1990). School refusal in anxiety-disordered children and adolescents. *Journal of the American Academy of Child and Adolescent Psychiatry, 29*, 31–35.

Last, C. G., Strauss, C. C., & Francis, G. (1987). Comorbidity among childhood anxiety disorders. *Journal of Nervous and Mental Disease, 175*, 726–730.

Lavigne, J. V., Gibbons, R. D., Christoffel, K. K., Arend, R., Rosenbaum, D., Binns, H., et al. (1996). Prevalence rates and correlates of psychiatric disorders among preschool children. *Journal of the American Academy of Child and Adolescent Psychiatry, 35*, 204–214.

Lavigne, J., LeBailly, S., Hopkins, J., Gouze, K., & Binns, H. (2009). The prevalence of ADHD, ODD, depression, and anxiety in a community sample of 4-year-olds. *Journal of Clinical Child and Adolescent Psychology, 38*, 315–328.

Lawson, J., Banerjee, R., & Field, A. P. (2007). The effects of verbal information on children's fear beliefs about social situations. *Behaviour Research and Therapy, 45*, 21–37.

Layne, A. E., Bernstein, G. A., Egan, E. A., & Kushner, M. G. (2003). Predictors of treatment response in anxious-depressed adolescents with school refusal. *Journal of the American Academy of Child and Adolescent Psychiatry, 42,* 319–326.

Lazaro, L., Bargallo, N., Castro-Fornieles, J., Falcon, C., Andres, S., Calvo, R., et al. (2009). Brain changes in children and adolescents with obsessive-compulsive disorder before and after treatment: A voxel-based morphometric MRI study. *Psychiatry Research, 172,* 140–146.

Lazarus, A. A., & Abramowitz, A. (1962). The use of "emotive imagery" in the treatment of children's phobias. *Journal of Mental Science, 108,* 191–195.

LeBaron, S., & Zeltzer, L. (1984). Assessment of acute pain and anxiety in children and adolescents by self-reports, observer reports, and a behavioral checklist. *Journal of Consulting and Clinical Psychology, 52,* 729–738.

Leckman, J. F., Grice, D. E., Barr, L. C., de Vries, A. L., Martin, C., Cohen, D. J., et al. (1994). Tic-related vs. non-tic-related obsessive compulsive disorder. *Anxiety, 1,* 208 –215.

Leckman, J. F., & King, R. A. (2007). A developmental perspective on the controversy surrounding the use of SSRIs to treat pediatric depression. *American Journal of Psychiatry, 164,* 1304–1306.

Leckman, J. F., Weissman, M. M., Merikangas, K. R., Pauls, D. L., Prusoff, B. A., & Kidd, K. K. (1985). Major depression and panic disorder: A family study perspective. *Psychopharmacology Bulletin, 21,* 543–545.

LeDoux, J. E. (1996). *The emotional brain.* New York: Simon and Schuster.

LeDoux, J. E., & Muller, J. (1997). Emotional memory and psychopathology. *Philosophical. Transactions of the Royal Society of London, 352,* 1719–1726.

Leger, E., Ladouceur, R., Dugas, M., & Freeston, M. (2003). Cognitive-behavioral treatment of generalized anxiety disorder among adolescents: A case series. *Journal of the American Academy of Child and Adolescent Psychiatry, 42,* 327–330.

Leitenberg, H., & Callahan, E. J. (1973). Reinforced practice and reduction of different kinds of fears in adults and children. *Behaviour Research and Therapy, 11,* 19–30.

Lenane, M. C., Swedo, S. E., Leonard, H., Pauls, D. L., Sceery, W., & Rapoport, J. L. (1990). Psychiatric disorders in first degree relatives of children and adolescents with obsessive compulsive disorder. *Journal of the American Academy of Child and Adolescent Psychiatry, 29,* 407–412.

Leonard, H. L., Goldberger, E. L., Rapoport, J. L., Cheslow, D. L., & Swedo, S. E. (1990). Childhood rituals: Normal development or obsessive-compulsive symptoms? *Journal of the American Academy of Child and Adolescent Psychiatry, 149,* 1244–1251.

Leonard, H. L., Lenane, M. C., Swedo, S. E., Rettew, D. C., Gershon, E. S., & Rapoport, J. L. (1992). Tics and Tourette's disorder: A 2- to 7-year follow-up of 54 obsessive-compulsive children. *American Journal of Psychiatry, 149,* 1244–1251.

Leonard, H. L., & Rapoport, J. L. (1989). Pharmacotherapy of childhood obsessive-compulsive disorder. *Psychiatric Clinics of North America, 12,* 963–970.

Leonard, H. L., & Swedo, S. E. (2001). Paediatric autoimmune neuropsychiatric disorders associated with streptococcal infection (PANDAS). *International Journal of Neuropsychopharmacology, 4,* 191–198.

Leonard, H. L., Swedo, S. E., Lenane, M. C., Rettew, D. C., Hamburger, S. D., Bartko, J. J., et al. (1993). A 2- to 7-year follow-up study of 54 obsessive-compulsive children and adolescents. *Archives of General Psychiatry, 50,* 429–439.

Leonard, H. L., Swedo, S. E., Rapoport, J. L., Koby, E. V., Lenane, M. C., Cheslow, D. L., et al. (1989). Treatment of obsessive-compulsive disorder with clomipramine and desipramine in children and adolescents: A double-blind crossover comparison. *Archives of General Psychiatry, 46,* 1088–1092.

Letamendi, A. M., Chavira, D. A., Hitchcock, C. A., Roesch, S. C., Shipon-Blum, E., & Stein, M. B. (2008). Selective mutism questionnaire: Measurement structure and validity. *Journal of the American Academy of Child and Adolescent Psychiatry, 47,* 1197–1204.

Leung, P., Se-fong, H., Ting-pong, H., Chi-chiu, L., Wai-sum, L., Chun-pan, T., et al. (2008). Prevalence of DSM-IV disorders in Chinese adolescents and the effects of an impairment criterion. *European Child and Adolescent Psychiatry, 17,* 452–461.

Levendosky, A. A., Huth-Bocks, A. C., Semel, M. A., & Shapiro, D. L. (2002). Trauma symptoms in preschool-age children exposed to domestic violence. *Journal of Interpersonal Violence, 17,* 150–164.

Lewin, A. B., Storch, E. A., Merlo, L. J., Adkins, J. W., Murphy, T., & Geffken, G. A. (2005). Intensive cognitive-behavioral therapy for pediatric obsessive-compulsive disorder: A treatment protocol for mental health providers. *Psychological Services, 2,* 91–104.

Lewinsohn, P., Holm-Denoma, J., Small, J., Seeley, J., & Joiner, J. (2008). Separation anxiety disorder in childhood as a risk factor for future mental illness. *Journal of the American Academy of Child and Adolescent Psychiatry, 47,* 548–555.

Lewinsohn, P. M. , Gotlig, I. H., Lewinsohn, M., Seeley, J. R., & Allen, N. B. (1998). Gender differences in anxiety disorders and anxiety symptoms in adolescents. *Journal of Abnormal Psychology, 107*, 109–117.

Lewis, S. (1974). A comparison of behavior therapy techniques in the reduction of fearful avoidance behavior. *Behavior Therapy, 5*, 648–655.

Libby, A. M., Orton, H. D., & Valuck, R. J. (2009). Persisting decline in depression treatments after FDA warnings. *Archives of General Psychiatry, 66*, 633–639.

Liddell, A., & Murray, P. (1989). Age and sex differences in children's reports of dental anxiety and self-efficacy relating to dental anxiety. *Canadian Journal of Behavioral Science, 21*, 270–279.

Lieb, R., Wittchen, H. U., Höfler, M., Fuetsch, M., Stein, M. B., & Merikangas, K. R. (2000). Parental psychopathology, parenting styles, and the risk of social phobia in offspring. *Archives of General Psychiatry, 57*, 859–866.

Liebowitz, M. R., Turner, S. M., Piacentini, J., Beidel D. C., Clarvit, S. R., Davies, S. O., et al. (2002). Fluoxetine in children and adolescents with OCD: A placebo-controlled trial. *Journal of the American Academy of Child and Adolescent Psychiatry, 41*, 1431–1438.

Liddell, A., & Lyons, M. (1978). Thunderstorm phobias. *Behaviour Research and Therapy, 16*, 306–308.

Linning, L. M., & Kearney, C. A. (2004). Posttraumatic stress disorder in maltreated youth. *Journal of Interpersonal Violence, 19*, 1087–1101.

Lipsitz, J. D., Barlow, D. H., Mannuzza, S., Hofmann, S., & Fyer, A. J. (2002). Clinical features of four DSM-IV specific phobia subtypes. *The Journal of Nervous and Mental Disease, 190*, 471–478.

Lipsitz, J. D., Martin, L. Y., Mannuzza, S., Chapman, T. F., Liebowitz, M. R., Klein, D. F., et al. (1994). Childhood separation anxiety disorder in patients with adult anxiety disorders. *American Journal of Psychiatry, 151*, 927–929.

Lonigan, C. J., Phillips, B. M., & Richey, J. A. (2003). Posttraumatic stress disorder in children: Diagnosis, assessment, and associated features. *Children and Adolescent Psychiatric Clinics of North America, 12*, 171–194.

Lonigan, C. J., Shannon, M. P., Taylor, C. M., Finch, A. J., & Sallee, F. R. (1994). Children exposed to disaster: II. Risk factors for the development of post-traumatic symptomatology. *Journal of the American Academy of Child and Adolescent Psychiatry, 33*, 94–105.

Lowry-Webster, H. M., Barrett, P. M., & Dadds, M. R. (2001). A universal prevention trial of anxiety and depressive symptomatology in childhood: Preliminary data from an Australian study. *Behaviour Change, 18*, 36–50.

Lowry-Webster, H. M., Barrett, P. M., & Lock, S. (2003). *A universal prevention trial of anxiety symptomatology during childhood: Results at one year follow-up*. Unpublished manuscript, Griffith University.

Loxton, H. (2009). Monsters in the dark and other scary things: Preschoolers' self-reports. *Journal of Child and Adolescent Mental Health, 21*, 47–60.

Lu, W., Daleiden, E., & Lu, S. (2007). Threat perception bias and anxiety among Chinese school children and adolescents. *Journal of Clinical Child and Adolescent Psychology: The Official Journal for The Society of Clinical Child and Adolescent Psychology, American Psychological Association, Division 53, 36*, 568–580.

Macaulay, J. L., & Kleinknecht, R. A. (1989). Panic and panic attacks in adolescents. *Journal of Anxiety Disorders, 3*, 221–241.

MacFarlane, J. W., Allen, L., & Honzik, M. P. (1954). A developmental study of the behavior problems of normal children between twenty-one months and fourteen years. In *University of California Publications in Child Development* (Vol. 21, pp. 61–87). Berkeley: University of California Press.

MacMaster, F., Russell, A., Mirza, Y., Keshavan, M., Banerjee, S., Bhandari, C., et al. (2006). Pituitary volume in pediatric obsessive-compulsive disorder. *Biological Psychiatry, 59*, 252–257.

Macy, R. D., Macy, D. J., Gross, S., & Brighton, P. (2006). *Classroom-camp-community-culture based intervention: Basic training manual for the 9-session CBI*. Boston: Center for Trauma Psychology.

Maikovich, A. K., Koenen, K. C., & Jaffee, S. R. (2009). Posttraumatic stress symptoms and trajectories in child sexual abuse victims: An analysis of sex differences using the National Survey of Child and Adolescent Well-Being. *Journal of Abnormal Child Psychology, 37*, 727–737.

Manassis, K., Bradley, S., Goldberg, S., Hood, J., & Swinson, R. (1995). Behavioural inhibition, attachment and anxiety in children of mothers with anxiety disorders. *Canadian Journal of Psychiatry, 40*, 87–92.

Manassis, K., Fung, D., Tannock, R., Sloman, L., Fiksenbaum, L., & McInnes, A. (2003). Characterizing selective mutism: Is it more than social anxiety? *Depression and Anxiety, 18*, 153–161.

Manassis, K., & Kalman, E. (1990). Anorexia resulting from fear of vomiting in four adolescent girls. *Canadian Journal of Psychiatry, 35,* 548–550.

Manassis, K., Mendlowitz, S., Kreindler, D., Lumsden, C., Sharpe, J., Simon, M., et al. (2009). Mood assessment via animated characters: A novel instrument to evaluate feelings in young children with anxiety disorders. *Journal of Clinical Child and Adolescent Psychology: The Official Journal for the Society of Clinical Child and Adolescent Psychology, American Psychological Association, Division 53, 38,* 380–389.

Manassis, K., Mendlowitz, S. L., Scapillato, D., Avery, D., Fiksenbaum, L., Freire, M., et al. (2002). Group and individual cognitive-behavioral therapy for childhood anxiety disorders: A randomized trial. *Journal of the American Academy of Child and Adolescent Psychiatry, 41,* 1423–1430.

Mancini, C., Van Amerigen, M., Szatmari, P., Fugere, C., & Boyle, M. (1996). A high-risk pilot study of the children of adults with social phobia. *Journal of the American Academy of Child and Adolescent Psychiatry, 35,* 1511–1517.

Manicavasagar, V., & Silove, D. (1997). Is there an adult form of separation anxiety disorder? A brief clinical report. *Australian and New Zealand Journal of Psychiatry, 31,* 299–303.

Manicavasagar, V., Silove, D., & Curtis, J. (1997). Separation anxiety in adulthood: A phenomenological investigation. *Comprehensive Psychiatry, 38,* 274–282.

Manicavasagar, V., Silove, D., Curtis, J., & Wagner, R. (2000). Continuities of separation anxiety from early life into adulthood. *Journal of Anxiety Disorders, 14,* 1–18.

Mann, J., & Rosenthal. T. L. (1969). Vicarious and direct counter-conditioning of test anxiety through individual and group desensitization. *Behaviour Research and Therapy, 7,* 359–367.

March, J. S. (1997). *Multidimensional anxiety scale for children.* Toronto: Multi-Health Systems.

March, J. S. (1999). Assessment of pediatric posttraumatic stress disorder. In P. Saigh & D. Bremner (Eds.), *Post-traumatic stress disorder* (pp. 199–218). Washington, DC: American Psychological Press.

March, J. S., Amaya-Jackson, L., Murray, M. C., & Schulte, A. (1998). Cognitive-behavioral psychotherapy for children and adolescents with post-traumatic stress disorder following a single-incident stressor. *Journal of the American Academy of Child and Adolescent Psychiatry, 37,* 585–593.

March, J. S., Biederman, J., Wolkow, R., Safferman, A., Mardekian, J., Cook, E. H., et al. (1998). Sertraline in children and adolescents with obsessive-compulsive disorder. *Journal of the American Medical Association, 280*, 1752–1756.

March, J. S., Franklin, M. E., Leonard, H. L., & Foa, E. B. (2004). Obsessive-compulsive disorder. In T. L. Morris, & J. S. March (Eds.) *Anxiety disorders in children and adolescents* (pp. 212–240). New York: Guilford Press.

March, J. S., & Mulle, K. (1998). *OCD in children and adolescents: A cognitive-behavioral treatment manual.* New York: Guilford.

March, J. S., Mulle, K., & Herbel, B. (1994). Behavioral psychotherapy for children and adolescents with obsessive-compulsive disorder: An open trial of a new protocol-driven treatment package. *Journal of the American Academy of Child and Adolescent Psychiatry, 33*, 333–341.

March, J. S., Parker, J. D. A., Sullivan, K., Stallings, P., & Conners, K. (1997). The Multidimensional Anxiety Scale for Children (MASC): Factor structure, reliability and validity. *Journal of the American Academy of Child and Adolescent Psychiatry, 36*, 554–565.

Marks, I. M. (1969). *Fears and phobias.* New York: Academic Press.

Marks, I. M. (1970). The classification of phobic disorders. *British Journal of Psychiatry, 116*, 377–386.

Marks, I. M. (1985). Behavioral psychotherapy for anxiety disorders. *Psychiatric Clinics of North America, 8*, 25–35.

Martin, C., Cabrol, S., Bouvard, M., Lepine, J. P., & Mouren-Simeoni, M. C. (1999). Anxiety and depressive disorders in fathers and mothers of anxious school-refusing children. *Journal of the American Academy of Child and Adolescent Psychiatry, 38*, 916–922.

Martin, J. L., & Thienemann, M. (2005). Group cognitive-behavioral therapy with family involvement for middle-school-age children with obsessive-compulsive disorder: A pilot study. *Child Psychiatry and Human Development, 36*, 113–127.

Masi, G., Favilla, L., Mucci, M., & Millepiedi, S. (2000). Depressive comorbidity in children and adolescents with generalized anxiety disorder. *Child Psychiatry and Human Development, 30*, 205–215.

Masi, G., Favilla, L., Mucci, M., & Millepiedi, S. (2001). Anxiety comorbidity in referred children and adolescents with dysthymic disorder. *Psychopathology, 34*, 253–258.

Masi, G., Millepiedi, S., Mucci, M., Bertini, N., Milantoni, L., & Arcangeli, F. (2005). A naturalistic study of referred children and adolescents with obsessive-compulsive disorder. *Journal of the American Academy of Child and Adolescent Psychiatry, 44*, 673–681.

Masi, G., Millepiedi, S., Mucci, M., Poli, P., Bertini, N., & Milantoni, L. (2004). Generalized anxiety disorder in referred children and adolescents. *Journal of the American Academy of Child and Adolescent Psychiatry, 43,* 752–760.

Masi, G., Mucci, M., Favilla, L., Romano, R., & Poli, P (1999). Symptomatology and comorbidity of generalized anxiety disorder in children and adolescents. *Comprehensive Psychiatry, 40,* 210–215.

Masia, C. L., Hofmann, S. G., Klein, R. G., & Liebowitz, M. R. (1999). *The Liebowitz Social Anxiety Scale for Children and Adolescents (LSAS–CA).* Unpublished manuscript, NYU Child Study Center, New York.

Masia, C. L., Klein, R. G., Storch, E. A., & Corda, B. (2001). School-based behavioral treatment for social anxiety disorder in adolescents: Results of a pilot study. *Journal of the American Academy of Child and Adolescent Psychiatry, 40,* 780–786.

Masia, C. L., Storch, E. A., Dent, H. C., Adams, P., Verdeli, H., Davies, M., et al. (2003). Recall of childhood psychopathology more than 10 years later. *Journal of the American Academy of Child and Adolescent Psychiatry, 42,* 6–12.

Masia-Warner, C., Klein, R., Dent, H., Fisher, P. H., Alvir, J., Albano, A. M., et al. (2005). School-based intervention for adolescents with social anxiety disorder: Results of a controlled study. *Journal of Abnormal Child Psychology, 33,* 707–722.

Masia-Warner, C., Storch, E. A., Pincus, D. B., Klein, R. G., Heimberg, R. G., & Liebowitz, M. R. (2003). The Liebowitz Social Anxiety Scale for Children and Adolescents: An initial psychometric investigation. *Journal of the American Academy of Child and Adolescent Psychiatry, 42,* 1076–1084.

Mason, T. B., & Pack, A. I. (2007). Pediatric parasomnias. *Sleep, 30,* 141–151.

Mattis, S. G., & Ollendick, T. H. (1997). Children's cognitive responses to the somatic symptoms of panic. *Journal of Abnormal Child Psychology, 25,* 47–57.

Mattis, S. G., & Ollendick, T. H. (2002). *Panic disorder and anxiety in adolescents.* London: British Psychological Society.

Mauer, A. (1965). What children fear. *Journal of Genetic Psychology, 106,* 265–277.

McCathie, H., & Spence, S. H. (1991). What is the revised Fear Survey Schedule for Children measuring? *Behaviour Research and Therapy, 29,* 495–502.

McClure, E. B., Monk, C. S., Nelson, E. E., Parrish, J. M., Adler, A., Blair, J. R., et al. (2007). Abnormal attention modulation of fear circuit function in pediatric generalized anxiety disorder. *Archives of General Psychiatry, 64,* 97–106.

McDonald, A. S. (2001). The prevalence and effects of test anxiety in school children. *Educational Psychology, 21,* 89–102.

McFarlane, A. C. (1987). Posttraumatic phenomena in a longitudinal study of children following a natural disaster. *Journal of the American Academy of Child and Adolescent Psychiatry, 26,* 764–769.

McGee, R., Feehan, M., Williams, S., & Anderson, J. (1992). DSM-III disorders from age 11 to age 15 years. *Journal of the American Academy of Child and Adolescent Psychiatry, 31,* 51–59.

McGee, R., Feehan, M., Williams, S., Partridge, F., Silva, P. A., & Kelly, J. (1990). DSM-III disorders in a large sample of adolescents. *Journal of the American Academy of Child and Adolescent Psychiatry, 29,* 611–619.

McKenna, J. J., & Gettler, L. T. (2008). Cultural influences on infant and childhood sleep biology and the science that studies it: Toward a more inclusive paradigm II. *Lung Biology in Health and Disease, 223,* 183–221.

McKnight, C. D., Compton, S. N., & March, J. S. (2004). Posttraumatic stress disorder. In T. L. Morris and J. S. March (Eds.), *Anxiety disorders in children and adolescents* (2nd ed., pp. 241–262). New York: Guilford Press.

McLaughlin, K. A., Fairbank, J. A., Gruber, M. J., Jones, R. T., Lakoma, M. D., Pfefferbaum, B., et al. (2009). Serious emotional disturbance among youths exposed to Hurricane Katrina 2 years postdisaster. *Journal of the American Academy of Child and Adolescent Psychiatry, 48,* 1069–1078.

McLaughlin-Crabtree, V., & Witcher, L. A. (2008). Impact of sleep loss on children andadolescents. In A. Ivanenko (Ed.), *Sleep and psychiatric disorders in children and adolescents* (pp. 139–148). New York: Informa Healthcare.

McMenamy, C., & Katz, R. C. (1989). Brief parent assisted treatment for children's nighttime fears. *Journal of Developmental and Behavioral Pediatrics, 10,* 145–148.

Meijer, A. M., Habekothe, R. T., & van den Wittenboer, G. L. (2001). Mental health, parental rules, and sleep in pre-adolescents. *Journal of Sleep Research, 10,* 297–302.

Meiser-Stedman, R., Smith, P., Glucksman, E., Yule, W., & Dalgleish, T. (2007). Parent and child agreement for acute stress disorder, posttraumatic stress disorder and other psychopathology in a prospective study of children and adolescents exposed to single event trauma. *Journal of Abnormal Child Psychology, 35*, 191–201.

Meiser-Stedman, R., Smith, P., Glucksman, E., Yule, W., & Dalgleish, T. (2008). The posttraumatic stress disorder diagnosis in preschool- and elementary school-age children exposed to motor vehicle accidents. *American Journal of Psychiatry, 165*, 1326–1337.

Meiser-Stedman, R., Yule, W., Smith, P., Glucksman, E., & Dalgleish, T. (2005). Acute stress disorder and posttraumatic stress disorder in children and adolescents involved in assaults and motor vehicle accidents. *American Journal of Psychiatry, 162*, 1381–1383.

Melamed, B. G., Yurcheson, R., Fleece, E. L., Hutcherson, S., & Hawes, R. (1978). Effects of film modeling on the reduction of anxiety-related behaviors in individuals varying in level of previous experience in the stress situation. *Journal of Consulting and Clinical Psychology, 46*, 1357–1367.

Mellman, T., Bustamante, V., Fins, A., Pigeon, W., & Nolan, B. (2002). REM sleep and the early development of posttraumatic stress disorder. *American Journal of Psychiatry, 159*, 1696–1701.

Mellman, T., David, D., Bustamante, V., Torres, J., & Fins, A. (2001). Dreams in the acute aftermath of trauma and their relationship to PTSD. *Journal of Traumatic Stress, 14*, 241–247.

Mellman, T. A., & Hipolito, M. M. (2006). Sleep disturbances in the aftermath of trauma and posttraumatic stress disorder. *CNS Spectrums, 11*, 611–615.

Meltzer, H., Vostanis, P., Dogra, N., Doos, L., Ford, T., & Goodman, R. (2008). Children's specific fears. *Child: Care, Health and Development, 35, 6*, 781–789.

Menzies, R. G., & Clarke, J. C. (1993). A comparison of in vivo and vicarious exposure in the treatment of childhood water phobia. *Behaviour Research and Therapy, 31*, 9–15.

Merckelbach, H., de Jong, P. J., Muris, P., & van den Hout, M. A. (1996). The etiology of specific phobias: A review. *Clinical Psychology Review, 16*, 337–361.

Merckelbach, H., Muris, P., & Schouten, E. (1996). Pathways to fear in spider phobic children. *Behaviour Research and Therapy, 34*, 935–938.

Merikangas, K. R., Avenenoli, S., Dierker, L., & Grillon, C. (1999). Vulnerability factors among children at risk for anxiety. *Biological Psychiatry, 46*, 1523–1535.

Micco, J., & Ehrenreich, J. (2009). Validity and specificity of the Children's Automatic Thoughts Scale in clinically anxious and non-clinical children. *Cognitive Therapy and Research, 33,* 532–536.

Milgrom, P., Manci, L., King, B., & Weinstein, P. (1995). Origins of childhood dental fear. *Behaviour Research and Therapy, 33,* 313–319.

Miller, L. C. (1983). Fears and anxieties in children. In C. E. Walker & M. C. Roberts (Eds.), *Handbook of clinical child psychology* (pp. 337–380). New York: Wiley.

Miller, L. C., Barrett, C. L., Hampe, E., & Noble, H. (1971). Revised anxiety scales for the Louisville Behavior Checklist. *Psychological Reports, 29,* 503–511.

Miller, L. C., Barrett, C. L., Hampe, E., & Noble, H. (1972). Comparison of reciprocal inhibition, psychotherapy, and waiting list control for phobic children. *Journal of Abnormal Psychology, 79,* 269–279.

Mindell, J. A., & Barrett, K. M. (2002). Nightmares and anxiety in elementary aged children: Is there a relationship? *Child Care and Health Development, 28,* 317–322.

Mindell, J. A., & Owens, J. A. (2003). *A clinical guide to pediatric sleep: Diagnosis and management of sleep problems.* Philadelphia: Lippincott Williams & Wilkins.

Mindell, J. A., Owens, J. A., & Carskadon, M. A. (1999). Developmental features of sleep. *Child and Adolescent Psychiatric Clinics of North America, 8,* 695–725.

Mineka, S. (1987). A primate model of phobic fears. In H. Eysenck & I. Martin (Eds.), *Theoretical foundations of behavior therapy* (pp. 87–111). New York: Plenum Press.

Mineka, S., & Cook, M. (1988). Social learning and the acquisition of snake fear in monkeys. In T. Zentall & G. Galef (Eds.), *Comparative social learning* (pp. 51–73). Hillsdale, NJ: Erlbaum.

Mineka, S., & Öhman, A. (2002). Born to fear: Non-associative vs. associative factors in the etiology of phobias. *Behaviour Research and Therapy, 40,* 173–184.

Mineka, S., Suomi, S. J., & Delizio, R. D. (1981). Multiple separations in adolescent monkeys: An opponent-process interpretation. *Journal of Experimental Psychology: General, 110,* 56–85.

Mineka, S., Watson, D., & Clark, L. A. (1998). Comorbidity of anxiety disorders and unipolar mood disorders. *Annual Review of Psychology, 49,* 377–412.

Mizuta, I. M., Zahn-Waxler, C., Cole, P. M., & Hiruma, N. (1996). A cross-cultural study of preschooler's attachment: Security and sensitivity in Japanese and U.S. dyads. *International Journal of Behavioral Development, 19,* 141–159.

Moffitt, T. E., Caspi, A., & Rutter, M. (2005). Strategy for investigating interactions between measured genes and measured environments. *Archives of General Psychiatry, 62,* 473–481.

Monk, C. S., Klein, R. G., Telzer, E. H., Schroth, E. A., Mannuzza, S., Moulton, J. L., et al., &. (2008). Amygdala and nucleus accumbens activation to emotional facial expressions in children and adolescents at risk for major depression. *American Journal of Psychiatry, 165,* 90–98.

Monk, C., Lovelenko, P., Ellman, L. M., Sloan, R . P., Bagiella, E., Gorman, J. M., et al. (2001). Enhanced stress reactivity in paediatric anxiety disorders: Implications for future cardiovascular health. *International Journal of Neuropsychopharmacology, 42* (Special Issue), 199–206.

Monk, C. S., Nelson, E. E., McClure, E. B., Mogg, K., Bradley, B. P., Leibenluft, E., et al., &. (2006). Ventrolateral prefrontal cortex activation and attentional bias in response to angry faces in adolescents with generalized anxiety disorder. *American Journal of Psychiatry, 163,* 1091–1097.

Montgomery, E., & Foldspang, A. (2006). Validity of PTSD in a sample of refugee children: Can a separate diagnostic entity be justified? *International Journal of Methods in Psychiatric Research, 15,* 64–74.

Moore, P. S., Whaley, S. E., & Sigman, M. (2004). Interactions between mothers and children: impacts of maternal and child anxiety. *Journal of Abnormal Psychology, 113,* 471–476.

Morer, A., Lazaro, L., Sabater, L., Massana, J., Castro, J., & Graus, F. (2008). Antineural antibodies in a group of children with obsessive-compulsive disorder and Tourette syndrome. *Journal of Psychiatric Research, 42,* 64–68.

Morin, C. M. (1993). *Insomnia: Psychological assessment and management.* New York: Guilford Press.

Morris, T. L., Hirshfeld-Becker, D. R., Henin, A., & Storch, E. A. (2004). Developmentally sensitive assessment of social anxiety. *Cognitive and Behavioral Practice, 11,* 13–28.

Mosing, M. A., Gordon, S. D., Medland, S. E., Statham, D. J., Nelson, E. C., Heath, A. C., et al. (2009). Genetic and environmental influences on the co-morbidity between depression, panic disorder, agoraphobia, and social phobia: A twin study. *Depression and Anxiety, 26,* 1004–1011.

Mowrer, O. H. (1947). On the dual nature of learning: A re-interpretation of "conditioning" and "problem-solving." *Harvard Educational Review, 17,* 102–148.

Mrakotsky, C., Masek, B., Biederman, J., Raches, D., Hsin, O., Forbes, P., et al. (2008). Prospective open-label pilot trial of mirtazapine in children and adolescents with social phobia. *Journal of Anxiety Disorders, 22*, 99–97.

Mufson, L., Weissman, M. M., & Warner, V. (1992). Depression and anxiety in parents and children: A direct interview study. *Journal of Anxiety Disorders, 6*, 1–13.

Muller, S. A. (1987). Trichotillomania. *Dermatology Clinic, 5*, 595–601.

Muris, P., du Plessis, M., & Loxton, H. (2008). Origins of common fears in South African children. *Journal of Anxiety Disorders, 22*, 1510–1515.

Muris, P., & Field, A. (2008). Distorted cognition and pathological anxiety in children and adolescents. *Cognition and Emotion, 22*, 395–421.

Muris, P., Huijding, J., Mayer, B., Leemreis, W., Passchier, S., & Bouwmeester, S. (2009). The effects of verbal disgust- and threat-related information about novel animals on disgust and fear beliefs and avoidance in children. *Journal of Clinical Child and Adolescent Psychology, 38*, 551–563.

Muris, P., Meesters, C., & Gobel, M. (2001). Reliability, validity, and normative data of the Penn State Worry Questionnaire in 8–12-yr-old children. *Journal of Behavior Therapy and Experimental Psychiatry, 32*, 63–72.

Muris, P., Meesters, C., & Knoops, M. (2005). The relation between gender role orientation and fear and anxiety in nonclinic-referred children. *Journal of Clinical Child and Adolescent Psychology, 34*, 326–332.

Muris, P., Meesters, C., Merckelbach, H., Sermon, A., & Zwakhalen, S. (1998). Worry in normal children. *Journal of the American Academy of Child and Adolescent Psychiatry, 37*, 703–710.

Muris, P., Merckelbach, H., & Collaris, R. (1997). Common childhood fears and their origins. *Behaviour Research and Therapy, 35*, 929–937.

Muris, P., Merckelbach, H., Gadet, B., & Moulaert, V. (2000). Fears, worries, and scary dreams in 4–12 year old children: Their content, developmental pattern, and origins. *Journal of Clinical Child Psychology, 29*, 43–52.

Muris, P., Merkelbach, H., Holdrinet, I., & Sysenaar, M. (1998). Treating phobic children: Effects of EMDR versus exposure. *Journal of Consulting and Clinical Psychology, 66*, 193–198.

Muris, P., Merckelbach, H., Ollendick, T. H., King, N. J., & Bogie, N. (2001). Children's nighttime fears: Parent-child ratings of frequency, content, origins, coping behaviors and severity. *Behaviour Research and Therapy, 39*, 13–28.

Muris, P., Merckelbach, H., Ollendick, T. H., King, N. J., Meesters, C., & van Kessel, C. (2002). What is the Revised Fear Survey Schedule for Children measuring? *Behaviour Research and Therapy, 40,* 1317–1326.

Muris, P., Merckelbach, H., Schmidt, H., & Tierney, S. (1999). Disgust sensitivity, trait anxiety, and anxiety disorders symptoms in normal children. *Behaviour Research and Therapy, 37,* 953–961.

Muris, P., Schmidt, H., & Merckelbach, H. (1999). The structure of specific phobia symptoms among children and adolescents. *Behaviour Research and Therapy, 37,* 863–868.

Muris, P., Steerneman, P., Merckelbach, H., & Meesters, C. (1996). The role of parental fearfulness and modeling in children's fear. *Behaviour Research and Therapy, 34,* 265–268.

Murphy, C. M., & Bootzin, R. R. (1973). Active and passive participation in the contact desensitization of snake fear in children. *Behavior Therapy, 4,* 203–211.

Murphy, T. K., Sajid, M., Soto, O., Shapira, N., Edge, P., Yang, M., et al. (2004). Detecting pediatric autoimmune neuropsychiatric disorders associated with streptococcus in children with obsessive-compulsive disorder and tics. *Biological Psychiatry, 55,* 61–68.

Murray, L., Cooper, P., Creswell, C., Schofield, E., & Sack, C. (2007). The effects of maternal social phobia on mother-infant interactions and infant social responsiveness. *Journal of Child Psychology and Psychiatry and Allied Disciplines, 48,* 45–52.

Murray, L., De Rosnay, M., Pearson, J., Bergeron, C., Schofield, E., Royal-Lawson, M., & Cooper, P. J. (2008). Intergenerational transmission of social anxiety. *Child Development, 79,* 1049–1064.

Murray, P., Liddell, A., & Donohue, J. (1989). A longitudinal study of the contribution of dental experience to dental anxiety in children between 9 and 12 years of age. *Journal of Behavioral Medicine, 12,* 309–320.

Nader, K., Blake, D., Kriegler, J., & Pynoos, R. (1994). *Clinician Administered PTSD Scale for Children (CAPS-C), Current and Lifetime Diagnosis Version, and instructional manual.* Los Angeles: UCLA Neuropsychiatric Institute and National Center for PTSD.

Nader, K., Pynoos, R., Fairbanks, L., & Frederick, C. (1990). Children's PTSD reactions one year after a sniper attack at their school. *American Journal of Psychiatry, 147,* 1526–1530.

Nalvern, F. B. (1970). Manifest fears and worries of ghetto versus middle class suburban children. *Psychological Reports, 27,* 285–286.

National Institutes of Health. (2003, July). *National sleep disorders research plan.* Retrieved January 1, 2010, from http://www.nhlbi. nih.gov/health/prof/sleep/res_plan

Nauta, M. H., Scholing, A., Emmelkamp, P. M. G., & Minderaa, R. B. (2001). Cognitive-behavioural therapy for anxiety disordered children in a clinical setting: Does additional cognitive parent training enhance treatment effectiveness? *Clinical Psychology and Psychotherapy, 8,* 330–340.

Nauta, M. H., Scholing, A., Emmelkamp, P. M. G., & Minderaa, R. B. (2003). Cognitive-behavioral therapy for children with anxiety disorders in a clinical setting: No additional effect of a cognitive parent training. *Journal of the American Academy of Child and Adolescent Psychiatry, 42,* 1270–1278.

Naylor, M. W., Staskowski, M., Kenney, M. C., & King, C. A. (1994). Language disorders and learning disabilities in school refusing adolescents. *Journal of the American Academy of Child and Adolescent Psychiatry, 35,* 1331–1337.

Neal, A. M., Lilly, R. S., & Zakis, S. (1993). What are African American children afraid of? *Journal of Anxiety Disorders, 7,* 129–139.

Neidhardt, E. J., Krakow, B., Kellner, R., & Pathak, D. (1992). The beneficial effects of one treatment session and recording of nightmares on chronic nightmare sufferers. *Sleep, 15,* 470–473.

Nelles, W. B., & Barlow, D. H. (1988). Do children panic? *Clinical Psychology Review, 8,* 359–372.

Newman, D. L., Moffitt, T. E., Caspi, A., Magdol, L., Silva, P. A., & Stanton, W. R. (1996). Psychiatric disorder in a birth cohort of young adults: Prevalence, comorbidity, clinical significance, and new case incidence from ages 11 to 21. *Journal of Consulting and Clinical Psychology, 64,* 552–562.

Nishida, M., Pearsall, J., Buckner, R. L., & Walker, M. P. (2009). Prefrontal theta during REM sleep enhances emotional memory. *Cerebral Cortex, 19,* 1158–1166.

Noll, J. G., Trickett, P. K., Susman, E. J., & Putnam, F. W. (2006). Sleep disturbances and childhood sexual abuse. *Journal of Pediatric Psychology, 31,* 469–480.

Obler, M., & Terwilliger, R. F. (1970). Pilot study on the effectiveness of systematic desensitization with neurologically impaired children with phobic disorders. *Journal of Consulting and Clinical Psychology, 34,* 314–318.

Ohmi, H., Kojima, S., Awai, Y., Kamata, S., Sasaki, K., Tanaka, Y., et al. (2002). Post-traumatic stress disorder in pre-school aged children after a gas explosion. *European Journal of Pediatrics, 161,* 643–648.

Okami, P., Weisner, T., & Olmstead, R. (2002). Outcome correlates of parent-child bedsharing: An eighteen-year longitudinal study. *Journal of Developmental and Behavioral Pediatrics, 23,* 244–253.

Olivares, J., Garcia-Lopez, L. J., Beidel, D. C., Turner, S. M., Albano, A. M., & Hidalgo, M. D. (2002). Results at long-term among three psychological treatments for adolescents with generalized social phobia (I): Statistical significance. *Psicologia Conductual, 10,* 147–164.

Olivares, J., Garcia-Lopez, L. J., Turner, S. M., Beidel, D. C., Albano, A. M., & Sanchez-Meca, J. (2002). Results at long-term among three psychological treatments for adolescents with generalized social phobia (II): Clinical significance and effect size. *Psicologia Conductual, 10,* 371–385.

Ollendick, T. H. (1979). Fear reduction techniques with children. In M. Hersen, R. M. Eisler, & P. M. Miller (Eds.), *Progress in behavior modification* (Vol. 8, pp. 127–168). New York: Academic Press.

Ollendick, T. H. (1983). Reliability and validity of the Revised Fear Survey Schedule for Children (FSSC-R). *Behaviour Research and Therapy, 21,* 685–692.

Ollendick, T. H. (1995). Cognitive-behavioral treatment of panic disorder with agoraphobia in adolescents: A multiple baseline design analysis. *Behavior Therapy, 26,* 517–531.

Ollendick, T. H., Birmaher, B., & Mattis, S. G. (2004). Panic disorder. In T. L. Morris and J. S. March (Eds.), *Anxiety disorders in children and adolescents* (pp. 189–211). New York: Guilford Press.

Ollendick, T. H., & Horsch, L. M. (2007). Fears in clinic-referred children: Relations with child anxiety sensitivity, maternal overcontrol, and maternal phobic anxiety. *Behavior Therapy, 38,* 402–411.

Ollendick, T. H., & King, N. J. (1991). Origins of childhood fears: An evaluation of Rachman's theory of fear acquisition. *Behaviour Research and Therapy, 29,* 117–123.

Ollendick, T. H., & King, N. J. (1994). Diagnosis, assessment and treatment of internalizing problems in children: The role of longitudinal data. *Journal of Consulting and Clinical Psychology, 62,* 918–927.

Ollendick, T. H., & King, N. J. (1998). Empirically supported treatments for children with phobic and anxiety disorders: Current status. *Journal of Clinical Child Psychology, 27,* 156–167.

Ollendick, T. H., King, N. J., & Frary, R. B. (1989). Fears in children and adolescents: Reliability and generalizability across gender, age and nationality. *Behaviour Research and Therapy, 27,* 19–26.

Ollendick, T. H., King, N. J., & Muris, P. (2004). Phobias in children and adolescents. In M. Maj, H. S. Akiskal, J. J. Lopez-Ibor, & A. Okasha (Eds.), *Phobias* (pp. 245–279). London: Wiley.

Ollendick, T. H., Matson, J. L., & Helsel, W. J. (1985). Fears in children and adolescents: Normative data. *Behaviour Research and Therapy, 23,* 465–467.

Ollendick, T. H., Mattis, S. G., & King, N. J. (1994). Panic in children and adolescents: A review. *Journal of Child Psychology and Psychiatry, 35*, 113–134.

Ollendick, T. H., & Mayer, J. A. (1984). School phobia. In S. M. Turner (Ed.) *Behavioral theories and treatment of anxiety* (pp. 367–411). New York: Plenum Press.

Ollendick, T. H., Ost, L., Reuterskiold, L., Costa, N., Cederlund, R., Sirbu, C., et al. (2009). One-session treatment of specific phobias in youth: A randomized clinical trial in the United States and Sweden. *Journal of Consulting and Clinical Psychology, 77*, 504–516.

Ong, H. S., Wickramaratne, P., Min, T., & Weissman, M. M. (2006). Early childhood sleep and eating problems as predictors of adolescent and adult mood and anxiety disorders. *Journal of Affective Disorders, 96*, 1–8.

Orton, G. L. (1982). A comparative study of children's worries. *Journal of Psychology, 110*, 153–162.

Osofsky, H. J., Osofsky, J. D., Kronenberg, M., Brennan, A., & Hansel, T. C. (2009). Posttraumatic stress symptoms in children after Hurricane Katrina: Predicting need for mental health services. *American Journal of Orthopsychiatry, 79*, 212–220.

Öst, L. G. (1985). Ways of acquiring phobias and outcomes of behavioral treatments. *Behaviour Research and Therapy, 23*, 683–689.

Öst, L. G. (1987). Age of onset in different phobias. *Journal of Abnormal Psychology, 96*, 223–229.

Öst, L. G., Fellenius, J., & Sterner, U. (1991). Applied tension, exposure in vivo, and tension-only in the treatment of blood phobia. *Behaviour Research and Therapy, 29*, 561–574.

Öst, L. G., Svensson, L., Hellstrom, K., & Lindwall, R. (2001). One-session treatment of specific phobias in youths: A randomized clinical trial. *Journal of Consulting and Clinical Psychology, 69*, 814–824.

Owen, P. R. (1998). Fears of Hispanic and Anglo children: Real-world fears in the 1990s. *Hispanic Journal of Behavioral Sciences, 20*, 483–491.

Owens, J. A. (2005). Insomnia in children and adolescents. *Journal of Clinical Sleep Medicine, 1*, 454–458.

Owens, J. A., Spirito, A., & McGuinn, M. (2000). The Children's Sleep Habits Questionaire (CSHQ): Psychometric properties of a survey instrument for school-aged children. *Sleep, 23*, 1–9.

Owens, J. A., Spirito, A., McGuinn, M., & Nobile, C. (2000). Sleep habits and sleep disturbance in elementary school-aged children. *Developmental and Behavioral Pediatrics, 21*, 27–34.

Owens-Stively, J., Frank, N., Smith, A., Hagino, O., Spirito, A., Arrigan, M., et al. (1997). Child temperament, parenting discipline style, and daytime behavior in childhood sleep disorders. *Journal of Developmental and Behavioral Pediatrics, 18*, 314–321.

Ozer, E. J., Best, S. R., Lipsey, T. L., & Weiss, D. S. (2003). Predictors of posttraumatic stress disorder and symptoms in adults: A meta-analysis. *Psychological Bulletin, 129*, 52–71.

Pace-Schott, E. F., Milad, M. R., Orr, S. P., Rauch, S. L., Stickgold, R., & Pitman, R. K. (2009). Sleep promotes generalization of extinction of conditioned fear. *Sleep, 32*, 19–26.

Park, S. Y., Belsky, J. U., Putnam, S., & Crnic, K. (1997). Infant emotionality, parenting and 3-year inhibition: Exploring stability and lawful discontinuity in a male sample. *Developmental Psychology, 33*, 218–227.

Parkinson, L., & Rachman, S. (1981). Part II. The nature of intrusive thoughts. *Advances in Behavioural Research and Therapy, 3*, 101–110.

Partridge, J. M. (1939). Truancy. *Journal of Medical Science, 85*, 45–81.

Pauls, D. L., Alsobrook, J. P., Goodman, W., Rasmussen, S., & Leckman, J. F. (1995). A family study of obsessive compulsive disorder. *American Journal of Psychiatry, 152*, 76–84.

Pauls, D. L., Towbin, K., Leckman, J., Zahner, G., & Cohen, D. (1986). Gilles de la Tourette syndrome and obsessive-compulsive disorder: Evidence supporting a genetic relationship. *Archives of General Psychiatry, 43*, 1180–1182.

The Pediatric OCD Treatment Study (POTS) Team. (2004). Cognitive-behavior therapy, sertraline, and their combination for children and adolescents with obsessive-compulsive disorder. *Journal of the American Medical Association, 292*, 1969–1976.

Perrin, S., & Last, C. G. (1993). *Comorbidity of social phobia and other anxiety disorders in children.* Paper presented at the Anxiety Disorders Association of America annual convention, Pittsburgh. March.

Perrin, S., & Last, C. G. (1997). Worrisome thoughts in children clinically referred for anxiety disorder. *Journal of Clinical Child Psychology, 26*, 181–189.

Pfefferbaum, B., Nixon, S. J., Tucker P. M., Tivis, R. D., Moore, V. L., Gurwitch, R. H., et al. (1999). Posttraumatic stress responses in bereaved children after the Oklahoma City bombing. *Journal of the American Academy of Child and Adolescent Psychiatry, 38*, 1372–1379.

Piacentini, J., & Bergman, R. L. (2001). Developmental issues in cognitive therapy for childhood anxiety disorders. *Journal of Cognitive Psychotherapy: An International Quarterly, 15*, 165–182.

Piacentini, J., Bergman, R. L., Jacobs, C., McCracken, J. T., & Kretchman, J. (2002). Open trial of cognitive-behavior therapy for childhood obsessive-compulsive disorder. *Journal of Anxiety Disorders, 16*, 207–219.

Piacentini, J., Bergman, R. L., Keller, M., & McCracken, J. (2003). Functional impairment in children and adolescents with obsessive-compulsive disorder. *Journal of Child and Adolescent Psychopharmacology, 13*(Suppl.), 61–69.

Piacentini, J., Peris, T. S., Bergman, R. L., Chang, S., & Jaffer, M. (2007). Functional impairment in childhood OCD: Development and psychometric properties of the Child Obsessive-Compulsive Impact Scale-Revised (COIS-R). *Journal of Clinical Child and Adolescent Psychology, 36*, 645–653.

Pina, A. A., Silverman, W. K., Alfano, C. A., & Saavedra, L. M. (2002). Diagnostic efficiency of symptoms in the diagnosis of DSM-IV: Generalized anxiety disorder in youth. *Journal of Child Psychology and Psychiatry, 43*, 959–967.

Pina, A. A., Silverman, W. K., Fuentes, R. M., Kurtines, W. M., & Weems, C. F. (2003). Exposure-based cognitive-behavioral treatment for phobic and anxiety disorders: Treatment effects and maintenance for Hispanic/Latino relative to European-American youths. *Journal of the American Academy of Child and Adolescent Psychiatry, 42*, 1179–1187.

Pina, A. A., Silverman, W. K., Weems, C. F., Kurtines, W. M., & Goldman, M. L. (2003). A comparison of completers and noncompleters of exposure-based cognitive and behavioral treatment for phobic and anxiety disorders in youth. *Journal of Consulting and Clinical Psychology, 71*, 701–705.

Pina, A. A., Villalta, I. K., Ortiz, C. D., Gottschall, A. C., Costa, N. M., & Weems, C. F. (2008). Social support, discrimination, and coping as predictors of posttraumatic stress reactions in youth survivors of Hurricane Katrina. *Journal of Clinical Child and Adolescent Psychology, 37*, 564–574.

Pina, A., Zerr, A., Gonzales, N., & Ortiz, C. (2009). Psychosocial interventions for school refusal behavior in children and adolescents. *Child Development Perspectives, 3*, 11–20.

Pincus, D. B., May, J. E., Whitton, S. W., Mattis, S. G., & Barlow, D. H. (2010). Cognitive-behavioral treatment of panic disorder in adolescence. *Journal of Clinical and Adolescent Psychiatry, 39*, 638–649.

Pine, D. S. (2007). Research review: A neuroscience framework for pediatric anxiety disorders. *Journal of Child Psychology and Psychiatry, 48*, 631–648.

Pine, D. S., Cohen, P., Gurley, D., Brook, J., & Ma, Y. (1998). The risk for early-adulthood anxiety and depressive disorders in adolescents with anxiety and depressive disorders. *Archives of General Psychiatry, 55,* 56–64.

Pine, D. S., Coplan, J. D., Papp, L. A., Moreau, D., Tancer, M., Dummitt, E. S., et al. (1995). *Noradrenergic function in youth and adults with anxiety disorders.* In *Scientific Proceedings of the 42nd annual meeting of the American Academy of Child and Adolescent Psychiatry,* Washington, DC.

Pine, D. S., & Grun, J. B. S. (1998). Anxiety disorders. In T. B. Walsh (Ed.), *Child psychopharmacology* (Vol. 17, pp. 115–144). Washington, DC: American Psychiatric Press.

Pine, D. D., Klein, R. G., Coplan, J. D., Coplan, J. D., Papp, L. A., Hoven, C. W., et al. (2000). Differential carbon dioxide sensitivity in childhood anxiety disorders and non-ill comparison group. *Archives of General Psychiatry, 57,* 960–967.

Pomnoppadol, C., & Todd, R. D. (1999). Trichotillomania responds to lithium therapy in a 13-year-old girl. *Journal of the American Academy of Child and Adolescent Psychiatry, 38,* 1470–1471.

Potts, N. L., Davidson, J. R., Krishnan, K. R. R., & Doraiswamy, P. M. (1994). Magnetic resonance spectroscopy in social phobia: Preliminary findings. *Psychiatric Research, 52,* 35–42.

Poulton, R., & Menzies, R. G. (2002). Non-associative fear acquisition: A review of the evidence from retrospective and longitudinal research. *Behaviour Research and Therapy, 40,* 127–149.

Poulton, R., Trainor, P., Stanton, W., McGee, R., Davies, S., & Silva, P. (1997). The (in)stability of adolescent fears. *Behaviour Research and Therapy, 35,* 159–163.

Powell, M. B., & Oei, T. P. (1991). Cognitive processes underlying the behavior change in cognitive behavior therapy with childhood disorders: A review of experimental evidence. *Behavioural Psychotherapy, 19,* 247–265.

Prins, P. J. M. (2001). Affective and cognitive processes and the development and maintenance of anxiety and its disorders. In W. K. Silverman & P. D. A. Treffers (Eds.), *Anxiety disorders in children and adolescents* (pp. 23–44). Cambridge, UK: Cambridge University Press.

Prior, M., Smart, D., Sanson, A., & Oberklaid, F. (2000). Does shy-inhibited temperament in childhood lead to anxiety problems in adolescence? *Journal of the American Academy of Child and Adolescent Psychiatry, 39,* 461–468.

Pruis, A., Lahey, B. B., Thyer, B. A., Christ, M. A. G., Loeber, R., & Loeber, M. (1990). Separation anxiety disorder and overanxious disorder: How do they differ? *Phobia Practice and Research Journal, 3,* 51–59.

Pynoos, R. S., Frederick, C., Nader, K., Arroyo, W., Steinberg, A., Eth, S., et al. (1987). Life threat and posttraumatic stress in school-age children. *Archives of General Psychiatry, 44,* 1057–1063.

Pynoos, R., Rodriguez, N., Steinberg, A., Stauber, M., & Frederick, C. (1998). *UCLA PTSD Index for DSM-IV.* Los Angeles, CA: UCLA Trauma Psychiatry Service.

Pynoos, R. S., Steinberg, A. M., Layne, C. M., Briggs, E. C., Ostrowski, S. A., & Fairbank, J. A. (2009). DSM-IV PTSD diagnostic criteria for children and adolescents: A developmental perspective and recommendations. *Journal of Traumatic Stress, 22,* 391–398.

Rachman, S. (1977). The conditioning theory of fear acquisition: A critical examination. *Behaviour Research and Therapy, 15,* 375–387.

Rachman, S. (1990). The detriment and treatment of simple phobias. *Advances in Behaviour Research and Therapy, 12,* 1–30.

Rachman, S. (1993). Obsessions, responsibility, and guile. *Behavioural Research and Therapy, 16,* 233–238.

Rachman, S., & de Silva, P. (1978). Abnormal and normal obsessions. *Behaviour Research and Therapy, 16,* 223–248.

Rao, P. A., Beidel, D. C., Turner, S. M., Ammerman, R. T., Crosby, L. E., & Sallee, F. R. (2007). Social anxiety disorder in childhood and adolescence: Descriptive psychopathology. *Behaviour Research and Therapy, 45,* 1181–1191.

Rapee, R. M. (2000). Group treatment of children with anxiety disorders: Outcome and predictors of treatment response. *Australian Journal of Psychology, 52,* 125–129.

Rapee. R. M. (2003). The influence of comorbidity on treatment outcome for children and adolescents with anxiety disorders. *Behaviour Research and Therapy, 41,* 105–112.

Rapoport, J., Elkins, R., Langer, D. H., Sceery, W., Buchsbaum, M. S., Gillin, J. C., et al. (1981). Childhood obsessive compulsive disorder. *American Journal of Psychiatry, 138,* 1545–1554.

Rapoport, J. L., Weissman, M. M., Greenwald, S., Narrow, W., Jensen, P. S., Lahey, B. B., et al. (2000). Childhood obsessive-compulsive disorder in the NIMH MECA study: Parent versus child identification of cases. *Journal of Anxiety Disorders, 14,* 535–548.

Rasmussen, S. A., & Eisen, J. L. (1990). Epidemiology of obsessive compulsive disorder. *Journal of Clinical Psychiatry, 53,* 4–10.

Reeve, E. A., Bernstein, G. A., & Christenson, G. A. (1992). Clinical characteristics and psychiatric comorbidity in children with trichotillomania. *Journal of the American Academy of Child and Adolescent Psychiatry, 31,* 132–138.

Reinblatt, S., & Riddle, M. (2007). The pharmacological management of childhood anxiety disorders: A review. *Psychopharmacology, 191,* 67–86.

Research Units on Pediatric Psychopharmacology Anxiety Study Group. (2002). The Pediatric Anxiety Rating Scale (PARS): Development and psychometric properties. *Journal of the American Academy of Child and Adolescent Psychiatry, 41,* 1061–1069.

Rettew, D. C., Swedo, S. E., Leonard, H. L., Lenane, M. C., & Rapoport, J. L. (1992). Obsessions and compulsions across time in 79 children and adolescents with obsessive-compulsive disorder. *Journal of the American Academy of Child and Adolescent Psychiatry, 31,* 1050–1056.

Reynolds, C. R., & Richmond, B. O. (1978). What I think and feel: A revised measure of children's manifest anxiety. *Journal of Abnormal Child Psychology, 6,* 271–280.

Reznick, J. S., Kagan, J., Snidman, N., Gersten, M., Boak, K., & Rosenberg, A. (1986). Inhibited and uninhibited children: A follow-up study. *Child Development, 57,* 660–680.

Riddle, M. A., Hardin, M. T., King, R., Scahill, L., & Woolston, J. L. (1990). Fluoxetine treatment of children and adolescents with Tourette's and obsessive-compulsive disorders: Preliminary clinical experience. *Journal of the American Academy of Child and Adolescent Psychiatry, 29,* 45–48.

Riddle, M. A., Scahill, L., King, R., Hardin, M. T., Tobin, K. E., Ort, S. I., et al. (1990). Obsessive compulsive disorder in children and adolescents: Phenomenology and family history. *Journal of the American Academy of Child and Adolescent Psychiatry, 29,* 766–772.

Ritter, B. (1968). The group desensitization of children's snake phobias using vicarious and contact desensitization procedures. *Behaviour Research and Therapy, 6,* 1–6.

Roberson-Nay, R., & Turner, S. M. (2002, November). *Behavioral treatment of emetophobia (fear of vomiting): A single case study.* Paper presented at the Association for Advancement of Behavior Therapy annual convention, Reno, NV.

Rosenbaum, J. F., Biederman, J., Gersten, M., Hirshfeld, D. R., Meminger, S. R., Herman, J. B., et al. (1988). Behavioral inhibition in children of parents with panic disorder and agoraphobia: A controlled study. *Archives of General Psychiatry, 45,* 463–470.

Rosenbaum, J. F., Biederman, J., Hirshfeld-Becker, D. R., Kagan, J, Snidman, N., Friedman, D., et al. (2000). A controlled study of behavioral inhibition in children of parents with panic disorder and depression. *American Journal of Psychiatry, 157*, 2002–2010.

Rosenberg, D. R., & Keshavan, M. S. (1998). A. E. Bennett Research Award: Toward a neurodevelopmental model of obsessive-compulsive disorder. *Biological Psychiatry, 43*, 623–640.

Rosenberg, D. R., Benazon, N. R., Gilbert, A., Sullivan, A., & Moore, G. J. (2000). Thalamic volume in pediatric obsessive-compulsive disorder patients before and after cognitive behavioral therapy. *Biological Psychiatry, 48*, 294–300.

Rosenberg, D. R., MacMaster, F. P., Keshavan, M. S., Fitzgerald, K. D., Stewart, K. D., Stewart, C. M., et al. (2000). Decrease in caudate glutamatergic concentrations in pediatric obsessive-compulsive disorder patients taking paroxetine. *Journal of the American Academy of Child and Adolescent Psychiatry, 39*, 1096–1103.

Rosenberg, D. R., MacMillan, S. N., & Moore, G. J. (2001). Brain anatomy and chemistry may predict treatment response in paediatric obsessive-compulsive disorder. *International Journal of Neuropsychopharmacology, 4*, 179–190.

Rosnay, M. D., Cooper, P. J. Tsigaras, N., & Murray, L. (2006). Transmission of social anxiety from mother to infant: An experimental study using a social referencing paradigm. *Behaviour Research and Therapy, 44*, 1165–1175.

Roussos, A., Francis, K., Koumoula, A., Richardson, C., Kabakos, C., Kiriakidou, T., et al. (2003). The Leyton Obsessional Inventory-Child version in Greek adolescents. *European Child and Adolescent Psychiatry, 12*, 58–66.

Roy-Byrne, P. P., Uhde, T. W., & Post, R. M. (1986). Effects of one night's sleep deprivation on mood and behavior in panic disorder. *Archives of General Psychiatry, 43*, 895–899.

Rubin, K. H., & Asendorpf, J. B. (1993). *Social withdrawal, inhibition, and shyness in childhood.* Hillsdale, NJ: Erlbaum.

Rubin, K. H., Hastings, P. D., Stewart, S. L., Henderson, H. A., & Chen, X. (1997). The consistency and concomitants of inhibition: Some of the children, all of the time. *Child Development, 68*, 467–483.

RUPP Anxiety Study Group. (2001). Fluvoxamine treatment of anxiety disorders in children and adolescents. *New England Journal of Medicine, 344*, 1279–1285.

RUPP Anxiety Study Group. (2002). Treatment of pediatric anxiety disorders: An open-label extension of the Research Units on Pediatric Psychopharmacology Anxiety Study. *Journal of Child and Adolescent Psychopharmacology, 12*, 175–188.

RUPP Anxiety Study Group. (2003). Searching for moderators and mediators of pharmacological treatment effects in children and adolescents with anxiety disorders. *Journal of the American Academy of Child and Adolescent Psychiatry, 42,* 13–21.

Ryan, N. D., Puig-Antich, J., Ambrosini, P., Rabinovich, H., Robinson, D., Nelson, B., et al. (1987). The clinical picture of major depression in children and adolescents. *Archives of General Psychiatry, 44,* 854–861.

Rynn, M. A., Riddle, M. A., Yeung, P. P., & Kunz, N. R. (2007). Efficacy and safety of extended-release venlafaxine in the treatment of generalized anxiety disorder in children and adolescents: Two placebo-controlled trials. *American Journal of Psychiatry, 164,* 290–300.

Rynn, M. A., Siqueland, L., & Rickels, K. (2001). Placebo-controlled trial of sertraline in the treatment of children with generalized anxiety disorder. *American Journal of Psychiatry, 158,* 2008–2013.

Sadeh, A. (1996). Evaluating night awakenings in sleep-disturbed infants: A methodological study of parental reports and actigraphy. *Sleep, 19,* 757–762.

Sadeh, A., McGuire, J. P. D., Sachs, H., Seifer, R., Tremblay, A., Civita, R., et al. (1995). Sleep and psychological characteristics of children on a psychiatric inpatient unit. *Journal of the American Academy of Child and Adolescent Psychiatry, 34,* 813–819.

Sagaspe, P., Sanchez-Ortuno, M., Charles, A., Taillard, J., Valtat, C., Bioulac, B., et al. (2006). Effects of sleep deprivation on color-word, emotional, and specific stroop interference and on self-reported anxiety. *Brain and Cognition, 60,* 76–87.

Saigh, P. A. (1987). In vitro flooding of an adolescent's posttraumatic stress disorder. *Journal of Clinical Child Psychology, 16,* 147–150.

Saigh, P. A. (1989). A comparative analysis of the affective and behavioral symptomatology of traumatized and nontraumatized children. *Journal of School Psychology, 27,* 247–255.

Saigh, P. A., Yasik, A. E., Oberfield, R. A., Green, B. L., Halamandaris, P. V., Rubenstein, H., et al. (2000). The Children's PTSD Inventory: Development and reliability. *Journal of Traumatic Stress, 13,* 369–380.

Salkovskis, P. M. (1989). Cognitive behavioural factors and the persistence of intrusive thoughts in obsessional problems. *Behaviour Research and Therapy, 27,* 677–682.

Salkovskis, P. M., & Harrison, J. (1984). Abnormal and normal obsessions: A replication. *Behaviour Research and Therapy, 22,* 1–4.

Sallee, F. R., & March, J. S. (2001). Neuropsychiatry of anxiety disorders. In W. K. Silverman and P. D. A. Treffers (Eds.), *Anxiety disorders in children and adolescents* (pp. 90–125). Cambridge, UK: Cambridge University Press.

Sallee, F. R., Richman, H., Sethuraman, G., Dougherty, D., Sine, L., & Altman-Hamamdzic, S. (1998). Clonidine challenge in childhood anxiety disorders. *Journal of the American Academy of Child and Adolescent Psychiatry, 37,* 655–662.

Sallee, F. R., Sethuraman, G., Sine, L., & Liu, H. (2000). Yohimbine challenge in children with anxiety disorders. *American Journal of Psychiatry, 157,* 1236–1242.

Sartor, C. E., Lynskey, M. T., Heath, A. C., Jacob, T., & True, W. (2007). The role of childhood risk factors in initiation of alcohol use and progression to alcohol dependence. *Addiction, 102,* 216–225.

Sauter, F., Heyne, D., & Michiel Westenberg, P. (2009). Cognitive behavior therapy for anxious adolescents: Developmental influences on treatment design and delivery. *Clinical Child and Family Psychology Review, 12,* 310–335.

Scahill, L., Riddle, M. A., McSwiggin-Hardin, M., Ort, S. I., King, R. A., Goodman, W. K., et al. (1997). Children's Yale-Brown Obsessive Compulsive Scale: Reliability and validity. *Journal of the American Academy of Child and Adolescent Psychiatry, 36,* 844–852.

Scheeringa, M. S., Peebles, C. D., Cook, C., & Zeanah, C. H. (2001). Toward establishing procedural, criterion, and discriminant validity for PTSD in early childhood. *Journal of the American Academy of Child and Adolescent Psychiatry, 40,* 52–60.

Scheeringa, M. S., Wright, M. J., Hunt, J. P., & Zeanah, C. H. (2006). Factors affecting the diagnosis and prediction of PTSD symptomatology in children and adolescents. *American Journal of Psychiatry, 163,* 644–651.

Scheeringa, M. S., & Zeanah, C. H. (2008). Reconsideration of harm's way: Onsets and comorbidity patterns of disorders in preschool children and their caregivers following Hurricane Katrina. *Journal of Clinical Child and Adolescent Psychology, 37,* 508–518.

Scheeringa, M. S., Zeana, C. H., Drell, M. J., & Larrieu, J. (1995). Two approaches to the diagnosis of posttraumatic stress disorder in infancy and early childhood. *Journal of the American Academy of Child and Adolescent Psychiatry, 34,* 191–200.

Scheeringa, M. S., Zeanah, C. H., Myers, L., & Putnam, F. W. (2003). New findings on alternative criteria for PTSD in preschool children. *Journal of the American Academy of Child and Adolescent Psychiatry, 42,* 561–570.

Scher, A. (1995). *Changes in maternal separation anxiety in the first year.* Paper presented at the biennial meeting of the Society for Research in Child Development, Indianapolis, IN.

Scher, A. (2008). Maternal separation anxiety as a regulator of infants' sleep. *Journal of Child Psychology and Psychiatry, 49,* 618–625.

Scher, A., & Blumberg, O. (1999). Nightwaking among 1-year-olds: A study of maternal separation anxiety. *Child: Health, Care and Development, 25,* 323–334.

Scherer, M. W., & Nakamura, C. Y. (1968). A Fear Survey Schedule for Children (FSS-FC): A factor analytic comparison with manifest anxiety (CMAS). *Behaviour Research and Therapy, 6,* 173–182.

Schmidt, L. A., Fox, N. A., Rubin, K. H., Sternberg, E. M., Gold, P. W., Smith, C. C., et al. (1997). Behavioral and neuroendocrine responses in shy children. *Developmental Psychobiology, 30,* 127–140.

Schneir, F. R., Johnson, J., Hornig, C. D., Liebowitz, M. R., & Weissman, M. M. (1992). Social phobia: Comorbidity and morbidity in an epidemiologic sample. *Archives of General Psychiatry, 49,* 282–288.

Schniering, C. A., Hudson, J. L., & Rapee, R. M. (2000). Issues in the diagnosis and assessment of anxiety disorders in children and adolescents. *Clinical Psychology Review, 20,* 453–478.

Schreck, K. A., Mulick, J. A., & Rojahn, J. (2005). Parent perception of elementary school age children's sleep problems. *Journal of Child and Family Studies, 14,* 101–109.

Schwartz, A. N., Campos, J. J., & Baisel, E. J., Jr. (1973). The visual cliff: Cardiac and behavioral responses on the deep and shallow sides at five and nine months of age. *Journal of Experimental Child Psychology, 35,* 239–243.

Schwartz, C. E., Snidman, N., & Kagan, J. (1999). Adolescent social anxiety as an outcome of inhibited temperament in childhood. *Journal of the American Academy of Child and Adolescent Psychiatry, 38,* 1008–1015.

Segool, N. K., & Carlson, J. S. (2008). Efficacy of cognitive-behavioral and pharmacological treatments for children with social anxiety. *Depression and Anxiety, 25,* 620–631.

Seligman, L. D., Ollendick, T. H., Langley, A. K., & Baldacci, H. B. (2004). The utility of measures of child and adolescent anxiety: A meta-analytic review of the Revised Children's Manifest Anxiety Scale, the State-Trait Anxiety Inventory for Children, and the Child Behavior Checklist. *Journal of Clinical Child and Adolescent Psychology, 33,* 557–565.

Seligman, M. E. P. (1971). Phobias and preparedness. *Behavior Therapy, 2,* 307–320.

Shannon, M. P., Lonigan, C. J., Finch, A. J., Jr., & Taylor, C. M. (1994). Children exposed to disaster: I. Epidemiology of post-traumatic symptoms and symptom profiles. *Journal of the American Academy of Child and Adolescent Psychiatry, 33,* 80–93.

Shapiro, F. (1995). *Eye movement desensitization and reprocessing.* New York: Guilford Press.

Sharkey, L., Mc Nicholas, F., Barry, E., Begley, M., & Ahern, S. (2008). Group therapy for selective mutism—A parents' and children's treatment group. *Journal of Behavior Therapy and Experimental Psychiatry, 39,* 538–545.

Sharp, W. G., Sherman, C., & Gross, A. M. (2007). Selective mutism and anxiety: A review of the current conceptualization of the disorder. *Journal of Anxiety Disorders, 21,* 568–579.

Shear, K., Jin, R., Ruscio, A., Walters, E., & Kessler, R. (2006). Prevalence and correlates of estimated DSM-IV child and adult separation anxiety disorder in the National Comorbidity Survey Replication. *The American Journal of Psychiatry, 163,* 1074–1083.

Sheslow, D. V., Bondy, A. S., & Nelson, R. O. (1983). A comparison of graduated exposure, verbal coping skills, and their combination in the treatment of children's fear of the dark. *Child and Family Behavior Therapy, 4,* 33–45.

Shirk, S. R., & Karver, M. (2003). Prediction of treatment outcome from relationship variables in child and adolescent therapy: A meta-analytic review. *Journal of Consulting and Clinical Psychology, 71,* 452–464.

Shortt, A. L., Barrett, P. M., & Fox, T. L. (2001). Evaluating the FRIENDS program: A cognitive-behavioral group treatment for anxious children and their parents. *Journal of Clinical Child Psychology, 30,* 525–535.

Shulman, S. T. (2009). Pediatric autoimmune neuropsychiatric disorders associated with streptococci (PANDAS): Update. *Current Opinions in Pediatrics, 21,* 127–130.

Siegel, A., & Bulkeley, K. (1998). *Dreamcatching: every parent's guide to exploring and understanding children's dreams and nightmares.* New York: Three Rivers Press.

Silva, R. H., Kameda, S. R., Carvalho, R. C., Takatsu-Coleman, A. L., Niigaki, S. T., Abilio, V. C., et al. (2004). Anxiogenic effect of sleep deprivation in the elevated plus-maze test in mice. *Psychopharmacology, 176,* 115–122.

Silverman, W. K., & Albano, A. M. (1996). *The Anxiety Disorders Interview Schedule for Children DSM-IV Child and Parent Version.* San Antonio, TX: Psychological Corporation.

Silverman, W. K., & Berman, S. L. (2001). Psychosocial interventions for anxiety disorders in children: Status and future directions. In W. K. Silverman & P. D. A. Treffers (Eds.), *Anxiety disorders in children and adolescents* (pp. 313–334). Cambridge, UK: Cambridge University Press.

Silverman, W. K., & Dick-Niederhauser, A. (2004). Separation anxiety disorder. In T. L. Morris & J. S. March (Eds.), *Anxiety disorders in children and adolescents* (pp. 164–188). Cambridge, UK: Cambridge University Press.

Silverman, W. K., Fleisig, W., Rabian, B., & Peterson, R. A. (1991). Childhood Anxiety Sensitivity Index. *Journal of Clinical Child and Adolescent Psychology, 20,* 162–168.

Silverman, W. K., & Ginsburg, G. S. (1995). Specific phobias and generalized anxiety disorder. In J. S. March (Ed.), *Anxiety disorders in children and adolescents* (pp. 151–180). New York: Guilford.

Silverman, W. K., & Hicks-Carmichael, D. (1999). Phobic disorders. In R. Ammerman, C. G. Last, & M. Hersen (Eds.), *Handbook of prescriptive treatments for children and adolescents* (2nd ed., pp. 172–192). Needham Heights, MA: Allyn & Bacon.

Silverman, W. K., & Kurtines, W. M. (1996). *Anxiety and phobic disorders: A pragmatic approach.* New York: Plenum Press.

Silverman, W. K., Kurtines, W. M., Ginsburg, G. S., Weems, C. F., Lumpkin, P. W., & Carmichael, D. H. (1999). Treating anxiety disorders in children with group cognitive-behavioral therapy: A randomized clinical trial. *Journal of Consulting and Clinical Psychology, 67,* 995–1003.

Silverman, W. K., Kurtines, W. M., Ginsburg, G. S., Weems, C. F., Rabian, B., & Serafini, L. T. (1999). Contingency management, self-control, and education support in the treatment of childhood phobic disorders: A randomized clinical trial. *Journal of Consulting and Clinical Psychology, 67,* 675–687.

Silverman, W. K., La Greca, A. M., & Waserstein, S. B. (1995). What do children worry about? Worries and their relations to anxiety. *Child Development, 66,* 671–686.

Silverman, W., & Ollendick, T. (2005). Evidence-based assessment of anxiety and its disorders in children and adolescents. *Journal of Clinical Child and Adolescent Psychology, 34,* 380–411.

Silverman, W., Pina, A., & Viswesvaran, C. (2008). Evidence-based psychosocial treatments for phobic and anxiety disorders in children and adolescents. *Journal of Clinical Child and Adolescent Psychology, 37,* 105–130.

Silverman, W. K., Saavedra, I. M., & Pina, A. A. (2001). Test-retest reliability of anxiety symptoms and diagnoses with the Anxiety Disorders Interview Schedule for DSM-IV-child and parent versions. *Journal of the American Academy of Child and Adolescent Psychiatry, 40,* 937–944.

Silvestri, A. J. (2005). REM sleep deprivation affects extinction of cued but not contextual fear conditioning. *Physiology and Behavior, 84,* 343–349.

Simard, V., Nielsen, T. A., Tremblay, R. E., Boivin, M., & Montplaisir, J. Y. (2008). Longitudinal study of preschool sleep disturbance. *Archives of Pediatric and Adolescent Medicine, 162,* 360–367.

Simeon, J. G., & Ferguson, H. B. (1987). Alprazolam effects in children with anxiety disorders. *Canadian Journal of Psychiatry, 32,* 570–574.

Simeon, J. G., & Ferguson, H. B. Knott, V., Roberts, N., Gauthier, B., Dubois, C., & Wiggins, D. (1992). Clinical, cognitive, and neuropsychological effects of alprazolam in children and adolescents with overanxious disorder and avoidant disorders. *Journal of the American Academy of Child and Adolescent Psychiatry, 31,* 29–33.

Simonian, S. J., Beidel, D. C., Turner, S. M., Berkes, J. L., & Long, J. H. (2001). Recognition of facial affect by social phobic children. *Child Psychiatry and Human Development, 32,* 137–145.

Siqueland, L., Kendall, P. C., & Steinberg, L. (1996). Anxiety in children: Perceived family environments and observed family interaction. *Journal of Clinical Child Psychology, 25,* 225–237.

Skowron, E., & Reinemann, D. H. S. (2005). Effectiveness of psychological interventions for child maltreatment: A meta-analysis. *Psychotherapy: Theory, Research, Practice, Training, 42,* 52–71.

Smith, P., Yule, W., Perrin, S., Tranah, T., Dalgleish, T., & Clark, D. M. (2007). Cognitive behavior therapy for PTSD in children and adolescents: A preliminary randomized controlled trial. *Journal of the American Academy of Child and Adolescent Psychiatry, 46,* 1051–1061.

Southam-Gerow, M. A., & Kendall, P. C. C. (2000). A preliminary study of the emotional understanding of youths referred for treatment of anxiety disorders. *Journal of Clinical Child Psychology, 29,* 319–327.

Southam-Gerow, M. A., Weisz, J. R., & Kendall, P. C. (2003). Youth with anxiety disorders in research and service clinics: Examining client differences and similarities. *Journal of Clinical Child and Adolescent Psychology, 32,* 375–385.

Sowell, E. R., Thompson, P. M., Tessner, K. D., & Toga, A. W. (2001). Mapping continued brain growth and gray matter density reduction in dorsal frontal cortex: Inverse relationships during post-adolescent brain maturation. *The Journal of Neuroscience, 21,* 8819–8829.

Spell, A. W., Kelley, M. L., Self-Brown, S., Davidson, K., Pellegrin, A., Palcic, A., et al. (2008). The moderating effects of maternal psychopathology on children's mental health post-Hurricane Katrina. *Journal of Clinical Child and Adolescent Psychology, 37,* 553–563.

Spence, S. H., Donovan, C., & Brechman-Toussaint, M. (1999). Social skills, social outcomes, and cognitive features of childhood social phobia. *Journal of Abnormal Psychology, 108,* 211–221.

Spence, S. H., Donovan, C., & Brechman-Toussaint, M. (2000). The treatment of childhood social phobia: The effectiveness of a social skills training-based, cognitive-behavioral intervention, with and without parental involvement. *Journal of Child Psychology and Psychiatry, 41,* 713–726.

Spence, S. H., & McCathie, H. (1993). The stability of fears in children: A two-year prospective study. *Journal of Psychiatry and Psychology, 34,* 379–385.

Spielberger, C. D. (1973). *State-trait anxiety inventory for children.* Redwood City, CA: Mind Garden.

Sroufe, L. A., Waters, E., & Matas, L. (1974). Contextual determinants of infant affective response. In M. Lewis & L. Rosenblum (Eds.), *The origins of behavior. Vol. 2: Fear* (pp. 49–51). New York: Wiley.

Staley, A. A., & O'Donnell, J. P. (1984). A developmental analysis of mothers' reports of normal children's fears. *Journal of Genetic Psychology, 144,* 165–178.

Stanley, M. A., & Turner, S. M. (1995). Current status of pharmacological and behavioral treatment of obsessive-compulsive disorder. *Behavior Therapy, 26,* 163–186.

Stavrakaki, C., Vargo, B., Boodoosingh, L., & Roberts, N. (1987). The relationship between anxiety and depression in children: Rating scales and clinical variables. *Canadian Journal of Psychiatry, 32,* 433–439.

Stein, B. D., Jaycox, L. H., Kataoka, S. H., Wong, M., Tu, W., Elliott, M. N., et al. (2003). A mental health intervention for school children exposed to violence: A randomized controlled trial. *Journal of the American Medical Association, 290,* 603–611.

Stein, M. B. (1998). Neurobiological perspectives on social phobia: From affiliation to zoology. *Biological Psychiatry, 44,* 1277–1285.

Stein, M. B. (2009). Neurobiology of generalized anxiety disorder. *The Journal of Clinical Psychiatry, 70*(Suppl. 2), 15–19.

Steinberg, M. J., Brymer, M. J., Decker, K. B., & Pynoos, R. S. (2004). The University of California at Los Angeles post-traumatic stress disorder reaction index. *Current Psychiatry Reports, 6*, 96–100.

Steinhausen, H. C., & Juzi, C. (1996). Elective mutism: An analysis of 100 cases. *Journal of the American Academy of Child and Adolescent Psychiatry, 35*, 606–614.

Steinhausen, H. C., Metzke, C. W., Meier, M., & Kannenberg, R. (1998). Prevalence of child and adolescent psychiatric disorders: The Zurich epidemiological study. *Acta Psychiatrica Scandinavica, 98*, 262–271.

Stemberger, R. T., Turner, S. M., Beidel, D. C., & Calhoun, K. S. (1995). Social phobia: An analysis of possible developmental factors. *Journal of Abnormal Psychology, 104*, 526–531.

Stewart, S. E., Geller, D. A., Jenike, M., Pauls, D., Shaw, D., Mullin, B., et al. (2004). Long-term outcome of pediatric obsessive-compulsive disorder: A meta-analysis and qualitative review of the literature. *Acta Psychiatrica Scandinavica, 110*, 4–13.

Stewart, S. E., Jenike, M. A., & Keuthen, N. J. (2005). Severe obsessive-compulsive disorder with and without comorbid hair pulling: Comparisons and clinical implications. *The Journal of Clinical Psychiatry, 66*, 864–869.

St-Onge, M., Mercier, P., & De Koninck, J. (2009). Imagery rehearsal therapy for frequent nightmares in children. *Behavioral Sleep Medicine, 7*, 81–98.

Storch, E. A., Lack, C. W., Merlo, L. J., Geffken, G. R., Jacob, M. L., Murphy, T. K., et al. (2007). Clinical features of children and adolescents with obsessive-compulsive disorder and hoarding symptoms. *Comprehensive Psychiatry, 48*, 313–318.

Storch, E. A., Masia-Warner, C., Dent, H. C., Roberti, J. W., & Fisher, P. H. (2004). Psychometric evaluation of the Social Anxiety Scale for Adolescents and the Social Phobia and Anxiety Inventory for Children: Construct validity and normative data. *Journal of Anxiety Disorders, 18*, 665–679.

Storch, E. A., Murphy, T. K., Lack, C. W., Geffken, G. R., Jacob, M. L., & Goodman, W. K. (2008). Sleep-related problems in pediatric obsessive compulsive disorder. *Journal of Anxiety Disorders, 22*, 877–885.

Storr, C. L., Ialongo, N. S., Anthony, J. C., & Breslau, N. (2007). Childhood antecedents of exposure to traumatic events and posttraumatic stress disorder. *American Journal of Psychiatry, 164*, 119–125.

Strauss, C. C. (1988). Behavioral assessment and treatment of overanxious disorder in children and adolescents. *Behavior Modification*, 12, 234–251.

Strauss, C. C., Lahey, B. B., Frick, P., Frame, C. L., & Hynd, G. W. (1988). Peer social status of children with anxiety disorders. *Journal of Consulting and Clinical Psychology*, 56, 137–141.

Strauss, C. C., & Last, C. G. (1993). Social and simple phobias in children. *Journal of Anxiety Disorders*, 7, 141–152.

Strauss, C. C., Last, C. G., Hersen, M., & Kazdin, A. E. (1988). Association between anxiety and depression in children and adolescents with anxiety disorders. *Journal of Abnormal Child Psychology*, 16, 57–68.

Strauss, C. C., Lease, C. A., Last, C. G., & Francis, G. (1988). Overanxious disorder: An examination of developmental differences. *Journal of Abnormal Child Psychology*, 16, 433–443.

Striker, G., & Howitt, J. W. (1965). Physiological recording during simulated dental appointments. *New York State Dental Journal*, 31, 204–206.

Suomi, S. J. (1986). Anxiety in young nonhuman primates. In R. Gittelman (Ed.), *Anxiety disorders of childhood* (pp. 1–23). New York: Guilford Press.

Suveg, C., Aschenbrand, S., & Kendall, P. (2005). Separation anxiety disorder, panic disorder, and school refusal. *Child and Adolescent Psychiatric Clinics of North America*, 14, 773–795.

Svensson, L., Larsson, A., & Öst, L. G. (2002). How children experience brief-exposure treatment of specific phobias. *Journal of Clinical Child and Adolescent Psychiatry*, 31, 80–89.

Swedo, S. E., & Leonard, H. L. (1992). Trichotillomania: An obsessive compulsive spectrum disorder? *Psychiatric Clinics of North America*, 15, 777–790.

Swedo, S. E., Leonard, H. L., Garvey, M., Mittleman, B., Allen, A. J., Perlmutter, S., et al. (1998). Pediatric autoimmune neuropsychiatric disorders associated with streptococcal infections: Clinical description of the first 50 cases. *American Journal of Psychiatry*, 155, 264–271.

Swedo, S. E., & Rapoport, J. L. (1991). Trichotillomania. *Journal of Child Psychology and Psychiatry*, 32, 401–409.

Swedo, S. E., Rapoport, J. L., Leonard H., Lenane, M., & Cheslow, D. (1989). Obsessive-compulsive disorder in children and adolescents. *Archives of General Psychiatry*, 46, 335–341.

Sweeney, M., & Pine, D. (2004). Etiology of fear and anxiety. In T. H. Ollendick & J. S. March (Eds.), *Phobic and anxiety disorders in children and adolescents: A clinical guide to effective psychosocial and pharmacological interventions* (pp. 34–60). New York: Oxford University Press.

Swenson, C. C., Saylor, C. F., Powell, M. P., Stokes, S. J., Foster, K. Y., & Belter, R. W. (1996). Impact of natural disaster in preschool children: Adjustment 14 months after a hurricane. *American Journal of Orthopsychiatry, 66*, 122–130.

Szabo, M., & Lovibond, P. F. (2002). The cognitive content of naturally occurring worry episodes. *Cognitive Therapy and Research, 26*, 167–177.

Szabo, M., & Lovibond, P. F. (2004). The cognitive content of thought-listed worry episodes in clinical-referred anxious and nonreferred children. *Journal of Clinical Child and Adolescent Psychology, 33*, 613–622.

Taghavi, M. R., Neshat-Doost, H. T., Moradi, A. R., Yule, W., & Dalgleish, T. (1999). Biases in visual attention in children and adolescents with clinical anxiety and mixed anxiety-depression. *Journal of Abnormal Child Psychology, 27*, 215–223.

Tal, A., & Miklich, D. R. (1976). Emotionally induced decreases in pulmonary flow rates in asthmatic children. *Psychosomatic Medicine, 39*, 190–200.

Tallis, F., & Eysenck, M. W. (1994). Worry: Mechanisms and modulating influence. *Behavioural and Cognitive Psychotherapy, 22*, 37–56.

Taylor, J., & Turner, R. J. (2002). Perceived discrimination, social stress, and depression in the transition to adulthood: Racial contrasts. *Social Psychology Quarterly, 65*, 213–225.

Teicher, M. H., Dumont, N. L., Ito, Y., Vaituzis, C., Giedd, J. N., & Andersen, S. L. (2004). Childhood neglect is associated with reduced corpus callosum area. *Biological Psychiatry, 56*, 80–85.

Teicher, M. H., Ito, Y., Glod, C. A., Andersen, S. L., Dumont, N., & Ackerman, E. (1997). Preliminary evidence for abnormal cortical development in physically and sexually abused children using EEG coherence and MRI. *Annals of the New York Academy of Science, 821*, 160–175.

Terr, L. (1983). Chochilla revisited: The effects of psychic trauma four years after a school-bus kidnapping. *American Journal of Psychiatry, 140*, 1543–1550.

Terr, L. C. (1991). Childhood traumas: An outline and overview. *American Journal of Psychiatry, 148*, 10–20.

Thapar, A., & McGuffin, P. (1995). Are anxiety symptoms in childhood heritable? *Journal of Child Psychology and Psychiatry, 36*, 439–447.

Thienemann, M., Martin, J., Cregger, B., Thompson, H. B., & Dyer-Friedman, J. (2001). Manual-driven group cognitive-behavioral therapy for adolescents with obsessive-compulsive disorder: A pilot study. *Journal of the American Academy of Child and Adolescent Psychiatry, 40,* 1254–1260.

Thomsen, P. H. (1993). Obsessive-compulsive disorder in children and adolescents: Self-reported obsessive-compulsive behaviour in pupils in Denmark. *Acta Psychiatrica Scandinavia, 88,* 2212–2217.

Thomsen, P. H. (1995). Obsessive-compulsive disorder in children and adolescents: A study of parental psychopathology and precipitating events in 20 consecutive Danish cases. *Psychopathology, 28,* 161–167.

Thomsen, P. H. (2000). Obsessions: The impact and treatment of obsessive-compulsive disorder in children and adolescents. *Journal of Psychopharmacology, 14*(2, Suppl. 1), S31–S37.

Thomsen, P. H., & Mikkelsen, H. U. (1993). Development of personality disorders in children and adolescents with obsessive-disorder. *Acta Psychiatrica Scandinavia, 87,* 456–462.

Thyer, B. A., Nesse, R. M., Cameron, O. G., & Curtis, G. C. (1985). Agoraphobia: A test of the separation anxiety hypothesis. *Behaviour Research and Therapy, 23,* 75–78.

Tolin, D., Franklin, M., Diefenbach, G., Anderson, E., & Meunier, S. (2007). Pediatric trichotillomania: Descriptive psychopathology and an open trial of cognitive behavioral therapy. *Cognitive Behaviour Therapy, 36,* 129–144.

Topolski, T. D., Hewitt, J. K., Eaves, L. J., Silberg, J. L., Meyer, J. M. J., Rutter, M., et al. (1997). Genetic and environmental influences on child reports of manifest anxiety symptoms and symptoms of separation anxiety and overanxious disorders: A community-based twin study. *Behavior Genetics, 27,* 15–28.

Torgersen, S. (1983). Genetics of neurosis: The effects of sampling variation upon the twin concordance ratio. *British Journal of Psychiatry, 142,* 126–132.

Toto, J., Cervera, M., Osejo, E., & Salamero, M. (1992). Obsessive compulsive disorder in childhood and adolescence: A clinical study. *Journal of Child Psychology and Psychiatry and Allied Disciplines, 33,* 1025–1037.

Townend, E., Dimigen, G., & Fung, D. (2000). A clinical study of child dental anxiety. *Behaviour Research and Therapy, 38,* 31–46.

Tracey, S. A., Chorpita, B. F., Douban, J., & Barlow, D. H. (1997). Empirical evaluation of DSM-IV generalized anxiety disorder criteria in children and adolescents. *Journal of Clinical Child Psychology*, 26, 404–414.

Tracey, S. A., Mattis, S. G., Chorpita, B. F., Albano, A. M., Heimberg, R. G., & Barlow, D. H. (1998, November). *Cognitive-behavioral group treatment of social phobia in adolescents: Preliminary examination of the contribution of parental involvement*. Paper presented at the annual meeting of the Association for Advancement of Behavior Therapy, Washington, DC.

Tramer, M. (1934). Elektiver mutismus im Kindes alter. *Zeitschrift für Kinderpsychiatrie*, 30–35.

Treadwell, K. R., & Kendall, P. C. (1996). Self-talk in youth with anxiety disorders: States of mind, content specificity, and treatment outcome. *Journal of Consulting and Clinical Psychology*, 64, 941–950.

Treffers, P. D. A., & Silverman, W. K. (2001). Anxiety and its disorders in children and adolescents before the twentieth century. In W. K. Silverman & P. D. A. Treffers (Eds.), *Anxiety disorders in children and adolescents* (pp. 1–22). Cambridge, UK: Cambridge University Press.

Tupler, L. A., & De Bellis, M. D. (2006). Segmented hippocampal volume in children and adolescents with posttraumatic stress disorder. *Biological Psychiatry*, 59, 523–529.

Turner, S. M., Beidel, D. C., & Costello, A. (1987). Psychopathology in the offspring of anxiety disordered patients. *Journal of Consulting and Clinical Psychology*, 55, 229–235.

Turner, S. M., Beidel, D. C., Dancu, C. V., & Stanley, M. A. (1989). An empirically derived inventory to measure social fears and anxiety: The Social Phobia and Anxiety Inventory. *Psychological Assessment*, 1, 35–40.

Turner, S. M., Beidel, D. C., & Epstein, L. H. (1991). Vulnerability and risk for anxiety disorders. *Journal of Anxiety Disorders*, 5, 151–166.

Turner, B. G., Beidel, D. C., Hughes, S., & Turner, M. W. (1993). Test anxiety in African American school children. *School Psychology Quarterly*, 8, 140–152.

Turner, S. M., Beidel, D. C., & Jacob. R. G. (1994). Social phobia: A comparison of behavior therapy and atenolol. *Journal of Consulting and Clinical Psychology*, 62, 350–358.

Turner, S. M., Beidel, D. C., & Larkin, K. T. (1986). Situational determinants of social anxiety in clinic and non-clinic samples: Physiological and cognitive correlates. *Journal of Consulting and Clinical Psychology*, 54, 523–527.

Turner, S. M., Beidel, D. C., & Roberson-Nay, R. (2005). Offspring of anxious parents: Reactivity, habituation, and anxiety-proneness. *Behaviour Research and Therapy, 43,* 1263–1279.

Turner, S. M., Beidel, D. C., Roberson-Nay, R., & Tervo, K. (2003). Parenting behaviors in parents with anxiety disorders. *Behaviour Research and Therapy, 41,* 541–554.

Turner, S. M., Beidel, D. C., & Wolff, P. L. (1996). Is behavioral inhibition related to the anxiety disorders? *Clinical Psychology Review, 16,* 157–172.

Twenge, J. M. (2000). The age of anxiety? Birth cohort change in anxiety and neuroticism, 1952–1993. *Journal of Personality and Social Psychology, 79,* 1007–1021.

Udwin, O., Boyle, S., Yule, W., Bolton, D., & Oryan, D. (2000). Risk factors for long-term psychological effects of a disaster experienced in adolescence: Predictors of post traumatic stress disorder. *Journal of Child Psychology and Psychiatry, 41,* 969–979.

Ultee, C. A., Griffioen, D., & Schellekens, J. (1982). The reduction of anxiety in children. A comparison of the effects of "systematic desensitization in vitro" and "systematic desensitization in vivo." *Behaviour Research and Therapy, 20,* 61–67.

U.S. Department of Health and Human Services. (2005). National healthcare quality report. Retrieved May 19, 2010 from http://www.ahrq.gov/qual/nhqr05/nhqr05.pdf

Valderhaug, R., Larsson, B., Gotestam, K. G., & Piacentini, J. (2007). An open clinical trial of cognitive-behavioral therapy in children and adolescents with obsessive-compulsive disorder administered in regular outpatient clinics. *Behaviour Research and Therapy, 45,* 577–589.

Valleni-Basile, L. A., Farrison, C. Z., Jackson, K. L., Waller, J. L., McKeown, R. E., Addy, C. L., et al. (1995). Family and psychosocial predictors of obsessive compulsive disorder in a community sample of young adolescents. *Journal of Child and Family Studies, 4,* 193–206.

Valleni-Basile, L., Garrison, C. Z., Jackson, K. L., Waller, J. L., McKeown, R. E., Addy, C. L., et al. (1994). Frequency of obsessive-compulsive disorder in a community sample of young adolescents. *Journal of the American Academy of Child and Adolescent Psychiatry, 33,* 782–791.

Valleni-Basile, L. A., Garrison, C. Z., Waller, J. L., Ady, C. L., McKeown, R. E., Jackson, K. L., et al. (1996). Incidence of obsessive-compulsive disorder in a community sample of young adolescents. *Journal of the American Academy of Child and Adolescent Psychiatry, 35,* 898–906.

Vandenberg, B. (1993). Fears of normal and retarded children. *Psychological Reports, 72*, 473–474.

Van den Oord, E. J., Boomsma, D. I., & Verhulst, F. C. (2000). A study of genetic and environmental effects on the co-occurrence of problem behaviors in three-year-old-twins. *Journal of Abnormal Psychology, 109*, 360–372.

Van der Kolk, B. A. (2005). Developmental trauma disorder. *Psychiatric Annals, 35*, 401–408.

Van Oort, F., Greaves-Lord, K., Verhulst, F., Ormel, J., & Huizink, A. (2009). The developmental course of anxiety symptoms during adolescence: The TRAILS study. *Journal of Child Psychology and Psychiatry, 50*, 1209–1217.

Varela, R. E., Sanchez-Sosa, J. J., Biggs, B. K., & Luis, T. M. (2008). Anxiety symptoms and fears in Hispanic and European American children: Cross-cultural measurement equivalence. *Journal of Psychopathology and Behavioral Assessment, 30*, 132–145.

Vasa, R., Roberson-Nay, R., Klein, R., Mannuzza, S., Moulton III, J., Guardino, M., et al. (2007). Memory deficits in children with and at risk for anxiety disorders. *Depression and Anxiety, 24(2)*, 85–94.

Vasey, M. W. (1993). Development and cognition in childhood anxiety: The example of worry. *Advances in Clinical Child Psychology, 15*, 1–39.

Vasey, M. W., & Daleiden, E. L. (1994). Worrying in children. In G. C. L. Davey & F. Tallis (Eds.), *Worrying: Perspectives on theory, assessment and treatment* (pp. 185–207). Chichester, UK: Wiley.

Vecchio, J. L., & Kearney, C. A. (2005). Selective mutism in children: Comparison to youths with and without anxiety disorders. *Journal of Psychopathology and Behavioral Assessment, 27*, 31–37.

Vecchio, J. L., & Kearney, C. A. (2009). Treating youths with selective mutism with an alternating design of exposure-based practice and contingency management. *Behavior Therapy, 40*, 380–392.

Velez, C. N., Johnson, J., & Cohen, P. (1989). A longitudinal analysis of selected risk factors of childhood psychopathology. *Journal of the American Academy of Child and Adolescent Psychiatry, 28*, 861–864.

Velosa, J. F., & Riddle, M. A. (2000). Pharmacologic treatment of anxiety disorders in children and adolescents. *Psychopharmacology, 9*, 119–133.

Venham, L., Bengston, D., & Cipes, M. (1977). Children's response to sequential dental visits. *Journal of Dental Research, 56*, 454–459.

Verduin, T. L., & Kendall, P. C. (2003). Differential occurrence of comorbidity within childhood anxiety disorders. *Journal of Clinical Child and Adolescent Psychology, 32*, 290–295.

Verhulst, F. C., van der Ende, J., Ferinand, R., & Kasius, M. C. (1997). The prevalence of DSM-III-R diagnoses in a national sample of Dutch adolescents. *Archives of General Psychiatry, 54,* 329–336.

Vernberg, E. M., La Greca, A. M., Silverman, W. K., & Prinstein, M. J. (1996). Prediction of posttraumatic stress symptoms in children after Hurricane Andrew. *Journal of Abnormal Psychology, 105,* 237–248.

Viana, A. G., Beidel, D. C., & Rabian, B. (2009). Selective mutism: A review and integration of the last 15 years. *Clinical Psychology Review, 29,* 57–67.

Vitiello, B., Behar, D., Wolfson, S., & McLeer, S. V. (1990). Diagnosis of panic disorder in prepubertal children. *Journal of the American Academy of Child and Adolescent Psychiatry, 29,* 782–784.

Vitulano, L. A., King, R. A., Scahill, L., & Cohen, D. J. (1992). Behavioral treatment of children and adolescents with trichotillomania. *Journal of the American Academy of Child and Adolescent Psychiatry, 31,* 139–146.

Von Korff, M. R., Eaton, W. W., & Keyl, P. M. (1985). The epidemiology of panic attacks and panic disorder. *American Journal of Epidemiology, 122,* 970–981.

Wagner, K. D., Berard, R., Stein, M. B., Wetherhold, E., Carpenter, C. J., Perera, P., et al. (2004). A multicenter, randomized, double-blind, placebo-controlled trial of paroxetine in children and adolescents with social anxiety disorder. *Archives of General Psychiatry, 61,* 1153–1162.

Wagner, U., Gais, S., & Born, J. (2001). Emotional memory formation is enhanced across sleep intervals with high amounts of rapid eye-movement sleep. *Learning and Memory, 8,* 112–119.

Wagner, U., Hallschmid, M., Rasch, B., & Born, J. (2006). Brief sleep after learning keeps emotional memories alive for years. *Biological Psychiatry, 60,* 788–790.

Walker, M. P. (2009). The role of sleep in cognition and emotion. *Annals of the New York Academy of Sciences, 1156,* 168–197.

Walkup, J . T., Albano, A. M., Piacentini, J., Birmahar, B., Compton, S. N., Sherrill, J. T., et al. (2008). Cognitive behavioral therapy, sertraline, or a combination in childhood anxiety. *The New England Journal of Medicine, 359,* 2753–2766.

Walsh, K. H., & McDougle, C. J. (2001). Trichotillomania: Presentation, etiology, diagnosis and therapy. *American Journal of Clinical Dermatology, 2,* 327–333.

Warren, R., & Zgourides, G. (1988). Panic attacks in high school students: Implications for prevention and intervention. *Phobia Practice and Research Journal, 1,* 97–113.

Warren, S. L., Gunnar, M. R., Kagan, J., Anders, T. F., Simmens, S. J., Rones, M., et al. (2003). Maternal panic disorder: Infant temperament, neurophysiology, and parenting behaviors. *Journal of the American Academy of Child and Adolescent Psychiatry, 42,* 814–825.

Warren, W. (1948). Acute neurotic breakdown in children who refuse to go to school. *Archives of Disease in Childhood, 23,* 266–272.

Waters, T. L., & Barrett, P. M. (2000). The role of the family in childhood obsessive-compulsive disorder. *Clinical Child and Family Psychology Review, 3,* 173–184.

Waters, T. L., Barrett, P. M., & March, J. S. (2001). Cognitive-behavioral family treatment of childhood obsessive-compulsive disorder. *American Journal of Psychotherapy, 55,* 372–387.

Waters, A. M., Mogg, K., Bradley, B. P., & Pine, D. S. (2008). Attentional bias for emotional faces in children with generalized anxiety disorder. *Journal of the American Academy of Child and Adolescent Psychiatry, 47,* 435–442.

Watson, D. (2005). Rethinking the mood and anxiety disorders: A quantitative hierarchical model for DSM-VI. *Journal of Abnormal Psychology, 114,* 522–536.

Watson, J. B., & Rayner, R. (1920). Conditioned emotional reactions. *Journal of Experimental Psychology, 3,* 1–14.

Watson, T. S., & Allen, K. D. (1993). Elimination of thumb-sucking as a treatment for severe trichotillomania. *Journal of the American Academy of Child and Adolescent Psychiatry, 32,* 830–834.

Weems, C. F., Berman, S. L., Silverman, W. K., & Saavedra, L. S. (2001). Cognitive errors in youth with anxiety disorders: The linkages between negative cognitive errors and anxious symptoms. *Cognitive Therapy and Research, 25,* 559–575.

Weems, C. F., & Costa, N. M. (2005). Developmental differences in the expression of childhood anxiety symptoms and fears. *Journal of the American Academy of Child and Adolescent Psychiatry, 44,* 656–663.

Weems, C. F., Costa, N. M., Watts, S. E., Taylor, L. K., & Cannon, M. F. (2007). Cognitive errors, anxiety sensitivity and anxiety control beliefs: Their unique and specific associations withchildhood anxiety symptoms. *Behavior Modification, 31,* 174–201.

Weems, C.F., Pina, A. A., Costa, N. M., Watts, S. E., Taylor, L. K., & Cannon, M. F. (2007). Predisaster trait anxiety and negative affect predict posttraumatic stress in youths after Hurricane Katrina. *Journal of Consulting and Clinical Psychology, 75,* 154–159.

Weems, C. F., Silverman, W. K., & La Greca, A. M. (2000). What do youth referred for anxiety problems worry about? Worry and its relation to anxiety and anxiety disorders in children and adolescents. *Journal of Abnormal Child Psychology, 28,* 63–72.

Weems, C. F., Silverman, W. K., Saavedra, L. M., Pina, A. A., & White-Lumpkin, P. (1999). The discrimination of children's phobias using the revised Fear Survey Schedule for Children. *Journal of Child Psychology and Psychiatry, 40*, 941–952.

Weems, C. F., Taylor, L. K., Cannon, M. F., Marino, R. C., Romano, D. M., Scott, B. G., et al. (2010). Posttraumatic stress, context, and the lingering effects of the Hurricane Katrina disaster among ethnic minority youth. *Journal of Abnormal Child Psychology, 38,* 49–56.

Weissman, M. M., Leckman, J. F., Merikangas, K. R., Gammon, G. D., & Prusoff, B. A. (1984). Depression and anxiety disorders in parents and children: Results from the Yale family study. *Archives of General Psychiatry, 41*, 845–852.

Weisz, J. R., Donenberg, G. R., Han, S. S., & Weiss, B. (1995). Bridging the gap between lab and clinic in child and adolescent psychotherapy. *Journal of Consulting and Clinical Psychology, 63,* 688–701.

Werry, J. S. (1991). Overanxious disorder: A review of its taxonomic properties. *Journal of the American Academy of Child and Adolescent Psychiatry, 30*, 533–544.

Westenberg, P. M., Gullone, E., Bokhorst, C. L., Heyne, D. A., & King, N. J. (2007). Social evaluation fear in childhood and adolescence: Normative developmental course and continuity of individual differences. *British Journal of Developmental Psychology, 25,* 471–483.

Westenberg, P. M., Siebelink, B. M., Warmenhoven, N. J. C., & Treffers, P. D. A. (1999). Separation anxiety and overanxious disorders: Relations to age and level of psychosocial maturity. *Journal of the American Academy of Child and Adolescent Psychiatry, 38,* 1000–1007.

Wever, C., & Rey, J. (1997). Juvenile obsessive-compulsive disorder. *Australian and New Zealand Journal of Psychiatry, 31*, 105–113.

Whaley, S. E., Pinto, A., & Sigman, M. (1999). Characterizing interactions between anxious mothers and their children. *Journal of Consulting and Clinical Psychology, 67*, 826–836.

Whitaker, A., Johnson, J., Shaffer, D., Rapoport, J. L., Kakikow, K., Walsh, B. T., et al. (1990). Uncommon troubles in young people: Prevalence estimates of selected psychiatric disorders in a nonreferred adolescent population. *Archives of General Psychiatry, 47,* 487–496.

Wicklow, A., & Espie, C. A. (2000). Intrusive thoughts and their relationship to actigraphic measurement of sleep: Towards a cognitive model of insomnia. *Behaviour Research and Therapy, 38*, 679–693.

Wilcox, H. C., Grados, M., Samuels, J., Riddle, M. A., Bienvenu, O. J., Pinto, A., et al. (2008). The association between parental bonding and obsessive-compulsive disorder in offspring at high familial risk. *Journal of Affective Disorders, 111*, 31–39.

Williams, C. E., & Jones, R. T. (1989). Impact of self-instructions on response maintenance and children's fear of fire. *Journal of Clinical Child Psychology, 18*, 84–89.

Williams, L. R., Degnan, K. A., Perez-Edgar, K. E., Henderson, H. A., Rubin, K. H., Pine, D. S., et al. (2009). Impact of behavioral inhibition and parenting style on internalizing and externalizing problems from early childhood through adolescence. *Journal of Abnormal Child Psychology, 27*, 1063–1075.

Wittchen, H. U., Stein, M. B., & Kessler, R. C. (1999). Social fears and social phobia in a community sample of adolescents and young adults: Prevalence, risk factors and co-morbidity. *Psychological Medicine, 29*, 309–323.

Wolpe, J. (1958). *Psychotherapy by reciprocal inhibition*. Stanford, CA: Stanford University Press.

Wolfson, A. R. (1996). Sleeping patterns of children and adolescents: Developmental trends, disruptions, and adaptations. *Child and Adolescent Psychiatric Clinics of North America, 5*, 549–568.

Wolfson, A. R., & Carskadon, M. A. (1998). Sleep schedules and daytime functioning in adolescents. *Child Development, 69*, 875–887.

Wood, J. (2006). Parental intrusiveness and children's separation anxiety in a clinical sample. *Child Psychiatry and Human Development, 37*, 73–87.

Wood, J. J., McLeod, B. D., Sigman, M., Hwang, W., & Chu, B. C. (2003). Parenting and childhood anxiety: Theory, empirical findings, and future directions. *Journal of Child Psychology and Psychiatry, 44*, 134–151.

Wood, J. J., Piacentini, J. C., Bergman, R. L., McCracken, J., & Barrios, V. (2002). Concurrent validity of the Anxiety Disorders Section of the Anxiety Disorders Interview Schedule for DSM-IV: Child and Parent version. *Journal of Clinical Child and Adolescent Psychology, 31*, 335–342.

Woodward, L. J., & Fergusson, D. M. (2001). Life course outcomes of young people with anxiety disorders in adolescence. *Journal of the American Academy of Child and Adolescent Psychiatry, 40*, 1086–1093.

Yeganeh, R., Beidel, D. C., Turner, S. M., Pina, A. A., & Silverman, W. K. (2003). Clinical distinctions between selective mutism and social phobia: An investigation of childhood psychopathology. *Journal of the American Academy of Child and Adolescent Psychiatry, 42*, 1069–1075.

Yoo, S. S., Gujar, N., Hu, P., Jolesz, F. A., & Walker, M. P. (2007). The human emotional brain without sleep—a prefrontal amygdala disconnect. *Current Biology*, *17*, 877–878.

Young, B., Beidel, D., Turner, S., Ammerman, R., McGraw, K., & Coaston, S. (2006). Pretreatment attrition and childhood social phobia: Parental concerns about medication. *Journal of Anxiety Disorders*, *20*, 1133–1147.

Yule, W., Bolton, D., Udwin, O., Boyle, S., O'Ryan, D., & Nurrish, J. (2000). The long-term psychological effects of a disaster experienced in adolescence: I: The incidence and course of PTSD. *Journal of Child Psychology and Psychiatry*, *41*, 503–511.

Yule, W., & Canterbury, R. (1994). The treatment of posttraumatic stress disorder in children and adolescents. *International Review of Psychiatry*, *6*, 141–151.

Yule, W., Udwin, O., & Murdoch, K. (1990). The "Jupiter" sinking: Effects on children's fears, depression and anxiety. *Journal of Child Psychology and Psychiatry*, *31*, 1051–1061.

Zitrin, C. M., & Ross, D. C. (1988). Early separation anxiety and adult agoraphobia. *Journal of Nervous and Mental Disease*, *176*, 621–625.

Zohar, A. H., & Felz, L. (2001). Ritualistic behavior in young children. *Journal of Abnormal Child Psychology*, *29*, 121–128.

Author Index

Subject Index